ASSOCIATIVE NETWORKS

Representation and Use of Knowledge
by Computers

ASSOCIATIVE NETWORKS

Representation and Use of Knowledge by Computers

Edited by

NICHOLAS V. FINDLER

Department of Computer Science
State University of New York at Buffalo
Amherst, New York

ACADEMIC PRESS New York San Francisco London 1979

A Subsidiary of Harcourt Brace Jovanovich, Publishers

ACADEMIC PRESS, INC.
111 Fifth Avenue, New York, New York 10003

United Kingdom Edition published by
ACADEMIC PRESS, INC. (LONDON) LTD.
24/28 Oval Road, London NW1 7DX

Library of Congress Cataloging in Publication Data
Main entry under title:

Associative networks.

    Includes bibliographies.
    1. Information theory.   2. Artificial intelligence.
3. Linguistics--Data processing.   4. Semantics.
I. Findler, N. V.
Q360.A87   001.53'9   78-31318
ISBN 0-12-256380-8

PRINTED IN THE UNITED STATES OF AMERICA

79 80 81 82   9 8 7 6 5 4 3 2 1

Let fourteen flowers bloom

CONTENTS

A PROCEDURAL SEMANTICS FOR SEMANTIC NETWORKS

Hector Levesque and John Mylopoulos

THE STRUCTURE AND ORGANIZATION OF A SEMANTIC NET FOR COMPREHENSION AND INFERENCE

Lenhart K. Schubert, Randolph G. Goebel, and Nicholas J. Cercone

Part II   THEORETICALLY ORIENTED EFFORTS

THE SNePS SEMANTIC NETWORK PROCESSING SYSTEM

Stuart C. Shapiro

A PREDICATE CALCULUS BASED SEMANTIC NETWORK FOR DEDUCTIVE SEARCHING

James R. McSkimin and Jack Minker

MAKING PREFERENCES MORE ACTIVE

Yorick Wilks

EXTENSIONAL SEMANTIC NETWORKS: THEIR REPRESENTATION, APPLICATION, AND GENERATION

Jürgen M. Janas and Camilla B. Schwind

Part III AREAS OF APPLICATION

A HEURISTIC INFORMATION RETRIEVAL SYSTEM BASED ON ASSOCIATIVE NETWORKS

Nicholas V. Findler

RE: THE GETTYSBURG ADDRESS
Representing Social and Political Acts

Roger C. Schank and Jaime G. Carbonell, Jr.

RULE FORMS FOR VERSE, SENTENCES, AND STORY TREES

Robert F. Simmons and Alfred Correira

ON REPRESENTING COMMONSENSE KNOWLEDGE

Benjamin Kuipers

REPRESENTATIONS TO AID DISTRIBUTED UNDERSTANDING IN A MULTIPROGRAM SYSTEM

Christopher K. Riesbeck

FIVE ASPECTS OF A FULL-SCALE STORY COMPREHENSION MODEL

Chuck Rieger

LIST OF CONTRIBUTORS

Numbers in parentheses indicate the pages on which the authors' contributions begin.

RONALD J. BRACHMAN (3),   Bolt Beranek & Newman Inc., Cambridge, Massachusetts 02138

JAIME G. CARBONELL, Jr.* (327),   Department of Computer Science, Yale University, New Haven, Connecticut 06520

NICHOLAS J. CERCONE (121),   Computing Science Department, Simon Fraser University, Burnaby, British Columbia, Canada

ALFRED CORREIRA (363),   Department of Computer Sciences, University of Texas, Austin, Texas 78712

NICHOLAS V. FINDLER (305),   Department of Computer Science, State University of New York at Buffalo, Amherst, New York 14226

RANDOLPH G. GOEBEL (121),   Department of Computer Science, University of British Columbia, Vancouver, British Columbia, Canada

GARY G. HENDRIX (51),   Artificial Intelligence Center, SRI International, Menlo Park, California 94025

JÜRGEN M. JANAS (267),   Institut für Informatik, Technische Universität München, München, Federal Republic of Germany

BENJAMIN KUIPERS† (393),   Division for Study and Research in Education, Massachusetts Institute of Technology, Cambridge, Massachusetts 02119

HECTOR LEVESQUE (93),   Department of Computer Science, University of Toronto, Toronto, Ontario, Canada

JAMES R. McSKIMIN (205),   Bell Laboratories, Columbus, Ohio 43213

JACK MINKER (205),   Department of Computer Science, University of Maryland, College Park, Maryland 20742

* Present address: The Computer Science Department, Carnegie-Mellon University, Schenley Park, Pittsburgh, Pennsylvania 15213
† Present address: Department of Mathematics, Tufts University, Medford, Massachusetts 02155

JOHN MYLOPOULOS (93),   Department of Computer Science, University of Toronto, Toronto, Ontario, Canada

CHUCK RIEGER (425),   Department of Computer Science, University of Maryland, College Park, Maryland 20742

CHRISTOPHER K. RIESBECK (409),   Department of Computer Science, Yale University, New Haven, Connecticut 06520

ROGER C. SCHANK (327),   Department of Computer Science, Yale University, New Haven, Connecticut 06520

LENHART K. SCHUBERT (121),   Department of Computing Science, University of Alberta, Edmonton, Canada

CAMILLA B. SCHWIND (267),   Institut für Informatik, Technische Universität München, München, Federal Republic of Germany

STUART C. SHAPIRO (179),   Department of Computer Science, State University of New York at Buffalo, Amherst, New York 14226

ROBERT F. SIMMONS (363),   Department of Computer Sciences, University of Texas, Austin, Texas 78712

YORICK WILKS (239),   Department of Language and Linguistics, University of Essex, Colchester, England

FOREWORD

The opening sentence of a recently published article at first, I must admit, shocked me. It reads: "The goal of Artificial Intelligence is to identify and solve *tractable* information processing problems" [emphasis added]. We all know that there are quite a few people from the "outside" who attack our methodology, our philosophy, our outlook on the world, even the problems we solve successfully. And then an "insider" accuses that we deal with only "tractable" problems, in other words, that we avoid all those areas not easily manageable and pretend to have established a bona fide discipline on the basis of working on some cheap tasks.

Even before I went on to read the rest of the paper (which turned out to be interesting and nontrivial), my shock gradually disappeared when I started to think that (a) the same statement, with proper but superficial substitutions, holds for all scientific endeavors; (b) every "solution" is only partial and leads to the most ill-defined concept of all, *knowledge of truth*.

I am sure every reader will agree that this book can, in a modest but substantial manner, be used as an argument that we deal with really *difficult* problems. (How tractable they are, only time will tell.) Intelligent computer programs must have both a *representation* of the knowledge they involve and some *mechanisms* for manipulating that knowledge for certain purposes. This book aims at giving a critical description of the current state of the art of this area. It does so partly by presenting some critical surveys of the work accomplished so far, partly by outlining certain theoretical and practical developments. Because of the very nature of this rapidly evolving field, the book must present a snapshot: this is what we have now. However, it also goes in both directions along the time coordinate. Historical background is well treated in many contributions (without undue repetitions, I am glad to say), and future areas of exploration are outlined as well.

The main theme of the book is *associative networks*. I have deliberately avoided the term *semantic networks* (but did not impose such a restriction upon the contributors) to indicate that the former are more general in objectives and, possibly, in structure than the latter. Semantic networks aim, I believe, at furnishing a representation for linguistic utterances to capture the underlying relations of words and to produce the information contained in text (the whole being more than the sum of the parts). Indirectly, they also reveal the intricacies and use of language, the need for which is clearly shown by the quasi-asymptotic quality of machine translation programs. Associative networks, on the other hand, could, but need not, be language-independent. They can be studied at three distinct levels: an information structure in the computer; a (corresponding) diagram on paper; a directed, labeled graph with user-defined equivalence between edges and nodes on one hand and relations, restrictions, objects, events, actions, states, properties, on the other.

Associative networks are constructed to serve as the *knowledge base* of programs that exhibit some operational aspects of understanding.[1] These programs would be capable of carrying out some or all of the following: paraphrasing, abstracting, and classifying a corpus of text; answering questions on the basis of commonsense reasoning; drawing deductive and inductive inferences; obeying commands; and the like.

It must be obvious even to the casual reader that approach and methodology vary a great deal from author to author. Although some people may consider this fact disturbing and a sign of an immature discipline, one should rather be content—innumerable roads lead to "knowledge," and we try to explore many of them.

Forewords are also the place for some historical overview and a characterization of the problems solved and still outstanding. Luckily, I do not have to follow that pattern; the articles in Part I provide such excellent background material that it would be hopeless for me to compete with them.

Finally, the affiliation and address of each contributor are listed. I am sure we all would welcome comments, questions, and criticism from readers.

NICHOLAS V. FINDLER
Amherst, New York

---

[1] I do not intend to get involved with the philosophical problems concerning the concept of "understanding." Readers interested in this area are referred to, for example, the articles by E. Dresher and N. Hornstein, R. C. Schank and R. Wilensky, and T. Winograd in the December 1976 and June 1977 issues of *Cognition*.

PREFACE

This book is intended to present a reasonably comprehensive view of the present state of the art of, I believe, one of the most promising and most exciting areas of research in computer science, *associative networks*. About twenty active and well-known workers in this field were invited to contribute to this treatise, but unfortunately not all could; the contents of this volume are not as complete as they could be. In a way, this was fortunate: we have a more easily manageable book and its price is lower.

As anyone who has ever done it can tell, the level of difficulty of editing a book is directly proportional to e^n, where n is the number of contributors. In spite of all the frustrations and anxieties I had about many things, I must say that I enjoyed the challenge of trying to integrate a variety of research objectives and approaches into a reasonably uniform book. In this endeavor, I owe a great deal of gratitude to each contributor—not only for his writing and rewriting efforts but also for having reviewed, meticulously and constructively, three other authors' work. These anonymous critiques have helped all of us to improve both the style and the contents of our contributions. The whole process required a lot of effort and was very time-consuming, but, I am convinced, was worth it: we have a much better book whose value may not be only momentary. It is hoped that it will not be used only by the cognoscenti but also by the (yet) nonpractitioners, students, and researchers of other areas of computer science, psychology, and linguistics. Their interest will be raised and some of them will possibly become contributors to a second or third volume. (May God give me strength. . . .)

N. V. F.

PART I

OVERVIEW AND GENERAL SYSTEMS

ON THE EPISTEMOLOGICAL STATUS
OF SEMANTIC NETWORKS*

Ronald J. Brachman

ABSTRACT

This chapter examines in detail the history of a set of network-structured formalisms for knowledge representation—the so-called "semantic networks." Semantic nets were introduced around 1966 as a representation for the concepts
underlying English words, and since then have become an increasingly popular
type of language for representing concepts of a widely varying sort. While these
nets have for the most part retained their basic associative nature, their primitive representational elements have differed significantly from one project to
the next. These differences in underlying primitives are symptomatic of deeper
philosophical disparities, and I discuss a set of five significantly different
"levels" at which networks can be understood. One of these levels, the "epistemological," or "knowledge-structuring," level, has played an important
implicit part in all previous notations, and is here made explicit in a way that
allows a new type of network formalism to be specified. This new type of formalism accounts precisely for operations like individuation of description, internal
concept structure in terms of roles and interrelations between them, and structured inheritance. In the final section, I present a brief sketch of an example of a
particular type of formalism ("Structured Inheritance Networks") that was designed expressly to treat concepts as formal representational objects. This language, currently under development, is called KLONE, and it allows the explicit
expression of epistemological level relationships as network links.

INTRODUCTION

The idea of a memory based on the notion of *associations* is apparently a
very old one—Anderson and Bower [1973] trace the idea back as far as
Aristotle. However, only in the last ten years has the associative memory
idea taken a firm hold with those interested in modeling human memory
or providing working memories for intelligent computer programs. Yet in

* Prepared in part at Bolt Beranek and Newman Inc. under contracts sponsored by the Defense Advance Research Projects Agency and the Office of Naval Research. The views and
conclusions stated are those of the author and should not be interpreted as necessarily representing the official policies, either express or implied, of the Defense Advanced Research
Projects Agency or the U.S. Government.

the short time since Ross Quillian first introduced the idea of a "semantic network" in his Ph.D. thesis [1966], network models of information and their computer implementations have become rampant.

While Quillian's original intent was to represent the semantics of English words in his nets, representations that looked very similar were soon being used to model all sorts of nonsemantic things (e.g., propositions, physical object structure, "gated one-shot state coupling"). Yet, virtually every networklike formalism that has appeared in the literature since 1966 has at one time or another been branded by someone a semantic net. The possibility of confusion over the real nature of the network slipped by virtually unnoticed, since everyone working in the area already "knew" with what they were working. But as interest has developed over the last two years in the semantics of the semantic net itself, the epistemological status of the representation has become increasingly suspect. This chapter is an attempt to clear up what we mean when we call our representations semantic nets, and to examine what claims about the structure of knowledge these so-called representations actually make.

To this end, I shall first examine the history of semantic networks, covering as broadly as possible in a limited space the major developments in associative memory models from 1966 through the present. I shall then attempt to explain why so many of the earlier formalisms are inadequate in several ways, and why the more recent ones approaching complete logical adequacy are perhaps not as useful for knowledge representation as it was hoped they might be. The substance of this analysis will be a close look at the kinds of entities chosen by designers to be primitive in their network schemes. By elucidating the different kinds of primitives employed in these nets, I hope to illustrate how there are at least five different kinds of knowledge that have become confusingly called "semantic" by their association with semantic networks. For the purposes of the analysis, I shall postulate and discuss five levels of semantic net primitive corresponding to these kinds of knowledge—the "implementational," "logical," "epistemological," "conceptual," and "linguistic" levels.

One of these levels has been less used and understood than the others, but may have significantly more utility in the near future for general knowledge representation tasks than the others. This is the *epistemological* level of knowledge representation—the one on which several new nonnetwork formalisms like KRL [Bobrow and Winograd, 1977] and FRL [Goldstein and Roberts, 1977; Roberts and Goldstein, 1977] are built, and the one dealing with things like "inheritance," "abstraction," and concept structuring. In Section 3, I examine some of the implications of this level of thinking, and show how it has influenced my own work on what I used to think of as semantic networks. I shall present some of the prominent aspects of a new netlike formalism—the "Structured Inheritance Network." A structured inheritance network (SI-Net) has a fixed set of node and link types (the number of which is small), thereby providing the basis for a fixed and well-defined interpreter. The links in this kind of net are used to explicitly express "epistemological" relationships between Concepts and their parts ("Roles" and "Structural Descriptions"), that is, structuring relationships between formal objects used to represent knowledge. SI-Nets can be used to illustrate the level of concern of epistemological formalisms in general, and I shall use a particular SI-Net language, called KLONE, to help elucidate some of the representational responsibilities of such formalisms.

1. A LOOK AT THE EVOLUTION OF SEMANTIC NETWORKS

The last ten years have seen a tremendous explosion in the number of efforts directed toward developing memory models that might be considered networks, and the literature has expanded to the point where only with extreme effort can one maintain familiarity with the entire field. To treat fairly all of the work that has led to our current state of knowledge about network knowledge representation would be a Herculean task, and one requiring far more space and time than is convenient here. Therefore, my analysis will begin with Quillian's [1966] work and will not discuss the many earlier efforts of Gestalt psychology, perception-by-reconstruction theories (especially Bartlett [1967] and Neisser [1967]), and artificial intelligence that have had significant effects on the current shape of semantic nets. I shall only briefly outline the various major contributions to the semantic network literature, and hope that the bibliography at the end of this chapter will provide sufficient direction for the reader more interested in historical trends and details on the representations sketched here. I shall not proceed strictly chronologically (many of these projects developed simultaneously), but shall instead broadly outline three major groups of work: the early nets that provided the basic structure, those which attempted to incorporate linguistic case structure, and several more recent important foundational studies.

1.1. The Early Nets

The idea of a semantic network representation for human knowledge is generally acknowledged to have originated in the work of Quillian [1966, 1967, 1968, 1969; Bell and Quillian, 1971]; Quillian proposed an associational network model of "semantic memory" in his Ph.D. thesis in 1966. His intent was to capture in a formal representation the "objective" part of the meanings of words so that "humanlike use of those meanings" would be possible [1966, p. 1]. The representation was composed of *nodes*, interconnected by various kinds of *associative links*, and closely reflected the organization of an ordinary dictionary. The nodes were to be considered "word concepts," and links from a concept node pointed to other word concepts, which together made up a definition, just as dictionary definitions are constructed from sequences of words defined elsewhere in the same volume. The structure thus ultimately became an interwoven network of nodes and links.

In Quillian's structure, each word concept node was considered to be the head of a "plane," which held its definition. Figure 1 [Quillian, 1968, p. 236] illustrates a set of three planes (indicated by solid boxes) for three senses of the word "plant." Pointers *within* the plane (the solid links in the figure) are those which form the structure of the definition. Quillian postulated a small set of these, which included *subclass* (e.g., the relationship of PLANT 2 to APPARATUS in the figure), *modification* (e.g., APPARATUS is modified by the USE structure), *disjunction* (labeled by OR), *conjunction* (labeled by AND), and *subject/object* (e.g., the parallel links from USE to PEOPLE (the subject) and to = A (the object)). Pointers leading *outside* the plane (the broken links in the figure) indicate other planes in which the referenced words are themselves defined. The fact that in Quillian's structure words used in definitions of other words had their own planes, which were *pointed to* by place-holder nodes within those definitions, corresponded to the important "type/token" distinction. Each word was defined in only one plane in the structure (the head of the plane being the "type" node), and all references to a word went through intermediate "token" nodes. Thus definitions were not repeated each time a word concept was referenced.

Quillian's desire of his semantic memory model was that it might serve as a general *inferential* representation for knowledge. He presented in his thesis several examples of an inference technique based on the notion of a spreading activation *intersection search*—given two words, possible relations between them might be inferred by an unguided, breadth-first search of the area surrounding the planes for the words; this search was carried out by a propagation of some kind of activation signal through the network. A search would fan out through links from the original two planes to all planes pointed to by the originals, until a point of intersection was found. The paths from the source nodes to the point of contact of the two "spheres of activation" formed by the search would indicate a potential relationship between the two word concepts.* Quillian hoped that in this way information input in one frame of reference might be used to answer questions asked in another. The use of information implicit in the memory, but not stated explicitly, was one of the important features of the memory model.

---

* The belief that properties of a node could be found by an expanding search led Quillian to the idea that a word concept's "full meaning" comprised *everything* that could be reached from the patriarchal type node (the head of its defining plane) by an exhaustive tracing process.

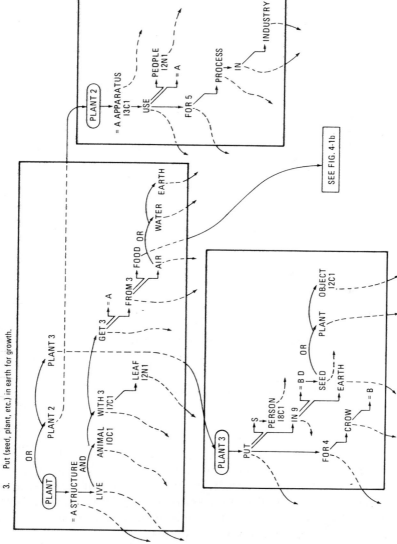

PLANT. 1. Living structure which is not an animal, frequently with leaves, getting its food from air, water, earth.
2. Apparatus used for any process in industry.
3. Put (seed, plant, etc.) in earth for growth.

Fig. 1. Quillian's planes. Reprinted from Quillian [1968], by permission of the MIT Press, Cambridge, Massachusetts. Copyright 1968 by the Massachusetts Institute of Technology.

Part of the reason that certain properties could be inferred from such a memory was its use of a link indicating a "subclass" relationship and a link specifying a "modifies" relation. A concept could be defined in terms of a more general concept (of which it was a subclass) and a modifying property, which was a combination of an attribute and a particular value for that attribute.* In this characterization, properties true of a class were assumed true of all of its subclasses, except for the modifications. As a result, the superclass chain extending upward from a concept embodied all of the properties true of that concept. Thus the semantic net represented the combination of two important types of memory feature—a superclass–subclass taxonomic hierarchy, and the description of properties (attribute/value pairs) for each class. Earlier work done by Lindsay (see Lindsay [1973] for a later discussion of Lindsay's original work) and Raphael [1968] can be seen to be the precursors of this important marriage.

Quillian later cleaned up his memory model a bit. He eliminated the type/token distinction by making everything in the net a pointer, and, in a project called the "Teachable Language Comprehender" (TLC) [1969], he investigated its utility as a knowledge base for the reading of text. In TLC, a property was formally defined to be an attribute (some relational concept), a value, and possibly some further "subproperties." Properties were used in the definitions of "units," which represented the concepts of objects, events, ideas, assertions, etc.: a unit was defined by its superset and a set of refining properties. For reading, an intersection technique was used to find relations between words encountered in a text (this was augmented by the application of certain "form tests" as syntax checks). Figure 2 [Quillian, 1969, p. 462] illustrates a simple unit. The unit being defined in this figure is the one for "client." The unit indicates that a CLIENT is a PERSON (i.e., PERSON is its superset), with a further qualification indicated by the second pointer from the unit to a restricting property. That property combines the attribute EMPLOY with a value PROFESSIONAL and the subproperty BY THE CLIENT.

While TLC was an interesting model for finding connections between word meanings, its success in reading was limited. TLC's failure to achieve understanding was at least in part due to its insufficient set of link types and the fact that the search did not take into account the meanings of the various links. Despite the many shortcomings of his model, however, Quillian's early papers contain the seeds of most of the important ideas that are today the mainstays of semantic nets.

Quillian's revised TLC format gave rise to two other important studies. With Collins, Quillian undertook a series of experiments to test the psychological plausibility of his network scheme [Collins and Quillian, 1969,

* Quillian claimed that his nodes corresponded "to what we ordinarily call 'properties'" [1966, p. 26].

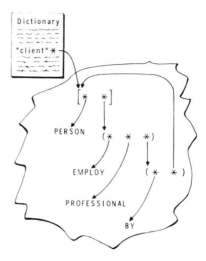

1970a,b, 1972a],* and the networks they used to check reaction time are easily recognized as the direct forerunners of recent networks (see Fig. 3 [Collins and Quillian, 1970a, p. 305]). The nets were simple superset hierarchies of concepts like *Animal, Bird,* and *Canary,* with each node having attached a set of properties defining its corresponding concept (e.g., "has skin," "has wings," "is yellow"). Since more general properties were supposedly stored higher up the generalization hierarchy, one would expect it to take more time to affirm a statement like "A canary has skin" than one like "A canary is yellow." The reaction time studies seemed to confirm the plausibility of a hierarchical model for human memory, although not conclusively. In any case, the experiments crystallized the notion of *inheritance of properties* in a semantic net (the passing of values like "has skin" from the general concept of *Animal* to the more specific one of *Canary*) and gave rise to a concrete notion of *semantic distance* between concepts (i.e., the number of links to be traversed between two nodes). More recently, Collins and Loftus [1975] have discussed in much detail the psychological implications of an extended version of this model, and have examined some experimental results in regard to their "spreading-activation" theory of processing (a sophistication of Quillian's semantic intersection technique). The reader is referred to that paper for some clarification of Quillian's original theory and a defense of the original experiments.

The other significant project arising directly from Quillian's TLC work was established by Carbonell [1970a,b] and attempted to use Quillian's

---

* The reader is also referred to an interesting article by Collins and Quillian called "How to make a language user" [1972b], in which they summarize many of the things that they learned from their experiments about language and memory.

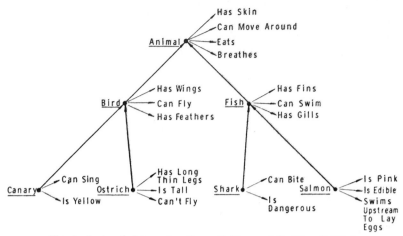

Fig. 3. A simple hierarchy. From Collins and Quillian [1970a].

networks as a data structure in an implemented computer-aided instruction program. The SCHOLAR program had a knowledge base that described in network terms the geography of South America. A student could participate in a "mixed-initiative" dialogue with the system, asking and being asked questions about the data base.

SCHOLAR's data base made some important new contributions to Quillian's nets. Carbonell began to distinguish "concept units" (like LATITUDE) from "example units" (like ARGENTINA), setting the stage for the later notion of *instantiation*.* In addition, a notion of Quillian's called *tags* was expanded and used extensively. Figure 4 [Carbonell, 1970b, p. 194] illustrates the SCHOLAR units for latitude and Argentina; in the text part of the figure, the name of a unit follows RPAQQ (a LISP value-setting function), and anything within the unit that follows a left parenthesis is an attribute. Tags on relations are indicated by parenthesized pairs following the attribute names [e.g., the SUPERP of LATITUDE is LOCATION, and has the tag (I 2)]. The most important of the tags in SCHOLAR was the *irrelevancy tag* (I-tag), which could explicitly increase the semantic distance between two nodes. I-tags were used to determine the relevance of certain facts in a given context, and allowed the system to start with the

---

* Instantiation has become one of the most well-known aspects of semantic net formalisms. The general idea is the association of a particular individual with the class of which it is a member, and in most notations, this is reflected by the construction of an individual description based on a generic description that the individual satisfies. Thus, while we primarily think of instances as things *in the world* that are manifestations of our abstract concepts, the term "instantiation" is very often used to refer to the production of a *description* of an individual based on a more general description. I shall later (Section 3) use the term, "individuation" (of description) for this latter intent, avoiding the potential confusion over what the term "instance" really means.

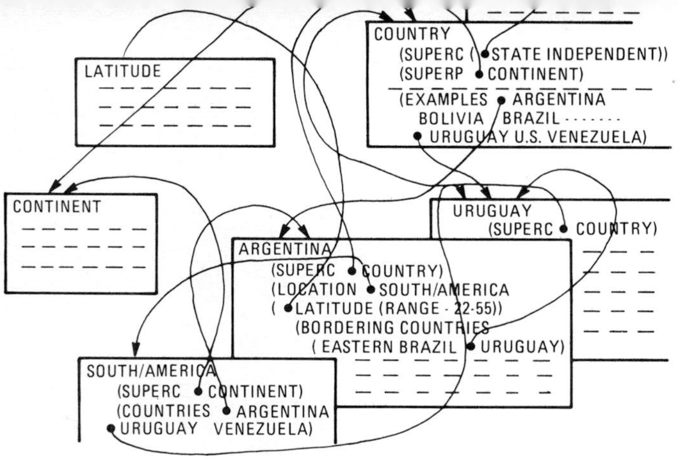

COUNTRY
(SUPERC (STATE INDEPENDENT))
(SUPERP CONTINENT)
(EXAMPLES ● ARGENTINA
    BOLIVIA BRAZIL.......
    URUGUAY U.S. VENEZUELA)

LATITUDE

CONTINENT

URUGUAY
(SUPERC COUNTRY)

ARGENTINA
(SUPERC COUNTRY)
(LOCATION SOUTH/AMERICA
    (LATITUDE (RANGE -22-55))
    (BORDERING COUNTRIES
        (EASTERN BRAZIL URUGUAY)

SOUTH/AMERICA
(SUPERC CONTINENT)
(COUNTRIES ARGENTINA
    URUGUAY VENEZUELA)

(RPAQQ LATITUDE (((CN LATITUDE)
    (DET THE DEF 2))
NIL
(SUPERC NIL (DISTANCE NIL ANGULAR (FROM NIL
    EQUATOR)))
(SUPERP (I 2)
    LOCATION)
(VALUE (I 2)
    (RANGE NIL -90 90))
(UNIT (I 2)
    DEGREES)))

(DET NIL DEF 2))
NIL
(SUPERC NIL COUNTRY)
(SUPERP (I 6)
    SOUTH\AMERICA)
(AREA (I 2)
    (APPROX NIL \ 1200000))
(LOCATION NIL SOUTH\AMERICA (LATITUDE (I 2)
        (RANGE NIL -22 -55))
    (LONGITUDE (I 4)
        (RANGE NIL -57 -71))
    (BORDERING\COUNTRIES (I 1)
        (NORTHERN (I 1)
            BOLIVIA PARAGUAY)
        (EASTERN (I 1)
            (($L BRAZIL URUGUAY
            NIL
                (BOUNDARY NIL URUGUAY\RIVER)) ─ ─ ─ ─ ─
(CAPITAL (I 1)
    BUENOS\AIRES)
(CITIES (I 3)
    (PRINCIPAL NIL ($L BUENOS\AIRES CORDOBA ROSARIO
        MENDOZA LA\PLATA TUCUMAN)))
(TOPOGRAPHY (I 1)
    VARIED
    (MOUNTAIN\CHAINS NIL (PRINCIPAL NIL ANDES
            (LOCATION NIL (BOUNDARY NIL (WITH NIL
                CHILE)))
            (ALTITUDE NIL (HIGHEST NIL ACONCAGUA
                (APPROX NIL 22000))))
        (SIERRAS NIL (LOCATION NIL ($L CORDOBA
            BUENOS\AIRES))))
    (PLAINS NIL (FERTILE NIL USUALLY)
        (($L EASTERN CENTRAL)
        NIL PAMPA)
        (NORTHERN NIL CHACO)))

Fig. 4. SCHOLAR units. From Carbonell [1970b].

most relevant aspects of a unit when describing a concept to the student. In addition, SCHOLAR introduced temporary, time-dependent tags. Also, while SCHOLAR's units looked much like Quillian's TLC units, the properties associated with a unit had as their first elements the *names* of attributes, rather than pointers (resurrecting the type/token distinction). Thus the precedent was set for *naming links*—associating arbitrary labels with the associations between units. In addition to several special attributes (SUPERC for superconcept, SUPERP for superpart, and SUPERA for superattribute), things like LOCATION, TOPOGRAPHY, CITIES, and UNIT were now being encoded directly into the network.* Another important precedent set in the SCHOLAR net was the intermixing of *procedures* with the declarative structure. LISP functions associated with units were used to actively infer properties that were not stated as declarative facts.

Another early effort, which proceeded independently of the Quillian/SCHOLAR work but made use of similar structures, was Winston's "structural descriptions" work at MIT [1970, 1975]. Winston created a program that could infer the "concept" of a physical structure such as an ARCH (see Fig. 5 [Winston, 1975, p. 198]), given encodings of a set of ex-

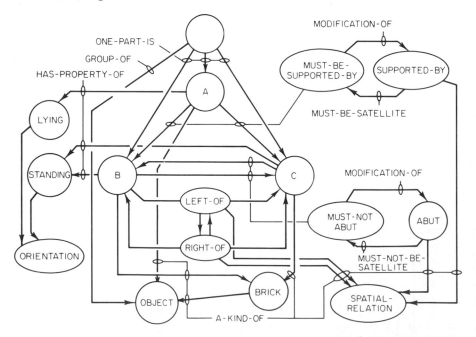

Fig. 5. Structural description of an ARCH. From Winston [1975]. Copyright 1975 by McGraw–Hill, Inc., New York. Used with permission of McGraw–Hill Book Company.

* While Carbonell claimed that no links were privileged [1970a, p. 112], that those like "*SUPERC*" are very special indeed is illustrated in Brachman [1978b].

amples of the structure in a network description language. The descriptions included nodes for concepts of physical objects (like BRICKs) in a scene, and labeled links representing physical relationships between the objects (e.g., LEFT-OF, SUPPORTED-BY). The interesting thing about Winston's networks (aside from the fact that he had actually written a program to induce generalizations from them) is that the relationships between concepts could themselves be modified or talked about as concepts. For example, in the very same notation, B could be described as LEFT-OF C, and LEFT-OF described as OPPOSITE RIGHT-OF. Winston also used the same language as his comparison language for determining differences between examples.

One problem with Winston's notation, as with each of the others mentioned so far, was its complete uniformity. While the notions of superconcept and instance were included in these nets, there was no acknowledgement of their difference from domain-specific notions like location and support. One could not "see" a hierarchy by looking at the structure, and important notions like inheritance were obscured by an overly uniform mixture of domain-specific and general "properties." However, with the groundwork laid by Quillian, Collins, Carbonell, and Winston, almost all of the semantic net apparatus used in the 1970s is already accounted for, and very little has really changed since then (at least until very recently, as Section 3 will attempt to show).

1.2. Case Structures

The work of Fillmore on linguistic case structure [1968] helped focus network attention onto *verbs*. Those interested in processing natural language with semantic nets began to think of a sentence as a *modality* coupled with a *proposition*, where a modality captured information such as tense, mood, manner, and aspect, and a proposition was a verb and a set of filled-in *cases*. There were believed to be a reasonably small number of cases (i.e., relationships in which nominals could participate relative to the verb of a sentence), and several people set out to incorporate this belief in network formalisms. The fact that properties in semantic nets were clustered around nodes made the nodes ideal places to anchor cases—if a node were thought of as a verbal concept, its associated attribute/value pairs could easily be case/filler pairs.

Simmons *et al.* [1968], Simmons and Bruce [1971], Simmons and Slocum [1972], Simmons [1973], Hendrix *et al.* [1973] used this notion very early in work that developed from the older Protosynthex system. Simmons' networks became centered around verbal nodes, with pointers labeled with case names to the participants in the action represented by the node (see Fig. 6 [Simmons and Bruce, 1971, p. 525]—the verbal node here is C1, a TOKen of the verb *Make*). The verbs themselves were grouped into "para-

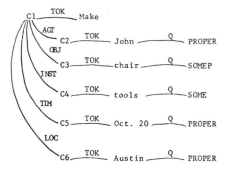

Fig. 6. A Simmons case structure. From Simmons and Bruce [1971]. Used with permission of International Joint Conferences on Artificial Intelligence, Inc.

digms," according to the sets of case relations in which they participated.

Simmons' networks focused on the understanding and generation of particular sentences—not much attention seems to have been given in the original work to the semantic network as a hierarchical classification device, nor to the place of general "world knowledge" in the overall scheme. Thus no classification of verbs, or nouns, for that matter, existed outside the similar case-frame grouping (the paradigms), and no definitions of general concepts seemed to exist at all. Recently, however, some sophistication has been added to these networks, including substantial use of superconcept and instance links. In addition, quantification and deductive mechanisms are discussed in Simmons and Chester [1977].

A similar incorporation of case structures into a network framework was achieved by Rumelhart *et al.* [1972], Norman [1972, 1973], Norman *et al.* [1975], and Rumelhart and Norman [1973]. Their attempt, spanning several years, included many of the features that Simmons had left out, although their orientation was more psychological and thus dealt with more aspects of memory. The Rumelhart *et al.* networks included nodes for concepts, nodes for *events,* and nodes for *episodes*—sequences of events clustered together. General definitions of concepts in the network were encoded in a straightforward manner, with caselike pointers indicating parts of nominal concepts and agents and objects of verbs, as illustrated in Fig. 7 [Rumelhart *et al.*, 1972, p. 224]. Unfortunately, their notation was also very uniform, so that all links looked the same. In addition, the infamous IS-A link (see Woods [1975] and Cercone [1975]) was used to indicate type–token relations as well as subset relations, and many other relations were not motivated or explained—the English mnemonics are all that we have to indicate their semantics. Relatively little attention was given to the structure at the foundational, logical adequacy level, so that the inheritance relations between concepts were not always clear.

On the other hand, the Rumelhart and Norman group made an effort to account for procedural-type information directly in their notation (using a link called IS-WHEN), and integrated case-type information with other

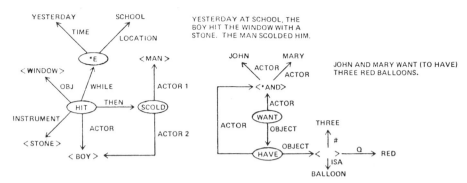

Fig. 7. Some Rumelhart *et al.* concepts. From Rumelhart *et al.* [1972].

"world knowledge." They included definitional as well as instantiated (propositional) constructs, and, all in all, they captured many good ideas in their nets.

Another important piece of work that deserves at least brief mention here is Schank's "conceptual dependency" representation [1972, 1973a,b; Schank *et al.*, 1973]. While Schank himself does not seem to believe in semantic memory [1974, 1975], his *conceptualizations* very much resemble concepts in systems like Simmons' and Rumelhart and Norman's, as evidenced in Fig. 8 [Schank, 1973b, p. 201]. A conceptualization consists of a *primitive act* and some associated cases, like "instrument" and "direction." In conceptual dependency diagrams, arrows with different shapes and labels indicate the case relations. For example, in Fig. 8 the R relation (a three-pronged arrow) indicates the recipient case, while the I relation indicates the instrument of the conceptualization (one interesting idea that is illustrated here is that the instrument of an action is itself a conceptualization). Each primitive act (e.g., TRANS, INGEST) has a particular case structure associated with it, and the higher-level verbs that one sees in the other notations must be broken down into canonical structures of primitives here. Thus, not only does Schank specify a set of primitive relations, he suggests a set of *knowledge primitives* out of which concepts

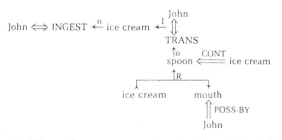

Fig. 8. A Conceptual Dependency conceptualization. From Schank [1973b]. Copyright 1973 by W. H. Freeman and Company.

should be built (this is in contrast to what we shall later refer to as *episte-mological primitives*, operations for structuring pieces of the represen-tation). Schank's contribution to the study of knowledge representation, while controversial, is an important one. His cases are "deeper" than those of Simmons, and begin to attack knowledge structure at the primi-tive level. Conceptual dependency was incorporated as the memory struc-ture of the MARGIE system, which was a natural language understanding system that could parse an input sentence into the deep conceptual struc-ture and rephrase it in a number of different ways. Schank and Rieger [1974] developed some important inferential properties for their memory structures, and their work has had a great influence on much of the later work in the field. The reader should consult Wilks [1974] and Cercone [1975] for two excellent expositions of Schank's work.

In more recent work, Rieger has attempted to deal in greater depth with the relations between actions and states [1975, 1976, 1977; Rieger and Grinberg, 1977]. Commonsense Algorithms (CSAs) capture information of a much more dynamic sort than that handled by the traditional, static concept networks. Rieger has nodes that represent not only primitive ac-tions, but states, statechanges, wants, and "tendencies" (a tendency in CSA representation is a kind of action that takes place without the effort of an intentional force; one such tendency, for example, is gravity). There is a small repertoire of primitive link types, which are used to represent the underlying dynamic relationships between the actions, states, etc. ("ten theoretical forms of inter-event causal interaction" [Rieger and Grinberg, 1977, p. 250]). CSA links stand for relations like causality, enablement, concurrency, and the like, with the primary emphasis on expressing the cause and effect relationships that make physical systems work. While the notion that causality can be captured in a single link is debatable, CSAs may provide a useful way to express dynamic information that in other systems is supposedly captured by unstructured relational links, and may do so in a complete enough way to allow the simulation of certain physical mechanisms, like the reverse-trap flush toilet [Rieger, 1975] and the rea-sonably complex home gas forced-air furnace [Rieger and Grinberg, 1977].

Two other important treatments of memory with verb-centered caselike systems surfaced in the early 1970s. Heidorn's thesis [1972] parlayed a simple hierarchical network and instantiation mechanism into a system (called NLPQ) which could "understand" a queuing problem described to it in English. From this description, NLPQ could produce both an English restatement of the problem and a complete program (written in GPSS) for simulating the situation described. By including in advance some simple case frame definitions of actions relevant to queuing situations (for ex-ample, "unload" takes an agent, a goal, a location, and a duration), Hei-dorn provided his system with a built-in definitional context for the description of a particular situation. During an initial conversation with the user, the NLPQ system would build an "internal problem description (IPD)." This IPD comprised a set of instances connected appropriately to the general definitions (see Fig. 9 [Heidorn, 1974, p. 95]). NLPQ could consult those definitions and tell when the problem description was incomplete; it could thus intelligently ask the user for missing information. Although Heidorn's network was very simple and uniform (it was not very deep, concepts had very simple structure, and the SUP link was used for both subconcepts and instances), he achieved a rather dazzling effect by incorporating it in a general grammar-rule language and by starting with a set of concepts well-matched to the simulation language in which the output was produced.

The other "case" study produced a strongly psychologically oriented memory structure called HAM (for Human Associative Memory) [Anderson and Bower, 1973, 1974]. The elements of HAM were *propositions*, binary trees that represented the underlying structure of sentences. A simple proposition of this sort is depicted in Fig. 10 [Anderson and Bower, 1973, p. 165]. Relations allowed between nodes in the trees included set membership (the E links in Fig. 10) and subset, some cases like subject (S in Fig. 10), object (O), location (L), and time (T), and some logical indicators like predicate (P), context (C), and fact (F)—all represented uniformly. Propositions in HAM had truth values, and were supposed to convey assertions about the world; Anderson and Bower's notation failed to account for the internal structure of nominal entities. There were many problems with this simple notation, some of which are discussed in Schubert [1976], a work whose detail on the logical structure of semantic networks in terms of predicates and propositions makes it clear that HAM's propositional notation is insufficient. However, Anderson and Bower produced an extensive investigation into the state of the relevant philosophical and scientific work at the time of their own work, and their detailed psychological discussions should be consulted. Although their model is admitted to be inadequate and the semantics of their representation is not thoroughly worked out, their book is a milestone of start-to-finish research in a field often plagued by less than thorough work.

1.3. Concern for the Foundations

Unfortunately, most of the early work covered above suffers from a lack of explicit acknowledgement of some fundamental principles of knowledge representation design. Authors are most often intuitive when describing the semantics of their representations,* and as the network no-

---

* For example, "Intuitively, the nodes in the tree represent *ideas* and the links *relations* or *associations* between the ideas" [Anderson and Bower, 1973, p. 139]; "In this system a large part of the information is about the words and concepts of the relevant domain of discourse . . . ." [Heidorn, 1972, p. 35].

18

Ronald J. Brachman

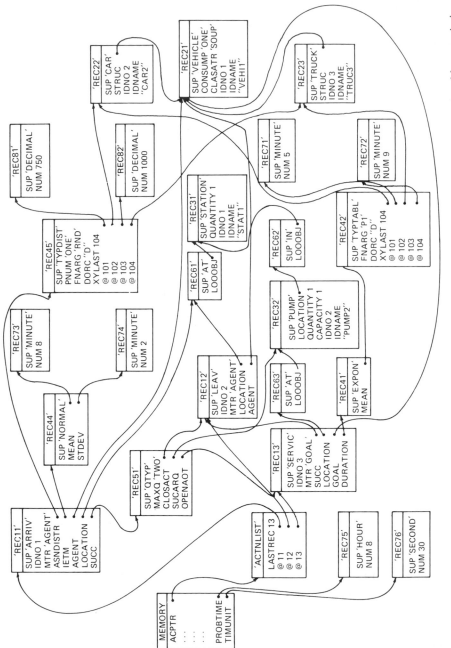

Fig. 9. Heidorn's IPD. From Heidorn [1974]. Copyright 1974. Association for Computing Machinery, Inc., reprinted by permission.

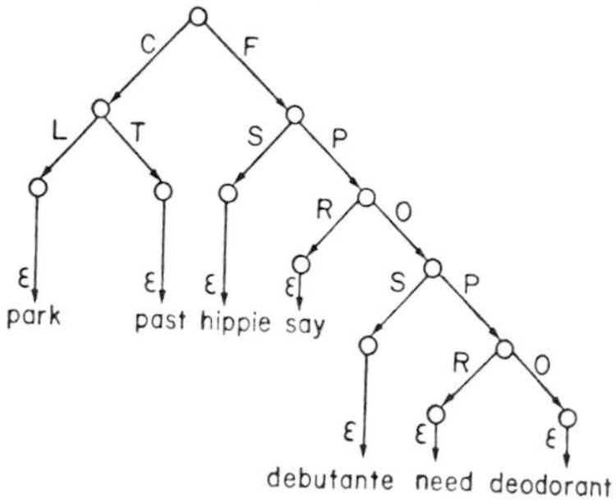

Fig. 10. A HAM proposition. From Anderson and Bower [1974]. Copyright 1974 by V. H. Winston and Sons, Inc., Washington, D. C. Used with permission of Hemisphere Publ. Co., and J. R. Anderson.

tations get more complex, more and more of the assumptions are left to the reader's imagination. Most of the early representations were not extensible in a general way (i.e., the system designer must intervene to add new case relations), and in general, the combination of set operations and descriptive concept operations that the semantic net is based upon has been poorly understood (see Brachman [1978b], especially Chapter 4, for details). All of the notations mentioned so far are seductively uniform— conceptual relations (e.g., agent, color, left-of) and underlying knowledge mechanisms (e.g., superset, "iswhen," member) are expressed in indistinguishable terms. In Section 2, I shall contend that this homogeneity is misguided and confusing.

However, in addition to that described in Section 3, some recent efforts have set out to remedy this inadequacy. Among the more important of the earlier and concurrent projects that attempted to deal with the expressive inadequacy of semantic nets are the work of Cercone and Schubert at the University of Alberta, and the work of Levesque and Mylopoulos at the University of Toronto, to which we turn in a moment. Several years earlier, however, Shapiro [1971a,b] introduced the important distinction between the "*item*," or conceptual level of network, and the "*system*" level—the structural level of interconnection that ties structured assertions of facts to items participating in those facts (i.e., indicates bindings). System relations are the labeled links in the network, and their semantics is determined by the set of processing routines that operate on them. Item relations are concepts that happen to be relational in nature, and are represented by nodes (items) just as are other, nonrelational concepts. Thus, a relationship like LOVES would appear not as a link in the net, but as a node. Particular assertions of the relationship would also be nodes, with AGENT and OBJECT system links to nodes for the participants, and a VERB link back to the node for LOVES (see Fig. 11 [Shapiro, 1971a, p. 43]. In Fig. 11, the top three nodes are assertions of particular LOVES relationships). Shapiro makes no suggestion as to how the general verb itself should be defined in network terms (that is, what makes a concept LOVES as opposed to any other verb with a similar case frame).

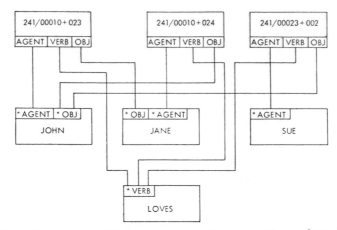

Fig. 11. Separating system relations from item relations. From Shapiro [1971a]. Used with permission of the author.

Shapiro's distinction explicitly separates underlying primitive cases from all other (conceptual) relations. He also explains how rules for deduction can be encoded directly in his formalism, and discusses at length a language for doing retrieval from his network structure. His early work gives us no guidelines for what the set of system relations should be (his examples suggest linguistic cases), nor does he talk about the semantics of items, except to imply through his search mechanism that sets are important. Shapiro's claim is only that what he has given us is an epistemologically neutral structure, a general language on top of which many models of knowledge might be constructed. This in itself, however, represents a significant advance over previous networks in the distillation of two very different levels of representation.

Between the time of Shapiro's thesis [1971a] and the more recent work to which I have alluded, others have tried to resolve some of the inadequacies of the homogeneous standard evolved from Quillian's Semantic Memory. Hays [1973a,b], in his "cognitive networks," has attempted to differentiate some of the semantics of network notations, and to be more formal than earlier authors about network structures (he specifies four node types, including "modalities," and five major link types). Among other things, his work has contributed the distinction between a "manifestation" of an object and an "instance."*

Hendrix [1975a,b, 1976], in attempting to provide an adequate quantification mechanism for semantic network concepts, introduced what has become a very broadly utilized facility—*partitions,*† or formal

---

* Objects in Hays' epistemology are permanent. However, they do change over time (e.g., a person is at various times an infant, a child, an adolescent, an adult, etc.). Manifestations are different concepts of the same object at different places or stages of its existence.

† Scragg [1975] has, apparently independently, introduced a very similar mechanism, which he calls "planes."

groupings of concept nodes. Figure 12 [Hendrix, 1975a, p. 239] illustrates the use of partitions (indicated by rectangular dashed boxes) to represent "Every city has a dogcatcher who has been bitten by every dog in town." In this figure, the two larger "spaces" hold the scopes of the universal quantifiers: the "form" link points to a space representing the scope of the universally quantified variable, which is encoded by a node pointed to by a "for all v" link. The node labeled "p" is an implicitly existentially quantified node, representing the particular dogcatcher for any given town.

Partitioning has many potential uses; for example, it can be used to provide a context mechanism, whereby entire areas of memory may be opened up or sealed off at relevant times (this allows reasonable groupings of beliefs). It should be pointed out that the nodes in many of Hendrix's nets represent sets as well as "prototypes", and the introduction of case-like properties for concept nodes makes them susceptible to the same confusions as all of the older, uniform nets (this is evidenced by relations like "creature" and "assailant" being directly encoded as links in his nets). Apparently, however, different space-types are used to distinguish different uses of the same link, and the nonlogical links are not really primitive in the system—they are introduced by "delineations" associated with general verbal concepts like OWNINGS. This is not obvious in some of the earlier papers, but see Hendrix (this volume) for the supporting details.

Partitions have become a mainstay of many recent semantic nets and are an indisputably helpful mechanism for representing higher level phenomena like quantification, context, and structural "plots" [Grosz, 1977]. When viewed as a *mechanism*, with no epistemological claims about their expressive adequacy (which depend on each individual's use of them), partitions do not come under the jurisdiction of our criticisms in Section 2. When partitions implement mixed sets of relationships (like "creature"

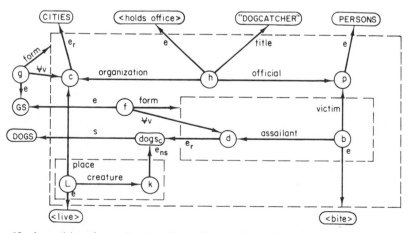

Fig. 12. A partitioned set of nodes. From Hendrix [1975a]. Used with permission of the author.

and subset), then they are open to the kind of complaint we shall lodge in that section. That is, each partition (space) type used in a system is open to its own epistemological constraints, just as is each use of the simple, general notion of a node.

In 1975, a very important paper by Woods appeared; this study of "what's in a link" for the first time seriously challenged the logical adequacy of previous semantic network notations [Woods, 1975]. Woods pointed out the *intensional* nature of many of the things we call upon nets to represent (see also Chapter 5 of Brachman [1978b]), and discussed in detail several important challenges for network notations that had not been previously acknowledged, let alone successfully met. We were asked to begin to consider the *semantics of the representation itself*, and to be held accountable for things previously brushed aside under the auspices of "intuition." The work to be described in Section 3 is, to some extent, a broader and deeper investigation in the same spirit as the Woods paper, a continuation of the semantic investigative work only begun there. It is hoped that many of Woods' challenges have been overcome by the structures illustrated in that section and in [Brachman, 1978b].

Some of the issues raised by Woods—the more logically oriented ones— have been recently treated in a series of papers by Cercone and Schubert [1978], Cercone [1975], and Schubert [1976]. In their attempts to extend the expressive power of network notation, Schubert and Cercone have expended considerable effort in the investigation of the underlying logical content of the node-plus-link formalism. Many of the issues of knowledge representation that were emphasized in my thesis [Brachman, 1978b] were raised in various papers from Alberta; in particular, an excellent criticism of the naive notion of the existence of a small number of "conceptually primitive relations" (i.e., cases) reflects a similar intuition about roles (see Section 5.1.3.1 of Brachman [1978b], Schubert [1976, pp. 168–170], and Cercone [1975, pp. 79–80]).

The notation developed by Schubert and Cercone is *propositional*—an important basic node type in the network is the predicative concept node, which is instantiated by conjoining at a *proposition node* a pointer to the predicate and a pointer to each argument of the predicate (see Fig. 13 [Cercone, 1975, p. 36]). The links used are all predefined system links, used only to point out the particular predicate invoked and to order the arguments. All of the conceptual work is done by the particular predicates pointed to with PRED links from the proposition nodes. Schubert and Cercone claim also to have concept nodes for *individuals* and *sets*, although it is not clear from the notation where these interpretations are expected. Given the propositional nature of the notation, a series of logical connectives and quantification conventions can be unambiguously (and explicitly) represented. In addition, Schubert and Cercone provide facilities for lambda-abstraction and various other intensional operations, and include time primitives for certain types of predicates. Schubert [1976] discusses

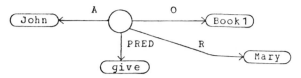

Fig. 13. A proposition node. From Cercone [1975]. Used with permission of the author.

the clear correspondence of his notation to predicate calculus, providing for the first time a clear standard of reference for network (logical) adequacy.*

While the work of Cercone and Schubert begins to answer some of the questions raised in Woods' paper, theirs is still only a neutral logical language. This notation, as all others discussed so far, offers no guidelines to its users on how to structure concepts in terms of the primitives of the notation. The language is as general, uniform, and low-level as predicate calculus and it is up to the designer of the particular network how to structure his world in terms of predicates and propositions. While Schubert's notation unambiguously accounts for many of the underlying logical operations of the semantic network, something more seems to be needed for it to be a truly useful representation of knowledge. This seems to involve looking at network structures at a slightly "higher" level.

Some hints on higher level primitives have been afforded us by some more recent efforts in network formalisms. Fahlman [1977] has designed a network system comprising two major parts: a parallel memory scheme, which allows propagation of markers through a network composed of special-purpose hardware, and a language (called NETL) for representing knowledge on top of the parallel memory. There are several important things to note about Fahlman's work. His is perhaps the first attempt to account for network-implementing hardware in its own right. The marker propagation and detection mechanism eliminates much of the costly search intrinsic to previous, nonparallel systems. Further, he introduces the idea of a "virtual copy" as a dominant organizing concept. This is a convenient way to think about inheritance in semantic nets, since it lets us assume that all properties at a parent node are (virtually) available at its subnodes. When a real copy is needed, as, for instance, when a property is to be explicitly modified, Fahlman has us create a MAP-node. The parallel-processing scheme makes virtual copy and map links act as short circuits in the appropriate circumstances, thereby allowing any inherited definitions to be immediately available.

Further, Fahlman introduces the "role" as a type of individual, whose universe of existence is another concept. While he at times, I believe, confuses the notion of a functional role (like AGENT) with that of a role *filler* (like PERSON), he seems to be on the right track in terms of the structure

* See also Simmons and Bruce [1971] for an earlier discussion of the correspondence between semantic nets and predicate calculus.

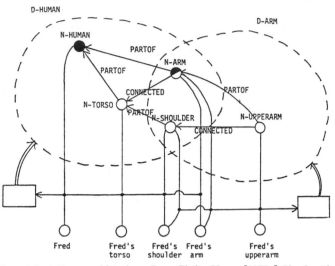

Fig. 14. Hayes' depictions and binders. From Philip Hayes [1977a]. Used with permission of the author.

of concepts. In my own work (see Section 3 here), I have found this role notion to be critical, and have what amount to MAP-nodes also. A good deal of Fahlman's foundations could be used to support other network schemes.

Role-nodes as parts of structured descriptions also constitute a critical element in the work of Philip Hayes [1977a,b]. Hayes' networks have two levels of structure, just as those to be presented in Section 3 have: the internal structure of "depictions" (concepts), and relationships between depictions as wholes. Briefly, a depiction expresses the structure of an entity through a set of PART-OF and CONNECTED relationships between other entities that make up its parts. For example, in Fig. 14 [Philip Hayes, 1977a, p. 93], the depiction D-HUMAN (indicated by dashed lines) partially expresses the structure of a human (represented by the node N-HUMAN) in terms of an ARM and a TORSO. In the depiction D-HUMAN, N-ARM acts as a depic*ter*; at the same time, in D-ARM, N-ARM is the depic*tee*—the subject of the depiction.* Thus, while it is a thing unto itself in one structure, it acts as the specifier of a role to be filled in another. In some cases, Hayes contends (and I concur), the role can only exist within the larger context. For example, an arm cannot exist without implying the existence of some human; in that case, N-ARM would be an SQNODE for D-HUMAN, and the dependency would be expressed in an SQN structure (for *sine qua non*) involving D-ARM and D-HUMAN.

---

* While N-ARM is the same node in both depictions, links to it are only "visible" from the depiction from which it is viewed. That way various uses of ARM from more than one context can be kept distinct.

While Hayes does not distinguish the role itself from the role filler (see Section 3), and CONNECTED is much too simplistic to capture relations between roles, the very fact that Hayes has roles at all is significant. Concept structure involving roles is strictly enforced in instantiation, using a structure called a "binder." In Fig. 14, there are two binders (indicated by the rectangular boxes, the arrows coming in to them, and the dots at intersections), representing Fred and Fred's arm. The binder captures the fact that roles are inherited *as part of a structure.* There are explicit connections between role definitions (in the depictions) and role filler/instance pairs (in the binders), just as I propose in Section 3 (although the exact nature of the relationships is not spelled out in Hayes' structure). The explicit acknowledgement of these relationships is a very important development in the history of semantic networks.

Finally, a joint concern for higher-level (nonlogical) structures and their semantics in a semantic network formalism has surfaced in the work of Levesque and Mylopoulos at Toronto [in this volume; Levesque, 1977]. Their efforts attempt to provide a procedural semantics for the relations in a network by associating with a class (concept) a set of four operations: *add* an instance, *remove* an instance, *fetch* all instances of the class, and *test* for being an instance of the class. Classes are given internal structure with slots; parts fill these slots, generating a "PART-OF hierarchy." The classes themselves are organized in an "IS-A hierarchy," which expresses generalization relationships between classes and subclasses.

In addition to these two hierarchies, the system of Levesque and Mylopoulos also has an "instance hierarchy." Every class is itself an instance of the class CLASS, which is termed a "metaclass." Adding this distinction allows a precise account of inheritance and of relations often mistaken in more uniform schemes—including the descriptions of the programs themselves. Levesque and Mylopoulos also provide (in this volume) nice accounts of the distinctions between *structural* and *assertional* properties and between property *attributes* and property *values,* and account with their procedures for the interdependencies between pieces of a structure. As such, their account would provide a good set of tools for exploring the semantics of the representation to be presented in Section 3. The only major shortcoming is the lack of an explicit representation of the relationships between the parts of a class, since their dependencies are only implicitly accounted for in the four programs associated with a class definition.

2. "ONE MAN'S CEILING IS ANOTHER MAN'S FLOOR"*

Given this rich and interesting history, what, can we conclude, is a "semantic net"? About the only thing in common among all of the above-

---

* Copyright 1973, Paul Simon. Used by Permission. "One Man's Ceiling Is Another Man's Floor" provided courtesy of CBS Records.

discussed formalisms is their connectivity—the fact that they all claim to be made of links and nodes. But these two kinds of entity are really just descriptive of implementations—they have nothing to say about the epistemological import of these networks. While Hendrix states, "Broadly speaking, any representation interlinking nodes with arcs could be called a semantic network . . ." [Hendrix, 1977, p. 984], I believe that there is something amiss in this interpretation. Hendrix's definition is indistinguishable from that of a *graph*—and there is nothing inherently "semantic" about a graph.

The "semanticness" of semantic nets lies in their being used in attempts to represent the semantics of English words. Besides nodes and links, the common thread that has held together the many efforts described in Section 1 is the fact that most of the networks were to be used in understanding natural language. Semantic nets have become a popular meaning representation for use in natural language understanding systems.

Despite the fact that virtually all semantic networks have been used to represent the "concepts" corresponding to words and sentences, there has been very little agreement on how to factor such knowledge. The most important disagreement—as evidenced by the fact that we find no two sets of links the same in the literature—has to do with the structural decomposition of a concept. While only the most recent work [Brachman, 1978a,b; Levesque and Mylopoulos, in this volume; Smith, 1978] has dealt with concept-structuring *per se*, every network implicitly embodies a theory of the primitive elements that make up a concept. Structural links holding together the arguments of a logical predicate, "deep semantic cases," and even conceptual relations that are supposed to exist between objects in the world have all been proposed as semantic network links.

Consider the following statements:

(1) The distinction between these alternatives *appears* to be a significant one since logical forms are clearly formal *languages* within which meanings of surface strings are represented, whereas the latter are *labelled graphs* which somehow represent these same meanings. This distinction quickly evaporates, however, the moment one observes that a network is basically a particular choice of representation (at the *implementation* level) for some (*conceptual* level) logical form. [Nash-Webber and Reiter, 1977, p. 121]

(2) If someone argues for the superiority of semantic networks over logic, he must be referring to some other property of the former than their meaning . . . [Pat Hayes, 1977, p. 561]

(3) A semantic network purports to represent concepts expressed by natural-language words and phrases as nodes connected to other such concepts by a particular set of arcs called semantic relations. Primitive concepts in this system of semantic networks are word-sense meanings. Primitive semantic relations are those that the verb

of a sentence has with its subject, object, and prepositional phrase arguments in addition to those that underlie common lexical, classificational and modificational relations. [Simmons, 1973, p. 63]

How are we to rationalize such disparate views of what has always seemed to be a single formalism?

2.1. Will the Real Semantic Network Please Stand Up?

The key issue here is the isolation of the *primitives* for semantic network languages. The primitives of a network language are those things that the interpreter is programmed in advance to understand, and that are not usually represented in the network language itself. While there is, of course, no one set of primitives that is *the* set, for any single language there should be one fixed group of primitive elements. Only with a fixed set of primitives can a fixed interpreter be constructed.* It would be difficult to justify an interpreter in which the set of primitives changed meaning, or for which it was expected that new primitives were to be added in the course of interpretation.

The view I shall take here is that the history of semantic nets and their utility as a representational device can best be understood by carefully examining the nature of the primitives that have been proposed. Since the semantics of any given language is dependent on the interpretation of the primitive elements and a set of rules for combining them into nonprimitive elements, the "well-definedness" of a network language rests heavily on the set of node and link types that it provides. While it is difficult to make simple, clear-cut comparisons of primitives from one language to the next, it is possible to distill a small number of distinctive types of nodes and links from the formalisms discussed in Section 1. Each of these types can be considered to form a consistent conceptual "level"; I shall therefore propose a set of levels, or viewpoints, with which to understand the range of semantic network primitives that have been used in the past. Each of the levels will have a set of link types whose import is clearly distinct from those of other levels.

Any network notation could be analyzed in terms of any of the levels, since they do not really have any absolute, independent "existence." For example, a particular concept might be structured with semantic cases. These cases can be understood as sets of logical predicates, which in turn are implemented with some set of atoms and pointers. However, each network scheme does propose an *explicit* set of primitives as part of the language, and this is the set that is actually supported by the language's in-

---

* It is probably also desirable to have this set as small as possible. However, at the current stage, we shall settle for any set that is adequate. One of the purposes of this chapter (see Section 3) is to begin to circumscribe what would be an adequate set of primitives, and therefore, an adequate interpreter.

terpreter. The particular sets of primitives that are proposed in particular languages are the ones of interest to us here. Understanding past problems with semantic nets and what one is getting when one uses a particular semantic net scheme are both facilitated by looking closely at these explicit primitive sets.* As we shall see, one set of difficulties has arisen because most network notations freely intermix primitives of different types.

The diverse opinions on the primitives of semantic networks expressed both explicitly in the literature and implicitly in the style of existing networks indicate that there are at least four main levels of primitive to be considered. The first view, expressed by the quote from Nash-Webber and Reiter above, considers a semantic network to be an implementational mechanism for a higher-level logical language. This view we might call the *implementational* form of semantic nets. In implementation level networks, links are merely pointers, and nodes are simply destinations for links. These primitives make no important substantive claims about the structure of knowledge, since this level takes a network to be only a data structure out of which to build logical forms. While a useful data-organizing technique, this kind of network gives us no more hint about how to represent (factor) knowledge than do list structures.

A second view sees a semantic network as a set of logical primitives with a structured index over those primitives. In this type of *logical* level net, nodes represent predicates and propositions. Links represent logical relationships, like AND, SUBSET, and THERE-EXISTS. The above quote from Pat Hayes expresses a viewpoint that is essentially the same as those implicitly expressed in networks by Schubert and Hendrix, to some extent Shapiro, and to a lesser extent Woods. In this point of view, logical adequacy, including quantificational apparatus, is taken to be the responsibility of semantic network representations of knowledge. The aforementioned efforts express a tacit dependence on predicate calculus for knowledge factoring and espouse network schemes as useful organizing principles over normally nonindexed predicate calculus statements. In doing so, they make at least some claim about how knowledge can be meaningfully factored. It is interesting to note that almost all of the "foundational" work on semantic networks has been done at this logical level of interpretation.

The most prevalent view of networks is reflected in Simmons' above statement and almost all of the work discussed in Section 1. This is, in some sense, the "real" semantic net—a network structure whose primi-

---

* The assignment of a notation to a particular level should not be taken as a value judgment (very few formalisms can, in fact, be assigned to a single level). Different level notations are useful for different tasks. Here it is asked only that one become aware of the level at which one stops decomposing concepts, and understands the meaning of one's primitives as potentially decomposed into "lower" level ones.

tives are word-senses and case relations. As Simmons notes, in these *conceptual* level nets, links represent semantic or conceptual relationships. Networks at this level can be characterized as having small sets of language-independent conceptual elements (namely, primitive object- and action-types) and conceptually primitive relationships (i.e., "deep cases") out of which all expressible concepts can be constructed. The strongest view at this level is that of Schank and followers, which picks a small set of act types (e.g., GRASP, INGEST, PTRANS) and cases (e.g., IN-STRUMENT, RECIPIENT) and claims that this set is adequate to represent the knowledge expressed in any natural language.* Weaker views are embodied in the Norman and Simmons nets, where it is difficult to tell if there are any truly primitive knowledge pieces. In these nets, the belief in cases, and the particular sets settled upon, seem to be the unchanging elemental units.

Finally, going one step higher, we might consider networks whose primitive elements are language-specific. The only formalism that I know of at the current time that embodies this view is OWL, whose elements are expressions based on English.† In such a formalism, one would presumably "take seriously the Whorfian hypothesis that a person's language plays a key role in determining his model of the world and thus in structuring his thought" [Martin, 1977, p. 985]. In OWL there is a basic concept-structuring scheme (see Hawkinson [1975]) that is used to build expressions, and strictly speaking, the principles of "specialization," "attachment," and "reference" are the primitives of the language. However, these primitives are neutral enough to be considered implementational, and thus the knowledge itself can be considered to form the structure of the data base. This seems operationally reasonable when OWL is looked at in detail—the two expressions (HYDRANT FIRE) and (MAN FIRE), while both specialized by FIRE, can have the specializations "mean" different things based on the rest of the network structure. This *linguistic* level represents perhaps the most radical view of semantic nets, in that the "primitives" are language-dependent, and are expected to change in meaning as the network grows. Links in linguistic level networks stand for arbitrary relationships that exist in the world being represented.

It should be obvious that each of the above viewpoints implies a set of primitive relationships substantially different from the others. Relationships between predicates and propositions (e.g., AND, ARGUMENT1, PRED) are distinctly different than those between verbs and associated "cases" (e.g., AGENT, INSTRUMENT, RECIPIENT). Both of these are not

* In general, a characteristic of this level is that it should be language-independent.
† "We have taken English as the basis for our knowledge representation formalism" [Szolovits *et al.*, 1977, p. 2]. Not surprisingly, the view of the OWL group is that their "Linguistic Memory System" is a semantic network: "The most novel aspects of OWL are the structure of the semantic net (Hawkinson, 1975) . . ." [Martin, 1977, p. 985]

the same as arbitrary relationships between things in the world (i.e., relations between the entities that the concepts are supposed to denote, e.g., COLOR, HIT). And further, none of these is the same as the relations between the parts of an intensional description, to which we now turn.

2.2. The Missing Level

While this characterization of the levels of semantic network representations covers virtually all of the work that has been done, there appears to be at least one level missing from the analysis. That this is the case is suggested by some of the more recent phenomena appearing in network languages, including "partitions," "delineations" [Hendrix, 1975a,b, 1976], and "binders" [Philip Hayes, 1977a,b].* These features suggest the possibility of organizations of conceptual knowledge into units more structured than simple nodes and links or predicates and propositions, and the possibility of processing over larger units than single network links. The predominant use of concepts as intensional descriptions of objects in a world also hints that there is a class of relationship that is not accounted for by the four levels already discussed. This kind of relationship relates the parts of an intension [Carnap, 1947] to the intension as a whole, and one intension to another. Intensional descriptions can be related directly by virtue of their internal structures, or indirectly by virtue of their corresponding extensions.† In addition, even the single most common trait of semantic networks—"inheritance"—suggests a level of knowledge structure between the logical and conceptual ones described above. Inheritance of properties is not a logical primitive; on the other hand, it is a mechanism assumed by almost all conceptual level nets, but not accounted for as a "semantic" (deep case) relation.

There must be some intermediate level at which a precise formal account of such notions can be constructed. The very attempt to give conceptual units more structure than that of uniform configurations of links hints that at least some network designers have been thinking about "concepts" as formal objects, with predetermined internal organization that is more sophisticated than sets of cases. The formal structure of conceptual units and their interrelationships *as conceptual units* (independent of any knowledge expressed therein) forms what could be called an *epistemology*. I shall propose, then, an intermediate level of network primitive that embodies this formal structuring. This will be called the *epistemological* level, and it lies between the logical and conceptual levels.

The epistemological level of semantic network permits the formal def-

---

* Nonnetwork languages, like KRL [Bobrow and Winograd, 1977], have similar types of mechanisms playing a more and more prominent part.

† KRL has also focused intensively on the issue of description—most notably, what constitutes a description, and how descriptions in the above sense are inherently partial.

inition of knowledge-*structuring* primitives, rather than particular knowledge primitives (as in the Schank networks). Note that networks at the next higher level (conceptual) take as their primitives pieces of semantic knowledge and cases, but with no explicit accounting for their internal structure. While there is no universal agreement on what cases there are, everyone agrees that there are probably at least *some* cases, and they all seem to have a feel for what a case is. The basis for this agreement on the concept of case (or "slot") and the inheritance of cases in a network is provided by the epistemological level, which explains the meaning of cases in general and provides a defining mechanism for particular ones.

In Section 3, I shall touch on some of the other operations that nets built out of explicit epistemological primitives should account for. In that section, I shall also introduce a formalism expressly based on those notions. Briefly, relations at the epistemological level include those used to structure intensional descriptions and those used to interrelate them. The former involves piecing together aspects of a description, including descriptions of the conceptual subpieces of an object and how they intertwine. One such type of conceptual subpiece is a case, the meaning of which is taken to be something built out of epistemological primitives. The latter type of relation specifies inheritance of subdescriptions between descriptions.

Table I summarizes our discussion of the five levels. The examples listed with the levels are suggestive of the philosophy of those levels; none is really a "pure" example of a single primitive type. Although a desirable goal (as we shall see below), it is not clear that a pure network at any level is attainable. Our task here, then, is to understand as well as possible each

TABLE I

Levels of "Semantic" Networks

Level	Primitives	Examples (nonexclusive)
Implementational	Atoms, pointers	Data structures
Logical	Propositions, predicates, logical operators	[Schubert, 1976] [Cercone, 1975] [Hendrix, 1975a,b]
Epistemological	Concept types, conceptual subpieces, inheritance and structuring relations	[Brachman, 1978a,b]
Conceptual	Semantic or conceptual relations (cases), primitive objects and actions	[Schank, 1972] [Simmons, 1973] [Norman *et al.*, 1975]
Linguistic	Arbitrary concepts, words, expressions	[Szolovits *et al.*, 1977]

type of primitive so that the semantics of any formalism can be clearly and completely specified, even if it mixes elements of more than one level.

2.3. Neutrality, Adequacy, and Semantics

Despite the fact that we have isolated five distinct types of semantic net, there are some universal notions that can be applied equally well to each type of network. These are *neutrality, adequacy,* and *semantics.* Each of these can be used as a criterion for judging the utility and formality of a given network language. It is desirable that a formalism be as pure as possible, adequate to handle its appointed representation task, and have a clean, explicitly specified semantics.

A network implemented at some level should be *neutral* toward the level above it. For example, logical nets are "epistemologically neutral," in that they do not force any choice of epistemological primitives on the language user. Making "concepts" in logical nets, then, is a mixing of levels. Conceptual level nets must support many different linguistic systems and should be linguistically neutral (as Schank puts it, "the principal problem that we shall address here is the representation of meaning in an unambiguous language-free manner" [1973b, p. 187]). By the same token, of course, epistemological formalisms must be neutral in regard to particular semantic relationships. It is the job of the epistemological formalism to provide case-defining facilities—not particular cases.

A formalism at any of the four lower levels that is neutral toward the one above is a useful tool for designers of those at higher levels. Epistemological neutrality, for example, ensures flexibility in the design and definition of particular cases or nonstandard types of inheritance. It should be clear, then, that one of the main problems with many of the older formalisms was their lack of a clear notion of what level they were designed for. Almost universally, semantic networks have mixed primitives from more than one level (for example, particular cases were links in the same systems in which set membership was a link). In terms of neutrality, these formalisms were all less flexible than they could have been in serving knowledge base designers who were building structures on top of them. Decisions were forced at more than one level at a time; the simultaneous freedom on some issues and lack of flexibility on others (at the same level) has been a constant source of confusion for network language users throughout the history of semantic nets.

Any level network can also be judged on its *adequacy* for supporting the level above it. If a semantic net can somehow support all possible linguistic systems of knowledge, then it has achieved conceptual adequacy. While the particular features of conceptual adequacy are open to debate, the notion of adequacy for the logical level is well understood (see Shubert [1976], for example). At the current time, it is less clear

what it would take for a network representation language to be epistemologically adequate. This is a subject (as, for example, treated in Brachman [1978b]) that is ripe for study, and to which I would like to draw the
reader's attention. Treatments of criteria for epistemological adequacy
have heretofore been missing from network studies. Yet it seems that
the understanding of knowledge representation languages in general will
depend intimately on an understanding of what the elements of epistemological adequacy are, and how well given languages handle them. We
shall look at some aspects of this in the next section.

Thinking in terms of adequacy gives us another reason why previous
semantic networks have been difficult to assess. Given networks that
mixed levels of primitives, it was impossible to tell what exactly the networks were adequate for. The recent push toward completely logical networks was in part motivated by the desire to achieve for the first time a
network that was demonstrably adequate in a well-understood way.

Finally, each type of network language must be held accountable for its
semantics—what, formally, do each of its elements mean, and what are the
legal operations on them?* In this respect, the attempts to define logically
adequate nets (Schubert, Cercone, Hendrix, etc.) have a clear advantage
over all of the others: once a mapping to predicate calculus is established,
a formal semantics (i.e., Tarskian truth-theoretic) is available, essentially
for free. This requirement, on the other hand, makes a formal semantics
for linguistic level nets almost impossible to achieve, since it would require a formal semantics to be defined for the particular natural language
involved. For conceptual level nets, only Schank and Rieger [1974] have
provided a well-defined semantics, in that they have, in advance, specified sets of "inferences" for each of their predetermined primitive acts.
Thus an act is defined in terms of its inferences, and there are rules for
combining inferences into interpretations of larger, nonprimitive structures, based only on the primitives out of which they are built. Other conceptual level nets do not have fixed primitives, thereby making it difficult
to provide an acceptable semantics.

Formal semantics for epistemological level languages are currently
under study; studies of such semantics must however be done in parallel

---

* The reader should be warned here that I am using the term "semantics" in its currently
popular AI sense, wherein the meaning of a primitive is provided by the programs that
operate on it. While the notion of links being meaningful by virtue of the programs that use
them seems intuitively clear and reasonably precise, there is a lot more to be said on the
issue. Semantics deals with the relationship between a symbol and what it denotes. Therefore not only should we take careful account of what here is a symbol (e.g., some marks on a
piece of paper, an arrow with a word next to it, a set of bits in a computer), but we must also
be precise about what these symbols denote (i.e., what are "epistemological relations" anyway?). Smith treats these problems in insightful depth in his Master's thesis [1978]. See also
Fodor [1978] for a recent critique of "procedural semantics."

with those attacking epistemological adequacy, since the nature of the epistemological primitives is not yet understood, which therefore makes it hard to define a semantics. Three particular studies are of note here:

(1)   In Brachman [1978b], I attempt to ferret out the meaning of a network language by making each basic relationship available as a link, and then explaining in detail the epistemological significance of each link.

(2)   The work of Levesque and Mylopoulos at Toronto [in this volume; Levesque, 1977] investigates a procedural semantics in a similar manner—except that the nature of the procedures themselves is being dealt with in a general, network-expressible way.

(3)   Smith [1978] is working on a comprehensive paradigm for knowledge representation languages in general, which includes a noncircular explanation for the interpreter of the procedures,* as well as accounts of "meta-description," structured inheritance, believing as an active process that denotes, etc.

3.   AN EPISTEMOLOGICALLY EXPLICIT REPRESENTATION

In this final section, I hope to illustrate what a network formalism at the epistemological level of knowledge representation should be concerned with. Such a formalism should have a clean, well-understood semantics, should not depend in any way upon the domain to which it is applied, and should adequately handle the significant epistemological relationships of concept structuring, attribute/value inheritance, multiple description, etc.

In order to make the ideas more concrete, I shall discuss epistemological primitives in terms of a particular type of formalism called *Structured Inheritance Networks* (SI-Nets) [Brachman, 1978a,b]. SI-Nets were developed expressly to address the above cited epistemological issues and to provide a useful explanatory tool for semantic level languages. SI-Nets constitute a class of network languages whose links represent epistemologically primitive relations. For the purposes of this discussion, we shall use a paradigmatic example of this class, called KLONE. While KLONE will be discussed only briefly here, details are available in Brachman [1978a,b].

The basic elements of KLONE (as they are in most semantic net schemes) are *Concepts*. Concepts are formal objects used to represent objects, attributes, and relationships of the domain being modeled. A Concept is thought of as representing an intensional object, and no Concepts

---

* The account of the procedures of Levesque and Mylopoulos is, of necessity, circular since the procedures are being defined in the same network for which they attempt to provide the semantics.

are used to represent directly extensional (world) objects. There are two main Concept types—generic and individual. Generic Concepts represent classes of individuals by describing the characteristics of a prototypical member of the class. Individual Concepts represent individual objects, relationships, etc. by *individuating* more general Concepts. Individuation is a relationship between Concepts. The term "instance" has been used in many network models to refer to an individuating description, as well as to the thing in the world that the individual description describes. Here, however, we shall use "instantiation" *only* as a relationship between a thing in the world and a Generic Concept, and not as a relationship between Concepts. Thus, the Arc de Triomphe (i.e., the one in Paris) is an "instance" of the Concept ARCH; the Individual Concept (call it ARC-DE-TRIOMPHE) that denotes the Arc de Triomphe "individuates" the Concept ARCH. The relationship between ARC-DE-TRIOMPHE and the real Arc is "denotation." See Fig. 15 for a schematic picture of this three-way relationship.

3.1. Internal Concept Structure

The key observation of SI-Nets is that objects in the world have complex relational structure—they cannot, in general, be usefully taken as atomic entities or mere lists of properties (see Brachman [1977, 1978b] for detailed justification). A Concept must therefore account for this internal structure as well as for the object as a wholistic entity. The KLONE formal entities that support this view of structured objects are *Role/Filler Descriptions* (Roles) and *Structural Descriptions* (SDs). Roles represent the conceptual subpieces of an entity, while SDs account for the structuring relationships between them.

The Roles represent the various kinds of attributes, parts, etc. that things in the world are considered to "have." These include, for example,

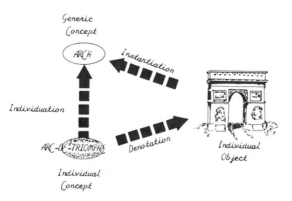

Fig. 15. A sketch of the individuates/instantiates dichotomy.

such things as parts (e.g., fingers of a hand), inherent attributes of objects and substances (e.g., color), arguments of functions (e.g., multiplier and multiplicand of a multiplication), and "cases" of verbs in sentences (e.g., "agent").* Any generalized attribute of this sort has two important pieces: (1) the particular entity that becomes the value for the attribute in an instance of the Concept, and (2) the functional role which that entity fills in the conceptual complex. A Role is a formal entity that captures both of these aspects in a structured way, by packaging up information about both the role filler and the functional role itself.

In KLONE, the substructure of a Role indicates the following: the type of entity that can fill the functional role, how many fillers of that role are to be expected, whether it is important in some way to have the role filled in an instance, and the name of the functional role itself. Notice, then, that the formal entity, Role, is somewhat more than a description of either the potential filler or the functional role alone. It is a very special type of epistemological entity that ties together the functional role, the context in which that role is played, and the (set of) filler(s) of the role. Figure 16 schematically illustrates the internal structure of a Role and its place in a Concept (Roles will henceforth be pictured as small squares, while Concepts will be depicted as ovals).

As just mentioned, while the "internal" Role structure indicates information about the particular fillers in themselves, the Role itself is the meeting place for information about how those fillers fit into the entire conceptual complex. It is the Concept's set of Structural Descriptions (SDs) that is the source of information about how role fillers interact with each other. Each SD is a set of relationships between two or more of the Roles. Just as a Role indicates that for any instance of the Concept there will be the appropriate number of fillers (with the corresponding characteristics) for the given functional role, an SD indicates that any instance of the Concept will exhibit the relationships specified in that SD. So, for example,

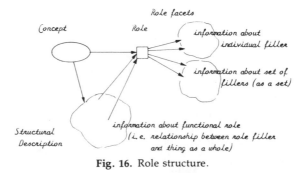

Fig. 16. Role structure.

---

* I have in the past [Brachman, 1978a,b] referred to the generalization of this kind of conceptual subpart as a "dattr." Here I shall use the term, "generalized attribute."

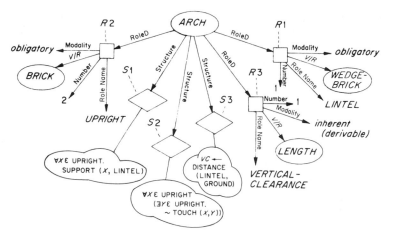

Fig. 17. A simple KLONE concept.

the Concept for a simple arch, which has three bricks as its parts, might be
factored as in Fig. 17 (SDs are indicated by diamonds).

In this figure, Role R1 expresses the fact that this kind of arch has one
LINTEL, which must be a WEDGE-BRICK. The *RoleD* link expresses the
relationship between the Concept ARCH and one of its Role descriptions;
the *V/R* (Value Restriction) link points to the type predicate that must be
true of the eventual role filler; the *Number* link indicates the restriction on
the number of fillers of the role; the *Modality* link indicates the importance
of the attribute to the Concept; and finally, the *RoleName* link names the
relationship (conceptual, not epistemological) between the filler and the
whole. R2 similarly indicates that any example of this type of object has
two UPRIGHTs, which are BRICKs. R3 defines the generalized attribute of
VERTICAL-CLEARANCE. The *Modality* INHERENT means that, while
every arch has one of these, knowing its value is not critical to the recognition of some object as an ARCH.* In addition, DERIVABLE means that the
value can be computed from the values of the other Roles, once they are
found. As for the SDs, S1 is a set of relationships that expresses how every
UPRIGHT supports the LINTEL, S2 specifies that no two UPRIGHTs touch
each other, and S3 embodies the definition of the VERTICAL-
CLEARANCE in terms of the LINTEL and an Individual Concept,
GROUND. We now turn briefly to the internal structure of these relational
parts of the Concept.

Let us say that we want to define the VERTICAL-CLEARANCE of an
ARCH to be the distance between its lintel and the ground. There will
thus be some Concept related to DISTANCE in one of the SDs of ARCH.

---

* There is a general problem here, of mixing recognition information with more neutral
descriptive information. This aspect of the representation is currently under scrutiny.

To determine the exact nature of this Concept, let us look at the way that we have expressed the relationship in English: first, the definite determiner for "ground" indicates that we mean a unique individual.* To reflect this, our network would have an Individual Concept, GROUND, which corresponded to that "constant." Further, there should be some individuator of the DISTANCE Concept with one of its Roles satisfied by GROUND. In Fig. 18, we illustrate this partial state of affairs—D1 is an individuator of DISTANCE (indicated by the *Individuates* link), and the fact that its TO Role (R1) is satisfied is captured by R2, whose *Satisfies* link indicates the appropriate Role, and whose *Value* link points to the filler. Now—back to our English description—we have still to account for "its lintel" and "the distance." By "its," we mean that for each arch, there is one lintel, and that is precisely what we meant by the Role R1 in Fig. 17. The "the" with "distance" then follows as saying that for each instance of ARCH, there is one unique distance involving the lintel of that arch. Thus, what we thought was an individuator of DISTANCE, is not quite—it has Role fillers tied down to lintels, but not to a single constant one.

The fact that the FROM Role of D1 is to be "filled" not by a constant, but by a type of existential, makes it a different sort of entity than R2. It is not quite a general Role, since it can only be filled by the lintel of a particular arch; nor is it a filled Role. Instead, it is an argument of a Concept that is parameterized by another Concept—D1, parameterized by ARCH. Once a particular arch is selected, the filler of the corresponding DISTANCE's FROM Role is fixed. We call this type of Concept a "Parametric Individ-

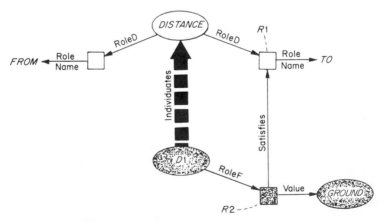

Fig. 18. Partially specified DISTANCE.

---

* To be precise, this use of "the" probably means "the ground under the arch." Let us assume that in this world all ground is at the same level and is, in fact, all one large individual entity, and therefore allow "the ground" to refer to that individual. Otherwise, the treatment of GROUND would be analogous to that of LINTEL.

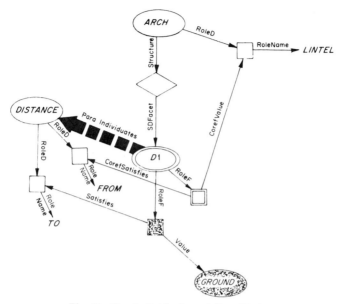

Fig. 19. ParaIndividuals and Coref Roles.

ual" (ParaIndividual), and express it as in Fig. 19. In this figure, the double oval represents the ParaIndividual, which is linked to DISTANCE by a *ParaIndividuates* link. The double square is a "Coref Role," which equates (as coreferential) the filler of the FROM role of the particular distance in some instance of ARCH with the filler of the LINTEL role for that same arch. *CorefValue* links the equated Roles, and *CorefSatisfies* performs an analogous task to that of *Satisfies* in an ordinary filled Role.

3.1.1. Epistemological Relations for Structuring Concepts

Our notions of Concept, Role, and SD give us the picture of structured conceptual objects schematically illustrated in Fig. 20. This structure implies that a knowledge representation language that is based on structured conceptual objects must account for at least the following relationships:

(1) the relationship between a Concept and one of its Roles,
(2) the relationship between a Concept and one of its SDs,
(3) the "internal" structure of a Role—the relationship between a Role and one of its facets,
(4) the "internal" structure of an SD,
(5) relationships between parts of SDs and Roles.

In SI-Nets, we account for these explicitly as link types, most of which were illustrated in the above figures. Thus, the primitives in this notation are epistemological (knowledge-structuring) relationships that compose

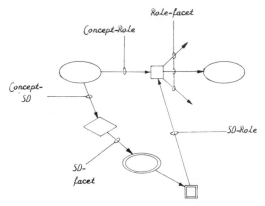

Fig. 20. Schematic Concept structure.

formal representational objects. It should be clear at this point that there is no sense to having links like COLOR and ASSAILANT in the same formalism with links for epistemological operations (nor links like AND and PRED, for that matter). The relationship between a Concept and a Role/Filler structure is *not* the same as that between the object that the Concept represents and the thing that fills the functional role for that object.

The semantics of each of these links is, of course, built into the interpreting functions that operate over the network structure. While I shall not detail that interpreter here (except briefly; see Section 3.4), it should be noted that with a small, predetermined set of link types, a fixed interpreter can, at least in principle, be designed. In languages that claim to have no primitives at all, the status of an interpreter is in question.*

3.2. Epistemological Primitives for Inheritance

One type of epistemological relation that we have so far glossed over is that which connects formal objects of the same type—Concept to Concept, Role to Role, and SD to SD. This type of link is a critical one in the SI-Net scheme, since it accounts for *inheritance*. For example, as mentioned, individuation is a relationship between Concepts, such that there is always some description (Concept) that is being individuated. That Concept is composed of various subdescriptions, all of which must be satisfied by the individuating Concept. Not only is there a relation between the two Concepts involved (i.e., *Individuates*), there is a set of subrelations between the generalized attribute descriptions (Roles) of the parent Concept and the values of those attributes in the individuator (i.e., the relation *Satisfies* expresses this in the above examples).

---

* See Smith [1978] for a philosophical account of the place and nature of interpreters in knowledge representation schemes.

The notion of inheritance is broader, however, than just the defining of an Individual Concept by a more general Generic Concept. "Subconcepts," themselves also Generic, can be formed from Generic Concepts by restricting some of the subparts of the description embodied by the Generic Concept. As we have seen in the history of semantic nets, the formation of more and more specific descriptions is an important common feature, and taxonomic hierarchies depend on this for the backbone of their structure. There has generally been a single link (e.g., IS-A) to specify inheritance along sub/superconcept chains, and the assumption has been that everything relevant to a general class (e.g., MAMMAL) is relevant to its more specific subclasses (e.g., DOG, CAT). Looking at this with our epistemological eye, however, we find this to be an oversimplification of a multifaceted relationship.

The Roles and SDs of a parent Concept each contribute to the inheritance of a subConcept. Thus the inheritance link is effectively a "cable" carrying down each of these to the inheritor; the Roles and SDs must be transmitted as a group, since they do not have an existence independent of the Concept of which they are parts. Just as Fahlman's "virtual copy" link implies that all parts of the structure are immediately available at a subconcept, we think of inheritance as a *structured* epistemological relationship between Concepts.

Further, properties are usually not all inherited intact, but instead are often modified so as to give the subConcept a more restricted definition than the parent Concept.* In that case, each of the modifications must be represented in an explicit and precise way. Figure 21 sketches the set of epistemological relations between a parent Concept and one of its descendants. For each Role and SD that is to be modified in some way, we must say precisely what type of modification applies, and what Role or SD the modification applies to. The latter is indicated by an inter-Role or inter-SD link stating the relationship between the original Role or SD and

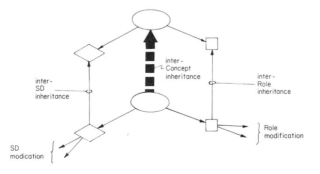

Fig. 21. Inter-Concept structured inheritance.

* In addition, further properties can be added to form more specialized Concepts, e.g., PRIME-NUMBER from NUMBER.

the new, modified one. The modification itself is then indicated just as if the modifying Role were a new Role description. KLONE currently allows three types of Role modification (satisfaction, or filling; differentiation, or the creation of subRoles; and restriction of the Role constraint). At the moment, only one type of SD modification (preempting) is provided. These relationships are explicitly indicated by appropriate links with unambiguous interpretations.

The reader should consult Brachman [1978a] for further details on KLONE. Here I have attempted only to illustrate the flavor of relationship for which it is necessary to account. More specifically, it is the job of an epistemological level formalism to provide internal Concept-, Role-, and SD-structuring relationships, and inheritance-specifying inter-Concept, inter-Role, and inter-SD relationships.

3.3. The "Conceptual Coat Rack"

In many of today's representation languages, there is a way for the knowledge base designer to go directly to the language in which the system is implemented (e.g., LISP) in order to express certain facts or associate certain procedures with network structures. Such "escape" mechanisms are used either when the knowledge to be expressed is too complex to be represented in the network itself, when knowledge about the network itself is to be encoded, or when certain procedures are to be triggered by operations on the data base. With the work of Smith [1978], the epistemological import of "procedural attachment" is now clear. There are, according to Smith, *two* different types of attachment that are most often confused under the guise of "procedural attachment": (1) "metadescription," wherein knowledge about knowledge is expressed in the same network language as the primary knowledge; and (2) interpretive intervention, in which direct instructions to the interpreter are expressed in the language that implements the interpreter itself.

In the case of metadescription, the interpreter is being asked to make a type or level jump when processing a Concept.* Metainformation is information about a Concept (or Role or SD) as a formal entity, and is not information about the thing(s) that the Concept describes. To support this kind of information, KLONE provides an explicit link to a node representing a separate sense of the Concept as a formal entity. This link is called a *"metahook,"* and it can attach to a Concept, a Role, or an SD. Metahooks always point to Individual Concepts, and those Individual Concepts express knowledge in the normal KLONE way—except that their "referents" are formal entities in the net, and not objects in the world.

KLONE provides another kind of hook, the "interpretive hook" (*ihook*), for attaching interpreter code directly to a Concept, Role, or SD. The code

---

* This is the case in the Levesque and Mylopoulos "instance hierarchy," for example.

pointed to by an ihook must be constructed from interpreter primitives (e.g., functions like "CreateConcept," "SatisfyRole"), and the ihook must specify the place in the interpreter from which the code is to be invoked. These hooks are not intended as escapes in which arbitrary information can be encoded when the formalism makes it hard to express a fact about the world, but as a means of direct advice to the interpreter with clear import.*

The two kinds of hooks express important relationships between the KLONE interpreter and data base. These relationships are different in nature from those expressed by the intensional, structure-building links discussed above. They allow us to look at the part of the network built out of those links as a structure on which to hang knowledge about knowledge or advice to the interpreter—as kind of a "conceptual coat rack." The knowledge-structuring relationships can be thought of as forming a representation "plane" out of which hooks emerge orthogonally.

3.4. Interpreting KLONE Structures

While I have given the impression that there is a single KLONE interpreter that deals with the node- and link-types described, that is a bit misleading. KLONE is implemented (in INTERLISP) as a set of interpreter primitives, all of which together, in some sense, form an "interpreter." However, these primitive functions for building, accessing, and removing structure are not organized into a single cohesive program. Instead, they may be used in combination by higher-level functions (matching, reasoning by analogy, deduction, etc.) to construct and maintain a KLONE data base. Each function guarantees structural integrity, and the set of functions together constitute the only possible access to the KLONE structures. In this way, Concepts, Roles, and SDs are like abstract data types in CLU [Liskov and Zilles, 1974]. The functional interface provides a clean, implementation-independent definition for the types of entities that KLONE supports.

The principal motivation for providing a set of primitive functional pieces out of which "higher-level" procedures can be built, and not a particular set of matching, deduction, etc. procedures, is that it is felt that we do not have a clear enough understanding of these issues to allow us to provide powerful procedures at this higher level. Experience with matchers in the field in general has been equivocal, and we have chosen instead to provide a basic set of tools for building different variants on an experimental basis. Since there is no general understanding of things like matching and reasoning by analogy, it seems wise not to commit the basic package to some ad hoc set of processing routines. This does not mean to

---

* See Smith [1978] for details on the interaction of interpretive "planes" and meta-descriptive "layers."

say, however, that there do not exist such higher-level routines for KLONE—we have, in fact, been experimenting with a variety of approaches to structure-matching, paraphrasing, question-answering, and situation recognition. KLONE is well-suited to some of these tasks, and where possible, we have provided the obvious functions. With some of these, we are investigating the use of "parallel" marker-passing algorithms (see Woods and Brachman [1978], for example).

The KLONE functions depend on the fact that the set of connections between Concepts, Roles, and SDs is fixed in advance. In order to implement, say, a function that finds a (possibly inherited) facet of a Role, we need to be able to anticipate all possible forms of inheritance that will be encountered. The function can then look for immediately accessible values, and if not found, can call a variant of itself recursively, depending on the type of Role inheritance connector it encounters. A complete set of Role inheritance functions, including the provision for multiple super-Concepts and multiple super-Roles, has been implemented, based on the small set of possible inter-Role relationships.

Since the user of KLONE "sees" only abstract structures for Concepts, etc., it is not necessary to think of the network as a set of nodes interconnected by links, but instead to view Concepts as sets of Roles and SDs, etc. The functions deal only with those entities (and their "epistemological" relations), and never attempt to make or break simple local linklike connections. This is important, considering that *structured* inheritance is a central feature of KLONE; a "cable" contains many connections that are not independent. One problem with the traditional semantic network metaphor in general is the apparent independence of each link from all other links.

There are currently two significant uses being made of the KLONE interpreter package. One involves a natural language understanding system that combines general English ATN-based parsing with the benefits of "semantic grammar" [Brown and Burton, 1975; Burton, 1976]. A KLONE taxonomy has been built that encodes semantic categories for certain types of phrases, and the parser, guided by a very general grammar of English, interacts with this taxonomy to build up the representation of a sentence. The Concept–Role paradigm is ideal for expressing the relationships between categories like "person-NP" and its possible modifiers, since it provides a completely general case-definition facility. Further, the interpretations of sentences are built incrementally from their syntactic representations using the ihook and metadescription facilities to map syntactic structures into those of a conceptual network. The conceptual net expresses the relationships between the entities discussed in the sentences, which at the moment, include people, places, and research topics. Structural Descriptions play a large part in handling paraphrase utterances and determining answers to queries.

The other domain to which the package has been applied is the description of general graphics knowledge and how to use the display facilities of a bit-map terminal. This knowledge includes coordinate system transformations, projections of entities onto display surfaces, and interrelations between actual domain objects (like ships and land masses) and their corresponding display forms. For example, one might incorporate into the general knowledge base the desire to see ships displayed as circles with centers at their projected positions, and augment that with the instruction to display ships with radar with a special symbol. Once particular ships were described to the system (and incorporated into the portion of the network dealing with domain objects), their displays would be handled automatically. The knowledge is encoded in KLONE so that it will not only be useful in producing the displays, but will also be available for discussion and easy manipulation by the system's user.

CONCLUSIONS

In this chapter, I have examined the history of the "semantic" network, looking for the major conceptual breakthroughs that have made it such a popular representation technique. It was found that through that ten-year history, at least five different interpretations of nodes and links have crept together to create confusing languages with limited expressive power. In the last two years, efforts have been mounted to crack that expressive deadlock; these efforts have concentrated on the logical status of network primitives, and have begun to take a hard look at the foundations of network representations. At the same time, the field has begun to see higher-level structures (e.g., partitions, frames) imposed on nodes and links. These structures appear to be useful and significant, but no comprehensive effort has been made to understand exactly what their status is.

In Section 2, I postulated a set of conceptual levels for interpreting primitives in semantic networks. The four that were immediately apparent from the history of the semantic net were the *implementational, logical, conceptual,* and *linguistic* levels. Each of these has had at least one (perhaps implicit) proponent in the literature. In addition, to account for some more recent aspects of knowledge representation, and the standard descriptional use of network concepts, I proposed an intermediate level to account for the internal structures of Concepts, and the relations of inheritance that exist between them. I called this the *epistemological* level of knowledge representation.

Section 3 attempted to make more apparent the kinds of relationships that an epistemological level representation should express. It was noted that descriptions of functional roles in complex objects and descriptions of the fillers of those roles were a critical part of knowledge about the world, and that, in addition, the meaning of a functional role was bound up in a set of relationships between its fillers and the fillers of other roles in the object. Given this interpretation of structured objects, the set of epistemological relations that a formalism must account for becomes clear. Finally, I tried to illustrate how a network language might account for all of these relations with explicit epistemological links, and how the structure thus formed could be used to hang information for the network interpreter.

In conclusion, it is in general useful to try to produce a knowledge representation language that is built on a small, fixed set of primitive node and link types. Settling on a fixed set of primitives, with well-understood import in terms of the operations of a particular level, enables the network designer to construct a well-defined and fixed interpreter. In addition, consistency at a single level affords the best position from which to achieve adequacy toward the level above.

ACKNOWLEDGEMENTS

I would like to thank Norton Greenfeld, Austin Henderson, Rusty Bobrow, Bill Woods, and especially Martin Yonke, for their great help in understanding and implementing KLONE.

REFERENCES

[Anderson, J. R., and Bower, G. H., 1973]. *Human Associative Memory.* Holt, New York.
[Anderson, J. R., and Bower, G. H., 1974]. A propositional theory of recognition memory. *Memory and Cognition* **2**, No. 3, 406–412.
[Bartlett, F. C., 1967]. *Remembering: A Study in Experimental and Social Psychology.* Cambridge Univ. Press, London and New York (first published, 1932).
[Bell, A., and Quillian, M. R., 1971]. Capturing concepts in a semantic net. In *Associative Information Techniques.* E. L. Jacks (ed.). Am. Elsevier, New York, pp. 3–25.
[Bobrow, D. G., and Winograd, T., 1977]. An overview of KRL, a knowledge representation language. *Cognitive Science* **1**, No. 1, 3–46.
[Brachman, R. J., 1977]. What's in a concept: Structural foundations for semantic networks. *International Journal of Man-Machine Studies* **9**, 127–152.
[Brachman, R. J., 1978a]. Structured inheritance networks. In "Research in Natural Language Understanding." W. A. Woods and R. J. Brachman, Quarterly Progress Report No. 1, BBN Report No. 3742. Bolt Beranek & Newman, Cambridge, Massachusetts, 36–78.
[Brachman, R. J., 1978b]. "A Structural Paradigm for Representing Knowledge," BBN Report No. 3605. Bolt Beranek & Newman, Cambridge, Massachusetts.
[Brown, J. S., and Burton, R. R., 1975]. Multiple representations of knowledge for tutorial reasoning. In *Representation and Understanding.* D. G. Bobrow and A. M. Collins (eds.). Academic Press, New York, pp. 311–349.
[Burton, R. R., 1976]. "Semantic Grammar: An Engineering Technique for Constructing Natural Language Understanding Systems," BBN Report No. 3453 (ICAI Report No. 3). Bolt Beranek & Newman, Cambridge, Massachusetts.
[Carbonell, J. R., 1970a]. "Mixed-Initiative Man-Computer Instructional Dialogues," BBN Report No. 1971. Bolt Beranek & Newman, Cambridge, Massachusetts.
[Carbonell, J. R., 1970b]. AI in CAI: An artificial intelligence approach to computer-aided instruction. *IEEE Transactions on Man-Machine Systems* **MMS-11**, No. 4, 190–202.

[Carnap, R., 1947]. *Meaning and Necessity*. University of Chicago Press, Chicago, Illinois.

[Cercone, N., 1975]. "Representing Natural Language in Extended Semantic Networks," Technical Report TR75-11. Department of Computing Science, University of Alberta. Edmonton, Alberta, Canada.

[Cercone, N., and Schubert, L., 1975]. Toward a state based conceptual representation. *Proceedings of the 4th International Joint Conference on Artificial Intelligence, 1975* pp. 83–90.

[Collins, A. M., and Loftus, E. F., 1975]. A spreading-activation theory of semantic processing. *Psychological Review* **82**, No. 6, 407–428.

[Collins, A. M., and Quillian, M. R., 1969]. Retrieval time from semantic memory. *Journal of Verbal Learning and Verbal Behavior* **8**, 240–247.

Collins, A. M., and Quillian, M. R., 1970a]. Facilitating retrieval from semantic memory: The effect of repeating part of an inference. In *Acta Psychologica 33 Attention and Performance III*. A. F. Sanders (ed.). North-Holland Publ., Amsterdam, pp. 304–314.

[Collins, A. M., and Quillian, M. R., 1970b]. Does category size affect categorization time? *Journal of Verbal Learning and Verbal Behavior* **9**, 432–438.

[Collins, A. M., and Quillian, M. R., 1972a]. Experiments on semantic memory and language comprehension. In *Cognition in Learning and Memory*. L. W. Gregg (ed.). Wiley, New York, pp. 117–137.

[Collins, A. M., and Quillian, M. R., 1972b]. How to make a language user. In *Organization of Memory*. E. Tulving and W. Donaldson (eds.). Academic Press, New York, pp. 309–351.

[Fahlman, S. E., 1977]. A system for representing and using real-world knowledge. Ph.D. thesis draft, Artificial Intelligence Laboratory, MIT, Cambridge, Massachusetts.

[Fillmore, C., 1968]. The case for case. In *Universals in Linguistic Theory*. E. Bach and R. Harms (eds.). Holt, New York, pp. 1–88.

[Fodor, J. A., 1978]. Tom Swift and his procedural grandmother (unpublished ms., MIT, Cambridge, Massachusetts).

[Goldstein, I. P., and Roberts, R. B., 1977]. Nudge, a knowledge-based scheduling program. *Proceedings of the 5th International Joint Conference on Artificial Intelligence, 1977* pp. 257–263.

[Grosz, B. J., 1977]. The representation and use of focus in a system for understanding dialogue. *Proceedings of the 5th International Joint Conference on Artificial Intelligence, 1977* pp. 67–76.

[Hawkinson, L., 1975]. The representation of concepts in OWL. *Proceedings of the 4th International Joint Conference on Artificial Intelligence, 1975* pp. 107–114.

[Hayes, Pat J., 1977]. In defence of logic. *Proceedings of the 5th International Joint Conference on Artificial Intelligence, 1977* pp. 559–565.

[Hayes, Philip J., 1977a]. "Some Association-Based Techniques for Lexical Disambiguation by Machine," TR25. Department of Computer Science, University of Rochester, Rochester, New York.

[Hayes, Philip J., 1977b]. On semantic nets, frames and associations. *Proceedings of the 5th International Joint Conference on Artificial Intelligence, 1977* pp. 99–107.

[Hays, D. G., 1973a]. "A Theory of Conceptual Organization and Processing." State University of New York at Buffalo (unpublished draft).

[Hays, D. G., 1973b]. Types of processes on cognitive networks. *Paper presented at the 1973 International Conference on Computational Linguistics*.

[Heidorn, G. E., 1972]. "Natural Language Inputs to a Simulation Programming System," NPS-55HD72101a. Naval Postgraduate School, Monterey, California.

[Heidorn, G. E., 1974]. English as a very high level language for simulation programming. *ACM SIGPLAN Notices* **9**, No. 4, 91–100.

[Hendrix, G. G., 1975a]. "Partitioned Networks for the Mathematical Modeling of Natural Language Semantics," Technical Report NL-28. Department of Computer Science, University of Texas at Austin.

[Hendrix, G. G., 1975b]. Expanding the utility of semantic networks through partitioning. *Proceedings of the 4th International Conference on Artificial Intelligence, 1975* pp. 115–121.

[Hendrix, G. G., 1976]. The representation of semantic knowledge. In *Speech Understanding Research: Final Technical Report*. D. E. Walker (Ed.). Stanford Research Institute, Menlo Park, California.

[Hendrix, G. G., 1977]. Some general comments on semantic networks. *Proceedings of the 5th International Joint Conference on Artificial Intelligence, 1977* pp. 984–985.

[Hendrix, G. G., Thompson, C. W., and Slocum, J., 1973]. Language processing via canonical verbs and semantic models. *Proceedings of the 3rd International Joint Conference on Artificial Intelligence, 1973* pp. 262–269.

[Levesque, H. J., 1977]. "A Procedural Approach to Semantic Networks," Technical Report No. 105. Department of Computer Science, University of Toronto, Toronto, Canada.

[Lindsay, R., 1973]. In defense of ad hoc systems. In *Computer Models of Thought and Language*. R. C. Schank and K. M. Colby (eds.). Freeman, San Francisco, California, pp. 372–395.

[Liskov, B., and Zilles, S., 1974]. Programming with abstract data types. *ACM SIGPLAN Notices* **9**, No. 4, 50–59.

[Martin, W. A., 1977]. OWL. *Proceedings of the 5th International Joint Conference on Artificial Intelligence, 1977* pp. 985–987.

[Nash-Webber, B., and Reiter, R., 1977]. Anaphora and logical form: On formal meaning representations for natural language. *Proceedings of the 5th International Joint Conference on Artificial Intelligence, 1977* pp. 121–131.

[Neisser, U., 1967]. *Cognitive Psychology*. Appleton, New York.

[Norman, D. A., 1972]. "Memory, Knowledge, and the Answering of Questions," CHIP Technical Report 25. Center for Human Information Processing, University of California at San Diego, La Jolla, California.

[Norman, D. A., 1973]. Learning and remembering: A tutorial preview. In *Attention and Performance IV*. S. Kornblum (ed.). Academic Press, New York, pp. 345–362.

[Norman, D. A., Rumelhart, D. E., and the LNR Research Group, 1975]. *Explorations in Cognition*. Freeman, San Francisco, California.

[Quillian, M. R., 1966]. "Semantic Memory," Report AFCRL-66-189. Bolt Beranek & Newman, Cambridge, Massachusetts.

[Quillian, M. R., 1967]. Word concepts: A theory and simulation of some basic semantic capabilities. *Behavioral Science* **12**, No. 5, 410–430.

[Quillian, M. R., 1968]. Semantic memory. In *Semantic Information Processing*. M. Minsky (ed.). MIT Press, Cambridge, Massachusetts, pp. 227–270.

[Quillian, M. R., 1969]. The Teachable Language Comprehender: A simulation program and theory of language. *Communications of the ACM* **12**, No. 8, 459–476.

[Raphael, B., 1968]. SIR: Semantic Information Retrieval. In *Semantic Information Processing*. M. Minsky (ed.). MIT Press, Cambridge, Massachusetts, pp. 33–145.

[Rieger, C., 1975]. The Commonsense Algorithm as a basis for computer models of human memory, inference, belief and contextual language comprehension. In *Proceedings of the Workshop on Theoretical Issues in Natural Language Processing*. B. L. Nash-Webber and R. Schank (eds.). Bolt Beranek & Newman, Cambridge, Massachusetts, pp. 180–195.

[Rieger, C., 1976]. An organization of knowledge for problem solving and language comprehension. *Artificial Intelligence* **7**, No. 2, 89–127.

[Rieger, C., 1977]. Spontaneous computation in cognitive models. *Cognitive Science* **1**, No. 3, 315–354.

[Rieger, C., and Grinberg, M., 1977]. The declarative representation and procedural simulation of causality in physical mechanisms. *Proceedings of the 5th International Joint Conference on Artificial Intelligence, 1977* pp. 250–256.

[Roberts, R. B., and Goldstein, I. P., 1977]. "FRL Users' Manual," A.I. Memo No. 408. Artificial Intelligence Laboratory, MIT, Cambridge, Massachusetts.

[Rumelhart, D. E., and Norman, D. A., 1973]. Active semantic networks as a model of human memory. *Proceedings of the 3rd International Joint Conference on Artificial Intelligence, 1973* pp. 450–457.

[Rumelhart, D. E., Lindsay, P. H., and Norman, D. A., 1972]. A process model for long-term memory. In *Organization of Memory*. E. Tulving and W. Donaldson (eds.). Academic Press, New York, pp. 197–246.

[Schank, R. C., 1972]. Conceptual dependency: A theory of natural language understanding. *Cognitive Psychology* **3**, 552–631.

[Schank, R. C. 1973a]. The conceptual analysis of natural language. In *Natural Language Processing*. R. Rustin (ed.). Algorithmics Press, New York, pp. 291–309.

[Schank, R. C., 1973b]. Identification of conceptualizations underlying natural language. In *Computer Models of Thought and Language*. R. C. Schank and K. M. Colby (eds.), Freeman, San Francisco, California, pp. 187–247.

[Schank, R. C., 1974]. "Is There a Semantic Memory?" Technical Report 3. Istituto per gli Studi Semantici e Cognitivi, Castagnola, Switzerland.

[Schank, R. C., 1975]. The structure of episodes in memory. In *Representation and Understanding*. D. G. Bobrow and A. M. Collins (eds.). Academic Press, New York, pp. 237–272.

[Schank, R. C., and Rieger, C. J., III, 1974]. Inference and the computer understanding of natural language. *Artificial Intelligence* **5**, No. 4, 373–412.

[Schank, R. C., Goldman, N., Rieger, C. J., III, and Riesbeck, C., 1973]. MARGIE: Memory, analysis, response generation, and inference on english. *Proceedings of the 3rd International Joint Conference on Artificial Intelligence, 1973* 255–261.

[Schubert, L. K., 1976]. Extending the expressive power of semantic networks. *Artificial Intelligence* **7**, No. 2, 163–198.

[Scragg, G. W., 1975]. "Frames, Planes, and Nets: A Synthesis," Working Paper 19. Istituto per gli Studi Semantici e Cognitivi, Castagnola, Switzerland.

[Shapiro, S. C., 1971a]. "The MIND System: A Data Structure for Semantic Information Processing," Technical Report R-837-PR. Rand Corporation.

[Shapiro, S. C., 1971b]. A net structure for semantic information storage, deduction, and retrieval. *Proceedings of the 2nd International Joint Conference on Artifical Intelligence, 1971* pp. 512–523.

[Simmons, R. F., 1973]. Semantic networks: Their computation and use for understanding English sentences. In *Computer Models of Thought and Language*. R. C. Schank and K. M. Colby (eds.). Freeman, San Francisco, California, pp. 63–113.

[Simmons, R. F., and Bruce, B. C., 1971]. Some relations between predicate calculus and semantic net representations of discourse. *Proceedings of the 2nd International Joint Conference on Artificial Intelligence, 1971* pp. 524–529.

[Simmons, R. F., and Chester, D., 1977]. Inferences in quantified semantic networks. *Proceedings of the 5th International Joint Conference on Artificial Intelligence, 1977* pp. 267–273.

[Simmons, R. F., and Slocum, J., 1972]. Generating English discourse from semantic networks. *Communications of the ACM* **15**, No. 10, 891–905.

[Simmons, R. F., Burger, J. F., and Schwarcz, R. M., 1968]. A computational model of verbal understanding. *AFIPS Conference Proceedings* **33**, 441–456.

[Smith, B., 1978]. Levels, layers, and planes: The framework of a system of knowledge representation semantics. Master's thesis, Artificial Intelligence Laboratory, MIT, Cambridge, Massachusetts.

[Szolovits, P., Hawkinson, L. B., and Martin, W. A., 1977]. "An Overview of OWL, a Language for Knowledge Representation," MIT/LCS/TM-86. Laboratory for Computer Science, MIT, Cambridge, Massachusetts.

[Wilks, Y., 1974]. "Natural Language Understanding Systems Within the AI Paradigm," Memo. AIM-237. Stanford Artificial Intelligence Laboratory, Stanford, California.

[Winston, P. H., 1970]. "Learning Structural Descriptions from Examples," Project MAC TR-76. MIT, Cambridge, Massachusetts.

[Winston, P. H., ed., 1975]. *The Psychology of Computer Vision*. McGraw-Hill, New York.

[Woods, W. A., 1975]. What's in a link? Foundations for semantic networks. In *Representation and Understanding*. D. G. Bobrow and A. M. Collins (eds.). Academic Press, New York, pp. 35–82.

[Woods, W. A., and Brachman, R. J., 1978]. "Research in Natural Language Understanding," Quarterly Progress Report No. 1, BBN Report No. 3742. Bolt Beranek & Newman, Cambridge, Massachusetts.

ENCODING KNOWLEDGE
IN PARTITIONED NETWORKS

Gary G. Hendrix

ABSTRACT

This chapter discusses network notations for encoding a number of different kinds of knowledge, including taxonomic information; general statements involving quantification; information about processes and procedures; the delineation of local contexts, beliefs, and wishes; and the relationships between syntactic units and their interpretations.

Many of the encodings appeal to the concept of network partitioning in which a large net is partitioned into subnets and higher-order relationships among the subnets are defined.

Procedural mechanisms for constructing and using the various network formalisms are discussed as equal partners with the declarative structures.

I. INTRODUCTION

Over the past three years, several systems* have been constructed in *SRI International*'s Artificial Intelligence Center that make use of partitioned network† structures as a medium for recording knowledge. These systems perform such diverse tasks as translating natural language into formal structures, performing logical deduction, doing judgmental reasoning, reasoning about the structure of data in data bases, reasoning about processes, interrelating the sentences of a dialogue, and generating natural language descriptions of information that is stored in formal structures. This chapter looks at the network techniques used in the various projects

---

* A system for judgmental reasoning is described in Duda *et al.* [1977, 1978]. Systems for deduction, discourse analysis, natural language understanding, and natural language generation are discussed in considerable detail in Walker [1978]. By permission from its publisher, some of the examples and figures of the latter work are reproduced herein.

† Although I have used the term "semantic network" in the past, it is my intention to avoid its use henceforth. The term "semantics" is best used to refer to the relationship between linguistic structures (words, phrases, sentences, discourses) and their meanings. Because the networks described here are used primarily (but not exclusively!) to encode the *knowledge* conveyed by language, rather than the *relationship* of language to what it conveys, the term "knowledge network" or "K-net" seems more appropriate.

from a uniform perspective, describing both the encoding techniques that are common to most of the systems and the special techniques devised to handle specialized tasks.

II. BACKGROUND AND MOTIVATION

A. Why Use Nets

Before plunging into the details of how networks can encode information, it is worthwhile to reflect on the general reasons for selecting nets as a representation medium. Their attraction largely centers around two factors. First, it is believed that the expressive power of nets is sufficient to encode any fact or concept that is encodable in any other formal, symbolic system. This means that nets may serve as a common medium of representation for diverse kinds of knowledge. Second, and this is the point that distinguishes network structures from other formally complete systems, the network data structures that encode information may themselves serve as a guide for information retrieval. From a given node, nodes representing related entities are found simply by following pointers from the node to its neighbors. In this way, a network provides its own meaning-bearing indexing system. To the extent that the labels on arcs and nodes are meaningful to net-manipulating procedures, they provide guidance to help traverse the net in search of information relevant to a task.

B. Partners with Nets

The knowledge encoded in a network, being declarative, is somewhat like that stored in a book: it is available for the support of intellectual activity only if there exists some outside agent that can retrieve the knowledge and apply it. This outside agent embodies knowledge about how to manipulate the information in the net, and may have access to yet other bodies of information. To the extent that the information in the network is to be used, the network and its manipulator are mutually dependent partners. Therefore, in considering the network structures presented below, it is important to consider also the procedures that manipulate them.

C. Networks as a Medium for Integrating Skills

Just as the knowledge in a book may be accessed and applied by multiple agents, so may the knowledge in a network. In particular, information in a net may be used by a number of different procedures in performing a variety of tasks. For example, constraints on set membership recorded in a network may aid both the process of natural language understanding and the process of logical deduction.

But a net need not merely provide a static repository of information that is to be shared by multiple processes. Rather, it may serve as a medium of communication between processes. For example, natural language translation may create a network description of a question. A question answerer may then process the question's description to produce a network-encoded answer, which in turn is the input to an English generator. All of the intermediate structures may be examined by discourse analysis procedures that seek to build up a network-encoded model of an extended dialogue.

The point is that their representational power makes nets attractive both as a medium for encoding information needed by multiple skill modules and as a common language for communicating results among modules. Thus, nets may aid in two ways in the integration of multiple intelligence skills.

III. BASIC NETWORK NOTIONS

This section introduces the basic techniques used by our systems to encode information in networks. The representation builds upon such work as that reported in Simons [1973], Shapiro [1971], and Norman *et al.* [1975], but is tied more closely to the notions of conventional logic than most network systems.*

A.   A Preliminary Example

In its simplest form, a knowledge representation network consists of a collection of nodes interconnected by an accompanying set of arcs. Each node denotes an object (a physical object, situation,† set) and each arc represents an instance of a binary relation. For example, the nodes JOHN and MEN in Fig. 1 denote a man John and the set of all men, respectively. The arc labeled *e* from JOHN to MEN indicates that *John* is an element of the set of men and is thus some particular man.

Further details concerning how the interconnections among nodes and arcs can be used to encode knowledge may be seen by considering Fig. 1 systematically. At the top of the figure is the node UNIVERSAL. This node denotes the set *Universal*, the universal set of objects.‡ Arcs labeled *s*,

---

* The networks of Schubert [1976] and Kay [1973] are also closely tied to conventional logic, but do not use partitioning.

† McCarthy [1968] has used the term *situation* to refer to the complete state of affairs at some instant of time. I prefer to use the term *state of the world* to refer to this concept, and to use the term *situation* to refer to any event or state of being that occurs over an interval of time. Thus, my notion of a situation might be applied to such conditions or circumstances as Mary owning a car (a state of being) or Mary driving her car to town (an event).

‡ Symbols composed of all capital letters are used as the names of nodes. Entities denoted by nodes are given names in which only the first letter is capitalized.

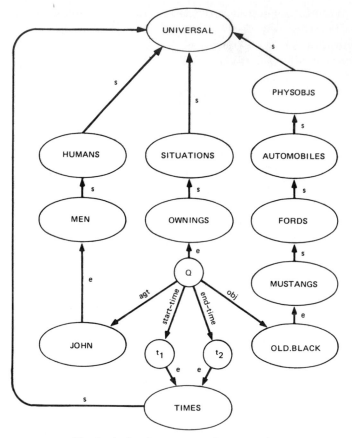

Fig. 1. A simple representation network.

called *s arcs,* are used to indicate subset relationships that exist between
Universal and other sets. In particular, the *s arc* from HUMANS to UNI-
VERSAL indicates that *Humans,* the set of all human beings, is a subset of
Universal. Similarly, *Situations, Times,* and *Physobjs* (the set of all physical
objects) are also indicated as being subsets of *Universal.* At the next lower
level, *Men* is shown to be a subset of *Humans.*

As indicated above, set membership is encoded in the network through
the use of *e arcs.* Thus, the network of Fig. 1 indicates that *John* is a man,
Old.Black is an automobile, and T1 and T2 are instants in time.

The node *Q* denotes an element of the set *Ownings,* the set of situations
in which an agent owns an object over some time period.* In turn,
Ownings is a subset of *Situations,* which is the set of all static conditions

---

* Methods for describing properties that are common to all elements of a set are discussed
subsequently.

and dynamic events. For the particular situation Q, *John* is the agent that owns the object *Old.Black* during the period from time T1 until T2. The components of situation Q are associated with it through *deep case* relationships. In general, a deep case (or slot or role) is a relationship between a situation (or other composite object) and a participant in the situation. For example, the agent of situation Q is indicated by the *agt arc* from Q to JOHN. (The notion of a deep case, which is a relationship between world objects, contrasts in the linguistic literature with the notion of a surface case, which is a relationship between syntactic units.)*

B. Useful Restrictions on Nodes and Arcs

Proponents of network structures have adopted a number of different conventions concerning what types of concepts may be encoded by nodes and what types of relationships may or should be encoded by arcs.† In creating our encoding structures, we have attempted to use constructs that are understood by appealing to such familiar mathematical systems as set theory and predicate calculus. Our nets place no restrictions on the types of objects that may be represented by nodes. However, arcs are restricted to the encoding of formal binary relationships, such as taxonomic (element and subset) relationships and deep case relationships.‡ Deep case relations must be functions. Thus, for example, any *Ownings* situation has exactly one start-time, but the same time T may be the start-time of many situations. Deep cases must also be constant over time and circumstance. Arcs are never, for example, allowed to encode relationships, such as ownership, that are time bounded.

Relationships that are not represented by arcs are represented by nodes having outgoing case arcs pointing to the participants in the relationship (such as node Q in Fig. 1). This representational convention allows an arbitrary amount of information to be stored with a relationship (using case arcs) and allows associative retrieval of the relationship using the network's indexing facilities (i.e., by following the arcs). Such relationships are grouped by type into sets and these sets are considered to be subsets of the set of all situations.

Some network systems have a small fixed number of arc labels, with each having a special meaning to the network processor. However, having many meaningful labels can be quite beneficial. Even our general-purpose routines that retrieve information from a network without special knowledge concerning the meanings of arc labels operate more efficiently when more case names are used, because an increase in the number of arc labels provides a finer index into the net.

* See Fillmore [1968] and Bruce [1973].
† For a useful perspective on these issues, see Woods [1975].
‡ The set of case relationships is open-ended. In particular, no fixed set such as {*agt, obj, goal, theme*} is especially known to the network system.

C. The Hierarchical Taxonomy

The presence of *e* and *s arcs* in a network serves to taxonomize the concepts represented by the various nodes in hierarchical form and is a key feature of the notation.* Because the knowledge of whether or not an item belongs to a given set is of central relevance in question answering and fact retrieval, the taxonomy itself often provides a natural and concise expression of major portions of the information about a task domain. The significance of the taxonomy is further enhanced by the fact that the members of many sets have a collection of properties in common. Any property that is characteristic of *all* members of a given set may be described at the set level and need not be repeated in the encoding of each individual set member. This set-level encoding, which requires the use of universal quantification, leads to great savings in storage.

To enhance the precision of the network encoding of taxonomies, the standard set theory notions of set membership and set inclusion, which are expressed by *e* and *s arcs,* may be supplemented by the more restrictive concepts of disjoint subsets and distinct elements.

Most sibling subsets described in taxonomies are disjoint. Arcs labeled *ds* are used to represent this disjointness property in a concise and easily interpretable manner. A *ds arc* from a node X to a node Z indicates that the set denoted by X is a subset of the set denoted by Z and that the X set is disjoint from any other set denoted by a node with an outgoing *ds arc* to Z. For example, the *ds arcs* in Fig. 2 emanating from the HUMANS and COMPANIES nodes indicate that the set of *Humans* and the set of *Companies* are disjoint subsets of the set of *Legal-Persons.*

Since each node in most taxonomies denotes a distinct entity, and in general an entity can be denoted by any number of nodes, arcs labeled *de* (for "distinct element") are used to indicate that each of two or more nodes denotes a different element of a set. In particular, a *de arc* from a node X to a node Z indicates that the entity denoted by X is an element of the set denoted by Z and that the X entity is distinct from any other entity denoted by a node that has an outgoing *de arc* to Z. For example, the *de arcs* in Fig. 2 emanating from G.M. and FORD indicate that G.M. and *Ford* are distinct members of the set of *Companies.*

To see the useful interplay between *de arcs* and *e arcs,* suppose Tom, Dick, and Harry went for a drive, and the driver wore a red cap. Tom, Dick, and Harry are distinct elements of the set of people who went for the drive, and their membership in the set would be recorded by three *de arcs.* The driver is also in this set, but could be any one of the three. Using a normal *e arc* to show the membership of the driver allows information about the driver (e.g., he wore a red cap) to be recorded while maintaining

---

* By using disjunction, certain ambiguities regarding the hierarchy may be encoded. For example, it is easy to represent the fact that John's pet is either a dog or a cat.

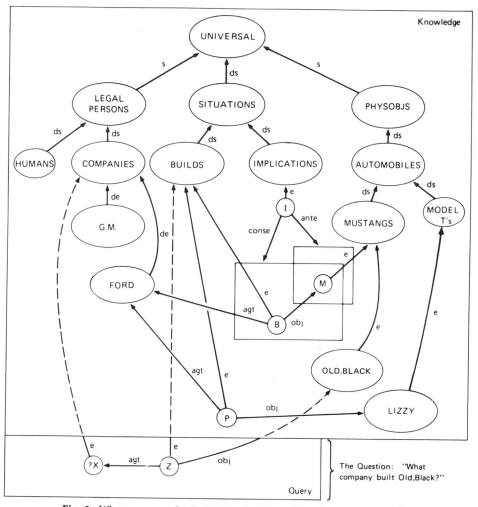

Fig. 2. What company built Old.Black? (From [Hendrix, G. G., 1978].)

the uncertainty as to which of the three set members the driver really is.

The use of *e, s, de,* and *ds arcs* in a more extended example is shown in Fig. 3. The network indicates that *US-Cities* and *P-US-Cities* are both subsets of each other. Hence, the nodes US-CITIES and P-US-CITIES may both be interpreted as denoting the set of all cities in the USA. The node US-CITIES is used to help taxonomize cities by state. The *ds arcs* to US-CITIES from CA-CITIES, TX-CITIES, and OK-CITIES indicate that the sets of cities in California, Texas, and Oklahoma are all subsets of *US-Cities* and are disjoint from one another. The node P-US-CITIES is used to help taxonomize cities by population into the disjoint sets *Major-Cities* and *Small-Cities.* Notice particularly that any of the disjoint subsets of *P-US-*

58   *Gary G. Hendrix*

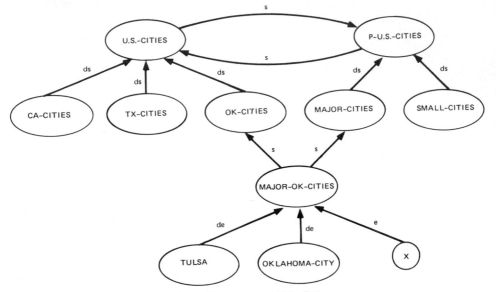

Fig. 3. Taxonomy of U.S. Cities.

Cities may (but in general need not) intersect with any of the disjoint subsets of *US-Cities*. In particular, the network shows *Major-OK-Cities* to be a nonempty subset of both *OK-Cities* and *Major-Cities*.

The membership of *Major-OK-Cities* includes *Tulsa, Oklahoma-City,* and *X. Tulsa* and *Oklahoma-City* are shown to be distinct. X might be either of these or yet some other city. If the cardinality of *Major-OK-Cities* is 2, then it is possible to deduce from the net that X is either *Tulsa* or *Oklahoma-City.* The very ambiguity regarding which distinct element of *Major-OK-Cities* is actually denoted by X is attractive for some applications (as shown in the Tom, Dick, and Harry example).

Note that distinctness and disjointness properties may be propagated through a network. In particular, if *A* has an outgoing *de arc* to *S1*, and *B* has an outgoing *de arc* to *S2*, and there are unbroken paths of *ds arcs* from both *S1* and *S2* to some common superset *S3*, then *S1* and *S2* are disjoint, and *A* and *B* are distinct. In fact, every element of *S1* is distinct from every element of *S2*.

The use of *ds* and *de arcs* increases the power of the taxonomy by making it possible to prove negative assertions. For example, with *Ca-Cities* and *OK-Cities* known to be disjoint, it is possible to show that *Tulsa* (or X) is not a California city. Information about nonintersection and nonequivalence can be encoded by other means, but the *de* and *ds arcs* allow much of this information to be encoded for the price of the hierarchical information alone, without additional structure.

IV. PARTITIONING

A. Spaces

A new dimension to the organizational and expressive power of representation networks may be added by extending the basic concept of a network as a collection of nodes and arcs to include the notion of *partitioning* [Hendrix, 1975a,b]. The central idea of partitioning is to allow groups of nodes and arcs to be bundled together into units called *spaces*, which are fundamental entities in partitioned networks, on the same level as nodes and arcs.*

Every node and every arc of a network belongs to (or lies in/on) one or more spaces. Associated with the data structure encoding a space is a list of all nodes and a list of all arcs that lie within the space. Likewise, associated with the data structures of nodes and arcs are lists of all the spaces upon which they lie. Nodes and arcs of different spaces may be linked, but the linkage between such entities may be thought of as passing through boundaries that partition spaces. Nodes and arcs may be created in (initially empty) spaces, may be transferred or copied (at a fraction of creation cost) from one space to another, and may be removed from a space.

An important application of spaces in language processing, which provides a convenient introduction to the partitioning concept, is in grouping together subparts of a network that are capable of being expressed by a single syntactic unit. For example, Fig. 4 shows a network containing

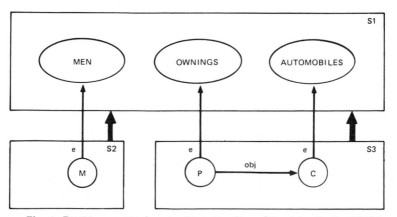

Fig. 4. Partitions around syntactic units. (From [Hendrix, G. G., 1978].)

---

* Aggregate structures similar to spaces have also been described by Scragg [1975b] and Hayes [1977], although their structures have not been applied in so wide a range of applications as have spaces.

three spaces, two of which correspond to syntactic units. Each space is represented by a rectangle that contains the name of the space in a corner. Thus, space *S1* is the space at the top of the figure. Diagrammatically, a node or arc is indicated as belonging to a space if its label is written within the rectangle associated with the space. Thus, node *M* and the *e arc* from *M* to MEN lie only in *S2*. Spaces *S1*, *S2*, and *S3* may be given concrete interpretations in the context of the sentence

"SOME MAN M OWNS A CAR C."

Space *S1* encodes background information (about men, owning situations, and automobiles) for the understanding of this sentence. Space *S2* encodes "some man *M*," the information that would be conveyed by the syntactic subject of the sentence. Space *S3* encodes aspects of an owning situation *P* in which the object owned is a car *C*. This corresponds approximately to the verb phrase of the sentence* ("owns a car *C*"). Figure 4 does not in fact indicate that *M* was the agent in owning situation *P*, but this omission is corrected below.

B. Vistas

It is often convenient to combine several spaces to form a composite bundle of nodes and arcs representing the aggregate of the bundles of the individual spaces. Such a combination of spaces is called a "vista," and is somewhat like a QLISP context [Reboh and Sacerdoti, 1973]. Most operations involving a partitioned network are performed from the vantage of a vista with the effect that the operations behave as if the entire network were composed solely of those nodes and arcs that lie in the spaces of the vista. All structures lying outside the vista are ignored.

The mechanics of partitioning allow vistas to be created freely from arbitrary combinations of spaces, but this freedom is seldom used. Rather, vistas are typically created in a hierarchical fashion by adding one new space to an existing vista or to the union of multiple existing vistas. A new vista created in this fashion inherits a view of (or access to) the information in the parent vista(s), and the newly added space is used for extending local information without altering the view of the parent(s). Such hierarchically created vistas are analogous to programming contexts with global and local variables. Information structures in the spaces of the parent vista(s) are global, relative to the new space. Because the new space *S* of a new hierarchically created vista *V* is so closely related to *V*, it will be convenient to talk about "viewing the net from the vantage of *S*" when the viewing is actually from *V*.

When new vistas are created hierarchically, they form a partial ordering of viewing capability. An example of such a partial ordering is depicted in

---

* Tense information is omitted.

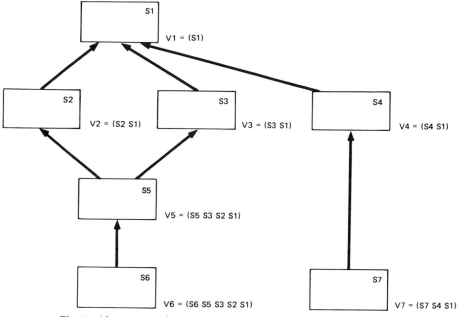

Fig. 5. Abstraction of vista ordering. (From [Hendrix, G. G., 1978].)

Fig. 5. The spaces that are included in the various vistas are represented by rectangles as before. To the right of each rectangle is a list notation (vistas are actually implemented as LISP lists) indicating the vista associated with the space. Heavy arrows indicate the inheritance of viewing capability. That is, from any point in the partial ordering, information is visible in any space that may be reached by following up heavy arrows.

Space *S1* at the top of the figure is associated with vista *V1*, which contains only space *S1*. From the vantage of *V1*, only the information in *S1* is visible. The vista of *S2* is *V2*, which contains both *S2* and *S1*. Thus, from the vantage of *V2*, all the information in both *S2* and *S1* is visible. However, the information in *S3* is not visible from *V2* (except to the extent that *S1* or *S2* contains some of the same nodes and arcs as *S3*). From the vantage of *V5* it is possible to see all the information in both *S2* and *S3*, as well as the information in *S5* and *S1*.

Figure 6 provides some indication of how vista hierarchies may be used. Again, the heavy arrows indicate which spaces are included in the vistas of spaces. From the vista of space *VP1*, it is possible to see information on spaces *VP1*, *V1*, *NP2*, and *BACKGROUND*. Thus, from the vantage of *VP1*, it is possible to see the background information and the structures used in creating a network interpretation of the verb phrase (*VP*) in the sentence "Some man *M* owns a car *C*." This view includes the information of space *V1* (which encodes the verb alone), space *NP2* (which encodes the

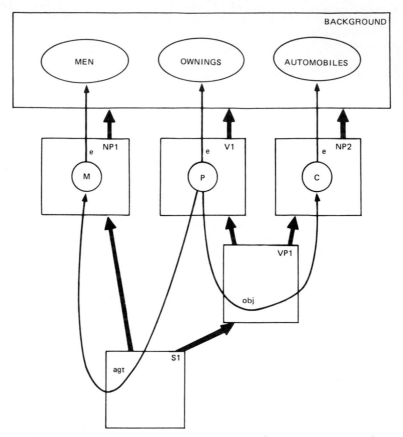

Fig. 6. Parsing "Some-man owns a-car." (From [Hendrix, G. G., 1978].)

direct object alone), and space *VP1* (which encodes the relationship between the verb and object). From this same vantage, the structures in spaces *NP1* and *S1* are invisible.

In subsequent diagrams, when a rectangle representing a space *S* is drawn completely within a rectangle representing a second space *S'*, then this indicates that the vista of *S* is an extension of the vista of *S'*. For example, (a) and (b) in Fig. 7 represent equivalent structures. If two rectangles overlap, but neither contains the other, then structures appearing in the overlap lie on both spaces. Examples of such overlaps occur in the section on quantification below.

C. Relating Spaces to Predicate Calculus

The collection of nodes and arcs composing a network encodes a body of information in much the same fashion as a set of propositions in predicate calculus. If a total network is regarded as a large set of propositions, then a

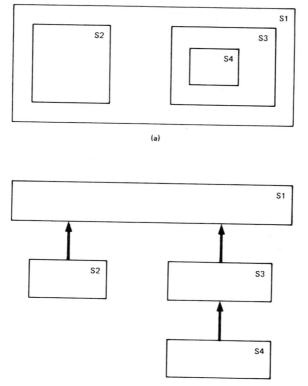

Fig. 7. Equivalence of enclosure and heavy arrow notation. (From [Hendrix, G. G., 1978].)

space may be regarded as a subset of the propositions, and a vista may be regarded as the union of a number of the subsets. Thus, for example, the vista consisting of spaces *VP1, V1,* and *NP2* of Fig. 6 contains the set of propositions that are conveyed by the verb phrase of the example sentence. This set of propositions may be thought of as a single proposition formed by conjoining the individual members of the set. Thus, the spaces and vistas may be regarded as propositions, that is, as *expressions* of information about the world. This, of course, is consistent with the notion that a network is an expression of information.

D. Supernodes

By bundling together a collection of representational structures, a space may be used as the aggregate expression of the information encoded by its internal nodes and arcs. For example, a certain space *S* might bundle together a collection of nodes and arcs that, when taken together, represent the set of things that some person has told about in a story, or believes to be true, or wishes to have happen. Each node and each arc represents some aspect of the belief (story, wish), but only the space is a representation of the aggregate of these aspects.

Because it is often necessary to relate other concepts in the network to the proposition encoded by a space, *supernodes* may be created to denote spaces. Supernodes have all the properties of ordinary nodes, and in particular may be pointed to by arcs.

When a supernode is formed to denote a space, a QUOTE-type operation takes place. The supernode comes to denote the *expression* of the information represented by the space. That is, the space represents information about the modeled domain, and the node denotes the representation.

An example supernöde is shown abstractly in Fig. 8. Node X represents a believing situation in which the believer (*agt* = agent) is JOHN and the thing believed (*thm* = theme) is a complex of information encoded by space S1. More precisely, the structures inside S1 (omitted in the figure) may be thought of collectively as a complex proposition that JOHN believes to be true. Moreover, the structures of the space represent objects and situations that JOHN believes to exist.*

It is important to note that by allowing the network to express information about expressions, the use of supernodes can lead to interesting inconsistencies and paradoxes, some of which are discussed by Montague

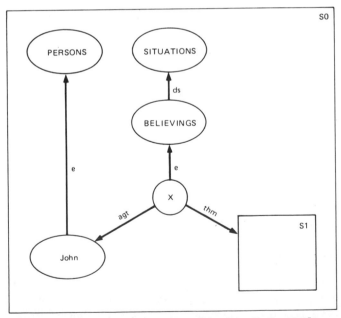

Fig. 8. The beliefs of John. (From [Hendrix, G. G., 1978].)

* A discussion of the use of partitioned networks in modeling belief structures is presented in Cohen and Perrault [1976].

[1974]. For example, the Liar Paradox ("this statement is not true") is easily expressed in a partitioned network. Fortunately, these problems have had little impact on our current work. This is because our systems that manipulate information about expressions currently limit their scope of activity to information about the standard logical connectives. For example, these systems know that if the disjunction of expressions *E1* and *E2* provides an ambiguous description of some aspect of a world *W*, then either the objects and situations described by *E1* or those described by *E2* exist in *W*.

V. STRUCTURES FOR LOGICAL DEDUCTION

Building upon the basic notions of nodes, arcs, spaces, vistas, taxonomies, situations, and deep cases, structures may be devised to meet the needs of various applications. This section describes how the basic notions may be extended to meet the needs of a system that does logical deduction. In particular, structures are described for handling logical connectives and quantification.

A. Logical Connectives

1. Conjunction

As the first logical connective, consider conjunction, which relates a number of components called "conjuncts." Thinking of each conjunct as a description of some condition, the conjunction itself is a complex description of the situation in which the conditions described by each of the individual conjuncts exist in unison.

The inherent bundling capability of spaces makes them a convenient medium for dealing with conjunction. In particular, a conjunction *C* corresponds to a space *S* upon which network structures are created corresponding to each conjunct of *C* (and only the conjuncts of *C*). Space *S2* of Fig. 9, for example, represents the information conveyed by the conjunction "Old.Black was built by Ford *and* Old.Black is owned by John." The subordination of *S2* under *S1* in the viewing hierarchy is rather artificial and was done here solely for exposition. Except for delimiting the conjunction (X & Y), the structures of *S2* might just as well have been encoded directly in *S1*. This ability to remove the partitioning of *S2* is the network analog of the ability to remove the embedded parentheses in the formula (A & (B & C)) to form (A & B & C).

2. Disjunction

A disjunction separates out a number of components called "disjuncts," each of which describes an alternative set of conditions. The inherent separating ability of spaces makes them a convenient medium for dealing

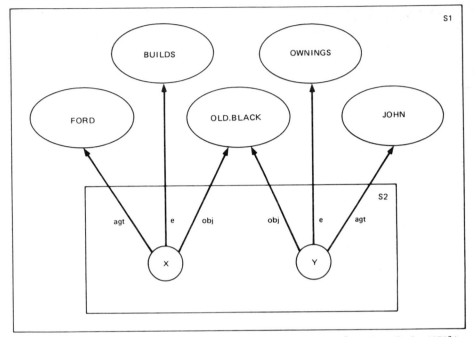

Fig. 9. Old.Black was built by Ford and is owned by John. (From [Hendrix, G. G., 1978].)

with disjunction. In particular, the information encoded by each of the *n* disjuncts of a disjunction *D* may be encoded on a different space and so kept (and reasoned about) in (relative) isolation.

Figure 10, for example, shows the network encoding of the disjunction *D* = "Either Old.Black was built by Ford, *or* Old.Black is owned by John." Node *D* denotes the disjunction itself. It is an element of the set *Disjunctions*, which might more properly be labeled *True-Disjunctions* because it denotes the set of sets of propositions in which at least one proposition represents entities that exist in the modeled world. That is, a disjunction like *D* can belong to *Disjunctions* in some world *W* only if the objects and situations described by at least one of its disjuncts exist in *W*. The disjuncts of *D* are represented by supernodes *S2* and *S3*. Since a disjunction may be regarded as a set of alternative disjuncts, the disjuncts of *D* are shown as distinct elements of *D*. Whenever a disjunction appears in the network, it is assumed that all members of the disjunctive set are explicitly encoded.

The entire disjunction structure is embedded in the conjunction of *S1*. *S1* provides a partial description of some world (i.e., a collection of objects and the interrelationships among them) and each structure in *S1* represents some object or situation that occurs in that world. Thus, when the

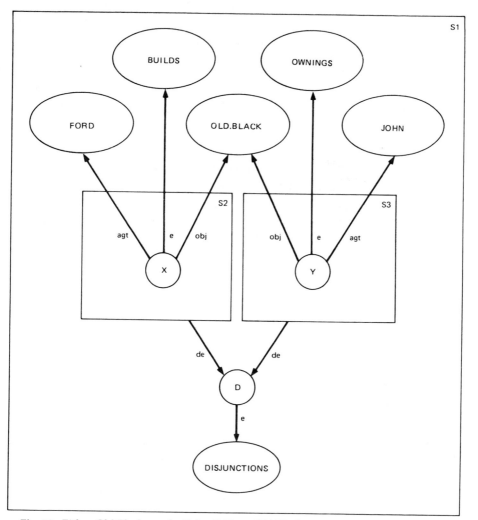

Fig. 10. Either Old.Black was built by G.M. or Old.Black is owned by John. (From [Hendrix, G. G., 1978].)

network is viewed from the vantage of *S1*, such entities as Old.Black and *D* are seen to occur. However, the structures in spaces *S2* and *S3* are not seen from the vantage of *S1* and are thus not asserted in the world modeled by *S1*. Since *D* does appear in the world of *S1*, it is known that the world of *S1* includes the situations described by at least one of the disjuncts of *D*. If *S2*, for example, were included, then the modeled world would include all situations described by structures that are visible from the vantage of *S2*. This view includes structures in *S2* and *S1*, but excludes structures in *S3*.

3. *Negation*

The network encoding of negation uses partitioning to separate the negative from the positive. Figure 11 shows the network encoding of the negation "G.M. did *not* build Old.Black." The negation, an element of *Negations,** is encoded by supernode S2. Space S2 is an (implicit) conjunction describing a set of conditions that cannot occur simultaneously in the context of the conditions described in *S1*. As in the disjunction example, the negated structures inside *S2* are not visible when viewing the network from the vantage of *S1*, although the negation itself is visible. That is, the *description* (denoted by supernode *S2*) of the negative conditions (described by space *S2*) exists in the world of *S1*, and the fact (denoted by the *e arc* from *S2* to NEGATIONS) exists in *S1* that this *description* encodes a nonexistent set of conditions for the world of *S1*. But entities described by *S2* do not (all) exist in *S1*.

4. *Implications*

Implications can be encoded by conversion to negations and disjunctions. ($A \Rightarrow C$ is the same as $\neg A \lor C$ in propositional logic.) However, it

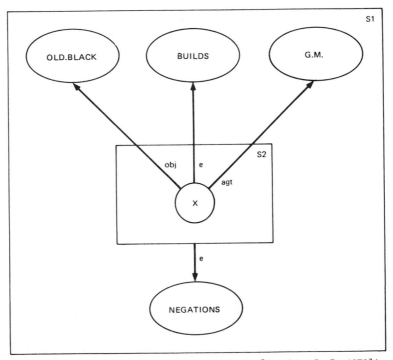

Fig. 11. Old. Black was not built by G.M. (From [Hendrix, G. G., 1978].)

---

* In a world *W*, *Negations* is the set of propositions that are not true in *W*.

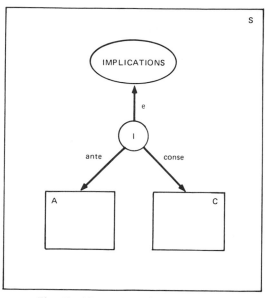

Fig. 12. Abstraction of an implication.

is also possible to encode implications directly, as shown abstractly in Fig. 12. An implication I occurring in space S is associated by case arcs with a collection of antecedent conditions, represented by a space A, and a set of consequent conditions, represented by a space C. As above, spaces A and C may be regarded as conjunctions.

B. Quantification

One of the important features of network partitioning is that it provides a facility for representing arbitrarily nested existential and universal quantifiers. Existential quantification is an implicit concept in the sense that the occurrence of a structure (i.e., a node or arc) in a space is taken to be an assertion of the existence with respect to that space of the entity represented by the structure. Existential quantification and negation could be used to represent any universally quantified formula $(\forall x \in X)P(x)$ by making use of the following transformation:

$$(\forall x \in X)P(x) \Leftrightarrow \neg\neg[(\forall x \in X)P(x)] \Leftrightarrow \neg[(\exists x \in X)\neg P(x)].$$

Although the network encoding suggested by this transformation is logically sound, it is cumbersome and unappealing intuitively. The following transformation suggests a more attractive representation:

$$(\forall x \in X)P(x) \Leftrightarrow (\forall x)[\text{member}(x, X) \Rightarrow P(x)].$$

That is, any universally quantified formula can be represented as an implication whose antecedent specifies the *typing* of the universally quantified variable and whose consequent specifies the statement that is being made about any entity that satisfies the type restrictions.

A distinguishing feature of the universally quantified variable x in this implication is that it occurs in both the antecedent and the consequent. Thus, in the network representation of an implication, if a node occurs in both the antecedent and the consequent space, it is considered to represent a universally quantified variable.*

Figure 2 shows the representation of a concrete example of such an implication, namely the statement "For all M in the set of *Mustangs*, there exists a B such that B is an element of the set of *Builds* situations, the agent of B is *Ford*, and the object built is M," or

$$\forall m[\text{member}(m, \text{Mustangs}) \Rightarrow \text{built}(\text{Ford}, m)].$$

When the main connective of a formula is an implication, it is not necessary to embed the formula in another implication to represent the universal quantification. That is,

$$(\forall x \in X)[Q(x) \Rightarrow R(x)]$$
$$\Leftrightarrow (\forall x)\{\text{member}(x, X) \Rightarrow [Q(x) \Rightarrow R(x)]\}$$
$$\Leftrightarrow (\forall x)\{[\text{member}(x, X) \ \& \ Q(x)] \Rightarrow R(x)\}.)$$

Arbitrary nesting of quantifiers may be achieved by placing implications in the consequent spaces of other implications. For example,

$$(\forall x \in X)(\exists y \in Y)(\forall z \in Z)P(x, y, z)$$
$$\Leftrightarrow (\forall x)\{\text{member}(x, X) \Rightarrow$$
$$(\exists y)[\text{member}(y, Y)\&(\forall z)(\text{member}(z, Z) \Rightarrow$$
$$P(x, y, z))]\}.$$

C. A Deduction Algorithm

The structures presented above are useful in deduction and question answering only to the extent that there exist procedures having the logical expertise needed to manipulate them. The general flavor of such procedures, which are discussed more extensively in Fikes and Hendrix [1977], is indicated by the following, highly simplified example.

The deduction system is given as input a QUERY space representing a question to be answered (theorem to be proved) and a KNOWLEDGE space representing the beliefs that are to be considered true while answering the question. In aggregate, the nodes and arcs of QUERY describe a set of objects and relationships whose existence is to be established in the world of the KNOWLEDGE space. If a set of such entities can be found, a

---

* Note that the constant K in $\forall x[P(x, K) \Rightarrow Q(x, K)]$ does not *appear* in both ante and conse spaces, but is *referenced* (i.e., pointed to by an arc) in both ante and conse. For example, FORD is referenced in the conse space of the implication of Fig. 2.

list of *bindings* that link the QUERY descriptions to their KNOWLEDGE instantiations is to be returned.

For example, Fig. 2 shows a QUERY and KNOWLEDGE space for the question "What company built Old.Black?" Given this problem, the system seeks an element (like Z) of the *Builds* situation set having both Old.Black as its object and an element (like ?X) of the *Companies* set as its agent. Looking for a match for Z, the system first looks only at structures in the KNOWLEDGE space. The *Builds* situation represented by node P is found by using the incoming e *arcs* to the BUILDS node as an index. However, P is rejected as a match for Z because the *obj arcs* from Z and P point to nodes that are members of disjoint sets, indicating that Z and P have different objects.

Because there are no other incoming e *arcs* to BUILDS in the KNOWLEDGE space, the system changes strategy and looks for elements of the *Builds* set that are buried in logical expressions. Indexing again on the incoming e *arcs* to the BUILDS node, the *theorem* "All Mustangs were built by Ford" is found. A unification process determines that the relevant instance of the theorem is one in which the universally quantified variable M is instantiated by *Old.Black*. The theorem allows a new *Builds* situation to be asserted if it can be shown that *Old.Black* is an element of the *Mustangs* set. A subproblem is created to find that *Element-Of* relationship, and when the subproblem is solved, a new *Builds* situation is asserted in KNOWLEDGE and the desired bindings are assigned. In particular, node ?X is bound to FORD and Z is bound to the newly derived *Builds* situation. Because node ?X is marked for questioning, its binding, FORD, is returned as the answer to the original question.

VI. INHERITING INFORMATION

A. The Contributions of Quantification and Case

The notion of a hierarchical taxonomy was presented earlier as a basic concept in nets used for the representation of knowledge. Although the taxonomy alone provides the information needed to answer several types of element/set/subset questions, the taxonomy's primary attraction is in supporting the "inheritance" of information. In particular, if certain properties P are known to be characteristic of all the members of a given set S, then it follows that all the members of the set's subsets also have the properties P and that each individual member of the set S and of its subsets has the properties as well. To explicitly reencode the properties P with each of the individual representations for S, its subsets, and its many individual members would be highly redundant. Instead, the properties P may be recorded solely with the representation of S and deduced for the subsets and individual members on demand. For example, if the fact that dogs have cold noses is recorded with the node representing the set of all dogs, then it is unnecessary to explicitly encode the fact that all members of the set of Hounds and the individual dog Fido have cold noses.

The procedures implementing deductions based on set membership and set inclusion may make very efficient use of the network data structures that encode taxonomic information. For example,* in looking for a property P of an object Q, these procedures may determine whether P is recorded with the data structure representing Q. If it is, no deduction need be done. If it is not, the procedures may work their way up the taxonomy above Q, checking to see if information about P is encoded with any of the sets and supersets to which Q belongs. Because such a search may be efficiently implemented, the deduction procedures make it appear as if the representation of object Q had inherited its own copy of information about P from supersets in the taxonomy.

Unfortunately, many network schemes have been devised that indicate inheritance either incorrectly or through a complicated system of ad hoc rules and structures. Various shortcomings are catalogued in Woods [1975] and in Brachman [1977]. Those systems that behave incorrectly suffer primarily from the failure to carefully distinguish properties of sets (such as cardinality) from properties of individual members of a set. For example, the individual members of a set of numbers may all be prime, but the set is not prime. Those systems that are clumsy or ad hoc fail to recognize that the encoding of information regarding all the individual members of a set inherently involves universal quantification.

In general, if a set S has some property Q, it should be encoded by the network formulation of $Q(S)$. Q might be encoded by a single arc or by a situation node with a case arc to S and other arcs to other participants in the situation coded by Q. If the individual members x of S all have property P, then this information should be encoded by the network formulation of $\forall x[\text{member}(x, S) \Rightarrow P(x)]$. Note particularly that P is not applied to S but to the values of the universal variable x that ranges over S.

Along with quantification, the notion of case plays an important role in "inheritance." Our explicit restriction that case arcs designate only instances of functions is a key (but often unrecognized) factor in network deduction. Suppose, for example, that it is known that

$$\forall x\{\text{member}(x, \text{Ownings}) \Rightarrow \exists t1,t2\ [\text{start-time}(x, t1)$$
$$\& \text{ end-time}(x, t2)$$
$$\& \text{ BEFORE}(t1, t2)]\}$$

$$\& \text{ member}(q, \text{Ownings})$$
$$\& \text{ start-time}(q, I)$$
$$\& \text{ end-time}(q, J)$$

---

* In this example, given particular object Q we ask if Q has property P. A more demanding application of the inheritance information, which is discussed in Moore [1975] and in Fahlman [1977], is to *find* an object Q that has property P.

From this information, is it possible to deduce that I, the start-time of q, is BEFORE J, the end-time of q? Certainly, the universally quantified statement (UQS) indicates that there exist $T1$ and $T2$, which are *a* start-time and *an* end-time for q with $T1$ BEFORE $T2$, but it is the fact that start-time and end-time are cases, and therefore functions, that indicates that $T1$ and $T2$ are necessarily identical to I and J respectively.

In general, for any case relation c, the function property brings with it the restriction that

$$\forall x, y, z\{[c(x, y) \ \& \ c(x, z)] \Rightarrow y = z\}.$$

The point here is that for a composite object (some object associated with cases), not only may the object itself "inherit" properties, but the associated objects that fill case roles may also inherit properties. That is, from a UQS of the form

$$\forall x\{\text{member}(x, S) \Rightarrow P(x) \ \& \ \exists y[c(x, y) \ \& \ Q(y)]\},$$

where c designates a case relation, it follows that

$$\text{If } A \text{ as in } S, \quad \text{then } P(A)$$

and

$$\text{If } c(A, B),^* \quad \text{then } Q(B).$$

B. Delineation

By indicating some common property P of members of a set S, a universally quantified statement serves to partially define and bound S. That is, by stating that all members of S have property P, a UQS indicates that *only* individuals having property P are in S. Thus, the UQS provides an indication of a limitation on the membership of S. Formally, this limitation arises as a consequence of the fact that

$$\{\forall x[\text{member}(x, S) \Rightarrow P(x)]\} \Leftrightarrow \{\forall x[\neg P(x) \Rightarrow \neg \text{member}(x, S)]\}.$$

For purposes of understanding natural language inputs, UQSs serving to limit the membership of situation sets are very important. In particular, it is useful for each situation set to have a UQS, called the set *delineation*, that names and restricts the participants of situations in the set. That is, the UQS specifies deep cases that are to be associated with situations of the type being delineated and indicates a possible set of values for each case. For example, the delineation of the set *Ownings* is shown in Fig. 13, and corresponds to the formula

$$\forall x\{\text{member}(x, \text{Ownings})$$
$$\Rightarrow \exists y, z, t1, t2[\text{member}(y, \text{Legal.persons}) \ \& \ \text{agt}(x, y)$$
$$\& \ \text{member}(z, \text{Physobjs}) \ \& \ \text{obj}(x, z)$$

---

* That is, if B fills the role c for A.

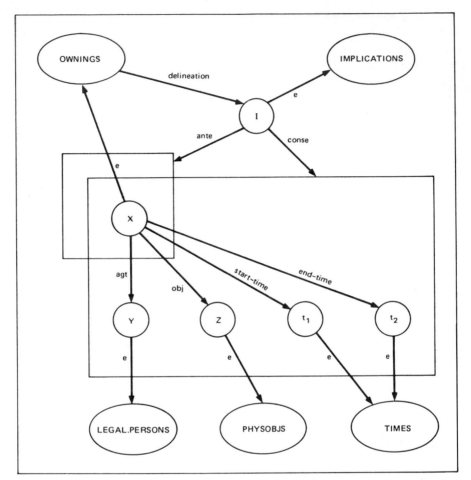

Fig. 13. The delineation theorem of Ownings. (From [Hendrix, G. G., 1978].)

$$\& \ member(t1, \ Times) \ \& \ start\text{-}time(x, \ t1)$$
$$\& \ member(t2, \ Times) \ \& \ end\text{-}time(x, \ t2)]\}.$$

This UQS indicates that all *Ownings* situations have an *agt*, *obj*, *start-time*, and *end-time*. Further, the *agt* must be a member of *Legal.persons*, the *obj* must be (in this system) a member of *Physobjs*, and the *start-time* and *end-time* must be elements of *Times*. More complex restrictions may also be added. For example, the *start-time* could be restricted to precede the *end-time*, and the *obj* could be excluded from the set of *Humans*.*

---

* The information that may be encoded by delineations appears to cover the information that is encoded on what Brachman [in this volume] calls the "epistemological" level of descriptions.

By using delineations, a speech or natural language understanding system is able to reject certain anomalous combinations of phrases that nevertheless meet syntactic and acoustic criteria for being joined. For example, if various indicators suggest that an input utterance mentions an ownership situation in which the role of *agt* (not *obj*) is played by an automobile, then the delineation of *Ownings* may be used to reject the hypothesis on the grounds that the role of *agt* may be filled only by elements of *Legal.persons*.

VII. STRUCTURES FOR JUDGMENTAL REASONING

There are a number of reasoning tasks that require an ability to deal with sketchy and/or uncertain information. For these tasks, the precise rules and two-valued logic of conventional deduction systems are too confining. However, such systems as MYCIN [Shortliffe, 1976] and PROSPECTOR [Duda *et al.*, 1977] have dealt successfully with uncertain reasoning by using judgmental production rules. For example, PROSPECTOR uses such rules as

"Limonite casts suggest the probable presence of pyrite."

Such rules resemble an implication

$$E1 \ \& \ E2 \ \& \ . \ . \ . \ \& \ En \Rightarrow H$$

where the *Ei* are individual pieces of evidence suggestive of a hypothesis *H*. Although the presence of evidence *Ei* seldom implies *H* with certainty, it is usually possible to give some rough estimate of both the necessity and the sufficiency with which some condition *Ei* indicates the existence of *H*.

Judgmental rules of this type may be encoded in partitioned networks by generalizing the structures used to encode logical implication. In particular, the *Ei* of a judgmental rule are placed in the implication's antecedent, the hypothesis is placed in the consequent, and the implication node is given two new case arcs indicating the necessity and sufficiency of the evidence in support of the hypothesis. (PROSPECTOR stores necessity and sufficiency on the node property list, rather than use the more expensive case arcs.)

Many judgmental rules are needed to produce a functional system. Moreover, because the hypothesis of one rule may be evidence for another, the antecedent and consequent spaces are effectively chained together into what may be called an *inference net*. When incoming information changes the probability of any piece of evidence, the probabilistic implications will ripple through the net, reassigning the probabilities of many hypotheses.

The use of partitioned networks to build inference nets and the processes for propagating probabilities are discussed in Duda *et al.* [1978].

VIII.   STRUCTURES FOR REASONING ABOUT PROCESSES

Systems, such as those described in Fikes *et al.* [1972], Hendrix[1973], Scragg[1975a], and Sacerdoti[1977], which do planning or other reasoning about processes, have made extensive use of state-of-the-world models (SWMs) and operators that describe how one state may be transformed into another. Partitioned networks offer attractive structures for encoding both SWMs and operators.

Hopefully, it is clear that a given world state can be modeled by a space containing structures representing the various conditions existing in the given state.* Relationships between states may be encoded by structures that point to the state descriptions as supernodes. To the extent that two states are similar, their encoding spaces may share common nodes and arcs.

Operators also may be encoded conveniently in networks, and are, in fact, needed to express much of the meaning of event situations. For example, Fig. 14 shows an abstraction of the delineation of the set *Exchangings*. As in the delineation of other situations, the various deep cases associated with an exchange are indicated. The delineation also contains an event descriptor D, which aids in encoding some of the dynamic aspects of an exchange. In particular, D indicates that any exchange U will be associated with certain preconditions P and certain effects E.

Both P and E are conjunctions of conditions that may reference the process parameters v, w, x, y, and t. For an instance of *Exchange* to exist with particular bindings for the variables, the preconditions must be met with the same bindings. If the exchanging does occur, then all of the effects (which may include disjunctions to represent uncertain outcomes) are implied just as if the implication

$$\forall v, w, x, y, t[\text{exchange}(v, w, x, y, t) \Rightarrow \text{effects}(v, w, x, y, t)]$$

had been encoded explicitly.

An important aspect of processes is that they usually may be decomposed into a sequence of subprocesses. The delineation of *Shopping* events, shown abstractly in Fig. 15, has provisions for such a decomposition. Preconditions and effects may be used to understand shopping at a coarse level of detail. For a finer look, the event descriptor includes a *plot* that shows how shopping decomposes into a sequence of subprocesses. This plot takes the form of a transition network, which is similar to the ATNs [Woods, 1970] used for parsing sentences. Rather than parse or generate sentences in a language, this transition net may be used to recognize or generate sequences of events that in aggregate constitute a shopping

---

* States of the world are represented in such systems as STRIPS [Fikes *et al.*, 1972] by sets of propositions, which are the predicate calculus analog of spaces.

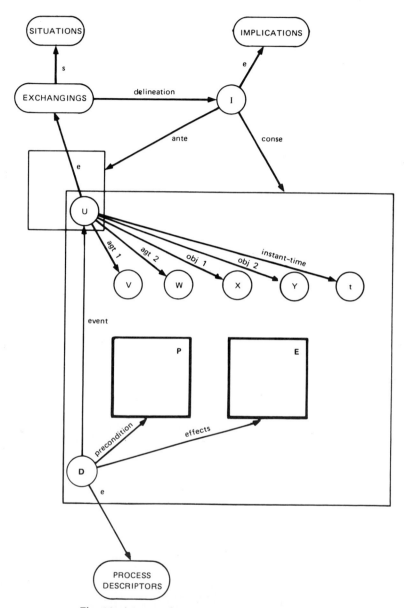

Fig. 14. A coarse description of exchange processes.

event. For example, one successful path through the *event grammar* is GO-STORE-1, GO-STORE-2, EXCHANGE (at STORE-2), GO-HOME.

Each node in the plot network is actually a variable indicating an element of some event set. Since each event set has its own delineation, the subevents may be understood either in terms of their preconditions and

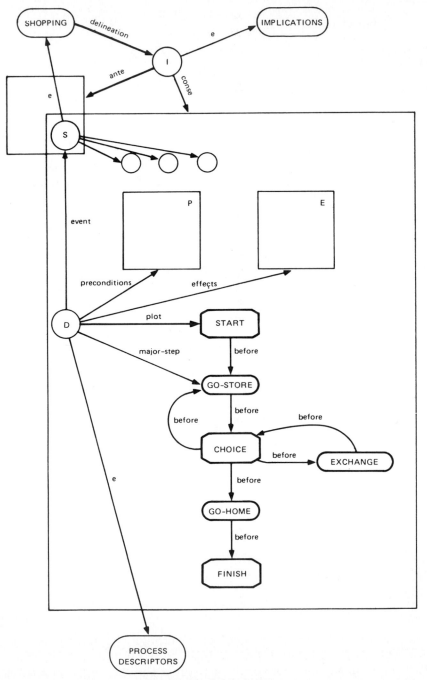

Fig. 15. Plot for shopping.

effects, or recursively, in terms of their own plots (when available). For example, the instance of *Exchangings* in Fig. 15 may be expanded through the delineation of *Exchangings* in Fig. 14.

IX. STRUCTURES FOR NATURAL LANGUAGE UNDERSTANDING

This section discusses the use of networks in a natural language understanding system (NLUS).

A. A Simple Example

To introduce the most basic aspects of using nets in a NLUS, consider the translation of the sentence

"SOME MAN OWNS A CAR."

The ultimate result of the literal translation process for this sentence is the network structure in space SCRATCH of Fig. 16. Structures representing inputs are constructed in scratch spaces to separate them from the system's model of the domain of discourse, which is recorded on a space labeled BACKGROUND. (Only a fraction of BACKGROUND appears in the figure.)

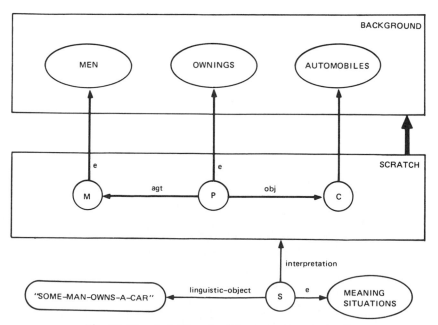

Fig. 16. Target structure for "Some-man owns a-car."

The interpretation of SCRATCH-space structures is quite simple: Node *M* denotes some man (an element of *Men*), *C* denotes some *Automobile*, and *P* denotes an *Ownings* situation in which the agent is *M* and the object is *C*. Because the input is understood through its relationship to previous knowledge, several arcs in the SCRATCH space link the interpretation of the new input to BACKGROUND anchor nodes. Also, because the SCRATCH space is meaningful only in the context of BACKGROUND, the vista of SCRATCH includes BACKGROUND.

As a supplementary feature, the figure also includes a node *S* that represents an element of the set of *Meaning Situations*. In particular, *S* associates the linguistic entity "some-man-owns-a-car" (i.e., the sentence itself) with its interpretation. Thus, the net encodes the semantics of the sentence in the conventional sense of "semantics" as a relationship between linguistic objects and their meanings.*

To suppress syntactic technicalities, assume the following highly simplified language definition:

GRAMMAR	LEXICON
R1: $S \Rightarrow NP \ VP$	NP: Some-man, A-car
R2: $VP \Rightarrow V \ NP$	V: Owns

In the translation process, spaces are created to represent the meanings of each grammatical constituent of the total utterance. These spaces are shown in Fig. 6, with heavy arrows indicating the visibility hierarchy.

At the start of processing, space BACKGROUND encodes both general and some specific knowledge about *Men, Automobiles,* and *Ownings* situations. This knowledge is referenced during the translation process. For example, upon spotting the noun phrase "some-man," the natural language understanding system (NLUS) sets up a structure representing the descriptive meaning of the phrase. In particular, a new space *NP1* is created below BACKGROUND in the viewing hierarchy. Within this space, a node *M* is created with an *e arc* to node MEN in BACKGROUND. Thus, node *M* represents some man and the *e arc* makes its membership in the set *Men* explicit. The new space *NP1* separates the structures built to represent the phrase from all other structures in the net. Similarly, new spaces *V1* and *NP2* are set up to encode other utterance constituents that correspond to explicit lexical entries. Note particularly that concepts conveyed by nouns and verbs are represented uniformly as elements of sets.

Once structures exist for lexical items, subphrases are grouped into

---

* The proposition denoted by the supernode SCRATCH captures only a small (but very central) part of the total meaning of the sentence. The proposition refers to concepts such as the set of *Men* and the set of *Ownings*. Clearly, the total meaning of the sentence must take into consideration what it means to belong to these sets. Moreover, a large number of inferences may be drawn from the information recorded on SCRATCH. These inferences, too, are a part of the extended meaning of the sentence.

larger units in accordance with the syntax. When syntax suggests combining *V1* ("owns") with *NP2* ("a-car") to form a larger phrase, a surface-to-deep-case map associated with the lexical entry for the verb "own" is consulted. This map indicates that an *NP* directly following the verb "own" generally specifies the deep *obj* case.*

Operating under this hypothesis, the NLUS consults the delineation of *Ownings* (see Section VI), which indicates that any *obj* of an *Ownings* situation must be a *non-Human Physobj*. The candidate for the *obj* is C of space *NP2*. Because C is an element of *Automobiles*, which in turn is a subset of *Physobjs* that is disjoint from *Humans*, C is accepted. (A combination such as "owns some-man" would be rejected.)

Once *V1* and *NP2* have passed the acceptability test, a new space *VP1* is constructed to help encode the resultant verb phrase. This new space contains an *obj arc* linking node P of *V1* to node C of *NP2*. The new arc, which constitutes the new component of meaning that *VP1* adds to *V1* and *NP2*, is visible from space *VP1*, but is not visible from either *V1* or *NP2*. This leaves the components seemingly unaltered and free to combine in alternatives to *VP1* if necessary.

Continuing the processing, when syntax rule *R1* suggests combining *NP1* with *VP1* to create an *S* phrase (sentence), acceptability tests similar to those described above are made. When these are passed, a new space, *S1*, is created as shown in Fig. 6, and an *agt arc* from P to M is placed in it. Because the new phrase is a complete sentence spanning the entire input, it is accepted as a legal interpretation.

The structure built during the translation process has two particularly interesting features. First, the partial ordering of spaces from *S1* to BACKGROUND is identical to that represented in Fig. 17, which, because of the choice of space labels, may be recognized as the syntax tree of the sentence. Second, the view from any space shows (after subtracting out BACKGROUND) the contribution of the associated phrase to the meaning

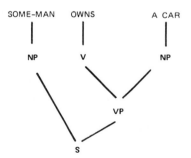

Fig. 17. Parse tree for "Some-man owns a-car."

---

* The NP following "own" is not always the deep *obj*. Consider "What John owns John keeps."

of the total input. For example, the view from *NP1* shows a man *M* and its relationship to *Men*. More importantly, the view from *S1* is identical to the view from SCRATCH of Fig. 16.

B. Quantification

After a structure of the form described above is constructed, a second phase of the translation process copies the various nodes and arcs of the translation from the spaces that reflect the input's syntax onto structures that reflect its quantification. Because the example sentence is purely existential, nodes and arcs are copied onto the single space SCRATCH. Following conventions described in Section V, this space represents the input as a conjunction of conditions expressed solely in terms of existential variables.

However, if the input is changed from "SOME-MAN OWNS A-CAR" to

"EVERY MAN OWNS A CAR"

then the situation is different. In particular, the property list of space *NP1* of Fig. 6 is marked to indicate its universal quantification for the routines that copy from syntactic to quantification structures. To express the universal quantification, the copying routines create an implication structure, as described previously. Structures from the space with the universal marking are placed in the antecedent space of the implication and all structures within their scope are placed in the consequent space. The "head node" of the marked space is placed in the overlap, resulting in the structure shown in Fig. 18.

Further details concerning the mechanics of this type of processing are contained in Hendrix [1978]. Some interesting theoretical problems in translating quantifiers are discussed in Hintikka [1973].

C. Resolving Definitely Determined Noun Phrases

The noun phrases in "SOME-MAN OWNS A-CAR" are indefinite in that they do not refer to any man or car in particular. However, the sentence

"JOHN OWNS THE-CAR"

contains the definitely determined noun phrases "John" and "the-car," which refer to particular objects that the hearer is expected to know about and recognize in context.

The structures built during the parsing of this sentence are shown in Fig. 19. Because "John" is a proper noun whose unique referent is known to the system, reference is made directly to node JOHN in BACK-GROUND. Space *NP1* encompasses JOHN to indicate the interpretation of

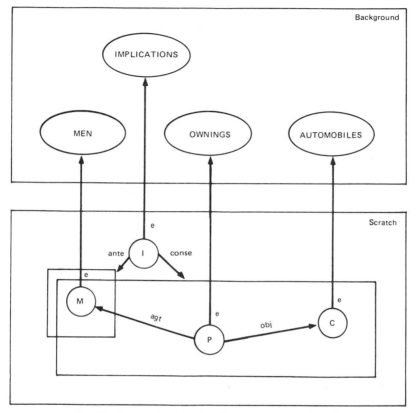

Fig. 18. Target structure for "Every man owns a car."

the noun phrase. Verb "own" produces space *V1* as before. The definitely determined noun phrase "the-car" initially produces a structure *NP2* paralleling that produced earlier for "a-car." But this time the "the" indicates that some particular car, the one currently in context, is being referenced. If *Old.Black* is the current topic of conversation, then *Old.Black* is "the-car." Hence, when *Old.Black* is determined to be "the-car" by means discussed below, space *NP2* becomes obsolete. In its place, the NLUS constructs a new space *D-NP2* around OLD.BLACK, just as it created *NP1* around JOHN.

Following the syntax rules, spaces *VP1* and *S1* are created as before, but this time with arcs pointing directly to nodes in BACKGROUND. The view of the interpretation from *S1* indicates that the new information conveyed by the sentence is that an owning situation *P* exists between previously known objects *John* and *Old.Black*.

The point of interest here is finding the referent of "the-car." Essentially, the problem is to find some object in BACKGROUND that both

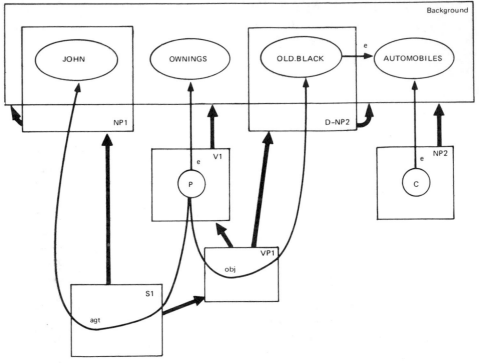

Fig. 19. Parsing "John owns the car."

matches the description given by the phrase and is "in context." To find objects meeting the phrase description, the NLUS looks for network structures in BACKGROUND that match the network structure representing the phrase. (This task may be nontrivial, because much BACKGROUND knowledge is recorded only implicitly. For example, an *e arc* from OLD.BLACK to AUTOMOBILES may be derived from an *e arc* from OLD.BLACK to MUSTANGS and an *s arc* from MUSTANGS to AUTOMOBILES. Were the problem to find "the car made by Ford," it would be necessary to derive that *Ford* made *Old.Black* from the fact that *Ford* made all *Mustangs*.) In general, there may be a great many objects in BACKGROUND meeting a given description, but only those currently in context are wanted.

The general problem of what objects should or should not be in the local context at any given point in an extended discourse has been investigated by a number of workers, most notably Grosz [1977], but is beyond the scope of this chapter. However, once a decision has been made concerning what belongs in a context, partitioning may be used to bundle together the objects of one context and separate them from those of another. In particular, space C2 of Fig. 20 shows OLD.BLACK and JOHN

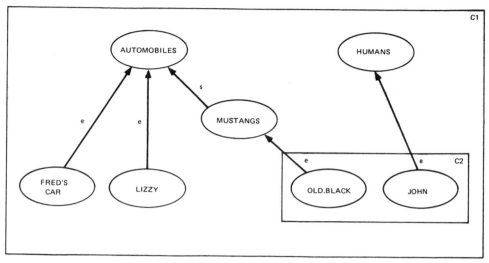

Fig. 20. Spaces encoding contexts.

grouped together into a local context that excludes such objects as FRED'S-CAR. Using vistas, a hierarchy of contexts may be defined. If the local context is encoded by space *C2*, and *C1* is in the vista of *C2*, then the objects in *Cl* may also be considered to be in context, but at a more global level. Objects in spaces outside the vista of *C2* are out of context. Following shifts in context during the course of a discourse is an important area of current research.

D.   Ambiguity

The structure built during the parsing of

"SOME-MAN GAVE A-DOG A-BONE"

is shown in Fig. 21. The point of interest here is that "GIVE A-DOG" is locally ambiguous in that it might mean that a dog was given to someone or that something was given to a dog. The structure of the figure reflects this ambiguity with *VP1* interpreting A-DOG as filling the *obj* case, and *VP2* interpreting A-DOG as filling the *rec* (recipient) case. Note that the viewing hierarchy allows both alternatives to share spaces *V* and *NP2* without confusion, the *rec arc* being invisible from *VP1* and the *obj arc* being invisible from *VP2*.

From the vantage of space S2, the correct interpretation of the total sentence is visible, with erroneous structures in spaces *VP1* and *S1* being effectively blocked out. Thus, partitioning enables networks to maintain alternative hypotheses concerning the use of input constituents and enables such competing hypotheses to share network subparts. Without

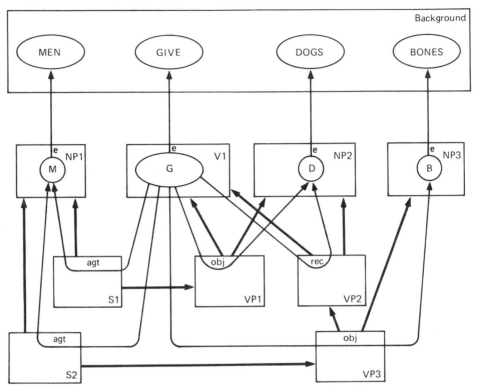

Fig. 21. Parsing "Some man gave a dog a bone."

partitioning or some similar technique, the back-linked nature of networks may cause a constituent to be altered when it is incorporated into a larger unit and hence render it unusable in alternative constructions.

X. LINEARIZED NET NOTATION

To provide a convenient formalism for communicating network structures to the computer, a linearized net notation, called the *LN2* language, has been devised as an extension of INTERLISP [Teitelman, 1975]. The syntax of LN2 was inspired by and bears some resemblance to the syntax of KRL [Bobrow and Winograd, 1977].

The flavor of this language is indicated by the following statement, which builds the network of Fig. 22:

```
(!SPACE S1
        [UNIVERSAL]
        [SITUATIONS (ARE UNIVERSAL)]
        [IMPLICATIONS (ARE SITUATIONS)]
```

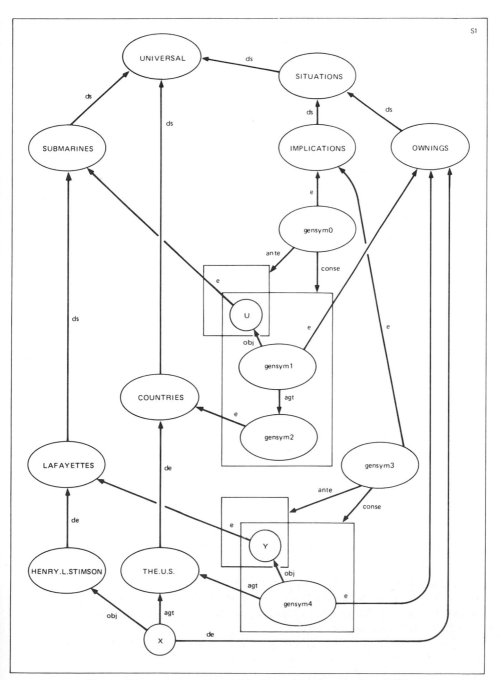

Fig. 22. Network created by LN2. (From [Hendrix, G. G., 1978].)

```
[OWNINGS (ARE SITUATIONS)]
[SUBMARINES (ARE UNIVERSAL)]
[LAFAYETTES (ARE SUBMARINES)]
[Henry.L.Stimson (A LAFAYETTE)]
[COUNTRIES (ARE UNIVERSAL)
                 (SINGULAR COUNTRY)]
[The.U.S. (A COUNTRY)]
[x (AN OWNING)
    {agt The.U.S.}
    {obj Henry.L.Stimson}]
(TURN.OFF.D)
(IMPLICATION
    ([u (A SUBMARINE)])
    ([[(AN OWNING)
       {obj u}
       {agt (A COUNTRY)}]]))
(LN2.SUB
    owns (OWNER OWNEE)
    [(AN OWNING)
    {agt OWNER}
    {obj OWNEE}])
(IMPLICATION
    ([y (A LAFAYETTE)])
    ((⟨owns The.U.S. y⟩))))
```

The total statement is a call to function !SPACE of the form (!SPACE name *e1 e2 . . . en*). Its first argument is a name to be given to a newly created space. All subsequent arguments are expressions to be executed in the context of the new space.

The first such expression is "[UNIVERSAL]," which read-macros expand into "(!NODE UNIVERSAL)." In general, calls to !NODE are of the form (!NODE optional-name *e1 e2 . . . en*). The function creates a new node on the current space, assigns it the optional-name, and then evaluates the various expressions *ei*. Thus, [UNIVERSAL] just creates a node named UNIVERSAL.

"[SITUATIONS (ARE UNIVERSAL)]" creates a node named SITUA-TIONS and then executes the expression "(ARE UNIVERSAL)," which creates a *ds arc* from the current node to UNIVERSAL. The next four !NODE expressions are similar.

"[Henry.L.Stimson (A LAFAYETTE)]" causes a node to be created named Henry L. Stimson. Function *A* produces a *de arc* from this node to LAFAYETTES, the node whose name is formed by adding "S" or "ES" to the argument of *A*.

Since COUNTRY has an irregular plural, the expression creating node

COUNTRIES has a call to function SINGULAR to note this fact. SINGU-LAR does the necessary bookkeeping so that the call to *A* in "[The.U.S. (A COUNTRY)]" works properly.

"[x (AN OWNING) {agt The.U.S.} {obj Henry.L.Stimson}]" creates node *x*, encodes *x* as a distinct element of *Ownings,* and then creates an *agt arc* to The.U.S. and an *obj arc* to Henry.L.Stimson.*

The expression "(TURN.OFF.D)" changes the operation of functions *A* and ARE so that *de* and *ds arcs* are replaced subsequently by *e* and *s arcs.*

Function IMPLICATION takes two arguments: a list of expressions for creating structures inside an implication ante space and a similar list for the conse space. IMPLICATION builds a new element of *Implications* with appropriate new spaces and then executes the lists of expressions. New structures created or referred to by both ante and conse are placed in the overlap.

In the first IMPLICATION of the example, the ante space expressions (there is only one) cause a node labeled *u* to be created with an *e arc* to SUBMARINES. The sole conse space expression calls for a node to be created and assigned a gensym name. The node represents an element of *Ownings.* The *obj* of this element is *u.* The *agt* is to be encoded by a newly created, gensym-named node with an *e arc* to COUNTRIES.

Function LN2.SUB creates no structure itself but defines an LN2 sub-routine for subsequent use. The example shown defines a subroutine called "owns" that may be used to create instances of *Ownings* situa-tions in terms of the local variables (formal parameters) OWNER and OWNEE. The remaining arguments to LN2.SUB are expressions to be evaluated when the "owns" subroutine is invoked. An invocation of the "owns" subroutine occurs in the conse of the last IMPLICATION. The delimiters ⟨ and ⟩ indicate that an LN2 subroutine is to be invoked. The first argument within the delimiters is the subroutine name (which must have been previously declared in a call to LN2.SUB) and the other arguments are actual parameters. Calls to LN2 subroutines are designed to resemble expressions of propositions in predicate calculus notation.

XI. IMPLEMENTATION

SRI's implementation of partitioned networks is written in INTERLISP [Teitelman, 1975] and makes extensive use of user data types. Nodes, arcs, and spaces are each represented by a separate record type.

A space record is a collection of four pointers referencing the list of nodes in the space, the list of arcs, the property list, and the node structure

* A delineation for the set of *Ownings* situations would be included in a more complete net-work, but is omitted here.

that encodes the space's nodelike properties if it is a supernode. The latter field is NIL for spaces that are not supernodes.

A node record is a collection of six pointers referencing the incoming arcs, the outgoing arcs, the node label (if assigned), the spaces upon which the node lies, the property list, and the associated space if the node is part of a supernode complex.

An arc record is a collection of five pointers referencing the arc label, the "from" node, the "to" node, the spaces upon which the arc lies, and the arc's property list.

The most recent versions of the net package, including one version that maintains large nets on secondary storage, where programmed by Jonathan Slocum, Ann Robinson, and Kurt Konolige. The largest partitioned net created to date contains some 4500 network structures (nodes, arcs, and spaces) and was used in the PROSPECTOR rule-based inference system. Models using in the neighborhood of 10,000 structures are under construction.

XII. CONCLUSION

This chapter has outlined the basic concepts underlying the encoding of knowledge in partitioned networks and has discussed structures used for a variety of specialized applications. The ability of networks to encode knowledge in a form convenient for a diversity of applications enhances the value of networks as a medium for integrating many skills in one coordinated system. Partitioning has increased the usability of networks for those applications in which a subportion of a network is to be treated collectively as a unit.

ACKNOWLEDGMENTS

Work on partitioned networks and their applications has been supported in part by the National Science Foundation under Grant No. MCS76-22004, the Defense Advanced Research Projects Agency under Contracts DAHC04-75-C-0005, DAAG29-76-C-0011, DAAG29-76-C-0012, and N00039-78-C-0060, and the Office of Resources of the U.S. Geological Survey under Contract No. 14-08-0001-15985. Thoughtful critiques of early drafts of this paper were given by Robert Moore. Virtually everyone in the Natural Language, Prospector, and Decision Aids projects at SRI International has made contributions to the development of partitioned networks. It is hoped that feedback from this community of users will continue to support the evolution of more powerful systems.

REFERENCES

[Bobrow, D. G., and Winograd, T., 1977]. An overview of KRL, a knowledge representation language. *Cognitive Science* **1**, 3–46.
[Brachman, R. J., 1977]. What's in a concept: Structural foundations for semantic networks. *International Journal of Man-Machine Studies* **9**, 127–152.

[Brachman, R. J., 1978]. "On the Epistemological Status of Semantic Networks." In the present book.

[Bruce, B. C., 1973]. A model of temporal references and its application in a question answering program. *Artificial Intelligence* **3**, 1–26.

[Cohen, P. R., and Perrault, C. R., 1976]. Preliminaries for a computer model of conversation. *Proceedings of the 1st CSCSI/SCEIO National Conference, 1976* pp. 102–111.

[Duda, R. O., Hart, P. E., and Reboh, R., 1977]. A rule-based consultation program for mineral exploration. In *Proceedings of the Lawrence Symposium on Systems and Decision Sciences, 1977* pp. 306–309.

[Duda, R. O., Hart, P. E., Nilsson, N. J., and Sutherland, G. L., 1978]. Semantic network representations in rule-based inference systems. In *Pattern-Directed Inference Systems*. D. A. Waterman and F. Hayes-Roth (eds.). Academic Press, New York, pp. 203–221.

[Fahlman, S. E., 1977]. A system for representing and using real-world knowledge. Ph.D. dissertation, MIT, Cambridge, Massachusetts.

[Fikes, R. E., and Hendrix, G. G., 1977]. A network-based knowledge representation and its natural deduction system. *Proceedings of the 5th International Joint Conference on Artificial Intelligence. 1977* pp. 235–246.

[Fikes, R. E., Hart, P. E., and Nilsson, N. J., 1972]. Learning and executing generalized robot plans. *Artificial Intelligence* **3**, 251–288.

[Fillmore, C. J., 1968]. The case for case. In *Universals in Linguistic Theory*. E. Bach and R. Harms (eds.). Holt, New York, pp. 1–88.

[Grosz, B. J., 1977]. The representation and use of focus in dialog understanding. Ph.D. dissertation, University of California at Berkeley.

[Hayes, Philip J., 1977]. Some association-based techniques for lexical disambiguation by machine. Doctoral thesis, Ecole Polytechnique Fédérale de Lausanne, Lausanne, Switzerland.

[Hendrix, G. G., 1973]. Modeling simultaneous actions and continuous processes. *Artificial Intelligence* **4**, 145–180.

[Hendrix, G. G., 1975a]. Expanding the utility of semantic networks through partitioning. *Advance Papers of the International Joint Conference on Artificial Intelligence. 1975* pp. 115–121.

[Hendrix, G. G., 1975b]. "Partitioned Networks for the Mathematical Modeling of Natural Language Semantics," Technical Report NL-28. Department of Computer Science, University of Texas, Austin.

[Hendrix, G. G., 1978]. Semantic aspects of translation. In *Understanding Spoken Language*. D. E. Walker (ed.). Am. Elsevier, New York, pp. 193–226.

[Hintikka, J., 1973]. Quantifiers vs. quantification theory *Linguistic Inquiry* **5**, 153–177.

[Kay, M., 1973]. The MIND system. In *Natural Language Processing*. R. Rustin (ed.). Algorithmics Press, New York, pp. 153–188.

[McCarthy, J., 1968]. Situation, actions, and causal laws. In *Semantic Information Processing*. M. Minsky (ed.). MIT Press, Cambridge, Massachusetts, pp. 410–417.

[Montague, R., 1974]. Syntactical treatments of modality, with corollaries on reflexion principles and finite axiomatizability. In *Formal Philosophy*. R. H. Thomason (ed.). Yale Univ. Press, New Haven, Connecticut, pp. 286–302.

[Moore, R. C., 1975]. "Reasoning from Incomplete Knowledge in a Procedural Deduction System," Technical Report 347. Artificial Intelligence Laboratory, MIT, Cambridge, Massachusetts.

[Norman, D. A., Rumelhart, D. E., and the LNR Research Group, 1975]. *Explorations in Cognition*. Freeman, San Francisco, California.

[Reboh, R., and Sacerdoti, E. D., 1973]. "A Preliminary QLISP Manual," Technical Note 81. Artificial Intelligence Center, Stanford Research Institute, Menlo Park, California.

[Sacerdoti, E. D., 1977]. *A Structure for Plans and Behavior*. Am. Elsevier, New York, 1977.

[Schubert, L. K., 1976]. Extending the expressive power of semantic networks. *Artificial Intelligence* **7**, 163–198.

[Scragg, G. W., 1975a]. Answering questions about processes. In *Explorations in Cognition* D. A. Norman and D. E. Rumelhart (eds.). Freeman, San Francisco, California, pp. 349–375.

[Scragg, G. W., 1975b]. "Frames, Planes and Nets: A Synthesis," Technical Note 19. Instituto per gli Studi Semantici e Cognitivi, Castagnola, Switzerland.

[Shapiro, S. C., 1971]. A net structure for semantic information storage, deduction and retrieval. *Advance Papers of the 2nd International Joint Conference on Artificial Intelligence, 1971* pp. 512–523.

[Shortliffe, E. H., 1976]. *Computer-Based Medical Consultations: MYCIN*. Am. Elsevier, New York, 1976.

[Simmons, R. F., 1973]. Semantic networks: Their computation and use for understanding English sentences. In *Computer Models of Thought and Language*. C. Schank and K. M. Colby (eds.). Freeman, San Francisco, California, pp. 63–113.

[Teitelman, W., 1975]. "INTERLISP Reference Manual" (xerox). Palo Alto Research Center, Palo Alto, California.

[Walker, D. E., ed., 1978]. *Understanding Spoken Language*. Amer. Elsevier, New York.

[Woods, W. A., 1970]. Transition network grammars for natural language analysis. *Communications of the ACM* **13,** 591–606.

[Woods, W. A., 1975]. What's in a link: Foundations for semantic networks. In *Representation and Understanding*. D. G. Bobrow and A. M. Collins (eds.). Academic Press, New York, pp. 35–82.

A PROCEDURAL SEMANTICS
FOR SEMANTIC NETWORKS

Hector Levesque   *and*   *John Mylopoulos*

ABSTRACT

In this chapter, we describe an approach to the representation of knowledge that formalizes traditional semantic network concepts within a procedural framework. The basic entities of the representation are classes and (binary) relations, and their semantics are provided by a small set of programs. Two organizational principles are offered by the representation: the IS-A and PART-OF hierarchies, which allow the specification of generalization and whole–part relationships, respectively. The concept of a metaclass is also introduced (i.e., a class of classes), and it is shown how it can be used to explain certain features of the representation within itself. Properties of classes are then classified as structural or assertional and it is demonstrated that each type must have different inheritance rules, which can be expressed quite simply in the representation. Finally, a representation for programs is proposed in terms of the IS-A and PART-OF hierarchies. The benefits of such an organization of programs and the relationship between the representation and others such as KRL and FRL are also discussed.

1. INTRODUCTION

In this chapter, we describe an approach to the representation of knowledge that attempts to capture traditional semantic network concepts within a generally procedural framework. Much of what is presented here is derived from Levesque [1977] although some simplifications have been made. Extensions and refinements to the representation continue in Schneider [1978] and the effort remains a topic of on-going research.

The original motivation for our work was the development of a consistent notation for semantic networks. Typically, a semantic network is described using diagrams of directed labeled graphs with little or no indication as to what exactly these diagrams are intended to represent. To interpret this diagram as a model of a data structure within a computer memory simply postpones the problem since we must now ask what the data structure represents. Clearly, a diagram is simply a notational convenience* and what is required is a semantic theory accounting for how configurations in the network represent aspects of the domain being modeled.

One possibility for a theory of semantic networks is to interpret a network in terms of the semantics of classical *logic*. Although this approach has many advantages and proponents, it has at least two drawbacks. First of all, the specification of concepts whose properties change over time tends to be quite cumbersome. This is a substantial problem since semantic networks are normally incomplete models of evolving worlds. Such models must be prepared to receive new information, determine its acceptability, and modify themselves accordingly. Second, and more important, the truth-value semantics of classical logic does not intrinsically concern itself with the control issues involved in *using* a representation. For example, there is no distinction between an inference rule that *can* be used and one that *should* be used.† Whether in fact semantics should remain at the level of "competence" or instead deal explicitly with resource limitations and other "performance" issues is a current topic of debate, and probably largely a matter of taste. Suffice it to say that any computational scheme must deal with performance at some level; failure to treat the issues is merely a willingness to accept *poor* performance.

A second possibility for a theory of semantic networks, and the approach taken by our work, is to base such a theory on *programs*. In this case, semantics involves the notion of *behavior* under certain operations, where the control issues mentioned in the last paragraph will be addressed explicitly. Thus, the thrashing common to an overly declarative representation can be minimized. This so-called procedural semantics view of representation has already had a profound impact on many areas of AI research (e.g., Winograd [1976]).

Any representation must interact with programs at some level. The approach generally taken in semantic network systems is to treat the network as a data structure and provide a general global interpreter to query, mod-·ify, and search this structure. Our approach, on the other hand, is to effectively distribute the global interpreter by associating directly with each component of a semantic network the programs necessary to perform the operations defined on the component. Every component consequently acts for itself (in the ACTOR [Hewitt, 1973] sense) and is responsible for its behavior under its defined operations.

In the next section, we examine the components of a semantic network

---

* The fact remains that diagrams have often hindered semantic network theory in that representational concepts were rejected or accepted solely in terms of their two-dimensional visualizations.

† This is precisely the point made by languages like PLANNER [Hewitt, 1972], which provide a weaker version of classical logic where the inference rules are severely restricted and controlled.

and attempt to categorize their operations. Section 3 investigates methods of organizing and structuring a semantic network within a procedural framework. In Section 4, we introduce the concept of a metaclass and show how this can be used to explain certain features of a semantic network within the representation itself. Section 5 describes the inheritance of properties in terms of the preceding sections, attempting to avoid the logical pitfalls quite common with this topic. Finally, in Section 6, we show how programs can be integrated into semantic networks in terms of the organizational facilities of Section 3, and what benefits are accrued from this effort.

Instead of presenting a formalism in which semantic networks can be built and manipulated, diagrams are used for the examples throughout. These diagrams should be understood by the reader as convenient visual aids, not to be confused with the representation itself (defined by the operations of a formalism) or a possible implementation of this representation (defined by an interpreter of the formalism). It is not claimed that the diagrams capture all the features of our formalism, which is described in considerable detail in Levesque [1977] and Schneider [1978].

It is perhaps worth acknowledging at the outset that many readers will question the usefulness of developing yet another representation of knowledge without having a very specific application area in mind. While sympathetic to this viewpoint, we still feel that there are enough unresolved representation issues to warrant research of a more fundamental nature. Obviously, our final goal is to actually use the representation, and detailed applications of our approach can be found in Kidd *et al.* [1977] and Cohen [1978]. For the purpose of this chapter, however, the reader is invited to assume that *his* domain of interest is the intended application area, and judge the utility of the representation accordingly.

2. COMPONENTS

Traditionally, a semantic network is viewed as a directed labeled graph where the nodes represent concepts and the edges represent relationships between these concepts. For example. Fig. 1 might represent the fact that John is a brother of Jim. However, in one reading of Figure 2, the "brother" edge is redundant in the sense that the relationship it represents can be inferred from the other two. If a semantic network is implemented as a data structure, the possibility of storing all relevant relationships including redundant ones is clearly impractical. Moreover, it misses completely the generalizations that can be made about, for example, transitive relationships (see Fig. 3). A major problem in many semantic network schemes is the inability to express this kind of interaction between the components.

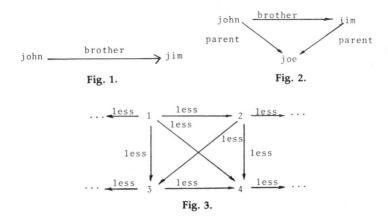

Fig. 1.   Fig. 2.

Fig. 3.

In our opinion, a method of *defining* certain kinds of concepts and relationships is required. For example, a brother of a person x is any other
person that is a son of x's parents. Similarly, a son of a person is any male
having the person as parent. One possible way of defining a concept or relationship type in a semantic network scheme (where the network is
treated as a data structure), is to incorporate rules of inference within the
global interpreter that manipulates the data structure. Thus the interpreter
would know how the "brother" and "parent" relationships interact. This
has the distinct disadvantage of anchoring the interpreter to the types of
concepts and relationships in a particular application. Moreover, for a
large evolving system, the interpreter may become unmanageable as concepts and relationships proliferate. Our solution is to take a more modular
approach consistent with the ideology of abstract data types (e.g., Liskov
and Zillies [1974]) and associate programs with each type of concept and
relationship independently. These programs will provide an interpretation for the operations on the concepts or relationships of this type.

To accommodate clearly this notion of type within our representation,
we use the terms *class* and (binary) *relation* to represent respectively concept type and relationship type, reserving the terms "node" and "edge"
for our diagrams. Particular concepts are represented by *instances* of
classes, while relationships between concepts are formulated as *assertions*.
Finally, the term *object* is used to denote any component of the semantic
network. To illustrate these features graphically, we shall change our notation to be, for example, as shown in Fig. 4. Here, PERSON and
NUMBER are classes, AGE is a relation, the unlabeled edges indicate the
type of the component, and the edges labeled domain and range are special associations explained in Section 4.*

---

* For the time being, these can be treated simply as diagrammatic notation and will occasionally be omitted.

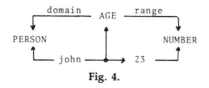

Fig. 4.

The operations on a semantic network therefore decompose naturally into those involving relations and those involving classes. There are four basic operations on relations:

(1) assert that a given relation holds between two objects;
(2) assert that a given relation no longer holds between two objects;
(3) fetch all objects related to another by a given relation.

These correspond, of course, to the assert, erase, and fetch operations of CONNIVER [Sussman and McDermott, 1972]. The fourth operation is

(4) test whether a given relation holds between two objects.

This may be quite different from the fetch operation, as we will soon see. Similarly, there are four operations on classes, which are

(1) create an instance of a class (or assert that an existing object is an instance of a class);*
(2) destroy an instance of a class (or assert that an object is no longer an instance of a class);
(3) fetch all instances of a class;
(4) test whether an object is an instance of a class.

There are therefore four basic operations on classes and four on relations, and the semantics of a class (or relation) are specified by indicating the behavior of the class (or relation) under the four operations using programs.

For example, to express the fact that the semantics of the PROFIT relation is such that the profit for a product is the price minus the cost, we could provide a program for the fetch operation of PROFIT that would fetch the price and the cost of a product and compute the difference (see Fig. 5). Thus the assertion relating "bread" and "7" is inferred from the

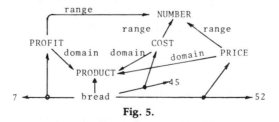

Fig. 5.

* This, of course, implies that an object may be an instance of more than one class.

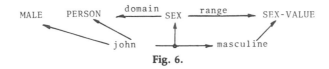

Fig. 6.

other two. Similarly, one way of expressing the semantics of MALE is to specify a program for the create operation that says that to assert that something is a male is to assert that he is a person whose sex is masculine (see Fig. 6). Note that the presence of an edge in the above diagram between john and MALE only implies that these two objects are related but says nothing about whether this information can be retrieved directly (i.e., is stored explicitly) or must be inferred. For that matter, the same holds true of the edges between john and PERSON or john and masculine. These will depend on the operations of PERSON and SEX.* This is quite different from the approach taken by PLANNER/CONNIVER, where assert and erase operations always manipulate the database regardless of the antecedent or erasing theorems. Only the retrieval operations allow a completely procedural specification (i.e., consequent theorems). This assumption forces all stored classes and relations to be stored in exactly the same way, whereas in our case some classes may be stored in tables, some using pointer structures, and still others interfacing with a completely separate database system. Hence, where the three methods of CONNIVER are referred to as "if-added," "if-removed," and "if-needed," a more suitable description of our four is *to-add, to-remove, to-test,* and *to-fetch.*

The main reason for proposing four operations instead of the three of CONNIVER is simply that in terms of programs, a testing operation can often be specified without considering the results produced by a retrieval operation even though these two operations must be consistent. For example, consider the relation FACTOR holding between two numbers if one number is a factor of another. Determining if a number is a factor of another may be much simpler than generating all the factors of a number, since the former can be done using only a division and a test for remainder of zero.

The semantic network representation we are considering is not as hierarchical as the above would imply. First of all, if no program is specified for some operation of a class or relation, a default program is provided. In this case, the class has the "standard" semantics for the operation.† More-

---

* In fact, a class can only interact with other classes or relations in terms of their four operations. The actual mechanism used to achieve the operation is private to the class or relation in question. This quality, known as *semantic data independence* [Abrial, 1974], corresponds to the abstract data type idea of separating a representation (e.g., a stack) from its implementation (e.g., an array).

† Adding involves storing in a database, removing involves undoing the storage, while testing and fetching consist of searching the database.

over, as we shall describe below, classes and relations can be organized to allow the semantics to default in a natural sort of way. In addition, facilities are provided for having partial defaults so that existing programs can be augmented and refined. In fact, although this is contrary to the spirit of the representation, programs need never be supplied for *any* class or relation; a standard semantic network is simply a special case of our representation. Thus, depending on the application and the personal preferences of the user, the network can range from very declarative (many defaults used) to very procedural (few defaults used). It is our feeling that the procedural/declarative issues are best dealt with by this kind of flexibility.

In summary, let an *object* be any single conceptual unit that can be referred to as a whole. Our semantic network representation is centered around *classes, relations,* and *programs* that are all (but not the only) objects:

(1)   A class is a collection of objects sharing common properties; these objects are said to be *instances* of the class and may themselves be classes (as discussed in Section 4).

(2)   A relation is a mapping from one class, its *domain,* to another, its *range;* relations can be considered as classes with *assertions* as instances (as discussed in Section 3).

(3)   A program is a class whose instances are called *processes* and correspond to program activations (as discussed in Section 6).

There are four basic operations defined on classes and relations: *add* an instance to a class, *remove* an instance from a class, *fetch* all instances of a class, and *test* for being an instance of a class. These operations are defined by attaching four programs to each class or relation. The *semantics* of a class or relation is its behavior under these operations.

3.   ORGANIZATION

An argument could certainly be made for the descriptive adequacy of the semantic network scheme considered in the last section. Indeed, one would be hard pressed to discover situations that could not be treated at some level in terms of classes, relations and programs (as is done in Abrial [1974], for instance). Furthermore, the representation shares with ACTORS an extreme form of modularity, allowing for very flexible interactions among the various components. However, the fact remains that programs were introduced to account for the interdependence among many of the components, and this interdependence is often of a very stereotyped nature not requiring the full power inherent in explicit programs. Moreover, if the representation offers just the tools introduced so far, it will be extremely difficult to extract the relationships that may exist between the definitions of two classes or relations since these will be hidden within programs. In this section, we present organizational principles for semantic networks as a way of *implicitly* describing stereotyped relationships among definitions.

To see the usefulness of this idea, consider, for example, any programming language offering patterns and pattern matching. The effect of these constructs can normally be achieved otherwise in terms of explicit programs. However, since the patterns themselves imply these programs, many unnecessary details are suppressed. Thus the semantics* of the language itself is enriched by the presence of a new operation (pattern matching), distinct from the combination of old operations used to achieve the effect.

Hence we view the organization of a semantic network as basically an *abstraction mechanism* in terms of which details from a lower level of representation are suppressed. This is a crucial issue when dealing with large semantic networks—just as structuring techniques are important in the development of large programs. We have begun the investigation of two abstraction mechanisms corresponding to generalization/specialization and aggregation/decomposition. In the first case, details are suppressed concerning the similarity between objects; in the second, details are suppressed concerning the relationships between objects. It should be noted at the outset that we do not preclude other organizational principles or other approaches to these two. Further discussion and extensions can be found in Schneider [1978].

The first abstraction mechanism we consider (and the most commonly used with semantic networks) is the organization that derives from splitting classes into *subclasses* generating a taxonomy of classes known as an *IS-A hierarchy*. This defines a partial ordering of classes where each instance of a subclass is (unless otherwise noted) considered an instance of the superclasses. The IS-A hierarchy is graphically described by its Hasse diagram (see Fig. 7). The unlabeled double edge represents the superclass (IS-A) relationship. The top of the hierarchy is the special class OBJECT, which is the class of all objects and thus a superclass of every class. Similarly, relations can be organized into an IS-A hierarchy as shown in Fig. 8. Here, John is the oldest child of Joe in addition to also being simply a child of Joe. The top of this hierarchy is the relation ASSERTION, which is a superclass of every relation.

Aside from the conceptual gains inherent in having a taxonomy of classes, the main purpose of this categorization is for what has been called the *inheritance of properties*, discussed in Section 5. In fact, the IS-A hierarchy expresses a simple but prevalent form of quantification. In terms of the four operations on classes and relations, the IS-A hierarchy allows the

---

* We are using the term semantics as it was defined in the preceding section: behavior under certain operations.

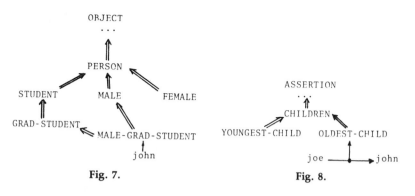

Fig. 7.   Fig. 8.

addition and deletion operations to affect the testing and retrieval operations of not only the immediate class or relation, but all the more generic classes and relations. This, of course, must be taken into account by the default programs for classes and relations.

The second abstraction mechanism we consider involves composing groups of interrelated objects into single functional units. Consider the following example: let GRADE be the class of all grades (for all students in all courses) and PUPIL, LESSON, and MARK be relations mapping grades into students, courses, and numeric values, respectively. Moreover, let grade23 be the object denoting John's grade in the course csc374. Thus Fig. 9 represents the fact that John's grade in csc374 was 78. Now the relations PUPIL and LESSON are quite different from the relations we have seen so far. For example, the relation PUPIL *always holds* between a grade and a single student in the sense that a grade is always for a particular student. Moreover, the mapping *remains fixed* throughout the lifetime of the object grade23. If in fact, we could assert that grade23 was to be associated to another student, then we would be changing the meaning of grade23 in that it would no longer represent John's grade in csc374. This is not the case with the relation MARK since the mark of a grade can be changed without altering what the grade is intended to represent. In some sense, john and csc374 determine which grade is being referred to, quite independently of whether this grade is a pass or fail, who is allowed to examine it, whether it was assigned fairly, etc. Following Woods [1975] and Brachman [1977], we refer to properties like PUPIL and LESSON as *structural properties* and properties like MARK as *assertional properties*.

To represent the fact that PUPIL and LESSON are structural properties

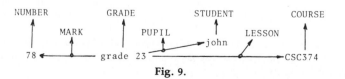

Fig. 9.

of grades, instead of defining these properties as relations having GRADE as domain (which would be done with assertional properties), we associate directly to each grade a *structure:* a group of named objects. These objects are said to be the *parts* of the structure, generating an organization called the *PART-OF hierarchy.* Thus, grade23 is a structure having john as its pupil part, and in general grades have a pupil part (a student) and a lesson part (a course). We represent this graphically in Fig. 10. Here, the labeled edges pupil and lesson indicate the parts of a grade, while ⟨pupil⟩ and ⟨lesson⟩ are placeholders called *slots*. Each instance of GRADE is specified by filling the slots by particular parts.

The fact that we have now represented grades as having both structural and assertional properties does not imply that any other arrangement is somehow incorrect.* We have merely indicated that the definition of grades depends on the two parts and that the two properties are not important enough to be defined independently as relations. In fact, structural properties have no semantics in isolation—they are simply associations between objects. The role played by a part of a structure is determined by the usual four programs of the class. This is quite different from relations that are *independent* units accounting for their own behavior procedurally. Consequently, any structural property can be treated as a relation given appropriate programs (as in our first representation of grades). Conversely, if the mapping represented by a relation is such that for each instance of the domain it is fixed to a single instance of the range, then this relation can usually be treated as a structural property.† The reason why the mapping represented by a relation can change over time is that programs will exist to interpret the change; if, however, the mapping is fixed

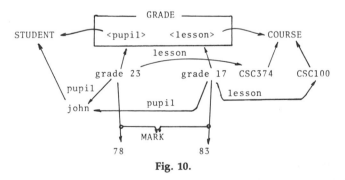

Fig. 10.

---

* In fact, the distinction between structural and assertional properties is far from being clear-cut on purely philosophical grounds. For example, as argued in Wittgenstein [1958], it is doubtful whether there could ever be general agreement on a "correct" set of structural properties for a class like GAME.

† For example, the relation MARK could be a structural property of grades provided that each grade had a single unchanging mark by definition. In this sense, the binding between a slot and its filler is similar to lambda-binding.

for some property, the programs of relations are unnecessary and can be suppressed by making the property structural.

Just as the IS-A hierarchy expresses a simple universal quantification, the PART-OF hierarchy implicitly expresses an existential quantification, since for each instance of the class, there exist objects constituting its parts. To help state exactly what can be part of the instances of a class, slots, in addition to having a type, can have a *default,* which is the expected slot filler (used if no other is provided), and *dependencies,* which are constraints associating the slot to other objects (including other slots).

For example, the following structure defines grades as having four parts (see Fig. 11):

(1)   a pupil, which is a student;
(2)   a mark, which is a positive number less than 100;
(3)   a lesson, which is a course, usually csc100; and
(4)   a prof, which is a professor, the instructor of the lesson.

Although structures now begin to take on the appearance of "frames" [Minsky, 1975; Roberts and Goldstein, 1977], it is important to stress that these structures must still be interpreted by programs. In particular, the dependencies of a structure have a number of *possible* procedural interpretations. For example,

(1)   When creating an instance of the class, the relations specified by the dependencies are tested and if they are not satisfied, the instantiation fails (prerequisite).

(2)   When creating an instance of the class, these relations are simply asserted of the given slot fillers (side-effect).

(3)   When creating an instance of the class with some of the structure provided, the relations can be accessed to infer the rest of the structure (slot filling).

(4)   The testing operation of the class can use the structure to recognize as an instance any object satisfying the dependencies (pattern matching).

Having examined structures, we can now state why relations can be

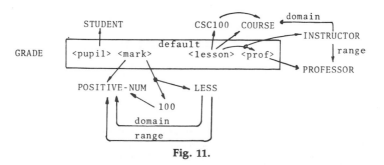

Fig. 11.

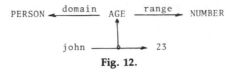

Fig. 12.

treated as classes. For example, the relation AGE (see Fig. 12) could also be interpreted (assuming appropriate programs) as a structure in Fig. 13. Moreover, this view of relations has the advantage of treating assertions as explicit objects (e.g., age243) to which properties can be attached.* For example, as discussed in Levesque [1977], by associating a truth-value with each assertion and certain cardinality information with each relation, it is possible to distinguish in a natural way between something that is not known (due to incomplete information) and something that is false.

In this section, we have been concerned with organizing a semantic network along two orthogonal hierarchies: IS-A and PART-OF. Although it must be admitted that our approach to these abstraction mechanisms is often simplistic, it should also be understood that we wish to avoid incorporating powerful but intransigent facilities into the representation at a primitive level. For instance, many recent semantic network proposals include elaborate techniques for dealing with fully general quantification (arbitrary nestings of quantifiers, etc.). Rather than introduce such specialized machinery over and above the IS-A and PART-OF hierarchies, we prefer to treat quantification procedurally (i.e., constructively) as in PLANNER. Our view is to have the IS-A and PART-OF hierarchies provide a convenient declarative supplement to the usual procedural definitions.

4. METACLASSES

In the previous sections, we have made the assumption (typical of many semantic network schemes) that every object is either a class (relation, program) or an individual instance of some class (relation, program). This

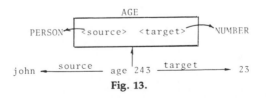

Fig. 13.

---

* Typical properties that could be attached to assertions are a confidence level as to the reliability of the assertion, other assertions that support the assertion, and the context in which the assertion is held to be true. In fact, although the notion of context (in the CONNIVER sense) is not discussed here, it is treated in detail in Levesque [1977].

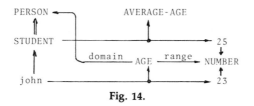

Fig. 14.

is a restrictive assumption and, in this section, we shall consider a more general interpretation where *every* object is an instance of some class.

Consider a situation where the average age of every person known to be a student is 25. Clearly, the property "average-age" is not a property of particular persons but rather of collections of persons. In this case, the average age being 25 is a property of a particular collection of persons, the class of students (see Fig. 14). One could certainly envisage the fetch operation of the relation AVERAGE-AGE in terms of generating the instances of a class, fetching their age, and computing the average, but the question remains as to what is the domain of this relation. Just as john can have an age because he is an instance of the domain of AGE, STUDENT can have an average age because it is an instance of the domain of AVERAGE-AGE. Hence AVERAGE-AGE maps classes of people into numbers just as AGE maps people into numbers (see Fig. 15). Thus PERSON-CLASS represents the class of all collections of persons, and its properties (such as AVERAGE-AGE) are properties of classes of persons. A class whose instances are also classes is called a *metaclass*. Thus we can distinguish between properties of students and properties of the collection of students itself. Needless to say, such a distinction is not possible in a semantic network scheme that does not discriminate between subclasses and instances (or, alternatively, between types and tokens).

Since metaclasses are classes, they can be organized along an IS-A hierarchy such as shown in Fig. 16. Here, CARDINALITY means the number of instances of a class (e.g., MALE-STUDENT has 247 instances). The top of the hierarchy is the special class CLASS, the class of all classes.* Hence every metaclass is a subclass of CLASS, and every class (including every

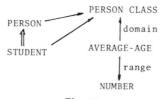

Fig. 15.

* The problem of Russell's paradox is addressed in Levesque [1977]. There is in fact no inconsistency here because all definitions are procedural (constructive).

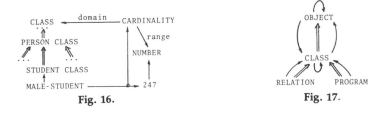

Fig. 16.   Fig. 17.

metaclass) is an instance of CLASS. Similarly, the class RELATION and the class PROGRAM represent the class of all relations and the class of all programs, respectively. We therefore have the situation shown in Fig. 17. Note that OBJECT and CLASS are instances of themselves as well as of each other. Consequently, there is no need to go "higher up" and speak of metametaclasses, etc.* It follows from the definition of metaclasses, that objects are organized along an *instance hierarchy* as well as an IS-A and a PART-OF one (see Fig. 18).

In addition to clarifying the operation of inheritance (see next section), metaclasses can also be used to explain certain aspects of our semantic network representation. For example, we can account for the edges labeled domain and range in terms of the structure of relations (see Fig. 19). Thus every relation has two classes as parts. Similarly, we can now describe the association between a class and the four programs that specify its semantics. In fact, since these programs determine which class is being referred to, they constitute the structural parts of the class (see Fig. 20). Here, PROG1 and PROG2 are specific programs. Thus defining a class† consists of filling the slots of the class CLASS by particular programs. Moreover, the fact that an operation of a class can default to a standard program can be explained in terms of the programs that are the defaults of these slots.

Both a class and its instances may therefore have a structure.‡ For example, STUDENT will have programs as parts while students may have

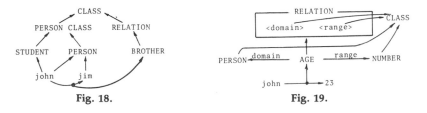

Fig. 18.   Fig. 19.

---

* The class METACLASS of all metaclasses, for example, would be a subclass of CLASS.
† Relations, of course, also have a similar structure in addition to a domain and a range.
‡ Since CLASS is an instance of itself, it must have four programs as parts. In this case, both CLASS and its instances (i.e., classes) have similar structures.

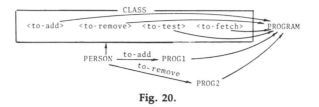

Fig. 20.

student numbers, departments, etc. as parts (see Fig. 21). Hence distinguishing between assertional and structural properties on the one hand, and properties of an object vs. properties of its instances on the other hand, there is a total of four kinds of property information that can be associated with a class. We shall refer to specific properties of an object as *property values* of the object and properties of its instances as *property attributes* of the class (for which instances have property values). Figure 22 shows this through our example of above. Thus we have

   (1)   assertional property values (e.g., the average age of students is 25);
   (2)   structural property values (e.g., the to-add program is PROG5);
   (3)   assertional property attributes* (e.g., students can take courses);
   (4)   structural property attributes (e.g., students have a department).

In the next section, we shall treat the inheritance of properties in terms of this categorization.

5.   INHERITANCE

As we noted in Section 3, the main feature of the IS-A hierarchy is the inheritance of properties defined for the classes that constitute it. In fact, it is this inheritance that serves as an abstraction mechanism since we suppress details concerning the *similarity* of objects and define objects by noting how they differ from existing, more general objects. In this section, we shall investigate how the inheritance of properties depends on not only the IS-A hierarchy, but the PART-OF hierarchy as well.

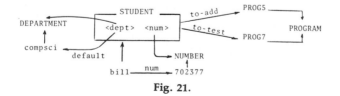

Fig. 21.

* Note that if P is an assertional property attribute of a class C, then C is the domain of P and consequently is a structural property value of P.

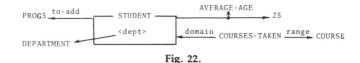

Fig. 22.

We have already implicitly dealt with a simple version of inheritance in terms of the defaults for slots in structures. For example, in Fig. 23 john will inherit compsci as his dept part from STUDENT. Note that john must have the attribute dept before we can consider giving this attribute a particular value. Thus john cannot inherit an average age of 25 since AVERAGE-AGE is not an attribute of individual students. Moreover, john can have certain attributes without necessarily inheriting a value (e.g., num and COURSES-TAKEN). Consequently, we can speak of *inheriting attributes* (having a given property) separately from *inheriting values* (having a particular value for some property) although inheriting a value always presupposes the inheritance of the corresponding attribute.

Every object necessarily has the properties shared by instances of its type. Hence when an object is an instance of more than one class, it will inherit attributes from all of them. In this sense, the inheritance of attributes is *cumulative*. In particular, if an object is an instance of a class that is a subclass of another, it will inherit attributes of both classes. In terms of structural attributes, another way of saying this is that a class implicitly has the structure of all its superclasses. Thus, with respect to the IS-A hierarchy, the inheritance of attributes can be treated as a phenomenon occurring between classes. A class can therefore treat its inherited slots as if they were its own and provide new defaults* or additional dependencies peculiar to the class. For example, in Fig. 24 a Ph.D. student, in addition to having a student number and a department, also has an external examiner and a supervisor, which is a tenured professor employed by the department. Thus the inheritance of attributes provides a convenient method of viewing a class as an extension or refinement of an existing class,† assuming the usual programs provide an appropriate interpretation. In the next

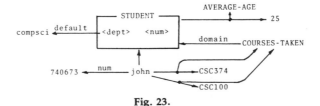

Fig. 23.

---

* For example, the metaclass RELATION inherits the attributes of CLASS, that is, the four program slots, but specifies new defaults: the four standard programs for relations.

† There are, of course, many other ways in which a class can be viewed as a specialization of another, for example, restricting a slot of a superclass to a single value. Thus a math student is a student whose dept slot is restricted to the value math.

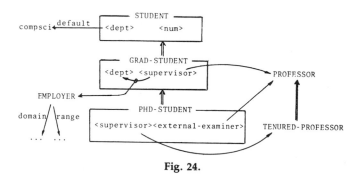

Fig. 24.

section, we discuss how programs themselves can be used to augment or refine definitions.

If we now turn our attention to the inheritance of values, we note a number of differences from the inheritance of attributes. For one, the inheritance of values is *preemptive* in the sense that an object will not inherit all possible values for a given property but rather a single value. Moreover, this inheritance can always be explicitly overwritten. For example, in Fig. 25, john inherits compsci as his department part, whereas bill does not. The question remains as to whether all inheritance of values involves defaults from the slots of an object's type. It might be convenient to say that the property values of two objects are sufficiently similar that one object could inherit from the other rather than inheriting the general defaults of the class itself. For example, perhaps John and Jim are quite similar as students so that the property values for student attributes of John should default to those of Jim and/or vice-versa. Needless to say, this would require introducing additional facilities to the representation.* We can, however, deal with a less general inheritance of values, by capitalizing on the expected similarity between a class and its superclasses. The rationale is that, if a class is a subclass of another, the properties of the former will often be trivial modifications of the properties of the latter. Thus, having no further evidence, a reasonable assumption is that the property values of the subclass are the same as those of the superclass. For example, in Fig. 26, OLDEST-CHILD being a relation, it inherits the attri-

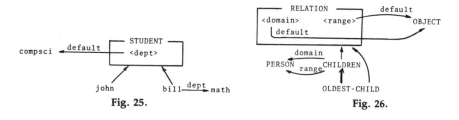

Fig. 25.   **Fig. 26.**

* It should be clear, however, that establishing a "similarity network" [Minsky, 1975] would not be unusually difficult within our procedural framework.

butes domain and range from RELATION. However, being a subrelation of CHILDREN, it inherits PERSON as its domain and range rather than the general default OBJECT. Let us now consider an assertional property value such as that shown in Fig. 27. Although GRAD-STUDENT will have the attribute AVERAGE-AGE (since it is a class of persons), it will *not* inherit from STUDENT an average age property value of 25. The reason for this is based on our structural/assertional distinction of Section 3. The inheritance of values depends on the notion of similarity, and although subclasses will usually be similar to their superclasses in definition (structural properties), they may have radically different incidental features (assertional properties). Furthermore, it is the responsibility of a relation to manage an assertional property with its four defining programs. If these values were inheritable, the interpreter would be infringing on the basic behavior of the relation. Consequently, the decision as to whether a given property is structural or assertional can be based on whether the property values are inheritable or not, in addition to the criteria mentioned in Section 3.*

Thus, unlike the inheritance of attributes, the inheritance of values involves only structural properties. Furthermore, it is important to reassert that the inheritance of values always presupposes the inheritance of attributes. Consider Fig. 28. Although SPOUSE is a symmetric relation and HUSBAND is a subrelation of SPOUSE (since every husband assertion is also a spouse assertion), HUSBAND is not a symmetric relation. Consequently, HUSBAND does not inherit any symmetric relation attributes. Thus, although HUSBAND can inherit property values of relations from SPOUSE, it cannot inherit property values of symmetric relations from SPOUSE. In other words, although a class will always inherit the structure of its superclasses, it may not inherit certain values from its superclasses because it may not be an instance of the same metaclasses as its superclasses.

Since the four programs of classes (and relations) constitute the structural properties of classes, a class can inherit particular programs from its superclasses. Consider now Fig. 29. Here, SAP, SRP, STP, and SFP are the standard default programs of classes. The to-add program of STUDENT

Fig. 27.   Fig. 28.

---

* It should also be noted that values for certain assertional properties could not be inherited anyway, because the relation may associate *many* values to a single object (e.g., the relation COURSES-TAKEN).

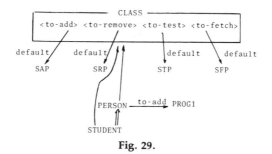

Fig. 29.

will default to that of PERSON (i.e., PROG1) rather than to the standard to-add program (i.e., SAP). Thus creating a student defaults to simply creating a person. The inheritance of programs allows the semantics of a class to default in a natural way to that of other classes. It is our feeling that this type of controlled interaction between essentially modular components is crucial when dealing with large semantic networks.

The inheritance rules can be summarized as follows: let C be a class, B one of its subclasses, and c one of its instances.

1. Inheritance rules along the instance hierarchy are

(a) if p is a (structural or assertional) property value of C, it is not inherited by c;

(b) if p is an assertional property attribute of C, c can have zero or more corresponding property values;

(c) if p is a structural property attribute of C, c has a corresponding property value.

2. Inheritance rules along the IS-A hierarchy are

(a) if p is a (structural or assertional) property attribute of C, it is inherited by B;

(b) if p is an assertional property value of C, it is not inherited by B;

(c) if p is a structural property value of C, it is inherited preemptively by B provided that B is an instance of the metaclass having the corresponding property attribute.

Note that according to these rules, properties are inherited only one level down instance relationships.

Thus, we view the inheritance of properties as a generalization of the defaults of slots where many levels of defaulting are possible. As such, it provides a convenient method of specifying how the definition of one class is related to the definition of another. On a different level, the inheritance of properties is the interaction between the IS-A and PART-OF hierarchies since IS-A determines the inheritance paths while PART-OF determines the inheritable values (structural properties). Of course, there are many problems left to be solved with inheritance, such as choosing between competing inherited values when a class has more than one superclass. For an approach to some of these problems, the reader is referred to Schneider [1978].

6. PROGRAMS

A common tendency in many semantic network proposals is to provide a programming facility through access to the implementation language being used (e.g., LISP). Although this approach has the advantage of expediency, programs should not have to be written in a language that does not support the conceptual data structures being manipulated. It should be clear by now that our representation relies heavily on the use of programs. It is therefore desirable to have a programming formalism that is uniquely suited to the kinds of processing required by the representation. Fortunately, this need not entail an excessive amount of additional machinery since programs can be incorporated directly into the semantic network. Moreover, this allows the full descriptive power of the representation to be applied to the specification of programs.

So far, the standard behavior of classes and relations in our scheme has been described in terms of eight primitive programs. To extend the basic semantics of a class or relation, a method of augmenting or restricting an existing program is required. This, in turn, can only be done once the relevant features of programs have been isolated. Our concern, therefore, is to find the most important kinds of programs and their most important parts, that is, to investigate the organization of programs along the IS-A and PART-OF hierarchies. In this section, we shall present a first step in such an analysis of programs based on Levesque [1977]. For two slightly different approaches to the same problem, see Wong et al. [1977] and Cohen [1978].

There are two distinct varieties of programs required for the specification of the behavior of classes and relations: *procedures*, which perform actions such as the addition and deletion operations, and *functions* (including *predicates*), which return values for the testing and retrieval operations.

In general, a procedure can be decomposed into the following parts:

(1)   Determine the acceptability of the proposed action by considering the conditions that must be true before the action can be performed. For example, to assert that a relation holds between two objects requires that the objects be instances of the domain and range respectively. If any of these conditions are false, the action is refused and a failure occurs.

(2)   Assuming the initial conditions are satisfied, the action itself must be performed. This can involve primitive actions such as storing results in a table, or more complex actions that pass the buck to other classes and relations. These actions may themselves fail.

(3)   Given that the action is successful, there may be additional inferences to be drawn as a result of this success, requiring further actions.

(4)   If the action is unsuccessful, however, in view of the fact that the initial conditions were satisfied, there may be steps that can be taken to remedy the situation at this level, rather than relinquishing control and allowing the procedure itself to fail.

A similar decomposition applies to programs that are functions (or predicates). In this case, the initial conditions are presuppositions that must be true before the requested information can be retrieved. Once the values are obtained, it may be convenient to perform actions such as storing the results for redundancy purposes. If, on the other hand, no value can be found even though the initial conditions are satisfied, it may still be possible to recover and return a value.

The programs we are considering, then, can be characterized by the following four parts:*

(1)   *prerequisite,* a logical expression that must be true before the body can be executed;

(2)   *body,* an action for procedures or an expression for functions;

(3)   *effect,* an action performed after a successful completion of the body;

(4)   *complaint,* an action or expression to be used after an unsuccessful completion of the body.

We can express this factorization of programs in terms of the metaclass PROGRAM as shown in Fig. 30. Here, EXPRESSION and STATEMENT are classes representing the constructs in terms of which programs are formulated. Consequently, each specific program is defined by filling the slots of these metaclasses. For example, a function of no arguments that always returns the object john can be defined as in Fig. 31. The identity function would be described as shown in Fig. 32. Note that programs are classes whose slots are the arguments. To describe the value of a function

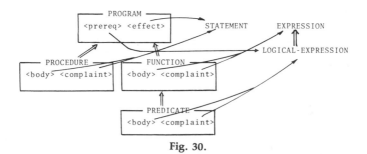

Fig. 30.

---

* The prerequisite/effect portions of a program were inspired by the antecedent/consequent distinction of PLANNER, while the complaint component is based on a similar notion of ACTORS.

Fig. 31.

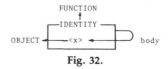

Fig. 32.

that requires additional functions, we shall use a notation like in Fig. 33. Here, times is a special placeholder for the function TIMES called a *form*. Just as slots are placeholders for instances of classes, forms are placeholders for instances of programs. An instance of a program is defined by filling the slots of the program (i.e., providing a value for each parameter of the program). This is illustrated in Fig. 34.

Thus identity0013 and identity0029 are particular instances of the program IDENTITY. Instances of programs, called *processes*, can be executed and hence correspond to program activations. However, a process need not be actively executing and can be suspended in the coroutine sense.* Moreover, the execution of a process may involve creating and destroying other processes. For example, the above function TIMES-TWO requires an instance of the function TIMES for each activation (see Fig. 35). The relation DYNAMIC maps a process onto its dynamic father. Thus, the execution stack is represented by a chain of DYNAMIC assertions (or a tree of assertions in the presence of coroutines). For example, let us consider the function FACTORIAL in Fig. 36.† For a process with the slot filled by 2, at the deepest level of the composition, we have the DYNAMIC chain of Fig. 37, where the execution of the first FACTORIAL process requires the execution of an IF, which requires a TIMES, which requires another FACTORIAL, and so on.

Since programs are classes, they can be organized along an IS-A hierarchy and benefit from the inheritance of properties. For example, in Fig. 38, both ITERATIVE-FACT and RECURSIVE-FACT will inherit the attribute (or parameter) n from FACTORIAL while ITERATIVE-FACT provides an additional slot. Similarly, both functions inherit a particular prerequisite

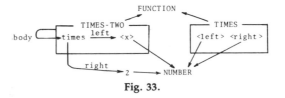

Fig. 33.

---

* This property of programs is required for functions that return many values. For example, the retrieval programs of classes generate values one at a time.

† We assume the availability of functions like LESSP and SUB1. In particular, the function IF allows programs to be defined recursively.

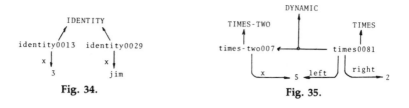

Fig. 34.   Fig. 35.

part (the greaterp form) as a value.* If the argument to these functions is ever less than 1, no value will be returned. Moreover, if the body of RECURSIVE-FACT does not return a value (presumably because it calls itself recursively with an improper argument), RECURSIVE-FACT will return 1, the "complaint" value.

There are many other aspects of programs that should be discussed. For example, we have not explained how expressions and statements are constructed, nor have we given any examples of procedures or of programs that deal with classes and relations (like ASSERT and FETCH). For a much more detailed presentation that includes an elaborate syntax and some of the machinery involved in the execution of processes, see Levesque [1977].

To apply the organization of programs to the definition of classes and relations, we need only realize that a program for an operation on a class is a subprogram of the corresponding program of the superclass. The process of instantiating a student, for example, is always implicitly a process of instantiating a person (see Fig. 39). Hence the program PROG5 can be defined by specifying special cases of prerequisites, effects, etc. applicable to students while allowing all the other components to default to those of PROG1 for persons. In particular, we could define PROG5 without knowing how persons are stored (the body of PROG1). Moreover, the top of the hierarchy for classes and relations have, as programs, the default programs for classes and relations (see Fig. 40). Consequently, any class or

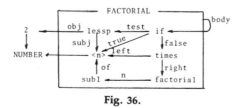

Fig. 36.

---

* This assumes as before the ITERATIVE-FACT is similar to FACTORIAL as a program and hence that they share common parts. This can be extended to processes, since when one process creates another during its execution, the two will often share common parts (i.e., have the same values for their arguments). Consequently, we can inherit values up the DYNAMIC chain as is done in LISP.

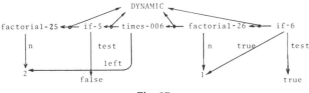

Fig. 37.

relation can build on the standard programs accumulating restrictions and inferences along the IS-A hierarchy, as was done with structures in Section 3.

For example, the assertion program for the relation CHILDREN might be the standard operation except for the "effect," which would assert the PARENT relation with the arguments reversed. Now the assertion program for OLDEST-CHILD can default to this program with an added prereq that there does not already exist a child that is older than the one being considered.

Thus the eight standard programs for classes and relations play a special role in our scheme since they are the programs that all classes and relations may ultimately inherit. Since many of the interdependencies between classes and relations can be expressed procedurally in terms of prerequisites and effects, the bodies of the eight programs are typically inherited by many classes and therefore provide an important interface between the representation and a physical implementation.

In summary, we see two major benefits arising from the integration of programs along the IS-A and PART-OF hierarchies. First of all, the factorization of programs into four components allows the inheritance of properties to be much more flexible than it would be otherwise since, in fact, a program can partially default to another. This is not only true of programs, but, more importantly, of classes whose semantics are specified procedurally. Secondly, with respect to programs themselves, it is our feeling that almost any organization is useful in the attempt to understand programs (by people or other programs). At worst, we have replaced one black box by four equally black boxes; at best, the introduction of "declarative"

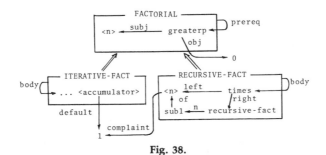

Fig. 38.

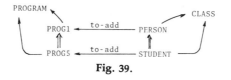

Fig. 39.

structure into programs allows them to be analyzed more readily. By the same token, the IS-A hierarchy of programs allows a program to be viewed as an extension or refinement of another, hopefully better understood program. Of course, it remains to be seen just to what extent the two hierarchies facilitate this understanding by other programs. We are, in effect, attempting to deal with the "complexity barrier" by making programs more declarative (and open to examination) and with the "combinatorial explosion" by making data more procedural (and subject to control).

7. CONCLUSIONS

Among most recent efforts to provide a semantic theory for semantic networks, Schubert [1976] and Hendrix [1976] have selected predicate calculus as a basis for their theory and, as a result, address themselves to a different set of issues than those treated here. On the other hand, the representations advocated by the knowledge representation languages KRL [Bobrow and Winograd, 1976], MDS [Irwin and Srinivasan, 1975], and FRL [Roberts and Goldstein, 1977] share with our formalism the use of a class concept (*unit* in KRL, *template* in MDS, *frame* in FRL) with an internal structure consisting of slots and constraints on the values the slots can take. Moreover, these representations offer facilities for a hierarchical organization of the classes constituting a knowledge base. The hierarchy is clearly an IS-A hierarchy in the case of FRL and (something like) an instance hierarchy for MDS and KRL (KRL-0). All three representations offer structural properties, possibly with defaults, but none of them appear to make the structural/assertional distinction between properties. Their inheritance rules are analogous to ours, although MDS offers special facilities, which allows an inheritance across more than one level of the in-

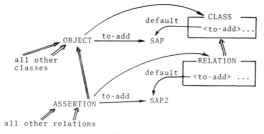

Fig. 40.

stance hierarchy. Another point of similarity between the three representations and ours is the heavy use of procedural attachment. Their programs, however, are LISP functions and, as such, are not treated as classes.

Another proposal of a theory for semantic networks appears in Brachman [1977]. This proposal organizes semantic networks in terms of concepts (analogous to our classes) that have structural properties and associated constraints. These properties are similar to ours; for example, they define the essential components of a concept and are inherited along an IS-A hierarchy. At the same time, these properties are treated as concepts in their own right, have a modality component that specifies their number of instances for each concept being described, and are presumably organized into an IS-A hierarchy. These are all characteristics of assertional properties in our formalism since structural ones obtain their semantics from the concept they are associated with. Brachman's framework also includes a number of features not in our formalism, for example, it defines a concept by analogy to (rather than as a subconcept of) another. Moreover, constraints are expressed in terms of a semantic network representation of logical expressions. Finally, Brachman's graphic notation appears to be much more than a notational convenience, as it is in our work, and is treated instead as the language for defining (unambiguously) a semantic network.

Overall, we claim the following contributions for our formalism:

(1)   It provides a semantic foundation for semantic networks using programs and shows how the representation can then be compared to other procedural approaches like ACTORS or CONNIVER.

(2)   It offers an IS-A and an instance hierarchy and provides explicit rules for inheritance along either hierarchy.

(3)   It differentiates between structural and assertional properties and explores the characteristics of the two types of properties (e.g., the source of their semantics and their inheritance).

(4)   It offers the concept of a metaclass as a method of representing certain aspects of the representation within the representation itself and shows how this can be used to solve some inheritance problems.

(5)   It integrates programs directly into the representation as classes having all the usual characteristics (e.g., inheritance). Consequently, an interpreter for the representation can be given in the formalism itself, allowing a completely self-contained specification of the representation (as in pure LISP). Moreover, since processes are explicit, alternative control regimes like backtracking or parallelism can also be represented (unlike pure LISP).

Needless to say, there are open questions regarding our formalism that will require further research. Among them, we note the following:

(1) inheriting values for classes having multiple superclasses;

(2) enforcing mutual consistency among the four programs of a class;

(3) treating slots and forms as objects in their own right, independently of structures;

(4) allowing for exceptions within our implicit quantification rules.

Most of these issues, and others, are treated in Schneider [1978].

The representation described in this chapter has been used for the definition of a knowledge base on income tax forms [Kidd *et al.*, 1977] and another involving belief spaces [Cohen, 1978]. A formal implementation of portions of the representation, expressed in the formalism itself, appears in Levesque [1977]. An earlier version of the work described here can be found in Levesque *et al.* [1976] and an overview given in Levesque and Mylopoulos [1977].

REFERENCES

[Abrial, J. R., 1974]. Data semantics. In *Data Management Systems*. J. W. Klimbie and K. L. Koffeman (eds.). North-Holland Publ., Amsterdam, pp. 1–60.

[Bobrow, D. G., and Winograd, T., 1976]. "An Overview of KRL, a Knowledge Representation Language," Technical Report CSL-76-4 (xerox). Palo Alto Research Center, Palo Alto, California.

[Brachman, R., 1977]. A structural paradigm for representing knowledge. Ph.D. thesis, Harvard University, Cambridge, Massachusetts.

[Cohen, P., 1978]. On knowing what to say: planning speech acts. Ph.D. thesis, Department of Computer Science, University of Toronto, Toronto, Canada.

[Hendrix, G., 1976]. The representation of semantic knowledge. In *Speech Understanding Research*. D. Walker (ed.), Final Technical Report. Stanford Research Institute, Stanford, California, pp. *V*-1–*V*-99.

[Hewitt, C., 1972]. Description and theoretical analysis (using schemata) of PLANNER: A language for proving theorems and manipulating models in a robot. Ph.D. thesis, MIT, Cambridge, Massachusetts.

[Hewitt, C., 1973]. A universal ACTOR formalism for artificial intelligence. *Proceedings of the 3rd International Joint Conference on Artificial Intelligence, 1973* pp. 235–245.

[Irwin, J., and Srinivasan, C., 1975]. "Description of CASNET in MDS," Report CBM-TR-49. Rutgers University, New Brunswick, New Jersey.

[Kidd, R., Schneider, P., and Vassiliou, Y., 1977]. "Using AI to Fill Out Your Individual Income Tax Return," AI Memo 77-3. University of Toronto, Toronto, Canada.

[Levesque, H., 1977]. "A Procedural Approach to Semantic Networks," Technical Report 105. Department of Computer Science, University of Toronto, Toronto, Canada.

[Levesque, H., and Mylopoulos, J., 1977]. An overview of a procedural approach to semantic networks. *Proceedings of the 5th International Joint Conference on Artificial Intelligence, 1977*, p. 283.

[Levesque, H., Mylopoulos, J., McCalla, G., Melli, L., and Tsotsos, J., 1976]. A formalism for modelling. *Proceedings of The 1st CSCSI/SCEIO Conference, 1976* pp. 243–254.

[Liskov, B., and Zillies, S., 1974]. Programming with abstract data types. *ACM SIGPLAN Notices* **9**, No. 4.

[Minsky, M., 1975]. A framework for representing knowledge. In *The Psychology of Computer Vision*. P. Winston (ed.). McGraw-Hill, New-York, pp. 211–277.

[Roberts, R., and Goldstein, I., 1977]. "The FRL Primer," AI Memo 408. MIT, Cambridge, Massachusetts.

[Schneider, P., 1978]. "Organization of Knowledge in a Procedural Semantic Network Formalism." M.Sc. thesis [and TR 115], Department of Computer Science, University of Toronto, Toronto, Canada.

[Schubert, L., 1976]. "Extending the expressive power of semantic networks". *Artificial Intelligence* **7**, 163–202.

[Sussman, G., and McDermott, D., 1972]. From PLANNER to CONNIVER: A genetic approach. *Proceedings of the FJCC* **41**, Part 2, pp. 1171–1180.

[Winograd, T., 1976]. "Towards a Procedural Understanding of Semantics," SAIL Memo AIM-292. Stanford University, Stanford, California.

[Wittgenstein, L., 1958]. *Philosophical Investigations.* 3rd ed. Macmillan, New York.

[Wong, H., Mylopoulos, J., and Bernstein, P., 1977]. "A Preliminary Report on TAXIS: A Language for Interactive Information Systems Designs," Technical Report. CCA, Boston, Massachusetts.

[Woods, W., 1975]." What's in a link? Foundations for semantic networks". *In Representation and Understanding.* D. G. Bobrow and A. M. Collins (eds.). Academic Press, New York, pp. 35–82.

THE STRUCTURE AND ORGANIZATION OF A SEMANTIC NET FOR COMPRE- HENSION AND INFERENCE

Lenhart K. Schubert, Randolph G. Goebel, and Nicholas J. Cercone

ABSTRACT

We have developed a network representation for propositional knowledge that we believe to be capable of encoding any proposition expressible in natural language. The representation can be regarded as a computer-oriented logic with associative access paths from concepts to propositions. Its syntax is closely modeled on predicate calculus but includes constructs for expressing some kinds of vague and uncertain knowledge. The representation allows the encoding and efficient use of caselike semantic constraints on predicate arguments for the purpose of language comprehension: these constraints are simply implications of the predicates concerned. Our approach to language comprehension is based on nonprimitive representations. We argue that primitive representations of simple propositions are often extremely complex, and offer no real advantages. We have demonstrated these ideas with a mini-implementation capable of mapping certain kinds of declarative sentences into the network representation. The implementation emphasizes the proper handling of iterated adjectival modifiers, especially comparative modifiers. More recently, we have worked on the problem of rapid access to the facts that are relevant to a query. Our solution involves the use of back-link structures from concepts to propositions, called "topic access skeletons," which conform with general topic hierarchies in memory. For example, the proposition "Clyde is grey" is classified under the "coloring" topic for Clyde, which is subsumed under the "appearance" topic, and in turn under the "external quality" topic, and finally under the "physical quality" topic for Clyde. The form of a query (or of an assertion) can be used to determine what concepts in memory should be accessed as starting points, and what paths in the associated access skeletons should be followed in order to access the relevant information. We have demonstrated the feasibility of building such hierarchies, inserting information into them automatically, and accessing the inserted information with a second experimental implementation. The hierarchic organization appears capable of providing order-of-magnitude improvements in question-answering efficiency, with only a doubling in storage costs.

121

1. INTRODUCTION

Since Quillian's introduction of a self-contained semantic net formalism [Quillian, 1968, 1969], semantic nets have gained increasing acceptance as propositional representations in understanding and reasoning systems. They have proved particularly useful for language understanding (e.g., Schank [1972]), concept learning (e.g., Winston [1970]), and deductive reasoning (e.g., McSkimin and Minker [1977]). They have also been influential in psychological theories of cognition (e.g., Anderson and Bower [1973]; Norman and Rumelhart [1975]; Wilson [1979]).

We have argued previously [Schubert, 1976] that semantic net *notation*, i.e., the graphical symbolism used by semantic net theorists, is a variant of traditional logical notation. If this is so, what are the special advantages of semantic nets at the implementation level? We shall answer with a brief characterization of distinctive semantic net features, and the intuitive reasons for their advantages. With this as background, we shall give the motivation for our own work and an overview of the following sections.

1.1.   What Are Semantic Nets?

The distinctive characteristic of semantic nets was succinctly stated by Shapiro [1971]: "All the information about a given conceptual entity should be reachable from a common place." He went on to explain that "a conceptual entity is anything about which information can be given. That is, anything about which one can know, think, or believe something; anything we can describe or discuss or experience." In other words, the network concepts are the intuitively *meaningful* entities, and knowledge about these entities is *directly attached to them.** In practice, the repertoire of meaningful entities typically includes particular concepts (individuals), generic concepts (properties and relations), and propositions. The knowledge attached to a concept is the set of propositions in which it participates plus, possibly, relevant procedures.

In networks without proposition nodes (e.g., those of Winston [1970] or of Mylopoulos *et al.* [1973]), this concept-centered organization is an immediate consequence of representing binary relationships as pointers from concepts to concepts.† In networks with proposition nodes, i.e., addressable points of attachment for the participants in a relationship, the concept-centered organization is achieved by *back-linking* the participants

---

* We claim that this is *all* that distinguishes nets from other propositional representations. Thus the term "semantic" is somewhat pretentious, but by now firmly established. Another well-established abuse, which we shall help perpetuate, is the substitution of "proposition" for "sentence."

† However, the inverse of each relationship needs to be added to make it "visible" from the target concept.

to the proposition nodes. These back-links are complementary to the "forward links" from propositions to their participating concepts. We should observe that the concept-centered organization is lacking in PLANNER-like data bases and in lists of predicate calculus formulas—two standard alternatives to semantic nets for representing propositional information. In neither representation is it possible to retrieve all propositions involving a given entity without scanning many irrelevant propositions. We should be aware, however, how easily the necessary linkages could be added to transform these representations into semantic nets.

1.2. Why Semantic Nets?

In a semantic net, the bidirectional connections between concepts and the information about them establish a "semantic vicinity" for each concept, consisting of the concepts and relationships reachable from the concept by traversing a small number of links. For example, if John loves Mary and Mary lives in Calgary, then the concepts "John" and "Calgary" lie close together in a semantic net, since each can be reached from the other by traversing only two relationships.

The fundamental assumption in the use of semantic nets is that *the knowledge required to perform an intellectual task generally lies in the semantic vicinity of the concepts involved in the task.* This is most easily seen for descriptive tasks such as "Describe Mary's appearance." Here it is essential to have access to knowledge in Mary's semantic vicinity, without distraction by semantically remote knowledge. For example, Mary's height and weight would probably be contained in propositions directly involving Mary, and her hair and eye color in propositions two or three steps away from Mary. Any more remote propositions are unlikely to be concerned with Mary's appearance, or any other aspect of Mary.

The advantages of a concept-centered organization can also be seen in tasks requiring simple inference. For example, suppose that it is known that John loves Mary and that John and Mary live in Edmonton and Calgary, respectively, and that lovers like to be in the same place as their beloved. Then the question "Where would John like to be?" can be answered deductively using only propositions lying within one or two steps of the concepts involved in the question. Note that the generalization about lovers lies two steps away from "John," because the concept "loves" is shared between the generalization and "John loves Mary." Also, the generalization is directly linked to the concept "likes" that occurs in the question. What this suggests is a "breadth-first" inference strategy that works in widening circles away from the concepts activated by the inference task. This sort of idea inspired Quillian's network design in the first place, and has remained a major theme in semantic net research (e.g., Shapiro [1971]; Collins and Loftus [1975]; Fahlman [1975]).

Despite these apparent advantages of semantic nets, we do not see nets as "the solution to the representation problem." Rather, we see them as a uniform representation that can *mediate between specialized representations appropriate to particular task domains*. For example, special representations are undoubtedly needed to reason efficiently about pictures and about physical objects moving through space (e.g., see Baumgart [1974]). A language for artificial intelligence under development at the University of Alberta is designed to permit links between semantic net concepts and special representations of these concepts [Gray, 1976]. We expect that these will become particularly important for representing spatial and linguistic knowledge.

1.3. Overview

In Section 2, we motivate and explain our network formalism. Our emphasis is on *expressive adequacy*, i.e., the ability to represent any proposition that a human being is capable of understanding. We also defend the view that networks should be formally interpretable, in a Tarskian sense, and comment on Woods' [1975] suggestion that "extensional and intensional entities" be distinguished syntactically.

In Section 3, we take positions on several basic questions about network form and content. These questions go beyond the mere choice of network syntax, but need to be answered early in the design of comprehension and inference mechanisms. We argue that the propositional representation of natural language text should separate the propositional content of the text from its pragmatic aspects; that the representation should be nonprimitive; and that in the interest of efficient property inheritance, a propositional "normal form" should be used, in which universal implicative statements are partitioned into sets sharing universally and existentially quantified variables. Within each set, the implicative antecedents are related by a generalization hierarchy.

In Section 4, we consider the organizational needs of simple inference, and find the basic network structure lacking. Our earlier example of the request to "Describe Mary's appearance" indicates the nature of the difficulty. How do we access all and only the propositions concerned with Mary's appearance? The concept-centered organization usefully limits the number of propositions to be scanned but fails to distinguish appearance-propositions from other propositions. Furthermore, we shall show by example that simple inference involves frequent scans of the propositions about a particular concept in search of propositions *of some restricted type*, such as appearance-propositions, coloring-propositions, location-propositions, or size-propositions. To facilitate these searches, we replace the simple lists of back-links from concepts to propositions by hierarchic "topic access skeletons," which conform with a general "topic hierarchy" stored in semantic memory.

In Section 5, we briefly describe two experimental implementations. The first is a LISP program designed to translate some kinds of English declarative sentences into our network representation. A notable feature is its sophisticated handling of comparatives. The second implementation is a C program for classifying, inserting, and retrieving propositions in a topically organized net.

In the concluding section, we assess our work and outline promising areas for future research. Our implementations lag behind our theoretical ideas, but we believe that our current emphasis on theoretical issues will prove advantageous in the long run. It is true that programming invariably brings to light unforeseen difficulties but we prefer to deal with the plainly foreseeable difficulties before launching on a major implementation effort. Some of the most important remaining problems are the integration of propositional nets with special-purpose representations, the expansion of the parser, and the detailed design of the inference processes that utilize the topically organized net. One of the most interesting features of our network organization is its adaptive potential. Our final remarks concern this feature.

2. A COMPREHENSIVE NETWORK FORMALISM

In this section, we recapitulate the network formalism we have presented and used in earlier reports [Schubert, 1975, 1976; Cercone, 1975a, 1977b; Cercone and Schubert, 1975; Goebel, 1977]. In our formalism, it is possible to represent n-ary relationships ($n = 1, 2, 3, . . .$), logical connectives, modal operators, functions, quantifiers arbitrarily embedded relative to each other and relative to propositional operators, and lambda abstraction. The semantics of the formalism, i.e., the intended *meaning* of the propositional nets, is clear and self-consistent. This is a result of its correspondence to predicate calculus, from which it inherits *formal* interpretability. We defend the desirability of this feature against objections raised in the AI literature. In addition, we take issue with Woods' [1975] contention that "intensional and extensional entities" must be distinguished in the network syntax. These arguments appear in slightly expanded form in Schubert *et al.* [1978].

2.1. The Requirement of Interpretability

Often network formalisms are put forward that are not systematically interpretable. For example, it is common practice to introduce an IS-A relation and to give examples of its application such as

Rufus —— IS-A ⟶ dog —— IS-A ⟶ mammal

Now exactly what does IS-A mean, i.e., what does it tell us about its conceptual arguments? It would seem from "Rufus IS-A dog" that if "x IS-A P" then x is a member of the set of Ps. But this leads to the absurd conclusion that the *generic* concept "dog" is a member of the set of mammals. Perhaps, then, the interpretation of IS-A depends on the type of its arguments, i.e., if both arguments are generic concepts then the interpretation is that every *instance* of the first concept is an *instance* of the second concept. But now how can we represent a second-order predication such as "Blue is a color"? Since both "blue" and "color" are generic, "Blue IS-A color" presumably comes out as "Anything blue is an instance of a color." This kind of confusion is compounded by the indiscriminate application of such relations as HAS-AS-PART to both particular and generic concepts. Generic concepts do not have parts; only their instances do. It is easy to understand why people fail to notice and remedy this sort of semantic incoherence in their networks, and will defend the faulty notation adamantly: network expressions can be read as pidgin-English (DOG IS-A MAMMAL, MAMMAL HAS-AS-PART LEG, NUMBER-OF (LEG) = 4) and as such are perfectly understandable. This is what Pat Hayes [1977] calls the "pretend-it's-English" analysis of meaning. However, a meaning representation is self-defeating if it retains the ambiguity and looseness of the surface text.

Pat Hayes [1977] has put the case for formal interpretability, in the logician's sense, very lucidly. We would add that one can believe in the value of model theory without believing in the existence of a formal model isomorphic to "reality." Reality may well be unformalizable in that sense, but at least logic "works" in idealized domains and is free from the elementary inconsistencies and ambiguities so common in network formalisms. If nothing else, logic and model theory are useful as diagnostic tools. For example, the above difficulties with IS-A and HAS-AS-PART are immediately revealed when one tries to supply a simple extensional model of these predicates.

Wilks [1976b] rejects model-theoretic semantics on the grounds that truth-conditions are not "computable." Similarly, Woods [1975] proposes to replace Tarskian truth conditions with effective criteria for determining sentential truth. However, this proposal confuses truth conditions with *assertability* conditions, i.e., conditions under which assertion of a sentence is warranted. We may reasonably demand that assertability conditions be computable, since we would like to have *effective* criteria for deciding when the available evidence warrants assertion of a sentence, but we cannot expect the same of truth conditions. As Fodor [1978] points out, computable truth conditions would enable us to judge the truth of such sentences as "positrons are made of quarks" or "I will marry an Armenian" merely by virtue of having learned English. We recommend

Fodor's paper, as well as Tarski [1944] for illuminating discussions of these issues. Also, we find Hobbs' [1978] paper on a computational analog of Montague's formal theory of language a useful antidote to Wilks' [1976b] indictment of Montague's "logical approach" to language and meaning (e.g., Montague [1970]). We feel that Montague's approach is not nearly as remote from AI approaches as Wilks maintains, and more generally, that valuable lessons in the systematic construction and analysis of meaning representation languages can be learned from the "philosophical logicians."

2.2. The Requirement of Expressive Adequacy

Many net formalisms restrict the representation to *binary* relationships between objects, where the name of the relation is used as an arc label. This causes problems not only for the representation of such polyadic relationships as *x* gives *y* to *z*, but also for the formation of *compound* propositions such as "either block1 supports block2 or block2 supports block1," or "Bill knows that John loves Mary." The difficulty derives from the lack of *proposition nodes* in such representations. Also, many formalisms lack adequate means for representing quantification in a manner that permits arbitrary nesting of quantifier and operator scopes. For example, the two readings of "John wants to marry a blonde" or of "Someone calls Mary every day" cannot be distinguished in many formalisms. None of these shortcomings can be tolerated in a general propositional representation.

2.3. Extension and Intension

Woods [1975] has made many points concerning networks similar to those made by Schubert [1975, 1976], especially concerning *n*-ary predicates, the distinction between cases and relations, quantification, and lambda abstraction.

There are two issues, however, on which we differ with Woods. One is the issue of what should be represented, which we discuss in Section 3. The other is the distinction between extension and intension, and its implications for network representations.

"Extension" and "intension" are the terms used to distinguish between that to which a designator refers or applies and its *meaning*. Thus, for example, "human" and "featherless biped" apply to the same things in the world (if "featherless" is taken as "naturally featherless"), but do not mean the same thing: their extensions, but not their intensions, coincide [Carnap, 1947]. Woods argues that since extensions and intensions are different, they must be represented by different sorts of nodes or subnets in semantic networks.

We take the position that terms (nodes, subnets) *already have both exten-sions and intensions.* In Carnap's words,

> it is essential to abandon the old prejudice that . . . an individual
> expression must stand either for an individual or an individual con-
> cept but cannot stand for both. To understand how language works,
> we must realize that every designator has both an intension and an
> extension. [Carnap, 1947, p. 202]

In this view, what is needed is not a syntactic distinction between extensional and intensional entities, but an explanation of the conditions
under which a term contributes to the truth value of a sentence through its
intension rather than through its extension only. The explanation lies in
the distinction between opaque and transparent contexts generated by
certain operators (such as "believes"), and the scopes of quantifiers binding variables in those contexts. An example is the distinction between the
two senses of "John wants to marry a blonde." For the sense "There is a
blonde whom John wants to marry" the truth value depends only on the
extension of "blonde," while for the sense in which John has no particular
blonde in mind, the truth value depends on the intension of "blonde."
The syntactic distinction lies in the relative scopes of the "wants" operator
and the existential quantifier for the "blonde." Semantic nets for propositions of this type can be found in Schubert [1975, 1976] and Cercone
[1975a].

We explain our representation of *n*-ary relationships, functions, time,
logical connectives, quantifiers, and uncertainty in the following sections.
Our representation also permits lambda abstraction, but we shall not repeat the description of its syntax here. The interested reader is referred to
Schubert [1975, 1976] and Cercone [1975a].

2.4. *n*-ary Relationships

Figure 1 illustrates the form of atomic propositions, using predicates of
one, two, and three arguments, and also how the network notation can be
abbreviated. The top net states "Mary is a girl" and involves three nodes:
a central *proposition node*, which stands for the proposition as a whole, and
two *concept nodes* linked to the proposition node. One of the concept
nodes denotes the particular concept "Mary" and the other the generic
concept "girl." (Throughout this chapter we use lower-case names, possibly with numerical suffixes, for concepts; for particular concepts, we
capitalize the first letter of the name.) Since "girl" is the predicate of the
proposition, the link to "girl" is labeled PRED. The label A on the link to
"Mary" simply means "first argument of the predicate." In the abbreviated notation (Fig. 1b), this is omitted since there is only one argument.

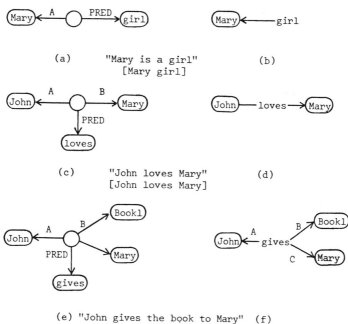

(a)   "Mary is a girl"   (b)
        [Mary girl]

(c)   "John loves Mary"   (d)
        [John loves Mary]

(e) "John gives the book to Mary" (f)
    [John gives Book1 Mary]

Fig. 1. Atomic propositions, in full and abbreviated.

Also, in the abbreviated notation, the proposition node is represented by the *name* of the predicate used in forming the proposition. It is important to remember that this name serves as a place-holder for the *proposition* node, *not* the predicate node; the link to the predicate node is now implicit.

The network diagrammed in Fig. 1c,d expresses the relationship "John loves Mary." Again, we have a central proposition node and a link to a generic node, but in this case the generic concept "loves" is used to relate the *ordered pair* of particular concepts John, Mary. The appropriate order is indicated by the link labels A, B. Again, the notation can be abbreviated by omitting the link to the generic node and using its name as a place-holder for the proposition node. The link labels can be omitted as well since the order of the arguments of "loves" are indicated by eliminating the arrowhead on the link to the *first* argument. Thus we get a notation very much like that of Winston [1970] for binary relationships.

Finally, in Fig. 1e,f we have a predication about three individuals, namely John, a specific book with the name Book1, and Mary. As before, the link to the predicate node is labeled PRED, and argument order is indicated by the link labels A, B, C. Also as before, the PRED link can be omitted in the short notation, and the proposition node is replaced by the name of the predicate used to form the proposition. Notice, however, that we cannot drop the link labels when we have three or more arguments.

Back-links from concepts to proposition nodes are not shown in the diagrams but are essential in a computer implementation of the nets. Specifically, there might be INSTANCE pointers from each generic concept to the atomic propositions in which it is used as predicate, and PROP pointers from each concept to the atomic propositions in which it appears as an argument of a predicate. In our first implementation [Cercone, 1975a], all back-links were of the same type (PROPOSITION), but in our second implementation [Goebel, 1977], we used the topically organized back-link structures that are the subject of Section 4.

The atomic propositional structure we have described so far is essentially that introduced by Shapiro [1971] and used, for example, by the RLN group [Rumelhart *et al.*, 1972]. Instead of link labels A, B, C, . . . , we could have followed Schank and others in using labels suggestive of the *role* played by each argument in a proposition, such as AGENT, OBJECT, RECIPIENT. However, like Shapiro, we regard the link labels as uninterpreted syntactic markers ("system relations").

In Fig. 1, we have also introduced an infix form of predicate calculus, which we shall use throughout. Propositions are of the form [arg1 predicate arg2 arg3 . . .], i.e., the predicate follows the first argument and precedes the rest, if any. This is a little more readable than prefix notation because it follows the structure of simple English declaratives, for example, compare

$$[[John\ happy]\ because\ [John\ knows\ [Mary\ loves\ John]]]$$

with

$$because\ (happy\ (John),\ knows\ (John,\ loves\ (Mary,\ John))).$$

Also, it aligns the syntax of predication with the conventional syntax of conjunction, disjunction, and other binary compounds. Sandewall [1971] went much further in developing an "English-like" form of predicate calculus, but this is not our purpose.

2.5. Functions

Although our original network formalism did not include any special representation for functions (which can be represented as relations), such a special representation appears to be useful (see Cercone [1975a]; Goebel [1977]).

The syntax of functions is analogous to the syntax of propositions. While the application of a predicate to a tuple of arguments produces a proposition, the application of a function to a tuple of arguments produces a concept (individual or generic) as its value. This is illustrated for the functions "age-of" and "father-of" in Fig. 2a,b. Note the FUNC link from the value of the function to the function node itself, which is the analog of the PRED link in an atomic proposition.

The corresponding relational representations are shown in Fig. 2c,d. This raises the question whether we should have two nodes for each single-valued relation, one for its use as a predicate and one for its use as a function. The answer is negative, since the PRED and FUNC links already make the necessary distinction in the *use* of the single-valued relation to which they point.

Our predicate calculus notation also allows this dual usage of single-valued relations, as indicated in the figure. Unlike propositional expressions, functional expressions are enclosed in round brackets and are in *prefix* form. This is a natural syntax since use of a single-valued relation as a function generally involves "elimination" of the first argument. For example, [Bill father-of John] becomes [Bill = (father-of John)] (see Fig. 2b,d); [x cosine-of y] becomes [x = (cosine-of y)]; etc.

Higher-order functions (or relations), i.e., functions that map generic concepts into generic concepts, appear to be essential in the representation of natural language text. For example, many adjectives must be interpreted as higher-order functions. The sentence "Snoopy is a big

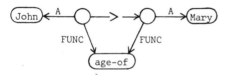

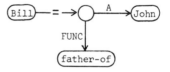

(a) "John is older than Mary"
　　[(age-of John) > (age-of Mary)]

(b) "Bill is the father of John"
　　[Bill = (father-of John)]

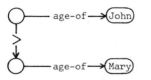

(c) "John is older than Mary"
　　[Age1 age-of John][Age1 > Age2],
　　[Age2 age-of Mary]

(d) "Bill is the father of John"
　　[Bill father-of John]

Fig. 2. Function notation, explicit and relational.

beagle" cannot be seriously represented as [[Snoopy beagle] & [Snoopy big]], since a big beagle is, for example, still a small hound. A satisfactorily interpretable representation is [Snoopy (big beagle)], in which "big" functionally transforms the generic concept "beagle" into the generic concept "(big beagle)." The network representation of this (atomic) proposition is shown in Fig. 3a.

A more "detailed" representation of the above sentence can be obtained from the paraphrase "Snoopy's size is (significantly?) greater than the typical size of a beagle." This approach to implicit comparatives was taken in Cercone [1975a]. However, a higher-order function is still required, namely, a "typical-value-of" function applicable to the generic concepts "size-of" and "beagle" to produce a numerical value of the typical size of a beagle. The corresponding representation is shown in Fig. 3b.

Higher-order functions are also required in the meaning representation of certain manner adverbs, such as "gracefully," "skillfully," or "quickly." It is sometimes suggested that these operate on action predicates much as adjectives operate on nominal predicates (see, for example, Bartsch and Vennemann [1972]). According to this view, for example, "skillfully" could be thought of as transforming the predicate "is playing chess" into the new predicate "is playing chess skillfully." However, this is not a genuine predicate, since it can be both true and false of a given agent at a given time, depending on the standard of comparison (e.g., amateur play or master level play). An additional generic argument is needed (for ex-

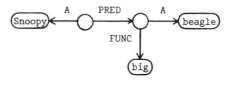

(a) "Snoopy is a big beagle"
    [Snoopy (big beagle)]

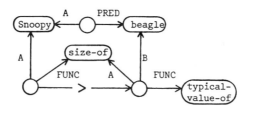

(b) "Snoopy is a big beagle"
    [Snoopy beagle],[(size-of Snoopy) >
    (typical-value-of size-of beagle)]

Fig. 3. Superficial and detailed representations of comparative adjectives.

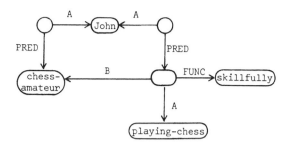

(a) "John is playing chess skillfully, for an amateur"
[John (skillfully playing-chess chess-amateur)],
[John chess-amateur]

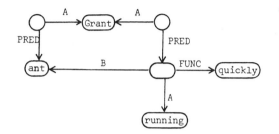

(b) "Grant (the ant) is running quickly"
[Grant ant], [Grant (quickly running ant)]

Fig. 4. Manner adverbs as higher-order dyadic functions.

ample, "chess amateur") to bring in this standard of comparison, as illustrated in Fig. 4a. This aspect of adverbial function is easily missed, since the standard of comparison usually defaults to the "type of object" of the agent (see Section 4.4) without explicit mention of that type. For example, when we are telling the story of Grant the ant and say at one point that "Grant was running quickly" (Fig. 4b), we naturally mean that he was running quickly by ant standards, not by cheetah standards. For attempts to construct more detailed meaning representations of manner adverbs, much as in the case of adjectives, see Cercone and Schubert [1975] and Cercone [1975a, 1977b].

2.6. Time

Because of the special status of time in the structure of events, our representation includes a special syntax for time. We assume that each predicate over physical entities has a time argument, which may be an instant or interval of time. In the logical notation, an instant of time is indicated by appending a time constant or variable in angle brackets to the predicate

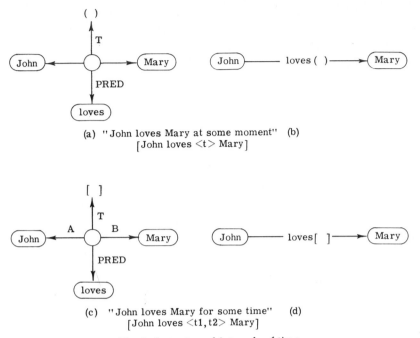

(a) "John loves Mary at some moment"   (b)
[John loves <t> Mary]

(c) "John loves Mary for some time"   (d)
[John loves <t1,t2> Mary]

Fig. 5. Instants and intervals of time.

name, and an interval of time by appending a pair of such variables in angle brackets (the beginning and end of the time interval). For example [John loves⟨t⟩ Mary] and [John loves⟨t1,t2⟩ Mary] say respectively that John loves Mary at time t, and that he loves her from time t1 to time t2. In the graphical notation (Fig. 5), time-instant nodes are represented by pairs of round brackets and time-interval nodes by pairs of square brackets.

Figure 6 shows the representation of "John first hugged and then kissed

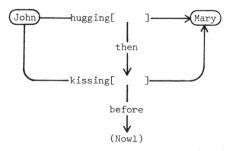

"John first hugged and then kissed Mary"

[John hugging<t1,t2> Mary], [John kissing<t2,t3> Mary],

[t3 before Now1]

Fig. 6. Representation of events.

Mary" as an illustration of the use of time relations to structure events. Networks for much more complex propositions, such as "The cow jumped over the moon" are shown in Cercone and Schubert [1975] and Cercone [1975a].

2.7. Logical Connectives and Modal Operators

Logical connectives are applied to one or more propositional arguments to form compound propositions, much as predicates are applied to one or more conceptual arguments to form atomic propositions. This is illustrated in Fig. 7.

At the top (Fig. 7a,b) we have an example of negation. The proposition node labeled p1 represents the atomic proposition "John loves Mary." The *denial* of this proposition is represented by node p2. This *compound* proposition is formed from two components: the propositional operator ⌐ and

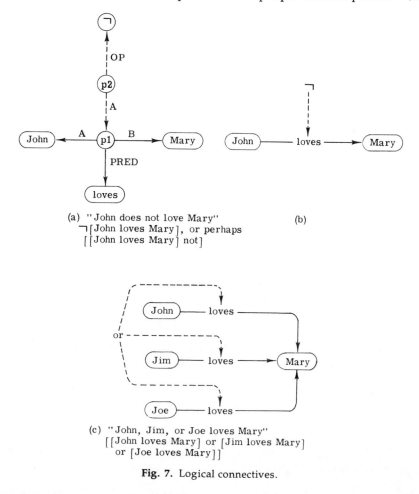

(a) "John does not love Mary"
⌐[John loves Mary], or perhaps
[[John loves Mary] not]

(b)

(c) "John, Jim, or Joe loves Mary"
[[John loves Mary] or [Jim loves Mary]
or [Joe loves Mary]]

Fig. 7. Logical connectives.

its operand p1. This is completely analogous to a predication about one argument, such as the earlier "Mary is a girl." But instead of a PRED link, we now have an OP link to the appropriate logical operator, and instead of a conceptual argument, we have a propositional operand. Notice that broken lines have been used for the links of the compound proposition. This is just to make logical compounds stand out visually. The same types of abbreviations can be used for compound propositions as for atomic propositions. The link to the operand is omitted, and the name of the operand is used to establish the proposition node.

Figure 7c illustrates disjunction in abbreviated form. In this case we are forming the compound proposition p4 ("John, Jim, or Joe loves Mary") by applying the disjunction operator to propositions p1, p2, and p3.* We are regarding disjunction as an operator that takes arbitrarily many operands. The links to these operands do not need to be distinguished since disjunction is associative and commutative.

In the same way, we can introduce conjunction, implication, equivalence, and other logical operators. In the graphical notation, a convenient form of implication is one that allows multiple antecedents and consequents; for example, (p1, p2, p3) implies (p4, p5, p6). Examples will be seen shortly. Similarly, a convenient form of equivalence is one that allows a set of implicity conjoined propositions to be equivalenced to another such set. However, we have found binary implication and equivalence combined with explicit conjunction more convenient in the internal representation [Goebel, 1977].

Unlike predicates, operators are not back-linked to their operands. There seems little point in having, for example, sequential access to all instances of disjunction.

Modal operators follow the same network syntax as logical connectives, except for the use of unbroken links in diagrams. Examples are shown in Fig. 8. The operator "believes" takes an individual first argument and propositional second argument. In these examples, as well as in Fig. 7, we take a proposition to be asserted if and only if it is not embedded in another proposition, i.e., if and only if its proposition node is not pointed to. Thus in Fig. 7a,b "John loves Mary" is not asserted; in Fig. 7c, the disjuncts are not asserted; and in Fig. 8a,b "Mary is happy" is not asserted. However, embedded propositions can still be asserted indirectly as shown in Fig. 8c. Here "Actually, Mary is happy" is asserted, which entails the truth of the embedded proposition "Mary is happy." The affirmative "actually" (or "in fact," or "it is the case that") can be represented by monadic conjunction or disjunction, or even double negation.

---

* It may be felt that an exclusive-or is more appropriate here. However, this would make "John, Jim, or Joe loves Mary" *false* if both John and Jim love Mary. For a nice discussion of this point, see Pelletier [1977].

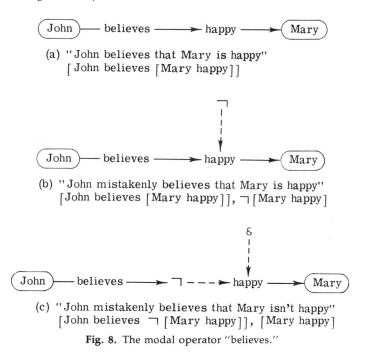

(a) "John believes that Mary is happy"
[John believes [Mary happy]]

(b) "John mistakenly believes that Mary is happy"
[John believes [Mary happy]], ¬[Mary happy]

(c) "John mistakenly believes that Mary isn't happy"
[John believes ¬[Mary happy]], [Mary happy]

Fig. 8. The modal operator "believes."

2.8. Quantifiers

A network syntax allowing arbitrary nesting of quantifier and propositional operator scopes is essential. The first complete representation for quantifiers was introduced by Shapiro [1971]. He treated "every" and "some" as relations between sentences and individuals (the variables being quantified) occurring in those sentences. Thus a quantified statement such as "Everyone loves Mary" involves two proposition nodes: one for the open sentence $[[x \text{ person}] \Rightarrow [x \text{ loves Mary}]]$, and another for the proposition that the relation "every" holds between x and the open sentence.

This method of quantification is syntactically complete but seems semantically unsatisfying, since unbound variable nodes, open sentence nodes, and relations over such nodes are not intuitively meaningful.

Kay [1973] was first to suggest the use of Skölem functions to represent quantification in networks. This approach dispenses with variable-binding operators and thus introduces no meaningless nodes. Skölem functions represent existentially quantified variables functionally dependent on universally quantified variables. For example,

$$(\forall x)(\exists y)[y \text{ bigger-than } x]$$

becomes

$$[y(x) \text{ bigger-than } x].$$

The universal quantification of x is implicit, and $y(x)$ is the Skölem function supplying a specific individual that is "bigger-than" x corresponding to each x.

Figure 9 shows the representation of the propositions "There is a man who likes all women" and "All men like some woman," respectively. The existentially quantified node for "a man" in Fig. 9a becomes a constant upon skölemization, since it does not lie within the scope of any universal quantifier. Hence its representation is identical to that of other individual constants such as "Mary." Universal quantification is indicated by the use of a broken line for the universally quantified node. Notice also the use of implication to form the compound sentence "If y is a woman, then x likes y," where y is the universally quantified variable. The antecedents of an implication are always attached to the back of the implication arrow, and the consequents to the front of the arrow.

In the second proposition, the existentially quantified node for "some woman" is a Skölem function of the universally quantified node. This dependency is expressed by the dotted *scope inclusion link* from the universally quantified node to the dependent existentially quantified node. In general, there are scope inclusion links (and/or their inverses) from each universally quantified node to each dependent existentially quantified node.

These conventions assume that propositions are in *prenex* form, i.e., the quantifiers have been "moved to the front" of propositions, so that the scopes of the quantifiers include those of the operators in a proposition. In Schubert [1975, 1976], a more general method of skölemization was proposed that allows arbitrary nesting of quantifier and operator scopes. Es-

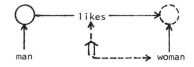

(a) "There is a man who likes all women"

[Man1 man], (∀x)[[x woman] => [Man1 likes x]]

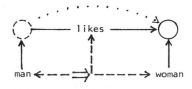

(b)   "Every man likes some woman"

(∀x)(∃y)[[x man] => [[y woman] & [x likes y]]]

Fig. 9. Quantifiers.

sentially, the method uses standard skölemization for *sequences* of consecutive quantifiers, and then ties the initial existential and all universal quantifiers of each sequence into the scope of the immediately superordinate operator, if any.

Three simple examples are shown in Fig. 10. Figure 10a shows the proposition "No one likes John" in nonprenex form, i.e., with an existential quantifier within the scope of a negation operator. (Negation with multiple operands is to be interpreted as negation of the conjunction of operands.) Figure 10b shows the proposition "John believes that everyone likes him." Here, the universal quantifier lies within the scope of the modal operator "believes." Figure 10c shows the proposition "John believes that everyone likes someone" in which a ∀∃ sequence of quantifiers is tied into the scope of the "believes" operator. Note that scope inclusion links establishing operator precedence over quantifiers run from *proposition* nodes to variables, not from *operator* nodes to variables. Expansion of the diagrams in Fig. 10 to full form would make this explicit.

The generalized scope syntax is necessary since certain modal propositions cannot be put in prenex form. For example, the proposition [John believes (∃x)[x witch]], i.e., John believes that some witch exists,

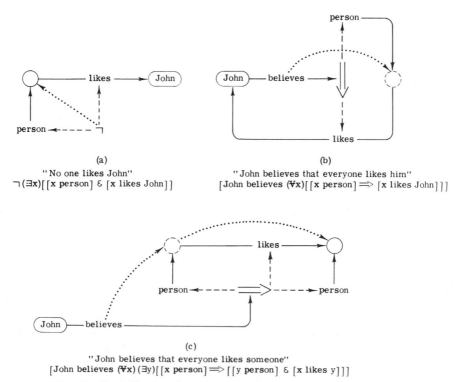

(a)

" No one likes John"

¬(∃x)[[x person] & [x likes John]]

(b)

" John believes that everyone likes him"

[John believes (∀x)[[x person] ⟹ [x likes John]]]

(c)

" John believes that everyone likes someone"

[John believes (∀x)(∃y)[[x person] ⟹ [[y person] & [x likes y]]]]

Fig. 10. Generalized scope notation allowing nonprenex propositions.

cannot be rewritten in prenex form as $(\exists x)[$John believes $[x$ witch$]]$, i.e., there is an individual that John believes to be a witch.

Furthermore, the generalized scope syntax solves a problem with Skolemization noted by Woods [1975], viz., the need to change all quantifiers and Skölem functions when a negation operator is applied to a proposition. For example, the negation of

$$(\forall v)(\exists w)(\forall x)(\exists y)[\overline{v\ P\ w\ x\ y}]$$

is

$$(\exists v)(\forall w)(\exists x)(\forall y)\neg[v\ P\ x\ w\ y]$$

and involves the Skölem dependency $x(w)$ instead of the original dependencies $w(v)$, $y(v, x)$. However, in the general scope syntax, the negation can be left in the form

$$\neg(\forall v)(\exists w)(\forall x)(\exists y)[v\ P\ w\ x\ y],$$

and all that is required is an additional scope link from the negated proposition to v.*

Numerical quantifiers can be represented with the aid of set functions and relations. For example, "five apples" can be represented as a set of apples with cardinality 5. "Exactly two-thirds of all cigarette smokers" can be represented as a subset of the set of all cigarette smokers, where the cardinality of the subset is $2/3$ times that of the superset.

Similarly, *vague quantifiers* such as several, many, and most can be represented with the aid of set functions and relations and *vague number predicates*. For example, "several apples" can be represented as a set of apples whose cardinality satisfies the vague predicate "several." "Most people" can be represented as a subset of the set of all people, where the cardinality of the subset is "considerably more than half" the cardinality of the superset. Network representations of such vaguely determined sets within the context of propositions have been shown in our previous work [Schubert, 1975; Cercone, 1975a]. In these representations, we are taking for granted that vague predicates can be satisfactorily interpreted. We briefly discuss vagueness below.

Finally, we should mention that our representation of quantification extends readily to quantification over predicates and over whatever additional entities are admitted into the domain of discourse (for examples, see Schubert [1976]).

2.9.   Uncertain and Vague Information

An obvious way to express uncertainty about truth values of propositions in any propositional representation is to introduce a propositional

---

* Then how do we know that $(\forall x)$ is within the scope of the negation operator? Because w, which is subordinate to v, does not depend on x and hence is superordinate to it.

function C, where $C(p)$ denotes the credibility (subjective certainty, degree of confirmation, likelihood) of proposition p, with values ranging over some subset of $[0, 1]$ including the endpoints of the interval.* Then "certainly not p" and "certainly p" can be expressed as $C(p) = 0$ and $C(p) = 1$, respectively. Note that explicit introduction of such a function as part of the object language, i.e., its use in propositions of the form $C(p) = r$, is not the same as attachment of numerical certainties to propositions (for example, Schank and Rieger [1974]; Shortliffe [1976]; Trigoboff and Kulikowski [1977]). With the explicit certainty function, it is possible to represent *relative* certainties, as in "It is more likely that John loves Mary than that she loves him." This belief might be represented as in Fig. 11a. Note that if we are *told* the English sentence, we need not arrive at the corresponding belief. We might have *prior* beliefs relevant to the proposition, which prevent us from adopting the informant's subjective degrees of certainty, no matter how truthfully, from the informant's point of view, they have been expressed.

This suggests that we really need a second function $D(x, p)$ denoting individual x's degree of belief in proposition p. Then the "face-value" meaning of an input such as "It is doubtful that Mary is happy" could be based on the paraphrase "The informant considers it doubtful that Mary is

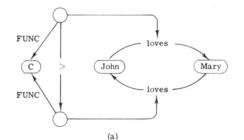

(a)

"It is more likely that John loves Mary than that she loves him"
[(C [John loves Mary]) > (C [Mary loves John])]

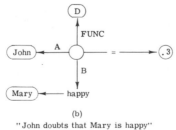

(b)

"John doubts that Mary is happy"
[(D John [Mary happy]) = .3]

Fig. 11. Expressing degrees of certainty.

* The formal semantical status of such a function is problematic but its intuitive semantics is clear enough.

happy." The attachment of some new C-value to "Mary is happy" would then be an *inference*. The function D is useful in any event, since sentences such as "John doubts that Mary is happy" explicitly (though vaguely) attribute a degree of belief to some individual. A corresponding semantic net is shown in Fig. 11b. Because of the vagueness of "doubts," the choice of a numerical degree of belief is rather arbitrary.

If credibilities are regarded as subjective *probabilities*, then it should be possible to compute credibilities of propositions obtained from natural language input or from reasoning processes on Bayesean principles. However, detailed development of this idea requires a theory of *vagueness* since "probabilistic hedges," such as "probably," which surely have an effect on credibilities, are also vague. Such a theory is required in any case since virtually all content words of natural language are more or less vague. Vagueness is a frequently discussed topic in the philosophy of language (for example, Alston [1964]; see also *Synthese* **30** [1975]), but its implications for AI remain unclear. In Schubert [1978] a probabilistic analysis of some vague terms is attempted. Reasons for preferring the probabilistic to Zadeh's [1975, 1977] "possibilistic" approach are given there, and some experimental evidence is presented that favors the probabilistic approach over both Zadeh's theory and Fine's [1975] "precisification" theory. The basis of the probabilistic approach is the *uncertainty* introduced into natural language communication by *variations in application* of vague terms (for example, Black [1937]). For example, when an informant states that there are several apples on the table, it is uncertain to what range of numbers the informant considers "several" applicable. The theory has so far been developed only for adjectives expressing gradable attributes, but appears to be generalizable to other types of vague terms.

3. NETWORK FORM AND CONTENT

In the early stages of building a language understanding or reasoning system, one has to make several fundamental commitments about the propositional representation that go beyond the mere choice of a propositional syntax.

With regard to language understanding, the first question is what should be represented. Should we just extract the "propositional content" of sentences, or should our representation also reflect such aspects of meaning as focus, presupposition, invited inference, connotation, and speaker intention, or even style and phrasing?

Further, we need to decide on a *level* of representation. Should we restrict ourselves to a small number of primitive predicates, or should we use word-related concepts? Schank [1975a,b] and Wilks [1974] have argued in favor of primitives, and their views are buttressed by some of the most impressive natural language understanding systems built to date.

Finally, propositional form can have a profound effect on the efficiency of inference. Should propositions be in some sort of normal form (such as conjunctive normal form), or should we allow their storage in "free form"?

The answers we give in this section are (1) that the semantic net representation of a sentence should isolate its "propositional content" from other aspects of meaning; (2) that the representation of sentences should be at the level of word-related (and even phrase-related) concepts; and (3) that propositions should be in a normal form determined by the generalization hierarchy.

3.1. What Should Be Represented?

Woods [1975] discusses relative clauses in definite descriptions, and concludes that a special syntax is needed for relative clauses. For example, he argues that the sentences

$$\text{The dog that bit the man had rabies} \qquad (3.1)$$

and

$$\text{The dog that had rabies bit the man} \qquad (3.2)$$

should not have identical representations. This is easy enough to accept. But Woods goes on to reject what he calls the "transient-process account" of the distinction, according to which the description "the dog that bit the man" in the first sentence is used to locate a node in memory and is then discarded; and similarly, the description "the dog that had rabies" serves a transient purpose in the second sentence. He points out that no suitable referent for a description might be found, in which case a new node satisfying the description needs to be created.

This is still unobjectionable. However, Woods insists that even when a new node is created, those of its properties expressed by the relative clause must be distinguished syntactically from those expressed by the main clause. (He proposes the use of "EGO links" to distinguish descriptive properties.) His reason, apparently, is that sentences (3.1) and (3.2) intuitively mean different things *even if no prior referents are available* for the definite descriptions occurring in them, as might be the case, for example, for an eavesdropper on a conversation.

At this point, we would like to propose a distinction between the *propositional content* of a sentence and its *pragmatic aspects*. The propositional content consists of the *explicitly mentioned properties of explicitly mentioned entities*. By "properties," we mean "true propositions about," i.e., those whose truth is asserted or implied in the sentence. For example, in sentence (3.1), two entities are mentioned, say *a* and *b*, and their explicitly

mentioned properties are [a dog], [b man], [a bit b], and [a had rabies].*
The propositional content of (3.2) is exactly the same. In other words, sentences (3.1) and (3.2) contain exactly the same information *about their subject matter* (the dog and the man).

The pragmatic aspects of a sentence typically concern discourse structure and speaker intentions and assumptions. For example, sentence (3.1) presupposes that the hearer knows about a dog that bit a man, and that this knowledge is sufficiently fresh in his mind for its unambiguous retrieval via the given description. By contrast, sentence (3.2) presupposes that the hearer knows about a dog that had rabies, etc.

We claim that it is the differences in *pragmatic* aspects that account for the intuitive meaning differences between sentences (3.1) and (3.2). From this point of view, Woods' position is that the internal representation of a sentence should reflect both its propositional content and is pragmatic aspects. In the very general sense that the pragmatic aspects should not be ignored or lost, this position is undoubtedly correct. However, we believe that it is a mistake to mingle the two sorts of information. First, such a policy is likely to encumber the comprehension and inference processes which utilize the acquired knowledge. For example, if some time after occurrence of either sentence (3.1) or (3.2) reference is made to "the dog with rabies that bit the man," or to "the man that was bitten by the dog with rabies," the matching processes seeking suitable referents will have to inspect sets of propositions with and without EGO links; some of the EGO links of the description to be matched will correspond to EGO links in memory, and some will not, depending very much on the phrasing of the original natural language text. Schank [1975b] has given good reasons why an internal representation should be in a canonical form that is relatively independent of surface wording and phrasing.

Equally important, the mingling of the two sorts of information disperses the pragmatic information associated with a particular segment of discourse over the propositional data base. Valuable information about discourse structure and speaker assumptions and intentions become buried in knowledge about dogs, people, etc. We feel that a *separate* model of discourse status and speaker and hearer attitudes needs to be maintained, and that such a model is the proper place for the kind of pragmatic information that Woods would combine with the propositional information.

Here we should also comment on Nash-Webber and Reiter's [1977] logical representation of natural language, which is highly dependent on the phrasing of the source text. There is an appealing elegance in the way their logical translations mirror the syntactic structure of the source text. More-

---

* We ignore time relationships for simplicity. There is, or course, a strong suggestion in both sentences that the dog had rabies *at the time* it bit the man.

over, the translations provide insight into anaphoric reference mechanisms in English. From a practical point of view there is, of course, the question of how easily such translations could be obtained computationally. But more important in the present context is the question of whether such translations are appropriate as final and permanent meaning representations. In view of our preceding discussion, we deny that they are. However well they might capture the pragmatic aspects of discourse, all but the propositional content should be stripped away before they are committed to long-term memory.

3.2. Primitives or Words?

Another crucial decision confronting the designer of a natural language understanding system is what predicates to use in the representation. The fundamental question is whether to admit a large number of highly specific predicates, comparable to the number of words in the language, or only a small number (perhaps dozens) of very general *primitive* predicates. Primitives would have to be chosen so as to allow *reconstruction* of all word senses. Schank, has been the most explicit advocate of primitive predicates (for example, Schank [1975a,b]). Wilks [1974] has argued for "deep" representations and, going beyond Schank, has developed a representation based wholly on primitives. However, he appears now to favor reinstatement of nonprimitive predicates [Wilks, 1975a].

Schank [1975a] enumerated the following advantages of his own primitive-based meaning representation:

(i)   Paraphrase relations are made clearer.

(ii)   Similarity relations are made clearer.

(iii)   Inferences that are true of various classes of verbs can be treated as coming from the individual [primitive] ACTs. All verbs map into a combination of ACTS and states. The inferences come from the ACTs and states rather than from words.

(iv)   Organization in memory is simplified because much information need not be duplicated. The primitive ACTs provide focal points under which information is organized.

We shall attempt to show on general principles that these advantages are not attributable to the use of primitives, but are equally available in systems that admit predicates expressing arbitrarily complex actions, relationships, or properties. The small-scale implementation to be described in Section 5 strengthens these arguments. Moreover, we contend that the further the reduction to primitives is carried, the more computational cumbersome the resulting representations become.

To begin with, advantages (i) and (ii) derive from the fact that Schank represents meanings in *canonical form*,* and not from his use of primitives. For example, each of the sentences

$$\text{John hit Mary} \tag{3.3}$$

$$\text{John struck Mary} \tag{3.4}$$

$$\text{John gave Mary a blow} \tag{3.5}$$

$$\text{Mary was hit by John} \tag{3.6}$$

etc., could be represented canonically as [John hit Mary z], i.e., John hit Mary with z, without decomposing "x hits y with z" into "x PROPELs z from x toward y, causing z to be in physical contact with y" [Schank, 1973]. Use of the nonprimitive predicate "hit" would allow recognition of synonymy for (3.3)–(3.7) and also of the similarities between (3.3) and

$$\text{John slapped Mary} \tag{3.7}$$

$$\text{John clubbed Mary} \tag{3.8}$$

$$\text{John kicked Mary} \tag{3.9}$$

$$\text{John punched Mary} \tag{3.10}$$

$$\text{John butted Mary} \tag{3.11}$$

etc., where the differences lie in the objects that make impact with Mary.

In the dispute surrounding level of representation, it is customary to advance an argument for primitives based on psychological evidence that people cannot recall the actual wording of a text (see Wilks [1976a]). Although we are not particularly concerned about psychological validity, we feel that the argument loses force once it is recognized that a nonprimitive canonical representation need not echo the wording of the original text. For example, we doubt that any advocate of nonprimitive representations would want to represent "John gave Mary a blow" as $(\exists x)[[x \text{ blow}] \& [\text{John gave Mary } x]]$. The representation would more likely involve a canonical "hit" predicate.

Now let us turn to points (iii) and (iv), according to which the use of primitives avoids duplication of information shared by related concepts, especially their implications. Our counterargument is best made by example. Consider the concepts "drinks" and "eats," which among other things entail the transfer of the stuff drunk or eaten from the outside to the inside of the agent. In Schank's primitive-based representation, this property is obtained not from "drinks" and "eats" but as an inference from the primitive act INGEST, which is the nucleus of the lexical formulas for

---

* By "canonical form," we mean "partially canonicalized form," in Woods' [1975] phrase. As Woods rightly points out, there is no effective way of transforming propositions into a canonical form in which the transforms of any two propositions are the same if and only if the propositions are *logically* equivalent. However, when Schank argues for canonical form, he surely has in mind a weaker notion of equivalence, such as paraphrase equivalence, in some psychological (rather than logical) sense.

"drinks" and "eats." Our point is this: we do not actually have to *replace* "drinks" and "eats" by their formulas in order to achieve this kind of inference-sharing. In our approach the fact that if *"x* drinks *y"* then *"x* ingests *y* through its mouth" is stored as an implication of the "drinks" concept, and similarly for "eats." In turn, the fact that if *"x* ingests *y* through *z"* then *"y* is transferred from the outside to the inside of *x"* is stored as an implication of the "ingests" concept. Thus the inference that if *"x* drinks *y"* then *"y* is transferred from the outside to the inside of *x"* could easily be obtained from the implications of the immediate supercon- cept of "drinks," i.e., "ingests." Note incidentally that we do not regard "ingests" as primitive since its meaning can be "explained" through its implications just as that of "drinks" can.

Argument constraints of predicates, which play a crucial role in the parsing process, are also easily accommodated within a nonprimitive rep- resentation. We treat them as monadic predications about the arguments of a given predicate. For example, the constraints for *"x* drinks *y"* are [*x* animate] and [*y* liquid] (more accurately, *y* is a *quantity* of liquid).

While we see no disadvantages in the use of nonprimitive concepts, we do see a major disadvantage in their elimination, namely, the resultant need for *matching* complex primitive representations of originally simple propositions. For example, suppose that a primitive-based system proc- esses the sentence "John dined at a restaurant," reducing this to a primi- tive representation using, say, the restaurant script of Schank and Abelson [1975]. John's action is thus stored in memory as a sequence of "scenes" (entering the restaurant, ordering, eating, and exiting) each of which con- sists of several successive conceptualizations built around primitive ac- tions. This collection of conceptualizations is then embedded in the epi- sodic memory. Suppose that the language understanding system is later asked "Did John dine at a restaurant?" Once again the previous sort of representation is built up, this time in the form of a pattern to be matched, but matching this pattern is a nontrivial task. Not only is the structure to be matched complex but its structural constituents, if these are primitive, will match huge numbers of identical constituents in memory.

Now, in fact, the question-answering system of Lehnert [1977] for a conceptual-dependency memory does not get bogged down with matching. Part of the reason is that *only* action concepts are decomposed into primitives so that very specific, topically revealing predicates, such as "restaurant," "table," "menu," and "waitress," are left in the represen- tation. More important, the system relies on *script summaries* in per- forming matching searches. These amount to nonprimitive represen- tations of complex actions. In Wilks' [1973] system, which is completely primitive-based, a serious matching problem is not encountered because the system is designed for sentence-by-sentence translation rather than question answering.

Moreover, the particular meaning formulas proposed by Schank and by

Wilks for nonprimitive concepts such as "drinks" and "walks" tremendously oversimplify the actual complexity of these concepts, and hence the complexity of matching them. For example, according to Schank [1973], to "walk" is to PTRANS oneself by MOVEing one's feet in a particular direction. This formula is equally applicable to running, skipping, hopping, shuffling, and even skating. The rejoinder that the formula is only a rough-and-ready definition that could easily be refined by adding a few additional conceptualizations is seriously mistaken: any adequate representation of what "walking" means to people is *at least an order of magnitude more complex* than the proposed definition. We previously suggested [Cercone and Schubert, 1975; Cercone, 1975a] that most people possess at least the following knowledge about human walking (irrespective of how well they can verbalize this knowledge):

Each foot of the walker repeatedly leaves the ground, moves freely in the walking direction for a distance comparable to the length of the walker's legs (while staying close to the ground), then is set down again, and remains in position on the ground, supporting the walker, while the other foot goes through a similar motion. The repetition rate is of the order of one repetition per second. The legs remain more or less extended. The body remains more or less erect and is carried forward at a fairly constant rate. (Further details could be added about flexing motions of feet, knees, and hips, and the slight up-and-down motion of the body, typical arm motions, and forces exerted on the ground.)

We showed as much of this "definition" in semantic net form as we could fit on a page. In part, our point was to show that our semantic net formalism was equal to the task. More importantly, however, we wanted to dramatize the *actual* complexity of ordinary concepts in contrast with the primitive-based definitions of Schank and Wilks. We should add that "walking" is òne of the simpler action concepts, in comparison with "dancing," "playing hopscotch," or "writing a PL/1 program," say.

Why, then, are Schank and Wilks able to process language effectively with such simplified definitions? The reason is that their definitions single out the properties *most frequently needed* for comprehension and routine inference. In this sense, their definitions capture the major properties of the concepts defined, and we have merely added minor details. But reliance on meaning caricatures ensures that comprehension will be of a crude sort, and will fail when the less important properties of concepts are needed. Consider the following passage:

Obeying a childish whim, he matched his stride to the cracks in the cement sidewalk, treading on a crack with every alternate step. He was keeping time with the brassy tune which rang from the loudspeakers of the nearby fairground. His small daughter skipped alongside, barely able to keep up.

It is hard to see how a conception of walking as "moving oneself by moving one's feet" could permit real comprehension of this passage (for example, how could we infer that one of the man's feet touches each cement slab at its approximate center, and how do we interpret the phrase "keeping time with the brassy tune"?)

If meanings are as complex as we maintain they are, then it should be clear that reduction of propositions to primitive form is impractical with regard to storage economization and the computational complexity of pattern-directed retrieval. The way to obtain the advantages of the Schank–Wilks meaning formulas without sacrificing either subtlety or efficiency, it seems to us, is to permit nonprimitive predicates within the semantic representations and to provide lists of the most frequently needed properties of each predicate. Thus the most significant properties of a concept become independently accessible, without being regarded as full meaning definitions. The complexity of a concept does not interfere with its matchability in such a scheme, since it is matchable by name.

3.3. What Normal Form, If Any?

In general, a concept P is characterized (though not defined) by its implications, i.e., those properties of x implied by $P(x)$ for all x. We want to consider the choice of logical form for universally quantified statements of this sort.

It is clear that any system designed for reasoning about the real world must efficiently exploit *property inheritance* within generalization (IS-A) hierarchies. What complicates this problem is that conceptual entities typically consist of many *components*, for example, the parts of an object, the participants in an action, or the departments of an organization. We need not only efficient *property* inheritance but also *relationship* inheritance from components to corresponding components.

For example, in a "bird" subhierarchy, it should be sufficient to specify the attachment relationships between head, neck, body, legs, and tail at the top level, and this information should be "visible" from each particular kind or instance of a bird. To see the difficulty, consider the following fragments of bird knowledge:

$$(\forall r)[[r \text{ bird}] \Rightarrow (\exists s)(\exists t)[[s \text{ part-of } r] \ \& \ [t \text{ part-of } r]$$
$$\& \ [s \text{ head}] \ \& \ [t \text{ neck}] \ \& \ [s \text{ joins } t]]]$$
$$(\forall u)[[u \text{ owl}] \Rightarrow (\forall v)(\forall w)[[[v \text{ part-of } u] \ \& \ [w \text{ part-of } u]$$
$$\& \ [v \text{ head1}] \ \& \ [w \text{ neck1}]] \Rightarrow [v \text{ big}] \ \& \ [w \text{ short}]]]$$
$$(\forall x)[[x \text{ emu}] \Rightarrow (\forall y)(\forall z)[[[y \text{ part-of } x] \ \& \ [z \text{ part-of } x]$$
$$\& \ [y \text{ head2}] \ \& \ [z \text{ neck2}]] \Rightarrow [y \text{ small}] \ \& \ [z \text{ long}]]].$$

We assume that in addition the subconcept relationships owl $\square\!\!\Rightarrow$ bird (an owl is necessarily a bird), emu $\square\!\!\Rightarrow$ bird, head1 $\square\!\!\Rightarrow$ head, head2 $\square\!\!\Rightarrow$ head, etc., are available. (The symbols $\Rightarrow$ and $\square\!\!\Rightarrow$ were proposed in Schubert [1976] as a means for expressing contingent and necessary universal statements, respectively.) The reasons for having a particularized owl's head concept head1 and similarly neck1, head2, etc., are partly intuitive ("owl's head" seems to evoke its own image, distinct from "bird's head") and partly anticipatory. We shall need a separate concept for each part of a thing as a point of attachment for knowledge peculiar to it.

This collection of propositions is very disjointed and redundant. Furthermore, nontrivial inference is required to transfer relationships from the "bird" context to the "owl" and "emu" contexts. Here the only relationship, besides part-of relationships, is that the head is joined to the neck. However, there would be many such relationships in a system knowledgeable about birds.

Now consider the following alternative arrangement of these facts:

$$(\forall x)(\exists y)(\exists z)$$
$$[[[x \text{ bird}] \Rightarrow [[y \text{ part-of } x] \& [z \text{ part-of } x]$$
$$\& [y \text{ head}] \& [z \text{ neck}] \& [y \text{ joins } z]]]$$
$$\& [[x \text{ owl}] \Rightarrow [[y \text{ head1}] \& [z \text{ neck1}] \& [y \text{ big}] \& [z \text{ short}]]]$$
$$\& [[x \text{ emu}] \Rightarrow [[y \text{ head2}] \& [z \text{ neck2}] \& [y \text{ small}] \& [z \text{ long}]]]].$$

Through *variable-sharing*, we have eliminated all redundancies. Moreover, parts relationships for birds now transfer trivially to owls and emus. This is essentially the scheme proposed by Philip Hayes [1977], although he describes it in terms of his network formalism (which unfortunately suffers from all the usual problems of interpretation). He points out that shared nodes change character depending on the "viewpoint." For example, in our bird propositions, x represents any bird from one point of view, any owl from another, and any emu from a third. Similarly, y and z represent different kinds of heads and necks depending on the point of view.

Note that we have simplified matters in our example by ignoring the fact that a bird has just one head and neck. One way of dealing with this would be to add the consequent

$$(\forall v)[[[v \text{ head}] \& [v \text{ part-of } x]] \Rightarrow [v = y]]$$

to the implications of $[x \text{ bird}]$, and similarly for "neck." A simpler way would be to combine "head" and "part-of" into a relation "head-of" (for example, $[y \text{ head-of } x]$), which we would treat as single-valued in its first argument.

Back-linking from shared variables to propositions should be suppressed, as there is no benefit in having uniform access to all propositions in which such nodes participate. It is more useful for general knowledge to be accessible via the participating predicates, such as "owl" or "head1."

Generalizing from our examples, we conclude that the knowledge associated with a generalization hierarchy should be stored as a set of implicative propositions sharing one universally quantified node and any number of existentially quantified nodes dependent on the universally quantified node. The antecedents of the implications involve the universally quantified node as argument, and correspond to the concepts making up the generalization hierarchy. In Section 4, we shall propose a hierarchic organization for the knowledge about each concept. With this organization, the implicants of each concept would be accessible by topic, instead of being part of a long conjunction, such as [y head1] & [z neck1] & [y big] & [z short] & . . . .

The shared-variable form of generalization hierarchies complicates the process of assimilating new information. New facts such as $(\forall x)[[x \text{ owl}] \Rightarrow [x \text{ predator}]]$ cannot simply be "added" to the net by creation of a new variable node. Instead, this information must be inserted at the appropriate place in the appropriate hierarchy, with x replaced by the universal node of that hierarchy. To date, we have not implemented such an insertion mechanism.

In the above we have considered only monadic concept hierarchies. It seems possible to organize relational concepts hierarchically as well. These will share more than one universal node, as exemplified in the following fragment of an "ingests" hierarchy:

$$(\forall x)(\forall y)(\exists u)(\exists v)(\exists w) \ . \ . \ .$$
$$[[[x \text{ ingests } y] \Rightarrow [[u \text{ orifice-of } x] \& [v \text{ place}] \& [w \text{ place}]$$
$$\& [v \text{ outside } x] \& [w \text{ inside } x]$$
$$\& [y \text{ moving } v \ w] \& \ . \ . \ .]]$$
$$\& [[x \text{ eats } y] \Rightarrow [[y \text{ food}] \& [u \text{ mouth-of } x]]]$$
$$\& [[x \text{ drinks } y] \Rightarrow [[y \text{ liquid}] \& [u \text{ mouth-of } x]]]$$
$$\& [[x \text{ snuffs } y] \Rightarrow [[y \text{ powder}] \& [u \text{ nose-of } x]]]$$

We have suppressed time relations and other subtleties for simplicity.

How many hierarchies are there? We imagine that the most general concept in each hierarchy should be of the order of generality of Schank's or Wilks' primitives (this may be the real significance of primitives). Thus, there may be some dozens of hierarchies.

4. ORGANIZING PROPOSITIONS FOR INFERENCE

The AI programmer's ruin is the combinatorially explosive search for a "winning combination" among numerous alternatives. Such searches must be restricted either by clever design of the combinatory strategy or by drastic limitation of the number of alternatives that will be considered "relevant" to any particular search.

In the context of automatic reasoning, the former approach tends to delay but not avert the combinatorial explosion. Since networks are intended as repositories for very large amounts of knowledge, we need to ask what sort of organization of this knowledge will ensure that only a small number of highly relevant items are considered at any stage of a reasoning process. Is the concept-centered organization that is characteristic of networks sufficient to achieve the required narrowing of view?

We argue below that it is not, by focusing on the "symbol-mapping problem." Then we propose a hierarchic organization of network knowledge as a solution to the difficulties brought to light in the consideration of that problem. Essentially, we propose to interpose a treelike access structure between each concept and the propositions in which it participates. This makes the connection between concepts and knowledge about them slightly less direct; however, the knowledge organization remains concept-centered and access to propositions *relevant* to a task is greatly facilitated. For the most part, our discussion is based on the thesis by Goebel [1977]. Here we slightly modify our logical view of "topics" (reinterpreting them as 2-place instead of 1-place predicates), and attempt to supply a more adequate strategy for classifying propositions and a more realistic example of a topic hierarchy. Not all of the ideas we shall put forward in the following subsections have been implemented. A brief description of the experimental implementation will be given in Section 5.

4.1. The Symbol-Mapping Problem

Superficially, the "symbol-mapping problem" [McDermott, 1975a] is the problem of effectively mapping the properties of a concept onto its subconcepts and instances, i.e., property inheritance. Fahlman [1975] gives the following example:

> Suppose I tell you that a certain animal—let's call him Clyde—is an elephant. You accept this single assertion and file it away with no apparent display of mental effort. And yet, as a result of this simple transaction, you suddenly appear to know a great deal about Clyde. If I say that Clyde climbs trees or plays the piano or lives in a teacup, you will immediately begin to doubt my credibility. Somehow, "elephant" is serving as more than a mere label here; it is, in some sense, a whole package of properties and relationships, and that package can be delivered by means of a single IS-A statement.

We should first of all note that property-inheritance is much less of a problem in networks than in PLANNER-like data bases, which were McDermott's and Fahlman's prime concern. In networks, property inheritance is facilitated by generalization hierarchies. Thus Clyde's elephanthood immediately provides a handle on knowledge attached to the elephant concept. Some of the proposals made for solving the symbol-mapping problem can be seen as attempts to introduce networklike organizations into proceduralized representations. For example, McDermott's

[1975b] "packets" and Moore's [1975] "buckets" can be viewed in this way.

However, there is more to Fahlman's example than property inheritance. Mere *access* to elephant knowledge does not guarantee swift question-answering or consistency checking ("clash detection," as Fahlman calls it). Suppose that a network contains *hundreds* of facts about the concepts "Clyde" (for example, stories involving Clyde), "elephant," "mammal," and "animal." Is it practical to have an inference mechanism sift through all of them whenever it seeks the answer to a simple question such as "Is Clyde grey" or "Does Clyde live in a teacup"? What if two or three propositions need to be combined into an inference chain—will this lead to a combinatorial explosion?

Let us consider how the above questions could be answered within a "rudimentary" network, unembellished by any superimposed organization. This will provide the motivation for introducing concept-centered "topic hierarchies" to facilitate simple inference.

We wish to answer the question "Is Clyde grey?" Assuming that simple assertions have been hash-coded, we first look for [Clyde grey] in the hash table. Failing to find it, we access the "Clyde" node and sequentially scan the attached propositions, checking if any involve a color predicate. Failing again, we move up one step in the generalization hierarchy to the "elephant" node. We now scan the elephant propositions for color predications and return an affirmative answer if one of them says that elephants are (normally) grey. If there is no confirming or contravening color predication we move up another step in the hierarchy (to mammal, quadruped, animal, or whatever), and so on. If we fail to find any relevant predications, we generate the answer "I don't know."

The question "Does Clyde live in a teacup?" is more difficult. Even if a search of Clyde-propositions for Clyde's location yields the fact that Clyde lives in, say, a zoo, the possibility that Clyde's particular niche is a teacup within the zookeeper's cupboard is not immediately precluded. What we need, of course, is the inference that Clyde is too big to live in a teacup. To obtain this inference, we can assume that the inference mechanism does a certain amount of "forward inferencing" on the assumption that Clyde does indeed live in a teacup. The "major implication" lists described in the last section in connection with the problem of organizing propositions for comprehension might be useful for this purpose. Alternatively, it may be appropriate to associate a new type of proposition list with each concept, designed to single out those propositions likely to be useful for consistency checking. In any case, we assume that the "in" of the question is interpreted as "inside," and that [x inside y], with x bound to Clyde and y bound to the teacup, triggers the inference [y bigger than x]. This is checked against Clyde-knowledge and teacup-knowledge. To make any progress beyond this point, we need to assume that "bigger-than" is classified as a "size" predicate (say, in the lexicon), and that the knowledge about elephants and teacups contains similarly classified predications about the *absolute* sizes of elephants and teacups, respectively. We locate these predications by scanning Clyde propositions, then elephant propositions, and similarly teacup propositions. Then we "grind" the retrieved size predications against each other by some standard deductive method to obtain a contradiction, and hence a negative answer to the original question.

Two features are noteworthy in both of these examples. One is the need to classify propositions topically as color propositions, location propositions, size propositions, etc., to avoid explosive search for combinations of propositions that yield a desired conclusion. The other is the need for access to just those propositions about a concept that belong to one of the above topics. In the examples, this access was achieved by exhaustive scanning. Clearly this inefficient mechanism needs to be reorganized. Our approach is to structure the propositions associated with each concept in accordance with a *topic hierarchy*. For first hints at this kind of approach see the remarks of Bundy and Stone [1975].

Before describing the design and implementation of topic hierarchies, we should mention Fahlman's solution to the symbol mapping problem [Fahlman, 1975], which involves the use of hardware elements to represent concepts and relations between concepts. Each unit can store "marker-bits," which can be propagated in parallel, through a network of such elements. In this way, rapid searches for information satisfying specified constraints can be performed, with a minimum of organizational overhead.

We believe, however, that good serial solutions are possible and that the required organizational overhead may be a blessing in disguise: it provides a form of explicit self-knowledge within the system, and a basis for self-organizing processes.

4.2. Topic Hierarchies and Topic Access Skeletons

We define a topic as a *predicate over proposition-concept pairs*. For example, "coloring" is a predicate that is considered to be true for the proposition "a zebra has black and white stripes" in relation to the concept "zebra." In other words, the proposition is a coloring proposition *about* zebras. Another topic predicate that is true for that proposition in relation to "zebra" is "appearance." In fact, "appearance" holds for any proposition-concept pair for which "coloring" holds, i.e., "appearance" is a *supertopic* of "coloring," and conversely, "coloring" is a *subtopic* of "appearance."

Topic predicates are stored in the semantic net, linked by subtopic and supertopic relationships. Together, these form a *topic hierarchy* (or several topic hierarchies). A possible topic hierarchy for physical objects is shown in Fig. 12. This represents an attempt to provide a comprehensive classification of knowledge about physical objects, with as little overlap between categories as possible. The "specialization" topic is intended as a slot for subconcept relationships (i.e., necessary subsumption) as well as contingent subsumption relationships and *instances* of a concept. Similarly, the "generalization" topic encompasses predications that give the "type" of a thing (e.g., [Clyde elephant]), in addition to superconcept predications. We shall comment further on the physical objects hierarchy in Section 4.5.

Once a topic hierarchy has been defined for a particular kind of node, the propositions attached to any node of that kind can be organized in accordance with the hierarchy. This is accomplished by superimposing an

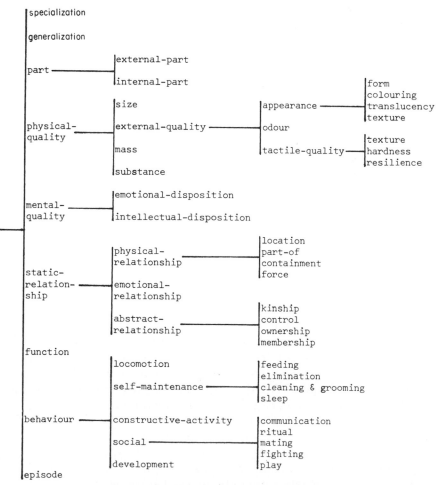

Fig. 12. A topic hierarchy for physical objects.

access structure called a *topic access skeleton* upon the attached propositions. A topic access skeleton "mimics" a part of the topic hierarchy,
namely that part needed to supply access paths to all the available propositions about the node, when these are attached to the appropriate terminal
topics.

For example, if the only facts known about Clyde are that he is an elephant and likes to eat peanuts, these would be attached to the access
skeleton:

```
                  ¦generalization
       Clyde ----¦
                  ¦behavior --- self-maintenance --- feeding
```

If elephants, in turn, are known to be very large, grey, rough-skinned
mammals and Clyde is a known instance, these facts would be attached to
the access skeleton:

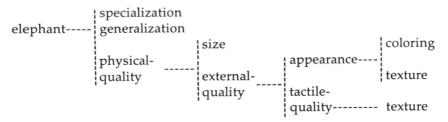

Note that "texture" appears twice, making the "rough-skinned" predication available both as an aspect of appearance and as a tactile quality. In
the implementation, a single "texture" node can be used, with pointers to
it from both the "appearance" and "tactile quality" nodes. Thus a topic
hierarchy and corresponding access skeleton need not be strictly tree-
structured.

4.3. Insertion and Retrieval of Propositions

How can semantic net propositions be inserted and retrieved in confor-
mity with a given topic hierarchy? To insert a proposition in the net, we
need to determine its place in the topic hierarchy in relation to each of its
participating concepts. For example, to insert the proposition "Clyde is an
elephant," we need to recognize it as a "generalization" proposition
giving the object type of "Clyde," and as a "specialization" proposition
giving an instance of "elephant." To insert the proposition "All elephants
are grey," we need to recognize it as a "coloring" proposition about "elephant" and as a "specialization" proposition about "grey."

We shall outline an approach to the automatic topical classification of
propositions in the next subsection. For the moment, we note only that
predicates in the semantic net can be marked as being indicative of a particular topic in relation to their arguments. This is achieved by means of

"indicator links" running from a predicate node to appropriate topic nodes. For example, the node for "grey" would have a indicator link to the "coloring" topic node.

Once a proposition has been recognized as belonging to a particular terminal topic in relation to one of its participating concepts, a complete topic access path is easily determined by ascending in the topic hierarchy encoded in the semantic net. For example, a "coloring" proposition about "elephant" can be classified immediately as an "appearance" proposition, and hence as an "external quality" proposition, and hence finally as a "physical quality" proposition. This sequence of topics can now be used in reverse, to travel down the topic access skeleton of "elephant".* The access skeleton will contain the complete access path if some "coloring" proposition is already present, and an initial fragment of the path (possibly empty) otherwise. In the latter case, the required extension of the access skeleton is built up in the process of inserting the proposition.

Retrieval of propositions satisfying a given "retrieval pattern" is achieved in much the same fashion. The only differences are (1) that a retrieval pattern may have indeterminate conceptual constituents (existentially quantified variables to be bound to constants in the process of matching); (2) that a retrieval pattern may explicitly mention a topic ("Describe the *appearance* of elephants"); and (3) that access skeletons are traversed but never modified during retrieval.

In general, retrieval might proceed from any of the concepts occurring in a retrieval pattern. For example, the retrieval pattern

[Clyde elephant]?

could lead to retrieval via Clyde (under the "generalization" topic) or via elephant (under the "specialization" topic). Of course, retrieval via Clyde is likely to be the better strategy in this case. In a general strategy, retrieval attempts might be made in a pseudo-parallel fashion via *all* candidate concepts, up to the point where a terminal topic is reached. A proposition count at terminal topics might then be used to determine further search priority.

When a pattern contains indeterminate constituents, the number of concepts usable for accessing is reduced. For example, the request

$(\exists x)[x \text{ elephant}]?$

can be answered only via "elephant."

When a retrieval request explicitly mentions a topic, as in "Describe the appearance of elephants," this topic can of course be used directly (i.e., without reliance on indicator links) to obtain an access path for traversal of topic access skeletons. In Section 5, we shall describe an explicitly topic-oriented form of retrieval request available in our implementation.

---

* The most recent implementation avoids the initial ascent in the topic hierarchy.

Once a list of proposition pointers has been reached at the "bottom" of a topic access skeleton in response to a retrieval request, the propositions pointed to can be examined one by one to determine if any of them match the required pattern, and possess whatever further properties are required for the purposes of the retrieval request.

4.4. Topical Classification of Propositions

We saw in the last section that an essential requirement for insertion and retrieval of topically organized network propositions is a mechanism for automatic topical classification of propositions. We shall sketch a mechanism that appears capable of correctly classifying many propositions about physical objects. For a fuller description, see Schubert *et al.* [1978].

First we need the notion of a *type predicate*, i.e., a monadic predicate that intuitively gives the "type of object" of its argument. Here we have in mind the kind of predicate that Quillian [1968, 1969] used for the "superset" of an object. For example, "elephant," "human," "mammal," and "computer" are type predicates, whereas "pet," "grey," and "pianist" are not; intuitively, the latter specify an abstract relationship, a color, and an occupation respectively, rather than a type of object. We assume that type predicates are distinguished in the semantic net by means of indicator links to the "generalization" topic node; i.e., type predicates are indicative of the generalization topic.

Propositions can be classified, with the aid of indicator links into topic categories other than "specialization" or "generalization" as follows. Relative to any monadic predicate with a universally quantified argument, a proposition is classified under all topics indicated by its *nontype* predicates. For example, the proposition "Fred likes everyone," i.e.,

$$(\forall x)[[x \text{ human}] \Rightarrow [\text{Fred likes } x]]$$

is classified relative to "human" under the "emotional relationships" topic indicated by "likes." Next, relative to each constant or existentially quantified argument, the proposition is classified under all topics indicated by nontype predicates applied to that argument. Thus, relative to "Fred" the above proposition is again classified under "emotional relationships."

This method is applied only to propositions equivalent to *clauses*, i.e., propositions that become pure disjunctions upon conversion to conjunctive normal form; otherwise, spurious classifications would result.

The methods for classifying propositions into the "specialization" and "generalization" topics also rely on clause form. A clause is classified as a specialization proposition relative to a predicate P if P occurs in unnegated form in the clause. For example, [Clyde animal] and $(\forall x)[\neg[x$

elephant] or [*x* animal]] are specialization propositions relative to "animal," while ⌐[Clyde animal] is not. The criteria for membership in the generalization topic are somewhat more complex and will not be given here (see Schubert *et al.* [1978]).

Our classification criteria are still very incomplete. Nevertheless, along with our pilot implementation, they are sufficient to indicate that automatic topical classification of propositions is feasible. We should mention that a proposition is, in general, not classified with respect to all of the concepts participating in it (in Goebel [1977] the concepts with respect to which a proposition is classified were called the *foci* of the proposition). For example, ⌐[Clyde animal] is not classified relative to "animal," as we have seen. Thus certain back-links are lost, if the topic organization is used to supplant the original system of back-links from concepts to propositions in which they participate. This seems unobjectionable to us. For example, it is hardly a useful fact about *animals* that Clyde is not one. When a connection is lost that we intuitively feel *should not* be lost, this simply indicates that the topic hierarchy or the classification mechanism is inadequate.

4.5. The Physical Objects Topic Hierarchy

Let us now return to the topic hierarchy for physical objects in Fig. 12. We have attempted to structure the hierarchy so that it would facilitate the kinds of inference processes about objects and animals that provided our motivation for the proposed network organization. For example, information about the color, size, and location of elephants, in general, and Clyde, in particular, is now made readily accessible. Propositions relating to the generalization hierarchy are distinguished by their membership in the top-level topics "generalization" and "specialization." Thus Clyde's main class membership is easily located.

If the sample hierarchy is to be adequate for knowledge about human beings as well as objects and animals, the "mental quality," "behavior," and "episodes" subhierarchies (and several other subhierarchies) will probably have to be considerably expanded. For example, "feeding," "communication," and "development" would each have to be further subdivided. Also, the accommodation of specialized scientific knowledge would require expansion of parts of the hierarchy.

Parts knowledge is essential for describing complex objects systematically, as many writers have recognized (for example, Brachman [1977]; Philip Hayes [1977]; Levesque and Mylopoulos [1977]). The parts topic in our sample hierarchy can provide an entry point for a full parts hierarchy. For example, the "external part" subtopic of "quadruped" might contain propositions to the effect that any quadruped has a head, neck, body, legs, tail, and hide as parts, while the "internal part" subtopic might contain propositions to the effect that any quadruped has a skeleton, musculature, nervous system, circulatory system, digestive system, respiratory system, and perhaps some other systems of internal organs, as parts. *Each of these parts would have its own topic hierarchy whose "parts" topic would in turn give access to further subparts.* In this way, parts knowledge at any level of detail could be accessed.

"Episodic" knowledge about a concept supplies specific event sequences involving the concept as a participant in the events. This would be a large category for many individual concepts and would require further subdivision in those cases. One possible substructure would be one that parallels that of the "behavior" topic, without regard for chronology. Since people seem to have more difficulty recalling events by their time of occurrence than by their conceptual content, we assume that a chronological hierarchy would be inappropriate, or in any case insufficient in itself. In the case of generic concepts, the episode topic would contain pointers to *scripts* [Schank and Abelson, 1975] in which the concepts play a role. Additional scripts could be attached to any of the terminals in the hierarchy. For example, there could be scripts for animal feeding behavior, mating behavior, or usage for particular purposes. Further scripts would be accessible indirectly via the parts hierarchy, for example, a script for digestive system function.

4.6. What Has Been Gained?

How much more quickly can simple questions be answered with a topically organized memory, in comparison with unmodified semantic nets, and what are the storage costs? If the sample hierarchy is any indication of what a realistic hierarchy for physical objects should look like, and the distribution of propositions over terminal topics is more or less uniform, then there should be a reduction by one or two orders of magnitude in the number of propositions considered relevant to an inference process. This should in turn have a dramatic effect on the efficiency of such processes. We make this point in greater technical detail in Schubert *et al.* [1978]. There, we also show that if access skeletons are stored in a contracted form in which nodes with single entering and leaving branches are omitted, then the storage overhead in comparison with simple back-linking is only a factor of two.

A further advantage of the topical organization is the fact that it permits gradual broadening of a search from an initial set of topics to "nearby" topics. For example, failure to find a useful piece of information under the "coloring" topic might prompt inspection of topically nearby information about form or texture.

Finally, we note that questions such as "What does an elephant look like?" can be answered much more easily with a topically organized net than with an unstructured set of elephant propositions. Essentially, we would reply with the propositions stored under the "appearance" topic of the "elephant" node. This type of question, requiring a descriptive answer, is important in human discourse but is rarely considered in question-answering research.

5. IMPLEMENTATIONS

In this section, we provide an overview of two mini-implementations. The first of these [Cercone, 1975a] is a small language understanding system for mapping certain declarative sentences into network propositions. Its design is based on the principles defended in Sections 3.1–3.2. The meaning representations produced for adjectival modifiers are unusually sophisticated. The system was written in LISP and ran under the MTS operating system on an IBM 360/67. The second mini-implementation [Goebel, 1977] demonstrates that the topical organization of knowledge proposed in Section 4 is effectively programmable. The system was written in the "C" language running under the UNIX operating system on a PDP11/45.

5.1. The First Implementation

For this implementation, we shall first describe the network structure and lexical structure, and then the operation of the parser.

Network nodes correspond to LISP atoms, and a node's links to other nodes are represented as indicator/value pairs on its property list. The indicators are the appropriate arc labels, such as PRED, ARG, and FUNC. All of the propositions in which a concept participates as argument or predicate are listed under a PROPOSITIONS indicator on the concept's property list. These back-links provide the concept-centered organization of knowledge, which is the definitive property of semantic nets.

At the time we implemented the parsing programs, we were uncertain about the best way to structure the generalization hierarchies and the knowledge associated with them (recall the discussion of logical form in Section 3). Also, we had not implemented the representation of quantification. Therefore, we decided to omit all general knowledge, i.e., propositions with universally quantified variables, from the net itself, putting such knowledge instead on the property lists of generic nodes.

For example, the implication

$$(\forall x)(\exists z)(\forall y)[[[x \text{ drink1 } y] \Rightarrow [[x \text{ ingest } y \text{ } z] \text{ \& } [z \text{ mouth of } x]]]$$

which is part of the meaning of "drink1" (the ordinary sense of drinking), is stored as the set of properties (ARGS $(x\ y)$), (P3 (ingest $x\ y\ z$)), (P4 (mouth-of $z\ x$)) on the property list of the "drink1" node. The remaining implications of "drink1" are stored in the same way. Needless to say, these propositions should ultimately be integrated into the net so that they can be properly used by inference processes. Note that z (the drinker's mouth) is Skölem-dependent on x (the drinker) in the above implication. In the property-list representation, we assume that all variables other than the ARGS are Skölem functions dependent on the ARGS, which are universally quantified. This leads to the minor inaccuracy of making the drinker's mouth z dependent not only on the drinker x but also on the stuff drunk y.

The property list of each predicative concept also contains the following items of "pragmatic" information: (1) one or more "templates" such as "x give y z" and "x give z to y" indicating the expected arrangement of arguments (and possibly certain prepositions) in the surface realization of the concept; (2) names of propositions that act as *argument constraints;* (3) names of *major implications* likely to be needed frequently for understanding discourse involving that concept (i.e., these correspond more or less to Schank's inferences from the primitive actions [Schank, 1973]); and (4) the name of a subsuming concept, if any.

The pragmatic and semantic information associated with the concept "drink1" is illustrated in Fig. 13. Note the constraints that the drinker should be animate and the stuff drunk liquid. The major implication that x ingests y (or the subsuming concept ingest) in turn provides access to the implications of ingesting. In this way, Schank-type inferences are made available through property inheritance.

Since "ingest" is not primitive in our representation, it also has associated pragmatic and semantic properties. These are illustrated in Fig. 14. Roughly, the semantic formula says that if x ingests y through z, then some unspecified state or event causes stuff y to move towards the opening z and this in turn causes y to assume a location inside x (we have not tried to be very sophisticated about this). Again, these propositions do not appear in the semantic net itself but only on the property list of "ingest."

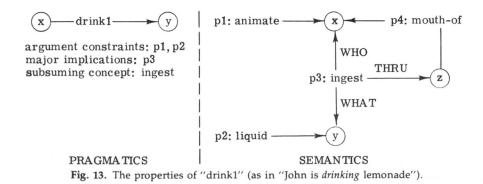

Fig. 13. The properties of "drink1" (as in "John is *drinking* lemonade").

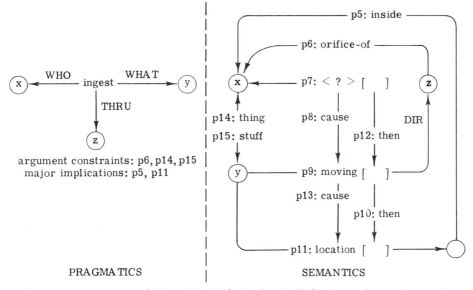

Fig. 14. The properties of "ingest" or "take in," as in "John *ingests* the medication," or "the car *takes in* gasoline."

The lexicon is an alphabetically organized list structure in which each letter of each word is embedded one level deeper than the previous letter. If the list structure is viewed as a tree, each path from the root to an intermediate node is an initial word fragment, and alternative paths from the node to leaf nodes are alternative completions of the initial fragment. The information at the leaves can thus be accessed by "CDRing" across and "CARing" down the tree; the time required is clearly bounded by a constant times word length. Words are accessed in the lexicon via their stems and irregular forms only. For a description of the morphological analyzer that obtains stems and affixes, see Cercone [1977a].

The lexicon contains syntactic information and pointers to word senses for each lexical item. For details of the syntactic information, see Cercone [1975a,b]. The word sense pointers provide access to the types of predicative nodes described above. In this way, the appropriate pragmatic and semantic information becomes available for each word sense.

We now turn our attention to the parser, which extracts the "propositional content" of declarative sentences in the sense of Section 3.1. Our approach to parsing relies on the mutual constraints of concepts selected as meaning candidates for surface words. This is a standard method and appears in the work of Schank and his associates (for example, Riesbeck [1975]; Wilks [1973]). The parser is not at present backed by any inference mechanism, so that no "world knowledge" can be used for disambiguation. However, we have already indicated how Schank-type inferences are made available in our representation.

The parser initially separates sentences into clauses (by a very unsophisticated process). Clauses are then "classified" as follows. Each word in a clause is morphologically analyzed to find its stem and affixes. The stem is located in the lexicon, and the possible syntactic roles of the word are extracted using the affix information. In this way, for example, the word "drinks" is found to be either a plural nominal (as in "He spilled the drinks") or an action with features "present" and "third person." Actually several action candidates are found corresponding to several senses of drinking: drinking liquid, drinking liquor, drinking habitually, and consuming liquid.

Once a clause has been classified, parsing proceeds as follows. An action candidate is located in a left-to-right scan. The various senses of the action are considered in an order determined by global and local frequency counts (the details need not detain us). The "templates" indicating the possible orderings of arguments of the concept are retrieved from the word sense pragmatics. In addition, the argument constraints are examined. Now the parts of the clause preceding and following the action candidate are searched for words of the appropriate lexical category to fill the argument slots of the action candidate. If there is no choice of words, or of senses of the words, which satisfies the argument constraints, another template is tried. If there are no more templates for the sense of the action candidate under consideration, the next sense is tried. If the senses of the action candidate have been exhausted, the next action candidate is tried.

In checking argument constraints such as [x animate] and [y liquid] the parser expects to find the appropriate predicate names (animate, liquid) directly on the property lists of the candidate argument concepts. This is an expedient shortcut that will eventually be replaced by *inference* of the constraints, by ascent in the concept hierarchy.

Once the main predication of a clause has been parsed, remaining modifiers are analyzed. The adjectival modifiers handled include *predicatives* (John is *short*), *adjectives* (Bill has a *yellow* car), *explicit comparatives* (Bill is *heavier* than John), *implicit comparatives* (*Big* Mary ate a *large* steak), and some functors (Joe is a *perfect* cook). Implicit and explicit comparatives are represented in terms of comparisons with "typical values" of base variables such as height and weight as explained in Section 2.5. The interpretation of functors can lead to the formation of lambda-abstracts to which the functor is applied (see Cercone [1975a]).

The propositions inserted in the semantic net for the sentence "Big John gave Mary a perfect cold drink" are shown in Fig. 15. Note that "big" has been analyzed as a comparative predication attributing greater than typical size to John relative to some unknown concept of which he is an in-

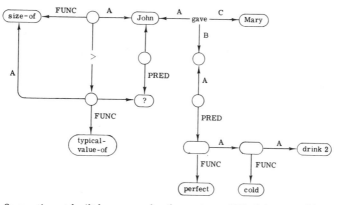

Fig. 15. Semantic net built by parser for the sentence "Big John gave Mary a perfect cold drink."

stance. "Cold" is not analyzed comparatively, since it acts more like a classifier (as in "grape drink") than a comparative in this context.

5.2. The Second Implementation

This system realizes the full network formalism of Section 2 and the topical organization of knowledge proposed in Section 4. The network is implemented as a set of link records and node records corresponding to network links and nodes. All generic concept and individual constant node records have a dictionary link field, a proposition back-links field, and a topic access skeleton field. In addition, generic concepts have a field for "indicator" links pointing to topics of which the concept is indicative. Proposition node records include fields for assertion time, constituent links (for example, to predicates, arguments, operators), scope links, and superordinate proposition links. Variable node records have only scope link and proposition back-link fields.

Although topic predicates and their supertopic/subtopic relations could be represented as generic concepts connected by superconcept/subconcept relations, they are in fact represented by topic node records with supertopic/subtopic link fields. This special format assures efficient traversal of the topic hierarchy, but the generic node format could be used to enable the system to reason *about* topics. Goebel's original implementation of topic access skeletons has recently been replaced by one based on preorder (depth-first) numbering of the nodes in the topic hierarchy. This permits retrieval of propositions without prior ascent in the topic hierarchy, and also allows skeletons to be represented in "contracted" form (see Section 4.6).

The system receives new propositions in the "English-like" predicate calculus notation that we have used throughout. Currently, the creation of new generic concepts and individual constants is prompted by their first appearance in a proposition as predicates and unquantified predicate arguments, respectively. New nodes are created for all variables (i.e., arguments bound with quantifiers).

Functional expressions such as "(father-of Fred)" are treated as references to existing nodes since indiscriminate generation of functionally specified nodes could quickly produce multiple copies of single concepts. For example, after asserting

[Sally sister-of Fred]

the functional expressions

(father-of Sally), (father-of Fred)

share identical referents (i.e., Sally and Fred's father), but reasoning is required to recognize this fact in order to refrain from creating two new nodes.

Conjunctions or disjunctions of arbitrary length are "normalized" by ordering their constituent terms according to the dictionary position of the predicate appearing in each constituent term. The need for inference to determine equivalence of two differently ordered conjunctions or disjunctions is thus usually avoided.

Any proposition may appear as an argument, for example,

[Fred believes [Bruce cat]],

and each proposition may be externally labeled and referred to in subsequent propositions by its assigned label.

Topic relations and indicator links are entered with a special syntax in accordance with their special internal format. For example,

{appearance SUPTOP coloring texture}

declares "appearance" to be a supertopic of "coloring" and "texture." The input

{coloring SUPTOP dark shiny}

causes insertion of indicator links from "dark" and "shiny" to "coloring."*

The "degree of relevance" of a topic to a supertopic can be specified as a cumulative probability distribution over degrees of relevance. This distribution supplies the probability $F(t)$ that the degree of relevance is *at most* t. These distributions represent an earlier attempt to combine a fuzzy logic model of vagueness with a probabilistic model of uncertainty. We are now

---

* "dark" and "shiny" (lowercase) may be thought of as degenerate topics distinct from the predicates DARK and SHINY (uppercase).

skeptical of such an approach but, since relevance is a matter of degree, *some* sort of relevance information should be included with topic hierarchies.

The propositions within a particular topic attached to a particular concept can be retrieved with a request of the form

$$\langle concept \rangle ; \langle topic \rangle$$

where ⟨concept⟩ serves as the primary index and ⟨topic⟩ as the secondary index. For example,

Clyde;appearance

yields a list of Clyde's appearance propositions. This mechanism could easily support a system for answering questions like "What does Clyde look like?", which are beyond the capabilities of the question-answering systems of which we are aware.

Figure 16 reproduces a terminal session that demonstrates the establishment of a topic hierarchy and insertion and retrieval of propositions in the hierarchically organized network.

6. CONCLUDING DISCUSSION

We attempt to sum up and assess our work in Section 6.1, and enumerate promising directions for further research in Section 6.2.

6.1. Assessment

We have shown that networks can be designed to be intuitively and formally interpretable, and expressively adequate with respect to the sort of propositional knowledge people are presumed to possess. This can be regarded as a corollary of the view that network formalisms are computer-oriented logics distinguished only by the inclusion of associative access paths from concepts to propositions.

With respect to language comprehension, we have argued that the propositional content of discourse should be separated from its pragmatic aspects in the representation; that primitive representations are cumbersome and unnecessary; and that predicate argument constraints and implications central to language comprehension can be stored as network propositions, but should be separately accessible to the parser. Our small implementation provides support for these quasi-theoretical claims; also its handling of adjectival modifiers does more justice to their meanings than other published systems.

With respect to inference, we made a proposal, not yet implemented, for storing general knowledge in a normal form that facilitates property and relationship inheritance among concepts. In this normal form, each prop-

```
*enter pdb system
*pdb empty
*?  input
*enter input mode
*input clear.
*?  A*x[[x DOG] => E*yE*t[[y CAT] & [x CHASES<t> y]] =X]
    .
    .
    (the  system replies with the names of the nodes created and
    confirms insertion of the subpropositions  PROP0000-PROP0003
    subordinate to the main proposition PROP0004)
    .
    .
*PDB insert PROP0004
*insert A*x[[x DOG] => E*yE*t[[y CAT] & [x CHASES<t> y]] =X]
*CONCEPT FOCI:  DOG  EXNODE0001  EXNODE0002  CHASES
*assert A*x[[x DOG] => E*yE*t[[y CAT] & [x CHASES<t> y]] =X]
*input clear.
*?  [[Fred DOG] & [Fred BELIEVES :X]]
    .
    .
*PDB insert PROP0007
    .
    .
*?  {appearance SUPTOP colour, texture, pattern}
    .
    (the  system  replies  with  the topic nodes created; it now
    prompts the user for cumulative probabilities  over  degrees
    of relevance)
    "
    "
appearance SUPER-TOPIC-OF colour
Enter values for truth distribution:
prob at 0.0?  0
prob at 0.1?  0
prob at 0.3?  0
prob at 0.5?  0
prob at 0.7?  0
prob at 0.9?  0
appearance SUPER-TOPIC-OF texture
Enter values for truth distribution:
    .
    .
appearance SUPER-TOPIC-OF pattern
Enter values for truth distribution:
prob at 0.0?  0
prob at 0.1?  0
prob at 0.3?  0
prob at 0.5?  0
prob at 0.7?  .2
prob at 0.9?  .2
*input clear.
*?  {colour SUPTOP grey, dark, shiny}
    "
    "
*?  {texture SUPTOP rough, smooth, shiny}
    .
    .
```

Fig. 16. Terminal session with the propositional data base system, showing insertion of propositions, establishment of topic hierarchies, and topic-oriented retrieval of propositions. The user entries are those immediately following a question mark. (Figure 16 continued on facing page.)

```
*?    {pattern SUPTOP spotted, striped}
         .
         .
*?    A*x[[ x ELEPHANT] => [ x GREY]]
         .
         .
*PDB insert PROP0010
         .
         .
*?   [Clyde SHINY]
         .
*PDB insert PROP0011
         .
         .
*?   Clyde;colour
*TOPIC categories scanned: colour grey dark shiny
*relevant propositions: PROP00 11
*input clear.
*?   Clyde;appearance
*TOPIC categories scanned: appearance colour texture pattern
         grey dark shiny rough smooth spotted striped
*relevant propositions: PROP0011
*input clear.
*?   ELEPHANT;texture
*TOPIC categories scanned: texture  rough  smooth  shiny
*no relevant propositions
*input clear.
*?   ELEPHANT;appearance
*TOPIC categories scanned: appearance colour texture pattern
         grey dark shiny rough smooth spotted striped
*relevant propositions: PROP0010
*input clear.
*?   A*x[[[ x TOE] & [ x PART-OF Clyde]] => [ x SHINY]]
         .
*PDB insert PROP0016
         .
         .
*?   Clyde;appearance
*TOPIC categories scanned: appearance colour texture pattern
         grey  dark  shiny  rough  smooth  spotted  striped
*relevant propositions: PROP0011  PROP0016
         .
         .
```

osition is embedded in some generalization hierarchy whose variables it shares with other propositions. We also argued that efficient reasoning requires rapid access to propositions relevant to any specified topic, and developed an organization capable of providing such access. The organization consists of back-link structures from concepts to propositions that conform with general topic hierarchies in memory. We described a procedure for classifying propositions in accordance with a topic hierarchy for physical objects. A partial implementation demonstrates the programmability of topically structured memories, and an analysis of time and storage requirements demonstrates their potential for dramatically improving question-answering efficiency. Moreover, by allowing retrieval of topically related propositions about any concept, such memories could support a mechanism for answering questions requiring *descriptive* answers.

The chief shortcoming of our representation is its lack of integration with any *procedural* knowledge base. This severely limits the present level of performance of our programs. Thus our comprehension program handles few constructions and is incapable of forming a causally connected representation of successive sentences. Similarly, our implemented topically organized net awaits the addition of inference procedures for a full demonstration of its potential. Essentially, what we have is an information retrieval system (organized according to the logical rather than statistical structure of the information), but no programs that utilize the retrieved information.

6.2. Future Directions

In the area of propositional representation theory, an important future task will be the integration of uniform propositional representations with special-purpose representations, such as those required for efficient spatial, linguistic, and numerical information processing. In addition, the difficult problem of representing vague and uncertain information in a clearly interpretable way, and using such information efficiently for inference, needs to be investigated further.

With regard to language comprehension, we need to transplant the parser to the topically organized net and expand it to handle at least noun phrase reference and to bring into play the "major implications" of verb concepts. This will be the acid test of our claims about nonprimitive representation, although we see no obstacle to the application of established parsing and inference techniques, such as those of Wilks [1975b] and Riesbeck and Schank [1976]. The target language for Riesbeck's parser and Schank's conceptual dependency representation differs from ours in only one essential respect, i.e., its use of primitives; and primitives, as we have argued, are more likely to hinder than help comprehension and inference processes. We also plan to implement an efficient technique for context-dependent sense and reference disambiguation utilizing "concept access skeletons," which are in a sense complementary to topic access skeletons. For an outline of this idea, see the discussion of "Nets and Frames" in Schubert *et al.* [1978].

With regard to knowledge organization, we plan to continue the detailed development of generalization and topic hierarchies to determine how readily the full range of human concepts and human knowledge can be systematized in this way. Also, we plan to elaborate the "variable-sharing" organization of concept hierarchies and study it experimentally.

But the most immediately rewarding extension of our work should be the implementation of inference processes along the lines described in Section 4.1 for the questions "Is Clyde grey?" and "Does Clyde live in a teacup?"—with the difference, of course, that retrieval of topically restricted propositions will rely on the topical organization we have described. Much detail is still lacking in our conception of question-answering and problem-solving processes, and the required procedural organization. We envisage a concept-centered organization of goal-oriented plans very much like the organization of propositional knowledge, i.e., with plans attached to tree-structured topic access skeletons rooted at concepts. To see how plans so organized might come to be used, consider a start-up plan for playing a piano. This might include a step that removes anything on the keyboard cover before raising it. In a use of the start-up plan, if a cat happens to be slumbering on the cover, this would occasion the retrieval and implementation of methods for removing cats via the "cat" node. Very different methods would be retrieved for removing, say, a cloth or a wineglass from the cover. Note that this sort of sensitivity to context would be very difficult to achieve in a PLANNER-like system using a universal CLEAR-OFF program. Our approach is similar to that embodied in KRL [Bobrow and Winograd, 1977], but will hopefully lead to simpler and more efficient mechanisms for selection of plans. In addition, we propose to attach "demons" to predicates, which are triggered whenever those predicates are instantiated, generating "guesses" for recognition purposes and "major implications" needed for comprehension, consistency-checking, and goal-oriented processes. The work of Charniak [1976], Kuipers [1975], Hobbs [1977], Havens [1977], and McCalla [1977], among others, appears to provide a good starting point for this work.

One of the most promising features of our topical network organization is its potential for learning. Methods for adaptive modification of both the topic hierarchy and the indicator links that determine propositional categories come to mind readily. For example, topics could be split when the knowledge subsumed under them becomes disproportionately large. The groupings of propositions under the split topics would be based on "co-usage" statistics, i.e., propositions that tend to be used together in the successful achievement of goals would stay within the same topic category. Conversely, distinct topics whose contents tend to be used together could be merged (and then perhaps resplit in a more favorable way). Similarly, the indicator links of predicates could be changed adaptively so that predicates in frequently co-used propositions would indicate the same topics.

However, pursuit of these more distant objectives must be deferred until the functional properties of topically organized nets have been more fully explored.

ACKNOWLEDGMENTS

The remarks on philosophical issues were influenced by discussions with Bernard Linsky and Jeffry Pelletier of the Department of Philosophy of the University of Alberta. We gratefully acknowledge their willingness to listen and react. The comments of Kelly Wilson and the referees helped to streamline the manuscript. We are also grateful for Judith Abbott's heroic performance in deciphering and typing multiple versions of the manuscript. The research was supported by the National Research Council of Canada under Operating Grant A8818.

REFERENCES

[Alston, W. P., 1964]. *Philosophy of Language*. Prentice-Hall, Englewood Cliffs, New Jersey.
[Anderson, J., and Bower, G., 1973]. *Human Associative Memory*, Holt, New York.
[Bartsch, R., and Vennemann, T., 1972]. *Semantic Structures*. Athenaeum Verlag, Frankfurt, Germany.
[Baumgart, D. G., 1974]. "Geometric Modeling for Computer Vision," Memo AIM 249. Report No. STAN-CS-74-463, NTIS Catalog No. AD/A-002 261. Stanford Artificial Intelligence Laboratory, Department of Computer Science, Stanford University, Stanford, California.
[Black, M., 1937]. Vagueness: An exercise in logical analysis. *Philosophy of Science* 4, 427–455.
[Bobrow, D., and Winograd, T., 1977]. An overview of KRL, a knowledge representation language. *Cognitive Science* 1, 3–46.
[Brachman, R. J., 1977]. A structural paradigm for representing knowledge. Ph.D. thesis, Harvard University, Cambridge, Massachusetts.
[Bundy, A., and Stone, M., 1975]. A note on McDermott's symbol-mapping problem. *ACM SIGART Newsletter* 53, 9–10.
[Carnap, R., 1947]. *Meaning and Necessity*. University of Chicago Press, Chicago, Illinois.
[Cercone, N. J., 1975a]. "Representing Natural Language in Extended Semantic Networks," Technical Report TR75-11. Department of Computing Science, University of Alberta, Edmonton, Alberta, Canada.
[Cercone, N. J., 1975b]. The nature and computational use of a meaning representation for word concepts. *American Journal of Computational Linguistics* 2 (Microfiche 34) 64–81.
[Cercone, N. J., 1977a]. A heuristic morphological analyzer for natural language understanding programs. *Proceedings of the 1st International IEEE Computers, Software and Applications Conference, 1977* pp. 676–682.
[Cercone, N. J., 1977b]. A note on representing adjectives and adverbs. *Proceedings of the 5th International Joint Conference on Artificial Intelligence, 1977* p. 139.
[Cercone, N. J., and Schubert, L. K., 1975]. Toward a state based conceptual representation. *Advance Papers of the 4th International Joint Conference on Artificial Intelligence, 1975* pp. 83–90. (A preliminary version appeared as Technical Report TR74-19, Department of Computing Science, University of Alberta, Edmonton, Alberta, Canada, 1974.)
[Charniak, E., 1976]. Inference and knowledge: II. In *Computational Semantics*. E. Charniak and Y. Wilks (eds.). North-Holland Publ., Amsterdam, pp. 129–154.
[Collins, A. M., and Loftus, E. F., 1975]. A spreading activation theory of semantic processing. *Psychological Review* 82, 407–428.
[Fahlman, S., 1975]. "A System for Representing and Using Real-World Knowledge," AI Lab Memo 331. MIT, Cambridge, Massachusetts.
[Find, K., 1975]. Vagueness, truth, and logic. *Synthese* 30, 265–300.
[Fodor, J. A., 1978]. Tom Swift and his procedural grandmother. *Cognition, 1978*.
[Goebel, R., 1977]. "Organizing Factual Knowledge in a Semantic Network," Technical Report TR77-8. Department of Computing Science, University of Alberta, Edmonton, Alberta, Canada.
[Gray, C., 1976]. ALAI: A language for artificial intelligence. M.Sc. thesis, Department of Computing Science, University of Alberta, Edmonton, Alberta, Canada.
[Havens, W. S., 1977]. A procedural model of recognition. *Proceedings of the 5th International Joint Conference on Artificial Intellience, 1977* p. 264.

[Hayes, Pat J., 1977]. In defence of logic. *Proceedings of the 5th International Conference on Artificial Intelligence, 1977* pp. 559–565.

[Hayes, Phillip J., 1977]. On semantic nets, frames and associations. *Proceedings of the 5th International Joint Conference on Artificial Intelligence, 1977* pp. 99–107.

[Hobbs, J. R., 1977]. Coherence and interpretation in English texts. *Proceedings of the 5th International Joint Conference on Artificial Intelligence, 1977* pp. 110–116.

[Hobbs, J. R., 1978]. Making computational sense of Montague's intensional logic. *Artificial Intelligence* **9,** 287–306.

[Kay, M., 1973]. The MIND system. In *Natural Language Processing.* R. Rustin (ed.). Algorithmic Press, New York, pp. 115–188.

[Kuipers, B., 1975]. A frame for frames: Representing knowledge for recognition. In *Representation and Understanding.* D. Bobrow and A. Collins (eds.), Academic Press, New York, pp. 151–184.

[Lehnert, W., 1977]. "The Process of Question Answering," Research Report No. 88. Department of Computer Science, Yale University, New Haven, Connecticut.

[Levesque, H. J., and Mylopoulos, J., 1977]. An overview of a procedural approach to semantic networks. *Proceedings of the 5th International Joint Conference on Artificial Intelligence, 1977* p. 283 (see also this volume).

[McCalla, G., 1977]. An approach to the organization of knowledge for the modelling of conversation. Ph.D. thesis, University of British Columbia, Vancouver.

[McDermott, D., 1975a]. Symbol-mapping: A technical problem in PLANNER-like systems. *ACM SIGART Newsletter* **51,** 4.

[McDermott, D., 1975b]. A packet-based approach to the symbol-mapping problem. *ACM SIGART Newsletter* **53,** 6–7.

[McSkimin, J. R., and Minker, J., 1977]. The use of a semantic network in a deductive question-answering system. *Proceedings of the 5th International Joint Conference on Artificial Intelligence, 1977* pp. 50–58.

[Montague, R., 1970]. English as a formal language. In *Linguaggi nella Tecnica e nella Società.* Visentini *et al.* (eds.). Olivetti, Milan, pp. 189–224.

[Moore, R. C., 1975]. A serial scheme for the inheritance of properties. *ACM SIGART Newsletter* **53,** 8–9.

[Mylopoulos, J., Badler, N., Melli, L., and Roussopoulos, N., 1973]. 1.PAK: A SNOBOL-based programming language for artificial intelligence applications. *Advance Papers of the 3rd International Joint Conference on Artificial Intelligence, 1973* pp. 691–696.

[Nash-Webber, B., and Reiter, R., 1977]. Anaphora and logical form: On formal meaning representations for natural language. *Proceedings of the 5th International Joint Conference on Artificial Intelligence, 1977* pp. 121–131.

[Norman, D. A., and Rumelhart, D. E., 1975]. *Explorations in Cognition.* Freeman, San Francisco, California.

[Pelletier, J. P., 1977]. Or. *Theoretical Linguistics* **4,** 61–74.

[Quillian, M. R., 1968]. Semantic memory. In *Semantic Information Processing.* M. Minsky (ed.). MIT Press, Cambridge, Massachusetts, pp. 227–270.

[Quillian, M. R., 1969]. The teachable language comprehender. *Communications of the ACM* **12,** 459–475.

[Riesbeck, C. K., 1975]. Conceptual analysis. In *Conceptual Information Processing.* R. C. Schank (ed.), Chapter 4. North-Holland Publ., Amsterdam.

[Riesbeck, C. K., and Schank, R. C., 1976]. "Comprehension by Computer: Expectation-based Analysis of Sentences in Context," Research Report 78. Department of Computer Science, Yale University, New Haven, Connecticut.

[Rumelhart, D., Lindsay, P., and Norman, D., 1972]. A process model for long term memory. In *Organization of Memory.* E. Tulving and W. Donaldson (eds.). Academic Press, New York, pp. 198–221.

[Sandewall, E. J., 1971]. Representing natural language information in predicate calculus. In

Machine Intelligence 6. B. Meltzer and D. Michie (eds.). Am. Elsevier, New York, pp. 255–277.

[Schank, R. C., 1972]. Conceptual dependency: A theory of natural language understanding. *Cognitive Psychology* **3**, 552–631.

[Schank, R. C., 1973]. "The Fourteen Primitive Actions and Their Inferences," Stanford AI Project, Memo. AIM-183. Stanford University, Stanford, California.

[Schank, R. C., 1975a]. The structure of episodes in memory. In *Representation and Understanding.* D. Bobrow and A. Collins (eds.). Academic Press, New York, pp. 237–272.

[Schank, R. C., 1975b]. The primitive ACTs of conceptual dependency. *Advance Papers of Theoretical Issues in Natural Language Processing Workshop, 1975* pp. 34–37.

[Schank, R. C., and Abelson, R. P., 1975]. Scripts, plans, and knowledge. *Advance Papers of the 4th International Joint Conference on Artificial Intelligence, 1975* pp. 151–157.

[Schank, R. C., and Abelson, R. P., 1977]. *Scripts, Plans, and Understanding.* Lawrence Erlbaum Associates, Hillsdale, New Jersey.

[Schank, R. C., and Rieger, C., 1974]. Inference and the computer understanding of natural language. *Artificial Intelligence* **5**, 373–412.

[Schubert, L. K., 1975]. Extending the expressive power of semantic networks. *Advance Papers of the 4th International Joint Conference on Artificial Intelligence, 1975* pp. 158–164. (This is a condensed version of Schubert [1976].)

[Schubert, L. K., 1976]. Extending the expressive power of semantic networks. *Artificial Intelligence* **7**, 163–198. (A preliminary version appeared as Technical Report TR74-18, Department of Computing Science, University of Alberta, Edmonton, Alberta, Canada, 1974.)

[Schubert, L. K., 1978]. On the representation of vague and uncertain knowledge. *COLING 78, Bergen, Norway, August.*

[Schubert, L. K., Cercone, N. J., and Goebel, R., 1978]. "The Structure and Organization of a Semantic Net for Comprehension and Inference," Technical Report TR78-1. Department of Computing Science, University of Alberta, Edmonton, Alberta, Canada.

[Shapiro, S. C., 1971]. A net structure for semantic information storage, deduction, and retrieval. *Advance Papers of the 2nd International Joint Conference on Artificial Intelligence, 1971* pp. 512–523.

[Shortliffe, E. H., 1976]. *Computer-Based Medical Consultations: MYCIN.* Am. Elsevier, New York.

[Simmons, R., 1973]. Semantic networks: Their computation and use for understanding English sentences. In *Computer Models of Thought and Language.* R. Schank and K. Colby (eds.). Freeman, San Francisco, California, pp. 63–113.

[Tarski, A., 1944]. The semantic conception of truth and the foundations of semantics. *Phil. and Phenom. Res.* **4**, 341–376 (reprinted in L. Linsky, ed., *Semantics and the Philosophy of Language.* University of Illinois Press, Urbana, 1952, pp. 13–47; also in H. Feigl and W. Sellars, eds., *Readings in Philosophical Analysis.* Appleton, New York, 1949.)

[Trigoboff, M., and Kulikowski, C. A., 1977]. IRIS: A system for the propagation of inferences in a semantic net. *Proceedings of the 5th International Joint Conference on Artificial Intelligence, 1977* pp. 274–280.

[Wilks, Y., 1973]. An artificial intelligence approach to machine translation. In *Computer Models of Thought and Language.* R. C. Schank and K. M. Colby (eds.). Freeman, San Francisco, California, pp. 114–151.

[Wilks, Y., 1974]. Do machines understand more than they did? *Nature (London)* **252**, 275–278.

[Wilks, Y., 1975a]. Primitives and words. *Advance Papers of Theoretical Issues in Natural Language Processing Workshop, 1975* pp. 34–37.

[Wilks, Y., 1975b]. A preferential pattern-seeking semantics for natural language inference. *Artificial Intelligence* **6**, 53–74.

[Wilks, Y., 1976a]. Parsing English II. In *Computational Semantics.* E. Charniak and Y. Wilks (eds.). North-Holland Publ., Amsterdam, pp. 155–184.

[Wilks, Y., 1976b]. Philosophy of language. In *Computational Semantics*. E. Charniak and Y. Wilks (eds.). North-Holland Publ., Amsterdam, pp. 205–233.

[Wilson, K. V., 1979]. *From Associations to Structure*. North–Holland Publ., Amsterdam (in press).

[Winston, P., 1970]. Learning structural descriptions from examples. Ph.D. thesis, MAC-TR-76. MIT, Cambridge, Massachusetts.

[Woods, W. A., 1975]. What's in a link: Foundations for semantic networks. In *Representation and Understanding*. D. Bobrow and A. Collins (eds.). Academic Press, New York, pp. 35–82.

[Zadeh, L. A., 1974]. The concept of a linguistic variable and its application to approximate reasoning. I and II. *Information Sciences* (*New York*) **8,** 199–249 and 301–357.

[Zadeh, L. A., 1977]. "PRUF-A Meaning Representation Language for Natural Languages," Memo. No. ERL-M77/61. Electronics Research Lab., College of Engineering, University of Calfornia, Berkeley.

PART II

THEORETICALLY ORIENTED EFFORTS

THE SNePS SEMANTIC NETWORK PROCESSING SYSTEM

Stuart C. Shapiro

1. INTRODUCTION

Semantic networks have been used as representations of knowledge since the mid 1960s. Quillian's 1966 semantic memory, described in Quillian [1968], is considered the first semantic network, but it had roots in Raphael's 1964 SIR [Raphael, 1968] and in the work of Reitman [1965]. An excellent historical review is in the chapter by Brachman in this volume.

One can define a semantic network as a labeled directed graph in which nodes represent concepts, arc labels represent binary relations, and an arc labeled **R** going from node **n** to node **m** represents that the concept represented by **n** bears the relation represented by **R** to the concept represented by **m**. Each concept represented in the network is represented by a unique node.

The notion of "concept" is vague, but one can think of it as including anything about which information can be stored and/or transmitted. Various semantic networks have included as concepts concrete and abstract individuals, prototypical and generalized individuals, actions, sets, propositions, facts, beliefs, roles, relations, hypothetical worlds, and others. Since Woods [1975] first pointed it out, it has been generally recognized that each node represents an intensional rather than an extensional concept. Furthermore, two concepts that are extensionally equivalent but intensionally distinct may be represented by different nodes.

Since each concept represented in the network is represented by a node, it follows that the relations represented solely by arc labels are not conceptual. I refer to such relations as *structural relations* since they are used to form the basic structure of the semantic network, and distinguish them from *conceptual relations*, which are represented by nodes. This distinction is discussed further in Shapiro [1971a,b], where structural relations are also called *item relations* and conceptual relations are also called *system relations*.

There are four levels at which semantic networks can be discussed: an

179

abstract graph level, a two-dimensional pictorial level, a one-dimensional symbolic level, and a computer implementation level. These levels, though related, are independent in the sense that two semantic networks can differ on one or more levels and be the same on the other levels. Often the levels are not clearly distinguished, and one must be careful not to conclude from a discussion at one level what another level must be like. Similarly, when comparing different semantic networks, one must be careful to note on which levels they differ and on which, if any, they are the same.

This chapter describes the SNePS semantic network processing system, which is a direct descendent of MENTAL [Shapiro, 1971a,b]. SNePS is currently implemented in ALISP [Konolige, 1975] and runs interactively on the CDC CYBER 173 at the State University of New York at Buffalo. Three levels of SNePS are described: the abstract graph level, the pictorial level, and the linear symbolic level. For the latter, the SNePS User Language, SNePSUL, is used.

2. BASIC REPRESENTATION

2.1. Abstract Graph Level

A SNePS semantic network is a labeled directed graph in which nodes represent concepts and arcs represent nonconceptual binary relations between concepts. Each concept is represented by a unique node. Whenever an arc representing a relation **R** goes from node **n** to node **m**, there is an arc representing the converse relation of **R**, **R**^{c}, going from **m** to **n**. An arc is labeled with a symbol intended to be mnemonically suggestive of the relation the arc represents.

I distinguish three kinds of arcs: *descending, ascending,* and *auxiliary*. For each relation represented by descending arcs, there is a converse relation represented by ascending arcs and vice versa. Together, descending and ascending arcs are the regular semantic network arcs referred to above. Auxiliary arcs are used for hanging nonnodal information on nodes and for typing the nodes as discussed below. If a descending arc goes from node **n** to node **m**, I say that **n** *immediately dominates* **m**. If there is a path of descending arcs from node **n** to node **m**, I say that **n** *dominates* **m**. If **R** is an arc label and **n** is a node, I shall use the notation **R(n)** for the set of nodes into which arcs labeled **R** go from **n**. In what follows, we shall often use the phrase "the relation **R**" when we mean "an arc labeled **R**."

There are three kinds of nodes: *constant, nonconstant,* and *auxiliary*. Auxiliary nodes are connected to each other and to other nodes only by auxiliary arcs. Auxiliary nodes do not represent concepts but are used by the SNePS system or the SNePS user to type nonauxiliary nodes or to maintain a reference to one or more nonauxiliary nodes. Constant nodes represent unique semantic concepts. Nodes that dominate no other node are called *atomic* nodes. Atomic constants are called *base* nodes and atomic nonconstants are called *variable* nodes or *variables*. Variables are distinguished by being in the auxiliary relation :VAR to the auxiliary node T. Variable nodes are used in SNePS like variables are used in normal predicate logic notations. Nonatomic nodes are called *molecular* nodes. They are often used for representing propositions. There is a set of descending relations called *binding* relations that act like quantifiers in normal symbolic logic formalisms. A molecular node that immediately dominates one or more variables and no other variable may have at most one binding relation to an arbitrary number of its dominated variables, which are referred to as *bound* by that molecular node. The remaining dominated variables are referred to as *free* in the molecular node, which has an auxiliary :SVAR to each of them. If a node **m** immediately dominates a set of variable nodes $\{v_1, \ldots, v_l\}$ and a set of molecular nodes $\{n_1, \ldots, n_k\}$ and $V = \{v_1, \ldots, v_l\} \cup {:}SVAR(n_1) \cup \cdots \cup {:}SVAR(n_k)$ is nonempty, **m** may have at most one binding relation, say **Q**, to one or more variables in **V**. These variables are referred to as bound by **m**. The remainder, $V - Q(m)$, are free in **m** and have the arc :SVAR to each of them from **n**. A node **n** such that :SVAR(**n**) is nonempty is a nonconstant molecular node and is called a *pattern* node. Pattern nodes are comparable to well-formed formulas with free variables. A molecular node **n** for which :SVAR(**n**) is empty is a molecular constant or *assertion* node.

Temporary molecular and variable nodes can be created. Temporary molecular nodes have no ascending arcs coming into them from the nodes they dominate. Temporary nodes are not placed on any permanent system list and are garbage-collected when no longer referenced. They are invisible to all the semantic network retrieval operations. I shall refer to nontemporary nodes as *permanent* nodes. Temporary nodes are used to build patterns of network structures, which can be matched against the network but do not match themselves. Occasionally, a structure of temporary nodes is used as a template for building a permanent structure resembling it.

2.2. Pictorial Level

The discussion so far has treated SNePS as an abstract graph. I can also discuss it diagrammatically or pictorially. In the diagrams, a base node is drawn as an oval inside of which is an identifier meant to be suggestive of the concept the node represents. A permanent assertion node is drawn as a circle inside of which is an arbitrary identifier of the form **Mn**; a permanent variable node as a circle inside of which is an arbitrary identifier of the form **Vn**; a permanent pattern node as a circle inside of which is an arbitrary identifier of the form **Pn**. A temporary variable node is shown as an identifier of the form **Qn**; a temporary molecular node as an identifier of the form **Tn**; an auxiliary node as a mnemonically suggestive identifier. Temporary and auxiliary nodes are drawn without enclosing circles. Figure 1 shows a network with various kinds of nodes and arcs. In future figures, the :VAR and :SVAR arcs will be omitted since they can be reconstructed from the information shown. For the same reason, the ascending arcs will be omitted.

2.3. Linear Symbolic Level—The SNePS User Language

At the linear symbolic level, I shall use the SNePS User Language, SNePSUL. Presentation of SNePSUL will give the reader an idea of what can be done in SNePS. It will also show the relationship between the linear symbolic form and the two-dimensional pictorial form, and will allow the former to be used in some examples, when the latter would be too complicated for easy understanding.

SNePSUL is embedded in LISP and consists of a set of functions for which the unquote convention (see Bobrow and Raphael [1974]) holds. An atom refers to itself unless it is unquoted. A list is either a reference to a SNePSUL function or a list of elements, which can be atoms, unquoted atoms, or SNePSUL function references.

SNePS itself is a read–evaluate–print loop, which assumes that each expression it reads is in SNePSUL. However, LISP may be accessed from SNePSUL and vice versa. Unless otherwise noted, all examples will show interaction with SNePSUL. The SNePSUL prompt is ** for the first line of an expression and * for subsequent lines.

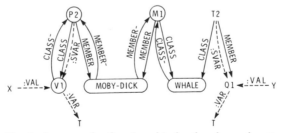

Fig. 1. An example of various kinds of nodes and arcs.

Descending arcs	MEMBER, CLASS
Ascending arcs	MEMBER-, CLASS-
Auxiliary arcs	:VAL, :VAR, :SVAR
Base nodes	MOBY-DICK, WHALE
Assertion node	M1
Variable node	V1
Pattern node	P2
Temporary variable	Q1
Temporary pattern	T2
Auxiliary nodes	X,Y,T

2.3.1. Defining Arc Labels

Since SNePS is not a particular semantic network but a system for building, operating on, and experimenting with semantic networks, the user is responsible for choosing arc labels. The function DEFINE declares the labels of descending and ascending arcs. The syntax is

$$(\text{DEFINE } \mathbf{R_1} \; \mathbf{R_1^C} \; \mathbf{R_2} \; \mathbf{R_2^C} \; . \; . \; .)$$

Here, $\mathbf{R_1}$, $\mathbf{R_2}$, etc., are declared to be labels of descending arcs, with $\mathbf{R_1^C}$, $\mathbf{R_2^C}$, etc., the corresponding ascending arc labels. An error message is given if any label is already in use. The system remembers the relationship between an arc label and the label of the converse arc by making each an auxiliary node with the auxiliary arc :CONV from each to the other. That is, for each i, :CONV$(\mathbf{R_i})$ = $\{\mathbf{R_i^C}\}$ and :CONV$(\mathbf{R_i^C})$ = $\{\mathbf{R_i}\}$.

When defining a set of arcs, one should keep in mind that it is a basic precept of semantic networks that all concepts, including assertions, are represented by nodes. Figure 2 shows three possible ways of representing "Socrates is a man," using ISA as an example of any binary relation. One can analyze the differences in these representations as follows. In Fig. 2a, there is a node representing Socrates and a node representing the set of men, but no node representing the assertion that Socrates is a man. SNePS retrieval functions will allow the retrieval of all members of the set of men and all the sets of which Socrates is a member, but not the specific assertion that Socrates is a man. In Fig. 2b, there are nodes representing Socrates, the set of men, and the assertion that Socrates is a man, but no node representing set membership as a conceptual relation. SNePS retrieval functions will allow the same retrievals as in Fig. 2a, plus the assertion that Socrates is a man, but not the relationship between Socrates and the set of men. In Fig. 2c, there are nodes representing Socrates, the set of

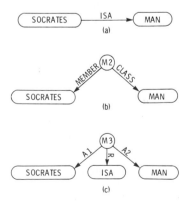

Fig. 2. Three ways of representing "Socrates is a man."

men, the ISA relation, and the assertion that Socrates is a man. SNePS retrieval functions will allow the same retrievals as in Fig. 2b, plus retrieval of the relationship between Socrates and the set of men. In this chapter, set membership will be represented as in Fig. 2b.

What SNePS retrieval functions can retrieve is coextensive with what the understander being modeled by SNePS can express (see the section on generating, below). Thus, although Fig. 2a represents the knowledge that Socrates is a man, it is inexpressible ("unconscious") knowledge. If it cannot be expressed by the understander, it cannot be expressed to the understander, and, indeed, the network of Fig. 2a cannot be built in SNePS, as will be explained in the discussion of BUILD.

The user chooses auxiliary arc labels by defining them with the function DEFINE-AUX, which takes a set of labels to be defined. Several auxiliary arcs are used by the system itself and are predefined as if

$$\text{(DEFINE-AUX :CONV :VAL :VAR :SVAR)}$$

had already been executed.

2.3.2. Adding Information

The main function for adding information to the network is BUILD, whose syntax is

$$\text{(BUILD } \mathbf{R_1} \text{ nodeset}_1 \text{ } \mathbf{R_2} \text{ nodeset}_2 \text{ . . .)}$$

Each $\mathbf{R}_i$ is the label of an ascending, descending, or auxiliary arc that has already been defined. Each **nodeset** is a node or set of nodes. BUILD creates a new node that has arcs $\mathbf{R_1}$ to the nodes of **nodeset**$_1$, $\mathbf{R_2}$ to the nodes of **nodeset**$_2$, etc. If the new node dominates any variable nodes, :SVAR arcs will be added automatically as appropriate. The identifier of the new node is created by the system, and a list of that identifier is returned as the value of BUILD. Table I shows the effect of the different possible forms for the **nodesets.**

Temporary nodes are created with the TBUILD function. The syntax is the same as that for BUILD, the only difference being that the newly created node is temporary rather than permanent. Figure 3 shows the SNePS session for building the network of Fig. 1.

Notice that when a new node is created by the **#atom, $atom,** or **%atom** form; **atom** becomes an auxiliary node with the auxiliary arc :VAL to the new node. This auxiliary node is called a *SNePSUL variable,* and is quite different from a variable node. Variable nodes are like variables in predicate logic. SNePSUL variables are like variables of a programming language. Another way to set the value of a SNePSUL variable is by appending to any **nodeset** an equal sign followed by the variable. At the top level, an enclosing set of parentheses is required. This technique is demonstrated in Fig. 4. (From now on figures will be cumulative and diagrams of the network will show new material enclosed by dashed lines.)

TABLE I

*Effect of the Different Possible Forms of **nodeset**$_i$ in the SNePSUL*
*Function Call (BUILD . . . **R**$_i$ **nodeset**$_i$ . . .)*

Form of **nodeset**$_i$	New node gets arc(s) labeled **R**$_i$ to
atom	the node whose identifier is **atom**
#atom	a new base node, which is also made the value of :VAL(**atom**)
$atom	a new variable node, which is also made the value of :VAL(**atom**)
%atom	a new temporary variable node, which is also made the value of :VAL(**atom**)
*atom	all the nodes in :VAL(**atom**)
list whose first element is the name of a SNePSUL function	the set of nodes returned as the value of the function call
list whose first element is not the name of a SNePSUL function	the set of nodes obtained by treating each element of the list as a form given in this table
(↑ LISP S-expression)	the set of nodes obtained by evaluating the LISP S-expression and treating the value as a form given in this table.

Several SNePSUL variables are maintained by the system:

NODES	the set of permanent nodes
VARBL	the set of permanent variable nodes
DRELST	the set of descending arc labels
ARELST	the set of ascending arc labels
AUXRELST	the set of auxiliary arc labels

There is no way in SNePSUL to add a nonauxiliary arc between two already existing nodes. This enforces the notion that any information given to the system is a concept and so must have a node representing it. The new node created by BUILD serves this purpose. Specifically, it is impossible to have a nonauxiliary arc between two nodes neither of whose identifiers were created by the system. For this reason the network of Fig. 2a could not exist in SNePS.

```
**(DEFINE MEMBER MEMBER- CLASS CLASS-)
(MEMBER MEMBER-)
(CLASS CLASS-)
(DEFINED)

**(BUILD MEMBER MOBY-DICK CLASS WHALE)
(M1)

**(BUILD MEMBER MOBY-DICK CLASS $X)
(P2)

**(TBUILD MEMBER %Y CLASS WHALE)
(T2)
```

Fig. 3. SNePS session building the network of Fig. 1.

**((BUILD MEMBER ORCA CLASS WHALE) = NEW)
(M3)

(a)

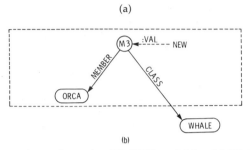

(b)

Fig. 4. Use of the equal sign for setting SNePSUL variables. (a) SNePSUL interaction; (b) modified network with the new material enclosed by dashed lines.

2.3.3. DUMP and DESCRIBE

Pieces of the network may be examined via the functions DUMP and DESCRIBE, which have the same syntax:

$$\left(\left\{ \begin{matrix} \text{DUMP} \\ \text{DESCRIBE} \end{matrix} \right\} \textbf{nodeset}_1 \ . \ . \ . \ \textbf{nodeset}_k \right)$$

For each node, DUMP prints the node's identifier, all arcs emanating from it, and the set of nodes to which each arc goes. DESCRIBE only prints descending and auxiliary arcs, but prints the information for all molecular nodes dominated by the nodes given. Figure 5 demonstrates the use of DUMP and DESCRIBE.

2.3.4. Deleting Information

There are three functions for removing information from the network.

(ERASE **node**$_1$ . . . **node**$_k$) removes each **node**$_i$ from the network along with any other nodes that thereby become isolated.

(REMVAR **variable**$_1$ . . . **variable**$_k$) unassigns each of the listed SNePSUL variables.

(DELREL **label**$_1$ . . . **label**$_k$) undefines each of the arc labels and their converses by removing them from the values of DRELST, ARELST, and AUXRELST. However, if any arcs with these labels already exist in the network, the arcs are not removed.

2.3.5. Finding Nodes

The function FIND performs a pattern match on the network and returns a list of the matched nodes. The syntax is the same as for BUILD, but specifies a node to be found rather than a node to be built. Figure 6 shows some simple uses of FIND.

**(DEFINE AGENT AGENT- VERB VERB- OBJECT OBJECT-)
(AGENT AGENT-)
(VERB VERB-)
(OBJECT OBJECT-)
(DEFINED)

**(DUMP(BUILD AGENT JOHN VERB KNOWS OBJECT *NEW) *NEW)
(M4(AGENT(JOHN))(VERB(KNOWS))(OBJECT(M3)))
(M3(MEMBER(ORCA))(CLASS(WHALE))(OBJECT-(M4)))
(DUMPED)

**(DESCRIBE M4)
(M4(AGENT(JOHN))(VERB(KNOWS))(OBJECT(M3)))
(M3(MEMBER(ORCA))(CLASS(WHALE)))
(DUMPED)

(a)

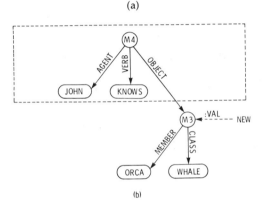

(b)

Fig. 5. Demonstration of DUMP and DESCRIBE. The material enclosed by dashed lines in (b) was added by the instructions of (a).

It should be noticed that (FIND R_1 **nodeset**$_1$ R_2 **nodeset**$_2$) finds all nodes with an R_1 arc to any node in **nodeset**$_1$ and an R_2 arc to any node in **node-set**$_2$. So (FIND **R** $(N_1 \ N_2)$) returns R^C (N_1) $\cup$ R^C (N_2), whereas (FIND **R** N_1 **R** N_2) returns R^C (N_1) $\cap$ R^C (N_2).

Besides the forms listed in Table I, a **nodeset** in a FIND may be of the form **?atom.** This represents a pattern variable that can match any node.

**(DESCRIBE (FIND MEMBER MOBY-DICK CLASS WHALE))
(M1(MEMBER(MOBY-DICK))(CLASS(WHALE)))

**(FIND MEMBER- (FIND CLASS WHALE))
(MOBY-DICK ORCA)

**(DESCRIBE (FIND VERB KNOWS OBJECT (FIND CLASS WHALE)))
(M4(AGENT(JOHN))(VERB(KNOWS))(OBJECT(M3)))
(M3(MEMBER(ORCA))(CLASS(WHALE)))

Fig. 6. Some examples of FIND.

```
**(FIND VERB KNOWS OBJECT(FIND MEMBER ?KNOWN-WHALE CLASS WHALE))
(M4)

** *KNOWN-WHALE
(ORCA)
```

Fig. 7. Simple use of a variable pattern in a FIND.

When SNePS has finished evaluating the top level FIND, the **atom** is given the list of nodes that it matched as its SNePSUL value. Figure 7 shows a simple use of this feature. Figure 8 shows a more complicated use of the pattern variable, where it is used to specify a node at the intersection of two paths.

A node may be found that satisfies one specification, but does not satisfy another with the aid of the infix set difference operator "-."

```
**(BUILD AGENT JOHN VERB KNOWS OBJECT M4)
(M5)

**(BUILD AGENT HENRY VERB KNOWS OBJECT M4)
(M6)

**(DESCRIBE(FIND AGENT ?X VERB KNOWS
*                     OBJECT(FIND AGENT ?X VERB KNOWS)))
(M5(AGENT(JOHN))(VERB(KNOWS))(OBJECT(M4)))
(M4(AGENT(JOHN))(VERB(KNOWS))(OBJECT(M3)))
(M3(MEMBER(ORCA))(CLASS(WHALE)))

** *X
(JOHN)
```

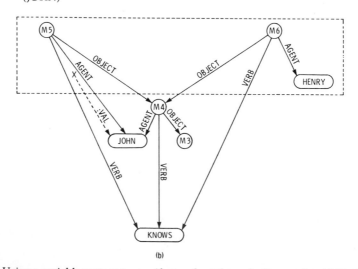

(b)

Fig. 8. Using a variable pattern to specify a node at the end of two paths. (a) The SNePSUL dialogue, (b) the network with material resulting from (a) enclosed by dashed lines.

**(FIND MEMBER- (FIND CLASS WHALE) - (FIND OBJECT- (FIND VERB KNOWS)))
(MOBY-DICK)

Fig. 9. A use of the set difference operator.

This operator is demonstrated in Fig. 9, where we find whales that no one knows are whales. One can also specify a set of nodes except those with certain arcs emanating from them, with the infix $\backslash$ operator. The value of (**nodeset** $\backslash$ ($\mathbf{R_1}, \ldots, \mathbf{R_k}$)) is (**nodeset** $- \{\mathbf{n}|\mathbf{R}_i(\mathbf{n}) \neq \phi, 1 \leq i \leq k\}$). Figure 10 demonstrates this operator.

The function (FINDORBUILD $\mathbf{R_1}$ nodeset$_1$ . . . $\mathbf{R_n}$ nodeset$_n$) first tries to find the specified node(s) but if none exist, it builds one. FINDOR-BUILD is used instead of BUILD when we wish to share nested molecular structures but are not sure if appropriate ones already exist.

3. INFERENCE

3.1. Representation of Deduction Rules

Automatic inference may be triggered by using the function DEDUCE, a generalization of FIND, or the function ADD, a generalization of BUILD. In order for these to accomplish anything, *deduction rules* must exist in the network. A deduction rule is a network structure dominated by a *rule node*. A rule node represents a propositional formula of molecular nodes, using one of the four connectives: $\bigvee$-entailment, $\bigwedge$-entailment, AND-OR, THRESH. A rule node $\mathbf{r}$ may also have either AVB($\mathbf{r}$) or EVB($\mathbf{r}$) nonempty, where AVB and EVB are the two binding relations representing universal and existential quantification, respectively.

This representation derives from that of Shapiro [1971a,b] and was further influenced by Kay [1973], Hendrix [1975a,b], and Schubert [1976]. It differs from the representation of Shapiro [1971a,b] by not using nodes to represent quantifiers, and from all the earlier work by the use of the new connectives, except for $\bigwedge$-entailment, which is the same as the generalized material implication of Schubert [1976, p. 173]. The match routine used by SNePS to locate relevant deduction rules is described in Shapiro [1977] and Shapiro and McKay [1979].

The four connectives all take sets of nodes as arguments and may be explicated as follows.

1. $\bigvee$-entailment: $\{\mathbf{A_1}, \ldots, \mathbf{A_n}\} \bigvee \rightarrow \{\mathbf{C_1}, \ldots, \mathbf{C_m}\}$ is true just in case each $\mathbf{A}_i$, $1 \leq i \leq n$, entails each $\mathbf{C}_j$, $1 \leq j \leq m$.

**(FIND MEMBER- (FIND CLASS WHALE) $\backslash$ (OBJECT-))
(MOBY-DICK)

Fig. 10. A use of the arc restriction operator $\backslash$.

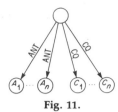 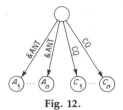

Fig. 11.   Fig. 12.

Fig. 11. The network representation of $\{A_1, \ldots, A_n\} \vee\!\!\rightarrow \{C_1, \ldots, C_n\}$.

Fig. 12. The network representation of $\{A_1, \ldots, A_n\} \wedge\!\!\rightarrow \{C_1, \ldots, C_n\}$.

2. $\wedge$-entailment: $\{A_1, \ldots, A_n\} \wedge\!\!\rightarrow \{C_1, \ldots, C_m\}$ is true just in case each C_j, $1 \leq j \leq m$, is entailed by the conjunction of the A_i, $1 \leq i \leq n$.

3.   AND-OR: $_n\!\!\times\!\!_i^j\{P_1, \ldots, P_n\}$ is true just in case at least i and at most j of the P are true.

4.   THRESH: $_n\Theta_i\{P_1, \ldots, P_n\}$ is true just in case either fewer than i of the P are true or they all are.

Figures 11–14 show how these connectives are represented in the network. Each choice of parameters for AND-OR and THRESH gives, in effect, a different connective. Some familiar ones are shown in Table II. Specifically, we shall abbreviate $_1\!\!\times\!\!_0^0(P)$ by $\sim P$.

Figure 15 illustrates how a negation can be stored in SNePS. In that figure, M7 represents "John loves Jane" and R1 represents "John does not love Jane." Since ARG^C (M7) is not empty, M7 is not considered "asserted in the network." Figure 16 shows a network for "Mary thinks that John loves Jane, but he doesn't." There, M8 and R1 are asserted in the network, while M7 is not. Figure 17 shows two alternative ways of representing "Mary thinks that John doesn't love Jane, but he does." In Fig. 17a, R2 acts as an assertion operator, asserting in the network that John loves Jane, while M9 asserts that Mary thinks that John doesn't love Jane. R1 is not asserted in Fig. 17. In Fig. 17b, M10 provides the assertion that John loves Jane. The technique of Fig. 17a has the benefit that it makes explicit that the very assertion (M7) that Mary thinks is not true is true. The technique

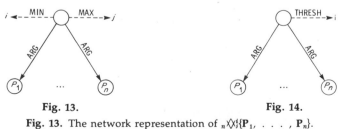

Fig. 13.   Fig. 14.

Fig. 13. The network representation of $_n\!\!\times\!\!_j^i\{P_1, \ldots, P_n\}$.

Fig. 14. The network representation of $_n\Theta_i\{P_1, \ldots, P_n\}$.

TABLE II

Some Familiar Connectives Represented by AND-OR and THRESH

Formula	Meaning
$_n\!\bigvee\!\!\bigwedge_n^n \{\mathbf{P}_1, \ldots, \mathbf{P}_n\}$	$\mathbf{P}_1$ and $\cdots$ and $\mathbf{P}_n$
$_n\!\bigvee\!\!\bigwedge_1^n \{\mathbf{P}_1, \ldots, \mathbf{P}_n\}$	$\mathbf{P}_1$ and/or $\cdots$ and/or $\mathbf{P}_n$
$_n\!\bigvee\!\!\bigwedge_0^0 \{\mathbf{P}_1, \ldots, \mathbf{P}_n\}$	neither $\mathbf{P}_1$ nor $\cdots$ nor $\mathbf{P}_n$
$_n\!\bigvee\!\!\bigwedge_1^1 \{\mathbf{P}_1, \ldots, \mathbf{P}_n\}$	exactly one of $\mathbf{P}_1$ or $\cdots$ or $\mathbf{P}_n$
$_n\!\bigvee\!\!\bigwedge_0^{n-1} \{\mathbf{P}_1, \ldots, \mathbf{P}_n\}$	not $(\mathbf{P}_1$ and $\cdots$ and $\mathbf{P}_n)$
$_n\Theta_1 \{\mathbf{P}_1, \ldots, \mathbf{P}_n\}$	$\mathbf{P}_1$ and $\cdots$ and $\mathbf{P}_n$ are all equivalent

of Fig. 17b, however, has the benefit that John loves Jane is asserted in the standard manner, namely, that there is a node in (FIND AGENT JOHN VERB LOVES OBJECT JANE) that is not dominated by any other node. In SNePS, R2 would be treated as a deduction rule capable of immediately deriving a node like M10. R1, if dominated by no other node, would also be treated as a deduction rule, but would derive itself, namely R1, the negation of M7. This discussion was motivated by the example of Scragg [1976, pp. 108–110], where "Peter said he went to the store, but he didn't" is handled as in Fig. 16, but "Peter said he didn't go to the store, although he did" is not discussed.

The LISP function (TOP? **N**) is provided, which returns T if the node **N** is asserted in the network, and NIL if it is not. The SNePSUL functions FORBTOP and FORBNOTOP are like FINDORBUILD but the former only finds nodes satisfying TOP?, while the latter only finds nodes not satisfying TOP? It is important to use FORBNOTOP when attempting to share dominated structures so that an asserted node does not become accidentally unasserted. Similarly, it is important to use FORBTOP when attempting to find-or-build a new asserted node.

A rule node that dominates one or more pattern nodes may have either AVB or EVB arcs to one or more of the variable nodes free in those pattern nodes. The restriction to either AVB or EVB arcs, but not both, is neces-

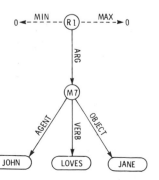

Fig. 15. "John does not love Jane."

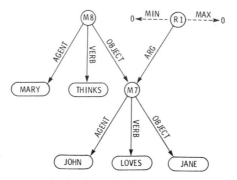

Fig. 16. "Mary thinks that John loves Jane, but he doesn't."

sary so that quantifier strings of the form $\forall\exists$ and $\exists\forall$ may be distinguished. Multiple AVB or EVB arcs are allowed since within quantifier strings of the form $\forall x_1 \cdot \cdot \cdot \forall x_n$ and $\exists x_1 \cdot \cdot \cdot \exists x_n$ order is irrelevant. Binding arcs may emanate only from rule nodes. This reflects the notion that in the formula $Q(x_1 \cdot \cdot \cdot x_n)A$, where Q is $\forall$ or $\exists$ and A is any formula, the quantifier clause $Q(x_1 \cdot \cdot \cdot x_n)$ may be associated with the main connective of A. If A has no main connective, either because it is atomic or because it is of the form $Q(y_1 \cdot \cdot \cdot y_m)B$, the formula can be represented as $Q(x_1 \cdot \cdot \cdot x_m)[\{\ \} \wedge\rightarrow \{A\}]$.

Figure 18 shows the SNePSUL instructions for building the deduction rules for "Every man loves some woman," and for the definition of transitive relations. A few comments are in order about the form chosen for these rules. If SNePS is asked to deduce instances of $R(x)$ using the rule, $\forall x(\{P(x)\} \vee\rightarrow \{Q(x), R(x)\})$, and $P(a)$ is true, it will build $R(a)$ in the network, but not bother building $Q(a)$. However, if the rule had been $\forall x(\{P(x)\} \vee\rightarrow {}_2\langle\!\langle\rangle\!\rangle_2^2\{Q(x), R(x)\})$ it would build both $Q(a)$ and $R(a)$. That is the reason for the form of the rule in Fig. 18a. If, for example, one asks whom Bill loves, one would not want to introduce a new Skölem constant **t** and record "BILL LOVES **t**" without also recording "**t** $\in$ WOMAN". When SNePS uses a rule of the form $\{P, Q\} \wedge\rightarrow \{R\}$, parallel processes are used to deduce **P** and **Q**. However, even though the rule $\{P\} \vee\rightarrow \{\{Q\} \vee\rightarrow \{R\}\}$ is formally equivalent, in this case SNePS establishes a process to deduce **Q** only after a deduction of **P** has been successful. The form of the rule in Fig. 18b forces SNePS to first check that a relationship is transitive before using the transitivity rule further. The way parallel processes are used to carry out deductions is discussed more fully in Shapiro and McKay [1979].

The rule in Fig. 18b looks like a second-order rule, but strictly speaking, it is not. Relations such as ON are represented by semantic nodes as are other individual concepts, and so variables can range over them. We can consider each *case frame*, i.e., each combination of descending arcs, to be a

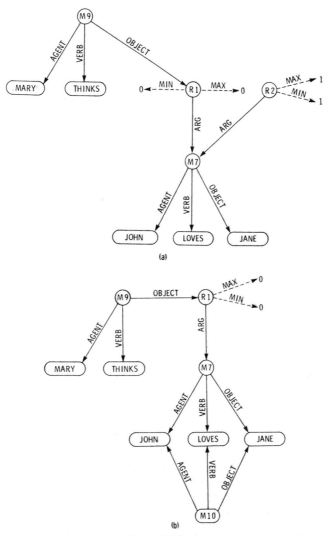

Fig. 17. Two ways of representing "Mary thinks that John doesn't love Jane, but he does."
(a) with an assertion operator, (b) with a duplicated molecular node.

different predicate in the network. Thus, if we represent the proposition
ON(BLOCK1,BLOCK2) by the node constructed by (BUILD AGENT
BLOCK1 VERB ON OBJECT BLOCK2), it is accurate to say that we are asserting the proposition AGENT-VERB-OBJECT(BLOCK1,ON,BLOCK2).
We never quantify predicates of the type of AGENT-VERB-OBJECT, even
though we do quantify individuals like ON that are used as predicates in
other notations.

```
**(BUILD AVB $X
        ANT(BUILD MEMBER *X CLASS MAN)
        CQ(BUILD EVB $Y MIN 2 MAX 2
                ARG((BUILD MEMBER *Y CLASS WOMAN)
                    (BUILD AGENT *X VERB LOVES
                           OBJECT *Y))))
(M11)
```

(a)

```
**(BUILD AVB $R
        ANT(BUILD MEMBER *R CLASS TRANSITIVE)
        CQ(BUILD AVB($X $Y $Z)
                &ANT ((BUILD AGENT ᵧX  VERB ᵧR  OBJECT ᵧY)
                      (BUILD AGENT *Y VERB *R OBJECT *Z))
                CQ(BUILD AGENT *X VERB *R OBJECT *Z)))
(M17)
```

(b)

Fig. 18. SNePSUL BUILDS for (a) Every man loves some woman: $\forall x(\{x \in MAN\} \vee\!\!\to \{\exists y\ _2\!\bigotimes_2^2\{y \in WOMAN,\ xLOVESy\}\})$. (b) The definition of transitivity: $\forall R(\{R \in TRANSITIVE\} \vee\!\!\to \{\forall(x,\ y,\ z)(\{R(x,\ y),\ R(y,\ z)\} \wedge\!\!\to \{R(x,\ z)\})\})$.

3.2. Backward Inference

Deduction rules are used for backward inference via the SNePSUL function (DEDUCE **numb** R_1 **nodeset₁** · · · R_n **nodeset**$_n$). This causes the temporary node (TBUILD R_1 **nodeset₁** · · · R_n **nodeset**$_n$) to be built and turned over to the deduction system, which uses a multiprocessing system to deduce both positive and negative instances of it. The parameter **numb** controls how many answers are desired. If **numb** is omitted, all answers are found. If **numb** is 0, the DEDUCE is equivalent to a FIND—only explicit answers are found. If **numb** is a positive integer, deduction ceases as soon as at least **numb** answers are found. Otherwise, **numb** is a list of two numbers (**npos nneg**), and deduction ceases as soon as at least **npos** positive instances and **nneg** negative instances are found. For example, to cease deduction as soon as three positive instances are found, **numb** should be (3 0); to stop as soon as one answer, either positive or negative, is found, **numb** should be 1. Since several instances may be found at the same time, the number of answers found may sometimes exceed the number requested. If fewer than the requested number of answers are deducible, all will be returned.

Table III summarizes the rules of inference used for each of the four connectives.

Figure 19 shows a deduction using the rule in Fig. 18a, and Fig. 20 shows a deduction using the rule in Fig. 18b to deduce four positive instances. When a deduction is interrupted, as in Fig. 20, sufficient information to resume the deduction is stored as the SNePS value of LASTINFER.

TABLE III

Rules of Inference for the Four Connectives

Deduction Rule	As soon as _____ are found	Deduce
$\forall x\{A_1(x), \ldots, A_n(x)\}$		
$\quad \vee\rightarrow\{C_1(x), \ldots, C_m(x)\}$	1 of $A_1(a), \ldots, A_n(a)$	$C_m(a)$
$\forall x\{A_1(x), \ldots, A_n(x)\}$		
$\quad \wedge\rightarrow\{C_1(x), \ldots, C_m(x)\}$	n of $A_1(a), \ldots, A_n(a)$	$C_m(a)$
$\forall x_n \bigvee\!\bigvee_i^i\{P_1(x), \ldots, P_n(x)\}$	j of $P_1(a), \ldots, P_{n-1}(a)$	$\sim P_n(a)$
	$n - i$ of $\sim P_1(a), \ldots, \sim P_{n-1}(a)$	$P_n(a)$
$\forall x_n \Theta_i\{P_1(x), \ldots, P_n(x)\}$	i of $P_1(a), \ldots, P_{n-1}(a)$	$P_n(a)$
	$i - 1$ of $P_1(a), \ldots, P_{n-1}(a)$	
	and 1 of $\sim P_1(a), \ldots, \sim P_{n-1}(a)$	$\sim P_n(a)$

The deduction may be resumed by evaluating

(RESUME **numb** *LASTINFER),

as shown in Fig. 21.

3.3. Restricted Forward Inference

When the multiprocessing deduction system uses an inference rule, an INFER process is created for each antecedent proposition. For example, if the rule $\forall(x, y)\ _n\!\bigvee\!\bigvee_{min}^{max}(P_1(x, y), \ldots, P_n(x, y))$ is to be used to deduce $P_n(a, z)$, an INFER process is created for each $P_i(a, z)$, $1 \le i \le n - 1$. Each INFER process is connected to a *data collector* process that stores all deduced instances of $P_i(a, z)$. While these processes are retained, if $P_i(a, y)$ becomes a subgoal of another deduction, the results stored in the data collector are used and repeated deduction of the same information is

```
**(BUILD MEMBER JOHN CLASS MAN)
(M18)

**(BUILD MEMBER HENRY CLASS MAN)
(M19)

**(DESCRIBE(DEDUCE AGENT %X VERB LOVES OBJECT %Y))
(M24(AGENT(HENRY))(VERB(LOVES))(OBJECT(M21)))
(M22(AGENT(JOHN))(VERB(LOVES))(OBJECT(M20)))
(DUMPED)

**(DESCRIBE (FIND CLASS WOMAN) \ (:SVAR))
(M23(MEMBER(M20))(CLASS WOMAN)))
(M25(MEMBER(M21))(CLASS WOMAN)))
```

Fig. 19. A use of rule Fig. 18(a), "Every man loves a woman." The data base includes the network of Fig. 16, but not of Fig. 17.

```
**(BUILD AGENT A VERB SUPPORTS OBJECT B)
(M26)
**(BUILD AGENT B VERB SUPPORTS OBJECT C)
(M27)
**(BUILD AGENT C VERB SUPPORTS OBJECT D)
(M28)
**(BUILD MIN 0 MAX 0
            ARG(BUILD AGENT B VERB SUPPORTS OBJECT E))
(M30)
**(BUILD MEMBER SUPPORTS CLASS TRANSITIVE)
(M31)
**(DESCRIBE(DEDUCE(4 0)AGENT %X VERB SUPPORTS OBJECT %Y))
(M32(AGENT(B))(VERB(SUPPORTS))(OBJECT(D)))
(M30(MIN(0))(MAX(0))(ARG(M29)))
(M29(AGENT(B)) (VERB(SUPPORTS))(OBJECT(E)))
(M28(AGENT(C))(VERB(SUPPORTS))(OBJECT(D)))
(M27(AGENT(B))(VERB(SUPPORTS))(OBJECT(C)))
(M26(AGENT(A))(VERB(SUPPORTS))(OBJECT(B)))
(DUMPED)
```

Fig. 20. A use of the transitivity rule Fig. 18b asking for four positive answers.

avoided. Processes are presently retained for the duration of the run in which they are created.

The SNePSUL function ADD is identical to FORBTOP, except that if a new node is built, it is matched against the network to find INFER processes for which the node is a new answer. If any are found, the new node is added to the appropriate data collectors from which it is passed to the deductions interested in it. In other words, structures built using ADD will cause forward inferences to be made just in case these structures are relevant to a question asked previously in the session. Figure 22 demonstrates this facility.

4. PARSING AND GENERATING

SNePSUL functions may be activated as actions on the arcs of an augmented transition network (ATN) grammar, so that natural language sentences can be parsed directly into SNePS networks. To facilitate this, the ATN interpreter was modified so that the nodes built while traversing an arc are deleted when back-tracking occurs on the arc.

The ATN interpreter was also modified so that when a SNePS node is

```
**(DESCRIBE (RESUME *LASTINFER))
(M34(AGENT(A))(VERB(SUPPORTS))(OBJECT(D)))
(M33(AGENT(A))(VERB(SUPPORTS))(OBJECT(C)))
(DUMPED)
```

Fig. 21. Resuming the deduction of Fig. 20.

```
**(DESCRIBE (ADD MEMBER SAM CLASS MAN))
(M37(AGENT(SAM))(VERB(LOVES))(OBJECT(M36)))
(M35(MEMBER(SAM))(CLASS(MAN)))
(DUMPED)

**(DESCRIBE (FIND MEMBER M36))
(M38(MEMBER(M36))(CLASS(WOMAN)))
(DUMPED)
```

Fig. 22. A demonstration of restricted forward inference.

given, ATN grammars can construct a natural language string that expresses the concept represented by the node. Space limitations preclude a further discussion of these facilities here. They are described in Shapiro [1975, 1979].

Tying the generator to the nodes is an important mechanism in enforcing the requirement that the set of intensional concepts represented in the network is coextensive with the set of constant nodes. If the system is to express a concept (an idea?), there must be a node representing it to give to the generator. Also, the generator must be able to create a string expressing the concept represented by each constant node.

5. AN EXAMPLE APPLICATION—CLUE

The development of SNePS has been carried out with concern for logical adequacy, for generality, and for the foundations of semantic networks as representations of knowledge. Nevertheless, tests of application domains are important. A SNePS-like collateral descendant of MENTAL [Shapiro, 1971a,b] is being used in SOPHIE, an AI-CAI system (see J. S. Brown *et al.* [1974]), and a version of SNePS is being used in a natural language graphics system [D.C. Brown *et al.*, 1977]. Example domains in medical information and art history are being planned. This section describes an application to the game Clue, implemented by Bill Neagle. This example illustrates the interaction of SNePSUL and LISP, and the use of AND-OR, FORBNOTOP, DEDUCE, and ADD.

Clue is a game of deductive reasoning marketed by Parker Brothers. The game equipment consists of a board representing a house of nine rooms (hall, study, billiard room, library, conservatory, ballroom, kitchen, dining room, lounge), six tokens representing suspects (Miss Scarlet, Professor Plum, Miss Peacock, Mrs. White, Mr. Green, Colonel Mustard), six pieces representing weapons (rope, revolver, candlestick, lead pipe, knife, wrench), one card for each of these 21 items, and an envelope. One room card, one weapon card, and one suspect card are placed in the envelope representing the location, weapon, and perpetrator of a murder. The remaining cards are shuffled and distributed to the players, each of whom uses one of the suspect tokens to move around the board (up to six people can play). The object of the game is to deduce which cards are in the envelope. Each player knows that the cards he holds are not in the envelope. Players roll dice to move from room to room along corridors. When in a room, a player may "suggest" that the murder was committed in that room by any of the suspects using any of the weapons. Beginning on the suggestor's left, each player either states that he has none of the cards or that he has at least one of them until a player states that he has at least one card. This player shows one of these cards to the suggestor, refuting the suggestion. The other players know only that one of the cards has been shown, not which one. There is no rule preventing the suggestor from including one or more of his own cards in his suggestion, so if every other player denies having any of the three cards, they are either in the envelope or held by the suggestor. The suggestor does not say whether he holds any of the cards. On his turn, a player may make an "accusation," stating which three cards he believes to be in the envelope. He then looks in the envelope. If he is right, he openly displays the cards and wins the game. If he is wrong, he replaces the cards in the envelope and ceases to participate in the game except for replying to other players' suggestions.

We have written a LISP/SNePSUL program that can be used by a player to deduce which cards are in the envelope. The initial game information is established by a call to the LISP function CLUE, which takes as its one argument an ordered list of the players. The following LISP lists are established:

PLAYERS	the ordered list of players
HANDS	the players and the ENVELOPE
SUSPECTS	(SCARLET PLUM . . .)
WEAPONS	(ROPE REVOLVER . . .)
ROOMS	(HALL STUDY . . .)
CARDS	a list of the 21 cards

The set of cards is also established in the SNePS network by evaluating the LISP expression

```
(MAPC CARDS (LAMBDA (CARD)
          (BUILD MEMBER ( ↑ CARD) CLASS CARD)))
```

Rules are built expressing such facts as that the envelope holds exactly one suspect, weapon, and room, that each card is held by exactly one hand, and that the kth player (of n players) holds exactly numdealt(player$_k$) cards, where

$$\text{numdealt(player}_k) = \lfloor 18/n \rfloor + \begin{cases} 1, & \text{if } k \leq 18 \bmod n \\ 0, & \text{otherwise} \end{cases}$$

These rules are built by the LISP function BUILD-BETWEEN, defined as follows:

```
(DE BUILD-BETWEEN (I J SET PRED)
   (BUILD MIN ( ↑ I) MAX ( ↑ J)
      ARG ( ↑ (MAPCAR SET
                 (LAMBDA(X)
                    (APPLY FORBNOTOP
                       (SUBST X '+ PRED)))))))))
```

This function builds a rule saying that between I and J elements, x, of SET are such that PRED(x). Rules of this sort suggest a parameterized existential quantifier, $\exists^i_j$. The rule $\exists^i_j(x) \; _2\!\land^2_2(A(x), C(x))$ would assert that at least i and at most j objects satisfy both $A(x)$ and $C(x)$. Inclusion of this quantifier in SNePS is planned.

The rules stated above are built as follows:

```
(BUILD-BETWEEN 1 1 SUSPECTS '(HOLDER ENVELOPE OBJECT +))
(BUILD-BETWEEN 1 1 WEAPONS '(HOLDER ENVELOPE OBJECT +))
(BUILD-BETWEEN 1 1 ROOMS '(HOLDER ENVELOPE OBJECT +))
(BUILD AVB $X
       ANT (BUILD MEMBER *X CLASS CARD)
       CQ ( ↑ (BUILD-BETWEEN 1 1 HANDS
                  '(HOLDER + OBJECT *X))))
(MAPC PLAYERS
       (LAMBDA (PLAYER)
          (BUILD-BETWEEN (NUMDEALT PLAYER)
                 (NUMDEALT PLAYER) CARDS
                 '(HOLDER ( ↑ PLAYER) OBJECT +))))
```

Note the use of the connectives $_n\!\land^1_k$ and $_n\!\land^k_k$. A great many clauses would be required to represent this information in a resolution-based theorem prover.

There are two ways of gaining information during the game. One is entered by the function

(SUGGEST **player suspect weapon room responder card**)

which asserts that **player** suggested that **suspect** committed the murder with the **weapon** in the **room**, that none of the players between **player** and **responder** had any of those cards, and that **responder** showed **player** the card **card**. If **player** or **responder** is the person using the program, **card** will be **suspect**, **weapon**, or **room**, otherwise it will be NIL. If no one responded, **responder** and **card** will both be NIL. The definition of SUGGEST is

```
(DF SUGGEST (PLAYER SUSPECT WEAPON
             ROOM RESPONDER CARD)
   (MAPC (BETWEEN PLAYER RESPONDER)
      (LAMBDA (PASSED)
```

```
            (HAS-NONE PASSED SUSPECT WEAPON ROOM)))
     (IF RESPONDER
       (COND (CARD (ADD HOLDER ( ↑ RESPONDER)
                         OBJECT ( ↑ CARD)))
             (T (ADD MIN 1 MAX 3
                      ARG((FORBNOTOP HOLDER ( ↑ RESPONDER)
                                     OBJECT ( ↑ SUSPECT))
                          (FORBNOTOP HOLDER ( ↑ RESPONDER)
                                     OBJECT ( ↑ WEAPON))
                          (FORBNOTOP HOLDER ( ↑ RESPONDER)
                                     OBJECT ( ↑ ROOM))))))))
```

where (BETWEEN **player1 player2**) returns a list of the people sitting between (clockwise) **player1** and **player2,** unless **player2** is NIL in which case it returns a list of all players except **player1.** Furthermore, HAS-NONE is the function

```
     (DE HAS-NONE (PLAYER SUSPECT WEAPON ROOM)
        (ADD MIN 0 MAX 0
             ARG ((FORBNOTOP HOLDER ( ↑ PLAYER)
                             OBJECT ( ↑ SUSPECT))
                  (FORBNOTOP HOLDER ( ↑ PLAYER)
                             OBJECT ( ↑ WEAPON))
                  (FORBNOTOP HOLDER ( ↑ PLAYER)
                             OBJECT ( ↑ ROOM)))))
```

The other way in which information may be gained during the game is if someone makes an accusation and is wrong. The accuser may be assumed not to have any of the cards in the accusation. This is handled by a call to HAS-NONE.

Below is the protocol of a reduced game in which the only cards were MUSTARD, PLUM, KNIFE, CANDLESTICK, HALL, LOUNGE, DINING-ROOM, and KITCHEN. The program's trace of its inferences is presented in English for ease of reading. Arrows point to the three statements that provide the solution. The program was being used by player "Don."

```
(CLUE '(DON CHUCK BILL STU))
(BUILD HOLDER DON OBJECT MUSTARD)
(BUILD HOLDER DON OBJECT KNIFE)
(DEDUCE (3 0) HOLDER ENVELOPE OBJECT %X)
Don holds Mustard.
Don holds knife.
Envelope doesn't hold Mustard.
```

→ Envelope holds Plum.
Stu doesn't hold Plum.
Bill doesn't hold Plum.
Chuck doesn't hold Plum.
Don doesn't hold Plum.
Stu doesn't hold Mustard.
Bill doesn't hold Mustard
Chuck doesn't hold Mustard.
Envelope doesn't hold knife.
→ Envelope holds candlestick.
Stu doesn't hold candlestick
Bill doesn't hold candlestick.
Chuck doesn't hold candlestick.
Don doesn't hold candlestick.
Stu doesn't hold knife.
Bill doesn't hold knife.
Chuck doesn't hold knife.
Don doesn't hold hall.
Don doesn't hold lounge.
Don doesn't hold dining room.
Don doesn't hold kitchen.
(SUGGEST STU MUSTARD KNIFE KITCHEN DON KNIFE)
(SUGGEST DON MUSTARD KNIFE DINING-ROOM STU
        DINING-ROOM)
Bill doesn't hold dining room.
Chuck doesn't hold dining room.
Stu holds dining room.
Envelope doesn't hold dining room.
Stu doesn't hold hall.
Stu doesn't hold lounge.
Stu doesn't hold kitchen.
(SUGGEST CHUCK PLUM CANDLESTICK LOUNGE BILL NIL)
Bill holds lounge.
Envelope doesn't hold lounge.
Chuck doesn't hold lounge.
Bill doesn't hold hall.
Bill doesn't hold kitchen.
(SUGGEST BILL PLUM KNIFE HALL DON KNIFE)
(SUGGEST STU PLUM CANDLESTICK DINING-ROOM NIL NIL)
(SUGGEST DON MUSTARD KNIFE HALL CHUCK HALL)
Chuck holds hall.
Envelope doesn't hold hall.
→ Envelope holds kitchen.

6. SUMMARY

I have given a brief introduction 'to semantic networks as representations of knowledge and pointed out that they can be discussed on four levels: an abstract graph; a two-dimensional pictorial diagram; a linear symbolic string; a computer implementation. SNePS, the semantic network processing system, was then discussed on the first three of those levels.

SNePS is a general system for building and manipulating semantic networks but, because of our view of semantic networks, certain features are provided and some restrictions are imposed. Nodes and arcs are partitioned into several types. Auxiliary arcs and nodes are used to type other nodes (e.g., to distinguish variable and pattern nodes), to maintain references to nodes (SNePSUL variables are auxiliary nodes), and to hang nonnodal information onto nodes (AND-OR and THRESH parameters are integers hung on rule nodes by MIN, MAX, and THRESH auxiliary arcs). Pattern and variable nodes do not represent constant concepts but are used to construct deduction rules. Temporary nodes are used by the DEDUCE function to construct templates of desired structures. Universal and existential quantifiers are represented by binding relations between rule nodes and variable nodes. Four nonstandard logical connectives—$\wedge$-entailment, $\vee$-entailment, AND-OR, and THRESH—are provided for building deduction rules that can be used for backward inference or restricted forward inference. The major restriction imposed by SNePS is that nonauxiliary arcs cannot be added between two pre-existing nodes. Each addition of information to the network must be accompanied by a new node. The normal use of BUILD is to have this new node be a molecular node representing the new information.

An application of SNePS to the deductive game Clue was discussed. It illustrated the use of deduction rules, especially the use of AND-OR and restricted forward inference. Further applications are planned along with the continued development of the SNePS system and the SNePSUL language.

ACKNOWLEDGMENTS

SNePS is a descendant of MENTAL [Shapiro, 1971a,b] and is presently implemented in ALISP [Konolige, 1975] on the CDC Cyber 173 at the State University of New York at Buffalo. For aid in the development and implementation of successive versions of SNePS and its associated systems, I am grateful to Nick Vitulli, Nick Eastridge, Jim McKew, Stan Kwasny, Steve Johnson, Ben Spigle, John Lowrance, Darrel Joy, Bob Bechtel, Don McKay, Chuck Arnold, Bill Neagle, and Rich Fritzson.

For their comments on an earlier version of this chapter, I am grateful to Nick Findler, David G. Hays, Don McKay, Chuck Arnold, Rich Fritzson, and three anonymous reviewers, authors of other chapters in this book.

REFERENCES

[Bobrow, D. G., and Raphael, B., 1974]. New programming languages for artificial intelligence. *Computing Surveys* **6**, No. 3, 153–174.

[Brown, D. C., Kwasny, S. C., Buttelman, H. W., Chandrasekaran, B., and Sondheimer, N. K., 1977]. NLG—natural language graphics. *Proceedings of The 5th International Joint Conference on Artificial Intelligence, 1977* p. 916.

[Brown, J. S., Burton, R. R., and Bell, A. G., 1974]. "SOPHIE: A Sophisticated Instructional Environment for Teaching Electronic Troubleshooting (An Example of AI in CAI)," AI Report No. 12. Bolt, Beranek & Newman, Cambridge, Massachusetts.

[Hendrix, G. G., 1975a]. Expanding the utility of semantic networks through partitioning. *Proceedings of the 4th International Joint Conference on Artificial Intelligence, 1975* pp. 115–121.

[Hendrix, G. G., 1975b]. "Partitioned Networks for the Mathematical Modeling of Natural Language Semantics," Technical Report No. NL-28. Department of Computer Sciences, Univ. of Texas, Austin, Texas.

[Kay, M., 1973]. The MIND system. In *Natural Language Processing*. R. Rustin (ed.). Algorithmics Press, New York, pp. 155–188.

[Konolige, K., 1975]. *ALISP User's Manual*. University of Massachusetts Computing Center, Amherst.

[Quillian, M. R., 1968]. Semantic memory. In *Semantic Information Processing*. M. Minsky (ed.). MIT Press, Cambridge, Massachusetts, pp. 227–270.

[Raphael, B., 1968]. SIR: A computer program for semantic information retrieval. In *Semantic Information Processing*. M. Minsky (ed.). MIT Press, Cambridge, Massachusetts, pp. 33–45.

[Reitman, W. R., 1965]. *Cognition and Thought*. Wiley, New York.

[Schubert, L. K., 1976.]. Extending the expressive power of semantics. *Artificial Intelligence* **7**, No. 2, 163–198.

[Scragg, G., 1976]. Semantic nets as memory models. In *Computational Semantics*. E. Charniak and Y. Wilks (eds.). North-Holland Publ. Amsterdam, pp. 101–127.

[Shapiro, S. C., 1971a]. "The MIND System: A Data Structure for Semantic Information Processing," Report R-837-PR. The Rand Corporation, Santa Monica, California.

[Shapiro, S. C., 1971b]. A net structure for semantic information storage, deduction and retrieval. *Proceedings of The 2nd International Joint Conference on Artificial Intelligence, 1971* pp. 512–523.

[Shapiro, S. C., 1975]. Generation as parsing from a network into a linear string. *American Journal of Computational Linguistics* (Microfiche 33), 45–62.

[Shapiro, S. C., 1977]. Representing and locating deduction rules in a semantic network. *ACM SIGART Newsletter* **63**, 14–18.

[Shapiro, S. C., 1979]. "A Generalization of Augmented Transition Networks That Allows for Parsing Graphs." Department of Computer Science, SUNY, Buffalo, New York.

[Shapiro, S. C., and McKay, D. P., 1979]. "The Representation and Use of Deduction Rules in a Semantic Network." Department of Computer Science, SUNY, Buffalo, New York.

[Woods, W. A., 1975]. What's in a link: Foundations for semantic networks. In *Representation and Understanding*. D. G. Bobrow and A. M. Collins (eds.). Academic Press, New York, pp. 35–82.

A PREDICATE CALCULUS BASED
SEMANTIC NETWORK
FOR DEDUCTIVE SEARCHING

James R. McSkimin   *and*   *Jack Minker*

ABSTRACT

A *semantic network* is described for use in the deductive portion of an inferential system. The semantic network uses the first-order predicate calculus as a framework. The notation of the predicate calculus is modified in order to accommodate semantic information concerning the domain of application. The modification corresponds to a many-sorted logic.

Four types of information are stored in the semantic network: (1) the *data base*, consisting of assertions and general rules, represented as a form of predicate calculus clauses; (2) the *semantic form space*, which defines how each argument of an n-ary predicate is constrained to be from a named subset (Boolean category expression) of the domain; (3) the *dictionary*, which defines for each domain element, function name, and predicate name, the semantic category of which it is a member; (4) the *semantic graph*, which defines the set-theoretic relationship between semantic categories.

The rationale for the form of the semantic network, and each of the components of the network is developed in the chapter. Several examples are presented to illustrate the concepts developed.

1. INTRODUCTION

Semantic networks have been the subject of extensive research since Quillian [1968] developed the concept. Work in this field has attempted to use a semantic net to understand natural languages so as to be able to translate a natural language into a form that can be understood by a computer. In this chapter, we describe how a semantic network may be used during the deductive phase of a problem-solving system. We use the first-order predicate calculus as a framework for the semantic network, and modify the notation of the predicate calculus so as to accommodate semantic information concerning the domain of the application. The semantic network has the full power of the predicate calculus as it handles functions and quantification. Predicate calculus and the notation used in automatic theorem proving is used throughout. McSkimin [1976a,b] and

205

McSkimin and Minker [1977]) describe the use of the semantic network during the deductive search process in detail. We refer to these prior publications in our discussions.

Previous efforts in deductive searching using the predicate calculus have been oriented primarily toward syntactic approaches. Such systems relied solely on syntactic pattern matching for retrieving assertions or axioms in attempting to solve a problem. As a result, for most reasonably large data bases of assertions and axioms, they often became deluged with an inordinate number of inferences and generally ran out of time or space before a problem had been answered. The work described herein is an attempt to improve upon the performance of such declarative systems by allowing the user to input semantic information about the domain in use.

Four types of information are stored in the *semantic network:* (1) the *data base*, consisting of assertions of facts and general inference axioms—represented as a form of predicate calculus clauses; (2) the *semantic form space*, which defines how each argument of an n-ary predicate and an n-ary function symbol is constrained to be from a named subset (called a Boolean category expression) of the domain in use; (3) the *dictionary*, which defines for each domain element, function name, and predicate name, the semantic category of which it is a member; (4) the *semantic graph*, which defines the set-theoretic relationships between semantic categories.

Each argument of a predicate is explicitly constrained to belong to a named sort, which we refer to as a Boolean category expression. Each sort is a member of the semantic network. Thus, we are dealing with a sorted logic, which is equivalent to the first-order predicate calculus. The use of a many-sorted logic requires that the unification algorithm of first-order logic be modified. This is described in Section 4. The purpose of introducing the many-sorted logic and semantic network is for its use in the deductive search process to restrict the search space. As described in Mc Skimin and Minker [1977] there are three primary uses of the semantic network:

(1)   to reject queries, data base assertions, and general inference axioms whose predicates have arguments that are not compatible with the semantic constraints specified in the semantic network;

(2)   to retrieve and apply only data base assertions and general rules semantically relevant to some part of the query;

(3)   to detect when all semantically possible answers for a query have been found; and if such a condition is detected, prevent the deductive search mechanism from searching for additional answers.

The following section is devoted to the concept of a *semantic graph*. The semantic graph defines interrelationships between named subsets of the domain and is the basis for the understanding of the semantic network.

Section 3 describes the semantic network and briefly alludes to its use. The semantic unification algorithm is presented in Section 4. Illustrative examples are presented in Section 5. Related work in semantic networks is presented in Section 6, and a summary of the work is given in Section 7.

2. SEMANTIC CATEGORIES

2.1. Unary Relations and Set Memberships

Two problems that arise in deductive systems are those of using irrelevant data or general rules to aid in the deductive process, and attempting to solve semantically meaningless problems.

An example of the first type of problem is the desire to find an x such that PARENT(JACK, x) is satisfied, and an axiom such as $\neg$MOTHER(u, v) $\lor$ PARENT (u, v) is to be applied to the negation of the query. Syntactically the general rule applies. However, in a domain in which JACK is known to be *male*, and the first argument of MOTHER(x, y) must be *female*, the general rule will never be on a path to a solution since JACK cannot be a mother of an individual in the particular domain of discourse. An example of the second type of problem is the desire to find a state x such that REPRESENT(SIRICA, x) is satisfied. If in the domain of discourse SIRICA is a *judge* and the first argument of REPRESENT must be a *senator* or a *representative*, again there will be no solution to the problem since judges cannot be members of Congress.

These problems are caused in large part by a failure to define explicitly the contents of the domain of discourse D, and the relationships in which various subsets of D may occur meaningfully. In the following discussion, we describe how the domain of discourse may be subdivided into various named subsets, and how each subset will be designated as a *semantic category*. We use the term semantic category, whereas the term *sort* is used in logic. Hence, the system that we are describing is equivalent to a many-sorted logic.

A hierarchy of semantic categories may exist for a particular domain as specified by a user. We do not propose a general, all-encompassing hierarchy since we do not believe in the existence of such a hierarchy for all problem domains. A hierarchy that is possible is specified in Section 2.2, and the user must particularize the relationships for the specific domain of interest.

Each element of the domain of discourse D can be given a list of properties that characterize the element. In addition, each predicate defined over D can be restricted to having arguments whose elements must possess certain properties. In previous predicate calculus representations, these properties have often been represented as unary predicates over the elements of the domain. For example, HUMAN(JOHN) and BALD(JOHN) might represent the fact that JOHN is a human and JOHN is bald, respectively. That is, the properties associated with the domain element JOHN, namely being human and being bald, are represented as unary predicates. The unary predicate representation is consistent with the notation used to describe relations among elements of the domain, for example, RESIDE(JOHN, MARYLAND) to denote that "John resides in Maryland".

We perceive a distinct difference between the two types of relations, however. In the first case what is being described is *set membership*, whereas in the second the *interactions* among domain elements or between sets is being described. As described in the following section, we have chosen to represent set membership relations as semantic categories and interaction relations as *n*-ary predicates. It should be emphasized that semantic categories (or unary relations) are simply labels for a set of objects that may have as complex a combination of properties as desired. Such labels are necessary in order to concisely refer to such a set without enumerating its properties at each reference.

There is no concensus on how relations should be represented. In fact, it has often been the case that the distinction between set interrelationships (i.e., subset) and other relations has been blurred. For instance, Simmons [1972] represents all information in his semantic network by binary relations. Rumelhart *et al.* [1972] represent human conceptual knowledge as a labeled directed graph. In particular, they use a relation termed IS-A to label an arc from one object to the objects that are its superset. On the other hand, Quillian [1968, 1969] does make a distinction between the superset relations and other properties by using separate pointers in the graph structure for his semantic network. Similarly, Winograd [1971] isolated the superset relations from all others and classified all objects in his block world into classes. The issue of how relations should be represented has yet to be settled as evidenced by other opinions [McDermott, 1975; Moore, 1975a].

It is our belief that the distinction between set interrelationships and interaction relations is significant and that they should be treated differently. In particular, it is believed that one way to help solve the problems encountered in inferential systems not employing user-supplied semantic information is to use a special semantic category representation for set interrelationships *separate* from that used for interaction relations. The need for developing more efficient representations and processing algorithms for set interrelationships is motivated by the following observations.

First, in order to specify set restrictions on arguments of an interaction relation R, a list of set relations must be appended to R and checked whenever a substitution is made into that argument. For example, if we wanted to find a member of the House who is old, male, and lives in Maryland, we could phrase this as the negated query

$$\neg\text{RESIDE}(x, \text{Maryland}) \ \vee \neg\ \text{OLD}(x) \ \vee \neg\text{MALE}(x)$$
$$\vee \neg\text{REPRESENTATIVE}(x)$$

This is a very long and cumbersome expression and would probably require a separate peripheral storage reference for each set relation retrieved. It is very desirable to develop a method to perform similar checks with much less overhead.

Second, if RESIDE(x, Maryland) were to be inferred rather than simply retrieved, a great deal of effort might be expended before realizing that all was in vain, since an inference rule was applied that itself had semantic restrictions that were incompatible with the set relations of the above query. For example, it is possible to infer the state of residence of a senator by knowing the state he or she represents, i.e.,

$$\neg\text{REPRESENT}(x, y) \ \vee \neg\text{SENATOR}(x) \ \vee \neg\text{STATE}(y) \ \vee \text{RESIDE}(x, y)$$

If this inference rule were applied to the subproblem $\neg$RESIDE(x, Maryland) from the above query, the following inference would be formed:

$$\neg\text{REPRESENT}(x, \text{Maryland}) \ \vee \neg\text{SENATOR}(x) \ \vee \neg\text{STATE(Maryland)}$$
$$\vee \neg\text{OLD}(x) \ \vee \neg\text{MALE}(x)$$
$$\vee \neg\text{REPRESENTATIVE}(x)$$

This is an invalid inference since x cannot be a REPRESENTATIVE (i.e., a member of the House) and a SENATOR simultaneously. Unfortunately, in such a representation, there is no easy way to detect this inconsistency. What is needed is some way to detect semantic conflicts *before* the axiom is applied. The semantic graph (Section 2.2) and the semantic unification algorithm (Section 4) have been developed to handle these problems.

Third, set membership relations, if appended to queries and general rules as above, could be satisfied by the retrieval of data base facts asserting the set membership of domain elements. However, it is often the case that a trivial *set inference* must be made in order to verify that a relation is true. For instance, transitive superset relations may be inferred. A more efficient mechanism is thus needed to perform set inferences.

A fourth disadvantage to the unary predicate approach is that whereas relations such as HUMAN(x) denote membership in a set, there is no efficient way to denote exclusion except by a proliferation of trivial axioms.

Inferences deriving set memberships are used constantly in everyday life. It is thus desirable to design a computer model of a knowledge base in which such information may be represented naturally and used efficiently.

In the following discussion, we provide a viable alternative to the use of set membership relations in a relational system. The proposed method uses what is termed a *semantic category graph* and avoids the above problems in what we believe is a straightforward and computationally efficient manner.

2.2.   The Semantic Graph

The representation developed for set interrelationships in a relational system is centered around the idea of *semantic categories* (sorts). A semantic category is a *name* given to a collection of *known* elements in the domain. For example, *male* is the semantic category that consists of all males that are listed in the data base. Other examples of categories might be: *senator, judge, bird, animate,* and *city.* In this discussion, the universe of discourse, or domain, will always be a category called *UNIV.* All semantic categories are subsets of the universal category. The names given to categories may be specified arbitrarily to the system, and are simply *syntactic* entities whose only meaning comes from their occurrence in various structures of the system. The semantic graph G_s is defined as follows:

Definition 2.1   A *semantic graph* G_s is a finite graph without cycles whose nodes are semantic categories. The nodes are interconnected by labeled arcs, which specify three set-theoretic relations:

(1)   Category c_i is a *superset* of category c_j, denoted $c_i \supseteq c_j$ iff $x \in c_j \Rightarrow x \in c_i$ for each x in the domain *UNIV.*

(2)   A category c_i *equals* c_j, denoted $c_i = c_j$ iff $c_i \supseteq c_j$ and $c_j \subseteq c_i$.

(3)   A category c_i is *disjoint* from c_j, denoted $c_i \phi c_j$ iff $c_i \cap c_j = \varnothing$, the empty set.

G_s is constrained as follows: Let c be a node of G_s and let $c_1, c_2, \ldots, c_n$ be the set of nodes that are incident to c such that $c \supseteq c_i, i = 1, \ldots, n$. Then c_i is incident to $c_j, i \neq j$, such that $c_i \phi c_j$. This constraint has the effect of forming a *partitioning* for c, defined below.

The terminal nodes of G_s have no superset arcs leaving them (i.e., they have no subsets) and are called *primitive* categories. The root node of G_s has no superset arcs entering it and is a distinguished node called the *universal category* abbreviated *UNIV.*

Figure 1 shows an example of G_s.

Some explanation is needed concerning the equality relation. Two categories are equal (i.e., *synonyms*) if they contain the exact same collection of objects from the domain *UNIV;* i.e., they are different names for the same set of objects. Equality relations are important since they permit the subdivision of a category c in various ways, each of which is called a *partitioning* of c.

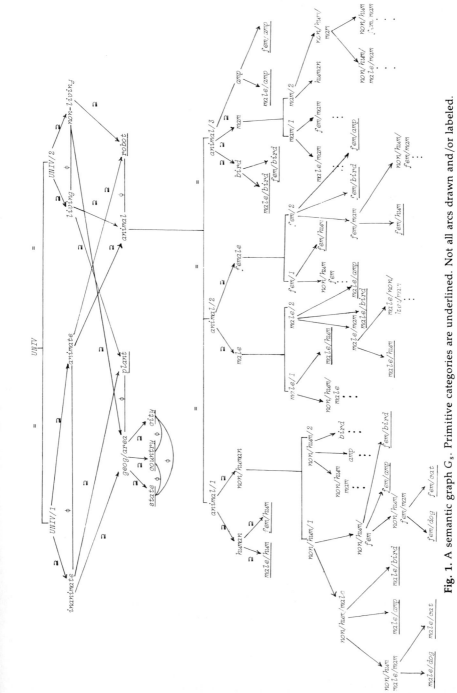

Fig. 1. A semantic graph G_s. Primitive categories are underlined. Not all arcs drawn and/or labeled.

Definition 2.2   A *partitioning* of a semantic category c is a subdivision of c into a finite number of subsets $c_1, c_2, \ldots, c_n$ such that the following two conditions hold true: (1) $\cup_{i=1}^{n} c_i = c$, and (2) $c_i \phi c_j$, for $i \neq j$.

Each partitioning represents a different way to describe category c and is a classification of c along different dimensions. Since the union of the subsets comprising a partitioning equals the original category c, it is intuitive to think of each different partitioning as a different "covering" for c.

For example, in Fig. 1, *animal/1* is the synonym for *animal*, which partitions it into *human* and *non/human*; whereas *animal/2* partitions it into *male* and *female*.

In general, the data base designer has complete freedom in constructing the semantic graph, and may put as much or as little information into the graph as desired. In particular, primitive categories need not be disjoint but may overlap. Since they cannot be expanded into their subsets, this means that it is not possible to identify precisely the elements contained in the overlap. This can lead to difficult problems, which are not discussed here but are treated in McSkimin [1976a,b]

2.3.   Boolean Category Expressions (BCE)

Although semantic categories are useful in their own right, it will often be the case that more complex expressions built up from categories will be needed to represent data base facts and general rules in a notation natural to a user of a relational system. Such expressions are called *Boolean category expressions* (BCE) and are combinations of categories using the operators of intersection ($\cap$), union ($\cup$), and complement ($-$). BCEs greatly increase the expressive power of semantic categories and are used extensively in all phases of the semantic processing algorithms to be described in the following sections. Examples of BCEs are *plant $\cup$ animal* and *senator $\cap$ old*.

Exactly how BCEs and the semantic graph are used will be outlined in this chapter and are discussed more extensively in McSkimin and Minker [1977]. The above discussion was given to familiarize the reader with the basis upon which semantic information is represented in the *semantic network*. A description of how our semantic network relates to other work in this field is given in Section 6.

3.   THE REPRESENTATION OF SEMANTICS— THE SEMANTIC NETWORK

3.1.   Introduction

To implement the semantic techniques specified in the introduction, suitable representations must be chosen for the data base of assertions and general rules, as well as for the necessary semantic information. In answering questions, the theorem prover has access to all such information and any part of it may affect the outcome of the search process. This total available information is termed the *semantic network*. One could also think of it as a world model since it defines the rules for deciding what facts and relations are true or false. In typical theorem-proving systems, this model is largely *implicit* since only syntactic assertions and general rules are provided; information describing the semantics of concepts is still in the mind of the person creating the data base but is missing from the computer model. To answer questions more efficiently by computer, this implicit model is made more explicit in the form of the semantic network.

The *semantic network* comprises four components:

(1)   the *data base* of assertions and general rules;
(2)   the *semantic form space*, which defines the semantics of each argument of n-tuples in the system;
(3)   the *dictionary*, which contains semantic information about predicates, functions, constants, and semantic categories;
(4)   the *semantic graph*, which specifies the set-theoretic relation between each pair of semantic categories in the graph G_s described in Section 2.

All of these components are closely related logically and are closely coordinated during all phases of system operation. Before defining each of the components of the semantic network, extended Π-clause notation is presented. This notation is used throughout the description of the network.

3.2.   Extended Π-Clause Representation

In large data base systems, one generally deals with sets of objects rather than individual objects. Because of this, Fishman [1973a,b] and Fishman and Minker [1975] developed the concept of a Π-clause, which facilitates the representation of sets of first-order predicate calculus clauses as a single Π-clause if they are sufficiently similar in structure. Specifically, a Π-clause $\mathfrak{C} = (T, \Phi)$ consists of two parts: a clause template T, which looks exactly like a first-order clause, (in that it is a disjunction of literals) but it contains no individual constants; and a set Φ of substitution *sets* in which *sets* of constants are substituted for variables of the template. For example, the first-order clauses

$\neg P(f(x, a), g(h(b, c))) \vee Q(a, b, c)$ $\neg P(f(x, l), g(h(b, c))) \vee Q(l, b, c)$
$\neg P(f(x, a), g(h(b, d))) \vee Q(a, b, d)$ $\neg P(f(x, l), g(h(b, d))) \vee Q(l, b, d)$
$\neg P(f(x, a), g(h(b, e))) \vee Q(a, b, e)$ $\neg P(f(x, l), g(h(b, e))) \vee Q(l, b, e)$

can be represented as a single Π-clause as

$$(\neg P(f(x, y), g(h(z, w))) \lor Q(y, z, w), \{\{[a, l]/y, [b]/z, [c, d, e]/w\}\}).$$

The bracket $[c, d, e]$ denotes that any one of the elements in the set consisting of c, d, and e can be substituted for w. Hence, the Π-clause represents six clauses in the first-order predicate calculus. In general, the number of clauses represented by a substitution set is the product of the number of elements in each of the bracketed sets within the substitution set denoted by braces.

An extended Π-clause is a notational variant of the above in which n-ary predicates are represented as $(n + 1)$-tuples in which the first argument is always taken as the predicate. Predicates are now represented as variables in the template T, and the predicate names are listed in the substitution sets of Φ. Thus, given the predicate $R(x, f(a, y), b)$, in Π-notation it is represented as $(R(x, f(z, y), t), \{\{[a]/z, [b]/t\}\})$, while in extended Π-notation it is written as $((\alpha, x, f(z, y), t), \{\{[R]/\alpha, [a]/z, [b]/t\}\})$.

Formal definitions of extended Π-clauses may be found in McSkimin and in Wilson [1976]. Informally, an extended Π-clause $\mathfrak{C}$ consists of an ordered pair: $\mathfrak{C} = (T, \Phi)$, where T is a clause template and Φ a *set* of extended Π-substitution sets φ_i. An extended Π-substitution set φ is a nonempty set of Π-substitution components,

$$\varphi = \{S_0/v_0, S_1/v_1, \ldots, S_m/v_m\},$$

where S_i are sets, and the v_i are variables and referred to as placeholder variables. Sets may be infinite or finite. If v_i is a variable that represents a predicate name in a template, then S_i must be finite.

Extended Π-notation achieves the following objectives. Structurally identical clauses are consolidated, thereby saving memory and permitting axiom schema to be represented. Structurally similar resolvents deduced by similar logical deduction paths in a conventional system are combined into a *single* parallel resolvent. Multiple and alternative queries are answered easily within the deduction mechanism without the need for any external control structure. Axiom schema are handled naturally, and questions such as "Are A and B in the relationship $\alpha(A, B)$, where α is a binary predicate name 'variable'?" may be handled conveniently.

Extended Π-notation is modified further in Section 3.3 to permit semantic information to be represented within clause substitution sets. As will be explained more fully, each variable in a template, each function symbol, and each constant will have a semantic category (sort) associated with it. In the above description of extended Π-notation, and in the first-order predicate calculus, the variables, functions and constants range over one domain, the universal domain. For conciseness, in the remainder of this chapter, we shall refer to extended Π-notation as simply Π-notation.

3.3. Data Base Assertions and General Rules—
Semantic Π-Clause Representation

The first part of the semantic network is the data base. There are two types of data base clauses: *assertions,* which are explicit facts about elements of the domain, and *general rules,* which are clauses that may be used to deduce assertions. Assertions are fully instantiated unit Π-clauses represented using a modification of Π-notation.

To be able to handle *semantic categories,* Π-clause notation has been modified to allow the restriction of argument positions of assertions and of rules to members from an *implicit* set of constants represented as a Boolean category expression. These may be arbitrarily complex Boolean category expressions or simply semantic categories. In standard Π-notation, a variable may only be quantified over an explicit set of constants, or over the entire (implicit) domain. This concept is extended to allow quantification over *subsets* of the domain *UNIV* (the universe of objects); the resulting notation is called Π-σ *clause representation.* By restricting arguments in this way, one may limit the application of a general rule R to those literals of search space clauses that are consistent with semantic preconditions for R; the application of the general rule has thus been made more restrictive. In addition, the expressive power of Π-notation has been increased considerably. This restriction is performed by a *semantic unification algorithm,* which allows the substitution of a semantic term (i.e., a constant, a function, a predicate name, or a Boolean category expression) t, where $t \in BCE_1$ for a variable v restricted by BCE_2 if and only if $BCE_1 \subseteq BCE_2$. Section 4 provides more details of this algorithm.

We now consider how the Π-clause representation has been modified for semantic restrictions. Recall that a Π-clause is of the form

$$\mathfrak{C} = (T, \Phi)$$

where T is the clause template containing only functions and placeholder variables, and Φ is a nonempty set of Π-substitutions $\{\varphi_1, \varphi_2, \ldots, \varphi_n\}$. We shall call the revised notation semantic Π-clause representation (abbreviated Π-σ). No changes are made in the definitions for the template portion given in Section 3.2. However, the definitions for the substitution sets are changed.

Definition 3.1 A Π-σ *substitution component** is an expression of the form $S/v = ([D^E, D^X], D')/v$, where D^E is a possibly empty finite set of constants *explicitly included* in S; D^X is a possibly empty finite set of constants *explicitly excluded* from S; D^X is a possibly empty set of constants represented as a BCE and implicitly included in S; and v is a placeholder.

---

* A Π-σ substitution component can be modified further to include counting information. Such information specifies the number of instances in which a given constant can appear in an n-tuple for the given predicate. (See McSkimin and Minker [1977] for details.)

A $\Pi\text{-}\sigma$ substitution component $([D^E, D^X], D^I)/v$ indicates that v is universally quantified over the set $D^E \cup (D^I \cap -D^X)$. The following conditions hold true:

(1) $D^E \cap D^I = \emptyset$
(2) $D^X \subseteq D^I$

The constants of D^X are distinguished from those of D^E by enclosing them in parentheses.

Example 3.1 Let $D^E = [\text{John, Joe}]$, $D^X = [(\text{Mary})]$, and $D^I = pretty \cap girl$. Then $S = ([\text{John, Joe, (Mary)}], pretty \cap girl)/v$ is a $\Pi\text{-}\sigma$ *substitution component*. That is, S is the set consisting of John, Joe, and all pretty girls except Mary (who, "by convention," must be a *pretty girl*). In addition $[\text{John, Joe}] \cap (pretty \cap girl) = \emptyset$. All explicit constants, whether included or excluded, are contained within square brackets, with excluded constants parenthesized.

The sets D^E, D^X, and D^I are used to represent information concisely in data base clauses. These sets are also used in general rules and queries to inhibit the substitution of constants into arguments of literals unless they are members of the set $D^E \cup (D^I \cap -D^X)$. That is, the expression $S = ([D^E, D^X], D^I)$ is the set of objects in D^E plus those implicitly specified by the Boolean category expression D^I except for those explicitly excluded by D^X.

D^E and D^I must be disjoint in data base clauses. If not, the clause would have redundant information, which makes it difficult to calculate the cardinality of S, needed for detecting when all answers semantically possible for a problem have been found. Likewise, D^X must be totally contained in D^I, and thus $D^X \cap D^E = \emptyset$.

If the disjointness conditions between D^I, D^E, and D^X were not imposed, we would have to establish the degree of overlap between D^E and D^I and only count it once, and in addition, find the degree of overlap between D^X and D^I as well as D^X and D^E so as to subtract the right number. This could be a long and cumbersome process to perform each time a new clause is generated (which occurs every time an inference is formed). This inefficiency may be avoided by checking clauses at input time to determine if they meet the above restrictions. That is, no constant in D^E may be contained in D^I. This is detected by comparing the semantic category of each constant in D^E against D^I, which is done by an algorithm termed CONFLICT (see McSkimin [1976a,b]). The CONFLICT algorithm plays a major role in semantic unification where one must determine whether or not the Boolean category expression of the two entities to be substituted for one another have a nonnull intersection. In the event that a query is rejected, it is possible to isolate the difficulty, and the user can be informed of the problem so that actions may be taken. We do not discuss this aspect here.

Definition 3.2 A Π-σ *substitution* φ is a possibly empty set of Π-σ substitution components:

$$\varphi = \{S_0/v_0, S_1/v_1, \ldots, S_m/v_m\}.$$

We denote the empty Π-σ substitution by ϵ.

Let $\varphi = \{([D^E, D^X], D')_0/v_0, \ldots, ([D^E, D^X], D')_m/v_m\}$. Then φ may be interpreted as all possible combinations of substitutions taking an element from D_i^E or D_i^I, $i = 1, \ldots, m$, MINUS the combinations of excluded substitutions from the excluded sets, D_i^X, $i = 1, \ldots, m$. Π-σ notation is a very compact way to represent information, and condenses many clauses in the first-order predicate calculus into a single clause in Π-σ representation.

Definition 3.3 A Π-σ *set* $\Phi = \{\varphi_1, \varphi_2, \ldots, \varphi_n\}$ is a finite nonempty set of Π-σ set substitutions.

Definition 3.4 A Π-σ *clause* C is a pair (T, Φ), where T is an extended Π-clause template and Φ a Π-σ set, where every predicate placeholder must occur in every Π-σ substitution of Φ. Equivalently, C may be written as $T\Phi$. A Π-σ clause represents n sets of clauses $T\varphi_1, \ldots, T\varphi_n$. A literal L of a Π-σ clause is a Π-σ literal denoted by $L = (L, \Phi)$ where $L \in T$.

Example 3.2 An example of an assertion is as follows:

$((\alpha, x, y), \{\{[\text{LIKE}]/\alpha, (little \cap boys)/x, ([\text{SANTA}], ice\ cream)/y\}\})$.

This may be interpreted to mean: "All little boys like Santa and all types of ice cream."

An example of a general rule is as follows:

$(\neg(\alpha, x, y) \vee (\beta, x, y), \{\{[\text{RESIDE}]/\alpha, [\text{REPRESENT}]/\beta, senator/x, state/y,$
$[\text{RESIDE}]/\alpha, [\text{REPRESENT}]/\beta, representative/x, state/y\}\})$.

This may be interpreted to mean "If x is a senator (representative) and y is a state and x resides in y, then x represents y."

3.4. The Semantic Form Space

An important kind of semantic information is the assignment of semantic category restrictions to arguments of predicates. These restrictions are stored in what is called the *semantic form space*, which is the second part of the semantic network. Obviously, a predicate is not necessarily true for all possible instantiations of its arguments. Rather, there is generally a subclass of objects from which there are some instantiations that may be substituted for each of its arguments that will make the predicate true. This is the purpose of the semantic forms. They explicitly state the name of the subclass from which instantiations may be drawn to make the predicate true, and thus make the semantics of the predicate explicit.

Semantic forms are stored in data structures identical to data base assertions and general rules, and can be retrieved in the same manner by the semantic unification algorithm. It is because of this similarity to data base clauses that semantic forms are stored as "clauses" rather than as part of a dictionary entry. Semantic forms are defined as follows:

Definition 3.5 A semantic form $F = (T, \Phi)$ is a Π-σ clause consisting of two parts: an extended Π-clause template T and a Π-set Φ. T is of the form $L \vee S$, where $L = (v_0, v_1, \ldots, v_m)$ is the *distinguished literal* of F used to determine if a query literal Q conforms with semantic category restrictions specified by Φ, and S is a Π-σ template of *semantic literals* appended to Q to check other relations between arguments of Q during the proof process. Each φ_i is of form

$$\{([F^E, F^X], F^I)_0/v_0, \ldots, 1[F^E, F^X], F^I], F^I)_t/v_t\}, \qquad t \geq m$$

where (as in Definition 3.3) F_0^E is an explicit set of *predicates*, F_0^X an explicit set of excluded predicates, and F_0^I an implicit set of included predicates. F_i^E, F_i^X, and F_i^I, $i \neq 0$, are defined similarly for the other arguments of the form containing sets of constants.

Semantic forms are used to perform semantic well-formedness tests on literals of queries, or data base clauses input by the system user. These tests determine whether the substitution of a predicate, function, constant, or BCE for a placeholder variable of some n-tuple input to the system occurs in a semantically consistent way in combination with other placeholder instantiations. More specifically, if a predicate is explicitly specified in F_0^E, then the placeholders $v_1, v_2, \ldots, v_m$ of the distinguished literal define what objects may be substituted for each argument of the predicate. In the next example, the FATHER relation may only take a male as its first argument in combination with an animal as its second argument.

Example 3.3

$$((\alpha, x_1, x_2) \{\{[FATHER]/\alpha, male/x_1, animal/x_2\}\})$$

i.e., argument 1 of the FATHER predicate must be male and argument 2 must be an animal.

Because semantic forms are similar to data base clauses, the semantic unification algorithm (Section 4) is used for detecting conflicts in query or data base clauses; this algorithm unifies two clauses both of which are in Π-σ notation. In this case, one clause is the query or search space clause and the other "clause" is a semantic form from the semantic net. Although not truly a clause, by placing the form in Π-σ notation, the unification algorithm can be applied nevertheless. A literal of the problem is tested for well-formedness by resolving it with the distinguished literal of a semantic form. If unification with some form F_i is successful, then the particular problem literal unified has constants or predicates substituted for its arguments that are consistent with the semantics stored. Otherwise, the problem is rejected, and the user may be informed of the reason for the rejection. An example of semantic well-formedness testing is presented in Section 5, following the description of the semantic unification algorithm.

There are many tests that can be made in checking well-formedness besides the argument tests using the semantic forms. Some of these tests are deferred to the proof procedure process. However, during the semantic well-formedness test, the conditions needed during the proof procedure process are specified. The additional conditions might demand, for example, that two arguments be equal, or unequal, or that both possess certain properties simultaneously.

The latter checks are specified by the Π-σ template S of semantic literals attached to the semantic form $L \vee S$. When a problem literal Q is resolved with L to check the well-formedness of Q, the unifying substitution is applied to S also. These literals are then appended to the problem and the checks are carried out *during the proof* by data retrieval, inference, or predicate evaluation in parallel with answering the query, instead of during a preprocessing phase. That is, all literals of S must be contradicted for Q to be answered. For more details on well-formedness, see McSkimin [1976a,b].

An example of a semantic form follows:

Example 3.4

$$F = L \vee S = ((\alpha, x, y) \vee \neg(\beta, x, z) \vee \neg(\beta, y, w) \vee \neg(\partial, z, w) \vee (\delta, x, y),$$
$$\{\{[PARENT]/\alpha, \ animal/x, \ animal/y, \ [AGE]/\beta,$$
$$integer/z, \ integer/w, \ [GRT]/\partial, \ [NE]/\delta\}\}).$$

The distinguished literal L is given by (α, x, y) and the remainder are semantic literals. The interpretation is that for individual x to be the parent of y, he/she must be older than y and not equal to y. In the semantic well-formedness test the literal (α, x, y) is resolved away, and the remaining literals, appropriately modified by substitutions are appended to the query. Each semantic literal must be removed by the proof mechanism and hence must be contradicted in the data base. If one of the literals appended is TRUE, the query is not well-formed.

3.5. The Dictionary

The representation of data base assertions and general rules, and the structures to be used for testing the well-formedness of input entries have been described. In addition, it has been shown how the universal domain may be structured to be consistent with the data base and semantic forms. It is now necessary to describe how the semantics of domain elements can be defined.

The primary purpose of the dictionary is to define the semantic categories assigned to constants, function domains and ranges, and predicates. In addition, the dictionary defines the *structure* of the semantic graph G_s. As discussed in Section 2.2, G_s defines how the domain is partitioned into named subsets, level by level. This subdivision of the domain is recorded in dictionary entries for semantic categories and is referenced by algorithms that perform semantic unification and semantic well-formedness tests.

The dictionary therefore contains information on the semantics of Boolean category expressions and semantic categories, constants, predicates, and functions.

3.5.1.   Dictionary Entries for BCEs and Categories

BCE entries contain the following information: the external *string* representation for the BCE/category; the internal representation for the BCE/category used in the BCE processing routines; for semantic category c, a BCE is stored that represents the composition of each of the partitions defined by the synonyms of c as occurring in the semantic graph G_s—these define the various ways in which c may be subdivided; for semantic category c, a BCE is stored that represents a list of those categories that are in the *complement* of c.

The internal form for both the expansion and complement expansion of a category c are BCEs of the form: $\cup_{i=1}^{n} c_i$, where c_i are mutually disjoint categories and are integer indices. These partitions are used to simplify BCEs of clauses given as input to the system and to detect semantic conflicts. They, together with the list of synonyms for a category c, define how c fits into the semantic graph G_s, defined by Definition 2.1 and illustrated by Fig. 1. Thus, each node of G_s is implemented as the dictionary entry for the semantic category labeling the node.

An example of the semantic category entry in a dictionary is given by the following example.

Example 3.5   A Semantic Category Entry (cf. Fig. 1)

external form of semantic category	*"animal"*
internal index for semantic category	*animal*
expansion of semantic category	∪*male female*
complement expansion of semantic category	∪*robot inanimate*
synonyms	*animal/1, animal/2, animal/3*

3.5.2.   Dictionary Entries for Constants and Predicates

To determine whether a constant or predicate k is a member of some arbitrary BCE, it is mandatory that its set membership be specified in advance. That is, the data base designer must specify that k is a member of some semantic category in G_s. As noted in McSkimin [1976a,b], it might be useful to demand that k be a member of a *primitive* category that is either a subset of or disjoint from any other BCE. If this is done, problems of decidability of set membership are avoided. Therefore, for the present time, and to avoid complications, we require that for both predicates and constants, the dictionary entry specifies its primitive category.

Predicates may be considered domain elements much like constants. It is possible to subdivide the domain *UNIV* into what may be classified as "relations" and what may be classified as "objects in the domain." Just as it is possible to create a hierarchy of sets for objects, it is also possible to do so for relations.

Constant and predicate entries contain the external string representation of the entry used in printing Π-σ clauses; the primitive semantic category of which the constant/predicate is a member; and for a predicate entry, the degree of the n-tuple in which it appears. This is shown in the following example.

Example 3.6   Predicate entry in the dictionary

external name	"LIKE"
primitive semantic category	*emotional-relation*
degree	3

All constants or predicates must be defined to the semantic network before attempting to answer a question about one. The rationale for this is that we must be sure that a query containing a constant k is *potentially* answerable. If k does not have a dictionary entry already, then there is no explicit information about k in the semantic model.

Under most circumstances when a constant does not appear in the dictionary, any query containing the constant should be rejected. However, this would be relaxed when it would be unreasonable to create dictionary entries for a large class of constants, such as the integers. In such a case, we may require that each constant be recognized either by its presence in an existing dictionary entry or by a special recognition procedure. Such a procedure would ascertain whether or not an input string were numeric, and if so, place its integer equivalent in the data structure for the input clause directly, rather than by a pointer to a dictionary entry.

3.5.3.   Dictionary Entries for Functions

The last type of dictionary entry to be discussed is the function entry. Functions occur only in the template portion of a clause or semantic form. Nevertheless, like predicates and constants, they must be compatible with the argument position into which they are substituted. Function entries are thus similar to the entries for predicates and constants. They contain the external string name for the function, the semantic category that defines the function range, the number of arguments of the function, and a functional form similar to that stored in the semantic form space for predicates that defines the semantic category of each argument of the function.

Functional forms are defined as follows:

Definition 3.7   A *functional* form is $F = (T_f, \varphi)$ where T_f is a function template of the form $(v_1, v_2, \ldots, v_n)$, where φ is a single substitution set of the form $\{F_1^I/v_1, F_2^I/v_2, \ldots, F_n^I/v_n\}$ for a function f of n arguments.

Unlike predicates whose semantic well-formedness is checked by the semantic unification algorithm [McSkimin, 1976a,b], which unifies clauses against the form in the semantic form space, functions are handled separately using a form in the dictionary. Π-σ unification *does* check to determine if a function may be substituted for a BCE, but checks only the outermost function symbol since it is the one that determines the range of the term. However, for checking the semantic well-formedness of functions in queries and data base clauses at the time of input, it is necessary to check the inner terms of a function also. This is the purpose of functional well-formedness. This recursive procedure scans each function and checks the compatibility of argument instantiations with the semantic forms and either accepts or rejects the term.

A brief word is required about Skölem functions. Let the following be the form to be Skölemized: $\forall x_1, \ldots, x_n \exists x_{n+1} P(x_1, \ldots, x_n, x_{n+1})$. This then becomes $\forall x_1, \ldots, x_n P(x_1, \ldots, x_n, f(x_1, \ldots, x_n))$. The variables $x_1, \ldots, x_n$ in the Skölem function inherit the semantic categories of the variables $x_1, \ldots, x_n$, while the semantic category of the range of the Skölem function is restricted to the semantic category of the variable x_{n+1}. Hence, Skölem functions are restricted to range over semantic categories and do not necessarily range over the entire universe as in the predicate calculus. The range of a Skölem function may vary because it represents an unknown.

3.6.   The Computer Representation for the Semantic Graph

In order to use a semantic graph G_s in an operational system, it is necessary to represent it in such a way that relations between any two categories may be retrieved efficiently so as to conserve time and space. Such relations are needed very frequently during the BCE translation routines and conflict-finding routines. Unfortunately, G_s explicitly stores only superset relations between a category c and the categories that partition it, equality relations, and disjoint relations between categories in the same partitioning. Many more relations (implicitly) exist that may be needed quickly by the above routines. For instance, the superset relation is transitive and many more superset relations exist than are explicitly stored in G_s. Similarly, if category c_i is disjoint from c_j, then c_i is also disjoint from all of the subsets of c_j. Overlap relations must also be derived since they do not occur at all in G_s. Two categories c_i and c_j overlap if superset, subset, disjoint, and equality do not hold but they have some elements in common.

These relations could be derived at run-time by scanning G_s and applying the above rules. This is inadvisable for two reasons: it would take a prohibitive amount of time, and since the relations are fixed once the graph is created, there is no need to keep recomputing the same relations every time they are needed.

Hence, the relations between *all* categories of G_s are derived at system creation, and stored in a special matrix G_m. It is anticipated that in most systems G_m will be small enough to store in core rather than on peripheral device. Even if all relations are computed in advance and stored in G_m, the advantage of doing so could be lost if each retrieval is to a slow (relative to core) peripheral device. If such is the case, it might be faster to rederive the relation between two categories c_i and c_j each time it is needed, even though this process itself could be lengthy.

Naturally, the size of G_m will be a function of the number of categories n. Since such a graph has never been implemented for a realistically large data base, it is hard to estimate a typical size for n and, therefore, the size of G_m. Nevertheless, there are several ways that storage may be saved. Conceptually, G_m is a square matrix of dimension n, where n is the number of categories in the system. However, since the universal category is the superset of every category, these n relations need not be stored. In addition, since all p primitive categories are by convention mutually disjoint, storing their interrelationships is also wasteful as is the storing of the diagonal (since any category equals itself). The largest savings results from the fact that either the relation $M(i, j)$ or $M(j, i)$ is stored but never both. This restriction saves approximately ½ of the space required for an $n \times n$ matrix.

Consequently, G_m has been stored as a *triangular* matrix, as shown in Fig. 2. It is defined formally as follows.

Definition 3.7 Let n be the number of category indices, p the number of primitive categories, and $n - p$ the number of nonprimitive categories. Then G_m is a lower triangular matrix indexed 3, . . . , n and 2, . . . , $n - 1$ such that the triangular section indexed by $n - p + 1$, . . . , n and $n - p + 1$, . . . , $n - 1$ is VOID. The relation between category i and j is contained in

$$\text{element } M(i, j), \text{ if } i > j; \quad \text{else in element } M(j, i).$$

The following relations are stored:

(1) i is the superset of j ($i \supseteq j$),
(2) i is the subset of j ($i \subseteq j$),
(3) i is disjoint from j ($i \phi j$),
(4) i overlaps j ($i \theta j$).

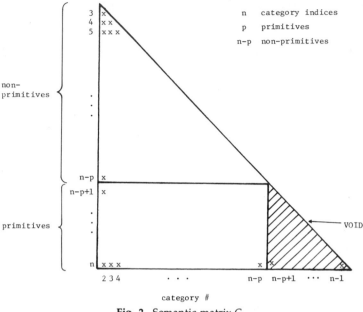

category #

Fig. 2. Semantic matrix G_m.

The universal category *UNIV* is assigned index number 1. If both $i \geq n - p + 1$ and $j \geq n - p + 1$, then $i \, \phi \, j$ holds.

Notice that the equality relation is absent. This is because two categories that are equal have the *identical* set of relations with all other categories and need not be stored twice. Thus, all synonyms of G_s are mapped onto the same index number of G_m.

The void section of G_m is not needed since all relations corresponding to that section are those between primitives, which are mutually disjoint. As a result, significant storage savings may be realized, depending on the number of primitives vs. nonprimitives.

The semantic matrix G_m is the last part of the semantic network to be described. The axioms, dictionary, semantic form space, and graph are all separate pieces of the net, which perform separate functions but which must be closely coordinated in order to perform the many semantic functions of the system developed. Above all, they must be consistent within themselves and among themselves in order for the system to operate smoothly. The responsibility for determining consistency is primarily the system designer's, although some built-in consistency measures exist (e.g., the semantic forms help detect inconsistent data base clauses). Precisely how the semantic network may be used for such consistency checking and other functions is given in McSkimin and Minker [1977].

4. SEMANTIC UNIFICATION

The use of the many-sorted logic and Π-σ notation requires that the unification algorithm developed by Robinson [1965] be modified. Fishman and Minker [1975] have shown how to perform unification when Π-notation is used.

Before presenting the semantic unification algorithm, it will be well to explain the modifications that are necessary. Consider the following templates and attendant substitution sets that are to be matched:

$$(\{P(x_1, x_2, f(x_1, x_2), x_4), P(y_1, y_2, y_3, y_4)\},$$
$$\{\{[a, b, d]/x_1, [d, e]/x_2, male/x_4\},$$
$$\{[a, b, c, e]/y_1, female/y_2, human \cap tall/y_3, human \cap tall/y_4\}\}).$$

To unify the two literals, the template forms must be made to match. In scanning the literals, the placeholders x_1 and y_1 can be substituted for one another provided that the two sets have a nonnull intersection. Since they do ($[a, b, d] \cap [a, b, c, e] = [a, b]$), unification can continue. Now, x_2 and y_2 must be made to match provided that the constants $[d, e] \in female$. Assuming that $[d] \in female$ and $[e] \notin female$, the resultant substitution could replace x_2 and y_2 by z_2, where z_2 is bound to the constant d. To determine the semantic category for d and e, the dictionary entries are accessed. Now, for $f(x_1, x_2)$ to replace y_3, the placeholder y_3 must range over a semantic category. For, if it did not, it would be replaced by an explicit set of constants, and the function $f(x_1, x_2)$ could not be made to match. Since y_3 is a BCE, the range of $f(x_1, x_2)$ must be a subset of the BCE for y_3. Hence, an algorithm is required to analyze $f(x_1, x_2)$ to determine if its range belongs to $human \cap tall$. For x_4 to match y_4, the semantic categories must overlap. Assume that in this case, one finds from the semantic graph that $male \subset human$. This is found by accessing the dictionary entries for $male$, for $human$, and for $tall$, and tracing the semantic graph to determine that $male \subset human$. Hence, the restricted semantic category becomes $male \cap tall$. Thus, the unified literals become,

$$(P(z_1, z_2, f(z_1, z_2), z_4), \{\{[a, b]/z_1, [d]/z_2, male \cap tall/z_4\}\}).$$

In the algorithm that follows, the various cases of matching two placeholder variables, a placeholder variable against a function, and two functions with one another are described. The testing of whether two placeholder variables semantically match is accomplished by the CONFLICT algorithm when one of the placeholder variables contains a BCE.

Because of space limitations, the CONFLICT algorithm will not be given here (see McSkimin [1976a,b]. The basic idea, however, is to find the set-theoretic overlap between two named, symbolic sets C and D, represented as BCEs. The potential advantage of using *symbolic* sets of objects rather than equivalent explicit sets is that the same set-theoretic overlap may be *symbolically* derived by using fewer symbol comparisons than required in performing more traditional explicit set intersections.

For example, if an intersection algorithm were to intersect two *explicit* sets C and D, each of cardinality 5000, the time required could be intolerably long. On the other hand, if C and D could each be represented as single semantic categories, then the entire intersection could be determined in one step if $C \supseteq D$, $C \subseteq D$, or $C \phi D$ since the relations may be easily retrieved from the semantic graph. Only if C and D overlap would C or D be broken down into its subsets so as to identify which are in common with the other category. This is done by retrieving the subset expansion of each category from its respective dictionary entry. Naturally, this is perhaps an oversimplified example, but the point is still valid that in many instances, performing *symbolic* intersections between BCEs will be faster than *explicit* set intersections. (See McSkimin [1976a,b] for details on the implementation of the semantic graph and the CONFLICT algorithm, as well as comparisons between explicit and implicit set intersection algorithms.)

The purpose of this section is to describe how the standard Π-unification algorithm has been modified to perform semantic tests on domain elements. The resulting algorithm is called the Π-σ unification *algorithm*. Perhaps the best way to describe the Π-σ unification process is in terms of nonparallel equivalences of Π-σ clauses. Recall that a Π-σ clause is a concise notation for a set of first-order clauses, some explicitly represented and others implicitly represented using BCEs. The set of nonparallel clauses to which the Π-σ clause $C = (T, \Phi)$ is equivalent is called the *nonparallel equivalence* of C.

It is also possible to talk about the set of equivalent *literal* instances for some Π-σ literal $\mathbf{L} = (L, \Phi)$ such that $L \in T$. This set is called the *nonparallel literal equivalence* of $\mathbf{L}$ and is simply the set of unique nonparallel literal instances resulting from the substitution of explicit or implicit constants from Φ for placeholder variables of L.

Given Π-σ literals $\mathbf{L}_1 = (L_1, \Phi_1)$ and $\mathbf{L}_2 = (L_2, \Phi_2)$ with literal equivalences E_1 and E_2, respectively, then the Π-σ unification algorithm attempts to find the overlap between E_1 and E_2, namely,

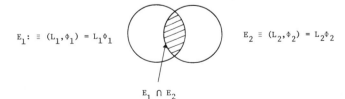

$$E_1: \equiv (L_1, \Phi_1) = L_1 \Phi_1 \qquad\qquad E_2 \equiv (L_2, \Phi_2) = L_2 \Phi_2$$

$$E_1 \cap E_2$$

The overlap instances of $\mathbf{L}_2$. In other words, we are trying to determine which instances of $\mathbf{L}_1$ *match* those of $\mathbf{L}_2$.

The set of matching literals between L_1 and L_2 is determined by the Π-σ unification algorithm, which creates a Π-σ unifier defined as follows:

Definition 4.1 Let Π-σ literal $\mathbf{L}_1 = (L_1, \Phi_1)$ have nonparallel literal equivalence E_1 and $\mathbf{L}_2 = (L_2, \Phi_2)$ have E_2. Then L_1 and L_2 have a Π-σ unifier (σ, Φ) iff the following conditions hold:

(1) $L_1\sigma = L_2\sigma = L$, and
(2) $(L_1\sigma, \Phi) = (L_2\sigma, \Phi) = (L, \Phi) \equiv E_1 \cap E_2$.

The unification algorithm has two basic steps: (1) the unification of the template literals L_1 and L_2, which produces a most general unifier (mgu) σ; and (2) a constructive process of building the Π-σ set Φ. The mgu σ is needed to eliminate any syntactic disagreement between L_1 and L_2 that may arise because of incompatible functions·or unequal variable names.

The process of making the template literals L_1 and L_2 equal is fairly straightforward and is really only first-order unification as described by Chang and Lee [1973]. The resulting most general unifier (mgu) σ between the template literals L_1 and L_2 is a specification of what functions or place-holder variables from L_1 should be substituted for variables of L_2 so as to make L_1 and L_2 identical. This is more precisely stated as follows:

Definition 4.2 Let $\mathbf{L}_1 = (L_1, \Phi_1)$ and $\mathbf{L}_2 = (L_2, \Phi_2)$ be Π-σ literals, where L_1 and L_2 are template literals and Φ_1 and Φ_2 are Π-σ sets. Let σ be the most general unifier for L_1 and L_2 such that $\{L_1, L_2\}\sigma = \{L\}$, a singleton. σ is of the form

$$\{t_1/v_1, t_2/v_2, \ldots, t_n/v_n\}$$

for terms t_i and placeholder variables v_i. Then each t_i/v_i is called a *unification task* of σ.

The application of all unification tasks of σ to L_1 and L_2 is the first step of the Π-σ algorithm. It corresponds to a *syntactic* unification of template literals L_1 and L_2 and does not take into account the sets substituted for placeholder variables in the template literals. Naturally, this must be done in order to find all common literal instances between L_1 and L_2. However, unifying L_1 and L_2 *before* intersecting sets can potentially save a great deal of time since they *must* themselves unify for there to be any common instances.

Each unification task of σ also indicates what sets from Φ_1 and Φ_2 should be intersected to determine the common instances for particular place-holder variables. Each task of σ must be applied to all *potential* substitution set combinations from Φ_1 and Φ_2.

Definition 4.3 Let $\Phi_1 = \{\delta_{11}, \delta_{12}, \ldots, \delta_{1n}\}$ and $\Phi_2 = \{\delta_{21}, \delta_{22}, \ldots, \delta_{2m}\}$. Then the set

$$\Phi = \{\delta_{11} \cup \delta_{21}, \delta_{11} \cup \delta_{22}, \ldots, \delta_{1n} \cup \delta_{2(m-1)}, \delta_{1n} \cup \delta_{2m}$$
$$= \{\varphi_1, \varphi_2, \ldots, \varphi_{mn}\}$$

is the set of *potential* $\Pi\text{-}\sigma$ *substitutions for a* $\Pi\text{-}\sigma$ *unifier involving* Φ_1 and Φ_2.

Since each δ_{1j} represents a set of nonparallel literal instances for L_1 and δ_{2k} similarly for L_2, we must examine all possible interactions of some δ_{1j} with some δ_{2k} and check for matching instances. This matching is done by applying each unification task of σ to each φ_i of Φ.

There are two cases that can occur for task t/v and substitution set φ. The first case is when t is a function and v is a placeholder variable occurring in φ and constrained by a set $S_v = ([S_v^E, S_v^X], S_v^I)$, where S_v^E is a set of explicitly included constants, S_v^X a set of explicitly excluded constants, and S_v^I a set of implicitly included constants. As defined in Definition 4.1, $S_v^E \phi S_v^I$, $S_v^X \subseteq S_v^I$, and $S_v^E \phi S_v^X$. Since t cannot match any explicit constant of S_v^E, S_v^E must be removed from φ. In addition, t must be checked (by calling the CONFLICT algorithm) to see if its function range is within $(S_v^I - S_v^X)$. If so, it matches $(S_v^I - S_v^X)$ and the template substitution was valid; the substitution components S_v^I and S_v^X must be then removed from φ. If a failure occurs, φ must be removed from Φ entirely since no semantically consistent matches exist for φ.

The second case occurs when t is a variable constrained by $S_t = ([S_t^E, S_t^X], S_t^I)$ and v is a variable of φ constrained as before. Applying t/v to φ amounts to finding $S = S_t \cap S_v$, where $S = ([S^E, S^X], S^I)$. S^E consists of the elements in the intersection of S_t^E and S_v^E, *plus* the elements of S_t^E that are in S_v^I but not in S_v^X, *plus* the elements of S_v^E that are in S_t^I but not in S_t^E that CONFLICT is again used to determine set memberships between a constant and a BCE. S^I is formed by calling CONFLICT with S_t^I and S_v^I, which returns $S_t^I \cap S_v^I$. The exclusions to S^I, namely S^X, consist of the elements of S_t^X that are in S_v^I plus the elements of S_v^X that are in S_t^I. Symbolically,

$$S = ([S^E, (S^X)], S^I) = S_v \cap S_t$$

where

$$S^I = S_v^I \cap S_t^I$$
$$S^X = (S_v^X \cup S_t^X) \cap S^I = S_v^X \cap S_t^I \cup S_t^X \cap S_v^I$$
$$S^E = S_v^E \cap S_v^E \cup S_v^E \cap (S_t^I - S_t^X)$$
$$\cup S_t^E \cap (S_v^I - S_v^X)$$

An example follows: Let

$$L_1 = ((\alpha, x, y), \{\{[P, Q]/\alpha, ([a, b, (c)], S_1^I)/x, [e, f]/y\}\})$$
$$= ((\alpha, x, y), \{\{\delta_{11}\}\})$$
$$L_2 = ((\beta, z, w), \{\{[P]/\beta, ([b, c, (f)], S_3^I)/z, ([(a)], S_4^I)/w\},$$
$$\{[Q]/\beta, S_5^I/z, S_6^I/w\}\})$$
$$= ((\beta, z, w), \{\delta_{21}, \delta_{22}\})$$

Assume that

$$a \in S_3^I, \quad \{a, b\} \phi S_5^I, \quad c \phi S_3^I, \quad c \in S_5^I, \quad \{e, f\} \subseteq S_4^I, \quad b \phi S_1^I,$$
$$e \phi S_6^I, \quad f \in S_6^I, \quad c \in S_1^I, \quad f \in S_1^I$$

$S_1^I \cap S_3^I$ is nonnull and $S_1^I \cap S_5^I$ is nonnull.

The steps taken are as follows:

1. The mgu σ between (α, x, y) and (β, z, w) is formed in a very straightforward manner, yielding $\sigma = \{\alpha/\beta, x/z, y/w\}$.

2. The set of potential Π-σ substitution sets is formed:

$$\Phi = \{\delta_1 \cup \delta_{21}, \delta_{11} \cup \delta_{22}\} = \{\varphi_1, \varphi_2\}$$

3. Assume that the unification tasks are processed on a left-to-right basis for simplicity. $\{\alpha/\beta\}$ is selected first.

4. $[P, Q] \cap [P]$ is formed and φ_1 modified to

$$\{[P]/\alpha, ([a, b, (c)], S_1^I)/x, [e, f]/y, ([b, c, (f)], S_3^I)/z, ([a]), S_4^I)/w\}$$

5. Similarly, φ_2 is modified to become

$$\{[Q]/\alpha, ([a, b, (c)], S_1^I)/x, [e, f]/y, S_5^I/z, S_6^I/w\}$$

6. $\{x/z\}$ is selected as the next task and it is applied to φ_1.

7. $S^E \leftarrow [a, b] \cap [b, c] = [b]$
   $S^E \leftarrow [b] \cup ([a, b] \cap S_3^I) = [b] \cup [a] = [a, b]$
   $S^E \leftarrow [a, b] \cup ([b, c] \cap S_1^I \cap - [(c)]) = [a, b] \cup \emptyset = [a, b]$

8. $S^I \leftarrow S_1^I \cap S_3^I$

9. $S^X \leftarrow [(f)]$ since $f \in S_1^I$. c is not part of S^x since $c \phi S_3^I$.

10. φ_1 is modified to

$$\{[P]/\alpha, ([a, b, (f)], S_1^I \cap S_3^I)/x, [e, f]/y, ([(a)], S_4^I)/'\}$$

11. φ_2 is similarly modified to

$$\{[Q]/\alpha, ([(c)], S_1^I \cap S_5^I)/x, [e, f]/y, S_6^I/w\}$$

12. The last task $\{y/w\}$ is selected and is applied to φ_1.

13. $S^E \leftarrow [e, f]$ since $[e, f] \subseteq S_4^I$.

14. $S^I \leftarrow \emptyset$ since no BCE occurs in δ_{11}.

15. $S^X \leftarrow \emptyset$ since $S^I = \emptyset$.

16. φ_1 is modified to

$$\{[P]/\alpha, ([a, b, (f)], S_1^I \cap S_3^I)/x, [e, f]/y\}$$

17. φ_2 is also modified to:

$$\{[Q]/\alpha, ([(c)], S_1^I \cap S_5^I)/x, [f]/y\}$$

The Π-σ unifier (σ, Φ) is thus

$$\sigma = \{\alpha/\beta, x/z, y/w\} \qquad \Phi = \{\varphi_1, \varphi_2\}$$

5. AN ILLUSTRATIVE EXAMPLE

5.1. Semantic Resolution

We now provide a brief example to illustrate the use of the semantic network in the deductive process. Consider the example in Fig. 3, taken from Moore, [1975b]. It consists of three boxes one on top of the other. The color of the top box is green and the color of the bottom box is blue. The color of the intermediate box is not specified. The facts also specify which boxes are on top of which other boxes and one general axiom that states that if a box is green, then it is not blue. The problem is to find if there is a box on top of another box such that the top box is green and the bottom box is not green.

Moore [1975b] discusses how a problem-solving system might handle the question. We note from Fig. 3 that a theorem-proving system with an-

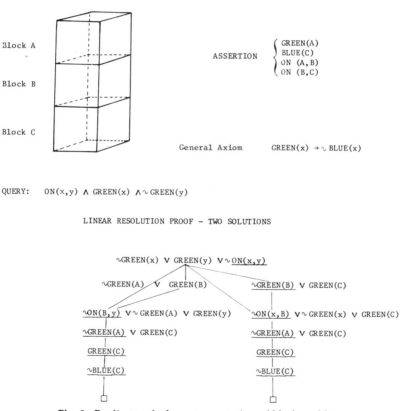

Fig. 3. Predicate calculus representation of block problem.

DICTIONARY

ASSERTIONS

$((\alpha,x,y),\ \{\{[ON]/\alpha,\ [A]/x,\ [B]/y\}\})$

$((\alpha,x,y),\ \{\{[ON]/\alpha,\ [B]/x,\ [C]/y\}\})$

A --- green
B --- color
C --- blue
color = blue U green

QUERY $((\beta,y,v),\ \{\{[ON]/\beta,\ (green)/u,\ (color \cap -green)/v\}\})$

PROOF - LINEAR RESOLUTION

$\sim((\beta,u,v),\ \{\{[ON]/\beta,\ (green)/u,\ (color \cap -green)/v\}\})$

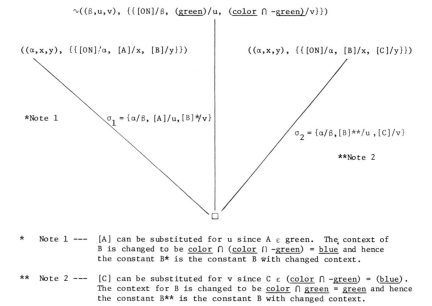

$((\alpha,x,y),\ \{\{[ON]/\alpha,\ [A]/x,\ [B]/y\}\})$

$((\alpha,x,y),\ \{\{[ON]/\alpha,\ [B]/x,\ [C]/y\}\})$

*Note 1

$\sigma_1 = \{\alpha/\beta,\ [A]/u, [B]\text{*}/v\}$

$\sigma_2 = \{\alpha/\beta, [B]\text{**}/u, [C]/v\}$

**Note 2

*   Note 1 ---   [A] can be substituted for u since A ε green. The context of
                    B is changed to be color ∩ (color ∩ -green) = blue and hence
                    the constant B* is the constant B with changed context.

**   Note 2 ---   [C] can be substituted for v since C ε (color ∩ -green) = (blue).
                    The context for B is changed to be color ∩ green = green and hence
                    the constant B** is the constant B with changed context.

Fig. 4. Π-σ representation of block problem.

cestry resolution would easily handle the problem. In particular, the example uses linear resolution [Loveland, 1968; Luckham, 1968] and uses ancestry resolution in the proof. Loveland and Stickel [1973] have discussed
the general implications of ancestry resolution in connection with a generalization of problem reduction representations.

In Fig. 4, a proof is provided using the methods described in this
chapter. Only one assertion is necessary, that of relating that A is on B,
and B is on C. The dictionary entries for A, B, and C are green, *color* (a set),
and blue, respectively. Since B does not belong to a primitive category, it

is treated as if it is a Skölem constant, and hence its semantic category can be modified during a proof. The set *color* = blue ∪ green. The query then requests whether there is an *x* on top of *y*, where *x* must be green, and *y* is in the set *color* ∩-*green*. Two solutions are found, one in which B is set to blue, and one in which B is set to green. As may be seen from Fig. 4, two answers are derived in different contexts. The first solution applies for A on B, and the second for B on C. If the set of all answers binding B to a particular context is considered, B = blue ∪ green. Hence, B ∈ *color* satisfies the query. Thus, a solution was found in one step, in contrast to the six steps of linear resolution, and the method proposed by Moore. The example illustrates the use of the semantic unification algorithm to restrict the context of a constant specified by a semantic category.

5.2. Semantic Well-Formedness Test and Inputs

The semantic form space serves to reject ill-formed problems to be solved. Such inputs are generally difficult to detect in conventional predicate calculus systems. Consider the semantic forms:

$$((\alpha, x, y)\{\{[FATHER]/\alpha, male/x,animal/y\}\})$$
$$((\beta, x, y)\{\{[MOTHER]/\beta, female/x,animal/y\}\})$$

The forms define permissible arguments for FATHER and MOTHER. Their purpose is merely to test inputs. We shall assume that the forms are unit clauses.

Consider the problem: "Does there exist an individual who is the father of an individual a, and the mother of another individual b?" Upon placing the negated question in clause form, a proof is attempted using *only* the query and the semantic form space. Input proofs are sufficient for this process. As may be seen from Fig. 5, a proof can be formed since the variable *u* is first bound to the set *female*. Upon attempting to unify the resul-

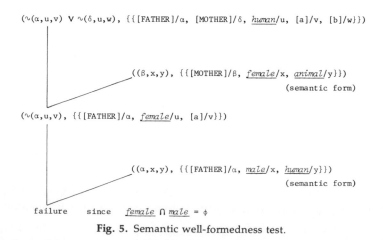

Fig. 5. Semantic well-formedness test.

tant clause against the father template, we find that *female* ∩ *male* = ϕ from the semantic graph, and there can be no proof. Hence, the question is rejected, and the user can be informed of the reason for the lack of a possible proof.

5.3. Filtering of Semantically Irrelevant Data Base Assertions and Axioms

One problem that often occurs when a query is answered in a system without sorts is that the search space is exhausted and/or the retrieval takes an unacceptably large number of peripheral accesses; both result in a disenchanted user. This is specially true for compound queries that have several parts, each of which must be satisfied before an answer is found for the entire query. What often happens is that many assertions that satisfy subquery Q_i are carried along by the search mechanism for several deduction steps only to be rejected at a later time because they do not satisfy some Q_j.

The system proposed herein uses semantic categories to restrict the arguments of queries so that the *very first* time an assertion is retrieved, it is passed through a "semantic filter" and rejected if incompatible. This has the effect of reducing I/O and storage utilization.

As an example, consider the following query in Π-σ representation:

$$(\neg(\alpha, x, y) \vee \neg(\beta, x, z)\{\{[\text{REPRESENT}]/\alpha, senator/x, [\text{NJ}]/y,$$
$$[\text{PHILOSOPHY}]/\beta, [\text{liberal}]/z\}\})$$

that is, "Who are the liberal senators from N.J."?

Assume that the following assertion is in the database:

$((\alpha, x, y),$ {[REPRESENT]/α, [Case, Williams, Patten, . . . , Meyner] ⊆ *representative*. Then the Π-σ unification algorithm would prevent the constants in [Patten, . . . , Meyer] from passing through the *senator* "filter" and be used in the rest of the deduction. This is because from the semantic graph G_m, it would be found that *representative* ∩ *senator* = ∅. This example illustrates perhaps the most significant use of the semantic network described in Section 3.

Although the above illustrates the use of semantic filtering for data assertions, the same considerations apply to general axioms.

6. RELATED WORK IN SEMANTIC NETWORKS

Semantic networks were introduced in the literature by Quillian [1968] as a means of modeling how semantic information is organized within a person's memory. A common definition of a semantic network is that it is a directed graph whose nodes represent individuals and whose arcs represent relationships between individuals [Deliyanni and Kowalski, 1978;

Shapiro-1977; Schubert, 1976; Woods, 1975]. An arc in such a graph is labeled by the name of the relation it represents. When viewed as a graph, they aid in the formulation, exposition, and visualization of the computer data structures they represent.

Schubert [1976] notes that semantic networks, "are variously thought of as diagrams on paper, as abstract sets of n-tuples of some sort, as data structures in computers or even as information structures in brains."

The above specification of semantic networks is restricted and cannot handle general statements, such as "if an object is animate, then the object is either a vegetable or an animal." Deliyanni and Kowalski [1968] have termed such semantic networks to be *simple semantic networks*.

A number of authors have defined extensions of simple semantic networks based on predicate logic (see, e.g., Hendrix, [1975] and Schubert [1976]. These extensions generally avoid extensional quantifiers by introducing functions. Fikes and Hendrix [1977] use a partitioned semantic network to combine the expensive capabilities of first-order logic with linkage to procedural knowledge and with full indexing of objects to the relationships in which they participate. Simmons and Chester [1977] have also devised a quantified predicate notation for semantic networks and an algorithm that uses the network for finding and distinguishing the meanings that are encoded.

The initial use of semantic networks, and a continuing one, has been for modeling human memory and for disambiguating and understanding natural language. Woods [1975] has analyzed semantic networks as they relate to the representation of natural language meanings, and has also noted some of the inadequacies of simple semantic networks. His primary concern is with understanding the semantics of the semantic network structures themselves.

The need to extend semantic networks to contain quantified information was perhaps proposed first by Shapiro [1971a,b]. Kay [1973] used an alternative representation to the one proposed by Shapiro. More recently, Deliyanni and Kowalski [1978] have defined an *extended semantic network* to consist of binary relations in which terms are represented as nodes. They use the clausal form of logic and show how general axioms in the form of clauses may be represented in such a network. A semantic network may then be viewed as a syntactic form of the clausal form of logic. Because of this relationship with logic, the extended semantic network is provided with a precise semantics, inference rules, and a procedural interpretation. Shapiro [1977] also uses a clausal type form to depict general rules that may be used in deductive searching.

The work described in this chapter bears many similarities to the work of Fikes and Hendrix [1977], Deliyanni and Kowalski [1978], and Shapiro [1977]. As with these efforts, and the one by Simmons and Chester [1977], we are concerned with deductive search and semantic networks in contrast to natural language. Instead of considering binary relations, we use

n-ary relations. In contrast to Kowalski, we use a sorted first-order logic to restrict arguments of variables. The semantic network consists of the n-ary relations and clauses where each variable in a clause belongs to a particular sort. The semantic graph is an integral part of the semantic network since it provides a means for handling information about what is commonly referred to as IS-A relations, such as "a male *is a* human." Part relationships, such as "a finger is a part of a male," are represented in the clausal form. As noted in Section 3.6, the semantic graph is effectively compiled in our system so that transitive IS-A relations can be retrieved efficiently without extensive searching. Fikes and Hendrix [1977] and Shapiro [1977] also consider variables to belong to particular sorts. The semantic form space is also considered as a part of the network and serves the purpose of providing integrity checks on the input data and queries. The extended Π-σ notation groups common relationships together. Thus, if one had the following information, where P, H, and W represent, respectively, parent, husband, and wife,

$$
\begin{array}{llll}
P(a_1, b_1) & P(a_2, b_1) & H(a_1, a_2) & W(b_4, c_4) \\
P(a_1, b_2) & P(a_2, b_2) & H(b_1, c_1) & \\
P(a_1, b_3) & P(a_2, b_3) & H(b_2, c_2) & \\
P(a_1, b_4) & P(a_2, b_4) & W(b_3, c_3) &
\end{array}
$$

the semantic graph could be depicted as

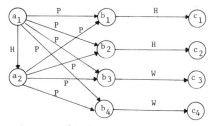

If Π-σ notation is used, one obtains

$$((P(x, y), \{\{[a_1, a_2]/x, [b_1, b_2, b_3, b_4]/y\}\})$$
$$(H(x, y), \{\{[a_1]/x, [a_2]/y\}, \{[b_1]/x, [c_1]/y\}, \{[b_2]/x, [c_2]/y\},$$
$$\{[b_3]/x, [c_3]/y\}, \{[b_4]/x, [c_4]/y\}\}).$$

The semantic graph would become:

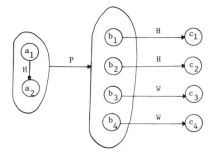

The semantic graph using the concept of Π-σ notation effectively collapses the graph by placing nodes together in a set.

7. SUMMARY

The primary purpose of this chapter has been to describe the elements that comprise the semantic network and to describe, briefly, its use in a deductive system. In Sections 5.1–5.3, we illustrated several uses of the semantic network. Another use, that of knowing when all solutions of a problem have been found, is described in detail in McSkimin and Minker [1977].

The following summarizes the major features of the semantic network.

(1) Set membership properties are represented as semantic categories rather than as unary relations and represent set membership. Semantic categories are incorporated into a semantic graph G_s. The semantic graph allows the domain D to be subdivided into a hierarchy of relationships.

(2) Π-σ representation has been introduced. It extends the Π-clause representation of Fishman and Minker and allows arguments of predicates and functions to be restricted to *Boolean category expressions* (BCEs). A BCE permits Boolean combinations of *semantic categories*. The representation allows economy of storage and permits many predicates to be retrieved in parallel.

(3) A *semantic form space* has been introduced. It permits the user to express semantic constraints on the arguments of predicates. Since entries in the semantic form space have the same form as assertions or general axioms, the same algorithms that apply to clauses may be used to apply to semantic forms. The major use of semantic forms is to check whether queries and data base clauses are incompatible relative to the world model. If such entries appear, rather than to process them, as would be done in a strictly first-order predicate calculus approach, they are rejected from consideration.

(4) Π-σ unification, an extension of the Fishman–Minker algorithm (which is an extension of the Robinson [1965] unification algorithm) has been developed to unify two Π-clauses that contain implicit constraints as well as explicit constants. Details may be found in McSkimin [1976a,b].

The primary use of the semantic network is to narrow the search space in a deductive search. We have shown how one may supply domain-dependent information and store it in a type of semantic network. Assertions and general rules are part of the semantic network and have been implemented as a form of predicate calculus statements. The semantic network and the algorithm for performing semantic well-formedness tests, operator selection, and semantic actions, all form a coherent system within the framework of the predicate calculus. Other semantic information may also be introduced into the search process to control the search space. This topic, however, has not been discussed here.

As of the writing of this chapter, a system termed MRPPS 3.0 has been implemented at the University of Maryland, which incorporates a semantic network. Experiments are currently in progress to determine its effectiveness. A more comprehensive description of how the semantic network is used is contained in McSkimin and Minker [1977]. We believe that techniques such as have been described here will be very useful for the development of operational deductive question-answering, and problem-solving systems.

ACKNOWLEDGMENTS

The authors wish to express their appreciation to the National Science Foundation, NSF GJ 43632, for providing the support to the University of Maryland that made this work possible. We would also like to express our appreciation to Dr. Gerald Wilson and Mr. Guy Zanon for their many suggestions concerning the semantic network.

REFERENCES

[Chang, C. L., and Lee, R. C. T., 1973]. *Symbolic Logic and Mechanical Theorem Proving.* Academic Press, New York.

[Deliyanni, A., and Kowalski, R. A., 1978]. Logic and semantic networks. *Preprints Workshop & Logic and Data Bases, Touloose, France, Nov. 16–18, 1977, XII*, pp. 1–31.

[Fikes, R., and Hendrix, G. G., 1977]. A network-based knowledge representation and its natural deduction system. *Proceedings of the 5th International Joint Conference on Artificial Intelligence, 1977* pp. 235–246.

[Fishman, D. H., 1973a]. *Experiments with a resolution-based deductive question-answering system and a proposed clause representation for parallel search.* PhD. dissertation, Department of Computer Science, University of Maryland, College Park.

[Fishman, D. H., 1973b]. Technical Report TR-280. Department of Computer Science, University of Maryland, College Park. (This is identical to Fishman [1973a].)

[Fishman, D. H., and Minker J., 1975]. Π-representation—a clause representation for parallel search. *Artificial Intelligence* **6**, 103–127.

[Hendrix, G. G., 1975]. Expanding the utility of semantic networks through partitioning. *Advance Papers of the 4th International Joint Conference on Artificial Intelligence, 1975* pp. 115–121.

[Kay, M., 1973]. The MIND system. In *Natural Language Processing.* R. Austin (ed.). Algorithmics Press, New York, pp. 155–188.

[Loveland, D. W., 1968]. A linear format for resolution. *IRIA Symposium on Automatic Demonstration, 1968* pp. 147–162. Springer-Verlag, Berlin and New York.

[Loveland, D. W. and Stickel, M. E., 1973]. A hole in goal trees: Some guidance from resolution theory. *Proceeding of the 3rd International Joint Conference on Artificial Intelligence, 1973,* pp. 153–161.

[Luckham, D., 1968]. Refinement theorems in resolution theory. *IRIA Symposium on Automatic Demonstration, 1968* pp. 163–190. Springer-Verlag, Berlin and New York.

[McDermott, D., 1975]. Symbol mapping: A technical problem in PLANNER-like systems. *ACM Sigart Newsletter* **51**, 4–5.

[McSkimin, J., 1976a]. *The use of semantic information in deductive question-answering systems.*

Ph.D. dissertation, Department of Computer Science, University of Maryland. College Park.

[McSkimin, J., 1976b], Technical Report TR-465. Department of Computer Science, University of Maryland, College Park. (This is identical to McSkimin [1976a].)

[McSkimin, J., and Minker J., 1977]. The Use of a Semantic Network in a Deductive Question-Answering System," Technical Report TR-506. Department of Computer Science, University of Maryland, College Park.

[Moore, R. C., 1975a]. A serial scheme for the inheritance of properties. *ACM Sigart Newsletter* **53**, 8–9.

[Moore, R. C., 1975b]. "Reasoning from Incomplete Knowledge in a Procedural Deduction System," Report TR-347. Artificial Intelligence Laboratory, MIT Cambridge, Massachusetts.

[Quillian, M. R., 1968]. Semantic memory. In *Semantic Information Processing*. M. Minsky (ed.). MIT Press, Cambridge, Massachusetts, pp. 227–270.

[Quillian, M. R., 1969]. The teachable language comprehender: A simulation program and theory of language. *Communications of the ACM* **12**, pp. 459–476.

[Robinson, J. A., 1965]. A machine oriented logic based on the resolution principle. *Journal of the ACM*, **12**, 25–41.

[Rumelhart, D. E., Lindsay, P. H., and Norman, D. A., 1972]. A process model for long-term memory. In *Organization of Memory*. E. Tulving and W. Donaldson (eds.). Academic Press, New York.

[Schubert, L. K., 1976]. Extending the expressive power of semantic networks. *Artificial Intelligence* **7**, 163–198.

[Shapiro, S. C., 1971a]. The MIND System: A Data Structure for Semantic Information Processing," R-837-PR. The Rand Corporation, Santa Monica, California.

[Shapiro, S. C., 1971b]. A net structure for semantic information storage, deduction and retrieval. *Proceedings of the 2nd International Joint Conference on Artificial Intelligence, 1971* pp. 512–523.

[Shapiro, S. C., 1977]. Representing and locating deduction rules in a semantic network. *ACM SIGART Newsletter* **63**, 14–18.

[Simmons, R. F., 1972]. Some semantic structures for representing English meanings. In *Language Comprehension and the Acquisition of Knowledge*. R. Freedle and J. Carroll (eds.). Wiley, New York, pp. 71–79.

[Simmons, R. F., and Chester, D., 1977]. Inferences in quantified semantic networks. *Proceedings of the 5th International Joint Conference on Artificial Intelligence, 1977* pp. 267–273.

[Wilson, G., 1976a]. *A description and analysis of the PAR technique-an approach for parallel inference and parallel search in problem-solving systems*. Ph.D. thesis, University of Maryland, College Park.

[Wilson, G., 1976b]. Technical Report TR-464. Department of Computer Science, University of Maryland, College Park. (This is identical to Wilson [1976a].)

[Winograd, T. A., 1971]. Procedures as representation for data in a computer program for understanding natural language Ph.D. thesis, MIT, Cambridge, Massachusetts.

[Woods, W. A., 1975]. What's in a link? Foundations for semantic networks. In *Representation and Understanding*. D. G. Bobrow, and A. M. Collins, (eds.). Academic Press, New York, pp. 35–82.

MAKING PREFERENCES MORE ACTIVE*

Yorick Wilks

ABSTRACT

The paper discusses the incorporation of richer semantic structures into the preference semantics system. They are called *pseudotexts* and capture something of the information expressed in one type of *frame* proposed by Minsky. However, they are in a format, and subject to rules of inference, consistent with earlier accounts of this system of language analysis and understanding. Their use is discussed in connection with the phenomenon of *extended use:* sentences where the semantic preferences are broken. It is argued that such situations are the norm and not the exception in normal language use, and that a language understanding system must give some *general* treatment of them. A notion of *sense projection* is proposed, leading on to an alteration of semantic formulas (word sense representations) in the face of unexpected context by drawing information from the pseudotexts. A possible implementation is described, based on a new semantic parser for the preference semantics system, which would cope with extended use by the methods suggested and answer questions *about the process of analysis itself.* It is argued that this would be a good context in which to place a language understander (rather than that of question-answering about a limited area of the real world, as is usual) and, moreover, that the sense projection mechanisms suggested would provide a test bed on which the usefulness of frames for language understanding could be realistically assessed.

INTRODUCTION

This paper is intended to suggest how we might deal with *extensions of word-sense* in a language understanding system, one manipulating rich structures of meaning and knowledge, and do so in a general and systematic manner. But two preliminary points must be dealt with immediately. First, what I shall call new, or extended, use is the *norm* in ordinary language use and so cannot be relegated to some mode of special, but dispensible, treatment. Second, simply to *accept* extended uses, in the way I have shown that the preference semantics system does [Wilks, 1975a], is not sufficient, and we must seek ways to *interpret* those uses in an active manner.

Suppose we look at some perfectly ordinary sentence of newspaper text chosen, I promise you, at random:

*This chapter is reprinted with kind permission from *Artificial Intelligence* **11** (1978), 197–223, copyright North–Holland Publishing Co., Amsterdam, 1978.

239

(1)   Mr. Wilson said that the *line taken* by the Shadow Cabinet, that a Scottish Assembly should be *given no executive powers,* would *lead to the break up of the United Kingdom.* (Emphasis added.)

The Times: February 5, 1976

The sentence presents no problem whatever to the normal reader with a general grasp of British politics, and yet, if we start from the point of view of "selection restrictions" [Katz and Fodor, 1963] we notice that, at no less than four (underlined) places in a perfectly straightforward sentence, they are broken. That is to say, anyone setting out to write down the selection restrictions for the objects of the verb "take" would not want to write then in such a way that lines could be said to be taken, and so on for the other three actions in the sentence.

My first preliminary point is that, whether or not we want to call such usage "metaphorical," it is the *norm* in ordinary everyday language use, and cannot be relegated to the realm of the exceptional, or the odd, and so dealt with by considerations of "performance" in the sense of Chomsky [1965]. On the contrary it is, I shall argue, central to our language capabilities, and any theory of language must have something concrete to say about it. Even if the newspaper usages above are "extended," I would suggest that anyone who could not grasp these extensions could not be said to understand English properly (given adequate knowledge *from which* to extend, and we shall come to that later).

No claims are being made here about the murky matter of language *learning* beyond saying that, given some grasp of word-senses and some knowledge representation, a language understanding system should have mechanisms for extending that repertory of senses in a systematic way, and this is a much weaker claim than any general one about language learning as such. For it is only a claim about how to extend the language *from some given starting point.*

An additional argument for some such facility, as a glance at any dictionary shows, is that yesterday's extended use is today's normal sense of a word; in other words, sense-extension is part of the fundamental process underlying language development, and a natural language cannot be contained within a fixed repertory of senses, in the way that a logical language can, and this is a fundamental point of difference between the two.

My second preliminary point concerns the difference between *acceptance and interpretation* of extended use. In previous papers describing a programmed system of natural language understanding (e.g., Wilks [1975b]), I have described how rules operate on semantic descriptions of word-senses so as to build up text descriptions. The rules for inserting the word-sense descriptions are what I have described as "preferential," in that they seek preferred entities but will *accept* those that do not satisfy the preferences. For example, the action of drinking can be said to prefer an animate agent and so will correctly select as a the agent of

(2)   The adder drank from the pool

the snake and not the machine. However, in the case of

(3)   My car drinks gasoline

none of the senses available for "car" are animate, and so the system simply accepts what it is given. I contrasted this approach with that of selection restrictions, not so much as regards the content of the restriction (to animate in this case), nor as to the form of its coding, but as regards the form of the rule that operates on the restriction. I described a form of rule that would both make the discrimination required for (2) and accept (3), while the "selection restrictions" approach was specifically intended to *reject* (3).

However, it is clear that simply accepting the car as the agent of (3) is not enough, as far as "understanding the utterance" goes, which we may take as implying at least some of the structure derived for interpreting *later* stretches of text. In Wilks [1968], I described a feature of an early LISP program in which the system did make an attempt to interpret "preference-breaking" utterances like (3): by finding a coded sense for some *other* word (in the same text) that *did* satisfy the preference under examination, and substituting that for the sense that did not fit. In that way the sense repertory of the nonfitting word (such as "car" in (3)) was extended by one new sense representation. However, that heuristic depended very much on the semantically dense structure of the particular texts under examination, and was almost certainly not of any general application. So, for example, in a text containing (3) there is no reason to believe that there would be another (animative) drinker mentioned in the same text, such that "car" could plausibly be said to be being used to mean that animate drinker. We could easily construct texts to which such a heuristic *would* apply, viz.,

(4) Smith took the chair at the Board Meeting. Jones came in late, acknowledged *the chair* and crept to his seat.

Here, the underlined phrase is used to indicate Smith, who *would* in this example be an appropriate type of object for the action "acknowledge." Nonetheless, there is no reason to believe that such a heuristic would be much use in dealing with everyday language like (1).

Clearly something more is required. Let us return to (3) briefly and ask what an intelligent program might be expected to make of it. First, it should see that nonanimate entities may be said to drink, and be prepared to revise its agent preference accordingly in the future. Second, and more importantly, it should notice that cars can be said to drink *in virtue of something already known about cars,* namely, that they have a fluid (gasoline) injected into them in order to make them run. That is to say, the program should have access to a sufficiently rich knowledge structure for "car," and be able to notice that cars stand in a consumption relation to a particular fluid, that is of the same semantic structure (in the sense of that phrase yet to be defined) as the relation in which a drinker normally stands to a liquid to be drunk. All this may sound obvious, but it must surely be that on that similarity the successful metaphorical force of (3) rests.

It will also come as no surprise to those acquainted with recent artificial intelligence (AI) literature to know that the knowledge structures proposed will be within the recent paradigm by Minsky for larger knowledge structures that are normally called "frames" [Minsky, 1975]. However, the detailed structures to be proposed here are consistent with previous accounts of the preference semantics system (see Wilks [1976]).

A final point to be noted about (3) is that its normal force in English is to suggest not only that the car consumes gasoline but also that it consumes *a great deal* of it. We might distinguish that element in the interpretation as the *idiomatic* element, in that there is no way in which a reasoned basis could be established for deducing it. Like any idiom, it would have to be dealt with by crude listing of forms, just as we have to *learn* idioms in a foreign language simply because there is no way we could deduce them unless, by chance, they happen to match our own.

The next section is simply to recap the programmed form of the preference semantics system. A reader who is familiar with it should proceed directly to the following section, which is the nub of the present paper.

1. A BRIEF RECAP OF THE PROCESSES OF THE PREFERENCE SEMANTICS SYSTEM

The purpose of these general processes is to construct a unique semantic representation for a text. This representation, a *semantic block,* will consist of *template* structures tied together with various case, anaphora, and inference ties. Each template structure corresponds to a phrase or clause of the surface text and expresses its gist. A template consists of a network of *formulas* that represent word senses. Every structure in the system consists, directly or indirectly, of *semantic primitives* (drawn from a vocabulary of one hundred). In order to construct a unique semantic block for a text, that system may have had to make explicit semantic information not present in the surface text. This is done (see below) by inferring template-like objects (extractions) and adding them to the semantic block, even though they do not correspond to any surface clause in the text. This "deepening" of the representation is only done if necessary for the isolation of a unique representation.

The system assumes that every English *word-sense* in the dictionary has had a *formula* associated with it that expresses its meaning. Formulas are trees of semantic primitives. They consist, at the top level, of *case subfor-*

mulas. All dependency, within subformulas, and *of* subformulas on others, is left-on-right, with the result that the right-most primitive—the *head* of the formula—becomes its principal category. Here are two *action* formulas for two senses of the English "grasp," having heads THINK and SENSE, respectively:

(5)

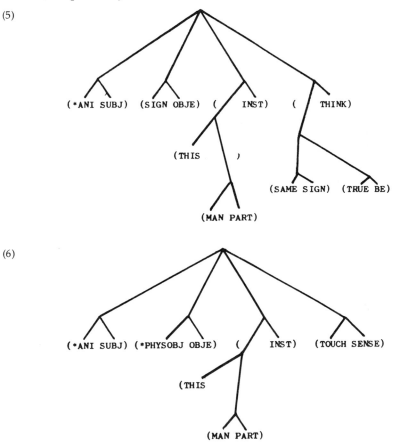

(6)

Primitives like *ANI (animate) indicate with the asterisk that they are equivalent to a *class* of other primitives. The above formulas can be loosely explicated as follows (a full syntax of formulas is given in Wilks [1977b]):

(5)   implies that grasping is a THINKing action, that the SAME SIGN is TRUE, an action preferably done by an ANImate agent to a SIGN (the same sign as earlier) OBJect, and with an INSTrument that is a particular PART of a MAN (human, i.e., the brain or mind).

(6)   implies that grasping is a SENSing action, TOUCH sensing, preferably done by an ANImate agent, and to a PHYSical OBJect, and again by an INSTrument that is a particular PART of a MAN (the hand this time).

Templates are the initial, shallow, semantic representations attached to clause or phrase-length fragments of text. They are networks of formulas consisting of at least an agent formula, an action formula, and an object formula, where other formulas may depend on each of those three, and any one of the three may be only a dummy in any particular example.

In what follows, square brackets enclosing English words will stand as shorthand for the above semantic formula trees and the template networks of them. Thus, [John] will indicate the formula for "John," and

(7)   [John grasped the+idea]

will indicate the template (of three formulas) for "John grasped the idea."

The process that constructs the templates is the first operation of "preference" in the system: the formulas function as active objects, each seeking to specify what its *neighboring* formulas in a template shall be. Thus the preference expressed by (5) for a SIGN (i.e., symbolic) object is satisfied if (5) goes at the central (action) node of (7), but *not* if (6) goes there. The principle of preference is that the template structure is assigned to a fragment in which *the most such preferences are satisfied*. By this method, "grasp" is correctly resolved in (7) to (5), not (6). However, preference-breaking templates are set up if there is no formula available to satisfy them.

Templates are then tied together by *paraplates*. These are structures, of no direct relevance to this paper (see Wilks [1975b] for details), with the form of an inference rule connecting two template skeletons. If the skeletons match two templates—one for a main clause, the other for a prepositional phrase—then whatever case name is attached to the inference arrow is the name of the case tie between the two templates in the semantic representation. Thus, the second phrase of

"John grasped the idea in the lecture"

would be tied to the first by a paraplate with a TLOCA (time location) inference arrow. But note that the paraplate is only a structure *by means of which* this case tie is assigned (and the ambiguity of "in" is resolved); it does not itself become part of the representation.

Pronoun ties, assigned on similar principles, complete this *basic mode* of the system. If a unique semantic block can be constructed in this way then that representation suffices, but in many cases it cannot and the representation must be *deepened*. For this, the system shifts to the *extended mode*. First, as many templates as possible are *repacked*, which means filling in their dummies by inference. So in the second template for

"John drank the whiskey from a glass,"

the dummy agent—prepositional phrase templates always have a dummy agent, with the preposition functioning as a "pseudoaction"—can be repacked by the formula [whisky], yielding a repacked template [whiskey from a+glass] that is also a true inference. More importantly, the representation is enlarged with *extractions:* template-like entities, not represented in the original surface text, but which are appropriate inferences from the structure of the original, shallow, template representation.

In what follows, we extend the "short form" of templates (obtained by writing square brackets around English words, clustered at three nodes to show the distribution of formulas in the full template) by writing extractions as English words inside *double* square brackets.

Let us consider

(8)   John fired at a line of stags with a shotgun.

The *result* of matching this with templates, applying paraplates, and then performing case extractions can be written in summary form as follows:

(9)

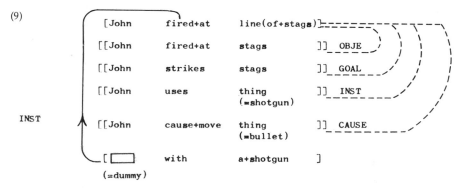

The extracted templates are tied by dotted lines to the source template from which they have been extracted, and the case name on the dotted line shows the case type of the extraction. The inferences cover both those that *must* be true (like the OBJE extraction, since to fire at a line of stags is necessarily to fire at stags) and those, like the GOAL extraction, that are only *likely*.

The extraction *mechanism* consists of a "specialist" (to use Winograd's term) for each case (and for CAUSE, which is treated as a semicase during extraction). An extraction, resulting in a new double-square-bracketed template, as in (9) above, is made for each case (or CAUSE) subformula at the top level of the formulas of each source template.

Let us see how the extractions in (9) are actually obtained. This will require that we give more of the content of the first source template in (9), and in particular the formula for "fire + at." (10) may be considered a semifull form of template for

"John fired at a line of stags"

in that the center node has been expanded to its formula but the other two nodes are left in "short form."

(10)

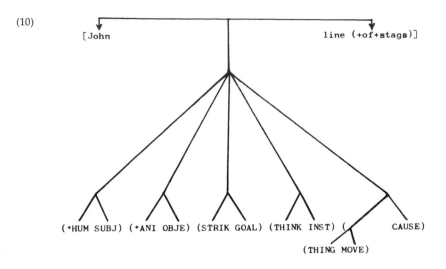

The dependent of OBJE case in (10) shows that "fire at" prefers an ANImate object, but the formula is in a template whose object is *not* animate (it is "line") and so we have a failed preference. However, an animate object (stags) is available as a dependent of the surface object in the template. The extraction process takes the form of filling *a new copy* of the source template, and *imposing* the available preferred animate object, to yield:

[[John   fired + at   stags]].

The repackings and extractions provided an extended or deeper representation and chains of *inference rules* are now constructed in order to resolve any outstanding pronoun or sense ambiguities. The inference rules, like paraplates, consist of two template skeletons and, again like the latter, do not become *part of* the representation into which they insert ties. But, unlike paraplates, they can be chained together, although the system always prefers the shortest inference chain it can construct between any two templates. An inference rule would typically express some inductive generalization such as, "If a human entity wants some object then it will try to obtain it." This would tie the two templates representing "John wanted a bicycle. He went to get his money box."

One structural change to the system should be mentioned briefly. In Wilks [1975b], it was suggested that, since there is no *theoretical* difference of any sort between the semantic primitives and English words, then more specific entities could be put into the formulas if necessary, *provided that they too were in the dictionary and had their own formulas there.* This would have the effect of making the formulas more compact.

In Wilks [1976], this notion was extended, and it was suggested that the formula dictionary should be thought of as imposing a *thesaurus* structure on the whole vocabulary.

A thesaurus, such as Roget's, is a grouping of English words into semi-synonymous *rows*, usually having the same part of speech type. These rows are grouped under one of about a thousand *heads* (not to be confused in any way with "head" meaning the right-most primitive of a formula), which are in turn grouped under about ten very general sections.

Thus, under the very general section †† **volition** we would find the *head*, say 22, †† **propulsion** and under that we would find a *subhead* †† 221 *firer*, attached to some row of "firer" words:

(11)   ** †† 221 *firer:* gun, bow, rifle, howitzer. . . .

Similarly, row "†† 222 **projectile**," say, would name a row of projectiles.

This organization is imposed by the formulas in the following way: each of the above is a word in the dictionary and has a formula, where the inclusion relations of the formulas *should reflect the head, subhead, rowmember* relation. Thus "gun," "bow," etc., are comembers of a row, and should have a common part to their formulas (all are THINKS, all have a *goal* of hitting something) and this common part *should be the (simpler, more general) formula in the dictionary for that row's subhead name* "†† *firer*" (which could also mean a person, of course, and ambiguous words will appear in the thesaurus under more than one head). This progressive generalization should extend right up the thesaurus to the general section names (†† **volition,** for example, would be associated only with the primitive elements GOAL and WANT).

Now, we see that the formula for "fire + at" in (11) could be made more specific if "††222 **projectile**" replaced the right-most THING in it, and "††221 **firer**" replaced the leftmost THING, to yield (11).

These thesaurus subheads would have their own dictionary formulas, hence (11) would now express more information. They would also, implicity, point to the thesaurus row each names, whose first member could, by convention, be an *even more explicit default:* "gun," say, for "††**firer**."

Thus in summary:

(i)   A *formula* is a binary tree representing a word sense. It is a dependency tree all of whose terminal nodes are *semantic primitives* or *nonprimitives*. Primitives come from a list of a hundred items with interpretations, and nonprimitives from a hierarchical *thesaurus*. Interpretation rules specify what trees are well-formed formulas and what their interpretations are.

(ii)   A template is a network of formulas representing a clause or phrase of text. It normally has an agent, action and object formula (in that order), and other formulas depending on these three nodes, though any of the main formulas may be a dummy. Again, interpretation rules specify which such networks are well-formed templates.

(iii) A *semantic block* is a text representation consisting of a network of

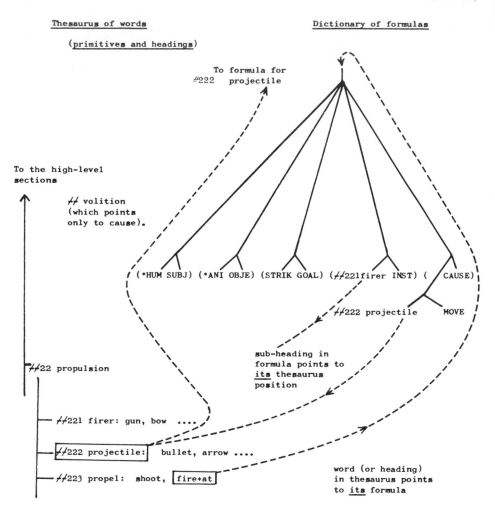

templates and *extractions*. The ties between the items of a semantic block may be imposed by *paraplates, inference rules,* or *extraction rules*.

(iv)   *Paraplates* are relations between template pairs and if a paraplate applies to a particular (usually contiguous) template pair, it imposes a *case relation* between them. A paraplate consists of six predicates which must apply to the three major nodes of the two templates if the relation is to hold.

(v)   *Inference rules* are also relations between template pairs, of the same form as paraplates, but they impose a relation not of a particular case but of CAUSE, REASON, or CONSEQUENCE.

(vi)   An *extraction* is identical to a template, except that it does not necessarily correspond to any clause or phrase of surface text (it is inferred from a template).

(vii)   An *extraction rule* produces, from any given template, a set of extractions. It contains a pattern which corresponds to a particular case and produces an extraction for each occurrence of that case in any formula in a template to which it applies.

2. PREFERENCE-BREAKING ALREADY ACCOMMODATED IN THE SYSTEM

The function of this paper is to discuss *new* ways of accommodating preference-breaking utterances, yet we should mention those preference breakers already dealt with by the processes described, and most particularly by the extraction process.

The standard ergative paradigm of verbs like "break" is dealt with in a uniform, though unconventional, manner. Utterances like

(12)   The window broke

and

(13)   The hammer broke the window

are well-formed English, but are preference breakers since "break" prefers an animated agent.

Thus (13), for example, yields *initially*

(14)   [the+window   broke   ]

Now, on extraction, the "SUBJ (agent) specialist" sees not only that (a) the surface subject (window) does not satisfy the (*ANI SUBJ) preference of [break], but (b) the same surface subject does satisfy the (*PHYSOB OBJE) preference of [break], which is filled by only a dummy in the source template (14). Thus the "SUBJ specialist" on extraction produces a copy template with the agency preference satisfied:

                  [[some+animate   broke   ]]

while "OBJE specialist" correspondingly produces

                  [[broke window]]

and these are immediately conflated, on the general preferences [Wilks; 1973] principle of producing the fullest representation possible, as the extraction

(15)   [[some+animate   broke   window]]

where the agent formula (now, of course, a true agent, not a surface subject) is *merely* (THIS *ANI), an extraction from the "break" formula. (12) is dealt with in a similar manner by the general extraction routine, with the added feature that [hammer] now cannot fit in the main template and will have to be inserted as object in the *INST*rument extraction from [break].

The standard type of extraction in the last example required the filling in a "new copy" template extracted from an *action* formula. Extractions are also made from substantive formulas (though only in the face of a preference violation) and these cover a range of examples like

(16)   John received a shock

where [shock] is

(17)

((NOT PLEASE * REAL)   OBJE)   SENSE)   (*HUM SUBJ))   POSS)(NOT GOOD) STATE)

and so is not the physical object that "received" would prefer. It indicates a shock is a not-good state possessed by a human who senses a not-pleasing real entity (a wider class than physical object).

The head of [received] is the primitive GET, and the extraction specialist for POSS (in [shock]) cued by the relation of POSS and GET can write out a "copy template" from the formula [shock], namely,

(18)   (*HUM) (SENSE) (NOTPLEASE *REAL)

whose agent, at least can be filled in from the context of the template for (16) to yield the extraction

(19)   [[JOHN (SENSE) (NOTPLEASE *REAL)]].

Here, this entity (19) can now seek further specifications in the text, if present, to fill its action and object which now have only a very general primitive form. It is important to see that the extraction is cued by the relation of GET and POSS: it would *not* have been cued by

(20)   John gave a shock to . . .

since [give] does not have the head GET.

It should be remembered during what follows that an *extraction* is a new template-like object, but present in the surface, or source, text, and which is produced by inference using *case-specialists* when there is a preference-breaking in a source template. This is quite consistant with the methods of Wilks [1975c], in which extractions were also produced to deal with problems of word sense ambiguity.

3. PSEUDOTEXTS: A SIMPLE PROJECTION SYSTEM

We shall now define a new operation in the system, *projection*, which requires a new form of coded knowledge, the *pseudotext* (PT).

A pseudotext is a structure of factual and functional information about a concept or item, and is intended to fall broadly within the notion of *frame* in the sense of Minsky [1975], Charniak [1977] and Schank [1975b].

Its form, in the terms developed so far, is simply that of a *semantic block:* a linear sequence of template forms tied by case ties, here taken to include CAUSE and GOAL (reason-for) ties inserted by the mechanisms of Wilks [1977a]. The linear order of the templates is taken by default to indicate normal time sequence. Thus a pseudotext for "car" might start:

(21)

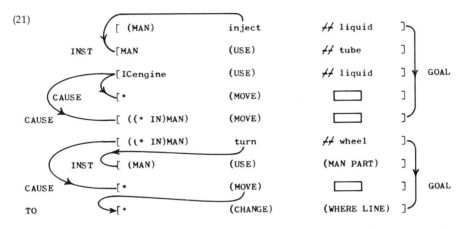

The first two lines refer to the insertion of fuel, the next three to the fact that the gas using engine moves the car, and the last four to the way the driver turning the wheel changes the direction of the car.

This entity is pointed to by "car" which *also*, of course, points to the formula [car]:

(22)

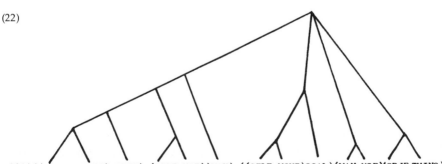

this says that a car is a thing that a person uses with the purpose of moving him or herself, by means of an engine part. Here, as with (11), ††**engine** in (22) points to both a formula for "engine" and to a *thesaurus row* of types of engines:

(23) ††**engine:** IC engine, turbine, electric motor . . . etc (IC = internal combustion)

just as "car" points to both (21) and (22) from *its* place in some thesaurus row under subhead ††**vehicle,** say.

The pseudotext can be extended to express as much detailed information about cars as is thought necessary, using exactly the same structure for text representation as was described in the earlier (recap) section, with the one addition that * indicates the formula [car] *from which we reached* this whole "pseudotext," so that ((* IN) MAN) indicates "a person inside the car" (i.e., the driver or passenger).

The entities in the templates of the pseudotext are either: dummies □; primitive elements (USE); formulas of primitive elements ((* IN)MAN); words which point to their own formulas in the thesaurus, such as "turn;" or words preceded by a sign †† **liquid,** which point to their formula in the thesaurus where it is a head or subhead formula. This notion will aid search in that it will indicate that the formula is not to be found at the bottom level of the thesaurus.

The pseudotext could clearly have this same information about the function of an engine, and steering, expressed in a number of different ways at different levels. For example, the third template in (21) indicates that an IC (internal combustion) engine uses a liquid, where [IC engine] is a word formula, but [††**liquid**] is a very general formula (FLOW STUFF), since ††**liquid** is a thesaurus subheading. It would have been possible to make the object of that template the more specific formula [gas] with an increase in specificity.

In general, these pseudotexts are intended to be as *specific as possible,* but, and this is why they are called pseudotexts, they have exactly the format of a text representation in preference semantics, and the intention is that *the processes that operate on such (dictionary) entities shall be identical with those operating on representations derived directly from surface texts.* The emphasis here is the reverse of the conventional one in this field: we stress the form of representation of *language* and seek to accommodate the representation of knowledge *to that,* rather than the reverse. And, of course, from a practical point of view, it means that, with our parsing procedures, "pseudotexts" could be input *as texts.*

Thus, (21) is not a copy of a text representation, or even a script for a possible text about cars—it *is* the representation of some, rather general, text about the basics of driving a car. Notice too, that ††**vehicle,** being a thesaurus subhead above "car," will point to a pseudotext more general than (21)—one we cannot assume is steered with a wheel, nor that is running by means of a liquid consuming engine—and so *the thesaurus imposes a hierarchy of pseudotexts as well as the associated hierarchy of formulas.* That is to say that, just as the thesaurus row members (as in (24)) stand in the row in virtue of the fact that their formulas have some common subformula (which should be also the formula for the subheading of the row itself), so should the pseudotexts of corow members be related. Thus, (21) as the pseudotext for car may be expected to have some *strong structural resemblance* to the pseudotexts for "truck," "railway train," "aeroplane," etc., which are plausible corow members with "car" in the row whose subheading is ††**vehicle**.

However, the relation may be more complex than can be expressed by any "single common subpseudotext" relation—as seemed possible with subformulas. Moreover, it may not be possible either to express the relation by saying that there are "slots" in the pseudotext for ††**vehicle** that are simply filled differently in the more specific pseudotexts for the members of the ††**vehicle** row, like "car." This has been suggested in Bobrow and Winograd [1977] but, although one might express, say, the third line of (21) by

(Propellant: liquid)
(Motor: IC engine),

here the right members could be replaced differently for "aeroplane," "railway engine," etc. It is not obvious that the whole content of (22) is easily captured by this format, although it may of course turn out that it is possible to do just that.

However, it is certainly possible to imagine the general structure of (21) being stored only *once* for the ††**vehicle** row, and a specific repacking function being assigned to each row that would construct its pseudotexts when and only when required. Thus, in (21) all the lines given would appear in the pseudotext for "aeroplane" except the sixth. Thus the repacking function for the row might well require that the row members were *ordered* so that their pseudotexts could be constructed from the one for the row subheading (like ††**vehicle**) so that as much pseudotext structure was "inherited" as possible as the repacking function was applied, let us suppose, rightward along the row. It is not yet clear, however, that row members could be simply ordered in terms of the relative generality of their pseudotexts in this way. There will also, of course, be more general "inheritances" of pseudotexts down the thesaurus hierarchy, but that is not brought out from the ††**vehicle** : car, etc., row because the head primitive of all the row members' formulas is THING, whose *own* pseudotext is pretty vacuous. However, the pseudotext for the high level primitive (i.e., thesaurus section) MAN would be highly complex. But note there is no "inheritance of property" problem in this system: the formula for "amputee" would have had MAN and would specify the loss of limbs and any inherited pseudotext from MAN—asserting "two legs"—would be modified by [amputee].

Since pseudotexts are text representations, it must be assumed that it will be possible to "deepen" them by the *extraction* and other inference procedures described in Wilks [1977a].

In this paper, we shall discuss a particular inference rule called projection that operates when extended use, in the sense of preference breaking, is encountered in the input surface text.

Projection results in the replacement of a template formula by a new one constructed by access to a pseudotext. Projection is operated *only in the presence of preference breaking,* so as to avoid assigning peculiar interpretations to wholly conventional utterances.

The need for such specific information as (21) provides can be seen if we think at an intuitive level about the understanding of (3). I suggest that we can understand (3), apart from its idiomatic element, noted already, in two ways:

(i)   We are made to feel that the car is in some way human-like as a drinker is.

(ii)   We know, more importantly, that "drink" is equivalent to "use" *because that is what car engines do with gasoline.*

Element (i) of the meaning might be important to the understanding of:

(24)   My car drinks gasoline. His thirst is never slaked.

Here, we might be helped to refer "his" to the car if we had simply projected the preferred (MAN) agent of [drink] as the head of [car]. In any case, this requires no more mechanism than the corresponding *extraction* from (3), which would yield a form [[(MAN) drink gasoline]].

The important notion (ii) is captured by accessing the pseudotext for "car" and *seeking the template in it with the closest match to the source template for* (3).

If we accept that that is the third one:

$$[\text{IC Engine}\quad(\text{USE})\quad \texttt{++liquid}]$$

then we would expect to project the formula [*use*] *in place of* [drink] to obtain as the new representation for (4):

(25)   [my+car   use   gasoline]

But now we notice that we cannot have a rule that produces the "projected" representation (25) for sentence (3) *solely* in virtue of the partial match of the original template for (3) with the third template of pseudotext (21) because that might lead to the same projection for "my car leaks gasoline" for which (25) would *not* be a suitable projected representation. So, the *general projection principle* of accommodating extended use with a pseudotext is PROJECT SENSE ONTO ACTIONS FROM A PSEUDOTEXT GIVING *WHAT WE NORMALLY* DO WITH THE ASSOCIATED OBJECT—but it must be modified somewhat in the light of "My car *leaks* gasoline."

We notice also that the template for (3) also matches the *first* line of (21), under an appropriate definition of match, in that [drink] and [inject] are both (MOVE CAUSE) formulas, but this is a weaker match than with the third line if we consider the agent and object terminals as yielding a stronger match given by *IC engine* being known as a car part from the structure of [car] (22), and ††**liquid** being the subheading of the row containing "gasoline" (which is simply the *extensional* idiom for saying that [gasoline] can be seen to contain [liquid], because (FLOW STUFF) is their common subformula).

So we may risk a new generalization: the projection represented by (25) is done in virtue of what I called the *general projection principle,* but requires confirmation by another weaker match, in the same pseudotext, on action not object/agent terminals. This would prevent an undesirable projection on "My car leaks gasoline" (although it might well be argued that since that sentence involves no preference breaking, we should not consider it as a problem for projection in any case, since this process, unlike extraction, would never be applied to it), as well as on the more distant "my car drinks *mud*" (which would not even achieve the agent/object terminal match), and "My car *chews* gasoline." The projected sense, "use" in (26), then, *carries over more than any alternative projection.*

A more complex case would be presented by a recent newspaper headline:

(26)   Britain tries to escape Common Market.

We would have the possibility of simply projecting the preferences of [escape] for a human escaper and a prison-like object—onto the agent and object formulas. The difficult aspect would be to get the [escape] formula replaced by something like [disassociate from]. This could not be done by, say, simplifying [escape] to a [leave] component because that is still *metaphorical.*

The interesting feature is that, although we might possibly have a historical pseudotext about Britain *joining* the Common Market, we would not have one about *disassociation.* Mere facts are sometimes not enough, even when highly structured as here.

We would, in fact, require a matching algorithm (as is argued for in Wilks [1975c]) that ignored negation in certain cases in favor of what one might call "mere relevance." That is, [joins] would have to be negated before being projected onto [escapes] as [disassociate from].

We would assume, too, that once having made a plausible projection in a text, the system should retain it, at least as a trial substitution, to other occurrences of the same word sense in the text.

In concluding to this section, it is important to reemphasize that it is anticipated that this projection rule will be required a great deal in the analysis of normal text, and not only for obscure examples. Those examples discussed here do have a nonstandard quality, and were chosen for their interest. However, the very same procedures and pseudotext would be required twice in so simple an example as "John's new car runs on diesel, but it does 100 m.p.h." for the preference failures of "run on" and "do."

The reader should note ways in which the newly defined *projection* operation differs from that of *extraction*. Extraction adds new template-like forms to a text representation, "copying them out of" formulas in *source templates* which are those actually matched with surface text. But the source templates remain as part of the representation. Moreover, extraction operates not only in response to preference-breaking.

In projection, on the other hand, *at least one formula of a source template is replaced* by a new formula constructed, either by rule from formulas in the source templates, or by access to "pseudotexts" and, as noted before, projection is operated *only in the presence of preference-breaking*.

Thus the two processes are distinct in the system though, as always with semantics, the phenomena covered may not divide so neatly. Thus, in dealing with (16) "John received a shock" *by extraction*, we added extraction (19) [[John (SENSE) (NOTPLEASE *REAL)]] to the text. It *could be* argued here that this is equivalent to the replacement of [received] in the template for (16) by a minimal formula consisting only of the primitive SENSE. Thus, in certain cases, projection may produce the same inferential effect as extraction.

4. SOME CONTROL ISSUES

The fact that the proposals of this paper have not yet been implemented in a working program rather limits discussion of control issues. Some can be foreseen but cannot be settled in advance: for example, any given preference-breaking template may contain a number of formulas pointing to pseudotexts, and it would seem reasonable that the matching algorithms outlined in the last section should apply to all of them. This is only a particular example of a problem that arises in all "frame using" systems but has not yet, to my knowledge, been solved in any of them: many frames are called but few can be chosen, and preferably only one! If different pseudotexts called by a given preference-break can yield rival projections, then some way will have to be found of choosing between them.

Again, the fact that the pseudotexts are only accessed by preference-breaking templates, and not by "normal" semantic structures, continues the "laziness" approach of the preference semantics system and remains a point of contrast with the frame systems of Schank and Abelson [1977] and Charniak [1977]. It is assumed that such structures should only be accessed when needed, and that a successful model of understanding will no more be able to tolerate "information overload" than we can. One specific aspect of that approach is that, although pseudotexts contain specific knowledge, the system will try to work with the *most general* pseudotext that it can.

Since it is intended that pseudotexts for bottom-level formulas in the thesaurus, like [car], will be constructed from more general ones, like [††vehicle], this means that the system will see how far it can get with matching into a pseudotext using only the one for the thesaurus subhead, like ††vehicle, and only construct the more specific pseudotext if no adequate match is found in the general one. This approach need not be inconsistent with the assumption stated earlier that "projection rests on specific knowledge," since the more specific pseudotext will in fact be *accessed via* the more general one, given the thesaurus structure.

It is important to all this that the thesaurus is not a "bad hierarchy," and it need not be, given that (a) it avoids bad property inheritance in the construction of specific pseudotexts as indicated earlier, and (b) the thesaurus contains *normal cross-referencing*, i.e., [knife] would appear under both [††tool] and [††weapon].

It is hoped that the "higher levels" of the thesaurus will play an important semantic role and explicate the obscure but important notion of what it might be to have the most specific possible information about very general concepts.

Let me give an example here. In the course of discussing the present system of language understanding in connection with extended use, Boden [1977] draws attention to a class of examples like:

(27)   I see what you mean,

where we might say that "see" is being used in an extended sense, at least with respect to its central sense formula in which it would express a preference for *PHYSOB or *REAL objects. We must say "with respect to" here, as always, because the metaphor in (27) might be considered so dead, so normal, as to deserve its own dictionary entry in virtue of having been learned by our culture. But let us consider how the system proposed might deal with (27) on the assumption that the dictionary does *not* explicitly anticipate it.

We must postulate two initial operations on the second template for (27), i.e., for "what you mean." The action "mean" can by extraction impose on the (dummy) object for the head SIGN (since the formula for "mean" shows that it prefers a SIGN object). This operation is covered by a simple extension of the extraction procedures discussed already, namely, in the presence of template dummies, formulas elsewhere in the template can impose their preferences on those dummies. Second, we must assume an operation for a relative clause template, like the one under discussion, in which the routines that tie templates together can postulate the head SIGN as equipollent with *the whole template*. This is a perfectly natural semantic analog of the fact that the phrase "what you mean" is the object of "see" in (27).

The important difference here from preceding examples is that the object of "see" is now given to us only as the semantic primitive SIGN, and not as the name for an entity (like "car" in (3)). Hence there is no question of accessing a *specific* pseudotext as we did for car, because there cannot be one.

If we wish to project an appropriate THINK head onto the formula for "see," in place of its normal SENSE, we shall have to use more general semantic procedures.

Now the *topmost* level of a thesaurus is that of the very general section names* equivalent to Human beings, Entities, etc., and these correspond directly to the primitives MAN, THING, etc., of our system. I have argued elsewhere that there is no *essential* difference between primitives and words (see Wilks [1975d]): MAN is just an English word, even though it happens to have a fundamental *organizing role* in the present system of meaning representation. But what would be "pseudotexts" for such general primitives?

It is, in fact, fairly clear what they would be : very general assertion forms, consisting wholly of heads, like:

> MAN HAVE THING
> MAN THINK SIGN
> MAN WANT THING

These are *very* general expressions of human activity† so general as to be almost vacuous. However, in the parsing procedures [Wilks, 1968, 1972, 1975b] of the present system these are the *bare template triples* which define the skeletons of well-formed templates. Yet it is here, as pseudotexts for the primitives themselves that they "really belong" in the knowledge structure of the system.

Now what might they do for us here? Well, if we now apply to (27) *exactly the same processes* that we applied to "My car drinks gasoline," we shall access the "pseudotext" of the preference-breaker and project from there. Here the preference-breaker is merely SIGN, and *its* "pseudotext" will be a stack of bare templates that list the primitive actions normally done to SIGN. The top‡ of the list of this will of course be THINK, which would also have an agent MAN matching the "I" of (27), since thinking is

---

* In Roget's thesaurus, the general section names are different, but again very close to primitives in the system, viz., ††**abstract relations** (GRAIN), ††**Space** (WHERE), ††**Matter (STUFF),** ††**Intellect** (THINK), ††**Volition** (GOAL), etc.

† In Minsky [1975], he writes of the top levels of a frame being "always true" in the sense of analytic postulates about the world in question. Most of these 3-primitive forms would express assertions of that type.

‡ The "top" here is loose, and the procedures of the earlier section, applied here, might well locate more than one "bare template" under SIGN that would have Agent MAN, viz., MAN CAUSE SIGN as well as MAN THINK SIGN. We must presume upon other, natural, determinants of closeness that will result in THINK being projected first: for example, SENSE, THINK, FEEL, etc., will already be grouped as the extension of a more general primitive *AFFEC (affections). These "high-order" primitives impose a tree-structure on the lower order ones.

what is normally done to and with SIGNS. This would enable us to project the desired THINK as the head of the (extended) "see" *using exactly the mechanisms we have already created for more specific knowledge examples.*

5. AN ENVIRONMENT FOR IMPLEMENTING THESE SUGGESTIONS

Having made a number of suggestions in this paper for restructuring the preference semantics system, it may be appropriate to give by way of conclusion a very brief sketch of the proposed implementation environment.

An important feature will be the attempt to make use of both local and global context as necessary, where any frame-type information can be thought of as a *global context,* and intratemplate preference as a paradigm of *local context.* It is well known that neither of these is adequate taken alone. In

(28)   John went hunting with four bucks in his pocket

we are misled about the sense of "buck" by using only the global context of "hunt." Conversely, in

(29)   John licked the gun all over and the stock tasted good

we are misled about the sense of "stock" by taking the (local) preference of "taste" and ignoring the global context given by "gun." With a little ingenuity one can produce a total *deadlock* between the two influences, as with "stock" in:

(30) I licked the gun all over after the soup course when the stock tasted particularly good.

In the implementation, local context will again be the operation of preference within and between templates via the operation of *paraplates* and *inference rules* [Wilks, 1975b, 1975c]. Global context will be the processes operating on the pseudotexts, the use of the thesaurus in determining topic context and its minimal ability to express a more *dynamic* notion of frame (see Wilks [1976]) than that dealt with here. The local and global context features will be, either directly or more likely by simulation, operated in parallel, so that they can independently, as it were, seek structures in the incoming text. But, as (30) shows, there can be no *guarantee* of a general solution.

The aim in doing this is twofold. First, to retain for the system the ability of doing *less than* all possible inference. If whatever problems of analysis the text presents can be settled without access to pseudotexts and other frames, so much the better. In processing terms, I have called this the operation of a lazy system.*

---

* A feature is now styled as "variable depth processing" [Bobrow & Winograd, 1977].

Second, retaining both local and global processing options, ideally in parallel, means that we can approach frames experimentally—to see what they do for us in practice. The ideal arrangement would be the facility in the HEARSAY [Reddy *et al.*, 1973] speech understanding system, where one can switch off one branch of the analysis, such as local context, to see if that makes any difference. We cannot assume *in advance* that extended use, say, *must** require access to frame-level knowledge. Our preliminary investigations in this paper suggest that sometimes it does and sometimes it does not.

Another feature of a desirable implementation will be some attempt to incorporate the sort of global rules of conversation investigated by Grice [1975]. As we shall see in the example that follows, such rules can override frame-like knowledge in certain situations.

The actual environment for the implementation will be an interactive question-answering facility in English *about* the construction of a semantic text representation, including accommodating "extended use." This methodology has the disadvantage that the *final semantic representation achieved,* though it remains available for some further task, is nevertheless in an internal linguistic representation rather than output in English.

However, it has the compensating advantage that the data base is non-trivial,† as is almost inevitable in the miniworld situations often chosen, and that the system will be that much more perspicuous if its semantic choices and inferences can be followed by a user.

Let us see, in sketch form, how such a system might work with a real example text:

(31)   An ambulance driver answering an emergency call, which turned out to be a hoax, went through red traffic lights and collided with a car, killing its driver. . . .

The Times: April 6, 1975

Readers of that sentence generally have no trouble seeing that the last mentioned driver is the car driver, and not the ambulance driver, though the inferences required to get that right are not easy to specify in any standard linguistic or logical terms. That professional language users sometimes use over-simple rules for noun–phrase reference is seen from the fact that the sentence appeared in *The Times* under the (wrong) headline: AMBULANCE DRIVER DIES IN HOAX CALL CRASH!

It will become clear that the understanding of the sentence requires inferences from both linguistic and real-world knowledge. In the ideal

---

* Though Fillmore seems to make this assumption about frames in Fillmore [1977].

† By that I mean no more than that question-answering implementations of frames *may* be no test of the analytic power of frames at all, but only of the *need of a data base*. That is, if you ask a system that has cinema-frames, "What do I buy during the movie intermission?," and get a suitable reply, you have not in any way shown the need for frames in *language understanding*.

dialogue that follows, the user interventions are in upper case, and notes
are preceded and followed by square brackets.

END OF TEXT INPUT

1. An ambulance answering an emergency call
2. S went through red traffic lights
3. and S collided with a car
4. S killing its driver
   [S marks missing template agents in the four fragments the text
   has been cut into for ease of reference]
   All fragments match templates.
   Template 2 fails preference for agent.
   Now repacking S slots:
2. The *ambulance driver and ambulance* went through red traffic lights.
   WHY?
   a driver and ambulance are mobile, a call not.
3. *The ambulance driver* and ambulance collided with a car.
   Suggest:
4. The ambulance driver killed ?its driver.
   [system unsure of S in (4) ?its is marked as a problem].
   WHY?
   active agent preferred for *kill* (ambulance inanimate).
      But now reinferring as follows:
   preference breaking in (2) drives inferences
      as follows:
   traffic lights are aperture (by extraction)
      or
   went through means passed (by projection)
   I select latter and *project* onto "went through"
      [straightforward extraction in (2),
      plus access to pseudotext* for "traffic lights"]
   examining preferences in
4. S killing ?its driver
   "It" is lights number wrong)
      or
      call
      or
      car
      or
      ambulance
   Prefer car or ambulance for "it"
      [calls don't have drivers]
   Confirm

---

* Notice that the pseudo-text is being used to analyse the text here, though no *general claim*
is being made, as in [Schank; 1975b] that the frame can be used as a basis for parsing the text.

4. *ambulance driver* kills *car's* driver
    WHY?
    First:
    from traffic lights pseudotext:
    passing red traffic lights can cause people hurt
       ["pass" has replaced "went through"
       by projection, remember].
       [pseudotexts can have a
       "cause tied" template *pair* read out].
    this confirms kills both car *and* ambulance
       drivers.
    Second:
       Calling *pragmatic override*
    its = cars
    means "its" not twice coreferential.*
       [A general pragmatics
       rule, as proposed by Grice, that maximises information
       in the fragment. If it = ambulance driver,
       writer would have used "killed himself"]
    Confirm its = cars.
    Representation complete.

The new point brought out of the hat at the end, as it were, shows the persistent need for general pragmatic principles at the highest level, just as we need preference at the lowest. The general interest here would be the possibility of two *clashing* general principles in the analysis of a given text: that of preference, seeking, in some sense, to minimize information (argued in Wilks [1975a]), and another seeking to maximize it.

6. RELATION TO OTHER SYTSTEMS

There has been little attempt to cope with preference-breaking in recent literature in artificial intelligence. Schank (in Schank and Colby [1973, p. 233]) allows nonfitting items to be inserted into his diagrams, marked with an asterisk, but gives no indication of how they are accommodated. Bobrow and Winograd [1977] refer to "forcing a match" in the KRL system but give no description of how it is to be done, over and above emphasizing that it would be a nice thing to do. An interesting thesis in Russell [1976] does tackle the problem. She describes a simple program, equipped with Schank-type conceptual information augmented in an important way. She provides, for the first time, conceptual coding of nouns for that

---

* A reader tempted to argue that "its" *must* refer to the car on syntactic grounds since it has been mentioned while the ambulance has not, should consider, "A bicycle rider passing a stationary truck swerved to avoid a dog and fell over buckling *its* wheel."

system (what we here call noun-formulas). Her program contains rules that attempt to draw inferences from input examples of "extended use." So, for example, the program would output (INK START BE IN CHAIR) from input (CHAIR DRINK INK), and quite properly give no output for (HE CLOSE INK). The program appears to have only simple conceptual structures, and to make no general claims over and above those contained in the extraction procedures of this paper and of Wilks [1973, 1975c]. But some of its output seems extremely interesting: divide the input–output pair: (HE CLOSE MIND), (HE (IPART:MIND) STOP POSSIBILITY-OF START-THINK.) However, this would, in the terminology of the present paper, almost certainly be *extraction* rather than *projection.*

Another interesting program, reported in Granger [1977], tackles the different but related task of inferring the sense of *unknown* words from semantic structures. However, it is not clear to this reader that his program does actually make use of script-like knowledge, since almost all his inferences seem to be from conceptual content (i.e., formulas), as are Weber's.

The pseudotext proposals, as regards the structure itself rather than its application, will have many points of similarity with those of Schank and Charniak, among others, who have also extended their "propositional representation" up one level to an *organization of* propositional representations (i.e., frames). For example, the case ties CAUSE and GOAL perform the same functions as Charniak's COMES-FROM and LEADS-TO ties Charniak [1977]. Unlike Charniak, these proposals emphasize the relation to parsing yet, as should be clear, the relation proposed is not that envisaged by Schank's "expectational" methods.

The notion of perspective, much emphasized by Bobrow and Winograd [1977], has always been present in the system as the possibility of multiple formulas for a word (such as "house as a point in space, a location, a destination" *and* "house as a container for people and their activities," where these two formulas do not correspond to a sense distinction), and is now made more general with the cross-referencing feature of the thesaurus. Here, as noted, a pseudotext and a formula for, say, knife, can be pointed to from the rows subheaded [††tool], [††weapon], etc.

7. DISCUSSION

This paper has not been a report on programs written nor on a working system of language understanding. It is, however, based on considerable experience with such a system, and is intended to indicate extensions to it that will be implemented and tested as soon as possible. The aim here has been to develop extensions of meaning and knowledge representation in a way consistent with the earlier assumptions of the preference semantics system, and to sketch out the sort of practical developments in the program that would facilitate their testing. It is also clear that some test of these suggestions for dealing with extended use need not wait upon the arrival of usable parallel processing.

There has been a great deal of attention given to examples in this paper, but there is intended to be a simple moral, or rather an (ultimately) testable maxim to the effect that much of what we call "understanding of language" may consist not merely in the correct and appropriate manipulation of precise knowledge—the "society of experts" view of knowledge and understanding—but in the manipulation of very general principles, possibly conflicting general principles, as here. Moreover, the ambulance driver example suggests that, on occasions, such principles may be needed *even where all possible detailed knowledge is available.*

It is a part of this view that the knowledge structures employed should, where possible, reflect language structure (hence the use of "pseudotexts" here for the frame-like objects) and that the system using them should make general claims about the nature of language and knowledge. If it does not, then no scientific phenomenon is being investigated and we have no claim to be scientists.

However, these general views can only be justified in the process of implementation and not by further general discussion. Moreover, a very important point will arise in such an implementation: the paper has emphasized both the role of *detailed* knowledge in projection (as in the *car* example) *and* the need to start at a general level in the hierarchy of pseudotexts when seeking a match in projection. There is no contradiction here but it leaves open the possibility that the rules as described will sometimes produce *very general* projections: in the Common Market example (27), the projection might produce a very *general* sense of "escape" as "exit from any enclosed space," rather than a fact-based one.

Again, it might project, rather than replace [drink] by USE in the analysis of (3), some very general sense such as "has fluid put into it". These will be matters to be worked out in practice, even though fundamental questions about meaning and understanding hang upon them. They will also require decisions on two other points:

(1)   Are the senses produced by projection to be stored or not? Are they to be tried as possible senses for further uses of the same word in the same text?

(2)   After projection has changed a template, should a copy of the original remain as part of the semantic block for the text, for fear that certain vital "surface" inferences will be blocked if it is not?

The last point is particularly important in connection with the issue of *how general* projections will turn out to be. The more general they are, the more it may be vital to keep a copy of the original template in the overall text representation.

Readers will also have remarked that the whole formula/pseudotext distinction rests on some intuitive meaning/factual distinction that cannot be formally justified. Why keep it rather than go over to a uniform notation for both, as KRL would suggest? I think one can only say that the meaning/factual distinction, even if not philosophically sound, does have some role in our understanding. And in this system, the formulas are basic to parsing, and that that is a procedural role that should have some reflection in the system's structure.

In conclusion, one could hope that the above techniques might produce some small additional understanding of text in this almost unchartered area. But optimism is almost certainly out of place where imaginative writing is concerned. Consider:

The sad colonel did not have a nervous breakdown because he had a friend and because he was too unimaginative to admit defeat. He poured Rembrandt a glass of his friend.

Pownall [1974, p. 195]

The interpretation of the last word is, alas, both straightforward and totally beyond the scope of any system conceivable at the moment.

REFERENCES

[Bobrow, D., and Winograd, T., 1977]. K.R.L.—an overview of a knowledge representation language. *Cognitive Science*, **1**, 3–46.
[Boden, M., 1977]. *Artificial Intelligence and Natural Man*. Harvester Press, Hassocks, Sussex, England.
[Charniak, E., 1977]. A framed PAINTING: the representation of a common-sense knowledge fragment. *Cognitive Science* **1**, 355–394.
[Chomsky, N., 1965]. *Aspects of a Theory of Syntax*. M.I.T. Press, Cambridge, Massachusetts.
[Chomsky, N., 1969]. *Language and Mind*. M.I.T. Press, Cambridge, Massachusetts.
[Fillmore, C., 1977]. Scenes and frames semantics. In *Linguistics Structures Process*. A. Zampolli (ed.). North–Holland Publ., Amsterdam.
[Granger, R. H., 1977]. "FOUL-UP, a Program that Figures Out Meanings of Words from Context." Department of Computer Science, Yale University, New Haven.
[Grice, H. P., 1975]. Logic and conversation. In *Syntax and Semantics*, Vol. 3. P. Cole and J. Morgan (eds.). Academic Press, New York.
[Katz, J., and Fodor, J., 1963]. The structure of a semantic theory. *Language* **39**, pp. 170–210.
[Minsky, M., 1975]. A frame-work for representing knowledge. In *The Psychology of Computer Vision*. P. Winston (ed.). McGraw–Hill, New York.
[Pownall, D., 1974]. *The Raining Tree War*. Heinemann, London.
[Reddy, R., 1973]. The *Hearsay* speech understanding system. *Proceedings of the 3rd International Joint Conference on Artificial Intelligence, 1973*, pp. 185–193.
[Russell, S., 1976]. Computer understanding of metaphorical verbs. *Amer. J. Comput. Lang.*, **44**.
[Schank, R., 1975a]. *Conceptual Information Processing*. North–Holland Publ., Amsterdam.
[Schank, R., 1975b]. Using knowledge to understand. In *Theoretical Issues in Natural Language Processing*. B.B.N., Cambridge, Massachusetts.
[Schank, R., and Colby, K., 1973]. *Computer Models of Thought and Language*. R. Schank and K. Colby (eds.). Freeman, San Francisco.

[Schank, R., and Abelson, R., 1977]. *Scripts, Plans and Goals.* Erlbaum Press, Hillside, New Jersey.

[Wilks, Y., 1968]. "Computable Semantic Derivations." Memo SP-3017. Systems Development Corp., Santa Monica, California.

[Wilks, Y., 1972]. *Grammar, Meaning and the Machine Analysis of Language.* Routledge, London.

[Wilks, Y., 1973]. "Natural Language Inference." Memo AIM-211. Artificial Intelligence Lab., Stanford, California.

[Wilks, Y., 1975a]. Preference semantics. In *The Formal Semantics of Natural Language.* E. Keenan (ed.). Cambridge Univ. Press, London and New York.

[Wilks, Y., 1975b]. An intelligent analyzer and understander of English. *Comm. ACM* **18**, 264–274.

[Wilks, Y., 1975c]. A preferential, pattern-matching semantics for natural language understanding. *Artificial Intelligence* **6**, 53–74.

[Wilks, Y., 1975d]. Primitives and words. In *Theoretical Issues in Natural Language Processing.* B.B.N., Cambridge, Massachusetts.

[Wilks, Y., 1976]. "De Minimis: The Archaeology of Frames." Artificial Intelligence Department, Univ. of Edinburgh.

[Wilks, Y., 1977a]. What sort of taxonomy of causality do we need for natural language understanding. *Cognitive Science,* **2**, 235–264.

[Wilks, Y., 1977b]. "Good and Bad Arguments for Semantic Primitives." Artificial Intelligence Department, Univ. of Edinburgh.

EXTENSIONAL SEMANTIC NETWORKS: THEIR REPRESENTATION, APPLICATION, AND GENERATION

Jürgen M. Janas   and   *Camilla B. Schwind*

ABSTRACT

This chapter introduces extensional semantic networks (ESNs), a new kind of semantic network that allows two different levels of interpretation, namely, the intensional and the extensional. We present the theoretical background on which these networks have been designed. In addition, we give both precise definitions and practical examples of ESNs and, finally, are concerned with application areas for and the automatic generation of the networks.

In an introductory section, we investigate the relationship between concepts and their extensions, i.e., the objects denoted by these concepts; a set of semantic relations that hold between concepts is introduced and some of their properties are derived. Section 2 contains a formal definition of the hierarchical ESNs that are constructed from concepts and relations. Furthermore, the two interpretations of an ESN, on the conceptual level and on the object level, are developed, including a treatment of negation and quantification. Section 3 is concerned with the use of these networks in information retrieval systems and demonstrates the appropriateness of their application in question-answering systems. In Section 4, we discuss how ESNs can be generated automatically from natural language discourse, emphasis being placed on a transparent description of the stepwise generation of a network.

INTRODUCTION

This chapter introduces a new kind of semantic network, which we call extensional semantic networks (ESNs). We must admit that this term might be a little misleading since it seems to be in contradiction to Woods' [1975] work on an intensional semantic representation but, in fact, it is not. ESNs are an augmentation of Woods' ideas on intensional representation. To illustrate this, we take Woods' example (originally by Frege) of the "Morning Star" and the "Evening Star," which both name the same physical object. Woods argues that "in the appropriate internal representation, there must be two entities (concepts, nodes, etc.) corresponding to the two different intensions, morning star and evening star. There is then

267

an assertion about these two intensional entities that they denote one and the same object (extension)." In an ESN, we have two entities for the morning star and the evening star. There is, however, a second level of interpretation, the extensional one, where the two different concepts appear as one and the same object. In other words, the purely intensional representation, which has to be augmented by additional assertions, is replaced by a representation that allows both an intensional and an extensional view. More precisely, our networks ought to be called "intensional and extensional semantic networks." However, since we share the opinion that intensionality is undoubtedly a constituent of any semantic network, we have chosen the name extensional semantic networks.

The general guideline in preparing this chapter was to meet the three main requirements for a semantic representation, as specified by Woods [1975]. These are the logical adequacy of the representation, the possibility of making inferences and deductions from the representation, and the ability of translating natural language text into the representation. In particular, the composition of the chapter is as follows. In an introductory section, we investigate the relationship between concepts and their extensions, i.e., the objects denoted by these concepts. We introduce a set of semantic relations that hold between concepts, investigate some of the properties of these relations, and discuss the extensional interpretation of the relations. The second section contains the formal definition of an extensional semantic network. We first introduce S-graphs, a kind of hierarchical, nonrecursive directed graph. S-graphs use the concepts and semantic relations described in Section 1 as nodes and arcs, respectively, and also have structure and node value restrictions imposed upon them. The extensional interpretation of semantic networks can then easily be introduced by augmenting the extensional interpretation of concepts and relations. Finally, we deal with quantification and negation in ESNs. Section 3 is concerned with the application of ESNs. We describe their use for both automatic indexing of natural language texts and question-answering systems. The final section shows how an ESN is generated from natural language discourse. We outline the techniques used and give an example of the process.

1. CONCEPTS AND RELATIONS

1.1. Concepts and Their Extensions

Extensional Semantic Networks (ESNs) are intended to represent the meaning of natural language. They are composed of concepts and of relations defined on these concepts. We are not concerned with providing a precise definition of concepts here. We assume that there is a set of concepts, the normative application of which is known. At the natural language level, concepts are denoted by single words or by sequences of single words (phrases). The words denoting concepts belong to different grammatical categories, namely, nouns, verbs, adjectives, and adverbs. Let C be the set of all concepts. It is the union of four disjoint subsets: C_N, the set of nominal concepts; C_V, the set of verbal concepts; C_A, the set of adjectival concepts; and C_{AV}, the set of adverbial concepts. C_N may also contain concepts that are not denoted by a proper word in natural language, such as the set of natural numbers. Many words may belong to several grammatical categories. For example, the word "partition" may be a noun or a verb. In such cases, we refer to different concepts, in the partition example, one concept belonging to C_N and the other to C_V. The respective word is then treated as a homonym. In almost all cases, to which category a concept belongs, in a particular context, is obvious for humans. How such a distinction can be made by a machine is discussed in Sections 3 and 4.

Every concept describes a set of objects or, in the case of a verbal concept, a set of actions. In contrast to the normative application of a concept, which we will call its intension, the set belonging to a concept is called its extension. "Extension" and "intension" in our use correspond to what Frege [1892] called *Bedeutung* (meaning) and *Sinn* (sense) (see also Carnap [1972]). To give an example, the extension of "tree" is the set of all trees; the intension of tree is what a human conceives of when he denotes something as a tree, i.e., some kind of "typical" tree. As an example of a verbal concept, consider the extension of "write" as the set of all writing actions, whereas the intension of write is the concept of what writing is. The importance of this distinction between extension and intension becomes obvious when we think of concepts with different intension but with the same extension. Consider "daughter" and "female." Every female is the daughter of someone and every daughter is a female. These two concepts are intended to be applied differently, they express different ideas, different intensions of the speaker. Although they have the same extension, they are not even synonymous.

Let T be the set of all "things" of some real world, namely a set of objects O and actions A, $T = O \cup A$. Let ϕ be the mapping relating concepts to their extensions, $\phi: C \rightarrow 2^T$. Here, 2^M denotes the power set of a set M; ϕ is a mapping because for every concept, there is exactly one set of objects belonging to this concept. ϕ is not injective because, as we have seen above, different concepts may describe the same set of objects. The distinction between concepts and their extensions is also important for the treatment of quantification because quantifiers usually refer to objects and not to concepts.

Semantic relations are subsets of C^n (M^n denotes the n-ary Cartesian product of set M). We assume the existence of n-ary relations although, in our later examples, we require only binary relations. As noted before, concepts may also be described by phrases composed of single word concepts. Phrases will later be shown to be representable by graphs. Therefore, the domain of relations is extended to graphs.

As we have stated above, semantic networks are intended to represent the meaning of natural language text. Many linguists have argued in the last few years (see, e.g., Schnelle [1973] and Montague [1970]) that meaning is closely related to subject areas (often called pragmatics). Consequently, a certain subject area is covered by a set of concepts and a set of relations defined on these concepts, and these sets are usually different for different areas. For example, we do not need a verb–subject relation for covering mathematics. Accordingly, we think of different semantic networks belonging to different subject areas. An extensional semantic network is a sort of frame structure as proposed by Minsky [1975] and Schank and Abelson [1975]. Within a complete and consistent set of concepts characterizing a certain subject, there will be some concepts that cannot be defined in terms of other concepts. These concepts are called prime concepts. All other concepts will be defined using the prime concepts. For example, in mathematics "set" and "element" are prime concepts. Consider the chains of concepts obtained by ordering concepts according to the relation "A occurs in the definition of B." Such a hierarchical concept structure is typically found within the languages of the exact sciences. Leibnitz [1840] already spoke of a hierarchical concept structure but he suggested that there is exactly one "greatest," most general concept. However, we believe that there is a set of several most general concepts that are not related hierarchically to each other.

1.2. Semantic Relations

In the following, we give an exemplary set of the relations that describe the subject area of computer science.

First, we define the superordinate relation SUP. The relation SUP_0 holds between a concept A and a concept B if B is directly superordinated to A. SUP_0 is defined for nominal and adjectival concepts only. Thus, $SUP_0 \subset (C_N \times C_N) \cup (C_A \times C_A)$. The relation SUP is defined to be the transitive closure of SUP_0. For example, both (RELATION, SET) and (BIJECTIVE, INJECTIVE) are elements of SUP. Theoretically, we could expand the relation SUP to verbs as one can see from examples like (TO SEQUENCE, TO ORDER). Since there are relatively few cases like this one, we omit them.

The referential relation REF holds between an adjectival concept A and a nominal concept B if B may have the property described by A. Thus, REF $\subset C_A \times C_N$. For every concept $A \in C_A$, there exists at least one concept $B \in C_N$ such that $(A, B) \in$ REF. Otherwise, it would not be reasonable to have A in C_A since A would be without meaning with respect to the particular subject covered by C. Examples here would be (CONTINUOUS, MAPPING) and (MAGNETIC, STORE).

The genitive relation OWN holds between two nominal concepts A and B if A may occur as a genitive attribute of B. Thus, OWN $\subset C_N \times C_N$. Strictly speaking, this relation combines several different semantic relations such as the possessive relation, as in (STATE OF A STORAGE), or the source relation, as in (ELEMENT OF A SET). Two exemplary elements of OWN then would be (STORAGE, STATE) and (SET, ELEMENT).

Prepositional relations hold between a nonadverbial concept A and a nominal concept B if B may be found as a prepositional adjunct of A or as a prepositional object of A. To avoid an overlap with the relation OWN, the linking preposition cannot be OF. We choose the name PREP to denote all prepositional relations. Thus, PREP $\subset (C_N \cup C_V \cup C_A) \times C_N$. A deeper distinction is not necessary with respect to the applications described in Sections 3 and 4. Some exemplary elements of PREP are (INSTRUCTION, PROGRAM), an instruction from a program; (DELETE, STORE), to delete in a store; and (CONTINUOUS, SET), continuous on a set.

The synonymy relation SYN holds between two nominal or adjectival concepts if they are synonymous, i.e., if they are identical in meaning and extension. Thus, SYN $\subset (C_N \times C_N) \cup (C_A \times C_A)$. It would be possible to expand SYN to verbal concepts. However, since cases of verbal synonymy are rare, we omit them. Two examples would be (NUMBER, NUMERAL) and (ALPHABETIC, ALPHABETICAL).

The antonymy relation ANT holds between two nominal or adjectival concepts if they are antonymous, i.e., if they have contrary meanings. Thus, ANT $\subset (C_N \times C_N) \cup (C_A \times C_A)$. Exemplary elements are (EQUIVALENCE, ANTIEQUIVALENCE) and (TRANSITIVE, INTRANSITIVE).

The adverb–adjective relation AVAJ holds between an adverbial concept A and an adjectival concept B if B may be modified by A. Therefore, AVAJ $\subset C_{AV} \times C_A$. This relation is the justification for the admission of adverbs as vehicles of concepts. Two exemplary elements of AVAJ are (TOTALLY, DIFFERENTIABLE) and (COUNTABLY, ADDITIVE).

The subject relation SUBJ holds between a verbal concept A and a nominal concept B if B may act as the logical subject of A. By definition, SUBJ $\subset C_V \times C_N$. The notion of "logical subject" refers to nonpassivized phrasings of sentences. Exemplary elements of the SUBJ relation are (CORRECT, CODE), as in a code that corrects errors, and (CONVERT, OPERATION), as in an operation that converts.

The object relation OBJ holds between a verbal concept A and a nominal concept B if B may act as the direct logical object of A. Therefore, OBJ $\subset C_V \times C_N$. The notion of "logical object" refers again to nonpassivized phrasings of sentences. Two exemplary elements of the OBJ relation are (CORRECT, ERROR), as in to correct an error, and (ADDRESS, LOCATION), as in to address a location.

Again, it has to be emphasized that the above set of relations is by no means an immutable component of the theory of ESNs. New relations may be introduced or existing relations may be decomposed whenever this seems to be advisable from the point of view of a particular application. Nevertheless, we feel that the above set provides a solid basis for a wide area of applications.

1.3. Properties of the Semantic Relations

In Section 1.2, we constrained the domains of the relations (e.g., the relation SUBJ may hold only between a verbal and a nominal concept). Here we deal with the properties that are imposed by the semantics of the relations.

ANT is a nonreflexive symmetric relation. Thus, if a concept A is antonymous to a concept B, then so is B to A. We denote the set of concepts that are antonymous to X by $ANT(X)$. In most cases, $ANT(X)$ will contain one element. Yet, we should not be dogmatic about this (cf. the concepts SOLID, LIQUID, and GASEOUS). SYN is an equivalence relation, i.e., it is symmetric, transitive, and reflexive. We denote the class of concepts that are synonymous to the concept X by $SYN(X)$.

Let us now consider the ordering of the relation SUP. For any two concepts A and B, from either C_N or C_A, at most one of the relations $(A, B) \in$ SUP and $(B, A) \in$ SUP may hold. Since $(A, A) \in$ SUP does not hold for any concept A, SUP is an irreflexive ordering relation. The concepts from C_N or C_A, for which no superordinated concept exists, are exactly the prime concepts (cf. Section 1.1).

Next, consider the compatibility of the relations REF and SUP. For a nonprime concept X, let $DEF(X)$ be the set of concepts from C needed to give a definition of X. For a prime concept X, let $DEF(X)$ be the empty set. Furthermore, we assume that $(A, N) \in$ REF and $(M, N) \in SUP_0$, where $A \in C_A$ and $M, N \in C_N$. Then $(A, M) \in$ REF holds if and only if $A \notin DEF(M)$ and $DEF(M) \cap (ANT(A) \cup SYN(A) \cup DEF(A)) = \varnothing$. This condition guarantees that relations like (BIJECTIVE, BIJECTION) $\in$ REF or (ISOMORPH, ANTIISOMORPHISM) $\in$ REF cannot be derived. On the other hand, if the relations $(A, B) \in SUP_0$ and $(A, N) \in$ REF are given, where $A, B \in C_A$ and $N \in C_N$, then $(B, N) \in$ REF may always be derived! For example, we may infer the existence of an (INJECTIVE MAPPING) from the existence of a (BIJECTIVE MAPPING). In the remaining two cases where $(A, M) \in$ REF and $(B, N) \in SUP_0$ or $(A, B) \in SUP_0$ and $(B, N) \in$ REF are given, the existence of the relation $(A, N) \in$ REF cannot be inferred. Examples of such disastrous inferences can easily be imagined.

Finally, let us consider the compatibility of SUP with other relations. Let K, M, and N be nominal concepts where the relations $(K, N) \in$ PREP and $(M, N) \in SUP_0$ hold. Then $(K, M) \in$ PREP may be inferred, i.e., if N is a prepositional adjunct for K, then so is any subconcept of N. For example, if (MAPPING, SET) $\in$ PREP and (GROUP, SET) $\in SUP_0$, then (MAPPING, GROUP) $\in$ PREP. Because of the similarity of these relations, the same property obviously holds for the relation OWN. Moreover, if $V \in C_V$ and $M, N \in C_N$ where $(V, M) \in$ OBJ and $(N, M) \in \mathrm{SUP_0}$, then $(V, N) \in$ OBJ is also valid. For example, if (STORE, PROGRAM) $\in$ OBJ and (SUBROUTINE, PROGRAM) $\in \mathrm{SUP_0}$, then (STORE, SUBROUTINE) $\in$ OBJ. A corresponding implication holds for the SUBJ relation. Throughout this and the previous section, we have expressed these conditions by the relation $\mathrm{SUP_0}$. They can also be extended to the relation SUP by induction.

1.4. Extensional Interpretation of the Semantic Relations

Among the relations that were introduced in Section 1.2, three classes may be distinguished, when viewed from the object level. The relations of the first class are SUP, SYN, and ANT. Whenever one of these relations holds between two concepts A and B, a corresponding relationship of the sets of objects $\phi(A)$ and $\phi(B)$ exists. From the definitions of these relations the following implications clearly result:

$$(A, B) \in \mathrm{SUP} \Rightarrow \phi(A) \subset \phi(B)$$
$$(A, B) \in \mathrm{SYN} \Rightarrow \phi(A) = \phi(B)$$
$$(A, B) \in \mathrm{ANT} \Rightarrow \phi(A) \cap \phi(B) = \varnothing$$

The second type of relation holds between two concepts A and B if these concepts may be combined to form a new concept. We denote such a new concept by $A \overset{\mathrm{REL}}{\rightarrow} B$, and the set of objects it stands for by $\phi(A \overset{\mathrm{REL}}{\rightarrow} B)$. Here, REL is the name of a particular relation. We may now specify the extensional interpretation of the relation REF by $\phi(A \overset{\mathrm{REF}}{\rightarrow} B) = \phi(A) \cap \phi(B)$. The validity of this definition becomes plausible from an arbitrary example. Let RED and DRESS be two concepts between which the relation REF holds, then a RED DRESS obviously denotes all objects that are red and that are dresses. A corresponding equation describes the extension of the relation AVAJ, i.e., $\phi(A \overset{\mathrm{AVAJ}}{\rightarrow} B) = \phi(A) \cap \phi(B)$. Things become more complicated when dealing with the relation OWN. In order to describe its extensional interpretation, we first introduce the relation $\overline{\mathrm{OWN}}$ between objects, $\overline{\mathrm{OWN}} \subset O \times O$. This relation holds between two objects if there is a possessive or a source relation (cf. Section 1.2) between the concepts to which these objects belong. The extension of OWN is then defined as

$$\phi(A \overset{\mathrm{OWN}}{\rightarrow} B) = \{o \,|\, o \,\epsilon\, \phi(B), \exists o' \,\epsilon\, \phi(A) \,[(o', o) \,\epsilon\, \overline{\mathrm{OWN}}]\}$$

Again, we illustrate this by giving an example. The concept TERM OF AN EXPRESSION would be denoted by EXPRESSION $\overset{\mathrm{OWN}}{\rightarrow}$ TERM, and the extensional interpretation of this concept, $\phi(\mathrm{EXPRESSION} \overset{\mathrm{OWN}}{\rightarrow}$

TERM), would be the set of all terms that are in an $\overline{\text{OWN}}$ relationship with an arbitrary expression. The example also clarifies why the objects denoted by $\phi(A \overset{\text{OWN}}{\rightarrow} B)$ are a subset of $\phi(B)$ rather than a subset of $\phi(A)$. Thus, a TERM OF AN EXPRESSION is a TERM, but not an EXPRESSION.

Quite similarly, the relation PREP can be treated as long as we restrict PREP to $(C_N \cup C_A) \times C_N$. For prepositions other than "of", we have relations $\overline{\text{PREP}}_i \subset O \times O$ describing the prepositional relationships between objects for particular prepositions or for classes of prepositions with similar semantics. For example, the prepositions "out", "from", and "off" may be collected in one class. The extension of the relation PREP then may be defined by $\phi(A \overset{\text{PREP}}{\rightarrow} B) = \{o | o \in \phi(B) [(o, o') \in \overline{\text{PREP}}_i]\}$, where $\overline{\text{PREP}}_i$ is chosen in accordance with the particular preposition which connects the concepts A and B.

The third type of relation is characterized by the fact that they are defined on C_V. As we stated before, the extensions of verbs are actions. Combining a verb on the conceptual level with a subject, a direct object, or a prepositional object means the restriction of the actions by the declaration of entities involved in these actions on the object level. Moreover for a nominal concept, its occurrence in a SUBJ relation also means a restriction to those of its denoted objects that may perform the corresponding action. Therefore, the extensions of the relation SUBJ and OBJ may be looked at in two different ways. In order to define this formally and to have the extensional interpretation of the relation PREP restricted to $C_V \times C_N$, we <u>first</u> have to introduce at the object level the relations $\overline{\text{SUBJ}} \subset A \times O$, $\overline{\text{OBJ}} \subset A \times O$, and $\overline{\text{POBJ}}_i \subset A \times O$. These are relations that hold between an action and an object if the extensional object acts as a logical subject, a logical object, or a prepositional object for the action, respectively. The extensions of the relations SUBJ and OBJ are then pairs of actions, and objects defined by;

$$\phi(A \overset{\text{SUBJ}}{\rightarrow} B) = (\phi(A) \times \phi(B)) \cap \overline{\text{SUBJ}}$$

$$\phi(A \overset{\text{OBJ}}{\rightarrow} B) = (\phi(A) \times \phi(B)) \cap \overline{\text{OBJ}}$$

We demonstrate this by giving another example. From the concept ERROR CORRECTING CODE, we may extract the relations (CORRECT, CODE) $\in$ SUBJ and (CORRECT, ERROR) $\in$ OBJ. $\phi(\text{CORRECT} \overset{\text{SUBJ}}{\rightarrow} \text{CODE})$ then consists of all pairs of correcting actions that are performed by codes, and the respective codes that have the ability to correct something. $\phi(\text{CORRECT} \overset{\text{OBJ}}{\rightarrow} \text{ERROR})$ consists of all pairs of correcting actions that are applied to errors and the respective errors that are corrected. Furthermore, we can now define the extension of PREP as

$$\phi(A \xrightarrow{\text{PREP}} B) = \{a \mid a \ \epsilon \ \phi(A), \ \exists o \ \epsilon \ \phi(B) \ [(a, o) \in \overline{\text{POBJ}_i}]\}$$

Here, A has to be an element of C_V, and $\overline{\text{POBJ}_i}$ is the relation that corresponds to the respective preposition. An example is the expression TO EXTRACT FROM A FILE, where the extension $\phi(\text{EXTRACT} \xrightarrow{\text{PREP}} \text{FILE})$ is the set of all actions of extraction pertaining to a file.

2. EXTENSIONAL SEMANTIC NETWORKS

Schwind [1972] has described the representation of semantic networks, based on conceptual relations, as hierarchical graphs. The graph structure of Fig. 1a shows a relation R that holds between two concepts A and B. The nodes are labeled with the concepts they are intended to represent and R is the label of the directed arc. Figure 1b shows the graph representation of (SET, ELEMENT) $\in$ OWN. If there is another concept referring to one of the nodes A and B, and if there is another relation R' that is "subordinated" to R, then the node is replaced by the appropriate graph to obtain a hierarchical graph. In the above example, if both (FINITE, SET) $\in$ REF and (GREATEST, ELEMENT) $\in$ REF are defined, we obtain the graph in Fig. 1c.

Thus, the original domain of a relation is extended to graphs in a natural way. Analogously, we can extend the definition of the extensions of concepts and relations to extensions of hierarchical graphs. In the following, we give a formal definition of hierarchical graphs (due to Pratt [1969]). A

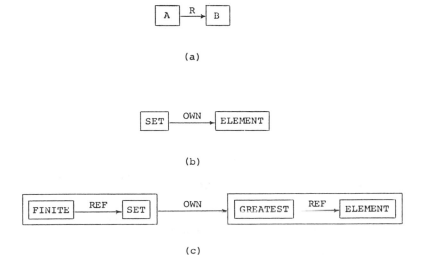

(a)

(b)

(c)

Fig. 1. (a) Graphical representation of $(A, B) \in R$. (b) Representation of (SET, ELEMENT) $\in$ OWN. (c) Substitution of (FINITE, SET) $\in$ REF for SET and of (GREATEST, ELEMENT) $\in$ REF for ELEMENT in (b).

graph will be called a network if it is intended to model a certain subject area. A network will be called an extensional semantic network if it comprises an extension function. Graphs have been widely used for the representation of natural language meaning. Formal definitions have been given by Boley [1977] and Fikes and Hendrix [1977]. Schwind [1972] introduced H-graphs, and formal grammars for their generation, for the representation of noun phrases.

2.1. S-Graphs

Definition 2.1.1 An extended directed graph G is a quadruple (N, L, E, n_0), where

(1) $N \neq \emptyset$ is a finite set of nodes,
(2) L is a finite set of labels,
(3) $N \cap L = \emptyset$
(4) $E \subset N \times L \times N$ is a set of arcs,
(5) $n_0 \in N$ is the entry node.

Definition 2.1.2 An H-graph is a quadruple $H = (\Omega, L, N, V)$, where

(1) $\Omega \neq \emptyset$ is a set of atoms,
(2) L is a finite set of labels,
(3) $N \neq \emptyset$ is a finite set of nodes,
(4) Ω, L, and N are pairwise disjoint,
(5) $V: N \rightarrow \Omega \cup G^*$ is a function (called the value function) with $G^* = \{G | G = (N', L', E', n_0')$, an extended directed graph with $N' \subset N$ and $L' \subset L\}$.

Pratt [1969] introduced H-graphs to represent the semantics of programming languages and programs. For our purposes, a restriction of this definition is required. It may be formulated after introducing the following content functions.

Definition 2.1.3 Let $H = (\Omega, L, N, V)$ be an H-graph. Then

(a) $C: 2^N \rightarrow 2^N$ is a function defined by

$$C(M) = \begin{cases} \emptyset, & \text{if } M = \emptyset \text{ or } M = \{n\} \text{ and } V(n) \in \Omega, \\ N', & \text{if } M = \{n\} \text{ and } V(n) = (N', L', E', n'), \\ \cup \{C(\{n\}) | n \in M\} & \text{if } |M| \geq 2, \end{cases}$$

where $M \subset N$.

(b) $C^k: N \rightarrow 2^N$ (with $k \geq 1$) is defined by

$$C^1(n) = C(\{n\}), \qquad C^{k+1}(n) = C(C^k(n)).$$

Definition 2.1.4 An H-graph $S = (\Omega, L, N, V)$ is called an S-graph if

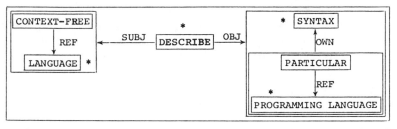

Fig. 2. Graphical representation of the sentence "A context-free language describes the syntax of a particular programming language."

(1) $\exists n \in N[\cup\{C^k(n)|k \geq 1\} = N\setminus\{n\}]$, and

(2) $\forall n \in N,\ \exists k \in \mathcal{N}[C^k(n) = \varnothing]$, where $\mathcal{N}$ is the set of natural numbers.

Part (1) of Definition 2.1.4 means that there exists a most exterior node and part (2) states that there are no recursive nodes. From these two, it can be easily derived that there is exactly one most exterior node. Figure 2 presents a representation of the sentence "A context-free language describes the syntax of a particular programming language." The entry node of a particular node is indicated by an asterisk.

For applying extensional semantic networks to question-answering systems, we require the following definition.

Definition 2.1.5 Given two S-graphs $S_i = (\Omega_i, L_i, N_i, V_i), i = 1, 2, S_1$ is a subgraph of $S_2, S_1 \subset S_2$, if

(1) $\Omega_1 \subset \Omega_2$,

(2) $N_1 \subset N_2$,

(3) $L_1 \subset L_2$, and

(4) if $n \in N_1$, then $V_1(n) = V_2(n)$ or $V_1(n) \subset V_2(n)$.

If $S_1 \neq S_2$, then S_1 is a proper subgraph of S_2. The graph of Fig. 2 has two subgraphs shown in Fig. 3.

One reason for having an entry node is to indicate the subnode of a node, to which arcs from the exterior can refer. This is particularly needed for the representation of relative clauses. Consider the graph in Fig. 4. It represents the sentence "The mother who drinks milk works in the factory." The entry node signals what concept is the subject of the superordinated sentence, whereas the sentence node restricts this subject in some

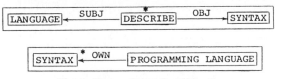

Fig. 3. Two subgraphs of Fig. 2.

```
┌─────────────────────────────────────────────────────────────────────┐
│ ┌──────┐  SUBJ  ┌──────┐  OBJ  ┌──────┐        SUBJ  ┌──────┐  IN  ┌────────┐│
│ │MOTHER│◄──────│DRINK │──────►│ MILK │◄───────────│WORK │────►│FACTORY││
│ └──────┘       └──────┘       └──────┘             └──────┘     └────────┘│
└─────────────────────────────────────────────────────────────────────┘
```

Fig. 4. "The mother who drinks milk works in the factory."

way. From the example in Fig. 4, we see that the entry node is not always the same for given graphs—it depends on how graphs are related to other concepts. Consider the sentence "The milk the mother is drinking is hot," represented by the graph in Fig. 5. The values in the sentence nodes in Figs. 4 and 5 differ only with respect to the entry node. In Fig. 4, the SUBJ arc refers to MOTHER but the REF arc in Fig. 5 refers to MILK. If a sentence is not a relative clause but the value of the most exterior node of an S-graph, we believe that the entry node should be the verb node of that sentence graph.

2.2. Semantic Networks

We use S-graphs for the representation of conceptually characterized subject areas. S-graphs therefore have concepts or actions as atoms and semantic relations as labels. Because the concepts and relations have a meaning dependent on the subject area to be characterized, it is clear that every structure arbitrarily generated from concepts and relations is not necessarily a meaningful one. Thus, for example, the source node of a SUBJ arc has to be a verb, the source node of a REF arc has to be an adjective or an element of the AVAJ relation. Furthermore, natural language allows the combination of both atomic and nonatomic concepts by the operators "and" and "or." We handle this phenomenon by including the respective concepts as isolated nodes in special "∧-nodes" and "∨-nodes." Thus, the sentence "The child is wearing a blue sweater and the mother's stockings" would be represented by the structure in Fig. 6. Since every arc referring to an ∧-node or an ∨-node refers also to each of its subnodes, it is not reasonable to assign entry nodes to such. In the following, we assume that every node can be an ∧-node or an ∨-node, composed of two other nodes of compatible types.

Graphs consisting of atoms from C, the set of all concepts, and relations from R, a set of relations, are restricted with respect to their structure as well as to their node values. First, we consider structure restrictions. The following list restricts the arc sets of graphs. A graph that is the value of

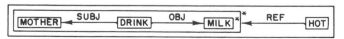

Fig. 5. "The milk the mother is drinking is hot."

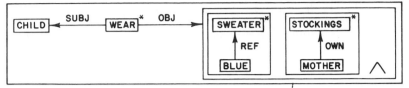

Fig. 6. "The child is wearing a blue sweater and the mother's stockings."

one of the nodes of an S-graph with atoms from C and labels from R must have one of the following arc sets:

(1) $E = \{(n_1, REL, n_2)|REL \in \{REF, AVAJ, OWN, PREP\}\}$, or
(2) $E = (n_0, R_1, n_1)$, where $R_i \in \{SUBJ, OBJ, PREP\}$.

These two types of restrictions are shown in Fig. 7a and 7b, respectively.

Next, we consider node value restrictions. In order to list the semantic restrictions concerning the combination of nodes depending on node values, we must first define the type of a node. A node n is of type

verb	if $V(n) \in C_V$,
noun	if $V(n) \in C_N$,
adj	if $V(n) \in C_A$,
adv	if $V(n) \in C_{AD}$,
rel	if $V(n)$ has the structure as in (1) above, or
s	if $V(n)$ has the structure as in (2) above.

Table I contains the semantic relation restrictions that belong to our set of relations and concepts.

Definition 2.2.1 An S-graph $S = (C_S, R_S, N, V)$ is called a semantic network over C and R if

(1) $C_S \subset C$ is a set of concepts,

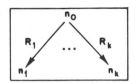

(a)

(b)

Fig. 7.

TABLE I

Semantic Relation Restrictions

Arc label	Type of source node	Type of target node
REF	adj, avaj	noun, ref, s
AVAJ	adv	adj, avaj
OWN	noun, ref	noun, ref, prep, own, s
PREP	noun, ref, verb	noun, ref, prep, own, s
SUBJ	verb	noun, ref, prep, own, s
OBJ	verb	noun, ref, prep, own, s

(2) $R_S \subset R$ is a set of semantic relations on C,

(3)   all node values and arcs satisfy the structure and node value restrictions given above.

2.3.   Relations and Operations on Semantic Networks

Because semantic networks may represent concepts, we extend the definition of SUP_0 to networks. Intuitively, a network S_1 is subordinated to another network S_2 if S_1 has the same structure as S_2 and if corresponding nodes have the same values or subordinated values.

Definition 2.3.1   (a)   Let $G_i = (N_i, L_i, E_i, n_i)$, $i = 1, 2$, be extended directed graphs. Then $G_1 \text{ SUP } G_2$ if

(1) $L_1 = L_2$,

(2)   there is a bijective mapping $f: N_1 \rightarrow N_2$ with $f(n_1) = n_2$, and

(3) $(n, e, m) \in E_1$ implies that $(f(n), e, f(m)) \in E_2$ and $n \text{ SUP } f(n)$ or $n = f(n)$.

(b)   Let $S_i = (C_i, R_i, N_i, V_i)$, $i = 1, 2$, be semantic networks. Then $S_1 \text{ SUP } S_2$ if there is a bijective mapping $f: N_1 \rightarrow N_2$ such that $\forall n \in N_1[V(n) \text{ SUP } V(f(n))]$.

Figure 8 contains an exemplary network.

Relation arcs within semantic networks join nodes whose values may be other graphs. As we have already noted, an arc that has such a complex node as target node or source node always refers to one of the content nodes. Thus, it is possible to obtain relations between atomic nodes from

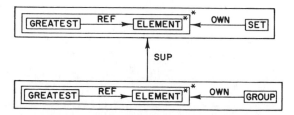

Fig. 8. An exemplary semantic network.

the relations between the complex nodes. If (n, e, m) is an arc occurring within a semantic network, then the relation denoted by e holds between the values of n and m, if n and m are atomic; and between the entry nodes of $V(n)$ and $V(m)$, if n and m have graphs as values. For the definition of the operation, the result of which is the relation between atoms within a semantic network, we define the following function. (Its domain is the set of nodes and its values are the atomic entry nodes.)

Definition 2.3.2 Let $S = (C_S, R\Sigma, N, V)$ be a semantic network. Then $*: N \to C_S$ is a function defined by

$$*(n) = \begin{cases} V(n) & \text{if } V(n) \in C_S, \\ *(V(n_0')) & \text{if } V(n) = (N', L', E', n_0'). \end{cases}$$

Definition 2.3.3 Let $S = (C_S, R_S, N, V)$ be a semantic network.

(a) $A(S) = \cup\{E' | \exists n \in N \text{ and } V(n) = (N', L', E', n_0')\}$ is the set of all arcs occurring within S.

(b) $\rho_0: A(S) \to C_S \times R_S \times C_S$ is a function defined by $\rho_0((n, r, m)) = (*(n), r, *(m))$.

(c) $\rho: \gamma \to 2^{C \times R \times C}$, γ being the set of semantic networks according to the set of concepts C, the set of relations R, and the restrictions of Section 2.2. ρ is defined by $\rho(S) = \rho_0(A(S))$.

The value of ρ for a semantic network S is the set of all triples $\rho_0(a)$ for an arc $a \in A(S)$. It is clear that $(A, \text{REL}, B) \in \rho(S)$ means $(A, B) \in \text{REL}$. For example, consider the network of Fig. 2. For that network, $\rho(S) = \{(\text{DES-CRIBE, SUBJ, LANGUAGE}), (\text{DESCRIBE, OBJ, SYNTAX}), (\text{PROGRAM-MING LANGUAGE, OWN, SYNTAX}), (\text{PARTICULAR, REF, PROGRAM-MING LANGUAGE})\}$.

2.4. Extensional Interpretation of Networks

In Section 1, we introduced extensions of concepts and relations. Because a semantic network is intended to represent objects and actions related to each other, we define its extension in terms of the extensions of its atoms and relations. We define the extension of a node n of type t as follows:

(1) If n is not of type s, then its extension is given by the extension of the appropriate relation or, if n is atomic, by the extension of the appropriate concept.

(2) If $t = s$ and $V(n)$ is a structure as in Fig. 9, then

$$\phi(n) = \Pi_{i_0}(\{(v, a_1, \ldots, a_k) | (v, a_i) \in \phi(n_0 \to n_i), 1 \le i \le k\}),$$

where Π_{i_0} is the i_0-th projection function applied to the whole domain and i_0 is the place of the entry node in $V(n)$.

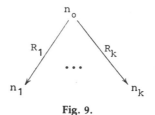

Fig. 9.

From the network in Fig. 10 and its associated relations, we have $\phi(n_1) = \Pi_4 (\{(\text{meet}_0, \text{John}, \text{Mary}, \text{garden}_0), (\text{meet}_1, \text{John}, \text{Mary}, \text{school}_0), (\text{meet}_2, \text{John}, \text{Kate}, \text{theater}_0)\}) = \{\text{garden}_0, \text{school}_0, \text{theater}_0\}$ and $\phi(n) = \phi(n_1) \cap \phi(\text{BEAUTIFUL}) = \{\text{theater}_0, \text{garden}_0\}$. Thus, the extension of this sentence graph is the set of beautiful places where a human is meeting a human.

Let $S = (C_S, R_S, N, V)$ be a semantic network, where $C_S \subset C$ is a set of concepts and $R_S \subset R$ is a set of semantic relations on C, and let ϕ be an extension function belonging to C and R. Then the extension of S is given by $\phi(S) = \phi(V(n_e))$, where n_e is the most exterior node of S.

Definition 2.4.1   An extensional semantic network (ESN) is a quintuple (C_S, R_S, N, V, ϕ), where (C_S, R_S, N, V) is a semantic network with $C_S \subset C$, $R_S \subset R$, and ϕ is an extension function for C and R.

2.5.   Quantification, Negation, and Network Expressions

Semantic networks, as described above, represent conceptual structures of a subject area. ESNs represent the facts underlying the appropriate conceptual structures. The extension of a network, like the network of Fig. 10, is the value of a projection function defined on a set containing tuples like $(\text{meet}_0, \text{John}, \text{Mary}, \text{garden}_0)$ and $(\text{meet}_2, \text{John}, \text{Kate}, \text{theater}_0)$. Such a tuple expresses the fact that "John meets Mary in the garden," i.e., constitutes a statement that may or may not be derivable from a given ESN. We

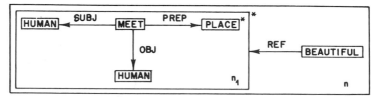

Fig. 10.   An exemplary network, where

$$\overline{\text{SUBJ}} = \{(\text{meet}_0, \text{John}), (\text{meet}_1, \text{John}), (\text{meet}_2, \text{John})\},$$
$$\overline{\text{OBJ}} = \{(\text{meet}_0, \text{Mary}), (\text{meet}_1, \text{Mary}), (\text{meet}_2, \text{Kate})\},$$
$$\overline{\text{PREP}} = {}^{\prime}(\text{meet}_0, \text{graden}_0), (\text{meet}_1, \text{school}_0),$$
$$(\text{meet}_2, \text{theater}_0)\},$$
$$\phi(\text{BEAUTIFUL}) = \{\text{theater}_0, \text{garden}_0, \text{flower}_1, \text{Kate}\},$$
$$\phi(\text{HUMAN}) = \{\text{John}, \text{Mary}, \text{Kate}, \ldots\},$$
$$\phi(\text{PLACE}) = \{\text{theater}_0, \text{garden}_0, \text{school}_0, \ldots\}.$$

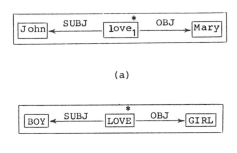

(a)

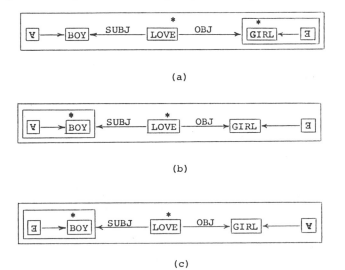

Fig. 11. (a) A network expression. (b) A semantic network.

(b)

call such statements, together with the network structure, network expressions. We represent network expressions by replacing the concepts in a network by objects that are in accordance with the extensions of the relations holding between two concepts. Such a network expression has the same structure as the underlying network. For example, the network of Fig. 11a is a network expression of the network structure of Fig. 11b.

Other kinds of expressions on the extensional level are statements with quantifiers. We represent quantification of a concept within a network by either replacing a node by a quantified structure or by appending a quantifier to a node. If a quantifier is appended to a node containing a graph, the quantifier is to refer to the entry node of the graph. Thus, quantifiers may appear on every level of a semantic network. By appropriate usage of the hierarchy, we can express mutual dependencies of quantified expressions.

From the network of Fig. 11, we may obtain the network expressions in Fig. 12. Figure 12a represents "Every boy loves a girl." The semantic net-

(a)

(b)

(c)

Fig. 12. (a) "Every boy loves a girl." (b) "There is some girl that all boys love." (c) "Every girl is loved by some boy."

work describes that possibly there are boys loving girls, whereas the network expression states that "Every boy loves some girl." The dependency of the quantified expression $(\exists x)[\text{Girl}(x)]$ on the quantified expression $(\forall y)[\text{boy}(y)]$ is expressed by means of the hierarchy. Thus, the "more inside" quantifier depends on the "more outside" one. Figure 12b represents "There is some girl that all boys love." Here, the universal quantifier is dependent on the existential. It should be noted that these differentiations by means of the hierarchies are only important for inner existential quantifiers because $\forall x \exists y \ldots$ is logically derivable from $\exists y \forall x \ldots$, whereas the converse does not hold. Thus, it is always possible to move the universal quantifiers on the top of a logical expression. We shall use this theorem when we formulate derivation rules for network expressions. It will then be sufficient to use only derivation rules such that universal quantifiers are always "out," whereas existential ones may be "out" or "in." Figure 12c represents "Every girl is loved by some boy." Thus, we can get any combination and it is clear what they mean.

Quantifiers may also appear within more complex expressions. The expression "Every intelligent boy who studies at some school owns a desk" is represented by the network in Fig. 13. In this example, the existential quantifier depends on the universal quantifier. In addition, the universal quantifier referring to a node that contains a graph refers to the entry node of that graph.

Because network expressions have the same structure as networks, we may define them formally in a similar manner.

Definition 2.5.1 A network expression is an S-graph $E = (T_E, R_E, N, V)$, where

    (1) $T_E \subset O \cup A \cup \{\exists, \forall\}$ is a set of objects, actions, and quantifiers,
    (2) $R_E \subset \{\text{REL}|\text{REL} \in R\} \cup \{\epsilon\}$ is a set of object relations belonging to conceptual relations and the ϵ label for appending quantifiers, and
    (3) $(n, r, m) \in A(E)$ implies $V(n) \in \{\exists, \forall\}$ if and only if $r = \epsilon$, i.e. quantifiers are always appended to a node by an ϵ arc. (It is noted that the ϵ label does not appear in the diagram.)

It should be pointed out that this approach to quantification resolves most of the problems mentioned in Woods [1975] and, due to the hierar-

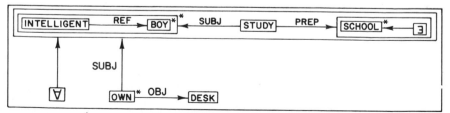

Fig. 13. "Every intelligent boy who studies at some school owns a desk."

chical structure of the networks, it also avoids the difficult notation, such as that in Schubert [1975] or Simmons and Chester [1977]. Moreover, the extension underlying a network gives us a natural means to determine quantifier domain restrictions. We give derivation rules for network expressions in the next section.

Negation can be expressed in an analogous fashion, namely, by appending "¬ nodes" to nodes and to arcs. Negation can be introduced for semantic networks, on the conceptual level, as well as for network expressions, on the extensional level. Negation within a semantic network means that the appropriate negated relation does not hold. An example for a covert negation is given by the incorporation of the ANT relation. In network expressions, it is possible to negate verb nodes in order to represent the negated network expression or to append a ¬ node to a quantifier to reverse its meaning. When a ¬ node is appended to a sentence node, it will change the quantifiers, if there are any, and will be appended to the verb node. We shall not outline the negation rules in detail but give examples of a negated network and of negated network expressions. Figures 14a and 14b are equivalent as well as Fig. 14c and 14d. We think that the examples show how such derivation rules may be applied and what may

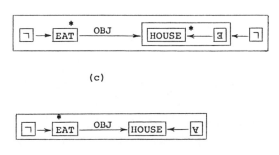

(a)

(b)

(c)

(d)

Fig. 14. Network examples of negation. (a) "It is not possible that houses are eaten." (b) "A house cannot be eaten." (c) "No house can be eaten." (d) "All things which are houses cannot be eaten."

be the result of their application. We are aware of the various difficulties posed by the introduction of such restrictions concerning the negation of conceptual relations, such as in Fig. 14b. Wilks [1977] discusses such problems in detail.

3. APPLICABILITY OF ESNs

ESNs provide a very general framework for meaning representation. Consequently, they can be used in all domains where it is necessary to reason in natural language. The special applications determine the choice of data structures for the representation of ESNs. We present examples of two applications. One uses only semantic networks and the other provides reasoning at both conceptual and extensional levels.

3.1. Semantic Networks as Scientific Languages and Their Use in Automatic Indexing

As mentioned in Section 1.1, the language of a scientific subject area is constructed systematically from prime concepts, which are used to define more specialized concepts. A definition of a concept usually consists of that concept and of a natural language text in which other concepts occur that have already been defined or are prime. Between all concepts of a definition, certain semantic relations hold. For example, a definition may contain superordinated concepts of a concept or referential concepts of an adjectival concept. Thus, it is possible to represent a definition by a semantic network. We call such a network a thesaurus. An example entry appears in Fig. 15.

It is possible to extract automatically these semantic relationships from text. Schwind [1971] describes an algorithm that automatically finds semantic relations from definitions in a mathematical textbook on general topology. Also, Schwind [1975] has shown that attributed grammars provide a very useful tool for the translation of definitions into semantic networks. We shall show in the next section how such translation algorithms may be generated with the help of a compiler–compiler.

A thesaurus is very important in documentation systems where the doc-

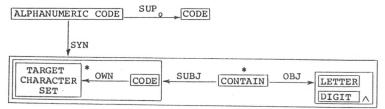

Fig. 15. "An alphanumeric code is a code whose character set contains both letters and digits."

uments consist of natural language text, such as abstracts in a library system. Here, an indexing device is needed that automatically extracts concepts from the documents to be stored in order to facilitate later retrieval. Braun and Schwind [1976] describe an indexing algorithm that extracts phrases, sequences of single-word concepts, from text, using a semantic network. Their idea is based on the observation that within every phrase certain semantic relations hold between the concepts in that phrase. Consequently, given a semantic network, including all the semantic relations of a particular subject area, it is possible to generate all phrases by combining the single-word concepts according to the relations (see Schwind [1972]). Taking into account this consideration, the indexing algorithm can find all phrases occurring in a text by combining the single-word concepts of the text by means of the semantic network. The algorithm proceeds as follows. From the single-word concepts occurring in a text, a set of start phrases is formed by combining two or more concepts if one of the semantic relations holds between them. Thus, starting phrases of the form X REF Y or X OWN Y are formed. Then these starting phrases can be inserted into each other according to specific rules. One such rule is that X REF Y can replace Y within Y OWN Z or within Z OWN Y.

Consider the sentence "A poset is a set in which a binary relation $x \leq y$ is defined which satisfies for all x, y, z the following conditions. . . ." We can generate the starting phrases BINARY REF RELATION, RELATION ON SET, and RELATION ON POSET. From these starting phrases, we obtain, by combination, the noun phrases ((BINARY REF RELATION) ON SET) and ((BINARY REF RELATION) ON POSET). It would be very difficult to find the phrases (RELATION ON SET) and (RELATION ON POSET) syntactically, but semantically we obtain (RELATION ON SET) directly from the network. By appropriate usage of the SUP relation, between broader and narrower concepts, which holds between SET and POSET, we obtain (RELATION ON POSET).

This algorithm has been applied to index mathematical texts via a network containing lattice theory concepts and, also, to index computer science abstracts via a network for computer science. The semantic relations that comprise the network have been realized in the following way. There is a dictionary containing all concepts C belonging to the network. For every dictionary entry, there are labeled pointers to other dictionary entries representing the semantic relations between single-word concepts. Since semantic relations may also hold between single-word concepts and phrases, there are also pointers from dictionary entries to semantic networks. Figure 16 shows such an entry.

The labeled pointers from dictionary entries to other concepts or semantic networks represent the following semantic relations. SUP_0 is specified in one direction only. Every concept has pointers to all directly su-

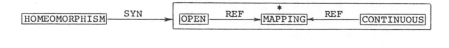

dictionary   semantic network

entry

Fig. 16. A dictionary entry that references a semantic network.

perordinated concepts or networks. The transitive closure SUP of SUP_0 may be calculated by following the SUP_0 chains. REF is also always specified in only one direction. Every adjective has pointers to all noun concepts or networks that it may modify. If the SUP relation holds between one of these concepts, the pointer is set to the most general one. The other concepts may be found by applying the right compatibility of REF and SUP, as mentioned in Section 1.3.

The relations OWN and PREP, as well as the verbal relations, are specified in only one direction. The prepositional supplements of a concept are given by pointers labeled with the appropriate prepositional relation names. For every verb, pointers are given to the appropriate noun concept or networks that may be subjects or objects of that verb. Here, too, only the most general concept is given, the others are found by following the SUP chains.

As described by Schwind [1974], semantic networks for mathematics can be presented in a very natural way by linear expressions. Schwind also defined an appropriate network manipulation language in the above referenced work.

3.2. Derivation of Networks and Network Expressions

A wide field of application, question-answering systems (QAS), uses semantic networks for the derivation of answers to questions. We propose a representation where the subject area of the QAS is given by a semantic network and the facts by its extension. The following derivation rules are formulated for ESNs.

The derivation of semantic networks is formulated by means of the SUP relation (cf. Section 2.3.1), which may hold between networks, and the subgraph relation (cf. Section 2.1.5) between networks. From a network, we may derive every subgraph that it contains. The following rules are dependent on the subject area that the network describes. We propose derivation rules for the domain whose semantic relations have been defined in Section 1.2. Thus, we have two rules, R1 and R2:

$$(R1) \quad N_1 \Rightarrow N_2 \quad \text{if } N_1 \subset N_2.$$
$$(R2) \quad N_1 \Rightarrow N_2 \quad \text{if } N_2 \text{ SUP } N_1.$$

For example, given the network in Figs. 17a and 17b, we can derive the

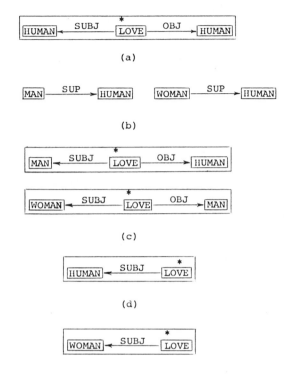

(a)

(b)

(c)

(d)

(e)

Fig. 17. Network derivations (see text).

two networks in Fig. 17c by R2. By R1, we can derive the network in Fig. 17d and, from it by R2, Fig. 17e.

As mentioned in the previous section, it is possible to obtain network expressions from networks by either replacing concepts by objects or appending quantifiers to nodes. Thus, we have our third rule,

$$(R3) \quad N \Rightarrow E \qquad \text{if } *(V(N_E)) \in \phi(N),$$

where $E = (T_E, R_E, N_E, V_E)$ and $\epsilon \notin R_E$. A network expression without quantifiers may be derived from a network if the object denoted by the network expression, which is the value of the $*$ function defined in Section 2.2.3, is an element of the extension of that network. For example, let $\phi(N) = \Pi_1(\{(l_1, \text{John, Mary}), (l_2, \text{Mary, John}), (l_3, \text{Kate, John})\})$, where N is the network in Fig. 17. Then the network expressions in Fig. 18 are derivable from N.

The following two rules provide for the appending of quantifiers to nodes. Let N be a network of type s, graphically displayed in Fig. 19a, where $R_i \in \{\text{SUBJ, OBJ}\}$ for $1 \leq i \leq k$. Then, we have the new rule R4 as depicted in Fig. 19b. R4 appends a universal quantifier to a subject or object node of a network, provided the extension of the network comprises

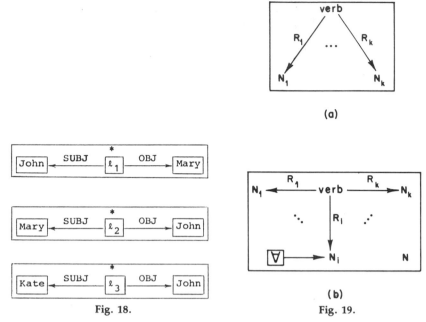

Fig. 18.   Fig. 19.

Fig. 18. Network expressions derivable from the network of Section 3.2.1.

Fig. 19. (a) A network of type s, where $R_i \in \{\text{SUBJ, OBJ}\}$.,(b) Rule R4 is applicable only if $\Pi_i(\phi(N)) = \phi(V(N_i))$.

all elements of the extension of the respective node. R5, as depicted in Fig. 20, appends an existential quantifier and can only be applied if the underlying extension is not empty. Again, from the network N of Fig. 17, we can derive the network N'' pictured in Fig. 21a by applying R5 twice. If $\phi(\text{MAN}) = \{\text{John, Robert}\}$ and $\phi(\text{WOMAN}) = \{\text{Mary, Kate}\}$, then we can derive the network in Fig. 21b by applying R2 to N, resulting in N'. Then, by applying R4 to the WOMAN node of N' and R5 to the MAN node, the network of Fig. 21c is obtained.

As another example, let N be the network of Fig. 22a, with $\phi(\text{MAN})$ and $\phi(\text{WOMAN})$ as in the previous example, and $\phi(\text{INTELLIGENT}) = \{\text{Mary, John}\}$, $\phi(\text{WORK} \overset{\text{SUBJ}}{\rightarrow} \text{MAN}) = \{\text{John}\}$. Then, we can derive the networks in Figs. 22b and 22c, representing "Every intelligent woman loves

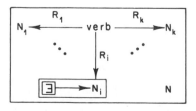

Fig. 20. Rule R5 is applicable only if the underlying extension is not empty.

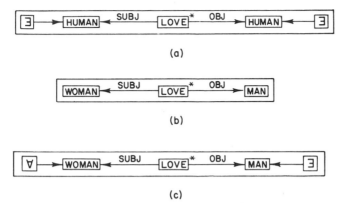

Fig. 21. (a) Network obtained by applying R5 twice. (b) Resultant network *N*, after applying R2. (c) Application of R4 to the WOMAN node and R5 to the MAN node of *N'*.

every man who is working" and "Every woman loves a man working," respectively.

It is also possible to derive network expressions from network expressions by replacing quantified nodes by elements of their extensions. In the following rules, E_1 and E_2 are network expressions:

(R6) $E_1 \Rightarrow E_2$, if E_2 is obtained from E_1 thorugh replacing the value of an "∃ node" by an element of the appropriate extension.

(R7) $E_1 \Rightarrow E_2$, if E_2 is obtained from E_1 by replacing the value of an "∀ node" by an arbitrary element of its extension.

For example, from the network in Fig. 21c, we can derive Fig. 23a by R6 and Fig. 23b by R7.

4. AUTOMATIC GENERATION OF SEMANTIC NETWORKS

Woods [1975] cites three main requirements for a semantic representation. Two of these, namely, the logical adequacy of the representation and the ability to make inferences and deductions from the representation, have been discussed in previous sections. In this section, we address the third requirement. We outline a procedure for translating natural language text into a semantic network. Therefore, we introduce the tools that are employed for the translation process and present a larger example for the translation.

4.1. Tools for the Translation Process

Any semantic network may be regarded as a language in which the meaning of certain facts is expressed. Thus, the translation of natural language text into a semantic network may be viewed simplistically as a translation from one language to another. As far as programming lan-

(a)

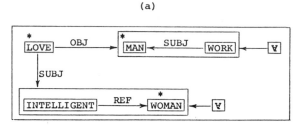

(b)

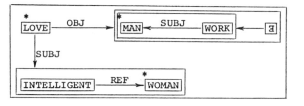

(c)

Fig. 22. (a) The Network *N*. (b) "Every intelligent woman loves every man who is working." (c) "Every woman loves a man working."

guages are concerned, such a translation is done by a compiler. A compiler may be either written by hand or may be generated by a program from a description of the source language, the target language, and the intended mapping from source to target language. Such a program is called a compiler–compiler. For our particular translation problem, where the source language is natural language, it is clearly preferable to use a compiler–compiler. The scope of the source language may be extended incrementally by merely adding new production rules to the grammar. Moreover, as the system grows, it does not become an incomprehensible

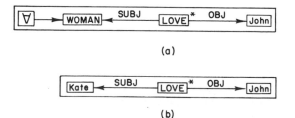

(a)

(b)

Fig. 23. (a) Derived from Fig. 21c by R6. (b) Derived from Fig. 21c by R7.

hulk, but still appears in the familiar shape of a formal grammar. As our main tool for the translation of natural language text into a semantic network, we chose the incremental compiler generating system MUG1. It was developed and implemented at the Technical University of Munich.

In the following, we present only a very brief overview of MUG1 (for details, see Ganzinger *et al.* [1976] and Ganzinger [1976]). MUG1 consists of four main generator modules, which correspond to the vertical fragmentation of the generated compiler (see Fig. 24). Nevertheless, the generated compilers are one-pass compilers because the generated modules, which realize the different compilation subtasks, work in an interleaved fashion. The scanner generator requires the definition of symbol classes. Its input symbols are elements of the source language. Symbols of the same symbol class are equivalent for syntactic analysis. Lexical analysis means the decomposition of the input string into a sequence of symbols. The parser generator accepts a context-free grammar as input and constructs a parser for it. The terminal symbols of the grammar have to correspond to the symbol classes defined for lexical analysis. As a means of describing semantic analysis, the attribute grammars (see Knuth [1968]), in the notation of affix grammars (see Koster [1971]) are used. Schwind [1975] showed the appropriateness of this approach for analyzing natural language. The input to the attribute handler generator consists of the definition of the attributes that are to be inserted into the grammar and the definition of the semantic actions, which are procedures for the manipulation of attributes. The symbols in the production rules are followed by a list of attached attributes. Different occurrences of the same symbol have to have the same attribute lists. For each attribute of a symbol, the direction of its transfer has to be defined. One must also specify whether an attribute receives its value from another attribute within the same production rule or delivers its value to one or more other attributes. The correct reference of the transfers is achieved by giving the same name to those attributes between which an assignment of a value has to take place. Calls to the semantic actions, the parameters of which are also attributes, are inserted into the

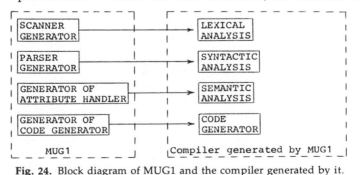

Fig. 24. Block diagram of MUG1 and the compiler generated by it.

production rules. Thus, at compile time, the attribute handler—upon calls
by the parser—effects the passing of the attributes, the administration of
an attribute stack, and the invocation of the semantic actions. The fourth
module of MUG1, the code generator, is not described here because it is
not required for our present purposes.

In trying to apply MUG1 to our translation task, we encounter a problem
with lexical analysis. The "symbols" of natural language are single words
and punctuation marks. For function words and punctuation, we may establish appropriate symbol classes. Because of the limited number of function words and punctuation marks, no problem is encountered here. The
remaining symbol classes have to be in accordance with those parts-of-
speech that are the vehicles for concepts. Yet, since a scanner of a compiler
designed for programming languages is not able to determine the part-
of-speech of an arbitrary English word represented by its corresponding
string, we have to add a "prescanner" to MUG1. The prescanner is a program designed for automatic recognition of grammatical categories for
English words. The program finds the category by analyzing endings and
by context analysis (see Janas [1975, 1977]) and supplies each word with a
marking of its part-of-speech, which is then evaluated by the MUG1 scanner. By means of the prescanner, the disambiguation of homonymous concepts (cf. Section 1.1) is achieved.

The main task of the semantic actions is to construct a network in parallel with the parsing process. For this purpose, we define the actions listed
in Table II.

TABLE II

Semantic Actions and Their Definitions

Action	Definition
CREATEATOM(*input* S; *output* N)	Creates a new atomic node N in the network whose contents is the concept denoted by the string S from the input text.
CREATENODE(*input* N1; *output* N2)	Constructs a new nonatomic node N2 in the network whose contents is the input node N1. N1 becomes the entry node of N2.
INSERT(*input* N1, N2)	Makes the node N1 a direct subnode of the nonatomic node N2.
SETRELATION(*input* N1, N2, REL)	Connects the two nodes N1 and N2 by an arc labeled with relation REL and directed from N1 to N2.
CHANGEENTRY(*input* N1, N2)	Makes N2, a direct subnode of N1, the entry node of N1.

The following sequence of semantic actions will construct the S-graph depicted in Fig. 25. Here, S_i is the string representing the concept C_i. The sequence of semantic actions is

> CREATEATOM (S3, N1),
> CREATEATOM (S4, N2),
> CREATENODE (N1, N3),
> INSERT (N2, N3),
> SETRELATION (N1, N2, R3),
> CREATEATOM (S1, N4),
> SETRELATION (N4, N3, R2),
> CREATEATOM (S2, N5),
> SETRELATION (N4, N5, R1),
> CREATENODE (N4, N6),
> INSERT (N3, N6),
> INSERT (N5, N6).

After execution of this sequence, the most exterior node of the S-graph may be addressed by means of the attribute of N6. Here, we have simplified the semantic actions and realize that others are also necessary. (The reason for the simplification is that we want the example in the next section to be clearly understandable.)

The network of a single sentence may be represented by two matrices, one of which is an adjacency matrix M1, and the other a "contents" matrix M2. The precise definition of M1 and M2 is contained in Table III. All other elements of M1 and M2 remain empty. The matrices corresponding to the S-graph in Fig. 25 are displayed in Fig. 26.

The network corresponding to an entire subject area is combined from networks constructed from single sentences and is stored in a data base according to CODASYL conventions. The representation in the data base depends to a high degree upon the application of the network and is not discussed here.

4.2. Example of Network Generation

In this section, we present an example of the translation of a particular sentence. We shall neglect the activities of the prescanner and the scanner,

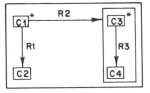

Fig. 25.

TABLE III

$M1_{ik} = R_j$	There is an arc from node N_i to node N_k with label R_j.
$M2_{ii} = C_j$	N_i is an atomic node containing the concept C_j.
$M2_{ik} = X$	N_i is a nonatomic node that contains the node N_k as its direct subnode.

and focus on the parsing and generation processes. Suppose we are given the simple context-free grammar in Fig. 27, where S is the start symbol and the terminal symbols are underlined. In Figure 27, NP, VP, and PP stand for nominal, verbal, and prepositional phrase, respectively. RC stands for relative clause and VGP for passive verb group. The terminal symbols *by* and *of* are symbol classes that contain the words "by" and "of," respectively, whereas *preposition* contains all other prepositions. Finally, *be-form* contains the words "is," "are," and "was." All other symbols are self-explanatory. Using this grammar, sentences like "A correct algorithm finds the solution of the equation that comprises an important result in a finite number of steps" can be parsed. The corresponding network representation is shown in Fig. 28.

We now complete the above grammar by including the attributes and the semantic actions so that the network of Fig. 28 may be obtained while parsing according to the grammar:

(1)   S: NP (n_1, e_1)
      VP (n, e)
          call SETRELATION (e, n_1, SUBJ)
          call INSERT (n_1, n)

To each nonterminal symbol, except the start symbol, there are two attributes attached. The first attribute denotes the node in the network corresponding to the actual occurrence of the symbol and the second stands for the entry node of the former node. Resulting from the call of SETRELATION, an arc between the entry node of the VP node and the NP node is established. Afterwards, the NP node is inserted into the VP node.

(2)   NP (n, e): NP1 (n, e)

The attribute values of n and e are transferred from the left- to the right-hand side. This is the case in all of the following production rules.

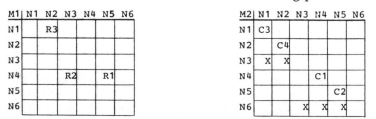

Fig. 26. The "adjacency" and "contents" matrices for the network of Fig. 25.

(1′)	S:	NP VP
(2′)	NP:	NP1
(3′)	NP:	NP1 RC
(4′)	NP1:	NP2
(5′)	NP1:	NP2 <u>of</u> NP2
(6′)	NP2:	NP3
(7′)	NP2:	<u>determiner</u> NP3
(8′)	NP3:	<u>noun</u>
(9′)	NP3:	<u>adjective</u> <u>noun</u>
(10′)	RC:	<u>by rel. pronoun</u> NP1 VGP
(11′)	VGP:	<u>be-form</u> <u>past-participle</u>
(12′)	VP:	<u>verb</u> NP PP
(13′)	PP:	<u>preposition</u> NP

Fig. 27. Sample grammar.

$$(3) \quad NP\,(n, e): NP1\,(e, e_1)$$
$$RC\,(n, e_2)$$
$$\text{call SETRELATION}\,(e_2, e, SUBJ)$$
$$\text{call INSERT}\,(e, n)$$
$$\text{call CHANGEENTRY}\,(n, e)$$

The beginning of the rule is quite similar to (1). In addition, the NP1 node is made the entry node of the relative clause node.

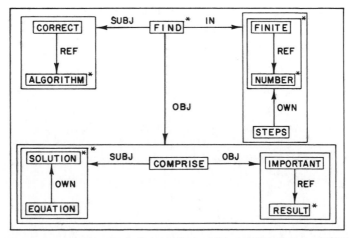

Fig. 28. "A correct algorithm finds the solution of the equation that comprises an important result in a finite number of steps."

(4)   NP1 (n, e): NP2 (n, e)
(5)   NP1 (n, e): NP2 (e, e_1)
            of
            NP2 (n_1, e_2)
                    call SETRELATION (n_1, e, OWN)
                    call CREATENODE (e, n)
                    call INSERT (n_1, n)

The node created becomes the value of the node attribute of NP1 and the first of the two NP2 nodes becomes its entry node.

(6)   NP2 (n, e): NP3 (n, e)
(7)   NP2 (n, e): *determiner*
            NP3 (n, e)

The presence or absence of a determiner does not influence the network structure.

(8)   NP3 (n, e): *noun* (s)
                    call CREATERATOM (s, n)
                    call ASSIGN (e, n)

The scanner delivers the string s, which denotes a nominal concept, and CREATEATOM builds a new node containing this concept. By the call of ASSIGN, the value of n is assigned to e, i.e., the entry node of an atomic node is the node itself.

(9)   NP3 (n, e): *adjective* (s_1)
                    call CREATEATOM (s_1, n_1)
            noun (s_2)
                    call CREATEATOM (s_2, e)
                    call SETRELATION (n_1, e, REF)
                    call CREATENODE (e, n)
                    call INSERT (n_1, n)
(10) RC (n, e): *by*
            rel. pronoun
            NP1 (n_1, e_1)
            VGP (e, e_2)
                    call SETRELATION (e, n_1, OBJ)
                    call CREATENODE (e, n)
                    call INSERT (n_1', n)

Note that the SUBJ arc leaving from the VGP node will be established by production rule (3).

(11) VGP (n, e): *be-form*
              past-participle (s)
                    call CREATEATOM (s, n)
                    call ASSIGN (e, n)

(12)   VP (n, e): *verb* (s)
             call CREATEATOM (s, e)
        NP (n_1, e_1)
             call SETRELATION (e, n_1, OBJ)
      PP (n_2, e_2, p)
             call SETRELATION (e, n_2, p)
             call CREATENODE (e, n)
             call INSERT (n_1, n)
             call INSERT (n_2, n)

The third attribute of the symbol PP indicates the particular preposition of the phrase.

(13)   PP (n, e, p): *preposition* (p)
        NP (n, e)

For further illustration, Fig. 29 displays the parse tree of the exemplary sentence above. The numbers in the tree refer to the sequence of substitutions while parsing in a bottom-up fashion. The numbers in parentheses refer to the numbers of the production rules of the grammar. Executing the semantic actions in the sequence determined by the parser causes the stepwise construction of the network. The reader may follow this process by referring to the full set of the production rules. We show two snapshots of the network under construction in Fig. 30a,b. Figure 30a displays the network at the time parsing has reached 4(2) in the parsing tree (see Fig. 29). Figure 30b refers to 14(10) in the parsing tree. At the end of the parsing process, we obtain the network that represents the whole sentence (see again Fig. 28). Recall that we did not intend to detail the translation of natural language text into a semantic network but only to outline the general approach.

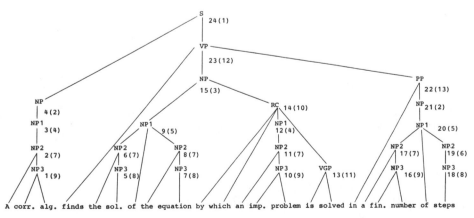

A corr. alg. finds the sol. of the equation by which an imp. problem is solved in a fin. number of steps

Fig. 29.

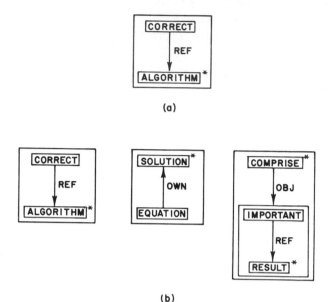

(a)

(b)

Fig. 30. The network under construction.

5. CONCLUSION

We have introduced a new kind of semantic network, which allows a clear differentiation between expressions at the conceptual level and statements at the extensional level. The former provides a framework for the representation of abstract semantic relations between concepts in order to formulate the semantics of particular subject areas. The latter is intended to represent the semantics of natural language expressions, which are statements about concrete objects of respective subject areas. These network expressions allow for the representation of quantification and negation. We believe that our approach to quantification largely resolves the problems generally imposed by the incorporation of quantifiers into semantic representations. The hierarchical structure of both the networks and network expressions allows a very natural and highly adequate representation of meaning. Concerning the representation, we have not yet attacked the problem of combining sentences by connectives other than "and" and "or." The main problem here will be how to express causality.

We have given examples for the application and the representation of ESNs. The advantage of using semantic networks in information retrieval systems has been demonstrated for the field of mathematics and computer science. The indexing algorithm described in Section 3.1 has been successfully applied to mathematical texts and to abstracts stored in a library documentation system. We have outlined how ESNs may be used in

question-answering systems by formulating derivation rules for both semantic networks and extensional semantic networks. Further work is required to obtain an efficient and reliable working system operating on
ESNs as the main component of a question-answering system.

The generation of semantic networks from natural language text is a
very important part of our research efforts. Attributed grammars have
been applied successfully to a mathematical textbook (Bourbaki: "General
Topology"). Because these texts are written in a very rigid and formalized
manner, this application area is quite limited with respect to the breadth
of natural language. The grammar used for this first application had to be
extended to be applicable to more general English text. Since we intend to
apply the method to arbitrary text, the extension of the grammar is not yet
completed. A problem still to be solved is how to distinguish automatically between natural language expressions at the conceptual level and at
the extensional level. Another problem currently being investigated is a
more precise distinction between the prepositional relations. In future research, we intend to develop a more powerful metalanguage for the
manipulation of ESNs than the one sketched in this chapter. This metalanguage will provide data structures corresponding to semantic nets
and operations on these data structures. It will be a necessary tool for the
maintenance of the networks.

ACKNOWLEDGMENT

This work was supported by the SFB 49 of the Deutsche Forschungsgemeinschaft.

REFERENCES

[Boley, H., 1977]. Directed recursive labelnode hypergraphs: A new representation-
language. *Artificial Intelligence* **9**, 49–85.
[Braun, S., and Schwind, C., 1976]. Automatic semantics-based indexing of natural language
texts for information retrieval systems. *Information Processing and Management* **12**, 147–153.
[Carnap, R., 1972]. *Bedeutung und Notwendigkeit.* Springer-Verlag, Berlin and New York.
[Fikes, R., and Hendrix, G., 1977]. A network-based knowledge representation and its natu-
ral deduction system. *Proceedings of the 5th International Joint Conference on Artificial Intel-
ligence, 1977* pp. 235–246.
[Frege, G., 1892]. Uber Sinn und Bedeutung. *Zeitschrift fur Philosophie und philosophische
Kritik* (1892), 25–50.
[Ganzinger, H., 1976]. "MUG1 Manual," Report 7608. Fachbereich Mathematik, Technische
Universität München.
[Ganzinger, H., Ripken, K., and Wilhelm, R., 1976]. MUG1—an incremental compiler-
compiler. *Proceedings of the ACM, 1976 1976* p. 415–418.
[Janas, J. M., 1975]. Ein Algorithms zur automatischen Wortartbestimmung in Texten eng-
lischer Sprache. Diplomarbeit, Technische Universität München.
[Janas, J. M., 1977]. Automatic recognition of the part-of-speech for English texts. *Information
Processing and Management* **13**, 205–213.

[Kamlah, W., and Lorenzen, P., 1967]. *Logische Propädeutik oder Vorschule des vernünftigen Redens.* Bibliographisches Institut Mannheim.
[Knuth, D. E., 1968]. Semantics of context-free languages. *Mathematical Systems Theory* **2**, 127–145.
[Koster, C. H. A., 1971]. Affix grammars. In *ALGOL 68 Implementation.* J. E. L. Peck (ed.). North-Holland Publ., Amsterdam, pp. 95–109.
[Leibnitz, G. W. von, 1840]. *Opera Philosophica,* Erdmann (ed.).
[Minsky, M., 1975]. A framework for representing knowledge. In *The Psychology of Computer Vision.* P. H. Winston (ed.). McGraw-Hill, New York, pp. 211–277.
[Montague, R., 1970]. Pragmatics and intensional logic. *Synthese* **22**, 68–94.
[Pratt, T., 1969]. A hierarchical graph model of the semantics of programs. *Proceedings of the AFIPS Spring Joint Conference, 1969* Vol. 34, pp. 813–825.
[Quine, W. van O., 1960]. *Word and Object.* MIT Press, Cambridge, Massachusetts.
[Schank, R. C., and Abelson, R. P., 1975]. Scripts, plans, and knowledge. *Advance Papers of the 4th International Joint Conference on Artificial Intelligence, 1975* pp. 151–157.
[Schnelle, H., 1973]. *Sprachphilosophie und Linguistik. Rororo Studium, Hamburg, 1973.*
[Schubert, L. K., 1975]. Extending the expressive power of semantic networks. *Advance Papers of the 4th International Joint Conference on Artificial Intelligence. 1975* pp. 158–164.
[Schwind, C., 1971]. Automatische Bestimmung von Begriffen und Beziehungen zwischen Begriffen in einem wissenschaftlichen Text. Diplomarbeit, Technische Universität München.
[Schwind, C., 1972]. "Automatische Erzeugung von Stichphrasen auf der Basis eines Beziehungssystems mathematischer Begriffe," Report 7224. Institut für Mathematik, Technische Universität München.
[Schwind, C., 1974]. "Eine einfache Sprache zur Manipulation eines Thesaurus," Report 7422. Institut für Mathematik, Technische Universität München.
[Schwind, C., 1975]. Generating hierarchical semantic networks from natural language discourse. *Advance Papers of the 4th International Joint Conference on Artificial Intelligence, 1975* pp. 429–434.
[Simmons, R. F., and Chester, D., 1977]. Inferences in quantified semantic networks. *Proceedings of the 5th International Joint Conference on Artificial Intelligence, 1977* pp. 267–273.
[Wilks, Y., 1977]. Knowledge structures and language boundaries. *Proceedings of the 5th International Joint Conference on Artificial Intelligence, 1977* pp. 151–157.
[Woods, W. A., 1975]. What's in a link? Foundations for semantic networks. In *Representation and Understanding.* D. G. Bobrow and A. M. Collins (eds.). Academic Press, New York.

PART III

AREAS OF APPLICATION

A HEURISTIC INFORMATION RETRIEVAL SYSTEM BASED ON ASSOCIATIVE NETWORKS

Nicholas V. Findler

ABSTRACT

The chapter describes an information retrieval system under development, which makes use of, rather than simulates, the strength and flexibility of humans in dealing with incomplete, uncertain, and inconsistent data. The interaction between the user and the system, for inputting, categorization, and retrieval of information, is in natural-looking English based on simple keyword analysis and the relational database model. A preprocessor makes it possible for the user to supply data for new or existing knowledge bases in a high-level manner, either in a uniformly structured or unstructured mode. The primary information structure built at input time is then converted into redundant list structures and associative networks. The system continually tests the data for consistency and completeness, and informs the user thereof.

Information is organized in a hierarchical fashion. At the lowest level, data are contained in atomic nodes. Certain retrieval queries may produce results that are worth storing in composite nodes. Bidirectional edges connect nodes, and are labeled with syntactic and semantic restrictions and other data to enhance the controlled traversal of nodes in the network. There is a multitude of descriptors associated with the information in the node, such as attribute–value pairs, synonyms, processes applicable to and by the item in question (actions involving the entity as an object and as an agent, respectively), supersets, subsets, processes capable of regenerating the item in question, and commonalities.

The user can select one of five automatic clustering algorithms that suits his needs best. The user may approve the outcome of the clustering process or initiate changes in it. A *cluster* contains one or several nodes characterized by some level of similarity or commonality. It can be created and recreated on-line to serve a family of retrieval requests. A *plane* contains one or several clusters and can also be dynamically created or recreated by the user. Both clusters and planes are labeled by data common to each of their constituents. The labels are compared with the retrieval query, and a program orders on this basis the planes and clusters to be entered according to the expected level of success of locating in them the item sought.

The retrieval request consists of a variety of descriptors, which may be fuzzy, incomplete, and even inconsistent. The user can specify the level of importance of each descriptor and how certain he is about its being true. These are then combined into a match factor, which is in turn used in computing the level of similarity between the item attached to a node and the one looked for to be retrieved. The most satisfactory item obtained in every cluster and plane entered so far is kept on record. The user may be satisfied with the result at any time and stop the search or else continue it until, eventually, the whole database is processed.

The expected power of the system is likely to make us pay a heavy price in terms of processing time and memory requirements. If feasible, we are willing to do so with the first version. The problems of tuning and optimization will be left for later efforts.

1. INTRODUCTION

Information retrieval systems in general perform two phases of processing on databases. First, they retrieve a subset of the records stored according to some composite search criteria specified by the user (usually different from the storage criteria). Second, they make computations that result in data reduction or data amplification. An instance of data reduction is a statistical calculation encompassing the records retrieved, such as the average value of the selected entities, whereas data amplification may be exemplified by linking the outcomes of the computation to a set of decisions contingent on the numerical values obtained previously.

It is also customary to distinguish between systems aiming at *document retrieval* and those performing *fact retrieval*. The former produces a document after a search based on a user request of a relatively simple nature, such as author's name, title, certain combinations of keywords or content identifiers (indices). Fact retrieval, in contrast, may analyze and synthesize the relevant pieces of information, rely on logical inferences, and in general, carry out complicated processes of decision-making. For an overview of the field, the reader is referred to Sparck Jones and Kay [1974] or Salton [1968, 1971, 1975].

Question-answering systems are a natural extension of fact retrieval programs and include, either as a necessary by-product or as *the* major research objective, a program that "understands" natural language. By this, I mean that the program can relate user utterances, both data inputs (new data or modification of already stored data) and queries, to information acquired before, in an intelligent and consistent manner—an activity often referred to as "common sense reasoning." It should, however, be noted as a fact of life rather than criticism that many of the projects in this area are characterized by the requirement that the supplier of the database and the user of the system (the two are often no longer the same person) adhere to a rather rigid and unnatural format in which data and search specifications are to be formulated. (At times, the published accounts of systems performance may give a somewhat misleading image of this aspect. Nevertheless, there is a noticeable, significant improvement toward more flexible user–system interaction as the technology of natural language processing advances.)

It is a truism that the *structure of knowledge representation* is in general of paramount importance and the success of the project concerned critically depends on it. "Plausible" and "esthetically pleasing" structures, moot as these terms may be, may lead to failure as far as computing time and memory requirements are concerned, and restrict the system to deal with only toy problems. I, personally, still consider such work very useful and feel that the limitation is due to a mismatch between the approach adopted and the architecture of the supporting hardware/software. Only such an ostensible fiasco can bring about progress toward future flexible architectures—as the history of microprogramming clearly indicates.

A successful and also plausible representational structure has emerged over the past ten years or so, the *associative* or *cognitive networks*. They satisfy the requirements of structural semantics, logic, and cognitive psychology namely, that the totality of information be represented by the concepts stored and their complex interrelationships. The format and interpretation of these networks vary from researcher to researcher, usually depending on processing need but, at times, also on personal taste or, if you like, philosophy. The present book should give a reasonable although far from exhaustive sample of the different approaches. Some of the efforts have the objective of providing a psychologically sufficient, explicatory model of human long-term memory, but the primary goal has more often been to construct a system capable of *common sense reasoning* in the processes of storing, modifying, and retrieving elements of knowledge. (See, for example, the works of Anderson and Bower [1973], Bell and Quillian [1971], Brachman [1977], Carbonell [1970a,b], Cercone [1975], Cercone and Schubert [1975], Collins and Quillian [1969, 1970a,b, 1972a,b], Hays [1973a,b], Heidorn [1972], Hendrix [1975], Hendrix *et al.* [1973], Levesque [1977], Norman [1973], Norman *et al.* [1975], Quillian [1966, 1967, 1968, 1969], Rumelhart *et al.* [1972], Rumelhart and Norman [1973], Schank [1972, 1973a,b], Schank and Rieger [1973], Schubert [1976], Scragg [1976], Shapiro [1971a,b, 1975], Simmons [1973], Simmons and Bruce [1971], Simmons *et al.* [1968], Simmons and Slocum [1972], Wilks [1974], Winston [1975], and Woods [1975].)

The investigation described in this chapter does not place emphasis on natural language processing. In fact, the tools used for such purpose are rather unsophisticated in comparison to those in most of the above efforts. The major thrust is directed toward a humanlike information retrieval method, which makes use of (rather than simulates) the strength of man in dealing with incomplete, inconsistent, and uncertain information.

2. ON SOME PRELIMINARY WORK

I shall describe in this section three pieces of work that form the starting points for the research being reported on.

First, we have developed the initial version of a simple conversational information retrieval system, MARSHA [Cipolaro and Findler, 1977]. It combines the keyword-oriented approach of ELIZA [Weizenbaum, 1966] and a relational database model. A preprocessor enables unsophisticated users to specify new databases or to add to existing ones, in a high-level language. Through this preprocessor, the system accepts scripts, simple responses to questions, synonyms, substitutions, and relations—all dealing with a particular topic of conversation. MARSHA is also able to keep track of the conversation by storing past relations and past values of the domains. There is no restriction with regard to the grammar and the vocabulary employed by the user in the conversation since parsing in the usual sense is not carried out by the system. If an unknown expression is used by the human, some ELIZA-like clichés bridge the gap of the text not comprehended.

This system can be expanded relatively easily so that, for example, a particular keyword combination could point to a procedure to be invoked, to a prompting question to be asked, or to a certain response to be given—depending on the results of past and current elements of the conversation.

The second work on which the present study is based is a particular programming language, AMPPL-II (Associative Memory, Parallel Processing Language, Version II). It is embedded, together with the Symmetric List Processor, SLIP, in FORTRAN IV [Findler *et al.*, 1972]. The language AMPPL-II simulates, from the user's point of view, a content-addressible memory for a variety of search processes, input/output, etc. Noninteracting data elements in this associative memory can be subjected to sequences of operations quasi-simultaneously. An information item can be accessed in an associative or content-adressible memory by being matched with a selectable field of a special item, the basis of search, rather than by an address. This matching process, as well as practically all other operations, takes place over all records in the memory at the "same" time, or so it appears to the user.

The programmer can utilize the characteristics of not only *exact associative memories,* in which the search processes are performed on the basis of finding the intersection of several sharply defined matching descriptors, but also *nonexact associative memories.* In these, spatial and temporal nearness, similarity, and rank ordering play an important role, too. Associations also connect statistically related entities. Partial and even conflicting information can serve as the basis of search. The search criteria can be either numerically or nonnumerically oriented and include the concepts of "most similar," "least similar," "greater than," "minimum," etc.

One of the basic data structures is the *relation-triple* in which the *relation* is connected to an *object* and a *value*, REL(OBJ) = VAL. Each of these three entities can be single items or different types of lists. REL is always symbolic; the other two, OBJ and VAL, can be either symbolic or numeric, simultaneously or separately. Furthermore, the entities can be primitive (atomic) or complex (defined). The latter means that an entity is expressed in terms of primitive (or previously defined complex) entities and operators. The operators, currently more than a dozen, are numerical (e.g., GREATER THAN), Boolean (e.g., AND), and other types (e.g., CONCATENATED). Powerful search processes built into the system can retrieve both atomic and defined entities along dynamically charted search paths, using single instructions. Similarly, items related by analogical relations are retrievable through a single program step.

The third basis on which the present work relies concerns a search strategy proposed for associative networks [Findler, 1972]. The user can specify partial, imprecise, or even inconsistent characteristics of the items to be looked for. He also states the estimated level of importance of each search criterion and his level of confidence about the search criterion being correct. These two are combined into a match factor that, in turn, participates in determining the level of similarity required to reach between individual items stored in the nodes of an associative network and the item satisfying the goals of the search. A heuristic hill-climbing method, appropriate for the irregular hypersurfaces representing similarity measures, leads to a "satisficing" solution—to use Simon's well-known term dealing with dynamically changing, subjective termination criteria of search processes (considering possibly some flexible aspiration levels of the user). Some additional aspects of this search strategy will be described in connection with the present investigations.

3. DESIGN PRINCIPLES OF IRUHS-1

The IRUHS-1 project (Information Retrieval Using Heuristic Search, Version 1) does not simulate but, rather, tries to make use of the high degree of flexibility humans display in:

(1) assimilating new information;
(2) responding to demands to categorize, sort, assess, revalue, identify, and/or discard elements of information at a variety of levels;
(3) recognizing and ignoring irrelevant and faulty data;
(4) finding sensible compromises in situations of conflict;
(5) distinguishing between more and less useful information;
(6) making global, inductive judgments on the basis of disjoint sample values;
(7) applying general principles and techniques to specific cases;
(8) discovering and utilizing partial similarities and analogies;
(9) constructing, adhering to and, when necessary, modifying plans.

The above capabilities improve with experience in humans and, of course, vary from individual to individual (see Collins *et al.*, [1975]). One cannot, however, fail to notice, for example, the great variety of ways in which certain information can be retrieved and how effortlessly (subconsciously?) the transformation from one information structure to another seems to take place (if at all). Similarly, we seem to have a range of error-detecting and -correcting mechanisms incorporated in our cognitive activity, which are reasonably tolerant and unobtrusive. They enable us to attain partial, conflicting, and fuzzy goals fairly effectively, in spite of the restrictions of human cognition, such as lack of precision, limited speed, and, probably, memory.

To approximate the above features in a computer system is a constant challenge for computer scientists who try to combine the best character-istics of man and machines. If, for example, such flexibility could be aug-mented by the speed and error-free operations of computers in informa-tion retrieval, an extremely powerful system could be generated. Our objective is to make a few steps in this direction. The following design features are being considered in the development of IRUHS-1:

(a) The user should be able to provide the input information, his search criteria, and the answers to systems questions in a relatively unrestricted natural language. If he transcends the limits of the allowed grammar and vocabulary, it must not cause an insurmountable systems error but only a graceful slowdown in the communication between him and the computer, which can then be corrected through a friendly collaborative effort.

The preprocessor, which accepts the user's high-level input, converts it into a somewhat redundantly organized structure (the *primary information structure*), which is then used for the first stage of checking the consistency and completeness of the information received. Such a check is carried out as early as possible but would also have to be continually performed later as search queries are formulated. Whenever the system finds that the input information or the search criteria are inconsistent and/or incom-plete, it poses the proper questions and issues warning messages when appropriate.

At input time, also the skeleton of a versatile information structure is es-tablished, consisting of both list structures and associative networks. These are gradually filled in with data obtained by means of different inference making mechanisms, which are employed in the course of answering queries. (It is wasteful to make "all" possible inferences at the start since some of them may never be needed [Findler and Chen, 1973].)

(b) Knowledge is organized *hierarchically*. A *node* in our associative net-work may contain "atomic" information, as provided by the user, or in-formation arrived at through computation over a number of other nodes. The nodes are conveniently interconnected so that traversing between them can be controlled easily and naturally (see Section 4.5). A number of nodes characterized by some degree of similarity are pulled together into a *cluster*. The next higher level agglomerate is a *plane*, which contains sev-eral clusters, again with some commonality among them. Most impor-tantly, this allocation of nodes to clusters and of clusters to planes is flexible and can be changed dynamically as a consequence of user–system interaction. Examples in Section 4.2 will clarify this concept.

A variety of clustering methods is available to the user, who not only selects the one most appropriate for his current needs but is also given the opportunity to review and modify, when so desired, the results obtained from clustering. The modification is such that it brings about the least amount of undesired side-effects. More will be said about it later.

(c) As stated above, nodes are selectively connected. The connections are bidirectional edges labeled with the syntactic and semantic restrictions that apply to traversing along the edge in question, and other data that concern the relationship between the information in the nodes (e.g., strength of "association," that is, likelihood of the two nodes being jointly referenced).

Each cluster and each plane also bears a label that describes the commonality among its constituents (similar properties and the like). Thus, whenever a retrieval request is specified, the search criteria are matched with these labels. The planes and, in them, the clusters are then ranked in an order of plausibility with regard to the expected level of success in locating the information item sought in the plane and cluster in question.

(d) The contents of a node, whether atomic or composite, can be described in a variety of different ways. Although the internal representation of the description modes is basically identical, the user is offered the following, nonexhaustive, options: attribute–value pairs, synonyms, processes applicable to and by the item stored in the node (actions involving the entity as an object and as an agent, respectively), superset and subset lists, processes that can regenerate the item, cases requiring exceptional treatment (as opposed to default values). As the examples later show, all these descriptor types can assume sharply defined or fuzzy values, dichotomic (yes/no) values, or strongly/weakly ordered rank number values. In fact, the scale may be based on counting (enumeration), ratios, intervals, ordinal numbers, and category subdivisions. The retrieval requests are usually answered on the basis of the information attached to one or a small number of nodes.

(e) Since the creation, modification, or augmentation of the database can be made on-line in an interactive manner, only the primary information structure is affected by the user directly. When necessary, a part of or all the subsequently constructed list structures and networks are destroyed and rebuilt. The fine tuning and optimization of this process is a major problem of its own, the best solution to which may not be found for some years to come.

(f) It has been stated before that when the user supplies a retrieval request, the system generates a list of planes and, in them, clusters—all ordered by levels of plausibility. The top (most likely) plane/cluster units are paged into the associative memory first. (There is a disk-resident, large

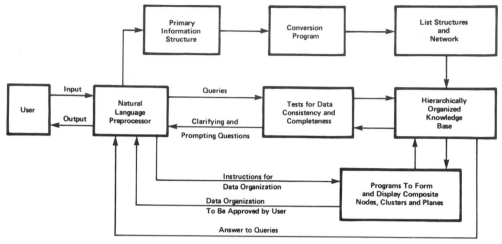

Fig. 1. The organization of the IRUHS-1 system.

"virtual" associative memory from which the "pages" are read.) In case of failure in locating the item sought, new clusters and then new planes replace the previous ones but the most satisfactory item in each subunit is kept on record. The user may cause, via continual interaction with the system, the search either to be continued, stopped at a certain level of success, or completely abandoned. In other words, the difference between the user's current aspiration level and degree of satisfaction with the so far best result controls the extent of the search process. The search therefore may not necessarily return the item from the whole database that best corresponds to the retrieval request.

(g) The responses of the system, whether prompting and clarifying questions or answering queries, are given in formatted but natural-looking English. MARSHA-II, a powerful descendant of the above referenced MARSHA, creates the framework for this two-way communication. It could also be noted that relatively little effort seems to be needed in order to change the language of communication from English to another (similarly structured) natural language.

A block diagram in Fig. 1 illustrates the organization of the IRUHS-1 system. The Appendix contains examples of dialogues we expect to be able to carry on.

4. SYSTEM DESCRIPTION

IRUHS-1 is under development and the following discussion reflects our present way of thinking about the system. It is impossible to foresee all the conflicts and difficulties we may encounter in our work as it evolves. We may set some objectives at too high a level and, in turn, we might accomplish, even in the first version, more than we plan for now.

The examples will be drawn mostly from the database we are using at this stage, achievements in modern Olympic Games. Although we try to develop IRUHS-1 in a database-independent manner, it is feasible that another database, richer or more demanding in some respects, could result in a more powerful system. (This caveat is not an apology or excuse, just a fact of life.)

4.1. The Input Operation

There are two rather different modes of providing information for the database. We call them BOOK and MENTAL. In the first case, the reader types it in from a book, in which the data are uniformly formatted and the order of presentation is constant for each item. In the second case, the user relies on his memory or some other relatively unstructured source of information.

The system does not ask prompting questions in the BOOK mode or expect more information than actually given during the input phase. However, the user may make typing errors or skip data accidentally. Therefore, tests for consistency and completeness have a meaningful role here, too. All information is considered to be given at 100% level of certainty— disregarding some exceptional cases in which the MENTAL mode must be used.

Before the data entered are transferred into the primary information storage, the contents of the input buffer is shown and approved by the user. (The user's response DISCARD is an inexpensive way of eliminating most of the erroneous input at this stage.)

4.2. The Hierarchical Organization of Knowledge

It is extremely important to incorporate in the system flexible and reasonably inexpensive algorithms that arrange and, when so instructed, rearrange the organization of knowledge. (A quick, preliminary reading of Section 4.5 may be helpful in understanding the material presented here.) At the lowest level, the creation of nodes with composite information must be described. In our exemplary database, a particular athletic event at a particular game is, for instance, an atomic piece of information. If the winner of that event happens to have won other events as well, the system will create a composite node, after a relevant query has been processed, that contains all the information concerning the athlete in question. Such selective recombination of data prompted by information requests en-

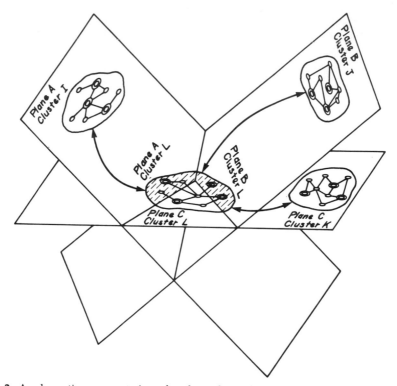

Fig. 2. A schematic representation of nodes, edges, clusters, and planes. Atomic nodes (○) and composite nodes (◎) are connected by edges to form the network. Each of the three planes in the diagram contain two clusters, one of which (cluster L) is shared by all three planes.

hances the responsiveness of the system and seems to be analogous to human information processing techniques. Section 4.5 describes the way in which the entity attached to a node is characterized.

At the next higher level, *clusters* are formed. The information in each cluster represents *some* similarity—a feature that is extremely useful in handling fuzzy retrieval requests. Another advantage of clusters is that the user can submit every component node of a cluster to a stream of identical information processes. For example, if the athletic events of the 1976 Montreal Olympic Games are associated with the nodes of a cluster, the user can change the location of all *yachting races* to Kingston, Ontario, using a small number of high level instructions that test for yacht races and, when appropriate, modify the value of the "place" attribute.

I shall come back to the problem of clustering algorithms shortly but, first, the next and highest level of information agglomerates, *planes*, need to be discussed. Each plane contains one or more "somewhat" similar clusters. It is important to realize that a node may belong to several clusters, and a cluster to several planes, at the same time. Each allocation—as initiated, defined, and approved by the user—serves some special *class* of retrieval requests. For example, the contents of a particular node may belong to one cluster representing water sports events in the 1956 Melbourne games, to another representing those meets in which past Olympic records were broken in 1956, and to a third one comprising races won by Australian girls, again in 1956. Similar multiple allocation of clusters to planes may be the case also for pragmatic reasons. The cluster of wrestling events in the 1908 London games may belong to the plane representing the 1908 Olympics, both Olympic Games held in London (in 1908 and 1948), and all wrestling events of modern games. Figure 2 contains a schematic representation of the knowledge base so organized.

4.3. How Planes and Clusters Are Formed

A plane is defined directly by the user, as consisting of a specified list of clusters named. There are, however, five ways of automatic cluster formation out of which the user selects the one most appropriate to his needs. He is then presented with the result of the clustering process; he either accepts it or makes changes—as described below.

4.3.1. Specification by Examples of Membership

The user provides a sample membership of each cluster he wants to be formed. The system first checks whether the extreme values of the attributes, in the numerical case, or the symbolic values of the attributes, in the nonnumerical case, overlap between members of different clusters. If not, distinct subranges tell the clusters apart. However, whenever there is some overlap, the system establishes simple Boolean combinations (ANDs, ORs, and NOTs) of the subranges, which are accepted until counterexemplary members cause redefinitions to be made (cf. concept formation).

4.3.2. Explicit Specification of Membership Criteria

In this case, the user gives the explicit Boolean combination of subrange values along the different descriptor dimensions for each cluster—results that have to be induced by the system under Section 4.3.1. This procedure implies that the user can deliberately or accidentally override aspects of similarity and relatedness (as may happen with the other methods, too). It is, therefore, very important that the result of clustering be submitted to him for approval or modification at the end of this activity. The system also checks whether the user-supplied formula is the simplest Boolean expression according to some criteria.

4.3.3. *Specifying a Constant Number of Members in All Clusters*

The system aims at determining the membership of clusters so that each cluster contains a constant number of nodes as a "natural" unit. This requirement means (now and in all following cases) that the Euclidean distance (using property coordinate values weighted according to the user's instructions) between each member of a cluster and its centroid is less than the distance between the member and the centroid of any other cluster. (Throughout this chapter, distance refers to the Euclidean distance as defined above.) The exhaustive method of performing this operation is, of course, extremely time-demanding, proportional to n^2, where n is the number of nodes, and heuristic techniques leading to satisfactory approximations of the optimal solution must be employed. The result would usually be such that clusters near the "fringes" end up with a membership less than the constant value specified.

4.3.4. *Specifying the Maximum Number of Members in Each Cluster and the Maximum Distance between Any Member and the Centroid of Its Cluster*

Again, the exact solution of this requirement is too expensive and heuristic methods can lead to "natural" cluster formation. If the requirement of "maximum member-centroid distance" is replaced with "minimum number of cluster to be formed," this problem becomes identical for all practical purposes with the problem of Section 4.3.3.

4.3.5. *Specifying the Number of Clusters to Be Formed*

The optimality requirement is expressed in the Chebyshev manner: the maximum member-centroid distance in each cluster is to be minimized.

4.4. The User–System Interaction in Clustering

Although there is a vast literature on clustering techniques (see, for example, Hartigan [1975] and Van Ryzin [1977]), the whole field is wide open for more research. The criteria listed above have mostly not been investigated. The heuristic methods studied would provide results of improving quality after each iteration. These are then presented to the user for his approval at regular times. His response can be of three kinds:

(a) He may *accept* the results as satisfactory or else he may want member X to belong to cluster A rather than to cluster B. He would, therefore, instruct the system to *change* either

(b) the *properties of node* X minimally so that it just qualifies for the necessary transfer, or

(c) the *properties of clusters A and B* minimally. It means that node X is now reassigned with *minimum side-effects,* that is, the smallest possible number of other nodes are affected by the change in their cluster assignments.

Figure 3a,b illustrates the respective changes.

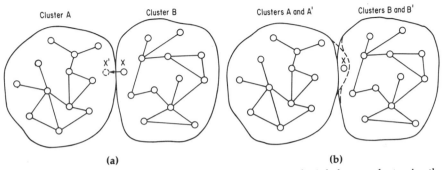

Fig. 3. (a) The user changes the properties of node X to make it belong to cluster A rather than cluster B. (b) The user changes the properties of clusters A and B so that node X, and only node X, may belong to cluster A rather than cluster B.

A few words should be said now about the allocation of nodes to clusters. The membership in a cluster is based on some level of similarity and relatedness among the node descriptors. This fact is utilized at the time queries are formulated. One or, depending on their size, several clusters, most likely to result in successful retrieval, are paged into the simulated associative memory (SAM) for the search process. The user may specify maximum resources (computation time and SAM size) for each stage of the search. When the system compares the label of a knowledge subunit (cluster or plane) with the search criteria, it may give the following responses as to their acceptability: yes; yes with some exceptions; probably yes; I do not know; probably no; no with some exceptions; no. The errors associated with the above judgments are due to wrong node assignments in the cluster considered. These errors are of two types, analogously to the errors concerning hypotheses in statistical decision-making:

(1) There are too many nodes, on the average, assigned to a cluster, and the nodes contain information irrelevant to a given retrieval request.

(2) The nodes relevant to given retrieval requests are assigned, on the average, to too many clusters.

The well-known measures of the quality of an information retrieval system, *precision* and *recall,* are directly related to the above sources of error. (Precision is the proportion of the retrieved material actually relevant to the query, and recall is the proportion of relevant material actually retrieved.)

Since our system is designed to have the flexibility of dynamic reassignment of nodes to new clusters and of clusters to new planes—as need for it arises in the user's view—a powerful correcting capability, relying on the information feedback to the user, exists in it. Finally, it is true in general that bigger clusters will result in lower precision and higher recall.

4.5. The Distribution of Knowledge over the Network

It was stated before that the bidirectional edges between the nodes are labeled with syntactic and semantic restrictions and other types of information. All this serves the efficiency of traversing the cluster from node to node. Let us discuss this question via an example.

Suppose a cluster contains all water sports events that took place in the 1972 Munich games. Nodes representing swimming meets are connected with each other pairwise by edges labeled with a higher association strength than those leading to nodes representing, say, water polo. A "syntactic" restriction could be the distinction between single competitor events and team efforts (relay swim), whereas a "semantic" restriction may refer to the fact that swimmers and divers are probably always different persons, and traversing from a "swimming" node to a "diving" node makes sense only when, for example, the task is to count the number of gold medals won by a particular country. (The distinction between syntactic and semantic restrictions is often, as now, rather moot.)

We have to consider now the variety of descriptors attached to a node. Again, examples will help in explaining their role. Some of these examples would look rather artificial but bear in mind that it may not be so with a different database.

4.5.1. *Attribute–Value Pairs*

This is the most common and most natural descriptor. If the exemplary node represents the 100 meter dash, one would have, say,

running time—9.9 seconds.

4.5.2. *Synonyms*

This descriptor enhances the system's conversational ability. We could have, for example,

Paavo Nurmi—the Flying Finn,

Bloody Olympics—the 1972 Munich games.

4.5.3. *Processes Applicable to the Entity in the Node*

Action attributes in which the entity is the object of the action:

athlete A—trained by coach B,

athlete C—disqualified by the Olympic committee for cheating.

4.5.4. Processes Applicable by the Entity in the Node

Action attributes in which the entity is the agent of the action:

athlete D—changed his nationality.

4.5.5. Superset and Part–Superpart Lists

athlete E—participated on relay team F and relay team G,

event H—member of events list I, in which past records were broken.

4.5.6. Subset and Set–Element Lists

athletes from country J—individual athlete K.

4.5.7. Processes That Can Regenerate an Item

number of gold medals won by Mark Spitz—test swimming events in 1972 and count the appropriate wins.

4.5.8. Cases Requiring Exceptional Treatment vs. Default Values

number of competitions Norway participated in 1972—
the Norwegian team left after the murder of Israeli athletes.

4.5.9. Commonalities

country L ⎫
country M ⎬ —English speaking
country N ⎭

As noted before, the values can be sharply defined or fuzzy, dichotomic (yes/no), strongly/weakly ordered rank numbers, counts, ratios, intervals, ordinal numbers or categories. Most of these do not have to be given as input directly but can be arrived at through computations.

Some of the knowledge must be given in terms of tables (e.g., year and location of games), special events (e.g., since 1964, West and East Germany have sent separate teams), and special definitions (e.g., the amateur status is lost after certain activities have been undertaken by an athlete).

Specific queries result in the recognition of certain facts, which again may be worth storing in a newly created node (e.g., the performance of East German swimmers in 1972) or attached as a label (e.g., the joint domination of swimming events by U.S. and East Germany) onto the edge connecting the affected nodes—if and when the user considers it important enough. Figure 4 contains a hypothetical example of a network segment.

4.6. On Some Problems of Retrieval

As stated before, the answering of questions is usually based on the information retrieved from one or a small number of nodes. (In addition,

The exemplary segment of the knowledge base depicts PLANE 17: Swimming, Diving and Water Polo (Men). The contents of the clusters are as follows:

CLUSTER 1: free style
CLUSTER 2: back stroke,
CLUSTER 3: breast stroke,
CLUSTER 4: butterfly,

CLUSTER 5: individual medley,
CLUSTER 6: relay,
CLUSTER 7: diving,
CLUSTER 8: water polo.

Cluster 1 is associated strongly with clusters 5 and 6, moderately strongly with clusters 2, 3 and 4 and weakly with clusters 7 and 8—expressing the probability of identical competitors in different cluster events. Each cluster carries the names and years of not-held events. In cluster 1, nodes 32 and 33, representing 400-meter free-style swimming events in 1956 and 1960, respectively, are very strongly connected because the winner of the gold medal was Murray Rose in both cases. Within each cluster, nodes representing identical distance events are connected moderately strongly. The different descriptors of the 1960 event in node 33 are:

attribute-value pairs:
  first athlete - Murray Rose,
  first time - 4:18:3,
  first athlete's nationality - Australian,
    ⋮

synonyms:
  400m - 437 yd. 1 ft.,
    ⋮

processes applicable to node:
  style chosen by first athlete - crawl,
    ⋮

processes applicable by node:
  nationality of first athlete changed from British to Australian,
    ⋮

superset lists:
  all free-style swimming events,
  all swimming events,
  all water sport events,
    ⋮

subset lists:
  none
regenerating processes:
  combination of event type, distance, style, times,
    participants' name and nationality,
    ⋮

commonalities:
  free-style,
  swimming,
  400-meter,
  water sports,
  first athlete identical to first athlete of same event in 1956,
  first and third athlete's nationality Australian,
  Olympic record set by first athlete,
    ⋮

Fig. 4. A verbal description of an exemplary segment of the knowledge base.

there are certain basic data tabulated in a redundant fashion, for reasons of economy. The narrative with the questions and answers in the Appendix illustrates this point via examples.) The first step in the search process is the retrieval of the *characteristic segment* of each plane. This contains the label of the plane and the labels of every cluster in that plane. The decision as to which cluster(s) shouls be "paged in" from the large "virtual" associative memory is based on the contents of the characteristic segments.

Since the mode of representation of the various descriptors is uniform (relation-triples), pattern matching is at the heart of all retrieval processes.

The knowledge embodied in the program control structure enables IRUHS-1 to consider partial, fuzzy, and conflicting information as well (see the definition of the *match factor* at the end of Section 2).

The reasoning processes, used in the deductive logic needed for the answers, are combined from elementary program-building blocks by pattern-invoked procedures. The limitations and the open-endedness of this approach represent the weakness and the strength of IRUHS-1, respectively. Only at the end of the project shall we know how well the system can handle the problems of quantification and anaphoric references; and how effective use can be made of the labels on the edges, clusters, and planes in the search processes.

5. OVERVIEW AND FINAL COMMENTS

It seems obvious from the discussion so far that we would have to pay a very high price for the power and flexibility we hope to attain. We feel the latter are worth the price expected—even if we must limit the size of the database below the one envisaged at present and even if the user–system interaction will be characterized by short bursts of computer output and long periods of waiting time, due to the big load from other users on our nondedicated computer.

Compared to the KRL project [Bobrow and Winograd, 1977] of somewhat similar objectives, we are sure that the language processing ability of IRUHS-1 will be much poorer but, we hope, its capabilities of retrieving information by handling uncertain, incomplete, partially matching, inconsistent and fuzzy data, will be better than those of KRL.

IRUHS-1 will be a significant step forward from those traditional systems based on inverted files, in which all possible queries had to be prespecified, the match had to be full and exact, the clusters were rigid and constructed according to principles alien to the class of retrieval requests expected.

APPENDIX

The following are some retrieval requests, formulated in possibly more natural-looking English than realistic, that we hope to be able to answer. Q means user's question, A is the answer by the system, and N is notes of explanation.

Q: What happened in London. . .
A: Please specify year. There have been two Olympic Games in London, in 1908 and 1948.
N: There is no need to enter the plane containing events in the London Olympic Games or even to consider the label attached to that plane. The information for the answer can be obtained less expensively from

tabulated data covering the ordinal numbers of the games, and the cities, countries, and years in which they were held.

Q: Which country won the greatest number of silver medals in the games when West and East Germany sent separate teams the first time.

A: The year was 1968 and the country in question was USSR with 56 silver medals.

N: The labels on the planes of both West and East Germany contain the information that up to and including the year 1964, the two countries sent joint teams designated as German. Tabulated data show that the Olympics next after the 1964 one was held in 1968. The program then enters the plane representing the 1968 events and an exhaustive counting process provides the answer. Following the finding of such datum, the latter is introduced into its appropriate place of a table.

Q: Who won the 100 meter dash in the games held in Asia the last time?

A: The games were in Tokyo in 1964 and the winner of 100 meter dash was R. Hayes of U.S.A.

N: Again the program looks up the tabulated data, starting in 1976 and going back in time. Every Olympic city is then located in a special cluster on geography (not the country because there are bicontinental countries, such as USSR and Turkey). Tokyo is the first one whose attribute "continent" has the value "Asia." The year 1964 had already been found in the table. The rest is then a simple search in the cluster covering running. It was also noted that "100 meter dash" is synonymous with "100 meter running."

Q: How many U.S. black athletes won gold medals in 1936?

A: I know of at least five, Jesse Owens, Ralph Metcalf, John Woodruff, "Corny" Johnson, and Archie Williams.

N: The plane for the 1936 Olympics contains a cluster representing U.S. athletes who won one or more medals. *Some* of the nodes in this cluster have the attribute–value pair "color: black," the others have no attribute "color." That is why the result of the counting process is preceded by "I know of at least . . ."

Q: How many gold medals were won by East German athletes in 1936?

A: East Germany entered the Olympic Games only in 1968.

N: The plane representing the 1936 games contains no participating nation called East Germany or its synonym German Democratic Republic. So the program looks up the plane associated with East Germany. (This is a somewhat redundant procedure but it can reduce the number of erroneous answers due to misplaced or faulty components in the database. Such a redundant procedure also yields, in general, more information than absolutely necessary—as seems to be the case with all answers.) The label on this plane says that the country began participating in the Olympics only in 1968. And 1968 > 1936. The apparent conflict is resolved. The program then makes use of the fact that East Germany has a "low priority" synonym, and also superset, called Germany. These are invoked only when such conflicts are encountered. The user is asked if he wants to receive the same results for Germany or the German team, athletes, etc.

Q: Who was the fastest runner in 1956?

A: I assume 100 meter running requires the highest performance. That was won by R. Morrow of U.S.A.

N: The keyword combination "fastest runner," "fastest swimmer," etc., without reference to a specific event (even anaphorically) immediately links to the shortest distance event in the respective cluster and makes use of the text as shown above.

Q: Are French athletes better than Italians?

A: If by "better" you mean more medals won over all modern games, then the answer is no.

N: The keyword "better" can be qualified by a single event at a given time and place, by a class of events, or by nothing at all. In each case, the phrase (in this instance, the above question) is changed internally to one involving the total number of medals won or, if meaningful, to a phrase involving numerical data of accomplishments.

Q: Who was the best Olympic swimmer?

A: If by "best" you mean the one who won the most gold medals, then the answer is Mark Spitz.

N: The keyword "best," similarly to the previous case, may or may not be qualified by a single event or a class of events (e.g., "the best Marathon runner in 1952" or "the best runner in 1952"). Again counting the number of medals or considering the achievements is called for (e.g., "best country in running in 1952" or "the best 100 meter runner over all games").

Q: Has Germany ever won the pole vault?

A: If you accept East Germany for Germany, the answer is yes, in 1972.

N: This procedure is similar to the one used four questions before. The program finds no German winner, considers the "low-priority" synonyms East German and West German, and gets the answer.

Q: Did a Ukrainian athlete win a weight lifting event in 1968?

A: I do not know. There were four winners from the Soviet Union: Kurentsov, Selitsky, Belayev, and Zhabotinsky.

N: No nation Ukraine appears in the weight lifting cluster of the plane for 1968. However, the special cluster for geography indicates that the Soviet Union, synonymous with USSR, is a superset of Ukraine. (Russia is not, although often used so mistakenly.)

Q: Were the Finns good runners in 1972?

A: I assume so. They won, for example, three gold medals in running in 1972.

N: The attribute "good" has many context-dependent synonyms. However, anybody winning at least one medal in a cluster is "good."

Q: Who won the 200 meter hurdle in Rome?

A: This event was not included after 1904 and the Rome games were in 1960.

N: The plane for running contains a cluster of nodes associated with hurdle events. The label of this cluster contains the fact (restriction) that the 200 meter hurdle was terminated after 1904. On the other hand, the year of the Rome Olympics is 1960 in the table of data. And 1904 < 1960 . . . The apparent conflict of not finding the information sought is resolved.

Q: How many games have been held in the U.S.?

A: Two, in St. Louis, 1904 and in Los Angeles, 1932.

N: A simple counting process over the tabulated data gives the answer.

ACKNOWLEDGMENTS

I am indebted to Obi Anizor and Andrew Chirwa for their ideas and programming effort, and to Stuart C. Shapiro for reading and commenting on an earlier draft. The National Science Foundation has given partial support to this project through Grant MCS76-24278.

REFERENCES

[Anderson, J. R., and Bower, G. H., 1973]. *Human Associative Memory*. Winston & Sons, Washington, D.C.

[Bell, A., and Quillian, M. R., 1971]. Capturing concepts in a semantic net. In *Associative Information Techniques*. E. L. Jacks (ed.). Am. Elsevier, New York, pp. 3–25.

[Bobrow, D. G., and Winograd, T., 1977]. An overview of KRL, a knowledge representation language. *Cognitive Science* 1, 3–46.

[Brachman, R. J., 1977]. What's in a concept; structural foundations for semantic networks. *International Journal for Man-Machine Studies* 9, 127–152.

[Carbonell, J. P., 1970a]. "Mixed-Initiative Man-Computer Instructional Dialogues," BBN Report No. 1971. Bolt, Beranek & Newman, Cambridge, Massachusetts.

[Carbonell, J. P., 1970b]. AI in CAI: An artificial intelligence approach to computer-aided instruction. *IEEE Transactions on Man-Machine Systems* 11, 190–202.

[Cercone, N., 1975]. "Representing Natural Language in Extended Semantic Networks," Technical Report TR75-11. Department of Computer Science, University of Alberta, Edmonton, Alberta, Canada.

[Cercone, N., and Schubert, L., 1975]. Toward a state based conceptual representation. *Proceedings of the 4th International Joint Conference on Artificial Intelligence, 1975* pp. 83–90.

[Cipolaro, J. K., and Findler, N. V., 1977]. MARSHA, the daughter of ELIZA—a simple program for information retrieval in natural language. *American Journal of Computational Linguistics* 14 (Microfiche 66), 4.

[Collins, A. M., and Quillian, M. R., 1969]. Retrieval time from semantic memory. *Journal of Verbal Learning and Verbal Behavior* 8, 240–247.

[Collins, A. M., and Quillian, M. R., 1970a]. Facilitating retrieval from semantic memory: The effect of repeating part of an inference. *In Acta Psychologica 33, Attention and Performance.III*. A. F. Sanders (ed.). North-Holland Publ., Amsterdam, pp. 304–314.

[Collins, A. M., and Quillian, M. R., 1970b]. Does category size affect categorization time? *Journal of Verbal Learning and Verbal Behavior* **9**, 432–438.

[Collins, A. M., and Quillian, M. R., 1972a]. Experiments on semantic memory and language comprehension. In *Cognition in Learning and Memory*. L. W. Gregg (ed.). Wiley, New York, pp. 117–137.

[Collins, A. M., and Quillian, M. R., 1972b]. How to make a language user. In *Organization of Memory*. E. Tulving and W. Donaldson (eds.). Academic Press, New York, pp. 309–351.

[Collins, A. M., Warnock, E. H., Aiello, N., and Miller, M. L., 1975]. Reasoning from incomplete knowledge. In *Representation and Understanding*. D. G. Bobrow and A. M. Collins (eds.). Academic Press, New York, pp. 383–415.

[Findler, N. V., 1972]. Short note on a heuristic search strategy in long-term memory networks. *Information Processing Letters* **1**, 191–196.

[Findler, N. V., and Chen, D. T., 1973]. On the problems of time, retrieval of temporal relations, causality and co-existence. *International Journal of Computer and Information Sciences* **2**, 161–185.

[Findler, N. V., Pfaltz, J. L., and Bernstein, H. J., 1972]. *Four High-Level Extensions of FORTRAN IV: SLIP, AMPPL-II, TREETRAN and SYMBOLANG*. Spartan Books, New York.

[Hartigan, J. A., 1975]. *Clustering Algorithms*. Wiley, New York.

[Hays, D. G., 1973a]. "A Theory of Conceptual Organization and Processing," Report. Department of Linguistics, State University of New York at Buffalo.

[Hays, D. G., 1973b]. Types of processes on cognitive networks. In *Computational and Mathematical Linguistics*, Vol. I. A. Zampolli and N. Calzolari (eds.). Leo S. Olschki Publishers, pp. 323–532.

[Heidorn, G. E., 1972]. "Natural Language Inputs to a Simulation Programming System," Report NPS-55HD72101a. Naval Postgraduate School, Monterey, California.

[Hendrix, G. G., 1975]. Expanding the utility of semantic networks through partitioning. *Proceedings of the 4th International Conference on Artificial Intelligence, 1975* pp. 115–121.

[Hendrix, G. G., Thompson, C. W., and Slocum, J., 1973]. Language processing via canonical verbs and semantic models. *Proceedings of the 3rd International Joint Conference on Artificial Intelligence, 1973*, pp. 262–269.

[Levesque, H. J., 1977]. "A Procedural Approach to Semantic Networks," Technical Report 105. Department of Computer Science, University of Toronto, Toronto, Canada.

[Norman, D. A., 1973]. Learning and remembering: A tutorial preview. In *Attention and Performance IV*. S. Kornblum (ed.). Academic Press, New York.

[Norman, D. A., Rumelhart, D. E., and the LNR Research Group, 1975]. *Explorations in Cognition*. Freeman, San Francisco, California.

[Quillian, M. R., 1966]. "Semantic Memory," Report AFCRL-66-189. Bolt, Beranek & Newman, Cambridge, Massachusetts.

[Quillian, M. R., 1967]. Word concepts: A theory and simulation of some basic semantic capabilities. *Behavioral Science* **12**, 410–430.

[Quillian, M. R., 1968]. Semantic memory. In *Semantic Information Processing*. M. Minsky (ed.). MIT Press, Cambridge, Massachusetts.

[Quillian, M. R., 1969]. A Teachable Language Comprehender: A simulation program and theory of language. *Communications of the ACM* **12**, 459–476.

[Rumelhart, D. E., Lindsay, P. H., and Norman, D. A., 1972]. A process model for long-term memory. In *Organization of Memory*. E. Tulving and W. Donaldson (eds.). Academic Press, New York, pp. 197–246.

[Rumelhart, D. E., and Norman, D. A., 1973]. Active semantic networks as a model of human memory. *Proceedings of the 3rd International Joint Conference on Artificial Intelligence, 1973*, pp. 450–457.

[Salton, G., 1968]. *Automatic Information Organization and Retrieval*. McGraw-Hill, New York.

[Salton, G., ed., 1971]. The SMART System—Experiments in Automatic Document Processing. Prentice-Hall, Englewood Cliffs, New Jersey.

[Salton, G., 1975]. *Dynamic Information and Library Processing.* Prentice-Hall, Englewood Cliffs, New Jersey.

[Schank, R. C., 1972]. Conceptual dependency: A theory of natural language understanding. *Cognitive Psychology* 3, 552–631.

[Schank, R. C., 1973a]. The conceptual analysis of natural language. In *Natural Language Processing.* R. Rustin (ed.) Algorithmic Press, New York, pp. 291–309.

[Schank, R. C., 1973b]. Identification of conceptualizations underlying natural language. In *Computer Models of Thought and Language.* R. C. Schank and K. M. Colby (eds.). Freeman, San Francisco, California, pp. 187–247.

[Schank, R. C., and Rieger, C. J., III, 1973]. "Inference and the Computer Understanding of Natural Language," Memo AIM-197. Stanford Artificial Intelligence Laboratory, Stanford, California.

[Schubert, L. K., 1976]. Extending the expressive power of semantic networks. *Artificial Intelligence* 7, 163–198.

[Scragg, G. W., 1976]. Semantic nets as memory models. In *Computational Semantics.* E. Charniak and Y. Wilks (eds.). North-Holland Publ., Amsterdam, pp. 101–127.

[Shapiro, S. C., 1971a]. "The MIND System: A Data Structure for Semantic Information Processing." Technical Report R-837-PR. The Rand Corporation; Santa Monica, California.

[Shapiro, S. C., 1971b]. A net structure for semantic information storage, deduction, and retrieval. In *Proceedings of the 2nd International Joint Conference on Artificial Intelligence, 1971* pp. 512–523.

[Shapiro, S. C., 1975]. "An Introduction to SNePS," Report. Department of Computer Science, Indiana University, Bloomington.

[Simmons, R. F., 1973]. Semantic networks: Their computation and use for undertanding English sentences. In *Computer Models of Thought and Language.* R. C. Schank and K. M. Colby (eds.). Freeman, San Francisco, California, pp. 63–113.

[Simmons, R. F., and Bruce, B. C., 1971]. Some relations between predicate calculus and semantic net representations of discourse. In *Proceedings of the 2nd International Joint Conference on Artificial Intelligence, 1971,* pp. 524–529.

[Simmons, R. F., and Slocum, J., 1972]. Generating English discourse from semantic networks. *Communications of the ACM* 15, 891–905.

[Simmons, R. F., Burger, J. F., and Schwarz, R. M., 1968]. A computational model of verbal understanding. *AFIPS Conference Proceedings* 33, 441–456.

[Sparck Jones, K., and Kay, M., 1974]. *Linguistics and Information Science.* Academic Press, New York.

[Van Ryzin, J., 1977]. *Classification and Clustering.* Academic Press, New York.

[Weizenbaum, J., 1966]. ELIZA—a computer program for the study of natural language communication between man and machine. *Communications of the ACM* 9, 36–45.

[Wilks, Y., 1974]. "Natural Language Understanding Systems Within the AI Paradigm," Memo. AIM-237. Stanford Artificial Intelligence Laboratory, Stanford, California.

[Winston, P. H., 1975]. Learning structural descriptions from examples. In *The Psychology of Computer Vision.* P. H. Winston (ed.). McGraw-Hill, New York, pp. 157–209.

[Woods, W. A., 1975]. What's in a link? Foundations for semantic networks. In *Representation and Understanding.* D. G. Bobrow and A. M. Collins (eds.). Academic Press, New York, pp. 35–82.

RE: THE GETTYSBURG ADDRESS
Representing Social and Political Acts

Roger C. Schank   and   *Jaime G. Carbonell, Jr.*

1. INTRODUCTION

At the last AI conference, one of us (RCS) was part of a panel on knowledge representation. The panel was asked to come prepared to discuss, among other things, problems that their systems found difficult or impossible to handle. For my part of the discussion, I suggested the Gettysburg Address was something that we had not the slightest idea how to handle.

Let us look at the beginning of the Gettysburg Address to see what kinds of problems we had in mind:

(1)   Four score and seven years ago . . .

There is no real difficulty here. This is just a grandiose way of saying 87 years ago. Although certain stylistic problems do come up, e.g., "Why do people say things in this way in speeches?" and certain artistic things come up, e.g., "Is this a pretty way of saying 87 years ago?" for the most part, this first phrase is not a part of the difficulties we were referring to.

(2)   our forefathers brought forth on this continent a new nation . . .

The problems here are numerous:

(a)   What is a "forefather"? To understand the concept of forefather, it is necessary to understand time and process notions; metaphors about fatherhood being bestowed on ideas and political entities as well as its literal meaning; and the general world of politics.

(b)   What does "brought forth" mean? Clearly this has to do with creation of some sort. Again we have a metaphor for "birth" and "fatherhood," etc. However, ascribing this to metaphor in no way solves the problem. How do we represent creation? The simplest (and most tempting) answer is to have a description, where first we have nothing and then we have something. This seems to miss something in the process of birth, however. More importantly, can the birth of a nation be

327

described this way? Certainly this is a very complicated idea (although perhaps no more complicated than the birth of a child).

(c)   What is a nation? Other than some simple rendering of a nation as *nation* or as type node in a semantic network, the concept of nation seems rather intractable. How do we deal with it?

(3)   conceived in liberty, . . .

Our birth metaphor continues on here. To analyze this we must understand how nations are like humans. We must also understand what liberty means. Saying something like "it means freedom" will not do. What are the primitive concepts by which we can get at ideas like this?

(4)   and dedicated to the proposition, . . .

Can a nation be dedicated? How does one dedicate it? Again, what does this really mean? It seems hard to even think about representing this in any conceptual dependency-like representational scheme. Neither does this seem tractable using scripts. Certainly there is no DEDICATION script, for example.

What is a proposition? In conceptual dependency, it is any ACTOR–ACTION–OBJECT construction, but how do we represent references to it? Texts that talk about texts must be represented in a fashion different from the texts themselves.

(5)   that all men are created equal.

If we can understand how to represent propositions like (5), we can represent anything. This is not a script or a series of conceptualizations describing equality. It seems like a simple idea and should be represented simply. On the other hand, how many people would agree in any detail about the meaning of (5)? One man's equality is probably not another's.

(6)   Now we are engaged in a great civil war, . . .

What is war? If we can really understand what war involves, we might be able to write a WAR script, but would that capture the purposes and aims of war? Who does the "we" refer to? Unless the concepts of *war* and *nation* are well understood, it becomes extremely difficult to disambiguate the referent. There are no general methods in the AI literature for disambiguating this type of referent, and we cannot envision any such methods without an adequate representation of the social or political situation.

In all the above kinds of problems, one thing seems clear. What we have had in conceptual dependency is a system for describing the physical world. Scripts, plans, and goals allowed us to look at the intentions and knowledge behind these physical events. What we need to handle a problem such as those found in the Gettysburg Address (though one would have no trouble finding them in a newspaper everyday) is a system for representing social and political actions and the knowledge and intentions underlying them. Such a system might parallel conceptual dependency in interesting ways, but it would not be identical to it. It is such a system that we shall seek to develop in this chapter.

2. TRIANGLES

Sometimes when one reads a newspaper it is possible to read only the headline and feel safe in ignoring the story. Although a headline is rather short it often can convey nearly the entire story, at least by inference. The following headlines taken from *The New York Times* illustrate my point:

(1) Catawba Indians Land Claims Supported.
(2) Integration Plan Deadline Met by Boards in Ohio.
(3) Lehigh University Uncovers Payments by Students to Alter Grades.

It is really not necessary to have read the stories underneath these headlines in order to know what the stories must have said. We can fill in the details of the stories ourselves. How?

Let us first point out that scripts do not solve the problem here. Scripts are a kind of knowledge structure meant to describe sequential events that are much more commonplace than land-claims or grade altering schemas. If we start admitting such things into the world of scripts, we essentially destroy the value of scripts by creating too many of them, thus making the process of searching for appropriate ones extremely cumbersome. Indian land claims and grade altering schemas are neither stereotypical nor well defined in terms of exactly what happens when they take place. We understand a grade altering schema more by its effects and likely consequences than by the precise method employed in altering the grades. Hence, it is not the sequential events described in a script that are of primary interest to the understander.

We have adopted, as a more general kind of knowledge structure, applicable where scripts are not, an elaborate scheme of plans, goals, and themes [Schank and Abelson, 1977]. However, this system, too, is inadequate to the task of rendering headlines into stories, this time for the opposite reason: that apparatus is too general to apply to the specific knowledge we use in these situations. We would not want to ask questions such as: What general goal did the Catawba Indians have in mind and what plan did they use to solve it? We really already know the answer to that in some detail, but from what?

The method by which we can fill in the details of headlines such as those given above is derived from our knowledge about sociopolitical situations. A child or a person naïve in politics or social organizations would have a great deal of difficulty discerning anything of substance from the above headlines. On the other hand, the more knowledgable one is in the general method by which societies operate, the easier it is to fill in the details. What we need then is a general apparatus for describing sociopolitical organizations and situations from which details of specific situations can be inferred.

Let us begin by looking at headline (1): Catawba Indians Land Claim Supported. The problem here is what exactly "land claim" and "supported" mean in a more general sociological point of view. That is, we know that a land claim is more than the set of physical acts done by the claiming party in service of establishing the claim. In fact, we do not often know, or need to know, the particular set of physical acts (that may be represented in conceptual dependency) in order to understand the social and legal implications of a land claim.

Something like "Indians MTRANS land be possessed by Indians" is possibly true, but it misses the point. A "land claim" is in a sense a petition to a higher authority to resolve a dispute between two parties. That is, the Indians are saying to the U.S. Government, "this land is ours." It may not be possible to infer the particulars of this land claim. Indians have been known to take the land by force, to file documents in government offices, to complain to newsmen, and so on. The important point here is that we really need not know, and in most cases a reader would not bother to worry about, exactly which method has been selected. Rather, a reader feels that he understands the story when he has been able to identify the relationships and aims of the parties involved.

In the case of (1) we can establish that a "land claim" is a type of petition to a higher authority to resolve a dispute about land ownership. We do not know who currently owns the land but we know enough about ownership of property to infer that there is probably a counterpetition of some sort. We also know about petitions to authority. They usually get resolved by the authority. In this case then, "supported" refers to the decision of the authority.

This information can be represented graphically by the kind of triangle in Fig. 1. In this triangle, (1) separates the dispute between the Indians and the owners of the land, (2) represents the appeal to authority to re-

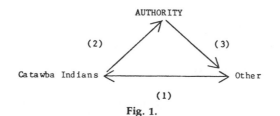

Fig. 1.

solve the dispute made by the Indians, and (3) represents the authority's decision.

Triangles of this sort are useful in representing disputes. For example, in (4) and (5) such triangles (Figs. 2 and 3, respectively) can also be constructed:

(4)   Burma appeals to UN to settle border dispute with Thailand.

(5)   John complained to Bill's mother that Bill hit him.

Of course, these triangles just suggest the basic relationships involved. In order to add substance to the bare bones of the triangles, we shall have to start discussing some representational issues that are being glossed over here. The important point at this juncture is that there is an essential similarity across (1), (4), and (5), that the similarity must be represented in some way, and that that similarity can be exploited for use in an understanding system.

3.   SOCIAL ACTs

The first representational problem we encounter in trying to make explicit much of what is implicit in the triangle representation is that we shall need to design a new set of ACTs to take care of the various relationships.

In the primitive ACTs of conceptual dependency [Schank, 1975], we have a system that represents physical actions by using a small set of basic actions that can combine in various ways to describe detailed or complex actions that underlie seemingly simple verbs and nouns.* The primitive ACTs do not account for intentionality and goals underlying physical action. To account for such things, we devised a complex apparatus discussed in Schank and Abelson [1977]. It should come as no surprise then that if we wish to account for social events, we shall need a system of basic social ACTs to represent the social actions that comprise the events. We term these "basic social ACTs" rather than primitive ACTs because in the

Fig. 2.   Fig. 3.

* It is not possible here to give a description of the notations and diagrams used by the conceptual dependency approach. The reader unfamiliar with them is referred to the article by Schank in, for example, Schank and Colby [1973]. The Appendix gives a concise summary only.   (*Editor*)

end most social ACTs have some physical manifestations, which are, however, of little relevance in representing sociopolitical interactions. For example, a government decision to resolve a dispute may be MTRANSed in a variety of ways to the several different parties concerned. The various details of the MTRANS or any of instrumental acts have little relevance to the social or political consequences of the government decision, which usually are of primary interest. The inferences resulting from the MTRANS (i.e., the actor of the MTRANS must have previously known the information he MTRANSed to the recipient; the recipient now has the new information) are true but of lesser significance than the inferences that can be drawn from the government decision itself. These inferences include the following: There must have been a dispute between two parties. One of the two parties probably asked the government to resolve their dispute. The dispute was probably resolved as a result of the governmental decision. The government is likely to enforce its decision if the parties concerned do not abide by the decision.

The most significant inference to be made from an authority's decision is that simply by virtue of that decision, something has actually happened. That is, a government authorization is a kind of societal performative ACT. Thus, if the government says some property is mine, or that a man is a criminal, then it is so by virtue of their saying it. Similarly, other authority figures have the same power. A professor can say a thesis is finished and a student has a Ph.D., and this is the case by virtue of his saying it.

Not all authoritys' decisions are like this, to be sure. Sometimes an authority gives an order and that order must be carried out for the decision to have effect. Frequently these orders come about as a result of a governmental decision or authorization. If the government says the land belongs to the Catawba Indians, then it does, but it may have to send in the National Guard to get the present owner off the property.

What we are proposing then is two basic social ACTs: AUTHORIZE (abbreviated AUTH) and ORDER. AUTH is something only an authority can do. This is actually a circular definition, since if one can AUTH then that defines one as an authority. In a sense, an authority is one whose AUTHs are recognized as legitimate by the parties involved, or one who has the power to effectively enforce his AUTHs with corresponding ORDERs.

We diagram AUTH in Fig. 4. A is the authority that can AUTHorize a DECREE. A DECREE is a statement about the state of the world, affecting

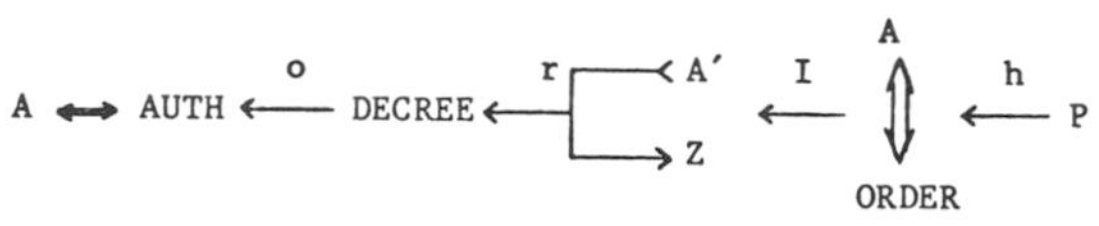

Fig. 4.

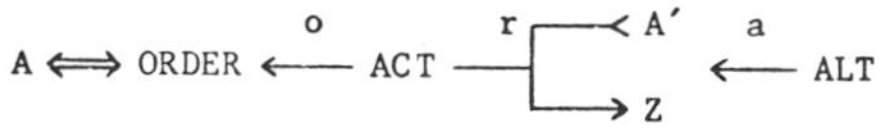

$$A \Longleftrightarrow ORDER \xleftarrow{\quad o \quad} ACT \xrightarrow{\quad r \quad} \begin{array}{c} \xrightarrow{\quad \ \ } <A' \xleftarrow{\quad a \quad} ALT \\ \to Z \end{array}$$

Fig. 5.

the recipient Z, that is true by virtue of it being AUTHed. Usually an AUTH signifies a change from the previous state of the world. The recipient can be a specific person, the parties involved in a dispute, or an entire nation (if A is a government). A' is the "real" authority on whose behalf A AUTHorizes the decree. For instance, a judge often AUTHorizes on behalf of the court; a business executive AUTHorizes on behalf of his company. It is often the case that A = A'. P is a measure of the relative degree of authority that A is able to exercise over Z, measured on a scale of 0 to 10 for convenience. The AUTHs of a dictatorial government over its citizens would all have P = 10 for example. On the other hand, an AUTH of the United Nations General Assembly over individual countries involved in a dispute would be more like P = 4. The social act ORDER often fills the instrumental case of an AUTH.

ORDER is a frequent inference of AUTH. The government can AUTH its army to fight a war, by means of declaring war on another country, but that does not, simply by virtue of the statement, imply that the army is fighting the war. A subsequent ORDER to the armed forces is required that carries with it the implicit punishments that are relevant in not carrying out an order. We diagram the ACT ORDER in Fig. 5.

The conceptual cases A' and Z are exactly the same ones of the AUTH, which preceded the ORDER. In a government, or any other hierarchical social structure, a lower authority may enforce the AUTH of a higher authority (A') via an ORDER. In other cases, the A who AUTHs is the same A who ORDERs. The ACT case of an ORDER is some action or sequence of actions carried out by the recipient (Z) in order to bring about the desired state of the world (the DECREE of the previous AUTH). ALT is the alternative open to Z if he decides not to do the ACT. ALT is usually a punishment, often left implicit in the ORDER, and hence it is an optional case of ORDER.

We might ask at this point, why we cannot do these things with the CD primitives we now have. What is the advantage of these new ACTs? To answer these questions, we need to look at the purpose of a primitive ACT. It is possible to represent ORDER in CD for example. The verb "order" means to MTRANS to someone that if they do not do a particular action or sequence of actions, then that will cause the actor of the MTRANS to do some other (unspecified) action whose result will be a negative state change on the part of the recipient of the MTRANS, and that this negative state change will cause the recipient to be more unhappy than any consequent state changes resulting from performing the MTRANSed acts. It must also be MTRANSed that if the MTRANS recipient does carry out the specified act(s), then the MTRANS actor will not do the action(s) resulting in a negative state change to the recipient. This representation is quite complete but extremely cumbersome. Is it necessary that we think of all the explicit details each time that we understand an order to have taken place?

The same question can be asked with respect to "authorize." We understand what authorization or governmental decision is but we need not access all that information each time we understand the word. Consider the problem of explaining the meaning of these words to a child, for example. It is very difficult to explain them precisely, because they are so complicated at the level of physical primitive ACTs. Yet these ideas are really not complicated at all at a social level of ACTs. Such simple concepts such as ORDER and AUTHORIZE form the basis of the organization of societies. What is complex at one level is simple at another. This idea of nested levels of complexity, each with its own set of primitives, is a very important one for the representation of information in artificial intelligence. By choosing a good set of primitives, we can effectively organize what we need to know. Thus, ORDER and AUTHORIZE have inferences that come from them just as the physical primitive ACTs do. The main difference is that these basic social ACTs are not primitive in the same sense. They can be broken down but we would rarely choose to do so.

The use of these new basic ACTs is much like the use of the original primitive ACTs. We can predict what will fill slots reasonably in a conceptualization and make inferences about slot fillers and consequent inferences as we would any conceptualization. Thus, in Figs. 6 and 7 we represent sentences such as the following using AUTH:

(7)   The Supreme Court decided segregation is illegal.

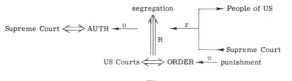

Fig. 6.

(8)   The cop gave the speeder a ticket.

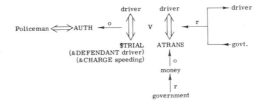

Fig. 7.

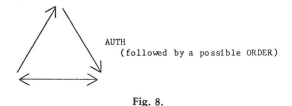

Fig. 8.

In (7), we have chosen to ignore representing segregation for the moment since it is obviously complex. Supreme Court decisions are AUTHs. They also carry with them (as do most AUTHs) an implicit ORDER for "punishment" if certain circumstances are met. The straightforward inference from (7) then is that someone practicing segregation can expect to be punished.

Policemen are authorities also. In (8), the ticket is a written manifestation of an AUTH that either puts the driver in a DEFENDANT role in a $TRIAL script or forces him to pay a fine under the guise of forfeiting bail. The instrument of the AUTH is the actual ATRANS of the ticket (left out here). The important point here is that we could represent part of (8) using ATRANS only. However, what we would be describing is the physical ACT itself when it is the social ACT that is significant here. [When I (RCS) was young there was much talk of bad kids getting "JD cards." I never understood what was so horrible about that. Couldn't they just throw them away?] The social significance of an ACT must be represented if it is understood.

Now that we have presented these two ACTs, we return to the triangle of Fig. 8. We have named one side of the triangle. The other sides represent ACTs as well. The complete triangle is as shown in Fig. 9.

The ACT PETITION represents an individual or group's act of requesting AUTH's from an authority. Thus a "civil suit" is a PETITION to the courts using some legal scripts. A protest demonstration is a PETITION to unstated authorities using some demonstration script. The point here is that we cannot do away with the scripts that describe the actual physical manifestations of these events. However, the scripts are instruments of the social ACT involved, i.e., PETITION. The most important inference from PETITION is, of course, that an AUTH is expected to resolve the issue that is the object of the PETITION. The ACT PETITION is diagrammed in Fig. 10.

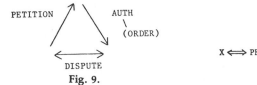

Fig. 9.

Fig. 10.

```
                       o                   c              s1
     X & Y ⟺ DISPUTE  ←── DISPUTEOBJ  ←── DISPCAT  ←── SOLX
                                                        s2
                                                       ←── SOLY
```

Fig. 11.

X is the instigator of the PETITION to the higher authority A. X′ is the
party on whose behalf X is petitioning; often X = X′. A lawyer hired by a
plaintiff does a PETITION on behalf of his client when he initiates court
proceedings. SOL is the change in the state of the world that X′ wants A to
AUTH. Hence SOL becomes the DECREE of the AUTH if A decides to
AUTH as PETITIONed by X. Often SOL is the solution desired by X to a
prior DISPUTE between X and another party (Y). SOL may have pointers
to a set of reasons presented by X to A that support SOL as a good solution
to a DISPUTE. Thus we have another social ACT, DISPUTE, whose existence often initiates one or more PETITIONS (Fig. 11). X and Y are the two
co-actors of the dispute, that is, the two parties at odds with each other.
The DISPUTEOBJ is that which is being disputed, such as ownership of an
object, political control of region, or more abstract items of dispute such as
the constitutionality of a law or policy (e.g., as in the Bakke case). The
DISPCAT is the classification or category of the dispute, for instance, military, economic, judicial, social, or political. The category of the dispute
seems useful in generating appropriate inferences (discussed in Section 7).
SOLX is the solution to the dispute that X wants (or will settle for); SOLY
is similarly defined. DISPUTE takes no recipient as it is not an inherently
directed ACT. It is the ACT of PETITION that directs it to a particular
authority who can AUTH something that will resolve it.

We are now ready to deal with sentence (1) (Catawba Indians Land
Claim Supported). The representation using the new social ACTs is given
in Fig. 12. Since this representation is not as easy to write as the triangular

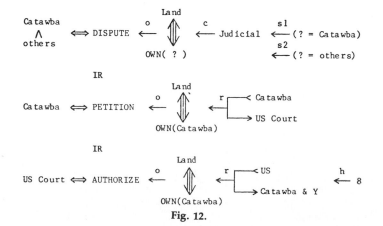

Fig. 12.

one, we shall continue to use triangles in the remainder of the paper. Thus (1) is given by Fig. 13. We shall leave out the arrows and the ACTS for diagrammatic purposes but the triangle of Fig. 13 should be understood as representing all the information given in Fig. 12. (Actually the triangles involve more information as we shall show later.)

Consider the following three sentences:

(9)   Egypt invites Israel to Cairo negotiations.

(10)   Russia invaded Czechoslovakia and replaced the premier.

(11)   Nader brought suit against GM, but the matter was settled out of court.

In each case we have a social or political dispute that does not involve PETITIONing a higher authority to AUTH a solution to the DISPUTE. Clearly, solution methods to disputes can be categorized into external (involving a third party to AUTH solutions) and internal solution methods (where the dispute is RESOLVEd directly by the disputing parties). Diplomacy is the resolution method in example (9) and military strength in (10). In example (11), there is a PETITION to authority but before the court can AUTH, Nader and GM RESOLVE their DISPUTE via arbitration. Hence, we have another social act, RESOLVE, diagrammed in Fig. 14.

The co-actors of the resolve, X and Y, are the same parties who were the co-actors of the original DISPUTE. The MEANS of resolving the problem can almost always be classified into negotiation, the application of force, or the threat thereof. SOL is the solution, a description of a change in the state of the world, which ends the DISPUTE. The way to RESOLVE a dispute is to make the SOLX and SOLY cases of the DISPUTE ACT equal to each other, that is, SOLX = SOLY = SOL. Thus RESOLVE represents negotiation to converge on a mutually acceptable solution or one party imposing a solution on the other by virtue of superior strength. RESOLVE is somewhat analogous to AUTH + ORDER; we need an ACT that initiates a RESOLVE in much the same way that PETITION initiates AUTH. We call this ACT INVOKE, which in turn is usually initiated by a DISPUTE. We diagram INVOKE in Fig. 15.

X initiates a course of action, on behalf of X', to RESOLVE a DISPUTE between X' and Y. Often X = X'. The MEANS case represents the course

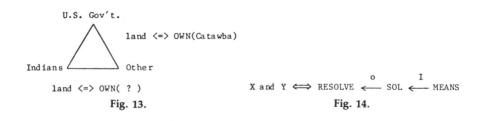

Fig. 13.   Fig. 14.

of action initiated to RESOLVE the DISPUTE; it is the same MEANS as in the RESOLVE ACT. SOLX is the solution that X intends to achieve as a result of INVOKING the MEANS. Y is the passive disputing party on whom the solution method is imposed. Consider the first conjunct of example (10) (Russia invaded Czechoslovakia). We can represent this as an IN-VOKE by letting X = Russian military, X' = Russia, Y = Czechoslovakia, SOLX = Russia increasing its political control over Czechoslovakia, MEANS = military strength. Clearly, from this INVOKE plus what we know of the relative military strengths of Russia and Czechoslovakia, we can infer the RESOLVE with SOL = SOLX and a DISPUTE that preceded the INVOKE.

Often if X INVOKEs a MEANS to resolve a DISPUTE with Y, then Y will also INVOKE the same MEANS. If country X uses military strength on country Y, then Y will probably also INVOKE military strength to defend itself, for instance. If GM offers to negotiate with Nader, then it is likely that Nader will also INVOKE negotiate with GM (at the very least he may listen to what GM is willing to offer).

We now have two basic types of triangles:

$$\text{DISPUTE} \rightarrow \text{PETITION} \rightarrow \text{AUTH} + \text{ORDER}$$

$$\text{DISPUTE} \rightarrow \text{INVOKE} \rightarrow \text{RESOLVE}$$

The DISPUTE ACT is the same in each case, and attempts at resolving the dispute can occur in either or both triangles in any given situation. We represent the RESOLVE triangle inverted below the AUTH triangle when both solution methods are active, as in Fig. 16.

As was the case for the upper triangle, the lower triangle should be interpreted to mean all that is contained in the three respective social acts. Now we can represent example (11) (Nader brought suit against GM but the matter was settled out of court) in Fig. 17.

There are some inferences that can be drawn from Figs. 16 and 17: the expected AUTH following the PETITION will not happen as a result of the RESOLVE; the DISPUTE no longer exists; GM was probably the ACTOR of the INVOKE.

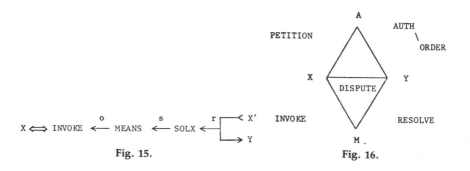

Fig. 15.   Fig. 16.

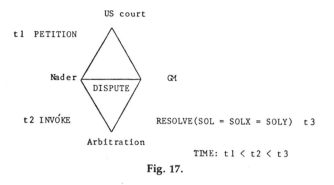

Fig. 17.

4. PROGRESS: STATIC DESCRIPTIONS

In the course of working on the problem of representing social actions, we happened across a statement by Secretary of State Vance that we found especially interesting for two reasons. First, it is real text, as are many of our previous examples, and superior to illustrative examples created for a specific purpose. Second, the statement by Vance is an alternative description of what is basically a very similar problem to the one we encountered in the Catawba Indians sentence. That is, it lends itself well to a triangle interpretation:

(12)　There will not be a Middle East treaty within a year, but there will be progress towards that goal.

To see how triangles relate here, we need to view relationships between governments as being not essentially different from relationships between individuals. That is, governments also engage in DISPUTEs. The difference is that there is frequently no obvious higher authority that will respond to PETITIONs with AUTHs. For our purposes, we can recognize three kinds of authorities to mediate between governments: the UN; world opinion; other more influential countries. The difference here is that the corresponding ACTs PETITION and AUTH cannot function in exactly the same way as they did when a government was the authority. In the case of the UN, the UN can be petitioned, and it can AUTH, but its AUTH does not always have corresponding ORDERs to carry out the AUTH. World opinion can be petitioned but it cannot AUTH at all. The RESOLVE triangle, by its very nature, works in exactly the same way for countries and individuals. The MEANS invoked to RESOLVE DISPUTEs are, in both cases, negotiation, threat, or application of force. In a political context, negotiation may be labeled "diplomacy," in a labor-relations context, it may be labeled "arbitration," but both terms fulfill identical roles in the social ACTs. Therefore, at our level of representation, the terms are synonymous.

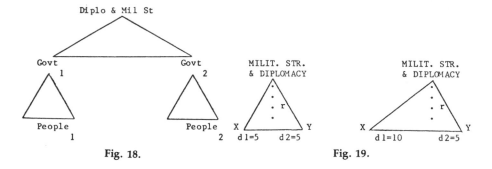

Fig. 18. Fig. 19.

Our triangles are useful for representing governmental relationships in a way analogous to those used previously. The base structure is given in Fig. 18. That is, people relate to their governments, and their governments relate to each other. In representing how governments relate, we can use the length of the base to describe the closeness of their relationship. Figure 19 illustrates two differing relations between countries X and Y. (For convenience we draw the RESOLVE triangle "upright" when there is no AUTH triangle to draw.)

We use the perpendicular (r) to divide the base of the triangle into two segments of lengths d_1 and d_2, respectively. We define two countries X and Y to be in a peaceful nonaggressive relationship if $d_1 = d_2 = 5$ with respect to military strength and diplomacy (Fig. 19, left). Two countries at war would have $d_1 = d_2 = 10$. If X declares war on Y, then we have a transition from $d_1 = d_2 = 5$ to $d_1 = 10$, $d_2 = 5$ (Fig. 19 right). Clearly, $d_1 \neq d_2$ represents an unstable situation. If one country changes its relationship to the other country, then there probably will be a complementary change on the part of the second country. The tendency of triangles to become isosceles generalizes to interpersonal and other social relations as well. Hence, from the triangle with $d_1 = 10$, $d_2 = 5$, we expect Y to do something causing $d_2 = 10$. One metaphor for countries getting more hostile toward each other is "drifting apart." We shall express that by the length of the base increasing relative to our normative length (5 for each segment). Similarly, two countries with very close diplomatic or military ties to one another would be represented with $d_1 = d_2 < 5$. When $d_1 = d_2$, we write d for d_1 and d_2 to simplify our notation.

Any triangle has a period of time for which it is true. This fact allows us to represent sentence (12) using triangles (Fig. 20):

(12a) There will be no Middle East treaty within a year:

The first triangle represents the stable (i.e., war is not imminent because no side is more aggressive than the other) but hostile [$d >$ norm (which is 5)] structure in the Middle East. The arrow represents a changing static description; NOT means will not change. The second triangle represents PEACE.

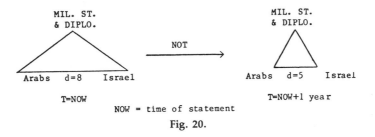

Fig. 20.

(12b)   but there will be progress towards that goal.

(See Fig. 21.) Thus, a series of collapsing triangles can be one method of representing successive state descriptions of progress toward a goal when the goal is a smaller triangle than we had at the beginning.

Using this representation method, we can represent (Figs. 22 and 23, respectively) the sociopolitical essence of conceptually complex sentences:

(13)   England and Poland signed a peace treaty.

(14)   Cambodia complained about Thailand's violation of their air space.

In (14), we have both of the facets of triangles available to us. The increased left segment of the base indicates an unstable situation caused by Thailand. In response, Cambodia has appealed to world opinion. We expect that such a situation will tend to stabilize, either by Cambodia turning toward MILITARY STRENGTH as an arbiter (making the triangle isosceles with a larger base) or by Thailand backing down [reducing the triangle to its basic isosceles form (base $d = 5$)].

The ACTs that world opinion and the UN can perform seem weak at best. The AUTH that is performed by an authority implies that the proposition AUTHed is now officially true and that an ORDER will follow if necessary to make the thing AUTHed happen. No such inferences could reasonably be said to follow from what world opinion or UN AUTHs.

A primary purpose of developing the social acts is to formulate a mechanism for making the inferences made by people reading about so-

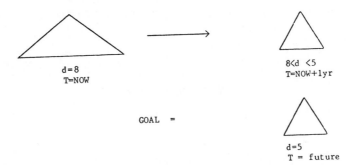

Fig. 21.

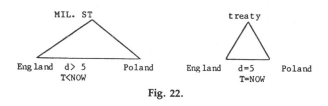

Fig. 22.

ciopolitical interactions. In this light, it seems important to be able to identify inferences as such. One way to recognize and analyze inferences is the "but" test. (The "but" test [Schank, 1975] is used to establish what is an inference from an ACT. If a phrase follows a "but" naturally, after an initial proposition, its negation is a reasonable inference.) For RESOLVE consider the following sentence:

(15)   Russia launched an attack on Albania because of a dispute concerning fishing rights in the Adriatic, but Albania won.

The "but" would not make sense here if we did not naturally assume that Russia had the stronger military. [Contrast (15) with the same sentence using the ending "but Russia won".] Since (15) is a bit unnatural as a sentence due to its curtness consider (16) as another example of the same effect:

(16)   Russia attacked Albania because of a dispute over fishing rights in the Adriatic, but Albania retained its rights when world opinion forced the Russian to back down.

What we have here is the diagram of Fig. 24. The diagram shows the initial state (t_i), the medial state (t_m) (the normal inference from the condition in t_i; this is what the "but" negates), and the final state (t_f) that is caused by the action of world opinion. We call that ACT PRESSURE. Its normal inferences are simply that the PRESSUREd party stops doing what it was doing that created a nonisosceles triangle. The triangle thus returns to normal.

PRESSURE is the most neutral of the three right sides of the triangle ACTs in that it does not imply direct actions of any sort. Why countries succumb to pressure is undoubtedly complex. That they do, needs to be

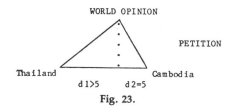

Fig. 23.

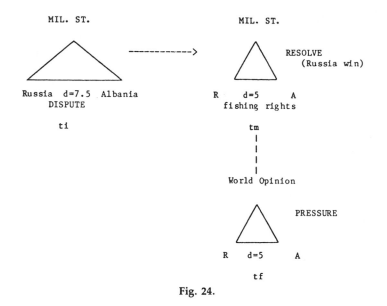

Fig. 24.

represented. The social ACT PRESSURE is diagrammed in Fig. 25. The conceptual cases of this social ACT should be interpreted in the following manner: Z applies PRESSURE to X on behalf of (or at the request of) Y in order to make X DO (or stop DOing) something to achieve SOL. PCAT is the type of PRESSURE applied by Z; economic, political, peer group are some of the more common types of PRESSURE in the sociopolitical domain.

PRESSURE has its analog in relationships between governments and their people, as we shall see in the next section.

5. RELATIONSHIPS BETWEEN AUTHORITIES AND THEIR CONSTITUENTS

One advantage of the triangle representation system is its use in explaining in a simple way such complicated concepts as power, democracy, and liberty. The ACT AUTH is the essence of the meaning of power, for example. Power means the ability to be the actor in an AUTH. The more AUTHs one can do over a wide range of subjects, the more power one has. A president of a company can AUTH in matters concerning his company.

$$Z \Longleftrightarrow \text{PRESSURE} \overset{o}{\longleftarrow} \text{SOL} \overset{c}{\longleftarrow} \text{PCAT} \overset{r}{\longleftarrow} \begin{matrix} \rightarrow X \\ < Y \end{matrix}$$

Fig. 25.

That is where his power is. A mother can AUTH over her children by virtue of her social role in the family. Children usually accept parental AUTHs without questioning their legitimacy; this essentially gives the parent the power to AUTH. As long as a parent has some psychological, emotional, or physical control over them, she can ORDER to enforce her AUTHs.

Democracy is clearly a very complex concept. A simple approximation of its meaning can be obtained using the triangle format. If a government is a system that AUTHs in response to petitions, then the correlation of PETITIONS to AUTHs would represent one measure of the workings of the government. For example, a dictatorship is a government where the AUTHs are motivated by the goals of the head of state rather than by petitions of the people. Ideally, a democracy is a government where all AUTHs are motivated by PETITIONs backed by a majority of the people. A responsive government is one where all PETITIONs result in AUTHs of one kind or another. A benevolent despot is one who issues AUTHs without regard for PETITIONs but in accord with what he believes the PETITIONs might be (or would be if the people knew how to best govern themselves).

Such simplistic definitions are, of course, just that. However, regardless of the inaccuracy of these definitions from a political scientist's point of view, it must be remembered that we are attempting to understand language. Furthermore, we are attempting to model the average person's understanding of a political situation since that is what is being referred to by the everyday language that is used to report on these situations. What we have here should in no way be assumed to be addressing the issue of what is "really" going on in political situations. We are not trying to simulate the understanding of the expert. Thus, a definition of equality in a country as "a government where every person gets to PETITION and where the PETITION has the same chance of resulting in an AUTH as any other person's PETITION" might be a more accurate way of describing what was meant by Lincoln when he said that all men are created equal than a method that dealt with physical or mental equality.

The relationship between people and their governments is one much touched upon in text. Thus any system of social–political representation can be evaluated by its ability to deal with such texts.

One of the first things to recognize is that, rather than one triangle to represent this relationship, what is needed is a hierarchy of triangles. That is, there are many avenues of appeal in a governmental system or in any power system. The notion of a "higher authority" must be represented.

To do this, we take advantage of another aspect of triangles, namely, their height. The taller the triangle, the more power (and more distance from the people) the authority at the top is said to have. Thus successive appeals might look like this:

(17)   John appealed the negative decision of the Lower Court to the Supe-

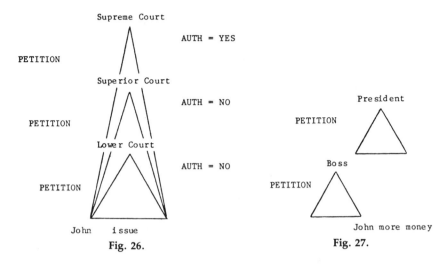

Fig. 26.

Fig. 27.

rior Court, which upheld the lower court's ruling, and finally to the Supreme Court, who overturned it.

The hierarchy in Fig. 26 looks a little different in the case where the authority in the first part becomes the petitioner's advocate in the second:

(18) John asked his boss for a raise. His boss took it up with the president of the company.

This agency relationship is shown in Fig. 27, for the case where the agent (Boss here) is also an authority over the petitioner. In the case where the petitioner uses an advocate who is not an authority (a lawyer, for example), we represent the situation as follows (Fig. 28):

(19) John had his lawyer ask the court for a ruling.

We shall call his relationship AGENT. This is a basic stative relationship that is used frequently. For example, in the Bakke case, Bakke was represented by lawyers hired by the YAF; UCD was represented by the California Regents, in the case before the Supreme Court. This is shown in Fig. 29.

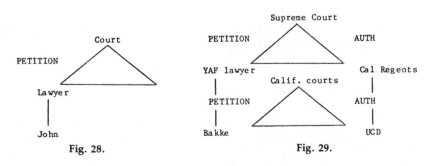

Fig. 28.

Fig. 29.

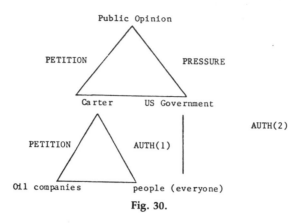

Fig. 30.

Higher authorities can be invoked by analogy to how governments relate to each other. Thus we can get a sentence like (17) (see Fig. 30):

(20)   Carter changed his energy policy as a result of public outrage.

6.   THE GETTYSBURG ADDRESS

We are now ready to discuss the representation of the beginning of the Gettysburg Address.

(21)   "Four score and seven years ago our forefathers brought forth upon this continent, a new nation . . .

(21) describes three states of triangles (Fig. 31). The initial state represents the two peoples being governed by the British. The second state shows that the initial triangle has split into two triangles (two governments). These governments are known to have been at war. This was not stated in (21) but since it was true, we have chosen to represent it. The creation of a new nation then is shown by one triangle becoming two.

(22)   conceived in liberty and dedicated to the proposition that all men are created equal.

(22) must be represented as the manner in which the authorities in the new government treat the people. Thus we have two propositions that are true of the new triangle (Fig. 32).

(23)   Now we are engaged in a great Civil War . . .

A civil war is a split in a triangle as before (Fig. 33). We have chosen here to represent the two different views of a civil war (we could have done it with the Revolutionary War, too, of course). The USA view has the triangle split with a war attempting to resolve the split. The CSA view has the

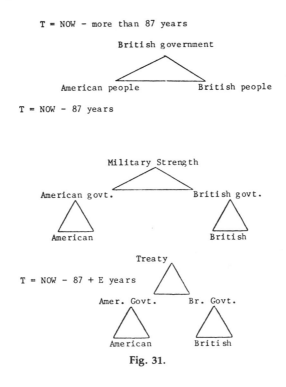

Fig. 31.

split having taken effect. There are thus two different countries at war in this view. The important point here is that when the war stops in the USA view, the split ceases and the triangle is whole. In the CSA view, if the war would stop, the two triangles could exist as two separate countries.

What we are doing here is not representing the Gettysburg Address so much as we are representing the political history surrounding the events

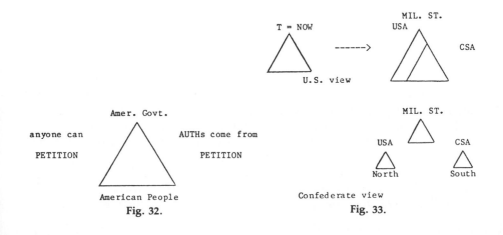

Fig. 32.

Fig. 33.

being discussed in the Gettysburg Address. We have thus left out the
birth metaphor we discussed earlier and have chosen to focus on understanding the content underlying the metaphor. We leave the value of the
metaphor to literary critics to analyze.

7. THE USE OF TRIANGLES

Triangles provide us with a method for representing the social significance of actions. As with any other representation scheme, the advantage
of the symbols we create can only be in the new symbols or actions that
they spawn. That is, the inferences that come from the triangles are of key
importance. When we created the original primitive ACTs, we said that
PROPEL was no more than the set of inferences that it fired off. The same
is true here, and so we must ask what these inferences are.

The first thing we can recognize about potential inferences here is that
they will come in two varieties. The first are the inferences that are fired
off from the new social ACTs that we have created. The second kind are
those that come from the triangles themselves. That is, there should be
patterns of triangles that are recognizable for the triangles they spawn as
well as a set of inferences that come from the fact that certain triangles
exist.

Authorize

We shall first analyze the inferences that are applicable to each social
ACT. For each ACT, there are inferences that state something that must or
may have occurred before the ACT took place, and inferences that describe relevant changes in the state of the world as a result of the ACT. The
latter category includes inferences that create expectations about future
ACTs that are likely to occur. We label our inference rules antecedent and
consequent, respectively, in order not to be confused with the PLANNER
deduction rules similarly labeled. We give a precise formulation of the
inference rules triggered from each social ACT after considering some illustrative examples.

Consider the plausible inferences that can be made from a typical AUTH
such as (1) (Catawba Indian land claims supported). We know that the
authority supporting the land claims is probably a U.S. court of law. We
are also quite certain that the Indians must have filed the land claim (a PE-
TITION), and that the ownership of the land is probably contested by another party (a DISPUTE, otherwise there would have been no need to file
the claim). If the other party claiming ownership of the land refuses to give
it to the Indians, we are fairly sure that the U.S. will do something to enforce its ruling (issue an ORDER). We would not be surprised to hear that
the Indians and the other party may have tried to resolve the issue before

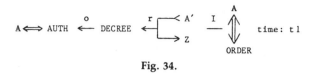

Fig. 34.

(or during) the judicial proceedings (INVOKE either negotiations or strength via occupation of the land). Indeed, some of us may suspect, from previous knowledge of Indian land disputes, that there was some sort of open confrontation. Are there other types of inferences that we can make from (1)? We have not yet considered the predictive inferences that might answer questions such as: What might the other party do at this point? How about the Indians? Will the court decision stand? Will it be obeyed? The Catawba Indians are probably satisfied with the court decision—how do we know that? We cannot say we have really understood example (1) unless we can answer most of these questions.

The goal that the Indians were striving for was ownership of the disputed land; we infer this from the fact that ownership of land was the object of their PETITION. Since the U.S. court ruled in their favor (i.e., AUTHed that which the Indians PETITIONed), we know that the Indians achieved their goal. Hence, we conclude that the Indians are satisfied and we predict no further acts on their part. The opposite is the case for the other party involved in the land dispute. Their goal, also ownership of the land, has been violated by the decision of the court. We expect that they might appeal the verdict (PETITION to a higher authority) or (less likely) try to hold on to the land by force (INVOKE strength) or possibly both. If there is no higher court to appeal to, we expect that the decision will stand and that the court may (through another branch of the government) enforce its ruling (ORDER).

The inference rules we illustrated in this example can be stated more precisely. We need the more exact formulation of our inference rules in order to build a computer system that can systematically apply them to understand stories such as the examples considered in this chapter. In our analysis of example (1), we applied most of the inference rules listed below for AUTH and two of the rules indexed under PETITION (see Fig. 34).

Antecedent inference rules:

(1) $Z \Leftrightarrow \text{PETITION} \overset{r}{\leftarrow} A$ (time: $t_2 < t_1$).
(2)   If DECREE = goal of Z then the $\overset{o}{\leftarrow}$ case of the PETITION probably = DECREE.
(3) Z & other $\Leftrightarrow$ DISPUTE (time: $t_3 < t_2$).
(4)   If Z & other $\Leftrightarrow$ INVOKE $\overset{o}{\leftarrow}$ MEANS then the MEANS failed in RESOLVING the DISPUTE (time: $t_4 < t_1$).

Consequent inference rules: (time $> t_1$):

(5) If Z does not accept the DECREE then expect A $\Leftrightarrow$ ORDER.

(6) If $h > 8$ or there is no authority higher than A to PETITION to (where h is a measure of the power that A may exercise over Z), then expect Z and the other party to accept the DECREE and end their DISPUTE. Otherwise consider rules 7 and 8.

(7) If DECREE = GOAL(Z), then expect the other party to PETITION an authority higher than A with the $\overset{s}{\leftarrow}$ case = GOAL(other). Also expect other $\Leftrightarrow$ INVOKE $\overset{\circ}{\leftarrow}$ MEANS to RESOLVE the DISPUTE directly. d_1 may decrease and d_2 may increase in the triangle (Fig. 35). This may balance a previously unstable situation, or it may unbalance an isosceles triangle. We need to reference the triangle itself in order to make other consequent or predictive inferences from the possible changes in d_1 and d_2.

(8) If DECREE = GOAL(other), then the converse of rule 7 applies.

(9) If DECREE = compromise, then possibly DISPUTE between Z and other will terminate. (It may prove difficult to recognize when a DECREE constitutes a compromise between two proposed solutions in our eventual computer implementation of these inference rules.)

Order

ORDER is an instrumental act to AUTH. As such, it is significant mostly because of the AUTH that can be inferred from it. Sometimes an ORDER appears explicitly in text; in other instances the ORDER itself must be inferred, as in the following example:

(24) The federal government suspended aid to the Chicago schools on grounds of continued segregation.

In example (24), we have a case where punishment is applied because an ORDER was not obeyed. We can infer that the government ORDERed the desegregation of the schools, with the (possibly implicit) punishment of cutting federal aid. Further inferences are triggered from the ORDER: The government must have AUTHed that segregation was illegal. If the government chose cutting aid as punishment, then it is probably the case that it is a worse consequence for the Chicago schools than the ORDERed desegregation. The Chicago schools will probably desegregate in the near future. The government AUTH that segregation is illegal will probably result in an end to (institutionalized) segregation. We can also generate a

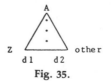

Fig. 35.

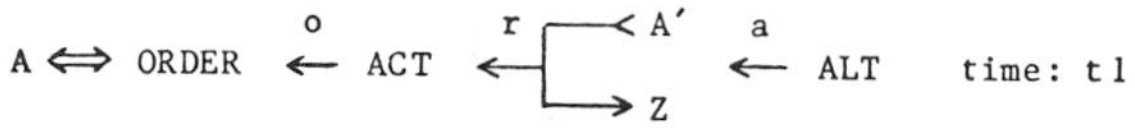

$$A \Leftrightarrow ORDER \overset{o}{\leftarrow} ACT \overset{r}{\leftarrow} \begin{array}{c} \overset{A'}{\prec} \\ \searrow Z \end{array} \overset{a}{\leftarrow} ALT \quad time: t\,1$$

Fig. 36.

large number of inferences from the AUTH, but we believe that these second-order inferences are usually not generated when a sentence like example (24) is understood.

The precise statement of the inferences triggered from ORDER is given below (see Fig. 36):

Antecedent inference rules:

(1) It must have been the case that $A' \Leftrightarrow AUTH \overset{o}{\leftarrow} DECREE \overset{r}{\leftarrow} Z$, where $Z \Leftrightarrow ACT$ or its result is the DECREE (time $t_2 < t_1$).

(2) If $A \neq A'$ then $A' \Leftrightarrow AUTH \overset{o}{\leftarrow} (A \Leftrightarrow ORDER) \overset{r}{\leftarrow} A$ (time $t_3 < t_1$).

Consequent inference rules:

(3) Z will probably do ACT.

(4) If Z does ACT then the DECREE of the preceding AUTH will be established as a change in the state of the world.

(5) In the case that Z does not do ACT, A will do ALT to Z (e.g., Jail or fine Z if A' is court of law.)

Petition

PETITION triggers a rather rich set of inferences. Some of these inferences are shared with INVOKE, but others can only be made from PETITION. Let us reconsider the first clause of example (11) (Nader brought suit against GM, but the matter was settled out of court). This is clearly a PETITION to a court of law. We can conclude that there must have been a DISPUTE of a judicial nature between Nader and GM. From the first clause, we infer that the US court will AUTH a solution to the DISPUTE. This inference is violated by the "but" construction in the second clause of (11). (Recall that the "but" test tells us that the second clause must be violating an inference triggered from the first clause.) Other inferences triggered from "Nader brought suit against GM" include: GM might bring a countersuit against Nader. GM might apply PRESSURE on Nader to drop his suit. GM might PRESSURE the US government to AUTH the court to drop the suit (e.g., lobby for legislation whose effect is to nullify the legal grounds on which Nader's lawsuit is based). Nader or (more likely) GM might INVOKE negotiation to RESOLVE their DISPUTE without waiting for the court proceedings to conclude. The second clause of example (11) states that this last inference is what indeed happened. In order to establish a causal connection between the two clauses in our example, it was essential to realize that the highly expected AUTH inference was violated and that the INVOKE negotiation inference was confirmed.

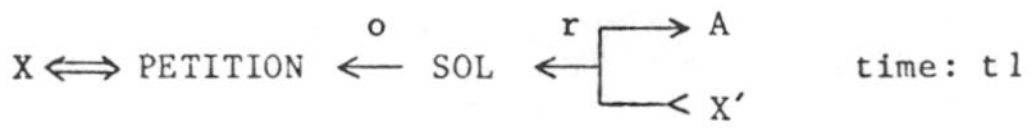

$$X \Longleftrightarrow \text{PETITION} \xleftarrow{o} \text{SOL} \xleftarrow{r} \begin{array}{l} \longrightarrow A \\ \longleftarrow X' \end{array} \qquad \text{time: t1}$$

Fig. 37.

The inferences just discussed are stated in more precise terms in the list below (see Fig. 37).

Antecedent inference rules:

(1)   There was probably a DISPUTE between X' and some other party (Y), with SOLX (of the DISPUTE) = SOL (of the PETITION). ($t_2 < t_1$) The words "probably" and "possibly" are used to convey an intuitive degree of certainty of the inference rule yielding true statements.

(2)   There may have been an $X \Leftrightarrow \text{INVOKE} \xleftarrow{r} Y$ that did not result in a RESOLVE.

Consequent inference rules:

(3)   A will probably AUTH a solution to X' (and any party involved in a DISPUTE with X') (time $t_3 > t_1$).

(4)   If $X \Leftrightarrow \text{PETITION} \xleftarrow{o} \text{SOL} \xleftarrow{r} B$ (where B is a lower authority than A) at time $t_4 < t_1$ then it was the case that $B \Leftrightarrow \text{AUTH} \xleftarrow{o} \text{DECREE}$ (where DECREE is NOT equal to SOL) (time t_5, where $t_4 < t_5 < t_1$).

(5)   Expect Y (where Y is the party in DISPUTE with X) also to PETITION A with SOL = SOLY (of the DISPUTE).

(6)   It is possible that $Y \Leftrightarrow \text{INVOKE} \xleftarrow{o} \langle \text{Strength} \rangle$ to force X to accept SOLY before A can AUTH (time $t_6 > t_1$).

(7)   It is possible that $Y \Leftrightarrow \text{INVOKE} \xleftarrow{o} \langle \text{negotiation} \rangle \xleftarrow{r} X$ to RESOLVE the dispute by creating a SOL = SOLX = SOLY [this entails a willingness on the part of X and Y to compromise on their original desired SOL(X or Y)] before A can AUTH a SOL $\neq$ SOLY (time $t_7 > t_1$).

Dispute

What can we infer from the statement of a DISPUTE? Let us analyze the following example:

(25)   Ethiopia and Somalia are in conflict over the Ogaden Desert.

We represent example (25) in Fig. 38. From the above DISPUTE, we may infer the following: Either country may PETITION the UN or world

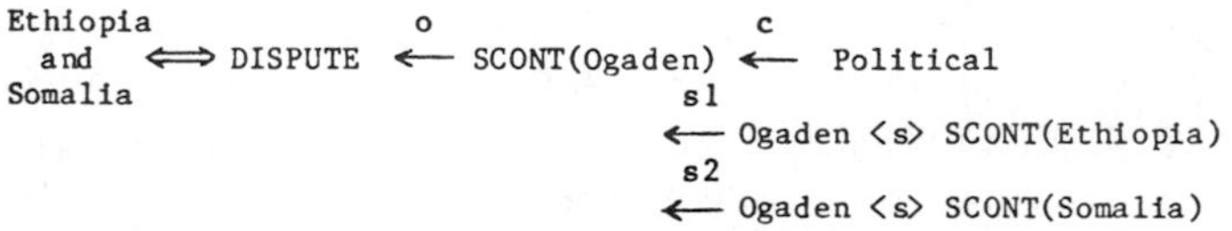

```
Ethiopia                o                     c
   and   ⟺ DISPUTE ⟵ SCONT(Ogaden) ⟵ Political
Somalia                              s1
                                     ⟵ Ogaden ⟨s⟩ SCONT(Ethiopia)
                                     s2
                                     ⟵ Ogaden ⟨s⟩ SCONT(Somalia)
```
Fig. 38.

opinion to AUTH a settlement. Either country may INVOKE negotiation or military strength; in the latter case the DISPUTE would escalate to a military category. A third country may be PETITIONed to PRESSURE one of the DISPUTING countries to either abandon the DISPUTE or partake in negotiations INVOKED by the PETITIONing country. The set of inferences presented in Fig. 39 for DISPUTE has a somewhat different flavor than those triggered from AUTH or PETITION.

Antecedent Inference Rules

There are no highly probable inference rules for inferring social ACTs that may have preceded a DISPUTE. We can infer that X has the GOAL of bringing SOLX about, similarly for Y, but this is hardly more than restating the definition of SOLX and SOLY. The cause of the DISPUTE may be inferred in terms of goal conflicts between the actors (for instance, see Carbonell [1978]) or violated inference rules triggered from other social ACTs. For example, the original DISPUTE in the Bakke case (analyzed in an earlier section) is largely caused by Bakke $\Leftrightarrow$ PETITION $\xleftarrow{}$ admittance $\xleftarrow{r}$ UCD, which did NOT RESULT in the desired AUTH by UCD (University of California at Davis). Hence, there was both a goal conflict between Bakke and the UCD affirmative action policy, as well as a violated expectation (or hope) on Bakke's part that his PETITION would be favorably AUTHed. It seems feasible to develop a more complete mechanism (e.g., a set of rules) to attribute causes to DISPUTEs, but this might require a more general formalism than the social ACTs (for instance GOALs and PLANs in Schank and Abelson [1977]).

Consequent Inference Rules

(1) X or Y may PETITION some authority (A) to AUTH a SOLution to the DISPOBJ. The PETITION SOL case will equal the SOL (X or Y, depending on who PETITIONs) case of the DISPUTE. Who X and Y are in conjunction with the DISPCAT determines what authority X or Y may appeal to. (For example, if X and Y are countries and their DISPUTE is economic, then A may equal World Bank; if their dispute is political, then A may equal the UN General Assembly.)

(2) X or Y may INVOKE a MEANS to RESOLVE their DISPUTE directly (without involving an authority). If DISPCAT = military then MEANS probably equals military strength. If DISPCAT = Social, judicial, or economic, then MEANS probably equals negotiation. If X is stronger than Y,

$$X \ \& \ Y \Longleftrightarrow DISPUTE \xleftarrow{o} DISPUTEOBJ \xleftarrow{c} DISPCAT \xleftarrow[s2]{s1} \begin{array}{l} SOLX \\ SOLY \end{array}$$

Fig. 39.

then X is more likely to use MEANS equal to (military or physical) strength than if Y is the stronger party.

(3) If the DISPUTE is not resolved after a PETITION and/or INVOKE, then it is likely that the DISPUTE will broaden to other DISPCAT in the following manner: Political DISPUTEs that remain unresolved may become Military DISPUTEs. Economic DISPUTEs between individuals may trigger judicial DISPUTEs. Economic DISPUTEs between nations may become political in nature. Ideological DISPUTEs tend to escalate to all other categories of DISPUTE.

Invoke

Recall example (10) (Russia invaded Czechoslovakia and replaced the premier). The first clause of this example is an INVOKE of military strength. We can infer that there probably was a DISPUTE between Russia and Czechoslovakia, and that this DISPUTE will probably be RESOLVEd by the use of military strength. Since we know that Russia is the stronger nation, we infer that Russia will win the confrontation and therefore dictate the terms of the RESOLVE. If we did not know the relative strengths of the two nations, we may still guess that Russia was the stronger because only thus could Russia hope to achieve its goals through INVOKing military strength. We may also infer that Czechoslovakia may PETITION the UN, world opinion, or other nations to PRESSURE Russia to stop its military actions. In order to establish the causal connection between the two clauses of example (10), we need to make the inference that Russia will achieve social control of Czechoslovakia (this is a result of RESOLVE by military means), and we need the rule that social control gives Russia the power to AUTH in Czechoslovakia. Russia was thus able to AUTH the change in government of Czechoslovakia. The inference rules triggered from INVOKE are given below (see Fig. 40):

Antecedent Inference Rules

(1) X' and Y were probably involved in a DISPUTE whose DISPCAT is commensurate with the MEANS INVOKEd to RESOLVE the DISPUTE.

(2) SOLX of the INVOKE = SOLX of the DISPUTE.

(3) If MEANS = (military or physical) strength, then probably X is stronger than Y.

(4) Possibly X ⟺ PETITION ⟵° SOLX ⟵ʳ A without getting the desired A ⟺ AUTH ⟵° SOLX.

$$X \Longleftrightarrow INVOKE \xleftarrow{o} MEANS \xleftarrow{s} SOLX \xleftarrow{r} \begin{array}{c} X' \\ Y \end{array}$$

Fig. 40.

(5)   Possibly Y $\Leftrightarrow$ PETITION $\xleftarrow{o}$ SOLY $\xleftarrow{r}$ A. Also X wants to RE-SOLVE the DISPUTE with Y before A $\Leftrightarrow$ AUTH $\xleftarrow{o}$ SOLY. This rule is not so far-fetched as it may seem at first glance; it is necessary, for instance, in understanding a version of example (11): Nader brought suit against GM, but GM offered to settle out of court. Rule 4 connects the two sentences by establishing the most probable reason why GM offered to settle their DISPUTE.

Consequent Inference Rules

(6)   Expect Y $\Leftrightarrow$ INVOKE $\xleftarrow{o}$ MEANS $\xleftarrow{s}$ SOLY, where MEANS is the same as in the original INVOKE.

(7)   Expect X & Y $\Leftrightarrow$ RESOLVE $\xleftarrow{o}$ SOL $\xleftarrow{I}$ MEANS.

(8)   If X & Y do NOT RESOLVE, then expect X $\Leftrightarrow$ PETITION or X $\Leftrightarrow$ IN-VOKE $\xleftarrow{o}$ other MEANS.

(9)   If MEANS = strength and Y is weaker than X, then expect Y to PE-TITION a third party to PRESSURE X into not forcing a RESOLVE.

Resolve

Let us again look at example (11) (Nader brought suit against GM, but the matter was settled out of court). The second clause is a RESOLVE by means of negotiation. We can immediately infer, just from the second clause, that there was a DISPUTE between Nader and GM, that the DIS-PUTE no longer exists, and that either Nader or GM INVOKEd negotiation to come to the settlement. Since the matter was RESOLVEd by negotiation (i.e., mutual agreement), then their settlement will probably not be challenged by either party. If there were any pending PETITIONs about the original DISPUTE, then their corresponding AUTHs will not take place. We can also make several less certain inferences, such as GM may have PRESSUREd Nader to negotiate or vice versa. The Government may AUTH that each side live up to its side of the agreement. More precisely, the list of inference rules for RESOLVE is given below (see Fig. 41):

Antecedent Inference Rules

(1)   It must have been the case that either

$$X \Leftrightarrow \text{INVOKE} \xleftarrow{o} \text{MEANS} \xleftarrow{s} \text{SOLX (time } t_2 < t_1)$$

or

$$Y \Leftrightarrow \text{INVOKE} \xleftarrow{o} \text{MEANS} \xleftarrow{s} \text{SOLY (time } t_2 < t_1).$$

$$\text{X and Y} \Longleftrightarrow \text{RESOLVE} \xleftarrow{o} \text{SOL} \xleftarrow{I} \text{MEANS} \quad \text{time: t1}$$

Fig. 41.

(2)   X and Y $\Leftrightarrow$ DISPUTE $\overset{s_1}{\leftarrow}$ SOLX $\overset{s_2}{\leftarrow}$ SOLY $\overset{c}{\leftarrow}$ DISPCAT (time $t_3 <$ $t_2 < t_1$). The SOLX and SOLY cases are the same as in the INVOKE. The MEANS is appropriate to the DISPCAT of the DISPUTE.

(3)   If MEANS = (military or physical) strength, then if X is stronger than Y, SOL = SOLX, else SOL = SOLY.

(4)   If MEANS = negotiation, then SOL is likely to be a compromise between SOLX and SOLY (hence acceptable to both X and Y).

Consequent Inference Rules

(5)   SOLX is now part of the state of the world. In a RESOLVE, there is no appeal to a higher RESOLVE as there is PETITION to a higher authority in many cases where X or Y is dissatisfied with the SOL of the AUTH.

(6)   The DISPUTE between X and Y has been eliminated.

(7)   If MEANS = application of strength, then the weaker party (say Y) may either PETITION an authority to AUTH an undoing of the RESOLVE, or PETITION a third party to PRESSURE X to undo the RESOLVE with Y.

Pressure

Social or political pressure can manifest itself in many forms, but there are some general inference rules triggered from social ACT PRESSURE that are independent of its physical manifestation. Let us list some inferences triggered from the following instance of PRESSURE:

(26)   The business community, fearing renewed inflation, forced Carter to reconsider his 1976 tax rebate bill.

There was an economic DISPUTE between the business community and some other economic group in the US (e.g., big labor). Carter had AUTHed a tax rebate. Carter may decide to yield to the business PRESSURE by reversing his AUTH. Carter may PETITION public opinion to PRESSURE the business community. We list below the inferences grouped under PRESSURE (see Fig. 42):

Antecedent Inference Rules

(1)   X & Y $\Leftrightarrow$ DISPUTE $\overset{c}{\leftarrow}$ DISPCAT with SOL = SOLY (time $t_2 < t_1$).

(2)   Either X $\Leftrightarrow$ INVOKE $\overset{o}{\leftarrow}$ Strength $\overset{s}{\leftarrow}$ SOLX or X $\Leftrightarrow$ PETITION $\overset{o}{\leftarrow}$ SOLX $\overset{r}{\leftarrow}$ A (time t_3; $t_2 < t_3 < t_1$).

(3)   Probably   Y $\Leftrightarrow$ PETITION $\overset{c}{\leftarrow}$ (Z $\Leftrightarrow$ PRESSURE) $\overset{r}{\leftarrow}$ Z   (time t_4; $t_2 < t_3 < t_4 < t_1$).

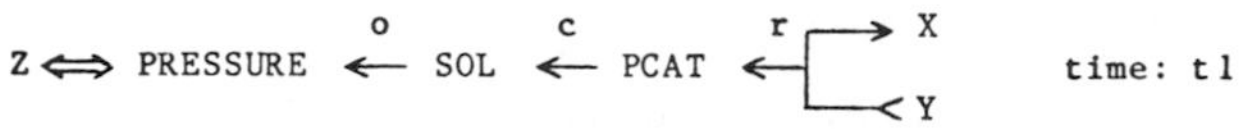

$$Z \Longleftrightarrow \text{PRESSURE} \overset{o}{\leftarrow} \text{SOL} \overset{c}{\leftarrow} \text{PCAT} \overset{r}{\leftarrow} \begin{array}{l} \rightarrow X \\ \prec Y \end{array} \qquad \text{time: } t1$$

Fig. 42.

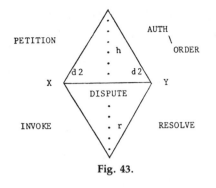

Fig. 43.

(4)   If X is an authority with respect to Y, then possibly Y ⇔ PETI-TION $\overset{o}{\leftarrow}$ SOL $\overset{r}{\leftarrow}$ X, but X did not AUTH $\overset{o}{\leftarrow}$ SOL.

Consequent Inference Rules

(5)   X is now more likely to INVOKE $\overset{o}{\leftarrow}$ negotiation to end his DIS-PUTE with Y.

(6)   Possibly Z & X ⇔ DISPUTE may arise.

(7)   Possibly X ⇔ PETITION $\overset{r}{\leftarrow}$ W to PRESSURE Y or to PRES-SURE Z.

There are, of course, many more inferences than the ones listed above for each social ACT; we listed the ones that yield information relevant in applying the social ACTs to understand sociopolitical events. There is a set of inferences triggered from the triangle structure itself. We diagram the complete AUTH and RESOLVE triangles with all relevant parameters in Fig. 43.

Recall that h is a measure of the degree of authority that A can exercise over X and Y; r is a measure of the effectiveness of M (the MEANS IN-VOKEd to RESOLVE the DISPUTE) with respect to X and Y. In the infer-ence rules listed below, DO represents any applicable social ACT. In accordance with our previous definitions, X can DO something to change d_1 and only d_1, and similarly for Y and d_2.

Let us consider the escalation of the Somali–Ethiopian conflict:

(27)   Somalia declared War on Ethiopia after the Ogaden conflict.

We can represent this situation by the sequence of triangles in Fig. 44

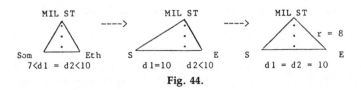

Fig. 44.

[although only the center triangle is explicitly stated in (27)]. The first and third triangle can be inferred from the central one; this is to say that from (27) we infer: Ethiopia and Somalia were NOT at war earlier (although they were involved in a political dispute). Ethiopia will probably also declare war on Somalia. The war will probably resolve the dispute over who controls the Ogaden desert. The rules applied to arrive at these inferences are listed below:

The triangle inference rules triggered by changes in the base are

(1)   If $d_1 \neq d_2$, then either X or Y must have PETITIONed or IN-VOKED $\xleftarrow{s}$ strength recently to unbalance a previously isosceles triangle.

(2a)   If X $\Leftrightarrow$ DO RESULT in $d_1 > d_2$, then expect Y $\Leftrightarrow$ DO RESULT in (probably) new $d_2 = d_1$ or (less likely) new $d_2 > d_1$.

(2b)   Same as (2a), reversing the roles of X & Y, and d_1 & d_2.

(3a)   If X $\Leftrightarrow$ DO RESULT in $d_1 < d_2$, then expect Y $\Leftrightarrow$ DO RESULT in (probably) new $d_2 = d_1$ or (less likely) new $d_2 < d_1$.

(3b)   Same as (3a), reversing the roles of X & Y, and d_1 & d_2.

Rules (1)–(3) express a balance principle in sociopolitical relations, to wit: Expect others to treat you as you choose to treat them. Rules 2 and 3 can be used to understand the escalation of a DISPUTE. X does something that causes d_1 to increase; Y, in turn, responds by making d_2 increase a little more than d_1; X, in turn, further increases d_1, etc. This principle is illustrated by a border skirmish escalating into a war, or the arms race between two countries (such as the US–USSR Cold War of the 1950s). Similarly, if one of two DISPUTing countries makes concessions reducing the differences between them, then it is likely that the other disputing party may follow up with similar actions.

There are some inference rules that are triggered by the h and r parameters. Recall that h is a measure of the power that A is able to exercise over X and Y; r is a measure of the effectiveness of M, the MEANS INVOKEd to RESOLVE the DISPUTE between X and Y.

(4)   If $h > 5$ (normative value), then A can AUTH and ORDER X & Y.

(5)   If $h < 5$, then A can only AUTH. X and Y may not respect the DE-CREE of the AUTH. (For example, a DECREE AUTHed by the UN General Assembly is often ignored by the recipient countries.)

(6)   If $h > 8$, then when A ORDERs, X and Y have no alternative action.

(7)   If $r > 5$, then if M is invoked, it is likely to RESOLVE the DISPUTE.

(8)   If $r < 5$, then if M is invoked, it may NOT RESOLVE the DISPUTE.

These inference rules from a static triangle structure are predictive in nature. There are also inference rules that are triggered from patterns matched by temporal progressions of triangles. For example, if X and Y are moving closer to each other, and Y and Z are drifting apart, then expect X and Z to also drift apart. This rule incorporates the sayings: "Friends of my enemies shall become my enemies" and "Enemies of my friends shall became my enemies." We can apply the rule to interpret the disputes involving Ethiopia, Somalia, and Russia: Russia and Somalia were at peace ($d = 5$), Russia allied itself with Ethiopia ($d < 5$). Ethiopia and Somalia started fighting a war ($d = 10$). Our rule would predict that relation between Somalia and Russia would worsen ($d > 5$). This is indeed exactly what is happening at the time of this writing.

8. CONCLUSION

We consider the seven basic social acts and the triangle representation to be a very useful set of tools in analyzing sociopolitical interactions. Each social act groups a set of inferences about the social situation it represents. A very large number of social conflicts, actions, and situations can be represented by combinations of this small set of social acts into causally connected structures. These larger structures, the triangles, are built from the social acts, their causal relations, plus some static information about the social situation not captured by the individual social acts (such as the overall relationships between two potentially conflicting parties). In this way, the basic social acts are closely analogous to the primitive physical acts of conceptual dependency (CD), and the triangles are rather loosely analogous to instantiated scripts comprised of causally connected sequences of CD diagrams.

There is, however, a significant difference between the *basic* social acts and the *primitive* physical acts of CD: Each social act may be decomposed into a structure built out of CD primitive acts, states, and causal connections. The primitive acts themselves are truly "primitive" in that there is no way to decompose them further from the point of view of a language understanding system. We envision a set of basic acts for analyzing and understanding most semantically rich domains, with each act grouping its own inferences and each set of acts being used as building blocks for larger structures analogous to the social triangles. The set of basic acts chosen for each domain would be theoretically decomposable into CD primitive acts, but one would rarely choose to do so since the more interesting inferences to the particular domain of analysis would be already grouped under each basic act or under each typical structure built out of the basic acts. It is very unlikely that either the CD-primitives or the basic social acts would be useful in codifying, for instance, the knowledge relevant to understanding chemistry or microbiology. These domains require their own basic knowledge organizing units.

There is nothing sacred about the particular social acts we chose nor about the fact that there are seven of them. As with the CD primitive acts, the important principle is that a very small number of basic acts are sufficient and useful in formulating canonical knowledge representations about the chosen domain by applying the inference rules to build larger, causally connected structures. The set of seven social acts that we chose is a particularly useful working set but we would not be terribly surprised if some new social acts were added or some of our present ones modified.

The development of social acts, or equivalent structures for a different domain, does not signify that we are abandoning the primitive acts of CD. Each representation is useful in its own domain of understanding. Our position has always been that one should choose the most useful units that organize knowledge about each particular domain. This position is further amplified in Schank and Abelson [1977] where yet another set of basic knowledge units is described for representing plans and goals (i.e., human intentionality). We strongly believe that organizing our knowledge into a small set of basic units, analyzing how these units interact to form larger structures, and developing an inferencing process to operate upon the new knowledge units is an extremely useful process for A.I. in understanding new knowledge domains.

In a sense, the initial choice of basic acts to represent knowledge and a new domain is necessarily *ad hoc*. We make an initial, tentative commitment to a set of basic acts in the new knowledge domain. In the process of codifying new knowledge, using the knowledge in computer programs that process text and answer questions, and in light of new theoretical considerations, we modify change or even replace our original choice of basic acts. We believe that this method rapidly converges upon a very useful set of basic units that organize the knowledge of the new domain in a useful and enlightening way.

Artificial intelligence is a strange business. We are in the position of attempting to codify all the knowledge of the world. Sometimes this knowledge is best encoded from the point of view of the expert. However, in our research (ordinary text understanding), we have had to rely on the point of view of the usual reader of the text. This means trying to assess what he knows and how he has organized it. We reiterate our belief that the best way to get at such knowledge is to forge ahead by creating basic knowledge units, and subsequently testing those basic acts for their use as the basis of inference rules and as a basis for the development of understanding programs. We are currently working on developing a system of computer programs to understand newspaper headlines and stories based on the social ACTs and their respective inference rules.

APPENDIX—CONCEPTUAL DEPENDENCY NOTATION

This section outlines the case structure of conceptual dependency (CD) diagrams. Some new notation was introduced in the representation of the basic social acts; these are also explained in this section. A brief explanation is given for each primitive act in CD. The reader is referred to Schank [1975] for a detailed explanation of the theory of conceptual dependency. The basic social acts are introduced and amply described in the body of this chapter.

CD is a theory of language-free meaning representation of concepts describing "overt" physical or mental activities. Each CD structure consists of a primitive act and a set of conceptual cases. Inference rules are grouped under the primitive acts. The small number of these acts helps to make the inference problem tractable.

Structure of a Conceptual Dependency Diagram

The ACT is one of the eleven primitive acts listed below. X is the actor who initiates and carries out the ACT. Y is the conceptual object, that which is acted upon. Z is the recipient of the act (e.g., the entity that receives possession of an ATRANSed object) or the directive case for the primitive act (e.g., the location toward which an object is PTRANSed). Each primitive act has either a recipient or directive case but not both. W is the source or initial location of the object acted upon. CD' is another CD structure that is instrumental in carrying out the act represented by the main CD structure. The instrumental case is optional. The arrows in Fig. A1 specify the conceptual case of the structure that follows them.

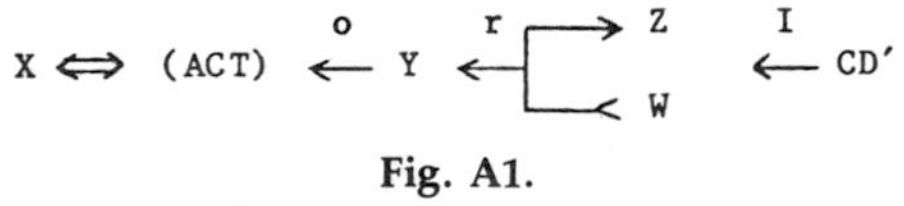

$$X \Longleftrightarrow (\text{ACT}) \overset{o}{\leftarrow} Y \overset{r}{\leftarrow} \boxed{\begin{array}{l} \rightarrow Z \\ < W \end{array}} \quad \overset{I}{\leftarrow} \text{CD}'$$

Fig. A1.

The following additional cases are used in the representation of the basic social acts: $\overset{s}{\leftarrow}$ denotes the goal (or solution) sought by the actor in performing the Social Acts. $\overset{a}{\leftarrow}$ denotes a set of alternative responses open to the recipient of the ACT. (This is an optional case.) $\overset{c}{\leftarrow}$ represents a category under which the Social Act may be classified. $\overset{h}{\leftarrow}$ denotes a strength value on a scale of 1 to 10, which signifies the ability of the actor to successfully complete the ACT once initiated. (This is an optional case.)

Primitive Acts in Conceptual Dependency

ATRANS   Abstract transfer of possession, ownership, or control of a physical object
PTRANS   Physical transfer of location
MTRANS   Mental transfer of information
INGEST   Bring a substance into the body of a person or an animal.
PROPEL   Apply a force to an object
ATTEND   Focus a sense organ (e.g., eyes, ears)
SPEAK   Verbally produce sounds

MBUILD   Mentally create a new conceptualization from previous knowledge
MOVE   Move a body part
GRASP   Close hand about an object
EXPEL   Expel a substance from the body of a person or an animal.

ACKNOWLEDGMENTS

This work was done at the Yale Artificial Intelligence Project, which is supported in part by the Advanced Research Projects Agency of the Department of Defense and monitored under the Office of Naval Research under contract N00014-75-C-1111.

The authors would like to acknowledge the following people: Danny Bobrow, who asked the question at the fifth International Joint Conference on Artificial Intelligence (IJCAI-5) that got one of us (RCS) to think about problems we had not tried to handle; Wendy Lehnert and Chris Riesbeck, who had some helpful insights; and most of all Joe Weizenbaum, who came up to RCS during IJCAI-5 and said how wonderful it was that I had admitted there were things that our systems could not do. I realized that what I meant by "could not" was "could not yet," and that this was probably not what he had in mind. Motivation comes in strange ways.

REFERENCES

[Carbonell, J. G., 1978]. Politics: Automated ideological reasoning. *Cognitive Science* **2**, No. 1.
[Charniak, E., 1972]. Toward a model of children's story comprehension. PhD. thesis, AI TR-266, pp. 56–82 and 154–198. MIT, Cambridge, Massachusetts.
[Schank, R. C., 1975]. *Conceptual Information Processing.* North-Holland Publ., Amsterdam, pp. 22–82.
[Schank, R. C., and Abelson, R. P., 1977]. *Scripts, Goals, Plans and Understanding.* Lawrence Erlbaum, Associates, Hillside, New Jersey.

RULE FORMS FOR VERSE, SENTENCES, AND STORY TREES

Robert F. Simmons and Alfred Correira

ABSTRACT

Rule forms and their interpreters are described for deriving sensible and nonsensical verse, for analyzing sentences into case structures, for generating sentences from case structures, and for generating story trees. A system of inference rules and assertions in the form of Horn clauses and their interpreter are presented as a computational method for generating narrative story trees that have the property that their terminal propositions form the story, while nodes closer to the root provide summaries. The story trees and their generator are proposed as a promising computational model for the macrostructure theorized by Kintsch and van Dijk to account for a human reader's memory and understanding of narrative text.

1. INTRODUCTION

A most significant problem in computational linguistics is to develop a formal definition of a computational structure that represents a human's understanding of a narrative or any other discourse. If such a structure is defined for a given text, it becomes possible to produce a computational model in the form of a grammar and an algorithm that applies the grammar to the input text to compute the representation of understanding. This assertion is more fully developed and supported in later sections.

A series of psychological studies (typified by Kintsch [1974] van Dijk [1975], Meyer [1975], Thorndike [1977], and Crothers [1972]) offers strong evidence for the hypothesis that a person, after reading a text, has developed a macrostructure that organizes the propositions of the text in a hierarchical form. The propositions highest in the hierarchy are more general than those that occur at the lower levels. When tested for recall, what a person remembers from reading a text are propositions at the higher levels. If asked to produce a summary, the person reports a set of high-level propositions also. Significantly, what a person remembers after a few

363

days is a set of propositions very similar to those produced by subjects asked to write summaries.

From a computational viewpoint, this hypothesized macrostructure can be represented as a tree where nodes closest to the root are the most important events, i.e., episodes in a narrative, or content categories in an expository text, and nodes closest to the leaves are concerned with details of the episodes or description. What a person remembers after a period of days or what a person reports as a summary is an organized set of nodes closest to the root—a small subset of all the nodes in the tree.

These findings lead us to the hypothesis that one effective computational model for a human's understanding of a discourse is the computation of such a tree so organized that the nodes closest to the terminals form a summary approaching the length of the text. The terminal nodes of this tree are the sentences or phrases of the text itself.

In purely linguistic terms, a similar hypothesis—that the content organization of folk tales could be described as a phrase structure tree or story grammar—was published by Propp in 1927. In the last decade, Propp's work has received wide recognition and has been a seminal influence on a whole subdiscipline of text linguists mainly in Europe, but now represented in the United States by Grimes [1975], Klein [1965], and Rumelhart [1975] among others. Earlier computational linguists including Klein and Simmons [1963] and Harper and Su [1969] studied the application of text grammars to computing stories and representations of story content, respectively, with limited success. Psychologists cited above adopted the notion of text grammars as a technique for representing the structure of discourse as a basis for measuring what human readers understood about a text.

In artificial intelligence work, comparable notions of macrostructure—frames, scripts, partitions, etc.—are found to be essential to provide representations that maintain connectivity among sentences in systems that use the organized content of dialogue or discourse for some computational purpose. Schank [1975b], Lehnert [1977], and Meehan [1976] have published demonstrations of the power of their script-oriented approach, and Bobrow and Winograd [1977] showed applications of frames to understanding dialogue. A related idea of partitioned semantic networks and focus spaces was shown to be useful in computing representations of dialogue by Hendrix [1976], Grosz [1977], and others. A selected survey of text understanding research by Young [1977] outlines much of the work in the psychological, linguistic, and artificial intelligence research in this area. Books by Charniak and Wilks [1976] and by Schank and Abelson [1977] develop more fully the notions of frames and scripts.

In an attempt to generalize the purely linguistic approach to include methods from artificial intelligence work, the next two sections describe some uses of grammars for generating and analyzing English sentences by using the derivation tree to direct the flow of control in generation and parsing procedures. Subsequent sections develop the idea of story trees and present an organized system of inference rules and assertions for generating simple stories and their summaries.

A necessary first step in computational understanding of a text is to define the structure that represents that understanding. By developing a system for generating story trees we believe we have accomplished that first step by defining a precise computational model for the macrostructure hypothesized by psychologists to account for human understanding of stories.

2. POGEN FOR SENSE AND NONSENSE

By 1960, Yngve had published a procedural description for a method of generating (i.e., computing) syntactically well-formed sentences from a grammar. This formed a basis for some early work by Klein and Simmons [1963] for generating coherent discourse where coherence was controlled by a dependency structure among words. The latter was derived from recording their usages from actual texts. The generation algorithm has proved useful over the years in teaching computational linguistics. It showed students how a text can be analyzed into a grammar form that can be used, together with appropriate vocabulary, classes, and variations on it, by a computer to generate that text.

Let us first consider a phrase structure grammar for a simple sentence:

(S1)   The little train goes toot, toot.

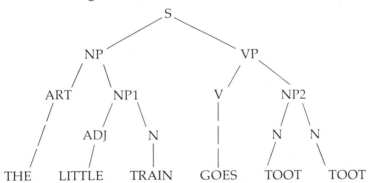

After constructing the above immediate constituent phrase structure tree, we can start with the root S and record the grammar for the sentence as follows:

$$S = NP + VP \qquad ART = THE$$
$$NP = ART + NP1 \qquad ADJ = LITTLE$$
$$NP1 = ADJ + N \qquad N = TRAIN$$

$$VP = V + NP2 \qquad N = TOOT$$
$$NP = NP2 \qquad V = GOES$$
$$NP2 = N + N$$

A sentence generation algorithm starts with the symbol S, selects a rule beginning with S from the grammar, rewrites the rule as its right side, and recurses until it reaches elements such as THE or TOOT, which have no rules associated with them and thus are terminal nodes. It lists these terminal nodes in the order in which they are achieved and thus outputs a sentence.

For example,

```
(GEN S) = (GEN NP) (GEN VP)
(GEN NP) = (GEN N) (GEN N)
(GEN N) = (GEN TRAIN)        = TRAIN
(GEN N) = (GEN TOOT)         = TOOT
(GEN VP) = (GEN V) (GEN NP)
(GEN V) = (GEN GOES)         = GOES
(GEN NP) = (GEN ART) (GEN NP1)
(GEN ART) = (GEN THE)        = THE
(GEN NP1) = (GEN ADJ) (GEN N)
(GEN ADJ) = (GEN LITTLE)     = LITTLE
(GEN N) = (GEN TOOT)         = TOOT
```

The result is the rightmost column, TRAIN TOOT GOES THE LITTLE TOOT, a syntactically well-formed nonsense sentence.

POGEN is a realization of this procedure as a LISP function shown in Fig. 1. This function expects each left part of a rule to have a list of right parts, as its VALue, and provides a random selection device CHOOSE to select one. If the left part also has the property REPLACE, a new right part is formed as a VALue with only the previously selected member of the left part. This procedural feature provides for controlled repetitions as illustrated in the next example.

The procedure can be used to control the coherence and sense of a text as well as to provide syntactic well-formedness. The last two lines of Keats' "Ode to a Grecian Urn" are:

```
(DEF
 (GEN (SYMB)
      (PROG (J)
            (COND ((NULL SYMB) (RETURN))
                  ((ATOM SYMB) (GO A)))
            (RETURN (APPEND (GEN (CAR SYMB)) (GEN (CDR SYMB))))
          A (COND ((SETQ J (GET SYMB "VAL))
                  (SETQ J (CHOOSE J))
                  (COND ((GET SYMB "REPLACE)
                         (PUT SYMB "VAL (LIST J))))
                  (RETURN (APPEND (GEN (CAR J)) (GEN (CDR J))))))
            (RETURN (LIST SYMB)))))
```

Fig. 1. LISP function for POGEN.

> Beauty is truth, truth beauty,
> That's all ye know on earth,
> and all ye need to know.

To obtain semantically controlled variations on this verse, we first form substitution classes named with arbitrary variables, as follows:

beauty	is	truth,	truth	beauty,
X	is	Y,	Y	X,
That's all	ye	know		on earth
T	P	K		L
That's all	ye	need to		know
T	P	N		K

We can then take each substitution class and augment it with items semantically similar to those of the original under the constraint that each new item maintain the syntax and the sense (to whatever extent desirable) of the original passage. One such set follows:

CLASS	ORIGINAL	SUBSTITUTES
X	beauty	life, this, knowledge, wisdom, love,
Y	truth	honor, all, joy, rapture, love,
T	(that's all)	(that's what), (it's all), (it's what)
P	you	Ye, I, we, some,
K	know	have, get, see, sense, meet
L	(on earth)	('til heaven), ('til hell), (for living),
N	(need to)	(want to), (have to), (ought to)

Since classes, X, Y, T, P, and K are all repeated in the verse, they are marked with the property REPLACE. Then the phrase structure grammar is formed as follows:

$$LINE1 = X \; IS \; Y, \; Y \; X,$$
$$LINE2 = T \; P \; K \; L,$$
$$LINE3 = T \; P \; N \; K,$$
$$VERSE = L1 \; L2 \; L3$$

The contents of the substitution classes are the terminal elements of the grammar. These data are set up as property list structures and POGEN is then called to generate a set of verses. The following results from this grammar:

(VARIATIONS ON TRUTH IS BEAUTY FROM KEATS)

(LOVE IS JOY, JOY LOVE)
(IT'S WHAT WE SEE FOR LIVING)
(IT'S WHAT WE HAVE TO SEE)

(KNOWLEDGE IS JOY, JOY KNOWLEDGE)
(IT'S ALL YOU SEE 'TIL HEAVEN)
(IT'S ALL YOU HAVE TO SEE)

(KNOWLEDGE IS HONOR, HONOR KNOWLEDGE)
(IT'S WHAT YE HAVE FOR LIVING)
(IT'S WHAT YE NEED TO HAVE)

(LOVE IS JOY, JOY LOVE)
(IT'S WHAT YE KNOW 'TILL HEAVEN)
(IT'S WHAT YE NEED TO KNOW)

(LOVE IS TRUTH, TRUTH LOVE)
(THAT'S WHAT WE GET ON EARTH)
(THAT'S WHAT WE NEED TO GET)

(WISDOM IS JOY, JOY WISDOM)
(IT'S WHAT WE MEET 'TIL HEAVEN)
(IT'S WHAT WE OUGHT TO MEET)

(WISDOM IS TRUTH, TRUTH WISDOM)
(THAT'S WHAT I HAVE ON EARTH)
(THAT'S WHAT I WANT TO HAVE)

(KNOWLEDGE IS TRUTH, TRUTH KNOWLEDGE)
(THAT'S ALL YE MEET ON EARTH)
(THAT'S ALL WE HAVE TO MEET)

(BEAUTY IS HONOR, HONOR BEAUTY)
(THAT'S ALL YE SEE ON EARTH)
(THAT'S ALL YE NEED TO SEE)

(LIFE IS TRUTH, TRUTH LIFE)
(THAT'S WHAT SOME SENSE ON EARTH)
(THAT'S WHAT SOME OUGHT TO SENSE)

The technique described above is well known in one form or another and it has been used to generate bales of computer verse. With minor changes to the procedure it is possible to control rhyme and meter as well. Judith Merriam (in a seminar assignment) provided one modification to produce the following:

VARIATIONS ON PRUFROCK

THE SULLEN HAZE
THAT STREWS HER LUST UPON THE HURRIED STREETS,
THE SULLEN AIR
THAT STREWS HER POISON ON THE HURRIED STREETS,
SLIPPED HER HEAD INTO THE CURRENT OF THE TWILIGHT,
SAUNTERED BENEATH THE EVES THAT SHADE DEFEATS,
LET REST AGAINST HER MOUTH
THE GRIT THAT RESTS IN STREETS,
PROWLED BY THE FOUNTAIN, LOOSED A MOCKING CRY,
AND SENSING THAT IT WAS SHRILL CICADA NIGHT,
SQUATTED LOW ALONG THE WALKS AND PACED THE SKY.

3. FROM SENTENCE TO NETWORK TO SENTENCE

POGEN is designed to accept a context-free phrase structure grammar and follow its flow of control to generate its terminal elements. Unfortunately, a pure context-free grammar is of little use for analyzing ordinary English text into underlying structures. Our goal in modeling macrostructures of discourse is to define methods for representing texts as structures suitable for providing summaries, retrieval capabilities, and translations. For this purpose, we must consider more complicated grammatical forms.

A 20-year preoccupation of natural language researchers has been to develop useful natural language question-answering systems. This led, among other approaches, to the development of quantified semantic networks as a useful method for classifying and representing factual data for sentence content or for data bases. A sentence such as "Rufolo loaded his ship and sailed to Cyprus" can be represented as follows:

(S2) (LOAD1 TENSE PAST AGT RUFOLO TH(SHIP1 OWNBY RU-
      FOLO)*AND SAIL1)
      (SAIL1 TENSE PAST AGT RUFOLO TH SHIP1 *TO CYPRUS1)

This can also be shown as the following graph:

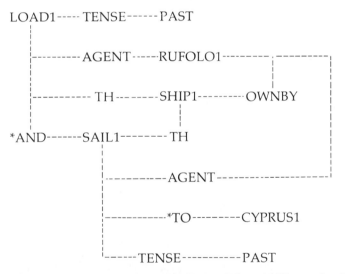

The arcs AGENT, THeme, INSTRUMENT, *TO, *AND, and others* are adopted originally from Fillmore's (1968) theory of case structure and have also developed independently with experimental study of semantic networks. The arcs are binary semantic relations that make explicit the ideas of agent or actor, theme or object of an act, instrument of an act, location,

* The * prefix distinguishes case relations such as *TO, to indicating a goal relation, from the word "to."

time, frequency, duration, etc., which are encoded in English mainly by morphology and word order (in German augmented by case endings).

The importance of semantic networks—or the equivalent linear form of S2, called case relations—is to provide a canonical representation of a sentence meaning in terms of explicit semantic relations between pairs of unambiguous conceptual elements. A given case relation may have several equivalent surface representations. In contrast to Schank's conceptual dependencies formulated at a level of primitive constructs, the case relations use word-senses as primitive concepts. This approach proves convenient for translation from surface to canonical structure and back to surface form, and also offers promise for translation between languages. It provides for the mapping of sense meanings onto variant character strings depending on the choice of the target language. (The question of what conceptual depth is most desirable for what purposes is, however, still open.)

To obtain the structure of S2 from the example sentence, an all-paths parser—a version of the Cocke–Kasami–Younger algorithm described by Pratt [1975]—applies a grammar whose rules are of the following form:

> (PHRASENAME (LIST OF SYNTACTIC CONSTITUENTS)
> (CORRESPONDING LIST OF SEMANTIC CONSTRAINTS)
> (TRANSFORMATION))

For example,

> (S(NP VP)(ANIM ACT)(2 AGT 1))

This rule applies to two constituents, an NP followed by a VP. If the NP has the semantic feature ANIMate and the VP has the feature ACT, then a new constituent is formed by combining the VP (i.e., the second constituent) and the NP (i.e., the first). They are connected by the semantic relation AGT, and the new constituent is labeled S. Thus, if the two constituents appear as

> NP = (RUFOLO ANIM T SING T)
> VP = (SAIL PAST T ACT T . . .)

then the new constituent S is formed,

> S = (SAIL PAST T ACT T . . . AGT (RUFOLO ANIM T SING T))

The symbol . . . indicates additional data in the constituent that are not relevant to the example.

Lexical rules follow the same form, and so

> (N(SHIP) T (1 SING T POBJ T))
> (N(CYPRUS) T (1 SING T PLACE T NAME T))
> (V(SHIP) T (1 3PS T ACT T))
> (N(RUFOLO) T (1 SING T ANIM T NAME T))
> (V(SAILED) T (SAIL PAST T ACT T))

(PREP(TO) T (1))
(POSSPRON(HIS) T (1 MASC T SING T POSS T))

The example lexicon accounts for the words of the sentence "Rufolo sailed his ship to Cyprus" and the following grammar rules apply:

(NP(N) T (1))
(VP(V) T (1))
(VP(VP NP) (ACT POBJ) (1 TH 2))
(VP(VP PP) (ACT (PLACE PREP TO)) (1 *TO 1))
(PP(PREP NP) T(2 PREP 1))
(NP(POSSPRON NP) (OK POBJ) (2 OWNBY 1))
(S(NP VP)(ANIM ACT)(2 AGT 1))

It can be noticed that the lexical rules contain semantic features that characterize the particular word sense, and that these features are included as the constituent is embedded in higher level constituents.

The complete result of the parse for "Rufolo sailed his ship to Cyprus" is as follows:

(S3)   (SAIL PAST T ACT T
          TH (SHIP SING T POBJ T OWNBY (HIS SING T MASC T
                                                            POSS T)
       *TO (CYPRUS SING T PLACE T NAME T PREP TO)
       AGT (RUFOLO SING T ANIM T NAME T))

The feature notation SING T, ANIM T, etc. is analogous to the linguistic feature markers + and −, where T is + and F is −. After parsing, the words of the structure are assigned subscripts and the semantic features may be discarded—unless they are needed for some additional linguistic processing, such as for the case of translation to another natural language.

Discarding the semantic features in this example the resulting semantic relation is

(S4)   (SAIL PAST T TH(SHIP SING T OWNBY(HIS SING T))
          AGT(RUFOLO SING T)
          *TO(CYPRUS SING T PREP TO))

This form is suitable for being converted to a knowledge base entry by subscripting the words, to give SAIL1, SHIP1, etc., and fitting it into the discourse network by discovering preceding referents for definite noun phrases and pronouns. It is appropriate to mention that this process of finding referents is still only partially understood and requires a human editor to assist the programs.

Once in the knowledge base, the concepts of the semantic relation are augmented by the network of general knowledge. Thus RUFOLO is a MAN, SHIP is a VESSEL, and SAIL implies MOVE; this particular SAILing followed a LOADing of the SHIP, etc. The relation of a word to the classification network is available through the lexical entry, and this serves as the primary basis for finding answers to questions. The process of answering questions is described elsewhere [Simmons and Chester, 1977]. This semantic representation system is easily capable of encoding, causal and coherency relations among sentences. However a single sentence parser cannot easily compute them.

Let us now suppose that relation S4 has been retrieved as an answer to some question such as "Where did Rufolo go?" We now wish to transform S4 into English. A generation procedure resembling POGEN but using a grammar sensitive to the case markers, accomplishes the task.

One convenient form for the generation grammar is as follows:

S = AGT:NP + VP	VP = VSTRNG + COMPL
NP = DET:NP + NP	VPAS = BE + VP
NP = MOD:NP + NP	VSTRNG = AUX + VSTRNG
NP = OWN BY:POSSPRON + NP	VSTRNG = *
NP = PREP:PP + NP	AUX = PAST
NP = *	AUX = *
PP = PREP + NP	COMPL = TH:NP + COMPL
PREP = *	COMPL = INSTR:PP + COMPL
S = INSTR:NP + VP	COMPL = *TO:PP + COMPL
S = TH:NP + VPAS	COMPL = #

In this grammar the three symbols, :, *, and # have the following effect on the generation algorithm:

ARCNAME	PHRASENAME
:	indicates that the phrase is to be generated from this relation only if the arc name is present
*	indicates that the head of the relation is to be realized as an English word
#	nothing need be generated; used to terminate a sequence of complements or PPs

Applying the above grammar to the relation,

(SAIL1 PAST T TH(SHIP1 OWNBY RUFOLO) AGT(RUFOLO SING T)
    *TO (CYPRÙS1 SING T))

the following steps result:

S = AGT:NP + VP	
NP = *	RUFOLO
VP = VSTRNG + COMPL	
VSTRNG = AUX + VSTRNG	
AUX = PAST	PAST

```
VSTRNG = *                      SAIL
COMPL = TH:NP + COMPL
NP = OWNBY:POSSPRON
POSSPRON = HIS                  HIS
NP = *                          SHIP
COMPL = *TO:PP + COMPL
PP = PREP + NP
PREP = *                        TO
NP = *                          CYPRUS
COMPL = #
```

When a word is to be generated, morphological routines are called to examine the SING/PLURAL markers, to decide on the desirability of constructing a pronoun or definite noun phrase, and to realize the English words. The result is the rightmost column, RUFOLO PAST SAIL HIS SHIP TO CYPRUS. A last pass on the sentence tenses the verb and adjusts agreements of subject, verb, etc.

It should be noticed that neither the analyzer nor the generator constructs a derivation tree. Instead, as in POGEN, the tree of derivation from the grammar is used only to direct the flow of control through the procedure. If the syntactic tree were needed for some purpose, a minor change in these procedures would record it.

Although the grammar shown above is a sufficient form for transforming simple semantic relations into single sentences, it offers no provision for constructing connected paragraphs to form an organized text. Nor does the recognition grammar provide capability beyond the single sentence level. Furthermore, it cannot organize sentences in a paragraph or discourse. This limitation is one of the reasons that the grammar cannot always find referents for pronouns or definite noun phrases. In this form, it does not even record from sentence to sentence what is being talked about.

A grammar relating sentences to each other must provide the connective tissue between the propositional elements of the text in order to remove these limitations of sentence analysis. It is our belief that if we can find a satisfactory structure for story trees we shall be able to write text grammars in the 4-tuple form described above. It can then be used to analyze text organization as well as sentence structure.

4. STORY TREES

Limitations of the single sentence grammar approach shown in the preceding section reveal much of the motivation underlying the invention of such procedural notions as scripts, implicational molecules, plans (see Schank and Abelson [1977]), partitions, focus spaces (see Hendrix [1976]

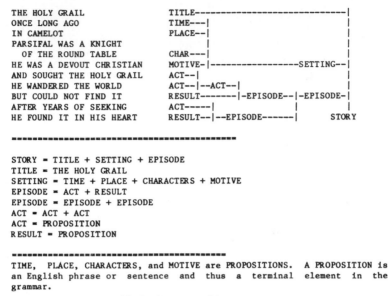

```
THE HOLY GRAIL              TITLE----------------------------|
ONCE LONG AGO               TIME---|                         |
IN CAMELOT                  PLACE--|                         |
PARSIFAL WAS A KNIGHT               |                        |
   OF THE ROUND TABLE       CHAR---|                        |
HE WAS A DEVOUT CHRISTIAN   MOTIVE-|-----------------SETTING--|
AND SOUGHT THE HOLY GRAIL   ACT--|                          |
HE WANDERED THE WORLD       ACT--|--ACT--|                   |
BUT COULD NOT FIND IT       RESULT-------|-EPISODE--|-EPISODE-|
AFTER YEARS OF SEEKING      ACT-----|              |         |
HE FOUND IT IN HIS HEART    RESULT--|--EPISODE------|    STORY
```

```
STORY = TITLE + SETTING + EPISODE
TITLE = THE HOLY GRAIL
SETTING = TIME + PLACE + CHARACTERS + MOTIVE
EPISODE = ACT + RESULT
EPISODE = EPISODE + EPISODE
ACT = ACT + ACT
ACT = PROPOSITION
RESULT = PROPOSITION
```

TIME, PLACE, CHARACTERS, and MOTIVE are PROPOSITIONS. A PROPOSITION is
an English phrase or sentence and thus a terminal element in the
grammar.

Fig 2. A story and its grammar.

and Grosz [1977]), and frames (see Minsky [1975], Bobrow and Winograd [1977], and Charniak and Wilks [1976]). The latter book also describes a rule-based approach of templates and paraplates by Wilks. Our own bias is toward a rule-based approach to the recognition and generation of English discourse, and we have sought for systems of rules that can more formally describe the organizations imposed by scripts, frames, etc.

Story grammars provide one basis for the approach. Generally, a story can be analyzed into a title and a setting followed by episodes, and an episode into actions and results. This analysis can be recorded as a phrase structure grammar as shown in Fig. 2.

All this grammar shows is that it is possible to organize the events of a story into SETTING, ACTS, RESULTS, and EPISODES. What has been gained is the conception that phrases and sentences at the story level can be "syntactically" classified in a manner analogous to words and phrases at the sentence level of analysis. However, the resulting tree appears to be lacking in the critical property required for the Kintsch–Van Dijk macrostructure [1975] that the nodes closest to the root should form a summary. Thus not just any grammar for a story will form a story tree, that is, a tree with the desired properties.

Figure 3 shows a story tree analysis and its grammar. The nodes of this tree are numbered to show their depth. When an episode is the rightmost member of a result rule, its level is assigned the same number as its ancestral episode. This feature insures that a sequence of episodes forms what is effectively a shallow tree, despite the deeply nested form of the

```
1 STORY ----- 2  TITLE -------------------------------- 3 THE HOLY GRAIL
     |
     |------- 2 SETTING ----- 3 CHAR ----------- 4 PARSEFAL WAS A KNIGHT
     |                           |
     |                           |---- 4 MOD ----- 5 OF THE ROUND TABLE
     |                           |
     |                           |---- 3 CIRCUM ----- 4 TIME ------------- 5 LONG AGO
     |                                      |
     |                                      |---- 4 PLACE --------------- 5 IN CAMELOT
     |                                      |
     |                                      |---- 4 ATTRIBS -------- 5 HE WAS A DEVOUT
     |                                                                      CHRISTIAN
     |
     |------- 2 EPISODE ----- 3 ACT --------- 4 HE SOUGHT THE HOLY GRAIL
     |                           |
     |                           |    4 ACT------------ 5 HE WANDERED THE WORLD
     |                           |
     |                           |--- 3 RESULT ----------------- 4 BUT COULDN'T FIND IT
     |                                   |
     |                                   2 EPISODE-- 3 ACT------- 4 AFTER YEARS OF SEEKING
     |                                                  |
     |                                                  |---- 3 RESULT---- 4 HE FOUND IT IN HIS HEART
     |                                                          |
     |                                                          |--------------------- 4 THE END
```

```
==================================================
STORY = TITLE + SETTING + EPISODE
TITLE = P
SETTING = CHAR + CIRCUM
CHAR = P + MOD
MOD = P
CIRCUM = TIME + PLACE + ATTRIBS
EPISODE = ACT + RESULT
ACT = P + ACT
ACT = P
RESULT = P + EPISODE
RESULT = P + THE END
==================================================
NOTES:
P means proposition, and TIME, PLACE, and ATTRIBS are rewritten
as P's.
Numbers on the tree are depth counters, the shortest summary can
be seen by reading the propositions marked 4 or less. The entire
story emerges at level 5.
```

Fig. 3. A story tree and its grammar.

grammar. If we read the propositions whose numbers are not greater than 3 from the tree, the only candidate is the title THE HOLY GRAIL. At the level not greater than 4, we read THE HOLY GRAIL: PARSEFAL WAS A KNIGHT, HE SOUGHT THE HOLY GRAIL, HE COULDN'T FIND IT, AFTER YEARS OF SEEKING HE FOUND IT IN HIS HEART, THE END. At level 5, the whole story can be read:

THE HOLY GRAIL: PARSEFAL WAS KNIGHT, OF THE ROUND TABLE, LONG AGO, IN CAMELOT, HE WAS A DEVOUT CHRISTIAN, HE SOUGHT THE HOLY GRAIL, HE WANDERED THE WORLD, HE COULDN'T FIND IT, AFTER YEARS OF SEEKING, HE FOUND IT IN HIS HEART, THE END.

Figures 2 and 3 show that if we want a story tree with the property that its higher nodes produce a summary, we must design a grammar that will place certain propositions at higher nodes in the tree than others. A better approach that will be developed in Section 6 is to include transformations at each node in the tree in such a manner that each node will provide a summary of the complex structure that lies below. These example story grammars also reveal the prominent weakness of the context free phrase structure approach. That approach is suitable for generating a sequence of propositions with such a system as POGEN, but it does not provide the semantic conditions or transformations required to derive a story tree from a sequence of propositions.

5. COMPUTATIONAL ASPECTS OF SEMANTIC NETWORKS AND STORY TREES

We believe Meehan's [1976] generation of stories about the interactions of the motives of talking animals may prove to be an excellent model for the human story-writing process. In his view, a story is a description of the events that occurred when a character attempted to achieve a goal or solve a problem. If we look at his work as an abstract problem-solving program, we can see that his approach was based on the use of a set of objects, such as bears, canaries, worms, trees, etc. (each object characterized as appropriate by conceptual dependency assertions of motives, personality characteristics, locations, etc.), and a set of rules in the form of plans that could transform properties of these objects. The rules were organized in plans and planboxes for easy access by appropriate goals. The action of a story developed as an exploration of paths through the rule tree when a character sought to satisfy a goal. The system for generating the story is a problem solver specialized to the use of indexed plans and conceptual dependency structures.

One significant aspect of Meehan's study was that, although his system was based on conceptual dependency networks, he found no necessity to draw graphs or deal explicitly with the network in his exposition. His system of plans and planboxes was adequately described in propositional form; his network was implicit in the chaining of subgoals leading to the accomplishment or failure of a plan. The interrelations among concepts, such as "bears like honey" and "bears live in caves," were similarly implicit in such common coreferential terms as "bear." In fact, the conceptual dependency system is an explicitly indexed network.

In previous papers (see Simmons [1978] and Simmons and Chester [1977]), semantic networks are defined as sets of nodes that represent verbal concepts, connected by arcs that represent semantic case relations between pairs of concepts. A single semantic relation is a node–arc–node triple. An English sentence or proposition is represented by a head node and a set of arc–node pairs. We call this a case predicate and usually write it as an n-tuple,

$$(\text{HD ARC1 VALUE1 ARC2 VALUE2 . . . ARC}n \text{ VALUE}n)$$

where the values refer to other n-tuples, that is, nodes. One natural computational form for this structure is an atom associated with a set of incoming arcs and a set of outgoing arcs. Let us consider these n-tuples as relations where the head is a predicate name and each arc identifies an argument by name. It is then apparent that in comparing two relations, each arc has a value that is a pointer to the location of the value of a relation's argument and no searching of the data base is required to find that value. The naming of arguments also allows the case predicate to list its arguments in any order and to represent only the arguments that are specified. Thus the named arcs in a semantic network serve two important purposes: (1) they provide indexing for directly accessing data, (2) they relax the constraint that a relation be represented as a strict n-tuple with an explicit position for every argument. Both of these properties are of significant value for dealing with large amounts of data derived from natural language statements.

An explicit semantic network is not the only way to represent the interrelations among case predicates; a simple list of the predicates provides exactly the information needed to compile the actual semantic network. We think of such a list as one that implies a network, i.e., as a virtual network. We have found it to be most convenient for representing rules containing free variables that in explicit representation could require infinite storage and computation. The connectivity of the virtual network is signified by the correspondence of values of arguments with names of other case predicates. This correspondence is discovered by searching the list of case predicates to find one that matches a given value. In other words, we can trade the memory required to represent the connectivity of the network for an increased amount of computation to explicate it by searching through the case predicates. We can also delete the case names and impose the constraint that every argument position be represented in the n-tuple. Thus we transform our semantic case predicates to ordinary logical relations of the form

$$(\text{HD ARG1 ARG2 . . . ARG}n)$$

whose elements are English terms (i.e., words and variable names). The connectivity of the virtual network remains the same. Other indexing schemes can also be provided to minimize the amount of computation required to explicate the connective properties.

In subsequent sections we shall use the strict n-tuples of English terms to represent the propositions and rules used in computing story trees. Excepting only the retrieval and direct matching steps, the computational procedures are the same as would be required for explicit semantic network representations. We sacrifice some of the indexing properties of the network, with consequent increased computation time and decreased memory requirements. What we hope to gain is easier readability for the rules and propositions, a more direct correspondence with a system of logic, and a simpler exposition of the essential steps in generating story trees.

From Meehan [1976], we understand that problem solving is an appropriate basis for developing a story. However, we have been interested in a method different from the use of conceptual dependency plans and plan-boxes. In his monograph "Logic for Problem Solving" [1974] Kowalski presents an attractive approach that allows the statement of problems, rules, and assertions as ordered sets of propositions. Although he interprets his logic in terms of resolution theory, various procedures are available to achieve flexible and efficient problem solving. Further relations of this system to semantic networks are developed in a later paper by Deliyanni and Kowalski [1977]. Using Kowalski's logic with strict n-tuple English notation, we are able to define sets of propositions and inference rules to describe a virtual network, which enables us to develop story trees and compute stories in a very general fashion.

The Kowalski logic for problem solving is based on Horn clauses. A Horn clause is a set of logical predicates

$$B0, \ldots, Bm <\!\!-\!\! A0, \ldots, An,$$

where m and n are equal to or greater than zero.

The clauses $Bi, \ldots, Bm$ can be called consequents, and $Ai, \ldots, An$, antecedents. If some clause $Bi, \ldots, Bm <\!\!-\!\! Ai, \ldots, An$ contains variables such as x, y, z, then the clause should be read:

For all x, y, z, $Bi, \ldots, Bm$ is true if $Ai, \ldots, An$ is true. A sentence $Ai, \ldots, An$ or $Bi, \ldots, Bm$ is read as the conjunction of its clauses Ai, Aj, Ak, etc.

Kowalski distinguishes four types of Horn clauses:

(1) $m = 0, n = 0$: the *null clause*.
(2) $m = 1, n = 0, B \leftarrow$ a Horn clause with no antecedents: an *assertion*.
(3) $m = 0, n \neq 0, \leftarrow Al, \ldots, An$ a Horn clause with no consequent: a *goal statement*.
(4) $m = 1, n \neq 0, B \leftarrow Al, \ldots, An$: every other Horn clause with a single element on the left is an *operator*.

Kowalski gives a complete development of this system as a resolution-based logic and shows its application to solving problems.

For example, a Horn clause procedure for doing sums in successor arithmetic is as follows:

(SUM 0 X X)←
(SUM (SUC X) Y Z) ← (SUM X (SUC Y) Z)
← (SUM (SUC(SUC 0)) (SUC 0) U)

The first clause says that the sum of zero and any y is y. This is an *assertion*. The second statement is an *operator;* it states that the sum of the successor of any x and any y is z if the sum of x and the successor of that y is z. The third clause states the *goal;* find the sum of the successor of the successor of 0 and the successor of 0 and its value will be the value of u.

The goal statement is matched to the elements that have an arrow to their right, i.e., consequents; it fails to match the assertion but it matches the operator. The values of argument positions in the goal are bound to those in the consequent and through into the antecedent. The consequent is detached and the antecedent is taken as a new goal until finally the goal is

← (SUM 0 (SUC(SUC(SUC 0))) Z)

which matches the assertion. The variable Z at that point takes on the value (SUC(SUC(SUC 0))) or 3. This brief outline of the problem solving use of Horn-clauses is sufficient only if the reader is acquainted with the use of such logical systems. Kowalski's description and exploration [1974] is recommended for a more complete and clear explanation.

Kowalski's logic is of interest here to show some relationships between problem solving and story generation. The basic method that Meehan used for story generation could be illustrated in this formalism but instead of using his complex world of motivated animals, let us use the familiar MIT robot and block world.

Suppose we command Winograd's [1972] robot (see Fig. 4) to PUT THE

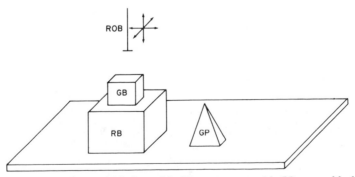

Fig. 4. Winograd's robot and block world. *GP*, green pyramid; *GB*, green block; *RB*, red block; *ROB*, robot's hand to pick up, move, and release objects; three degrees of freedom of movement.

GREEN PYRAMID ON THE RED BLOCK. This translates into a parenthesized Horn-clause as follows:

(a)   ← (PUT ROB GP ON RB)

Variables are recognized by being members of a special list, "S T U V W X Y Z" and other terms are constants. The robot's problem-solving system is encoded as follows:

(b)   (PUT ROB X ON Y) ← (Y IS CLEAR) (ROB PUTS X ON Y)
(c)   (Y IS CLEAR) ← (Z IS ON Y) (ROB REMOVES Z FROM Y) (ROB PUTS Z ON TABLE)
(d)   (ROB REMOVES X FROM Y) ← (ROB PICKS UP X) (A*(Y IS CLEAR))
(e)   ROB PUTS U ON W) ← (ROB HOLDS U)(W IS CLEAR) (A*(U IS ON W))
(f)   (ROB PICKS UP Z) ← (Z IS CLEAR)(A*(ROB HOLDS Z))
(g)   (ROB HOLDS X) ← (ROB PICKS UP X)
(h)   (RB IS ON TABLE) ←
(i)   (GB IS ON RB) ←
(j)   (GB IS CLEAR) ←
(k)   (GP IS ON TABLE) ←
(l)   (GP IS CLEAR) ←
(m)   (TABLE IS CLEAR) ←

The symbols GP, GB, RB, and ROB stand for GREEN PYRAMID, GREEN BLOCK, RED BLOCK, and ROBOT, respectively. Symbol A* is the name of the function ASSERT. When (X IS CLEAR) is asserted any (Y IS ON X) is deleted and when (ROB HOLDS X) is asserted any (X IS ON Z) is deleted. The initial assertions that the GREEN BLOCK IS ON THE RED BLOCK, THE RED BLOCK IS ON THE TABLE, THE GREEN PYRAMID IS ON THE TABLE, etc. are shown as (h)–(m). The robot accepts the command (PUT U GP ON RB) and proves it in the following steps:

(1)   Command (PUT U GP ON RB) matches the consequent of (b), and so (PUT ROB GP ON RB) is true if (RB IS CLEAR) and (ROB PUTS GP ON RB).
(2)   (RB IS CLEAR) matches (c).
(3)   (c) is true if (Z IS ON RB)(ROB REMOVES Z FROM RB) and (ROB PUTS Z ON TABLE).
(4)   (Z IS ON RB) matches assertion (i), (GB IS ON RB) and so
(5)   (ROB REMOVES GB FROM RB) is tried and found to match (d),
(6)   which is true if (ROB PICKS UP GB), which matches (f) and is true if (7) and (9),
(7)   (GB IS CLEAR)
(8)   (GB IS CLEAR) by (j), and so

(9)   (ROB HOLDS GB) is asserted by (f).

(10)   Statement (5) asserts (RB IS CLEAR) and is now true.

(11)   Statement (3) still requires that (ROB PUTS GB ON TABLE),

(12)   which matches (e), whose antecedents require

(13)   (ROB HOLDS GB), true by (9),

(14)   (TABLE IS CLEAR), true by (m),

(15)   and asserts (GB IS ON TABLE).

(16)   The remaining antecedent of statement (1) is (ROB PUTS GB ON RB),

(17)   which matches (e), whose antecedents require (ROB HOLDS GP)(RB IS CLEAR) and the assertion (GP IS ON RB);

(18)   (ROB HOLDS GP) matches (g), which is true if

(19)   (ROB PICKS UP GP), which matches (f), and is true since its antecedents,

(20)   (GP IS CLEAR) is true by (1), and

(21)   (ROB HOLDS GP) is then true by assertion.

(22)   Statement (17) still requires (RB IS CLEAR), which is true by the assertion in (10), and asserts

(23)   (GP IS ON RB) thus completing the procedure.

The proof tree for establishing the goal "PUT ROB GP ON RB" is shown in Fig. 5 as the tree BLOKSTAK.

Assertions are marked with the symbol *, while procedural clauses are left unmarked. The nodes SETTING and GOAL are simply added as labels to suggest a story tree. Actually, SETTING shows only the initial assertions; for some other purpose, it might include the whole inference system. Several summaries can be read from BLOKSTAK; the highest of

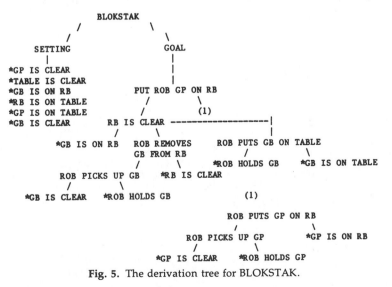

Fig. 5. The derivation tree for BLOKSTAK.

these is the GOAL-dominated node, which could be stated as THE ROBOT IS COMMANDED TO PUT THE GP ON THE RB. Next, the combination of two nodes can be read: THE ROBOT CLEARS THE RB THEN PUTS THE GP ON THE RB. The entire story primarily in terms of changes in world states is readable from the terminal leaves. Winograd took advantage of this hierarchical ordering to program his robot's reporting at successively deeper levels of what was done and why. A similar proof tree underlies the organization of each of Meehan's stories. A related approach is shown by Chester [1976] for translating from trees representing mathematical proofs into English paragraphs. It appears that some variation on this proof tree is what we are striving to compute when we attempt to understand a text.

An English description of what the robot did might take the following form:

(1)   Robot removed the green block from the red block.
(2)   He put the green block on the table,
(3)   picked up the green pyramid,
(4)   and put it on the red block.

These sentences suggest the scope of the text-understanding problem. From about 20 nodes on the derivation tree, four are selected to describe the series of events. The underlying motivation, that the robot wants to put the GP on the RB, is not explicitly stated. As readers, our knowledge of the blocks world gives us a context and the still inadequate theory of story trees gives us a basis for approaching the problem. However, until we can develop a theory of story or text grammars that approaches the completeness of our understanding of sentence structures and proof trees, we can only make informed guesses at what the underlying derivation tree might be for a given text.

Knowing the derivation tree for this example and following the constraints of story grammars, we can construct the story tree shown in Fig. 6.

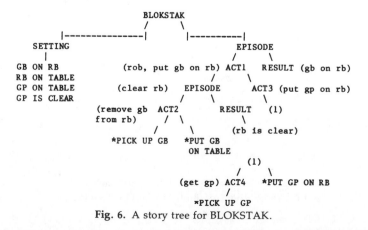

Fig. 6. A story tree for BLOKSTAK.

ACT1 corresponds to the derivation tree's top goal, ACT2 to the goal of clearing RB, ACT3 to the goal of putting the GP on the RB. The parenthesized lowercase expressions show what might be expressed as a description at each node in the tree and suggest the use of special comments for constructing summaries. The next section will show how useful rule systems can be prepared to generate story trees and summaries.

6. SOME RULES FOR STORY TREES

A general form for narrative grammars can be described in phrase structure rules as follows:

STORY = SETTING + EPI
SETTING = ACT
EPI = ACT + RESULT
ACT = ACT + ACT
ACT = T + . . . T
RESULT = TEST + EPI
RESULT = THE END

T + . . . T stands for a sequence of terminal assertions. Finer subdivisions in the grammar are possible and often desirable as was shown in Fig. 3. The notion of an episode being composed of an act and a result—often referred to as an act followed by a complication—is the main control branch of the story grammar. The result or complication is defined as a test to determine whether the story should continue with additional episodes or terminate at this point.

The phrase structure rules merely show the form of the story tree and reflect the flow of control in its generation. If we are to generate story trees from rules, we require the capability of testing whether a rule applies at a given point and of transfering the values of variables bound in one rule for use in another. We can use a phrase structure organization of Horn clauses to satisfy these requirements and to accomplish the generation.

In this form, the first three rules for a story grammar to generate a rather trite story, OLD WEST SAGA, appear as follows:

(OLD WEST SAGA) ← (SETTING GG BG L MOT OUTC)
                  (EPI GG BG L MOT OUTC)
(SETTING GG BG L MOT OUTC) ← (THE SHERIF IS GG)(THE BAD GUY)
     IS BG) (THE PLACE IS L) (SET MOT (PEACEFUL TOWN))
        (GG LIVES IN L) (BG RIDES INTO L)
(EPI GG BG L MOT OUTC) ← (ACT GG BG L MOT OUTC)
                  (RESULT GG BG L MOT OUTC)

The title, OLD WEST SAGA, stands for the node STORY. It is composed of a setting and an episode each of which is characterized by the variables

GG, BG, L, MOT, OUTC. The setting consists of a set of clauses—
sentences containing variables. Corresponding to some of these clauses,
the grammar contains the following assertions (the implication mark ← is
deleted for convenience):

(THE SHERIFF IS DESTRY)
(THE BAD GUY IS BLACKBART)
(THE PLACE IS DODGECITY)
(SET X X)

When the rule for SETTING is evaluated, each of its antecedents is
matched against the database of rules and assertions. When (THE
SHERIFF IS GG) is found to match (THE SHERIFF IS DESTRY), the vari-
able GG is bound to DESTRY for subsequent references within the rule.
The assertion (SET X X), which assigns a value to a variable, matches (SET
MOT (PEACEFUL TOWN)), and so MOTivation is bound to (PEACEFUL
TOWN). The result of evaluating the rule (SETTING . . .) gives the fol-
lowing:

(SETTING DESTRY BLACKBART DODGECITY (PEACEFUL TOWN)
OUTC)
    (THE SHERIFF IS DESTRY)(THE BAD GUY IS BLACKBART)
    (THE PLACE IS DODGECITY)(SET (PEACEFUL TOWN)
(PEACEFUL TOWN))
    (DESTRY LIVES IN DODGECITY)
(BLACKBART RIDES INTO DODGECITY)

This evaluation was a substep in evaluating the first rule, (OLD WEST
SAGA), and its values are bound back up into that rule as follows:

(OLD WEST SAGA) (SETTING DESTRY BLACKBART DODGECITY
(PEACEFUL TOWN) OUTC)
(EPI DESTRY BLACKBART DODGECITY (PEACEFUL TOWN) OUTC)

Thus the values of the variables have been established by the SETTING
rule and communicated through the antecedents of (OLD WEST SAGA)
into the EPI clause. The EPI clause is now evaluated and discovered to
match the EPI rule, and so the variables are bound through the EPI rule. It
appears as follows:

(EPI DESTRY BLACKBART DODGECITY (PEACEFUL TOWN) OUTC)
    (ACT DESTRY BLACKBART DODGECITY (PEACEFUL TOWN)
OUTC)
    (RESULT DESTRY BLACKBART DOGECITY (PEACEFUL TOWN)
OUTC)

The ACT antecedent is now to be evaluated. In the database, the following
rules are found to match the ACT antecedent:

```
(ACT GG BG L (PEACEFUL TOWN) (BG ROBS THE BANK))
(ACT GG BG L MOT (PEACEFUL TOWN))
    (GG DISCOVERS BANKROBBERY) (FIND GG BG)
```

These rules are in the above ordering and both are found to fit the ACT antecedent under the conditions that a variable matches a variable or a constant, and equal strings match. Thus DESTRY = GG, BLACK-BART = BG, DODGECITY = L, in both rules; (PEACEFUL TOWN) = (PEACEFUL TOWN) and OUTC = (BG robs THE BANK) in the first rule; and (PEACEFUL TOWN) = MOT and OUTC = (PEACEFUL TOWN) in the second. The first rule is selected. This rule is an assertion with the constant outcome that (BG ROBS THE BANK). Thus it is true and its OUTC value is bound back into the ACT above it. The RESULT rule is now evaluated with its OUTC = (BG ROBS THE BANK). In the database there are two result rules:

```
(RESULT GG BG L MOT OUTC) ← (EQ∗ MOT OUTC) (THE END)
(RESULT GG BG L MOT OUTC) ← (NEQ∗ MOT OUTC)
                           (EPI GG BG L MOT MOT)
```

Both are retrieved and the first one is tried. EQ∗ and NEQ∗ are functions for testing equality and nonequality, respectively. As a result of the last ACT, MOT = PEACEFUL TOWN and OUTC = BLACKBART ROBS THE BANK. Since MOT ≠ OUTC, the first RESULT rule fails and the second succeeds. It causes a new episode whose outcome is bound to the value of MOT, i.e., (PEACEFUL TOWN), and so the story will continue until the value of the MOT and OUTC arguments match. At this point, (THE END) will be asserted.

The interpreter that evaluates these Horn clauses has two modes, QUERY and ASSERT. In the QUERY mode, it is a problem solver that must show that all antecedents of a rule are eventually derivable from assertions in the data base. In this mode, it can be used to solve the Blocks world problem shown earlier. In the ASSERT mode, it is a tree generator and if an antecedent is not present in the data base, it can be asserted. Only functions such as EQ∗ and NEQ∗ can cause an antecedent to fail and, therefore, reject a rule whose consequent has been matched. The ASSERT mode is used in the above example. In it, such statements as (DESTRY LIVES IN DODGECITY) and (BLACKBART RIDES INTO DODGECITY) were asserted although not found in the database. In general, the ASSERT mode allows an author to place terminal assertions that he wishes to appear in his story directly in the antecedents of the rules that order the events of the story.

At this point, we can introduce one last important mechanism, the TF antecedent. This is a transformation statement that can be associated with each node to form a summary of what is happening. The TF antecedent allows the author to formulate such comments as were shown associated with nodes in the BLOKSTAK example of Fig. 6. The last antecedent in a statement may be a transformation and its arguments in the form (TF ( ) ( ) . . .). Let us add a TF antecedent to the SETTING rule:

(SETTING GG BG L MOT OUTC)
        . . . (TF (SHERIFF GG LIVES IN L A MOT UNTIL 7))

After binding, the whole expression appears as follows:

(SETTING DESTRY BLACKBART DODGECITY (PEACEFUL TOWN) OUTC)
(THE SHERIFF IS DESTRY)(THE BAD GUY IS BLACKBART)
(THE PLACE IS DODGECITY) (SET(PEACEFUL TOWN)(PEACEFUL TOWN))
(DESTRY LIVES IN DODGECITY) (BLACKBART RIDES INTO DODGE-CITY)
(TF(SHERIFF DESTRY LIVES IN DODGECITY A
                          (PEACEFUL TOWN)UNTIL 7))

```
(STORY OLD WEST SAGA)
*VALUE:
(OLD WEST SAGA (IN (THE DAYS OF THE OLD WEST) (THE SHERIFF IS DESTRY)
AND (THE BAD GUY IS BLACKBART) ; (DESTRY LIVES IN DODGECITY) HAPPILY
ENOUGH UNTIL (BLACKBART RIDES INTO TOWN)) (BLACKBART RIDES INTO
DODGECITY AND (BLACKBART ROBS THE BANK) (DESTRY DISCOVERS THE HEIST
AND (DESTRY SWINGS INTO THE SADDLE AND (GALLOPS AFTER BLACKBART) (
BLACKBART HIDES IN GREAT ROCK CANYON) (DESTRY RIDES INTO GREAT ROCK
CANYON) (DESTRY HEARS THE WHINNY OF A HORSE) (DESTRY DISMOUNTS AND
TRACKS BLACKBART) (DESTRY GETS THE DROP ON BLACKBART) THEN (BLACKBART
SURRENDERS) SO (DESTRY SHOOTS HIM) AND THERE IS A (PEACEFUL TOWN)) (
THE END))))
*TIME: 5821
(SAY PROOF 2)
*VALUE:
(OLD WEST SAGA (DESTRY KEEPS A (PEACEFUL TOWN) UNTIL BLACKBART ARRIVES
) (BLACKBART ROBS THE BANK (DESTRY HUNTS BLACKBART (THE END))))
*TIME: 265
(SAY PROOF 3)
*VALUE:
(OLD WEST SAGA (IN (THE DAYS OF THE OLD WEST) (THE SHERIFF IS DESTRY)
AND (THE BAD GUY IS BLACKBART) ; (DESTRY LIVES IN DODGECITY) HAPPILY
ENOUGH UNTIL (BLACKBART RIDES INTO TOWN)) (BLACKBART RIDES INTO
DODGECITY AND (BLACKBART ROBS THE BANK) (DESTRY DISCOVERS THE HEIST
AND (DESTRY SHOOTS BLACKBART TO MAKE A (PEACEFUL TOWN)) (THE END))))
*TIME: 329
(SAY PROOF 4)
*VALUE:
(OLD WEST SAGA (IN (THE DAYS OF THE OLD WEST) (THE SHERIFF IS DESTRY)
AND (THE BAD GUY IS BLACKBART) ; (DESTRY LIVES IN DODGECITY) HAPPILY
ENOUGH UNTIL (BLACKBART RIDES INTO TOWN)) (BLACKBART RIDES INTO
DODGECITY AND (BLACKBART ROBS THE BANK) (DESTRY DISCOVERS THE HEIST
AND (BLACKBART HIDES IN A CANYON (DESTRY RIDES INTO GREAT ROCK CANYON)
   (DESTRY HEARS THE WHINNY OF A HORSE) (DESTRY DISMOUNTS AND TRACKS
BLACKBART) (DESTRY GETS THE DROP ON BLACKBART) THEN (BLACKBART
SURRENDERS) SO (DESTRY SHOOTS HIM) AND THERE IS A (PEACEFUL TOWN)) (
THE END))))
*TIME: 459    (Note: Times are CP time in milliseconds.)
```
Fig. 7. Old West saga and summaries.

Notice that the TF expression had variables GG L and MOT, which were bound to values DESTRY, DODGECITY, and (PEACEFUL TOWN) when the expression was evaluated. It also contained the number 7, which remains. This number refers to the rule's seventh clause, (BLACKBART RIDES INTO DODGECITY). TF is a special interpreter function that will substitute the reference clause for the number when it is evaluated. The TF expression is treated as an ordinary clause when the rules are evaluated, but when the story tree has been computed, the function (SAY PROOF N) evaluates the TF functions at level N in the tree to form a summary or complete story.*

The complete story grammar for OLD WEST SAGA is not given here for lack of space. We note only that the function RAND* is used in one rule: it returns true or nil with a 0.5 probability to allow the author to include variations in his story. A story and its summaries derived from this grammar are shown in Fig. 7. The grammar provides a second story, which is shown with its summaries in Fig. 8.

Although the example stories are brief and uncomplicated, the problem-solving system, using Horn-clauses and including functions, is theoretically strong enough to support the generation of arbitrarily complex stories. In QUERY mode, it can solve a large class of problems and describe the solution path with the aid of the TF antecedents. Experimentation with the system for more complicated applications is continuing.

```
(STORY OLD WEST SAGA)
*VALUE:
(OLD WEST SAGA (IN (THE DAYS OF THE OLD WEST) (THE SHERIFF IS DESTRY)
AND (THE BAD GUY IS BLACKBART) ; (DESTRY LIVES IN DODGECITY) HAPPILY
ENOUGH UNTIL (BLACKBART RIDES INTO TOWN)) (BLACKBART RIDES INTO
DODGECITY AND (BLACKBART ROBS THE BANK) (DESTRY DISCOVERS THE HEIST
AND (DESTRY SWINGS INTO THE SADDLE AND (GALLOPS AFTER BLACKBART) (
BLACKBART HIDES IN GREAT ROCK CANYON) (DESTRY RIDES INTO GREAT ROCK
CANYON) (BLACKBART BUSHWHACKS DESTRY) AND (DESTRY DIES) AND BLACKBART
CONTROLS A (PEACEFUL TOWN)) (THE END))))
*TIME: 5453
(SAY PROOF 2)
*VALUE:
(OLD WEST SAGA (DESTRY KEEPS A (PEACEFUL TOWN) UNTIL BLACKBART ARRIVES
) (BLACKBART ROBS THE BANK (DESTRY HUNTS BLACKBART (THE END))))
*TIME: 230
(SAY PROOF 3)
*VALUE:
(OLD WEST SAGA (IN (THE DAYS OF THE OLD WEST) (THE SHERIFF IS DESTRY)
AND (THE BAD GUY IS BLACKBART) ; (DESTRY LIVES IN DODGECITY) HAPPILY
ENOUGH UNTIL (BLACKBART RIDES INTO TOWN)) (BLACKBART RIDES INTO
DODGECITY AND (BLACKBART ROBS THE BANK) (DESTRY DISCOVERS THE HEIST
AND (BLACKBART AMBUSHES DESTRY) (THE END))))
*TIME: 320
```

Fig. 8. Variant Blackbart story and summaries.

* Programmed by M. Kavanagh Smith.

7. AN INTERPRETER FOR STORY GRAMMARS

Systems of antecedent–consequent rules have been a frequent tool for
problem solving in artificial intelligence research, beginning with GPS.
Fischer Black in 1946 used a system of consequent–antecedent rules, pat-
terned partly after GPS, to demonstrate the efficacy of answering questions by proving theorems. He showed that his system mapped into Smul-
lyan's logic. We found his algorithm to be one of the most natural for
answering questions in quantified semantic networks [Simmons and
Chester, 1977]. It also applies to the interpretation of Horn clause representations of story grammars.

The interpreter offers two modes of operation, QUERY and ASSERT. In
the QUERY mode, it is an ordinary problem solver, which requires that a
problem or theorem be reduced to some combination of assertions and
theorems in the data base. In the ASSERT mode, it is a generator, so if a
theorem cannot be proved, it is asserted. This latter mode makes the procedure comparable to POGEN (see Section 2) concerning the flow of control. However, it binds variables in a different manner and computes a
syntactic derivation structure, the story tree.

The two basic functions GEN and GENLST incorporate the following
steps.

To Generate a Relation, SYM:

1. If SYM is null, return NIL.
2. If SYM is a function, return the value of the evaluated function.
3. Match SYM to the database of rules and assertions:
   1. If there is no match,
      1. if in the QUERY mode, return NIL,
      2. if in the ASSERT mode, assert SYM to database, return
      SYM.
   2. If SYM matches a database element R:
      1. if there is no right half to R, that is, R is an assertion, bind
      the constants of R through the variables of SYM and return
      SYM;
      2. if there is a right half, that is, R is a rule,
         1. bind constants of SYM through R,
         2. detach the first element of R—it is proved if the re-
         mainder is proved,
         3. for all the remaining elements $Ri = R1, \ldots, Rn$,
         Generate Ri; as each Ri is proved, bind its values
         through $R(i + 1), \ldots, Rn$ and reiterate from step
         3.2.2.2 until Rn is proved,
         4. bind the values of variables in R for the variables of
         SYM and return SYM.

The tree of instantiated rules forms the proof, and in the LISP procedure SYM is added to this tree in order to return both the answering relation and its proof.

The procedure above is a simplified first path version of the question-answering algorithm published in Simmons and Chester [1977]. It uses a list of rules and assertions as its database. In the more complete version, it consults a semantically organized network with significant savings in computation time. We have tested the semantically organized versions of this procedure for question answering and for several of the problems that Kowalski [1974] presents. It is our belief that it is a suitable interpreter for experimenting with many applications of predicate logic expressed in Horn clauses.

8. DISCUSSION AND CONCLUSIONS

The problem of most concern in computational linguistics is to compute a representation of the understanding of ordinary natural language text. Several psychologists, but particularly Kintsch and van Dijk [1975], have accumulated evidence that human readers construct a macrostructure above the level of the sentences that they read. This metastructure appears to organize the propositions of the text in a fashion similar to the way we might construct an outline. It is this macrostructure and its contents that appear best to account for the way human subjects remember, summarize, and forget what they read.

In developing a computational model of this theory, we have first presented a study of generating sense and nonsense from texts modeled in phrase structure grammars with more or less random selection of terminal elements. A considerable degree of control over the coherence of the resulting text has been demonstrated by the ability to generate reasonable variations on an author's verses.

We have then described a method for using more complex grammar rules for computing deep case structures from sentences and a corresponding rule-based method for reconstructing English sentences. It is expected that these semantically based grammars will ultimately prove adaptable to computing macrostructures that organize sentences into larger units of discourse.

We have defined a story tree as a phrase structure organization of text propositions. It has the property that the most general propositions were closest to the root. The test of "story-treeness" is that when the tree is truncated at a given depth above its leaves, the resulting terminals produce a summary. The leaves of the complete tree are the propositions of the entire story.

Meehan's use of plans and planboxes for writing stories was then considered as a model of the thought process that underlies the construction of a story. As a much simpler example, we have examined a story of Winograd's robot stacking a green pyramid on a red block. We have used Horn clauses, following Kowalski, to model the robot's problem solving for this task. We have then showed that the resulting derivation tree had the story tree's property of providing summaries at levels approaching the root. A similar tree ordered according to a story grammar was constructed from four sentences describing the robot's task.

This form of grammar, augmented with transformation rules, has then been used to organize Horn clauses so as to produce some simple stories and to demonstrate that the resulting story trees provide summaries. An interpreter for the story grammars has been described in terms of a problem-solving system with an ASSERT mode, which makes it a tree generator. In the QUERY mode, it can also prove ordinary AI examples written in Horn clauses.

In this study, we have defined a structure called a story tree, which is generated by assertions and inference rules. Its terminals provide the sequence of propositions comprising a story, while higher nodes contain transformations that describe summaries of the nodes below. As a result, truncation of the story tree at successively higher levels provides briefer and briefer summaries. This structure for representing narratives is presented as an initial computational model to account for aspects of human understanding and memory for stories.

Following Meehan, we have used a problem-solving approach, but in the form of Kowalski's logic of Horn clauses. A story tree is generated by using an inference procedure to generate a particular subtree of instantiated events in the microworld. All possible events in the microworld are modeled by a set of assertions and inference rules. These can imply an infinitely large network.

The microworlds that we use for defining narratives are comprised of such events as episodes, acts, results, TF-transformations, and propositions. These are obviously linguistic entities, which form models of possible text constituents—in contrast to microworlds, which model motivated characters and sequences of their problem-solving actions. Our analysis of the blocks problem as a story tree indicates that problem solving the in "blocks world" or in the "talking animals world" can also be organized to generate story trees.

Defining story trees by generating them is an initial step toward the goal of computing from English texts a representation of their meaning. If we could compute story trees from any arbitrary sequence of propositions in a narrative, we could claim a model of human understanding. Having established one form with properties that can model a human reader's understanding, our next step is to apply the network to infer the story trees, which account for a sequence of propositions comprising a story. In this recognition or parsing task, the inference rules will require many more antecedents. This way, they will specify tight semantic constraints on the realization of a story tree and minimize multiple interpretations.

Although it is clear that much work remains to be accomplished, we conclude that this approach to generating story trees provides a promising initial computational model for the macrostructure that appears to underly human understanding and memory for narratives.

ACKNOWLEDGMENT

This research is partially supported by NSF Grant MCS 77-0135 and RADC Contract F-30602-78-c-0132.

REFERENCES

[Black, F., 1969]. A deductive question answering system. In *Semantic Information Processing.* M. Minsky (ed.) MIT Press, Boston, Massachusetts.

[Bobrow, D. G., and Collins, A. M., eds., 1975]. *Representation and Understanding.* Academic Press, New York.

[Bobrow, D., and Winograd, T., 1977]. An overview of KRL, a knowledge representation language. *Cognitive Science* **1**, No. 1, 3–46.

[Charniak, E., and Wilks, Y., 1976]. *Computational Semantics.* North-Holland Publ., Amsterdam.

[Chester, D., 1976]. The translation of formal proofs into English. *Artificial Intelligence* **7**, No. 3, 261–278.

[Crothers, E., 1972]. Memory structure and recall of discourse. In *Language Comprehension and the Acquisition of Knowledge.* J. Carrol and R. Freedle (eds.). Wiley, New York. pp. 247–284.

[Deliyanni, A., and Kowalski, R., 1977]. *Logic and Semantic Networks.* Imperial College, University of London, London, England.

[Fillmore, C., 1968]. The case for case. In *Universals in Linguistic Theory.* E. Bach and R. Harms (eds.). Holt, New York. pp. 1–88.

[Grimes, J., 1975]. *The Thread of Discourse.* Mouton Publishers, The Hague, Netherlands.

[Grosz, B., 1977]. "The Representation and Use of Focus in Dialogue Understanding," Technical Note No. 151. Stanford Research Institute, Menlo Park, California.

[Harper, K., and Su, S., 1969]. "A directed random paragraph generator," Rand manuscript No. RM6053-PR. The Rand Corporation, Santa Monica, California.

[Hendrix, G. G., 1976]. Partitioned networks for modelling natural language semantics. Ph.D. Thesis, Department of Computer Science, University of Texas, Austin.

[Kintsch, W., 1974]. *Representation of Meaning in Memory.* Wiley, New York.

[Kintsch, W., and Van Dijk T., 1975]. "Recalling and Summarizing Stories" (unpublished mss. from the authors).

[Klein, S., 1965]. Automatic paraphrasing in essay format. *Mechanical Translation* **8**, Nos. 3 and 4, 68–83.

[Klein, S., and Simmons, R., 1963]. Syntactic dependence and the computer generation of coherent discourse. *Mechanical Translation* **7**, No. 2, 50–61.

[Kowalski, R., 1974]. "Logic for Problem Solving," Memo, 75. Department of Computational Logic, University of Edinburgh, Edinburgh, Scotland.

[Lehnert, W., 1977]. Question answering in a story understanding system. *Cognitive Science* **1**, No. 1, 47–73.

[Meehan, J., 1976]. The metanovel: Writing stories by computer. Dissertation, Department of Computer Science, Yale University, New Haven, Connecticut.

[Meyer, B., 1975]. *The Organization of Prose and its Effects on Recall*. North-Holland Publ., Amsterdam.

[Minsky, M., 1975]. A framework for representing knowledge. In *The Psychology of Computer Vision*. P. Winston (ed.). McGraw-Hill, New York, pp. 211–277.

[Pratt, V. R., 1975]. Lingol—a progress report. *Proceedings of the 4th International Joint Conference on Artificial Intelligence, 1975* pp. 422–428.

[Rumelhart, D. E., 1975]. Notes on a schema for stories. In *Representation and Understanding*. D. G. Bobrow and A. M. Collins (eds.). Academic Press, New York.

[Schank, R. C., 1975a]. *Conceptual Information Processing*. North-Holland Publ., Amsterdam.

[Schank, R. C., 1975b]. The structure of episodes in memory. In *Representation* and *Understanding*. D. G. Bobrow and A. M. Collins (eds.). Academic Press, New York.

[Schank, R., and Abelson, R., 1977]. *Scripts, Plans, Goals and Understanding*. Wiley, New York.

[Simmons, R. F., 1978]. Rulebased computations on English. In *Pattern-Directed Inference Systems*. R. Hayes-Roth and D. Waterman, (eds.). Academic Press, New York, pp. 435–468.

[Simmons, R., and Chester, D., 1977]. Inferences in quantified semantic networks. *Proceedings of the 5th International Joint Conference* on *Artificial Intelligence, 1977* pp. 267–273.

[Thorndike, P., 1977]. Cognitive structures in comprehension and memory of narrative discourse. *Cognitive Psychology* **9**, No. 1, 77–110.

[van Dijk, T. A., 1975]. "Recalling and Summarizing Complex Discourse (unpublished mss. from the authors). Department of General Literary Studies, University of Amsterdam, Amsterdam, The Netherlands.

[Winograd, T., 1972]. *Understanding Natural Language*. Academic Press, New York.

[Yngve, V., 1960]. A model and an hypothesis for language structure. *Proceedings of the American Philosophical Society* **104**, 444–466.

[Young, R., 1977]. "Text Understanding: A Survey," Natural Languages Report No. 33. Department of Computer Science, University of Texas, Austin. (Published in *Amer. J. Computational Linguistics* **14**.)

ON REPRESENTING COMMONSENSE KNOWLEDGE

Benjamin Kuipers

INTRODUCTION

Commonsense knowledge is knowledge about the world that "everybody knows." Everybody knows that water is wet, that round things roll downhill, that to drive somewhere you have to get in the car first, that if you insult someone he might be unhappy or angry. Everybody knows how to get home from work, where Florida is on the map, that the French Revolution was much longer ago than the Chicago riots, why the sea is boiling hot, and whether pigs have wings (apologies to Lewis Carroll).

Much of this knowledge is never taught: people just seem to pick it up without any effort. Some is learned in school, like facts about the French Revolution, but assuming the commonsense notion of "longer ago than . . . ." Commonsense knowledge is frequently wrong, but almost always "good enough" for commonsense purposes. Some people lack common sense for practical subjects like electricity or motors, but most people have it for active threats like open manholes or raging fires.

How can we account for the power and usefulness of commonsense knowledge? More technically, how can we represent commonsense knowledge in a computer? In this chapter, I explore some of the characteristics of representations that make them suitable for commonsense knowledge. The chapter arose from an attempt to capture some of the general features of representations that I used in constructing a computer model of commonsense knowledge of large-scale space [Kuipers, 1977, 1978]. In Sections I and II, I propose a definition for commonsense knowledge, list some of the performance constraints it must satisfy, and discuss what it means to *represent* knowledge on a computer. Section III presents a collection of design features that appear to be important for representations of commonsense knowledge. Sections IV and V discuss two representations in more detail: the partial order, and a route description. They discuss the performance characteristics of these representations and show how they tie into the larger structure of the TOUR model of commonsense knowledge of large-scale space.

393

I. WHAT IS COMMONSENSE KNOWLEDGE?

It would be desirable to have a definition of "commonsense knowledge" that characterized this concept precisely. This is not yet possible, and may never be, but the following definition is an attempt to distinguish commonsense knowledge from basic cognitive skills such as manipulation, vision, and language on the one hand, and expert knowledge of electronics, mathematics, or history on the other. The abundant qualifiers in the definition are necessary because of the fuzziness of the phenomenon itself:

> *Commonsense knowledge is knowledge about the structure of the external world that is acquired and applied without concentrated effort by any normal human that allows him or her to meet the everyday demands of the physical, spatial, temporal, and social environment with a reasonable degree of success.*

Commonsense knowledge is useful exactly because it is a description of the environment that is maintained at very low cost. Planning and action can then take place within a rich description of the context that need not be constructed for the particular occasion.

The above definition is superficially quite different from McCarthy's, "a program has common sense if it automatically deduces for itself a sufficiently wide class of immediate consequences of anything it is told and what it already knows" [McCarthy, 1968, p. 403]. McCarthy's definition is much more inclusive than mine, applying to any deductive process that does a significant portion of its work in response to new information. In both cases, however, the emphasis is on structuring a description of some environment from observations. The primary goal of McCarthy's Advice Taker research is to show how "interesting changes in behavior can be expressed in a simple way" [p. 404]. My observations here can be seen, in part, as an elaboration on one of the other features he ascribes to commonsense knowledge: "the machine must have or evolve concepts of partial success because on difficult problems decisive successes or failures come too infrequently" [p. 405].

The fact that commonsense knowledge is reasonably useful under real-world performance constraints without concentrated effort suggests an *opportunistic* way of operating. A system is called opportunistic if it performs computations only when information and processing resources are available and inexpensive, and functions adequately the rest of the time on partially processed information. Since commonsense knowledge is acquired and used under relatively unfavorable conditions, generally as a background to other more pressing activities, it seems forced to adopt an opportunistic mode of operation. Many kinds of knowledge do not lend themselves to opportunistic computation, and so cannot be commonsense knowledge. Vision and motor abilities cannot be opportunistic, for example; the importance to survival of quick recognition and physical activity is too high, implying that these processes must be able to demand resources when necessary. To make a different contrast, expert problem-solving often requires concentrated effort, and is very vulnerable to the destructive effects of interruptions.*

There are certain performance constraints (PCs) that are observably satisfied by human commonsense knowledge.† We must evaluate potential representations for commonsense knowledge against such performance constraints.

PC1.   Learning must be possible, i.e., it must be computationally feasible to combine new information with what is already known and store the result [Newell and Simon, 1972, p. 8].

PC2.   Performance must degrade gracefully under limitations of information and processing resources, rather than failing catastrophically [Norman and Bobrow, 1975; Marr, 1975].

PC3.   The amount of working memory (short-term memory) available to any process is limited and probably quite small [Miller, 1956].

PC4.   Processing time is subject to frequent interruptions, destroying some or all of the contents of working memory [Norman and Bobrow, 1975].

PC5.   Observational input is generally local and fragmented with respect to the scale of the overall phenomenon being described [Minsky and Papert, 1969].

PC6.   The contents of long-term memory are occasionally destroyed or lost.

There are two other constraints that seem very plausible to apply to knowledge representations, but their implications remain quite unclear at this time:

* It is not always possible to use the need for concentration to distinguish expert from commonsense knowledge. Many kinds of expertise apparently involve simply a more appropriate way of describing the world, for the purpose at hand. A representation for such expert knowledge would have exactly the same properties as a commonsense representation. Indeed, some experts consider their expertise to be simply "educated common sense." A doctor, for example, may make a preliminary diagnosis on the basis of evidence that appears obvious and compelling to him even at first glance, but might be missed entirely by the layman. On the other hand, a doctor's expertise also includes processes for considering and excluding possible alternative diagnoses by judging the interactions among multiple diseases and treatments, a process that can require sustained concentration.

† "Performance constraints" as used in this chapter have little to do with Chomsky's [1965] distinction between competence and performance. This chapter examines the implications of certain practical limitations of the real-world computing environment for the structure of useful representations of commonsense knowledge. Aside from inspiring the selection of constraints, the remarks here are independent of the properties of people. A "performance theory of common sense" (in Chomsky's sense) would be an enterprise of almost unbounded scope, attempting to explain what makes people use knowledge in practice the way they do.

PC7.   The same basic representational framework should accommodate the range of individual variation that is observable among human performances on the task [Hunt *et al.*, 1973].

PC8.   Development should be possible. There should be a sequence of representations by which adult performance can be reached without disastrous lapses of performance on the way as one representation is replaced by another [Howe and Young, 1976].

When discussing "graceful degradation of performance," we must outline the different kinds of potential disasters that we are trying to avoid. Listed below, in decreasing order of severity, are types of disasters that can befall a computational system as a consequence of an internal error. People and computer programs are both subject to such disasters (Ds) but computer programs incline toward the more severe ones, while people are able to restrict their computational disasters to the milder end of the spectrum.

D1.   The computational system attains an illegal state from which no further action is possible, and halts or "crashes." For example, a computer will halt if it is instructed to examine the contents of a nonexistent memory location.

D2.   Previously acquired and stored information is rendered worthless and must be discarded. For example, if an interruption occurs while an array is being shifted in place, and the working memory of the shifting process is lost, then the entire array has become inconsistent and must be discarded.

D3.   The current action cannot be continued and must be abandoned. For example, in evaluating an arithmetic expression, if a variable returns a nonnumerical value, or a function cannot return a value at all, evaluation halts. This is actually a version of D1, taking place within a larger context which can continue functioning when the current activity fails.

D4.   Available observations of interest cannot be represented and stored, and so are discarded. For example, in compiling a map of important features of an area, an observation of the heading of a remote landmark, without its ground position, cannot be represented and stored. When the map is used subsequently, information about that landmark is not represented.

D5.   A question cannot be answered, perhaps delaying the reorganization of a body of information. For example, the local coordinate frames of two places will not be combined if the curvature of the road connecting them is unknown.

II.   WHAT IS REPRESENTING KNOWLEDGE?

By Palmer's [1977] definition, a *representation* consists of two sets of objects and relations, and a correspondence between them. The two sets are known as the represen*ted* domain and the represen*ting* domain. The correspondence between them allows questions about the represented domain to be answered by examining the representing domain.

In normal usage, the objects and relations in the representing domain are often referred to as the "representation," with an implicit reference to the represented domain and the correspondence. The assumption in artificial intelligence is that computational objects and relations make a particularly good representing domain. In this case, the processes that examine the representing objects and relations to answer questions are also of interest, and so are referred to as part of the representation as well. Bobrow [1975] discusses a number of dimensions along which computational representations can be compared.

Notice that there are two different kinds of enterprises involved in representing commonsense knowledge in the computer. First, there is research attempting to find computational representations for objects and relations in the world that satisfy a given set of performance constraints like those in Section I. This research takes place in the fields of mathematics, computer science, and artificial intelligence. Second, there is empirical research in psychology that attempts to characterize the human phenomenon of commonsense knowledge by formulating and testing constraints like those above. The research presented in this chapter addresses the first of these questions. (Naturally, the two kinds of research cannot be kept as isolated as this simple dichotomy suggests since the concepts used in each endeavor can and do influence the investigations in the other.)

The mapping between a state of the world and its computational representation or description can fail to be unique, in both directions. The most commonplace version of this is the observation that there are many possible worlds that can satisfy any (consistent) description. Since a description captures only certain facets of the world, the same description can hold of situations that vary in the undescribed facets. Conversely, there can also be many different descriptions of the same world, capturing different facets of it.

It is also true, however, that a given facet of the world can have many different descriptions, corresponding to the states of knowledge an observer goes through while learning about its global structure from a series of local observations. This set of states of partial knowledge can have quite different properties from the set of states that the world itself can take on. That this point is nontrivial can be seen through a simple example.

Let the "real world" consist of a one-dimensional space S (e.g., a street) and a set P of points in S related by an order relation (e.g., places on the street):

$$\cdots A \cdots B \cdots C \cdots D \cdots$$

The "real world" satisfies the condition

$$x, y \text{ elements of } P \Rightarrow (x = y \text{ or } x > y \text{ or } y > x)$$

On the other hand, commonsense knowledge of one-dimensional order need not satisfy this condition. A state of knowledge may correspond to:

$$\cdots A \cdots \{BC\} \cdots D \cdots$$

with no order on $\{BC\}$. (It is easy to duplicate this example by asking people about the order relations of places on streets.) Thus, the relation in the "real world" is a total order, while the relation that makes up the corresponding commonsense knowledge is a partial order.

This example shows that a representation for commonsense knowledge (in this case 1-D order), if it is to support learning in a natural and efficient way, must be capable of expressing the intermediate states of knowledge that a person passes through as he learns the order from observations. Along with the other performance constraints, to be discussed below, this suggests that the properties of a representation may be quite different from the properties of the world being described.

III.   DESIGN FEATURES OF COMMONSENSE REPRESENTATIONS

In this section, I shall try to draw some conclusions about properties of commonsense representations from the performance constraints outlined above. Most of these conclusions are motivated by comparisons between examples that differ in whether or not they satisfy the various constraints rather than being deduced as logical consequences of the constraints. Ideally, the properties that are suggested by these comparisons will later be formalizable through more careful mathematical analysis.

Extracting some of the relevant characteristics of the performance constraints, we shall look at the ability of representations to function adequately in the face of:

(1)   Partial destruction of the represented information,
(2)   Premature demand for the result of an operation,
(3)   Resource limitations in (a) working memory, (b) computing time, (c) additional information.

The first property we want in a representation for commonsense knowledge is the ability to express intermediate states of the learning process. This property is motivated in part by resource limitations in additional information. A good illustration is the comparison between partial and total orders as representations for knowledge of one-dimensional order. If order relations are observed as sequences that are subsets of the order in the environment, then two possible representations for the description are the partial order and the total order. Suppose, for the sake of concreteness, that the current state of the description is (*ABCD*), and the observation is (*AEC*). If the representation can express any partial order, then (*A{BE}CD*) can be stored, perhaps with some cost in working memory and computing time; there is no cost in additional information. However, if only total orders can be stored, then an additional piece of information is required before (*AEC*) can be assimilated: either (*BE*) or (*EB*).

This requirement for additional information, gotten either from further observation or retrieved from elsewhere in memory, can be seen as a cost of the assimilation process, just like working memory or computing time. Furthermore, if the additional information must be gotten from further observation, or is not conveniently indexed in memory, it is a cost that can be quite hard to pay. Such a cost, and the corresponding delay in updating the long-term description of the environment, makes the system more vulnerable to interruptions that could destroy the temporary state and lose even the first observation. Thus, it is a valuable feature for a representation to be able to express the intermediate states of the learning process, corresponding to an arbitrary sequence of relevant observations.

The second property we want in a representation for commonsense knowledge is resilience in the face of partial destruction of the represented information. The performance constraints that motivate this property are the fact that commonsense operations are subject to frequent interruptions that destroy part of the state of working memory, and that long-term memory seems subject to some sort of destructive process. If part of the information in a description is destroyed, we would like the representation to degrade gracefully, suffering only from the actual information lost, rather than being utterly destroyed by violation of some global consistency condition.

As an example of loss of working memory under an interruption, compare three different kinds of tree search: breadth-first, depth-first, and "best-first." The transient state of a breadth-first search is a set of nodes that span the width of the tree, in that every path from root to leaf must intersect the set. Loss of a single element destroys this property and renders the rest of the set useless. (In fact, it is possible for a separate recovery procedure to "back up" the breadth-first search from the remaining fragments, to reach a previous state from which the search can be restarted.) The transient state of a depth-first search is a linked list of nodes connecting the current node with the root of the tree. Loss of a single link can carry with it an arbitrarily long tail of the list, depending on which link was lost, but the initial segment of the list remains a meaningful state for a depth-first search. Thus the depth-first search can be restarted immediately, having to repeat some work, but neither having to start over nor having to reconstruct its state from the remaining fragments. The transient state of a best-first search is a set of nodes judged to have the "best chance" of dominating the desired target. Loss of a single node from this set decreases the chance of success, but is still a meaningful state of a best-first search, and can be resumed without recovery procedures.

A similar example can be shown in the case of long-term memory by looking at the two familiar order representations: represent an order as a set of ordered pairs (which could be links in a semantic net or 2-tuples in a list). A partial order obeys only the global condition that no loops occur, while a total order also states that any two elements of the ordered set must be comparable. Loss of a single pair clearly leaves the condition on a partial order unaffected, but can render the total order meaningless. Notice that in both kinds of memory, the more resilient representations not only continue to function adequately after partial destruction of information but need not even explicitly detect the fact that an error has taken place. The remainder after destruction is a meaningful state of the representation that can be treated exactly like the complete version.

The third property we want in a representation for commonsense knowledge is the ability to express a meaningful response when a process is prematurely asked for the result of a computation. This property is motivated by the frequency of external interruptions, and by limitations in memory and computing resources that may stop a process before it has run to completion. This property refers at least as much to the ability of the surrounding context to use the response as to the ability of an interrupted process to return one.

The simplest response to a premature request for a result is "don't know." Many representations are not able to represent and store "don't know" as part of a description, and so a "don't know" response triggers an error and the system halts or the current activity is abandoned. This passes the problem onward in the hopes of finding a supervisory process resilient enough to treat "don't know" as a value. A simple case of using "don't know" effectively is the structure of a database that responds to an unsuccessful search by computing and storing the requested value, ensuring that searches appear never to be unsuccessful, and ensuring that computations are done as seldom as possible, at the expense of a larger database.

A more complex example of resilience in the face of premature demands for results comes from the taxonomic (or IS-A) hierarchy, used by a process attempting to identify some specimen. A classification tree for birds or plants is one familiar case and the human recognition system may be another [Quillian, 1968; Anderson and Bower, 1974]. A premature request for the identity of a specimen might produce "marsh bird" or "oak," rather than the actual species, but the larger category is as useful as the smaller in most contexts. This example suggests that the taxonomic hierarchy is useful not just as a convenient abbreviation technique that lets shared properties be associated with shared categories, but that it is es-

sential to providing commonsense resilience to interruptions in the identification process.*

It has been widely observed that severe time and working memory limitations must be met by processes that make up commonsense knowledge.
The mathematical analysis of algorithms (e.g., Knuth [1968]) provides a
rich collection of techniques for analyzing representations and procedures. Certainly, many kinds of tree search make excessive resource demands of this kind and cannot be considered serious candidates for operations on representations for large amounts of commonsense knowledge.

There are typically trade-offs of various kinds in the design of representations and algorithms: time vs. space and storage vs. retrieval are two
prominant examples. The kinds of disasters outlined in Section I, as well
as the observations of McCarthy [1968], suggest that a commonsense
knowledge representation should optimize storage of information—the
maintenance of an adequate description of the environment—even at the
expense of retrieval or the ability to solve each particular problem successfully. Since either kind of process will be vulnerable to interruptions, it is
important that the initial storage of observations be as efficient as possible, and that the subsequent assimilation process be made up of small
steps so as not to suffer excessively from interruptions.

IV. PARTIAL ORDER

The partial order is a mathematical structure that appears frequently in
attempts to devise a computational representation for knowledge. A partial order $(S, <)$ is a set S and a binary relation $<$ on the elements of S that
satisfies:

(1) for no x in S, $x < x$,
(2) for any x, y, z in S, if $x < y$ and $y < z$, then $x < z$.

A total order is a partial order that also satisfies:

(3) for any x, y in S, $x < y$ or $x = y$ or $y < x$.

A partial order can arise when representing a relationship, such as containment among subsets of a set, that is inherently partially ordered in the

---

* Thus we see a taxonomic hierarchy as a set of states of partial knowledge of identity;
useful in the recognition process. If this is true of people, we should find that its structure is
not determined by the number of shared characteristics among individuals (as would be required by economy of storage) but by the shared states passed through in the process of recognition. Thus, "whale" fits into the hierarchy under "fish" not because our ancestors
thought whales were fishes or even because they have many common characteristics but because the states of partial knowledge encountered in recognizing a whale have more in
common with "fish" than with "mammal."

world. Any set with more than one element has subsets that are not related by containment. On the other hand, a partial order can also arise when representing states of partial knowledge about a total order, such as the order of places on a street (as in Section II).

A partial order can be represented in the computer either as a distributed collection of pointers, or as a single complex data structure. The containment relation might be represented in a semantic network, for example, as a SUBSET-OF link between the nodes representing two regions. On the other hand, the node for a street may refer to a data structure representing, in one place, the current state of knowledge about the order of places on that street.

Two of the design features we want in commonsense representations are satisfied directly, because a partial order is the transitive closure of an *arbitrary* set of order relations. First, if an observation is a sequence of elements of S, then any set of observations can be represented by some partial order. This is clearly false of total orders, since there are some sets of observations that do not determine a total order uniquely. Second, if some of the order relations are lost, due to a destructive process acting on memory, the remaining information still constitutes a partial order, which furthermore is simply a less-specified version of the original.

Now let us examine a representation of a partial order in the computer. Let $(P, <)$ be a finite set with a partial order. Assume that we already have a representation for the elements of P, so that for each x in P, $f(x)$ is its computer representation. Now let S be a set of sequences of elements from $f(P)$. Define a new relation $<<$ on $f(P)$ by saying that $a << b$ for a and b in $f(P)$ if there is a sequence in S in which a precedes b, and let $<<^*$ be the transitive closure of $<<$. Then $(f(P), <<^*)$ is a partially ordered set, and S can be chosen so that

$$x < y \quad \text{iff} \quad f(x) <<^* f(y).$$

Thus, for an arbitrary, finite, partially ordered set, we can represent the order relation in the computer as a set of sequences.

Given the correspondence above, we can define access procedures that operate on the set-of-sequences data structure to answer questions about the represented partial order, and to change it as the partial order changes:

$$\text{ORDER}(a, b, S) = \begin{cases} +1, & \text{if } a <<^* b \\ -1, & \text{if } b <<^* a \\ \text{"don't know"} & \text{otherwise} \end{cases}$$

$\text{MERGE}(seq, S)$ = S with the side-effect that seq has been added to the partial order S

$\text{REORGANIZE}(S)$ = S rearranges and combines the sequences in S to make ORDER more efficient without changing its logical properties

The retrieval function ORDER can in general be quite inefficient, especially for pathological, highly branching partial orders. However, since the surrounding context must already be capable of dealing with a "don't know" response, an interruption or exhaustion of resources simply results in the least painful class of disasters D5.

MERGE needs only to append its sequence to S and do no extended computation, and so it is not very vulnerable to destructive interruptions and unlikely to lose observations (D4). Extended processing of input is left to REORGANIZE, which examines the set S of sequences, rearranging and combining them to achieve the minimum of branching. However, since the value returned by a call to ORDER is unaffected by REORGANIZE, it can operate completely in the background, freely interruptable by more urgent needs, but when resources are available making S suitable for more efficient access by ORDER.

In the TOUR model of commonsense knowledge of large-scale space [Kuipers, 1977, 1978], such a partial order data structure is part of the description of a street, representing the current state of partial knowledge about the order of places on the street. The observations provided are sequences of places observed when travelling along the street, and they are merged into the street's partial order. However, there is an ambiguity left in the correspondence between an observed sequence (ABC) of places, and the partial order data structure S associated with the street description. Does the observation of (ABC) mean $A <<^* B <<^* C$ or $C <<^* B <<^* A$?

Information must be provided by the global context to resolve this ambiguity. In the TOUR model, one element of the global context is the current one-dimensional orientation of the traveller on the current street. The 1-D orientation takes on the values $+1$, -1, and "don't know," exactly as provided by ORDER, and represents the correspondence between the dynamic order of observations and the static order associated with a street description. In case the 1-D orientation is "don't know," (ABC) is treated as $\{(A) (B) (C)\}$, and the order information is lost until it is observed again. Inference rules in the TOUR model specify how the 1-D orientation is obtained and updated, and how it guides the interpretation of observations such as these.

V. ROUTE DESCRIPTION

Sequential behavior is an important part of the life of any intelligent human or computer, and the learning of these sequences is an important aspect of commonsense knowledge. I shall present in this section an example of a representation for descriptions of routes through a large-scale space, intending to show how the gradual accretion of local observations produces several qualitatively different phases of behavior. (There are certainly attractive parallels with other kinds of learned sequential behavior, which bear further investigation in other contexts. However, it should also be observed that a representation such as this one is certainly inadequate for many other kinds of sequential behavior, such as language production.)

Let a *view* V be a description of an observable piece of the environment from one position, and let an *action* A be some motion that can be performed in the context of that piece of environment. To model the role of the environment in travel, let us define the function RESULT(V, A) = V', which is interpreted as "if performing action A in the context of the piece of environment described by V, the result will be the observation V'." Notice that RESULT does not model a mental operation; it models the physical fact that if you see one thing (V), then turn a corner (A), you will see something different (V').

I am thinking of a *view* as a visual image and an *action* as walking a distance or turning, although other interpretations are possible and reasonable. The internal structure of these descriptions is assumed to be extremely complex and data-rich, and fortunately is not of concern to us here. Assume that your eyes are capable of delivering a *view* description V that can be compared for identity with stored *views* V', V'', etc., and that an *action* A can be recorded if performed, and performed if recalled in the appropriate context.

With these preliminaries taken care of, we can define a route description as a set of triples (V A V'), where a triple may allow either the A or V' position to be unspecified. [For notation, (V A ?) leaves open the question of whether V' was specified, and (V A _) states that it was not.] As part of a route description, (V A V') represents the *imperative* of doing A when in the context described by V, and the *assertion* that RESULT(V, A) = V'.*

Three operations are permissible on a route description. If RD is a route description:

INSERT(*triple*, RD) = RD and adds *triple* to the set RD

$$\text{ASSOC}(V, \text{RD}) = \begin{cases} (V\ ?\ ?) & \text{if such a triple is in RD} \\ \text{"don't know"} & \text{otherwise} \end{cases}$$

A or V' can be added to a (V _ _) or (V A _) triple

In particular, the route description itself is a set with no sequential structure. That will arise as a property of the particular set of triples.

---

* The similarity of (V A V') triples to stimulus–response associations has not gone unnoticed but arose from the computational requirements of the problem, rather than being a theoretical principle that I brought to this design. However, a (V A V') triple is quite different from a stimulus–response pair in that it also acts as a symbolic assertion that can be the input or output of deductive procedures.

As information is gradually added to a route description, the behavior it supports goes through three phases:

(1) Considered simply as a collection of triples, a route description RD supports recognition of a previously observed view $(V \_ \_)$, knowledge of the action to take at that point $(V \; A \; \_)$, and even anticipation of the result of the action $(V \; A \; V')$. In the early stages of learning a route description, the set contains only a few partially filled triples and so it will support only occasional recognition and further acquisition of information but not self-guided travel.

(2) The first threshhold is passed when RD contains enough $(V \; A \; ?)$ triples to complete a sequence

$$V_0 A_0 V_1 A_1 \cdots V_n$$

connecting the beginning and end points of the route, satisfying

(a) $\mathrm{ASSOC}(V_i, RD) = (V_i \; A_i \; ?)$
(b) $\mathrm{RESULT}(V_i, A_i)$

This permits the route description to be followed as an imperative set of instructions, but only in conjunction with physical observation of the environment. The association between *view* and *action* is contained in the route description, while order information is contained in the physical structure of the environment.

(3) The second threshhold is passed when RD contains enough triples of the form $(V \; A \; V')$ so that the sequence:

$$V_0 A_0 V_1 A_1 \cdots V_n$$

can be constructed solely from

(c) $\mathrm{ASSOC}(V_i, RD) = (V_i \; A_i \; V_{i+1})$

In this case, the order information is now represented explicitly in the route description, and need not be acquired through physical interaction with the world. This level of organization supports planning and mental rehearsal of the route, which is valuable for constructing descriptions of larger spatial structures, as well as physical travel over that particular route.

This representation is interesting for a number of reasons. First, its performance undergoes two qualitative changes over a range of very simple information acquisition steps. Second, adding a new piece of information consists of either inserting a new triple into the set, or of filling an empty slot in a triple. Neither constitutes a heavy computational load or is likely to suffer much from destructive interruptions. Third, the only search involved is the associative retrieval from the set of triples.

This route description is also reasonably resilient in the face of various kinds of degraded performance:

(1) Extra information is no burden at all: associative retrieval simply overlooks information that is not needed.

(2) Loss of V' from a triple is not a barrier to physical travel (D3), but only to mental rehearsal of the route description, and therefore to some kinds of structure-building (D5).

(3) Loss of either A from a triple, or of an entire crucial triple, is a barrier to self-directed travel (D3), but not to recognition, and it does not render the remaining route description worthless (D2). Later observations can still fill the gap and restore full performance without an error ever having to be explicitly detected and recognized.

In the TOUR model, this route description bridges a gap between a plausible level of observational experience and the sequence of GO-TO and TURN instructions that formed the basis of the early formulations [Kuipers, 1977, 1978]. The further process of assimilation described there takes spatial information from the context of particular route descriptions and associates it with fixed features of the environment. Thus the egocentric *view* and *action* descriptions are assimilated into a nonegocentric *place* description whose local geometry summarizes the possible actions that can take place there. Similarly, order information that is implicit in the sequence of places encountered on a route is associated with *path* descriptions of the streets involved.

VI.   CONCLUSION

This chapter has essentially been about graceful degradation: how the performance of a representation for commonsense knowledge can survive the unpleasant computational environment of the real world. In particular, how it can minimize the level of disaster resulting from interruptions, destruction of information, and limitations in resources. Important properties of commonsense representations include (1) the ability to express intermediate states of the learning process, (2) resilience in the face of partial destruction of the represented information (preferably without even having to notice the destruction), and (3) the ability to express a meaningful response when a process is prematurely asked for the result of a computation. A number of examples were presented to illustrate different aspects of these properties.

The examples and properties give a qualitative description of the characteristics that are important in a commonsense representation, but they need to be supplemented by a quantitative, mathematical analysis.

How resilient is a representation under *what kinds* of destruction?

Which sequences of observations can and cannot be represented completely?

What kinds of partial results of procedures are usable by the process that made a premature demand for an answer?

How bad is a given class of disaster, for a given request in a given context?

For some of the questions ("how resilient," "how bad"), it is not even clear how to state the question mathematically or what form the answer would take. For other questions, the answer requires a precise description of the set of all possible observations, outputs, or items vulnerable to destruction.

Another intriguing class of mathematical questions that arises from these examples concerns the characterization of commonsense knowledge. How many computational representations are there? Infinitely many, of course, but can they be generated in some interesting way from a small basis, the way we describe cyclic groups? Of all these representations, how many satisfy the performance constraints we would like to apply to representations of commonsense knowledge? Even if we cannot generate all representations, perhaps we can generate all commonsense representations?

An alternative possibility is that there really are not very many commonsense representations at all, perhaps a dozen or two. Then we could catalog them in the way we catalog the "simple machines" out of which other mechanical devices are constructed. The wide use of metaphor from concrete physical and spatial knowledge to more abstract domains ends some plausibility to this curious notion. Perhaps one reason for the use of metaphor is that there are only a few suitable representations for commonsense knowledge, we learn them initially when learning about the physical world, then apply them metaphorically to get access to powerful representational devices in new domains.

ACKNOWLEDGMENTS

I would like to thank the reviewers for their helpful comments, and the inhabitants of the MIT AI Lab for their general inspiration. This chapter is based on research that was performed while the author was at the Artificial Intelligence Laboratory of the Massachusetts Institute of Technology. Support for the laboratory's artificial intelligence research is provided in part by the Advanced Research Project Agency of the Department of Defense under Office of Naval Research contract N00014-75-C-0643.

REFERENCES

[Anderson, J. R., and Bower, G., 1974]. *Human Associative Memory*, 2nd ed. Washington, DC: Hemisphere Publishing Corp., Washington, D.C.

[Bobrow, D. G., 1975]. Dimensions of representation. In *Representation and Understanding*. D. G. Bobrow and A. Collins (eds.). Academic Press, New York, pp. 1–34.

[Chomsky, N., 1965]. *Aspects of the Theory of Syntax*. MIT Press, Cambridge, Massachusetts.

[Howe, J. A. M., and Young, R. M., 1976]. "Progress in Cognitive Development," Research Report No. 17, Department of Artificial Intelligence, University of Edinburgh, Edinburgh, Scotland.

[Hunt, E., Frost, N., and Lunneborg, C., 1973]. Individual differences in cognition: A new approach to intelligence. *Psychology of Learning and Motivation* **7**, 87–122.

[Knuth, D. E., 1968]. *The Art of Computer Programming*. Vol. 1. Addison-Wesley, Reading, Massachusetts.

[Kuipers, B. J., 1977]. "Representing Knowledge of Large-Scale Space," TR-418. Artificial Intelligence Laboratory, MIT, Cambridge, Massachusetts. (Doctoral thesis, MIT Mathematics Department.)

[Kuipers, B. J., 1978]. Modelling spatial knowledge. *Cognitive Science* **2**, 129–153.

[McCarthy, J., 1968]. Programs with common sense. In *Semantic Information Processing*. M. Minsky (ed.). MIT Press, Cambridge, Massachusetts, pp. 403–418.

[Marr, D., 1975]. Early Processing of Visual Information. *Phil. Trans. Roy. Soc. B.* **275**, 483–524.

[Miller, G. A., 1956]. The magical number seven, plus or minus two. *Psychology Review* **63**, 81–97.

[Minsky, M. L., and Paper, S. A., 1969]. *Perceptrons*. MIT Press, Cambridge, Massachusetts.

[Newell, A., and Simon, H. A., 1972]. *Human Problem Solving*. Prentice-Hall, Englewood Cliffs, New Jersey.

[Norman, D. A., and Bobrow, D. G., 1975]. On data-limited and resource-limited processes. *Cognitive Psychology* **7**, 44–64.

[Palmer, S. E., 1977]. Fundamental aspects of cognitive representation. In *Cognition and Categorization*. E. H. Rosch and B. B. Lloyd (eds.). Erlbaum Press, Potomac, Maryland.

[Quillian, M. R., 1968]. Semantic memory. In *Semantic Information Processing*. M. Minsky (ed.). MIT Press, Cambridge, Massachusetts, pp. 227–270.

REPRESENTATIONS TO AID DISTRIBUTED UNDERSTANDING IN A MULTIPROGRAM SYSTEM

Christopher K. Riesbeck

ABSTRACT

Story understanding requires the application of many different kinds of knowledge: about language, about physical laws, about human intentionality, and so on. In implementations of story understanders at Yale, each set of rules is organized and applied by a different program. These programs communicate using conceptual dependency meaning representations to encode the inferences they have made. Using a few additional special forms, these representations can also encode directions for future inferencing from one program to another. Understanding text is thus a distributed process. Examples of simple texts requiring contributions from several different knowledge sources are given.

1. BACKGROUND

Understanding natural language texts requires knowledge—lots of it. It requires knowledge about language, about the physical world, about human intentionality, about stereotyped social situations, about story-telling conventions, and so on. Furthermore, each of these sorts of knowledge is associated with a particular style of processing. Checking for special cases is a useful technique in sentence processing [Becker, 1975], pattern matching is a useful tool for accessing information about stereotypical situations, and logical deduction is useful for calculating spatial relationships.

Thus, a reasonable model of a story understanding system is one with a number of autonomous subsystems working together. The idea of a community of "experts" working together has become more popular in recent years as it has become clear just how much work an intelligent system will have to do [Erman and Lesser, 1975; Hewitt, 1977; Lenat, 1975]. The problem then arises of how these subsystems talk to each other. There must be some internal language for interprocess communication, a "language for thinking."

409

Based on our experience at Yale with working story-understanding systems, this chapter suggests several simple types of messages that can be passed between the programs that we have developed. While the messages themselves are nothing new, they are surprisingly powerful when combined with other mechanisms that have already been developed. Most of the examples will deal with how the language analyzer talks to other programs but the message types themselves are not intended to be solely for that purpose.

2. THE YALE ARTIFICIAL INTELLIGENCE PROJECT

The artificial intelligence project at Yale has been involved for several years in the design and implementation of a number of natural language-understanding systems such as SAM and PAM [Schank, 1976]. These systems are story understanders. They take multisentence texts, apply various bodies of knowledge, and construct complex internal meaning representations that contain what the text said and what the text implied. These structures are then used to produce paraphrases, translations, and answers to questions.

These systems contain a number of different programs acting together, each with its own body of knowledge. The programs include:

1.   the language analyzer (ELI), which uses rules for understanding English [Riesbeck and Schank, 1976];

2.   the reference instantiator (TOK), which uses facts about various characters, objects, and places that have been mentioned

3.   the script manager (SCRIPT-APPLY), which uses knowledge about normal sequences of events in the real world, and which of these events have happened so far in the story [Cullingford, 1977];

4.   the plan manager (PLAN-APPLY), which uses knowledge about goals and plans for achieving them, and what characters have what goals and plans in the story [Wilensky, 1978];

5.   the generator (GEN), which uses rules about how to express concepts in English [Goldman, 1975];

6.   the question-answerer (QUALM), which uses rules about how to interpret and answer questions[Lehnert, 1977].

These various independent programs communicate with each other using conceptual dependency (CD) structures [Schank, 1972; Schank and Abelson, 1977]. CD forms represent conceptual meanings. They have been designed to be independent of constructs from English or any other natural language. Programs receive CD forms, build new ones, and send the results on. The analyzer and generator are special in that they also deal with text.

A typical flow of processing is for ELI to read an English text and pass to TOK a CD form representing the meaning of that text. TOK takes the CD form and replaces general descriptors like (#PERSON FIRSTNAME (JOHN)) with particular memory tokens, such as one representing some previously known person named John. The modified form is then passed to SCRIPT-APPLY, which uses it to determine the context of the event described by the form. The output of SCRIPT-APPLY is a full description of the events in the story, including events that were not explicitly mentioned but were inferred to have happened. This output is then used by the paraphraser to produce a set of CD forms describing the important events of the story. These forms are passed to GEN, which expresses them as English sentences.

A particular example is the following. The SAM system, after having processed "John was in a restaurant. A waiter came over," reads "He ordered a hamburger." When ELI sees the word "he," it produces the CD form (#PERSON GENDER MALE REF DEF), i.e., "some particular person who is male." TOK takes this form but cannot instantiate the reference because there is more than one male person known. TOK passes the uninstantiated form to SCRIPT-APPLY. SCRIPT-APPLY, looking at the whole conceptualization for "he ordered a hamburger," decides that "he" refers to "John" because John is a customer, and normally customers order, and not waiters. When GEN gets the output of SCRIPT-APPLY, it produces the sentence "*John* ordered a hamburger" (emphasis added).

The CD representation system has been worked on for over six years. It has undergone many changes, two of the most important being:

1.   the development of a small set of conceptual acts, which, in suitable combination, can represent most of the common activities that people do;

2.   the development of abstract knowledge structures (scripts, plans, themes, etc.), which organize the more concrete CD forms into coherent units.

3.   CHOOSING RESPONSES

CD representations are declarative. They describe concepts and their interrelationships rather than, as in the procedural semantics approach, procedures to execute in response to the input. For example, in a procedural semantics system, such as that of Woods and Kaplan [1971], questions are calls to information retrieval routines. In a question-answering task domain, this is quite reasonable.

However, we are interested in representing more than questions and also in being able to recognize when questions are being asked and when they are not. This was an important issue when Lehnert worked on a CD question-answering program for the SAM project [Lehnert, 1977]. Her program had to find out what the speaker really wanted when he asked a question or made a statement (WRONG: Q: "Do you know what time it is?" A: "Yes."). A question may not be a question (WRONG: Q: "What kind of fool do you think I am?" A: "I give up, what kind?") and an imperative may not be an imperative (WRONG: "Take my wife . . . please!"). A statement may call for an answerlike response ("Mary said you know where John is.") or an action to be performed ("That window is letting in a draft.")

In order to allow the choice of response to be made by whichever subsystem "expert" is appropriate, our system will have to be extended in several ways. First, the inferences produced by each high-level program (such as SCRIPT-APPLY and PLAN-APPLY) have to be passed to the other programs for possible processing. We could do this by allowing an indefinite number of cycles of messages from TOK to SCRIPT-APPLY to PLAN-APPLY to TOK, etc., after each analysis from ELI. In the current SAM system, only one pass from ELI to TOK to SCRIPT-APPLY occurs. The number of cycles of TOK, SCRIPT-APPLY, PLAN-APPLY, etc., would have to be restricted, on the basis of such factors as how many inferences a cycle produces, how important and/or certain they are, how much time is allocated for "pondering," and so on.

Second, the kinds of CD forms used by our system have to be extended to allow this kind of message passing. CD normally represents what is known or inferred about events, states, intentions, causes, physical objects, and so forth. However, sometimes an English phrase will contain information about information rather than about the real world. For example the word "who" in the sentence "Can you tell me who just came in?" obviously cannot refer to information that the speaker has. On the contrary, "who" refers to information that the speaker does *not* have and wishes to find out. In a somewhat different way, the sentence "Mary is the one who went to Boston" is information about information. It says that the descriptor "Mary" and the descriptor "one who went to Boston" refer to the same internal memory token. It is not a predication about two tokens since in fact it is understood that there is only one token involved.

We shall present several representational forms to allow us to handle these ideas. These forms are in use now as messages from ELI to the other programs, but not all the combinations here proposed are used nor is the repeating cycle of inferencing employed. For example, we shall talk about representing a question as "I want you to tell me . . . ." In this way, question-answering becomes part of the general task of finding a response in a conversation. "Where is John?" would be treated similarly to "I want to know where John is," which means that the motivation of the speaker as well as what he wants to know would be the basis of inferencing and response generation. Currently QUALM is given a simpler CD form for "Where is John?" that says "John is location = ?"

4. DISTRIBUTED UNDERSTANDING

In a complex system like the one being proposed, both understanding and response generation are distributed processes. Understanding a text, i.e., assigning a set of CD forms to it, is done in bits and pieces, each program in the system applying its knowledge to forms generated by other programs. Each program is able to leave notes for the other programs, indicating those parts left incomplete.

Thus, even after ELI takes care of specifically linguistic problems like word inflection, word order, and ambiguity, it may still be unable to complete a true CD form for a piece of text. This situation can arise if the text contains references to knowledge structures used by the other conceptual inferencing programs.

For example, the sentence "John is a good foreman" requires knowledge about what a foreman does before a set of CD forms describing John can be produced. Knowledge about foremen is scriptal knowledge, and it is in SCRIPT-APPLY and not ELI. If we do not want to require ELI to know everything about scripts, nor SCRIPT-APPLY to be able to analyze English, then we need some way that ELI can tell SCRIPT-APPLY "find out what foremen do, and assert that John does those things well."

"Doing things well," by the way, is only one of the meanings of "good." Choosing that meaning from the other possibilities (such as "John is a good person who is a foreman") is an English lexical ambiguity problem that ELI needs to solve. Determining what makes someone a good foreman is a language-independent problem requiring general world knowledge.

5. PROCESSING NOTES

When ELI cannot fill in all the parts of a CD form, it leaves *processing notes* where these parts should be. The convention is that whenever any program in the system sees one of these notes, it tries to replace it with a true CD structure. If it cannot, then the note is left for some other program to try.

A note embedded within a CD form referring to a script will probably be resolved by SCRIPT-APPLY, while a note embedded within a CD form referring to a plan will be handled by PLAN-APPLY. For example, ELI is not able to fill in the reference for "he" in the text "John went into a restaurant. The waiter came over and he ordered a steak." However the CD forms produced for "restaurant" and "waiter" mention the restaurant script; hence SCRIPT-APPLY looks at the form "someone ask for steak" in the restaurant script and finds that the customer (in this case, John) is the most likely person to be ordering [Cullingford, 1977].

5.1. The REF Note

The processing note used in the "he ordered a hamburger" example is called the REF note. The analysis produced by ELI for "he" is (#PERSON GENDER MALE REF DEF). The subpart REF DEF is not a concept. It is a processing note that guides TOK and SCRIPT-APPLY in their instantiation of the reference. ELI cannot find out who is ordering the hamburger because this involves scriptal knowledge, not rules of English. Instead, it leaves the REF DEF note for other programs to resolve. This note does not say which program should do the reference, and in fact different contexts will lead to different programs handling the note.

A REF DEF form is passed from program to program until one of them resolves it, i.e., replaces it with a true CD form or knowledge structure. If the text had been "John went into a restaurant. The midget came over," no program would resolve the REF DEF produced by "the midget." The system would know that it was supposed to have figured out how a midget fits into a restaurant script but in fact it could not.

REF INDEF notes are also used. When ELI sees the word "someone," it produces the form (#PERSON REF INDEF). When TOK sees this form it does not look for a previous referent but instead generates a new token. In processing the text "John went into a restaurant. A midget came over," ELI would produce a REF INDEF note for "a midget," TOK would generate a new token for this character with the appropriate properties, and there would be no unresolved note left, such as the one with "the midget".

5.2. The SPECIFY Note

The next kind of note that ELI can leave is commonly used when representing questions. The form ELI produces for a question like "Where is John?" or "What time is it?" says "I want you to tell me the fact X," where X is a CD form containing the atom SPECIFY. The note SPECIFY represents a hole in the CD form. If ELI puts a SPECIFY in some slot, then ELI is saying "fill this slot." The convention is that when an inferencing routine sees a SPECIFY and it knows the CD form that should fill that slot, then the routine replaces the SPECIFY note with that CD form.

For example, the representation of "Where is he?" is

```
(CON
        (ACTOR HEARER ⇔ MTRANS TO SPEAKER
              MOBJECT (ACTOR (#PERSON REF DEF)
                      IS (LOC VAL SPECIFY)))
     LEADTO
        (ACTOR SPEAKER TOWARD JOY INC 2))
```

This CD form says "If you tell me 'John is in location SPECIFY,' then I will be happier." QUALM, the question-answerer, looks for forms containing a SPECIFY atom embedded in the MOBJECT of the frame

```
(CON
        (ACTOR HEARER ⇔ MTRANS TO SPEAKER MOBJECT(. . .))
  LEADTO
        (ACTOR SPEAKER TOWARD JOY INC 2))
```

When QUALM sees such a frame, it takes the CD form in the MOBJECT slot. This represents what fact the speaker literally said he wanted to know. The note SPECIFY in that slot signals the part of the fact that is unknown to him.

5.3.   Representing "Trying"

With just these two kinds of notes, REFs and SPECIFYs, we can already represent complex messages. Consider the sentence "John is trying to get to Boston from New Haven." This sentence could describe a number of different situations. John may be looking for rides to Boston, he may be looking for plane or train connections, he may be hitch-hiking, etc. Maybe he wants to borrow a car. However the sentence is not vacuous. We would not guess that John is building a balloon to fly to Boston or that he is digging a tunnel there. We know reasonable ways of getting somewhere and this sentence is saying that John is trying one or more of those ways.

This knowledge about how to get somewhere is stored in PLAN-APPLY and SCRIPT-APPLY. PLAN-APPLY has general methods for changing location. SCRIPT-APPLY knows about specific means of transport like trains and busses and so on. By combining the general knowledge that PLAN-APPLY and SCRIPT-APPLY have with the specific knowledge that TOK has about John and Boston, the system can make guesses about what John might be doing.

In order for this combining to occur, however, ELI has to analyze "John is trying to get to Boston from New Haven" into something that will tell the other programs what they need to do. There are no explicit references in the text to scripts. What scripts are relevant has to be inferred by programs receiving ELI's interpretation. What ELI can tell them is that John has the goal of getting to Boston and he is doing actions that will help attain that goal. Note that ELI must specify that John's actions are goal-oriented. If the text had been "John is doing something because he likes being in Boston," then ELI's analysis would not suggest goal-oriented behavior. It would be very difficult (and probably unreasonable) to try and infer what John is doing.

ELI can use SPECIFY and REF to construct a CD form that says that John has a goal and that he is doing actions associated with attaining that goal. The goal is specified by the phrase "to get to Boston from New Haven."

The form saying that he is trying to attain that goal looks like this:

(CON
　　　　($GOAL VAL (ACTOR (#PERSON NAME (JOHN))
　　　　　　　　⇔ PTRANS
　　　　　　　　TO (#CITY NAME (BOSTON))
　　　　　　　　FROM (#CITY NAME (NEWHAVEN))))
　　REASON
　　　　(ACTOR (#PERSON NAME (JOHN)) ⇔ (SPECIFY REF INDEF))

(CON A REASON B) says "A is the reason why B was done." (ACTOR
X ⇔ Y) says "X is doing Y." In this case, Y is the form (SPECIFY REF
INDEF), i.e., John is doing unknown (to ELI) actions because he wants to
get to Boston.

The above form is passed around, from TOK to SCRIPT-APPLY, and
eventually to PLAN-APPLY. PLAN-APPLY reacts to references to goals.
When it sees them, it makes inferences about what actions are appropriate
for the goal. These inferences are used in story understanding to predict
(and hence help disambiguate) future event descriptions.

In examing the form produced by ELI for "trying to get to Boston,"
PLAN-APPLY discovers the ⇔ (SPECIFY REF INDEF) note that ELI left
behind. When PLAN-APPLY sees the REF INDEF, it "generates a new action" for John, just as TOK generated a new token when it saw (#PERSON
REF INDEF). Generating a new action means that PLAN-APPLY sets up
its own internal structures to represent the fact that John has initiated
some plan for getting to Boston. With just this much information,
PLAN-APPLY cannot say what John is doing for sure but it can make predictions about his actions.

Thus ELI's note led to PLAN-APPLY putting itself into the proper internal state. ELI did this without having to explicitly set PLAN-APPLY
variables or run PLAN-APPLY functions. In fact, ELI did not even have to
determine that PLAN-APPLY was the appropriate program.

5.4.　The EQUIV Note

The next processing note allows us to represent the idea of "this concept
refers to the same thing as that concept." For example, to represent the
meaning of "Mary is the one who went to Boston," we need to be able to
say that the concept referred to by (#PERSON NAME MARY) is the same
as the one referred to by

　　　(#PERSON REL (ACTOR (#PERSON)
　　　　　　　⇔ PTRANS TO (#CITY NAME BOSTON)))

We also want to be able to represent nonidentity for sentences like "Someone besides me ate the strawberries."

We represent referential equivalence with the forms (ACTOR X EQUIV Y) and (CON X EQUIV Y). ACTOR is used when X and Y are simple concepts like (#PERSON) or (#PHYSOBJ). CON is used when they are event conceptualizations like (ACTOR (#PERSON) ATRANS . . .). In either case, EQUIV says that the two CD forms refer to the same thing. To represent the idea that the two concepts refer to different things, we negate the EQUIV form.

For example, the representation of "Mary is the one who went to Boston" would be

```
(ACTOR (#PERSON NAME MARY)
EQUIV (#PERSON REF DEF
              REL (ACTOR "#PERSON"
                   ⇔ PTRANS
                   TO (#CITY NAME BOSTON)))
```

The form #PERSON in quotes is a notational convenience for this chapter. A CD form may contain references to itself. This circular self-reference will be noted here by the use of double quotes around some representative subpart of the CD form. Thus the quoted #PERSON form is a self-reference to the CD form that contains it, i.e., the form (#PERSON REF DEF . . .) that follows the EQUIV.

This representation produces different results in memory from the one produced for "Mary went to Boston," which is

```
(ACTOR (#PERSON NAME MARY)
 ⇔ PTRANS TO (#CITY NAME BOSTON))
```

When TOK sees this form, it adds the fact "went to Boston" to its token for "Mary." When TOK sees the EQUIV form, however, it looks for an existing token to match the CD form for "someone who went to Boston." (Organizing a large memory and searching it for tokens that satisfy certain properties is a task for which no one has a good solution yet, but it is one that we shall have to be able to do someday if we are to understand sentences like "That guy you told me about came in again.") If it finds such a token, TOK adds to it the information it has about Mary. If a token for "someone who went to Boston" cannot be found or if its properties conflict with those for Mary, then TOK cannot resolve the EQUIV note. If no one else resolves the note, then a problem in understanding exists.

For example, the text "John went to Boston. Mary went to Boston" does not cause any problems. TOK just adds the property "went to Boston" to both its "John" and "Mary" tokens. But the text "John went to Boston. Mary is the one who went to Boston" does cause a problem. The second sentence leads TOK to try and merge its "John" and "Mary" tokens. The conflict in names prevents this and TOK is unable to resolve the EQUIV note.

To represent the meaning of the sentence "Mary was not the one who went to Boston," we negate the EQUIV form thus:

```
((ACTOR (#PERSON NAME MARY)
   EQUIV (#PERSON REF DEF
                    REL (ACTOR "#PERSON"
                         ⇔ PTRANS
                         TO (#CITY NAME BOSTON)))
   MODE NEG)
```

We can also use EQUIV forms as fillers after REF, like INDEF and DEF. These are used for sentences that make passing mention of some referential equivalence. For example, the representation of "someone besides Mary went to Boston" would be

```
(ACTOR (#PERSON REF ((ACTOR "#PERSON"
                       EQUIV (#PERSON NAME MARY))
                      MODE NEG)
   ⇔ PTRANS TO (#CITY NAME BOSTON)))
```

5.5. A Meaning of "But"

With the EQUIV form, we can represent the equivalence and nonequivalence of concept descriptions. When applied to whole conceptualizations rather than simple concepts like "Mary," fairly complex messages can be passed.

Not surprisingly, some of the most complex messages come from the commonest words. In particular, developing representations for the various meanings of the word "but" that would be useful in an understanding system could occupy a doctoral thesis. This short section suggests the representation of one use of "but," primarily in order to show the functioning of the EQUIV note.

For example, consider the following pairs of sentences:

> *I looked for the book but couldn't find it.*
> *I looked for the book and couldn't find it.*
>
> *She asked him but he couldn't tell her.*
> *She asked him and he couldn't tell her.*
>
> *We voted for her but she lost.*
> *We voted for her and she lost.*

The events and states described by this second set of sentences are the same as those for the first set but intuitively they do not feel the same. This suggests that "but" and "and" are processed differently and that sometimes the same meaning is reached by different routes.

I would like to suggest that a good approximation to the meaning of "X but Y" as it is used in the above examples is "X and—contrary to goals—Y." Thus, not finding something is contrary to the goal of looking for it; no answer is contrary to the goal of asking; someone losing an election is contrary to the goal of voting for them.

This meaning of "but" is similar to but different from another meaning of "but," which is "contrary to expectations." Expectation is not the same as intention or plan, even when we allow "expectation" to refer ambiguously either to the expectations of the reader or of a person mentioned in the text. For example, you can clearly link winning to betting without expecting betting to lead to winning.

In order for the idea of "contrary to goals" to be useful, it has to be definable in terms that an understanding system can use. In our case, we can define "contrary to goals" in terms of scripts and plans.

A script has goals attached to it that describe what doing the script is supposed to accomplish. The script also contains various alternative event sequences. Some of these event sequences lead to the goal and others do not. We shall call those events that lead to goals *instrumental events.* The phrase "contrary to goals" refers to both the instrumental events and the goals to which they lead.

Hence, even though "but" often precedes unpleasant or unexpected events, this does not have to be true. If a script has an unpleasant instrumental event, "but" can precede a pleasant event that contradicts it. This is why "but" is acceptable in "John went to the dentist but he had no cavities."

Likewise, if a script has an event sequence that rarely succeeds, "but" can precede a predictable event that contradicts it. This is why we can say "John went to the race track but he lost."

For plans, instrumental events can be defined as the goals of the plan, the steps in the plan that lead to that goal, and the creation of the plan itself. "But" is *not* reasonable in a sentence where the first clause invokes a goal and the second clause describes an instrumental event. The following examples show this:

> *John planned to visit her but he finally made it.*
> *John was hungry but he looked for some food.*
> *John wanted to go home but he started his car.*

In summary, then one of the meanings of "but" in "X but Y" is "Y is not an instrumental event for the script or goal invoked by X." We can implement this meaning of "but" by having ELI attach a note to the CD form produced for "Y" that says "this form is not an instrumental event."

Depending on their internal data structures, this can have one of two effects on programs like PLAN-APPLY and SCRIPT-APPLY. If they have explicit alternatives to an expected instrumental event, then they can try matching against those alternatives first. If there are no known alternatives, then they can try matching for the negation of the expected instrumental events. In either case, the EQUIV form warns them not to try matching against the expected instrumental events.

Usually this warning is helpful but not necessary. We can understand "John ate at a restaurant. He couldn't pay." without a "but" linking the two sentences. However, there are times when the concept of "contrary to goals" is crucial for understanding.

For example, consider the sentence "John tried to flunk his draft physical but he failed." Most people would understand this sentence to mean John *passed* his physical. On the other hand, the interpretation of "John tried to flunk his draft physical and he failed." is ambiguous and can easily mean that he failed his physical (i.e., attained his goals). The difference between the two sentences can be explained if we assume that "but" rules out instrumental events and "and" does not.

Thus to represent this use of "but," ELI leaves the note "this concept is not EQUIV to an instrumental event." To represent an instrumental event, we use the SPECIFY atom and say "SPECIFY1 is an event that leads to SPECIFY2, which is a goal." The numbers following SPECIFY are used to distinguish the several different unknown elements involved.

For example, the representation of an instrumental event for the restaurant script is

```
(CON
     (SPECIFY1 REF INDEF)
LEADTO
     (SPECIFY2 REL ($RESTAURANT GOAL "SPECIFY2")
          REF INDEF))
```

The CD form says that an event (SPECIFY1) leads to another event (SPECIFY2), which is a goal of the restaurant script ($RESTAURANT). Thus SPECIFY1 in this form represents an instrumental event for the restaurant script.

To represent an event that is not a restaurant instrumental event, we use EQUIV and NEG and write

```
(SPECIFY3
REF ((CON "SPECIFY3"
          EQUIV (SPECIFY1
                    REL (CON "SPECIFY1"
                         LEADTO (SPECIFY2
                                   REL ($RESTAURANT
                                        GOAL "SPECIFY2")
                                   REF INDEF))))
     MODE NEG))
```

The atom SPECIFY3 is an event that is not an instrumental event, i.e., it is not equivalent to an event leading to a goal in the restaurant script.

The representation of "X but Y" therefore will be "X and Y, where Y is not an instrumental event." For example, the representation of "John went to a restaurant but he couldn't pay the check" would be two conceptualizations:

```
(ACTOR (#PERSON NAME JOHN) ⇔ PTRANS
 OBJECT (#PERSON NAME JOHN)
 TO (#BUILDING TYPE RESTAURANT))

((ACTOR (#PERSON NAME JOHN)
  ⇔ ATRANS OBJECT MONEY TO #MANAGEMENT)
 MODE CANNOT
 REF ((CON "ATRANS"
       EQUIV (SPECIFY1
              REL (CON "SPECIFY1"
                   LEADTO (SPECIFY2
                           REL ($RESTAURANT
                                GOAL "SPECIFY2")
                           REF INDEF))))
 MODE NEG))
```

The first CD form says that John went to a restaurant. The second says that John couldn't pay and, furthermore, that not being able to pay is not an instrumental event in the restaurant script. This tells SCRIPT-APPLY not to try to match the form against any instrumental events in the restaurant script. In fact, since the restaurant script also specifies failure events (e.g., the waiter takes a long time to come, the restaurant does not have what the customer wants, the food is burnt, the customer does not have enough money), it is a reasonable rule to first try and match events nonequivalent to instrumental events against the failure events. In this example, John's being unable to pay will be found in the set of standard failure events. It will be found faster than in the case when the "but" conjunction is not there to direct the search.

6. DISCUSSION

Our view of what understanding is has changed significantly over the years. Initially, understanding was defined as how to get from a natural language text to an unambiguous representation of the meaning of that text. Filling in gaps and resolving ambiguities were the central problems. Now, we can see the inadequacy of this concept of understanding. Understanding is not just a matter of filling in the gaps. Even more importantly, it involves finding larger structures within which to embed previously produced ones.

There is a big difference between how the MARGIE system [Schank *et al.*, 1975] understood "John went into a restaurant" and how SAM does it.

MARGIE stopped with the completed CD form representing "John moved himself to the interior of a restaurant building." SAM, however, *adds* the important information that John is probably hungry and is going to get some food. And even this interpretation is not final. In the system we have outlined, PLAN-APPLY would add a goal-plan structure linking John's goal of getting food with his use of the normal satisfy-hunger plan involving the restaurant script. And yet another program, knowing rules of conversation and text, would try to add an explanation of why John's trip to a restaurant was brought up, e.g., perhaps it was the beginning of a joke about John.

In order to understand in this additive manner, the conceptual inferencers have to analyze CD forms into their constituent parts, and pass around the results of these analyses. Story understanding and normal conversational dialogue requires contributions and interactions from all the inferencing programs. Each program applies its own special knowledge and produces CD forms representing what it has discovered. These results are then to be passed to the other inferencers to see if the new information affects them.

Along the way, processing notes are resolved. However, the same kinds of processes for resolution that we have been describing would also be invoked in our proposed system when processing notes were not created. For example, suppose we had the following story:

> *John went into Howard Johnson's. While waiting for a table, John saw someone he wanted to avoid. John left quickly.*

This story does not contain any processing notes but it still requires extensive interaction between the various programs.

When ELI reads "John went into Howard Johnson's," it determines that John went into some place associated with the name Howard Johnson. TOK finds in its memory a particular place, which is Howard Johnson's restaurant. SCRIPT-APPLY takes the CD form produced by TOK apart, discovers the reference to a restaurant, and uses a rule that says that going into a restaurant is sufficient reason for invoking the restaurant script. With this script invoked, SCRIPT-APPLY infers that John is hungry and is going to Howard Johnson's to eat. When PLAN-APPLY sees the CD forms for "John is hungry" and "John wants to eat," it sets up its own internal structures for John's goal of eating. Notice that PLAN-APPLY's inference depends on information from SCRIPT-APPLY, which in turn depends on information from TOK.

When the cycles of inferencing from the first sentence are finished, PLAN-APPLY will be ready for references to events relevant to John's goal of eating, and SCRIPT-APPLY will be ready for references to the stereotypical events that occur in restaurants, such as getting a table, a waiter coming over, and ordering.

When ELI reads "While waiting for a table," it produces a CD form satisfying one of SCRIPT-APPLY's expectations. From its knowledge about waiting for tables in restaurants, SCRIPT-APPLY infers that John is in some area of the restaurant outside the dining area and has not yet ordered or eaten.

When ELI reads "John saw someone he wanted to avoid," it produces a CD form that SCRIPT-APPLY cannot handle. It does not match any of the forms in the restaurant script nor does it contain any subpart referencing some other script. When this form reaches PLAN-APPLY on the other hand, it sees the goal "avoid person." Using the basic plan that one way to avoid being in contact with someone or something is to stay away from wherever they are, PLAN-APPLY infers that John may have the goal of not being in the restaurant and that he may leave.

When ELI reads "John left quickly," it produces a CD form that satisfies PLAN-APPLY's prediction. PLAN-APPLY therefore builds a CD form saying that the reason why John left is because he wanted to avoid the person he saw in the restaurant. This is an obvious inference but it is not explicitly stated in the text.

SCRIPT-APPLY now has the forms that say that John has left the restaurant and he does not intend to return. Since being in the restaurant is a precondition for eating there, SCRIPT-APPLY infers that John is no longer doing the restaurant script. Note that just knowing that John left would not have been sufficient to conclude that the script was no longer active. John might be leaving because he left something in his car. SCRIPT-APPLY's conclusion in this situation is dependent on the information that John does not want to come back. This information came from PLAN-APPLY.

At this point in the story, the system assumes that John is still hungry because neither PLAN-APPLY nor SCRIPT-APPLY ever saw anything to make them infer that John had eaten. Since no scripts are active the only predictions left are PLAN-APPLY's predictions that John will be trying to get food.

7. CONCLUSION

The process of story understanding naturally involves a continual passing of CD forms between the various programs. The addition of processing notes like REF, SPECIFY, and EQUIV fits in very well with this general mode of operation. The extended CD forms can then serve two roles in a multiprogram understanding system: to record the inferences produced by the various programs and to communicate directives for further processing. Understanding is a repetitive, piecemeal process in this model. It does not end with the language analysis nor with any other particular program in the system, but continues as long as there is some program with something to say.

ACKNOWLEDGMENTS

This work was supported in part by the Advanced Research Projects Agency of the Department of Defense and monitored under the Office of Naval Research under contract N00014-75-C-1111.

REFERENCES

[Becker, J. D., 1975]. The phrasal lexicon. *Proceedings of Theoretical Issues in Natural Language Processing, 1975* pp. 60–63.
[Cullingford, R. E., 1977]. Script Application: Computer Understanding of Newspaper Stories. Technical Report 116. Department of Computer Science, Yale University, New Haven, Connecticut.
[Erman, L., and Lesser, V., 1975]. A multi-level organization for problem solving using many, diverse, cooperating sources of knowledge. *Proceedings of the 4th International Joint Conference on Artificial Intelligence, 1975* pp. 483–490.
[Goldman, N., 1975]. Conceptual generation. In *Conceptual Information Processing*. R. C. Schank (ed.). North-Holland Publ., Amsterdam, pp. 289–371.
[Hewitt, C., 1977]. Viewing control structures as patterns of passing messages. *Artificial Intelligence* 8, No 3, 323–364.
[Lehnert, W., 1977]. Human and computational question-answering. *Cognitive Science* 1, No. 1, 47–73.
[Lenat, D., 1975]. BEINGS: Knowledge as interacting experts. *Proceedings of the 4th International Joint Conference on Artificial Intelligence, 1975* pp. 126–133.
[Riesbeck, C., and Schank, R. C., 1976]. Comprehension by Computer: Expectation-based Analysis of Sentences in Context, Technical Report 78. Department of Computer Science, Yale University, New Haven, Connecticut.
[Schank, R. C., 1972]. Conceptual dependency: A theory of natural language understanding. *Cognitive Psychology* 3, No. 4, 552–631.
[Schank, R. C., 1976]. Research at Yale in Natural Language Processing, Technical Report 84. Department of Computer Science Research, Yale University, New Haven, Connecticut.
[Schank, R. C., and Abelson, R. P., 1977]. *Scripts, Plans, Goals and Understanding*. Lawrence Erlbaum Associates, Hillsdale, New Jersey.
[Schank, R. C., Goldman, N., Rieger, C., and Riesbeck, C., 1975]. Inference and paraphrase by computer. *Journal of the ACM* 22, 309–328.
[Wilensky, R., 1978]. Understanding Goal-Based Stories. Technical Report 140. Department of Computer Science, Yale University, New Haven, Connecticut.
[Woods, W. A., and Kaplan, R. M., 1971]. The Lunar Sciences Natural Language Information System, BBN Report No. 2265. Bolt, Beranek & Newman, Cambridge, Massachusetts.

FIVE ASPECTS OF A FULL-SCALE STORY COMPREHENSION MODEL

Chuck Rieger

1. INTRODUCTION

The University of Maryland artificial intelligence (AI) group has been building a story comprehension system during the past year. Our purpose in undertaking the effort is primarily to gain some understanding of the global controls and information pathways in a full-scale story comprehension system. Of central interest are the control and interaction of a meaning-based parser, a reference mechanism, and inferences and predictions at a number of levels, ranging from the plot of the story to relatively mundane inferences about actions and causes.

In this article, I describe our conception of the architecture and important ingredients of a story comprehension model. Some of the ideas have been, or are in the process of being, implemented. The portions of the system which have been implemented form a working system we call GRIND-1. This current project has been based entirely upon a fairy tale by Walt Disney called "The Magic Grinder," available as a Book of the Month Club book. We chose this story because all of what we perceived to be its vital statistics perfectly matched our needs: it is long enough to be interesting (40 pages), it has a highly stereotyped plot and characters, it contains simple, yet content-rich English, and it calls for nontrivial intercharacter modeling.

Before beginning the discussion of our theory, let me put our work into perspective, both with respect to its philosophy and with respect to other work in the field. We feel that the thorough study of *one complete* story, in a vertically integrated fashion, is the only way to approach the construction of a theory of story comprehension. I use the term "vertically integrated" to suggest the coordination of the spectrum of processes from the lowest levels of language analyzers to the highest levels of plot inference and prediction. That we run the risk of building a useless, special purpose model is certainly a concern, but not a large one, since we feel we are building our theories upon reasonably flexible control paradigms and submodels.

425

The consideration of a complete control model for a single, realistically large story has not been the tradition of story comprehension research in AI, even though an important collection of ideas about the problems has gradually emerged. Charniak, for example, studied in considerable detail a procedural mechanism for making and confirming predictions, and data structures for storing dynamic information during comprehension. Recently, he has been investigating the topic of how problem solving cause–effect knowledge influences the understanding of stories involving that knowledge [Charniak, 1978], a topic in which our group [Rieger, 1978a,b], Schank and Abelson's group [Schank *et al.*, 1975], and Schmidt and his colleagues [Schmidt and Sridharan, 1977] have also invested considerable thought. Schank and Abelson have applied frame-like modules of stereotypical knowledge to the interpretation of stereotypical, paragraph-length "stories" in their systems called SAM [Schank *et al.*, 1975] and PAM [Wilensky, 1976], providing a simple, yet convincing illustration of how important preconceptions about a paragraph-length story's structure and content can be. Although Charniak, Schank, Abelson, and others (myself included) have been flirting with most of the concepts needed for a full-scale comprehension model, no one seems as yet to have made an attempt to connect all the pieces into an end-to-end model. Meehan [1977] has perhaps come the closest of anyone to this goal in his story generation system, TALE-SPIN; however, his techniques of generation do not seem for the most part to suggest inverse operations for analysis.

It seems to me, therefore, that someone needs to say: Here are a parser, a reference strategy, a character–character modeling strategy, a technique for generating the prediction set, a personality trait modeling strategy, a plot following strategy. . . , and here is how they interact, at least for *this* story. Whether or not the model is general, complete, adequate, or elegant is somewhat irrelevant at this stage; we simply need some benchmarks.

Our first attempt at such a statement, based on ongoing experience with GRIND-1, is the topic of this article. The discussion is organized around the five topics I feel are most essential in story comprehension:

1. meaning-based parsing;
2. representation of story text and inferences;
3. reference;
4. inference and inference conditioning from the plot and from story character models;
5. prediction/fulfillment pattern matching.

These five topics cut across what we feel are the spectrum of components required for full-scale story comprehension, listed in Fig. 1. I have attempted to cover the five selected topics in a way that addresses issues at both the theoretical and implementation level. Readers interested in more

1. Meaning-based parser
2. Reference Mechanism
3. Plot Follower and Plot-Level Inference Conditioner
4. Character-Character Relationship Modeller and Inference Conditioner
5. Single-Character Personality Trait Modeller and Inference Conditioner
6. Predictor/Fulfiller
7. Cause-Effect Inference System
8. Story Time Line Builder
9. Factual Data Base System

Fig. 1. Components of a story comprehender.

discussion on specific aspects of the Magic Grinder project are referred to and our group's other publications: Boose and Rieger [1977], Creeger [1978], Fauser [1978], Rieger [1976a,b], Rieger [1977], Rieger [1978a], Rieger [1978b], Salazar, and Small [1978].

2. PARSING: A NEW MODEL

The traditional approach to language analysis calls for assembling a collection of rules about syntax, semantics, and world knowledge, then applying those rules during the left–right scan of each input sentence. If the rules are an adequate reflection of the domain of discourse, they match pieces of the input sentence, suggest other rules, and produce outputs which are usually a nonlinear representation of the input—and usually in terms of less ambiguous symbols and relationships.

I feel the traditional, rule-based approach to meaning-based language analysis does not capture what I perceive to be the three fundamentals of language and language analysis:

1. language use and analysis relate more closely to individual words than to central collections of sentence-level rules of *any* form (syntactic, semantic, conceptual);

2. the processes of analysis and generation hinge on the application (in context) of individual word experts which encode large quantities of information about each word of each language;

3. human language knowledge is diffuse, spread throughout the system of word experts, each of which has evolved during the course of linguistic experience from a single word sense structure to a very elaborate multiple-sense discriminator/generator.

In short, most language phenomena follow from processes which organize and access expert knowledge about individual words; language phenomena relate only secondarily to central rule systems. The GRIND-1 parser is a more or less direct implementation of this notion that word sense discrimination in context is primary in language comprehension.

2.1. Word Sense Networks

Briefly, the organization of the parser, which we call the sense selection net (SSN) parser, is as follows. Every potentially ambiguous word of the language (i.e., virtually *every* word) is represented by an expert sense selection net. The structure of a sense net is such that each terminal node represents a conceptually distinct sense of the word, represented in GRIND-1's style of representation (discussed as the next topic). Each non-terminal node of a sense selection network contains one multiple-choice probe question about the context in which the word occurs. Perhaps the single most important feature of the sense net concept is that there is no

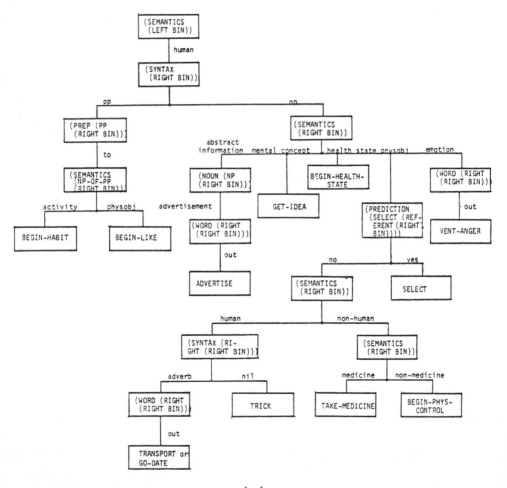

(a)

Fig. 2. (a) Illustrative sense net for some senses of the verb "take." (b) Sense selection networks (on facing page). (From Rieger [1978b].)

```
SENSE NETWORK INPUT SYNTAX

(SENSE-NET word
    (nodename (query1 ... queryN)
                    (response-vector1 successor-node optional-action ...)
                    (response-vector2 successor-node optional-action ...)
                    ...
                    (response-vectorK successor-node optional-action ...))
    ...
    (nodename TERMINAL action ... action)
    ...
)


EXAMPLE NET (TRIVIAL!)

(SENSE-NET WORK
    (1 ((SEMANTICS (LEFT BIN)) (SYNTAX (RIGHT BIN)))
       ((HUMAN PF) 2))
    (2 ((PREPOSITION (RIGHT BIN)) (SEMANTICS (NP-OF-PP (RIGHT BIN))))
       ((FOR HUMAN) 3))
    (3 TERMINAL (TRANSLATION 'WORK-FOR
                           (REFERENT (LEFT BIN))
                           (REFERENT (NP-OF-PP (RIGHT BIN)))
                           'UNKNOWN)))

SCHEMATIC SENSE NET INTERNAL REPRESENTATION
```

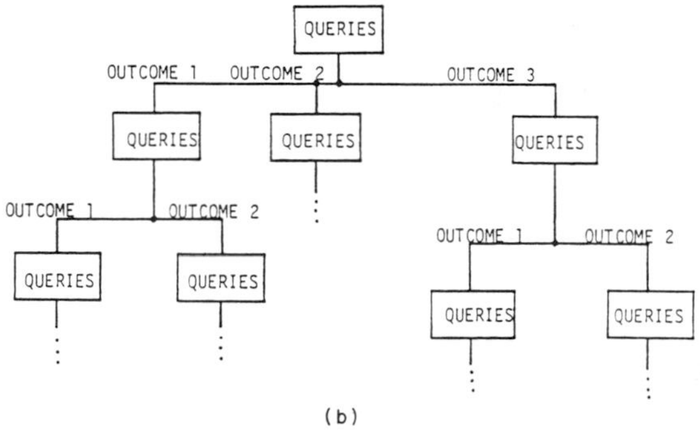

(b)

inherent restriction on the type of question a sense net nonterminal node can pose. Specifically, networks are free to ask questions not only about the word's local environment in the sentence (e.g., positional questions, syntactic questions, questions about the possible semantics of syntactically adjacent neighbors) but also questions about the current state of the comprehension model itself (e.g., factual and inferential knowledge already derived from the story, current predictions, current plot segment).

The abbreviated TAKE network of Fig. 2a (we have identified over 50 conceptually distinct senses of the verb form alone) serves to illustrate the structure and concept of word sense selection networks in the present model.* Figure 2b shows the schematic form of a sense net, its internal form, and a trivial illustration of the internal form. In this figure, the nodes

---

* Sense nets are implemented as data structures in the present model. Each net is a multiply-branching discrimination network which can be partially traversed, then suspended and later resumed. We will soon be converting the sense nets to a slightly more procedural form in which they will be regarded as processes and generators.

contain the context-elucidating questions which, if answered, would identify one of the terminal senses of the verb form of TAKE. (Terminals are represented in the figure only by descriptive words; in the model they are actually concept schemata.) The multiple branches out of each query, such as the PP (prepositional phrase) and NP (noun phrase) arcs from the second node, or the ACTIVITY and PHYSOBJ arcs from the bottom left query, represent the range of acceptable answers to each diagnostic question, and thereby help focus the question answerers in the model.*

Parsing with sense networks (Fig. 3) leads to a considerably different control paradigm from that of a conventional rule or pattern-based parser. As each (not necessarily syntactically well formed) sentence arrives, the sense net parser pages up copies of word sense experts, attaching them to the words of the sentence. The parser's workspace is a two-way linked list of "bins," each bin initially containing a word of the sentence and a pointer to the associated word sense expert. As the parse progresses, bins may be merged, deleted, suppressed, or suspended (see [Rieger, 1978b] for a more complete discussion).†

A parse begins with a call to the leftmost expert (i.e, applying the sense net for the first word of the sentence). This expert may complete, resulting in a translation (sense selection for the word the expert represents), or may suspend himself at any point, deciding to defer until more of the sentence has been seen by other experts. During the course of running, he may (and this is typical) request information that can only be answered by running other experts in the sentence, leading to a type of falling dominoes pattern of word expert invocation, left-to-right across the workspace. Any meaning products that a word sense expert extracts are attached on an appropriate bin in the workspace (typically the expert's own). In the absence of explicit wake-up calls from one expert to others farther right, the parse control forces the eventual left–right application of all word sense networks in the workspace.

---

* We have just completed a system by which naive users of the system can manually run and augment sense networks whose queries are all stored in English. In a typical interaction, a user approaches the system with a sentence illustrating a sense of some word with whose sense net he wishes to interact. By running the net, answering questions posed by the net's existing structure, he is either convinced of the net's adequacy for the example, or decides to augment or rearrange the network. Using this development aid, we will gradually amass a data base of sense nets from which we can abstract natural styles for sense net encoding before converting the system to machine-readable form. We expect to gain a better understanding of the range of diagnostic questions humans feel obliged to ask when manually sprouting and augmenting sense nets.

† Actually, the sentence has been preprocessed by a very dumb ATN syntactic reformatting grammar, so that bins can represent both words and highly stereotyped syntactic constructions such as noun and prepositional phrases. The ATN formatter does not perform a theoretical role; its purpose is to reduce the complexity of the input in "safe" ways that can be undone, if necessary, by the more intelligent sense net parser.

At the end of the first pass across the workspace, one of two conditions prevails: (1) all word experts completed successfully, or (2) one or several experts deferred and did not complete. In the first case, the parse is complete, and the various bins of the workspace cumulatively contain all extracted meaning assertions and language-based inferences. These assertions and inferences become the input to the inferential and predictive components of the model. In the second case, where not all word experts completed on the first pass, the parse controller rescans the workspace left–right to locate the first uncompleted expert, then reactivates him, hoping to advance the frontier of uncompleted sense nets. This type of relaxation parse control continues until all experts have successfully completed, or until no further progress is detected. In either case, as much meaning as possible is extracted, with relatively low likelihood of a total parse failure (i.e., the parser degrades gracefully, unlike many rule-based parsers). After parse termination, a process we call the "cherrypicker" scans the workspace, picking up all products of translation, and forwarding them to other parts of the model.

There seem to be some very interesting control possibilities for the coordination of this execution of experts (e.g., information passing among the sense nets, preconditioning of one net by another, suspension and later resumption of certain nets that cannot complete when first started, masking and merging of nets). Since the SSN parser is described in Rieger

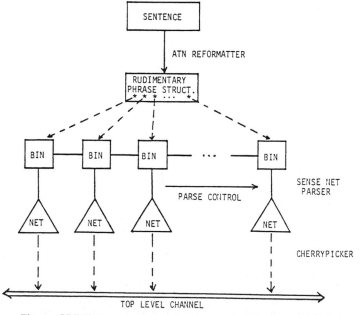

Fig. 3. GRIND-1 sense net organization. (From Rieger [1978b].)

[1978a,b] Small [1978], and since the parser is not a dominant topic of this article, I have included as Fig. 4 only an excerpted example and trace of the parser's behavior for the first sentence of the story, and in Fig. 5 the schematic representation of the SSN control paradigm.

One noteworthy feature of the SSN parse theory, beyond its potentially

```
Read the next sentence, calling the ATN parser:


EVAL:    (ns)
READING NEXT SENTENCE: ONCE THERE WAS A POOR MAID NAMED MINNIE.
CLEARING WORKSPACE
SETTING STATUS OF B1 TO UNEXAMINED
SETTING STATUS OF B2 TO UNEXAMINED
SETTING STATUS OF B3 TO UNEXAMINED
SETTING STATUS OF B4 TO UNEXAMINED
SETTING STATUS OF B5 TO UNEXAMINED
VALUE:    NIL


Call the sense-net applier to translate the workspace.


EVAL:    (tr)
TRANSLATING

SETTING STATUS OF B1 TO ACTIVE
RUNNING NET FOR BE AT BIN B1
BE NETWORK COMPLETION AT BIN B1
SETTING STATUS OF B1 TO TERMINATED
SETTING STATUS OF B2 TO ACTIVE
RUNNING NET FOR MAID AT BIN B2
MAID NETWORK COMPLETION AT BIN B2
RUNNING NET FOR POOR AT BIN B2
POOR NETWORK COMPLETION AT BIN B2
SETTING STATUS OF B2 TO TERMINATED
SETTING STATUS OF B3 TO ACTIVE
RUNNING NET FOR NAME AT BIN B3
SETTING STATUS OF B4 TO SUPPRESSED
NAME NETWORK COMPLETION AT BIN B3
SETTING STATUS OF B3 TO TERMINATED
SETTING STATUS OF B5 TO ACTIVE
SETTING STATUS OF B5 TO TERMINATED
VALUE:    NIL


Call the cherrypicker to gather the products of  the  translation
and pass them into the comprehension model.**


EVAL:    (cp)
CHERRYPICKING
CREATING NEW REFERENCE OBJECT G5
PLEASE DEDUCE (AGE G5 -X)
((t (-x.young)))
INJECTING (EXIST G5) ON MAIN CHANNEL
VALUE:    NIL
```

(a)

Fig. 4. Excerpted trace of SSN parse of first sentence (continued on facing page).

Take a look at the final state of the workspace. Note the markings SEMANTICS, MEANING, and REFERENT left by the translator and cherrypicker.

```
EVAL:   (ws)
B1
    MEANING: ((EXIST (REFERENT B2)))
    AFFIX: NIL
    INFL: (PAST)
    ADV: (THERE ONCE)
    AUX: NIL
    VERB: (BE)
    SYNTAX: VP
    STATUS: TERMINATED
B2
    REFERENT: G5
    SEMANTICS: (HUMAN ANIMATE)
    MEANING: ((CLASS -X HUMAN) (SEX -X FEMALE)
             (AMBIGUITY (SOCIAL-STATUS -X MONEY-POOR)
             (SOCIAL-STATUS -X MISTREATED)) (AMBIGUITY
             (SOCIAL-ROLE -X DOMESTIC-MAID) (SOCIAL-ROLE
             -X MEDIEVAL-MAIDEN)) (NAME -X MINNIE))
    ADJ: (POOR)
    DET: (A)
    NUMBER: (STEM)
    NOUN: (MAID)
    SYNTAX: NP
    STATUS: TERMINATED
B3
    AFFIX: (ED)
    INFL: (PAST)
    ADV: NIL
    AUX: NIL
    VERB: (NAME)
    SYNTAX: VP
    STATUS: TERMINATED
B4
    MEANING: NIL
    ADJ: NIL
    DET: NIL
    NUMBER: (STEM)
    NOUN: (MINNIE)
    SYNTAX: NP
    STATUS: SUPPRESSED
B5
    PUNCT: #PER
    SYNTAX: PUNCT
    STATUS: TERMINATED
VALUE:    NIL
```

(b)

Take a look at the model referent created to represent Minnie.

```
EVAL:   (ds g5)
(EXIST G5)
(AGE G5 YOUNG)
(NAME G5 MINNIE)
(AMBIGUITY (SOCIAL-ROLE G5 DOMESTIC-MAID)
          (SOCIAL-ROLE G5 MEDIEVAL-MAIDEN))
(AMBIGUITY (SOCIAL-STATUS G5 MONEY-POOR)
          (SOCIAL-STATUS G5 MISTREATED))
(SEX G5 FEMALE)
(CLASS G5 HUMAN)
VALUE:    NIL
```

(c)

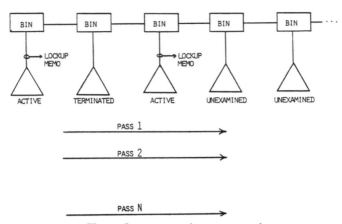

Fig. 5. Sense network parse control.

intense interaction via probe questions with all levels of the model, is that, since word experts can be potentially quite large and knowledgeable about the intricacies of each word's uses, they are capable of generating language-related inferences (i.e., secondary information), in addition to the primary mapping of word-in-context onto meaning structures. Thus, what we generally expect to find in the SSN parser's workspace after each parse is a collection of assertions reflecting not only the primary transla-tion but also language-based inferences, reference annotations, and anno-tations of remaining ambiguities (with associated denotations of the type of information the parser needed, but did not have) left behind by the word sense experts.

These products of meaning translation, deposited in the parser's work-space by the cooperative efforts of the word experts, flow into the rest of the model on the top-level model *channel* [Rieger, 1977] via the cherrypicker. It is to the top model channel that the various other GRIND-1 inferential and structure-building components are attached (Fig. 6). Although at the mo-ment of injection from the parser's workspace onto the model channel the information flow is one-way from the parser to the inferential compo-nents, the running of the word sense experts prior to that point will have in general resulted in interactions between the parser and the system's in-ternal question-answering and inference-making components. Thus, the GRIND-1 SSN parser is firmly knit into the inferential and plot-level seg-ments of the model. Readers interested in the extent of the interactions between the parser and the nonlinguistic components of the model are re-ferred to Rieger [1978b].

Structurally, all meaning assertions and inferences output by the parser are nested *n*-tuples representing partially or fully instantiated meaning

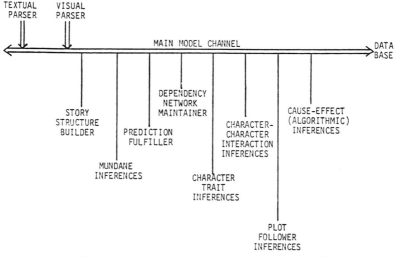

Fig. 6. GRIND-1 top level organization. (From Rieger [1978b].)

case frameworks of concepts. For example, the concept of person X working for person Y is encoded as:

$$(\text{WORK-FOR } X \ Y \text{ TASK})$$

where TASK is the service performed by X for Y (in return for monetary compensation). Since we have given considerable thought to the base representation for the comprehender, I want to discuss the GRIND-1 conceptual representation, and representation for story comprehension in general at this point.

3. MEANING REPRESENTATION OF LANGUAGE AND INFERENCE

In my view, there are two competing points of view for natural language meaning representation. They differ primarily in the degree to which they attempt to make explicit the details of meaning in the representation itself. I call the two schools of thought the "expansionists" and the "compressionists." The expansionist point of view advocates the decomposition of concepts into simpler concepts *explicitly* in the representation. This is in general tantamount to advocating the use of *large* structures, composed from small elements having some semantic role in the model, in representing nonelemental concepts. Such theories are inherently hierarchical, striving to make interrelationships among the higher-level concepts as explicit as possible in the data structure itself. A hallmark of expansionist theories is that their primitive symbols are generally low in information content and relatively context free.

The compressionist point of view, on the other hand, is that knowledge is best represented in more concise, less heavily composed forms that express higher-level concepts intrinsically. Characteristically, each predicate in a compressionist representation is information rich: it represents, all in one symbol, a compression of what would be a large schema in an expansionist theory.* Compressionist representations make heavier reliance on a system of inference for expressing interrelationships of knowledge, and make less of an attempt to have interrelationships be transparent from the data structures themselves.

There are practical and theoretical advantages of each style of representation for various types of modeling. However, in my opinion there is a clear-cut division between the classes of models for which expansionism and compressionism are best suited.

1.   Expansionism is most appropriate for models of such processes as analogical reasoning, paraphrase, and cross-language translation, where the goal is to discover similarities in global content, starting from similarities in structure and local content. Cross-language translation, for example, where the goal is to generate sentences in the target language that most closely express the concepts expressed by the sentences of the input language, is an ideal domain for expansionism. More generally, expansionism is called for where the model requires detailed analysis of the "microstructure" of concepts rather than their "macrostructure."

2.   Compressionism is most appropriate in models demanding heavy reliance on inference and problem solving, i.e., where the main enterprise is to discover or use important relationships among concepts, viewing them as terminals in the representation. For example, to know that "kissing is a symbol of affection" is to relate two concepts (kissing, affection) as units. To know this requires knowledge of neither the physics of kissing nor the psychology of affection. The relationship in this case is simply a cultural convention.†

There are compelling practical advantages of the two approaches that parallel their theoretical advantages. In expansionism, one does most of

* McDermott [1976] has humorously described a potential danger of compressionists representations which forget to define their impressive looking symbols via connections to the model's inference system. Clearly, it is incumbent upon the representer to define predicates of a compressionist system by referencing them adequately from the inferencing or problem solving component!

† Of course, it is quite possible that the microstructure of the two concepts "kiss" and "affection" provide some insight into why this relationship emerged (e.g. the microstructure of kiss might suggest that it is pleasurable). But, in general, knowledge of the concepts' microstructures is useful only when we *examine,* or try to justify the relationship, but less useful when we invoke it to comprehend at a macro, inferential level, where making the kiss–affection inference is only one small step in some larger comprehension unit.

the work of model building directly in the representation, leaving the control of the system up to uniform procedures that know how to manipulate that representation (e.g., uniform pattern matchers, data base retrievers, etc.). In compressionism, on the other hand, one essentially casts the burden of representation onto an inference and deductive system. In expansionism, one expects to be dealing constantly with rather large data structures, even for simple concepts. Hence, in an expansionist model, one expects that most of the model's intelligent behavior will derive directly from the manipulation and pattern matching of large, explicit structures. In the compressionist model, on the other hand, one expects most of the intelligent behavior to derive from processes that combine existing concepts to form new concepts (inference and deduction), and therefore wants the pattern matching which precedes this synthesis to be as direct and inexpensive as possible (since it does not account directly for the model's intelligent behavior).

In other words, if one's goal is to do inference or deduction at a powerfully high level, one should use a compressionist representation. If one's goal is to reason about the similarities of concepts, one should use an expansionist representation. Both are absolutely essential to a "full-scale" model of human intelligence but in practice a researcher is generally obligated to choose between them when he focuses on a specific topic.

Story comprehension is primarily concerned with discovering relations among concepts at the macro level (e.g., inference, prediction, connecting story concepts to plot concepts). It is my belief, therefore, that a compressionist representation is indicated.

3.1. Compressionism in the Magic Grinder

What compressionism translates to in the Magic Grinder project is simply that we use information-rich predicates and small data structures, rather than information-lean predicates and large data structures. This means that the bulk of the model's content will be on the processes that map language onto some representation, and on the inferences that deal with that representation, but not on the representation *per se*.

Following this philosophy, our representation technique is to choose predicates that are

1. semantically unambiguous,
2. semantically complete (i.e., each predicate's case framework is conceptually thorough, and all slots must be filled),
3. as close as possible to the concept as it is manifest in language (yet obeying (1) and (2) above),
4. consistent with all other predicates in the model.

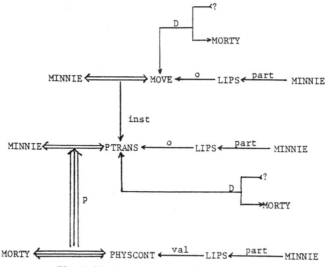

Fig. 7. Kissing in conceptual dependency.

So, for example, rather than use a conceptual dependency-like representation [Schank, 1972] of "kiss," as in "Minnie kissed Morty," that would probably take a form similar to that of Fig. 7, we will simply employ the predicate

(KISS ⟨kisser⟩ ⟨kissee⟩)

and let inferential processes decide on its significance in context (e.g., a sign of affection, a sign of derision, an attempt to be funny). (The same inferences would be required in a model that employs an expansionist representation; but in such a model, there is the additional burden of constantly pattern matching large data structures at every step.) Naturally, the concept represented by the predicate KISS might be reachable from many starting points of inference, so that sentences such as, "He pressed his lips against hers in a passionate. . . ," eventually lead to the same concept, but only after inferences keying on touching lips and passion have fired!

Figure 8 contains a representative subset of currently used predicates. Each is accompanied by its semantic case frame, excluding time and location slots (which are implied by the information's location in a separate GRIND-1 data structure that keeps track of story chronology).

To illustrate our representation, and the nature of the meaning and inference derived from the input sentences of the story, I have included as Fig. 9 the first page of story text and the associated meaning assertions (output of the SSN parser) that enter the inferential components of GRIND-1. It is to the style of representation shown in Fig. 9 that all inference and reference processes in the model are keyed.

```
(EXISTS <entity>)
(WORK-FOR <employee> <employer> <task>)
(SIT <actor> <loc>)
(DO-WORK <actor> <task>)
(GATHER <actor> <objecttype>)
(REMOVE <actor> <objecttype> <fromloc>)
(SEVER <actor> <object>)
(BRING-TO <actor> <object> <receiver> <fromloc> <toloc>)
(PLACE-UPON <actor> <object> <support>)
(SPEAK <actor> <message> <receiver>)
(REQUEST-GIVE <asker> <asked> <object>)
(SHOUT <actor> <message> <receiver>)
(LACKS <actor> <entity>)
(INTEFERES-WITH <conditon> <activity>)
(GO-TO <actor> <fromloc> <toloc>)
(EMPTY <container>)
(POSSESS <actor> <entity>)
(FAMILIAL <actor> <relative> <relation>)
(LOGICAL-CONSEQUENCE <event> <consequence>)
(WHEN <event1> <event2>)
(ANSWER-DOOR <actor> <door>)
(PEEK-AT <actor> <entity>)
(STOMACH-STATE <actor> <state>)
(WANTS <actor> <event> <time that actor wants event to occur>)
(EXCLAIM <actor> <message> <receiver>)
(LACK-AMOUNT-FOR <actor> <entity> <for what>)
(POSSESS-AMOUNT <actor> <entity> <amount>)
(EMOT-STATE <actor> <state>)
(ENABLES <condition> <event>)
(PASS-BY <actor> <entity>)
(RECEIVE-MESSAGE <actor> <message>)
(EMIT-SOUND <source> <noise>)
(THINK <actor> <thought>)
(STEP-INTO <actor> <entity>)
(LOCATION <entity> <loc>)
(MOANS <actor>)
(FALL <entity> <fromloc> <toloc>)
(NOT-EMOT-STATE <actor> <state>)
(STUCK-UNDER <entity> <object>)
(HELP-WITH <helper> <helpee> <algorithm>)
(MASS-OF <entity> <weight-tag>)
(MOVE-OBJECT <actor> <object> <fromloc> <toloc>)
(POINT-AT <actor> <entity>)
(SUPPORTED-BY <object> <support>)
(GIVE-TO <giver> <object> <receiver>)
(LISTEN-TO <actor> <sound-source>)
(TURN-HANDLE <actor> <mechanism>)
(IN-HEAD <actor> <knowledge>)
(GET-UNSTUCK <actor> <object> <algorithm>)
(UPRIGHT <entity> <loc>)
(DIG <actor> <tool> <loc>)
(LIFT <actor> <object>)
(MATERIALIZE <entity> <method>)
(STOP-ALG <actor> <algorithm>)
(CREATE <actor> <entity>)
(DONE-ALG <actor> <algorithm>)
(CAUSE <cause> <event>)
(THANKS <thanker> <thankee>)
(WAVE-BYE <waver> <wavee>)
(SPEAK-LOUD <speaker> <message> <receiver>)
(FORGET <actor> <item>)
(NOT-WANTS <actor> <item> <time not wants>)
(UNLESS <condition> <event>)
(CONTINUE <actor> <algorithm>)
(NOT-FORGET <actor> <item>)
(RUN <actor> <fromloc> <toloc>)
(SHOW <shower> <object> <actor>)
(LOOK-AT <actor> <object>)
(INQUIRE <questioner> <answerer> <queston>)
```

Fig. 8. Some compressionist predicates in GRIND-1.

4. REFERENCE

Textual references to characters and objects in the story must be connected, at both parse and inference time, with internal model symbols that
represent the model's concepts of those characters and objects. Otherwise,

```
Once there was a poor maid named Minnie.

(EXIST Gl)

    Gl:  (CLASS Gl HUMAN)
         (SEX Gl FEMALE)
         (NAME Gl MINNIE)
         (AMBIGUITY (SOCIAL-ROLE Gl DOMESTIC-MAID)
                    (SOCIAL-ROLE Gl MEDIEVAL-MAIDEN))
         (AMBIGUITY (SOCIAL-STATUS Gl MONEY-POOR)
                    (SOCIAL-STATUS Gl MISTREATED))


She worked for the greedy Lord Gurr.

(WORK-FOR Gl G2 UNKNOWN)

    G2:  (CLASS G2 HUMAN)
         (SEX G2 MALE)
         (NAME G2 GURR)
         (SOCIAL-STATUS G2 MEDIEVAL-LORD)
         (PERSONALITY G2 GREEDY)


While he sat in the shade all day, Minnie
and her nephews worked in his garden.

(CONCURRENT (SIT G2 G3) (DO-WORK G4 GARDEN-TASKS))

    G3:  (CLASS G3 XYREGION)
         (OUT-OF-DOORS G3)
         (LIGHT-INTENS LOW)

    G4:  (CLASS G4 SET)
         (MEMBERS G4 (Gl G5))

    G5:  (CLASS G5 UNDET-SET)
         (MEMBER-FEATURE G5 X
           (FAMILIAL-RELATION X Gl NEPHEW))


Minnie picked fruit and vegetables.

(GATHER Gl G6)

    G6:  (CLASS G6 UNDET-SET)
         (MEMBER-FEATURE G6 X
           (OR (CLASS X FRUIT) (CLASS X VEGETABLE)))


Morty and Ferdie pulled and cut weeds.

(REMOVE G5 G7)
(SEVER G5 G7)

    G7:  (CLASS G7 UNDET-SET)
         (MEMBER-FEATURE G7 X
           (CLASS X WEED))
```

Fig. 9. GRIND-1 representation style—the first page.

identities would be lost, plot role connections would be missed, and all the valuable associations among the characters and objects would be scrambled. Mapping textual descriptions onto model concepts is the *reference problem*, a problem that has received considerable attention in both the AI and linguistics literature (see [Nash-Webber, 1977], [Levin and Goldman, 1978], for example).

In GRIND, textual references, most typically via noun and pronoun phrases, are first converted into *descriptors*. Structurally, a GRIND descriptor has the form

$$(*D* \; \langle placeholder \rangle \; \langle feature\text{-}1 \rangle$$
$$\cdots$$
$$\langle feature\text{-}n \rangle)$$

where each $\langle feature \rangle$ describes one conceptual aspect of some model concept whose identification is sought. For example, the noun phrase "a poor maid named Minnie" results in the GRIND-1 descriptor

```
(*D* X (NAME X MINNIE)
     (CLASS X HUMAN)
     (SEX X FEMALE)
     (AMBIGUITY (SOCIAL-ROLE X MEDIEVAL-MAIDEN)
                (SOCIAL-ROLE X DOMESTIC-MAID))
     (AMBIGUITY (SOCIAL-STATUS X MISTREATED)
                (FINANCIAL-STATUS X POOR)))
```

and, in the next sentence of the story, "she" is represented by the descriptor*

```
(*D* X (CLASS X HUMAN)
     (SEX X FEMALE)).
```

Generally, a descriptor will reflect all the information present directly in the textual reference, as well as information that can be supplied by immediate language-based inference provided by the sense net experts as by-products of the parse.

Descriptors are constructed during sense net application, with noun, pronoun, and adjective sense nets playing central roles in their construction. To illustrate, when the SSN parser runs on the sentence containing the phrase "a poor maid named Minnie," the MAID network contributes two relatively certain features, namely (CLASS X HUMAN) and (SEX X FEMALE), to the descriptor under assembly in the parse workspace to represent "a poor maid." Then, unable to discriminate between two senses of "maid" in the context at that point (this is the first line of the story), the MAID network contributes the additional feature†

```
(AMBIGUITY (SOCIAL-ROLE X MEDIEVAL-MAIDEN)
           (SOCIAL-ROLE X DOMESTIC-MAID))
```

* More properly, this would be (CLASS X ANIMATE), rather than HUMAN. We use this form only for simplicity in the current model.

† MEDIEVAL-MAIDEN and DOMESTIC-MAID are concepts that occur in stereotypical world knowledge. Thus, when a connection is made from Minnie to one or the other of these, additional information about Minnie, derived from stereotypes, will become available. This is described shortly.

to the evolving descriptor representing this phrase (and associated with a bin in the SSN parser's workspace). When the POOR sense net is run, it is likewise unable to discriminate between two senses of "poor" in the current context, and hence contributes

$$\text{(AMBIGUITY (SOCIAL-STATUS } X \text{ MISTREATED)}$$
$$\text{(FINANCIAL-STATUS } X \text{ POOR))}$$

to the descriptor. When the NAME network (associated with the right-neighboring bin in the parse workspace representing the word "named") runs, it decides that "named Minnie" belongs with the descriptor being constructed for the entity represented by the entity to the immediate left. (This decision results from the NAME network realizing that it is occurring in past tense form, "named," with a construction representing an animate concept to its left, a construction that could be a proper noun to its right.) It thus adds the feature (NAME X MINNIE) by looking to its right neighboring bin to get MINNIE, then suppresses the "Minnie" bin and sends the newly built feature to its left neighbor's descriptor. The resulting descriptor is the one already shown above.

4.1. Reference Conversion

Descriptors form the input to the GRIND-1 reference mechanism, the process that locates model concepts as candidates for a given descriptor. From each input descriptor, the reference mechanism will either create a new model concept or identify an existing model concept. Creation is usually suggested by an indefinite textual reference ("a poor maid," "some shovels"), whereas identification is generally suggested by definite textual references ("the magic grinder," "the vegetables," "Minnie," "she").

4.1.1. Identification

When reference identification, as opposed to creation, is suggested by a definite article, the reference system attempts to locate all model concepts that match the descriptor, hopefully exactly one. If the model had perfect information at every point, this would amount simply to retrieving all model concepts lying in the intersection of the features. However, since the model seldom has perfect information (and never knows whether or not it does anyway), reference is a rather subtle topic, even after language has been reduced to a descriptor.

Our present referent identifier functions in the following way (Fig. 10). The list of descriptive features is scanned from the beginning, using each feature in turn as a candidate fetcher. This process stops at the first feature that successfully locates a nonempty candidate set. In case no feature can locate a nonempty candidate set, the identification fails, and a new model token is created to represent the descriptor. Otherwise, the candidates so located form a starting set of possible referents.

At that point, each candidate is examined in turn. For each candidate, starting with the first descriptor feature again, each descriptor feature is applied to the candidate. This results in one of three possible outcomes:

1. the candidate explicitly satisfies the feature;
2. the candidate is not compatible with the feature;
3. it cannot be determined whether or not the feature is compatible with the candidate.

Whenever case 2 applies, the candidate is immediately dropped from consideration, and the next candidate is examined. Whenever case 1 applies, the examination of the candidate successfully proceeds to the next descriptor feature. When case 3 applies, the examination proceeds to the next feature but a note is made that, if this candidate were to be adopted, the current feature would be a new piece of information. At the end of this process, survivor candidates (if any) will remain, each with annotations about the new information that would have to be incorporated if it were adopted. (If there are no survivors, a new model concept is created.)

The candidate that requires the introduction of the smallest amount of new information is then adopted. Each reference identification is explicitly noted as an event of potential significance to the model. This occurs via an assertion made into GRIND-1's data base of the form:

(REF-DECISION ⟨original descriptor⟩ ⟨adopted referent⟩
⟨story point⟩ ⟨other annotated candidates⟩).

We thus have a four-part record of the identification event recording the original descriptor, the chosen referent, a pointer to a point in GRIND-1's chronological story line (not described in this article), and the other candidates that were considered. As with all data base assertions, reference decisions come to be linked into GRIND-1's dependency network (to be described in a future report), a structure of pointers that makes explicit all logical dependencies among model decisions, facts and inferences generated or acquired during comprehension.* In case there is a tie among several candidates, their common features are extracted by an intersection algorithm, a new stop-gap token is created to represent the referent, and a note of the unsolved reference is made on a central list.†

Our algorithm for reference identification is far from complete but it embodies two natural principles: follow the path of least resistance, and do not falter on new information. The first principle guides the final selection

---

* Such a structure is vital when GRIND-1 must alter a decision, or when it discovers contradictory facts and must unravel parts of its reasoning sequences.
† This technique is described in more detail in Rieger [1974].

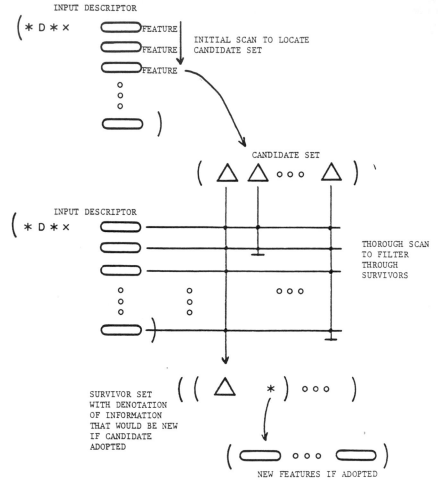

Fig. 10. Basic referent identification technique.

to the candidate requiring the fewest number of new model assumptions. The second principle, reflected in the initial candidate-locating scan, tolerates new information in descriptions of existing model concepts.

In practice, we are finding this reference strategy to be adequate for the simple reference requirements in the Magic Grinder. Fauser [1978] has recently suggested some interesting techniques that we will be incorporating in a more powerful reference mechanism.

4.2. GRIND-1's Deductive Component

In applying features to prospective candidates, the reference identifier calls GRIND-1's deductive component. Although this component is also a topic of a subsequent report, a brief description is included here.

GRIND-1 deductive strategies are separated into two groups, the global strategists and the specialists. The global strategists embody structural and semantic knowledge,* whereas the specialist strategies encode specific, domain-dependent rules of deduction. The deductive component is called via (DEDUCE ⟨pattern⟩ ⟨energy⟩), and returns one of three responses (at least for fully constant patterns, as required by the reference identifier): (1) YES, ⟨pattern⟩ is either explicitly believed or deducible, (2) NO, ⟨pattern⟩ is explicitly or deducibly false, or (3) DONT-KNOW, ⟨pattern⟩ cannot be determined to be either true or false, within the alotted energy budget. Energy is measured in terms of data base fetches, as demanded by various applicable deductive strategies. (It currently has no actual influence on deduction, since GRIND-1's deductive knowledge is sparse enough to result in quick terminations without any imposed limit!)

4.3. Referent Creation

Model referents are created either when suggested by an indefinite reference, or when the reference identifier fails to turn up a satisfactory model token. In creating a model token from a descriptor, a unique symbol is acquired, then each feature in the descriptor is asserted for the new symbol. Asserting a feature amounts to posting it on the top-level channel where inferential processes can have a chance to react to it.

A record of each model referent creation is made and linked into the dependency network in a fashion similar to that of REF-DECISIONS. The newly-created token is then passed through three higher levels of processing: the *flesher*, the *stereotyper* and the plot level *role connector* (Fig. 11). The basic idea behind these three processes is that new tokens must not be permitted to creep into the model without active scrutiny for possible plot-level role connections.

4.3.1. *The Flesher*

The flesher first types the new token with respect to its class membership in GRIND-1's semantic hierarchy, locating all superordinate concepts. (In the case of the new token for Minnie, for example, the hierarchy is (HUMAN ANIMATE PHYSOBJ THING).) Each concept in the semantic hierarchy has associated with it a set of features which are of sufficient significance to warrant seeking if they are not already explicitly known. These concepts are essentially frames (see, for example, Minsky [1975], Bobrow and Winograd [1977]), which define the knowledge about an entity

---

* There are six global strategists in the current model: symmetric predicate strategist, synonymous predicates strategist, antonymous predicates strategist, mutual exclusion strategist, negation strategist, and class inheritance strategist. The specialist strategies are organized into discrimination net structures keyed to individual meaning predicates. There are currently only a handful of specialists, as required to meet GRIND-1's needs in the first segment of the story.

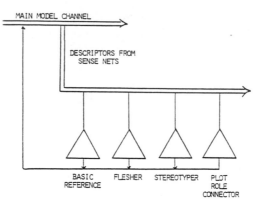

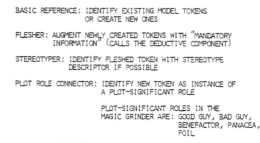

BASIC REFERENCE: IDENTIFY EXISTING MODEL TOKENS
OR CREATE NEW ONES

FLESHER: AUGMENT NEWLY CREATED TOKENS WITH "MANDATORY
INFORMATION" (CALLS THE DEDUCTIVE COMPONENT)

STEREOTYPER: IDENTIFY FLESHED TOKEN WITH STEREOTYPE
DESCRIPTOR IF POSSIBLE

PLOT ROLE CONNECTOR: IDENTIFY NEW TOKEN AS INSTANCE OF
A PLOT-SIGNIFICANT ROLE

PLOT-SIGNIFICANT ROLES IN THE
MAGIC GRINDER ARE: GOOD GUY, BAD GUY,
BENEFACTOR, PANACEA,
FOIL

Fig. 11. GRIND-1 reference hierarchy.

necessary to comprehend that entity fully. In the case of a human, for example, GRIND-1 is conditioned to believe that NAME, AGE, and SEX* are essential features of any newly introduced entity which is a HUMAN. Using this information, the flesher attempts to deduce any features not already explicitly present. Successful results are asserted on the main channel, and augment the new token. Unsuccessful results are sent to a global holding list for future action. (At present, no future processing occurs. However, this list of unanswered questions will eventually serve as a source of motivation in subsequent deduction and inference.)

4.3.2. The Stereotyper

After "fleshing," a new concept is passed through the stereotyper. The purpose of the stereotyper is to identify each newly identified token as an instance of a stereotype. Although all new tokens pass through this phase, the most interesting and useful stereotypes are those describing characters. For example, the model ought to be able to spot Lord Gurr as an evil

---

* These particular features are not necessarily advocated as complete or correct!

landlord, Minnie as a gentle, naive person. Making such identifications permits the new token to inherit potentially quite valuable, near-plot-level information, enhancing the chances of making relevant inferences and predictions about that character at a level that connects with the plot line.

The stereotyper is basically a best-fit match process. Stereotypes are represented by descriptor-like units that name the salient features of the stereotype. Any stereotype connections resulting from this step come to be associated with the new token by altering the token's class membership to point at the stereotype rather than the basic concept.*

4.3.3. The Plot Role Connector

The final phase of token creation, plot role connection, attempts to determine whether the new token can fill any plot-level roles not already satisfactorily filled. We presently believe that a plot-level role is best represented by a two-component description: a "personality trait profile" (described below), and an arbitrary function of one argument, a *role connector function*.

Initially, GRIND-1 is supplied with a list of plot role descriptions that correspond to expected participants in the story.† Each plot role connector function is capable of running on an arbitrary model concept passed to it from another part of the model. The result of applying a plot role function to a memory token is a yes–no–maybe decision about whether or not that token realizes the plot role. Internally, the plot role function is free to perform any computations necessary in making this decision.‡

There are three possible outcomes of a plot role connection attempt:

1. a definite connection is made;
2. no connection is made but the new token is of an interesting class, warranting further attempts;
3. no connection is made and the new token is probably not significant at the plot level.

---

* Stereotypes in GRIND-1 are similar in concept to KRL-0 specializations.

† The plot-significant roles in the Magic Grinder plot are "the good guy," "the bad guy," "the benefactor," "the foil," and "the panacea." Incidentally, these seem to be the same ones required for Cinderella and Snow White.

‡ Having to include an arbitrary procedural component in plot role descriptions stems from our present lack of understanding of abstract plot-level story representation. Plot roles need to be very loosely stated (e.g., "the good guy," "the bad guy," "the foil"). Declarative representations work adequately for basic reference and stereotype identification, since these levels deal with somewhat less abstract descriptions. Determining whether or not someone is good or bad, however, seems to call for more elaborate heuristic strategies (i.e., inference). For example, the bad guy is the one who does mean things, shouts menacingly, is greedy (or, in Walt Disney stories, one who exhibits *any* overtly negative characteristics), and so forth. In other words, the sources of evidence leading up to an identification of the bad guy can be quite diverse, and hence difficult to capture in reasonable declarative formats.

In the first case, an explicit assertion associating the new token with the plot role is made, e.g.,

(PLOT-LEVEL-GOOD-GUY ⟨Minnie's token⟩).

Here, PLOT-LEVEL-GOOD-GUY is simply the name of the connected plot role. A successful role connection will generally open a new realm of inferences for the connected character, permitting plot-driven predictions to diffuse through the model along with other lower-level inferences.

5. INFERENCE AND INFERENCE CONDITIONING

Inference is perhaps the most interesting aspect of story comprehension. It is the process that connects story events to model concepts and, via such connections, story events to other story events. The composite of such connections made during the reading of the story is the measurable product of story comprehension.

The language and reference systems of GRIND-1 make implicit inferences during the course of word sense discrimination and during the course of identifying model referents from textual references. In the case of word sense experts, most of the inferences are encoded implicitly in the structure and content of the sense nets, and are reflected indirectly in the form of commitments the system makes about word senses. We think of these implicit inferences as primarily language based, in that it is their job to extract meaning from the input text.

While the inferences and decisions made during parsing and reference are of considerable importance, they are not what one normally thinks of as the primary inferential component of a story comprehender. Instead, the inferences that occur *after* the system is reasonably certain of sentence meaning (e.g., the ones that build character models, predict actions, connect story events to the story plot) are the types of inference one normally thinks of as primary to comprehension. I will refer to these language-free inferences as *model inferences*.

In GRIND-1 we identify four tasks for model inferences:

1. to build single-character models for each story character, resulting in single-character *personality trait profiles;*
2. to build two-character interaction models, based on explicit and inferred power relationships (along various dimensions) between each pair of characters;
3. to generate relatively local inferences about actions: their causes, effects, and short-term predictions about them;
4. to connect characters and story events to plot roles and plot segments, respectively, via longer-term predictions.

I will refer to these four types of inference, respectively, as:

trait inferences;
interaction inferences;
algorithmic inferences;
plot inferences.

These four categories of inference comprise GRIND-1's theory of nonlinguistic inference, and are the topics of the following sections.*

5.1. Inferences about Character Personalities

Story comprehension is, to a great extent, a matter of understanding the story characters: their personalities, relationships, and problems. Because of this, we have emphasized single- and double-character modeling as important components in GRIND-1. In doing so, we have constructed a theory of character modeling based primarily on two concepts: *behavioral tags*, and *interaction patterns*. The global purpose of this modeling is to provide a mechanism for conditioning inferences and predictions in a way that reflects an awareness of both situation dynamics, and story character personalities. The following sections present our ideas about character modeling and its role in inference conditioning.

5.2. Behavioral Tags and Personality Trait Profiles

The basic organization of character models is as follows (Fig. 12). Each character's personality is defined via a collection of behavioral tags. Behavioral tags are in turn defined by pointers to interaction patterns which illustrate the tag. Since the purpose of interaction patterns is to spell out likely consequences of story events involving one or more characters, the trigger conditions of interaction patterns will be sensitive to both characters' personality traits and to story situations. The right-hand sides of interaction patterns are predictions. The most relevant interaction patterns will be dynamically promoted as more behavioral tags are associated with each character, resulting in a gradual conditioning of the model's prediction system.

5.2.1. Basic Behavioral Tags

Basic behavioral tags are objects which can be attached to model concepts for story characters. They roughly correspond to adjectival concepts used in everyday language to describe humans: GREEDY, MEEK, LAZY,

---

* With the exception of algorithmic inference, already described in considerable detail in Rieger [1976a,b]. In the following discussion of these categories of inference, I will use the term "inference" to describe information generated about the present or past (with respect to the "now" of the story), and the term "prediction" to refer to the future of the story "now."

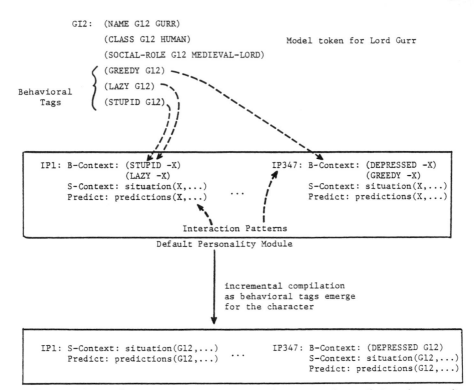

GI2:   (NAME G12 GURR)

       (CLASS G12 HUMAN)   Model token for Lord Gurr

       (SOCIAL-ROLE G12 MEDIEVAL-LORD)

       (GREEDY G12)

Behavioral   (LAZY G12)

   Tags   (STUPID G12)

IP1: B-Context: (STUPID -X)   IP347: B-Context: (DEPRESSED -X)
                 (LAZY -X)   (GREEDY -X)
      S-Context: situation(X,...)   ...   S-Context: situation(X,...)
      Predict: predictions(X,...)   Predict: predictions(X,...)

                           Interaction Patterns
                      Default Personality Module

                      incremental compilation
                      as behavioral tags emerge
                      for the character

IP1: S-Context: situation(G12,...)   IP347: B-Context: (DEPRESSED G12)
      Predict: predictions(G12,...)   ...   S-Context: situation(G12,...)
                                                        Predict: predictions(G12,...)

Fig. 12. Behavioral tags, interaction patterns, and incremental compilation of personality modules.

HONEST, and so forth. Each basic behavioral tag is defined as a collection of pointers to *interaction patterns*. Interaction patterns are encoded in a production rule style, having a collection of conditions as left-hand side, and a collection of predictions as right-hand side. The left-hand side conditions are further divided into two parts: a *behavioral context*, and a *situational context*. The behavioral context will make reference to behavioral tags (i.e., personality traits of characters), while the situational context will identify a set of story conditions. One of the interaction patterns attached to the basic behavioral tag SELFISH is shown in Fig. 13.

Semantically, each interaction pattern contributes to the definition of a basic behavioral tag by describing, in schematic terms, a situation in which the behavioral tag would be illustrated. The contribution of the interaction pattern of Fig. 13 to the definition of the basic behavioral tag SELFISH is to say that a SELFISH person who possesses an object someone else needs might keep it to himself solely because of his belief that the other person needs it.

The collection of interaction patterns attached to each basic behavioral tag therefore form the composite definition of the tag by describing nu-

```
Behavioral Context:  (SELFISH -X)

Situational Context: (POSSESS -X -OBJ)
                     (NEEDS -Y -OBJ -TASK)
                     (KNOWS -X (NEEDS -Y -OBJ -TASK))
                     (NOT NEED -X -Y -TASK1)
                     (REQUEST-GIVE -Y -X -Y -OBJ)
                     (KNOWS -X (REQUEST-GIVE -Y -X -Y -OBJ))

       Predictions:  (DENY-REQUEST -X (REQUEST-GIVE -Y -X -Y -OBJ))
```

Fig. 13. One of many interaction patterns for the behavioral tag SELFISH.

merous distinct schematic situations in which the tag would be illustrated.* A basic behavioral tag will typically require a number of interaction patterns to capture the underlying concept.

5.2.2. Inference Conditioning

From an operational point of view, basic behavioral tags, and hence personality trait profiles can be invoked in two directions:

1.   given that a basic behavioral tag has been associated with a character, to help predict how that character might behave in schematic situations;

2.   given that a basic behavioral tag has not yet been associated with a
character, to infer such an association on the basis of story events,
wherein the character behaves in ways that fully or partially match one or
more of the schematic situations in the tag's composite definition.

Use of basic behavioral tags in the first direction results in relatively
long-term inference conditioning in the following manner. Whenever a
basic behavioral tag is added to a character's personality trait profile,
GRIND-1 collects all the tag's defining interaction patterns, instantiates
them with respect to the newly tagged character, and deposits them in the
character's *personality module*. A character's personality module is therefore a reflection of the character's personality trait profile as a collection of
reactive interaction patterns tailored to (instantiated with respect to) the
character. Personality modules are one important source of dynamically-
conditioned predictions in GRIND-1.

5.2.3. Transient Behavioral Tags and the Default Personality Module

As each character token is introduced by the reference mechanism, a default personality module, the *basic behavioral module* is associated with it.
This default module consists only of the interaction patterns associated
with *transient behavioral tags*. A transient behavioral tag, while repre-

* This reflects the philosophy: Define by Illustration. This is the only reasonable approach
we can see in defining such amorphous concepts as GREED, SELFISHNESS, etc.

sented in the same format as basic behavioral tags, is temporal, representing transient states of characters: anger, sadness, joy, and so forth. Collectively, the purpose of the default personality module's interaction patterns
is to define nominal human behavior in terms of responses to emotional
transients. If and when *basic* behavioral tags emerge for the character, the
superposition of the basic tags on the default personality module refines
the module by masking some of its interaction patterns, and promoting
others. We think of the resulting personality module as having been conditioned in the long term by basic behavioral tags, yet modulated in the
short term by transient tags that are attached and detached from characters
as the story unfolds.

To illustrate, some (small) subset of the default personality module contains references to the transient behavioral tag ANGRY. This subset cumulatively defines the notion of anger. When a character is introduced by
the referent creator, the default personality module is attached to that
character. If we next learn that the new character is MEEK, the default personality module is altered, deleting any interaction patterns that make reference to behavioral tags which are incompatible with MEEK. (There is a
compatibility table for behavioral tags.) Even after only one conditioning,
the personality module will be quite a bit different from the one that
ASSERTIVE would have produced. That is, the expected behavior of a
person who is angry will vary according to what is currently known in the
character's personality trait profile: an ANGRY, MEEK character might in-
ternalize the ANGER, whereas an ANGRY, ASSERTIVE person might ex-
ternalize it. In the absence of basic behavioral tags, only general (often
multiple) predictions can be generated from the interaction patterns in the
default personality module. However, as basic tags begin to emerge for
each character, the default module can be refined by prunning out inap-
plicable patterns.

5.2.4. *Identification of Basic Tags*

Basic behavioral tags for a character emerge from three sources:

1.   observed and inferred story events;
2.   plot role descriptions;
3.   direct adjectives in the text.

The third source is an obvious one and easy to handle. For example, in the
second line of the Magic Grinder, we are told that Lord Gurr is greedy:
"She worked for the greedy Lord Gurr." Plot-based behavioral tags, the
second source above, come free from plot roles as various story characters
are identified as plot role fillers. (Lord Gurr inherits all the characteristic
Disney basic behavioral tags as soon as he is connected into the BAD-GUY
plot role.)

The first of these three sources, in which behavioral tags emerge from observed and inferred story events, demands a reverse use of interaction patterns. The mechanism of this reverse use is as follows. Our implementation of productions (demons) permits the maintenance of partially activated interaction patterns. Partial activation refers to the remembering of patterns whose left- or right-hand sides have been partially fulfilled by story events and inferences. For the purpose of inducing behavioral tags from story events and inferences, it is the right-hand side of interaction patterns that is of interest. As the system discovers behavior that partially or fully matches the right-hand side of interaction patterns, it continually makes and refines hypotheses about possible behavioral tags for each character. For example, if the story tells us that when an ANGRY character shouted at another character, and the other character shouted back, the interaction pattern that includes references to ANGRY(x), SHOUTING-AT(x, y) and ASSERTIVE(y) on the left-hand side, and a reference to SHOUT-AT(y, x) on the right-hand side, is partially or fully matched, providing supportive evidence for believing that the person shouted at is ASSERTIVE.

5.3. Two-Character Relationships

An important task in the comprehension of most stories is to understand relationships among the story characters. Specifically, a knowledge of each *pair* of intercharacter relationships is of immense importance to prediction and inference, and to inference conditioning. Suppose, for example, we believe that Gurr is physically, socially, and financially superior to Minnie, and that Minnie is intellectually superior to Gurr. When combined with single-character models, e.g., Gurr is GREEDY, LAZY, MEAN, Minnie is MEEK, GENTLE, KIND, this information can be quite powerful to a human comprehender in understanding interactions between each pair of characters. For example, if Minnie needs something that Gurr possesses, and asks him for it, we have a fairly clear idea of what to expect and (conversely) what would surprise us. If Gurr growls and slams the door, he is acting on schedule; if he smiles and hands over the item with no fuss, we are suspicious. Naturally, our "clear" picture concerning the nature of possible interactions between these two characters can be only schematic. The picture we form does not require fabrication of new inferences but, rather, the selection of the appropriate subset of existing ones.

5.3.1. Two-character Power Table

The personality modules gradually build up for each character as basic behavioral tags emerge are further conditioned by two-character modeling. In formulating two-character relationships, we think in terms of a two-character *power table*. The power table describes a set of relatively fixed relationships demanded by the structure of the table. We presently use five power relations: PHYSICAL-STATURE, INTELLECTUAL-STATURE, MATERIAL-STATURE, SOCIAL-STATURE, and FAMILIAL-SATURE. Although we think in terms of a "power table," where the rows correspond to the characters and the columns to these five relationships (Fig. 14), the information is in fact represented as a collection of data base assertions of the form

⟨⟨relationship⟩ ⟨character-1⟩ ⟨character-2⟩ ⟨value⟩⟩.

Here, ⟨value⟩ assumes one of four values: GREATER, LESS, EQUAL, and UNKNOWN. The point of thinking in terms of the power table is that it is important in theory to understand all relationships between every pair of characters. Because of this importance, one of the reference mechanism's tasks when a new character is discovered is to "fill in the power table" or, at least, to post background model goals for filling in the power table.

Two-character power relations are important for the same reasons personality trait profiles for individual characters are: they refine the person-

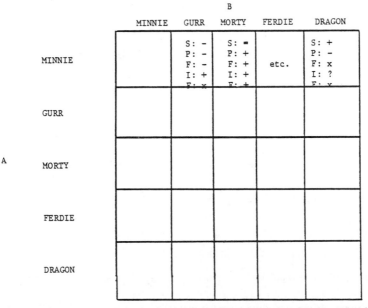

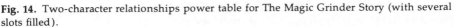

Fig. 14. Two-character relationships power table for The Magic Grinder Story (with several slots filled).

ality modules of individual characters by the same type of masking/promotion arrangement as for behavioral tags. To illustrate, a typical default interaction pattern relating to the transient behavioral tag ANGRY is

Behavioral Context:	(ANGRY X)
	(ASSERTIVE X)
	(MEEK Y)
	(SOCIAL-STATURE X Y GREATER)
Situational Context:	(NEEDS Y PHYSOBJ)
	(POSSESS X PHYSOBJ)
	(REQUEST-GIVE Y X PHYSOBJ)
Interaction Prediction:	(SHOUT-AT X Y)
	(DENY X Y PHYSOBJ).

If X is Lord Gurr, Y is Minnie, and we already know that Lord Gurr is assertive and Minnie is meek, then this interaction pattern will appear in the personality modules for both Minnie and Lord Gurr. That is it will have been "compiled" into the simpler form

Behavioral Context:	(ANGRY LORD-GURR)
	(SOCIAL-STATURE LORD-GURR MINNIE GREATER)
Situational Context:	(NEEDS MINNIE PHYSOBJ)
	(POSSES LORD-GURR PHYSOBJ)
	(REQUEST-GIVE MINNIE LORD-GURR PHYSOBJ)
Interaction Prediction:	(SHOUT-AT LORD-GURR MINNIE)
	(DENY LORD-GURR MINNIE PHYSOBJ).

Of course, there will in general be other competing interaction patterns in the current personality modules for Lord Gurr and Minnie. Some of these will reflect the same transient and fixed behavioral tag knowledge, but require different two-character power relations. Therefore, when we factor in knowledge about the physical and social superiority of Lord Gurr, some of the competing interaction patterns will drop out, some (this one being an example) will remain in further compiled form:

Behavioral Context:	(ANGRY LORD-GURR)
Situational Context:	(NEEDS MINNIE PHYSOBJ)
	(POSSESS LORD-GURR PHYSOBJ)
	(REQUEST-GIVE MINNIE LORD-GURR PHYSOBJ)
Interaction Prediction:	(SHOUT-AT LORD-GURR MINNIE)
	(DENY LORD-GURR MINNIE PHYSOBJ)

5.4. Why Bother?

The art of writing good interaction patterns will involve finding the correct level of generality at which to express knowledge about humans and human interaction. While the example above is typical of the patterns we are writing for GRIND-1, it is not yet clear that this is the correct level of abstraction. Obviously, if the system has too many patterns at this level of specificity, personality modules become costly to construct and expensive to store. Yet the basic tenet—that context-conditionable interaction patterns at some level of generality are a basic source of comprehension focus—seems inescapable. For, without some sort of constant inference conditioning (specifically, predictive inference conditioning via incremental compilation of personality modules), the system would always be a single-stratum mass of general rules about human behavior. Since (by definition) one of the primary phenomena of comprehension (and one by which it is relatively easy to gauge success of a comprehension model) is a prediction-fulfillment feedback cycle, it follows that a system with no *a priori* reasons to prefer one mode of character interaction over another will be incapable of accurate prediction, and, hence, of "accurate comprehension."

6. PREDICTIONS AND PATTERN MATCHING

The success of any cognitive model eventually devolves onto the success of its pattern matching. (This is a nearly tautological statement, of course, since it is easy to regard almost all computation in any model as some sort of pattern matching!) In story comprehension, for example, inference, reference, prediction, plot following, and character interaction modeling all are instances of pattern matching. However, one tends to associate different issues with each variety of pattern matching, and this leads to different intuitive feelings about the criticality of each variety.

I like to think in terms of two generic classes of pattern matching: *source* matching and *sink* matching. Source matching can be thought of as inference, in which the point is to produce conjectures about what is happening in the story. The patterns for source matching generally come from the left-hand sides of inference rules or from cause–effect patterns describing the world [Rieger, 1976a]. Source matching is part of a system's generative component. *Sink* matching, on the other hand, is the matching demanded by potential consumers of the information generated by the source matching processes. It is the matching that makes the connections between the hypothetical world of the model's producers, and the real world of the story text. Plot following, reference identification, and prediction fulfillment are examples of sink pattern matching.*

---

* The distinction between source and sink pattern matching is similar to the "antecedent vs. consequent" distinction in problem solving systems. The fundamental problem is to find a balance between the quantity of unsolicited inferential knowledge generated, and the comprehension needs of the potential consumers of that knowledge. In problem solving, the consumers are problem solving strategy experts; in story comprehension, they are inferences about characters' motives, plot role connections, and so forth.

The set of issues for source matching components and sink matching components of a system are somewhat different. Source matching components must deal with potentially vast combinatorial problems, e.g., the set of inferences generated from each input must be restricted in some way (say, by context conditioning). This is precisely the issue addressed by the interaction pattern conditioning I have described. Without the context-restricting influence of the character modelling, too many inferences would remain relevant too much of the time. The issue in source matching, therefore, is not so much *how* to generate information but, more, how to restrain a potentially overly prolific generative reflex. The adequacy of source matching will be closely related to the adequacy of the particular theory of knowledge it represents. It is somewhat less closely related to the absolute powers of the pattern matcher.

Sink matching is quite different. Since the point of sink matching is to make connections (e.g., between interaction predictions and subsequent story events), sink matching is sensitive to *two* input patterns rather than the one of source matching. (I am speaking conceptually here.) The issue in sink matching therefore is not how to restrict the generation of new patterns from an input pattern but how to seek out possible connections between two given patterns (e.g., a prediction and a subsequent story event or two inferences). Intuitively, the adequacy of sink pattern matching is less related to the adequacy of the theory of knowledge used in the system, and more related to abstract, pattern matching and deductive powers.*

To illustrate the problems of sink matching in the Magic Grinder, consider the following typical demand on the sink matcher. A plot-level prediction that is unmasked in the last plot step is that the bad guy suffers some sort of negative change. Although it is perhaps possible at the time this prediction is unmasked to refine it somewhat (e.g., that his negative change will somehow relate to his unrightful possession of the magic grinder), the prediction must be maintained in a reasonably general form since the number of ways to suffer a negative change is categorically large (e.g., physical, emotional, financial, etc.) and infinite in potential realizations. (Worse, what constitutes a negative change in one context might have a completely different interpretation in another context.) As it turns out, Lord Gurr finds himself buried under a mound of ice cream . . . hardly something that would occur to the reader *ab initio* as a realization of a negative change!

The problem in this example (and this is typical of sink matching

---

* The relative importance of source vs. sink matching probably varies with the domain. Lenat [1976], for example, relied on a powerful heuristic source matching component in his theory of mathematical discovery. I suspect that story comprehension will rely somewhat more on sink matching than this domain, since comprehension is less a process of discovery and more a process of relating new instances of known patterns to those patterns.

problems), then, is to answer the question: Do the patterns (I will finesse the representations here)

(BURIED-UNDER [LORD GURR] [MOUND OF ICE CREAM])
(NEGCHANGE [LORD GURR])

match? Clearly, some fairly subtle questions arise (is he enjoying it?), and must be posed by the sink matcher or some expert deductive strategist the sink matcher knows to call.

The problems of sink matching in a story comprehender seem to converge on one issue: How much work should be done by source matching components versus how much work should be left to the sink matching. The two ends of the spectrum of possible paradigms are:

1.   rely on a prolific source matching component that produces large, but flabby (in the sense that there is much wasted inference) targets for a relatively simple sink matcher;
2.   rely on a powerful sink matcher that is fed by small, concise clusters of output inference and prediction from a more constrained source matching component.

These ideas are expressed abstractly in Fig. 15.

Beyond this decision, there is the question of how to implement the sink matcher: should the sink matcher be reflexive (passive, demon-like) or purposive (goal directed)? In the former case, the prediction set would be implemented as a collection of trigger patterns capable of matching story events and firing at appropriate moments to make connections between those events and predictions. (This was essentially Charniak's strategy [Charniak, 1972].) With this design, one is left with the problem of deciding how exhaustive the trigger patterns should be. In my opinion, any passive system that ultimately relies on "direct hits" (e.g., the LISP function EQ tests in the limit) to trigger important predictions is doomed to failure, regardless of how exhaustive the trigger patterns are. There will always be near misses that escape a passive prediction/fulfillment scheme. Also, there is no ultimate remedy for the problem since, even though there may very well be expertise in the system for massaging the near miss into a hit, there is no way in a passive system of knowing to try to invoke that expertise. An important prediction pattern may simply never fire and a piece of the comprehension is lost.

In the second scheme, sink matching is a methodical, more "conscious" process, implementable in either of two forms. In the first form, as each new story event or story inference emerges, the prediction set is actively scanned, systematically calling the sink matcher once for each prediction in the current prediction set to determine which prediction patterns, if

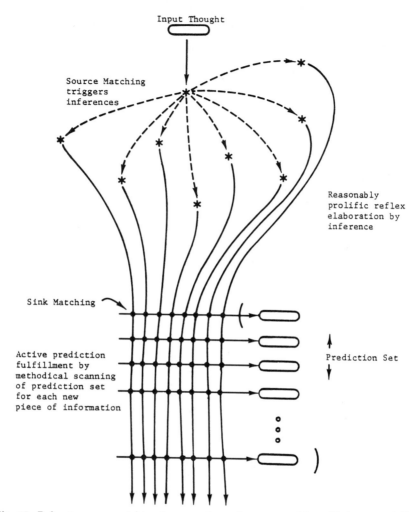

Fig. 15. Robust source matching to generate moderate quantities of inferences, followed by active sink matching.

any, match each newly produced piece of information from the source matcher.

In the second form, predictions are encoded as procedural experts who, when run, invoke both special-case knowledge as well as the powers of the general sink matcher to determine of an input whether or not it matches the prediction the procedure encodes. Fulfillment in this setting would amount to essentially the same methodical scanning (more properly, running) of the prediction set for each new input. (To "scan" a procedurally encoded prediction is to invoke the procedure, allowing it to decide whether or not it matches the input.)

I believe the correct mixture of strategies is the following:

1.   rely on a moderately prolific source matching component to generate reasonably large "spheres" of inference from each input;*
2.   implement an active, goal-directed sink matcher that scans a mixed prediction set of both declaratively and procedurally encoded predictions for each new input.

I am convinced of the importance of an active fulfillment mechanism because I see no other way of minimizing the near miss problem. With an agent in the system that is responsible for actively calling the sink matcher methodically to compare each new input to the model (factual, from the text, or inferential, from other parts of the model) against each prediction to seek out matches, most problems are at least focussed onto a central mechanism: a two-input matcher that can rely on abstract pattern matching and deductive techniques.

7.   SUMMARY AND CONCLUSION

I have outlined what our group perceives to be the main issues of full-scale story comprehension model architecture. I hope the five main points of the five sections have come across.

1.   Language analysis is best done by collections of relatively autonomous word sense experts who are assembled together on demand from each input utterance or sentence, and who probe all levels of the comprehension model in arriving at identifications of word senses (and hence of utterance or sentence meaning) in context.
2.   Meaning representation for a inferentially complex tasks is best done using a compressionist technique, in which concise, information-rich predicates with thorough case frameworks are used instead of larger graph structures built from information-lean "primitives;" relationships among concepts should be expressed more by inference patterns than by the representation of concepts themselves.
3.   Reference, and specifically referent creation, should be an active process that passes each newly created token through a hierarchy of pattern matching that culminates in attempts to connect the token to plot roles; model referents must not be allowed to creep into the comprehender without considerable scrutiny.
4.   Building and maintaining personality models of the characters in the story, and two-character relationship models between each pair of characters is vital for inference and prediction conditioning; incrementally compilable interaction patterns which model each character via personal-

---

* I have held this point of view since [Rieger 1974].

ity modules can be a major source of event-level and plot-level prediction conditioning.

5. Prediction fulfillment must be based on a sink pattern matching paradigm which actively rescans the prediction set each time a new fact or belief enters the model or is generated by the model's inferential component; passive prediction fulfillment schemes will fail because of near misses; source matching (the model's inferential component) should be fairly copious, elaborating each story event with inference to enhance the prediction fulfillment mechanism's chances for successful hits.

Although Salazar [1977] has produced a nice hand analysis of the first third of the Magic Grinder's plot by illustrating sequences of inferences that are required to connect the story events to plot segments, we still do not have a clear picture of plot representation, something we will need before the model can be fully tied together. Likewise, we do not have a clear idea of the requirements for the complexity of the sink pattern matcher. Our model presently relies considerably on the human to answer questions of the form: Does pattern X match pattern Y?," where "match" really means, "Does one pattern follow from another in the current context?," or, "Are the patterns part of the same, or related, larger patterns?"

Though we do not understand many of the problems yet, we are convinced that our methodology of studying one story from beginning to end is the only possible one for learning about story comprehension. Since we are attempting to incorporate submodels of language analysis, reference, inference, and inference conditioning that are motivated by a strong desire to understand humans, and not simply to solve the problems of this one story, we believe that the end product of the research will be a reasonable first approximation to human comprehension.

ACKNOWLEDGMENTS

I thank the members of the CSA group (Phil London, Milt Grinberg, Steve Small, Rich Wood, John Boose, Phil Agre, Albrecht Fauser, Bob Rosenschein, Sandy Salazar, Mache Creeger, Marty Herman, György Fekete, Jim Moulton) for the intellectual stimulation they provide. I also thank NASA for their support of this research under grant NSG-7253.

REFERENCES

[Bobrow, D., and Winograd, T., 1977]. An overview of KRL-0, a knowledge representation language. *Cognitive Science* **1,** 3–46.

[Boose, J., and Rieger, C., 1977]. "The Windows to the Soul: Character Behavior from Visual Inferencing in a Children's Story." TR-579, Computer Science Department, Univ. of Maryland.

[Charniak, E., 1972]. "Toward a Theory of Children's Story Comprehension. "AI Memo 266, Artificial Intelligence Lab, M.I.T., Cambridge, Massachusetts. (Doctoral Dissertation)

[Charniak, E., 1977]. Ms. Malaprop, a language comprehension program. *Procedings 5th International Joint Conference on Artificial Intelligence, 1977.*

[Charniak, E., 1978]. A framed PAINTING: the representation of a common sense knowledge fragment. *Cognitive Science* 1, 355–394.

[Creeger, M., 1978]. "Generating Perspective Through Belief." TR-634, Computer Science Department, Univ. of Maryland.

[Fauser, A., 1978]. "Pronoun Interpretation in a Story Comprehension Model." TR-636, Computer Science Department, Univ. of Maryland.

[Hawkinson, L., 1975]. The representation of concepts in OWL. *Proceedings 4IJCAI, Tbilisi, USSR, 1975.*

[Lenat, D., 1976]. "AM: An Artificial Intelligence Approach to Discovery in Mathematics as Heuristic Search." AI Memo 286, Stanford Univ.

[Levin, J., and Goldman, N., 1978]. "Process Models of Reference in Context." Information Sciences Inst. ISI/RR-78-72.

[McDermott, D., 1976]. Artificial intelligence meets natural stupidity. SIGART Newsletter 57, April.

[Meehan, J., 1977]. Tale-Spin, an interactive program that writes stories. *Proceedings IJCAI-77, Boston, 1977.*

[Minsky, M., 1975]. A Framework for Representing Knowledge. In *The Psychology of Computer Vision.* P. Winston (ed.). McGraw–Hill, New York.

[Nash-Webber, B., 1977]. "Anaphora: A Cross-Disciplinary Survey." Tech. Report CSR-31, Center for the Study of Reading, Univ. of Illinois and Bolt Beranek and Newman.

[Rieger, C., 1974]. "Conceptual Memory: A Theory and Computer Program for Processing the Meaning Content of Natural Language Utterances." AI Memo 233, Stanford Univ.

[Rieger, C., 1976a]. An organization of knowledge for problem solving and language comprehension. *Artificial Intelligence* 7, 89–127.

[Rieger, C., 1976b]. The representation and selection of commonsense knowledge for natural language comprehension. In *Georgetown University Roundtable on Language and Linguistics.* C. Rameh (ed.). Georgetown Univ. Press, Washington, D.C.

[Rieger, C., 1977]. Spontaneous computation in cognitive models. *Cognitive Science* 1, 315–354.

[Rieger, C., 1978a]. Viewing parsing as word sense discrimination. In *A Survey of Linguistic Science.* W. Dingwall (ed.). Greylock Publ., Stanford, Connecticut.

[Rieger, C., 1978b]. GRIND-1: first report on the Magic Grinder story comprehension project. *Discourse Processes* 1, No. 3.

[Salazar, S., 1977]. "Prediction/Fulfillment Application in a Frame-Based Story Comprehension System." TR-627, Computer Science Department, Univ. of Maryland.

[Schank, R., 1972]. Conceptual dependency: a theory of natural language understanding. *Cognitive Psychology* 3.

[Schank, R., 1976]. The structure of episodes in memory. In *Representation and Understanding.* D. Bobrow and A. Collins (eds.). Academic Press, New York.

[Schank, R., and Abelson, R., 1977]. *Scripts. Plans. Goals and Understanding.* Earlbaum Press, Hillsdale, New Jersey.

[Schank, R., et. al., 1975]. SAM—A Story Understander." Res. Report 43, Computer Science Department, Yale Univ.

[Schmidt, C., and Sridharan, N., 1977]. Plan recognition using a hypothesize and revise paradigm. *Proceedings IJCAI-77, Boston, 1977.*

[Small, S., 1978]. "Conceptual Language Analysis for Store Comprehension." TR-663 Computer Science Department, Univ. of Maryland.

[Wilensky, R., 1976]. Using plans to understand stories. *Proceedings Annual Conference of the ACM, New York, 1976.*